Circling Home

Circling Home:
Exploring Spirituality through a Unitarian Universalist Lens

Doug Kraft

Copyright 2010, 2018 Doug Kraft

First published in 2010 the Unitarian Universalist Society of Sacramento in celebration of the 10th anniversary of senior minister Doug Kraft's ministry with the congregation.

Updated version published in 2018 by Easing Awake Books,
1126 McClaren Drive, Carmichael, California, 95608
Cover photo by Duffy Brooks and distributed through www.unsplash.com.
Other photos and images by Doug Kraft.

Table of Contents

Table of Contents.. iii
Foreword vii
In Gratitude viii
Notes viii

Arriving

Getting Real.. 3
Dying into Life 7
Lines in the Sand: Creating a Self Through Boundaries........ 11
Beyond the Storyline.. 15
Anger 19
Compassion and Anger 24
Compassion.. 28
Spirituality of Despair 31
Fire Unbound by Longing 35
Consciousness and Morality.. 40
Forgiving Ourselves 44
Forgiving Others 49
Of Sisyphus and Groundhogs 54
Remorse and Guilt 58
Fallow Time 63
Wise Speech.. 67
Little Mind, Big Mind 71
Loving Your Consciousness 76
Being Who We Are: Playing Golf in Calcutta 81
Deep Listening 86
Self as Trance 90

Presence

Sànùk: Fun 97
Conflict and Ill Will... 101
Conflict and Goodwill 106
Conflict and Community 110
Discontentment.. 114
Contentment 118
Bad Reality, Good Reality 122
Generosity I 125

Generosity II 130
Cultivating Happiness 135
Seeing Simplicity 139
Our Divine Vulnerabilities I 143
Our Divine Vulnerabilities II 148
Our Divine Vulnerabilities III 152
Experiments in Truth 156
Ethical Lapses 160
Killing a Friend 165
Joy, Enjoying, and Being In Joy 167

Everyday Practices

Light Beyond the Scrim 175
Love-Truth 179
Loving Kindness 183
Taking Refuge 188
Resting in the Tempest 193
Mindfulness I: Wat Life 197
Mindfulness II: Transformation 202
Spiritual Eyes 206

Religious Experience

Deep Connection 213
God and the Power of Surrender 218
Atheism and the Wisdom of Uncertainty 222
Paradise and the Struggle for Harmony 227
The Pursuit of Happiness 231
Peaceful Heart 235
Joy and Formless Wellbeing 240
Forgiveness 244
Nibbana I: Unbound by Longing 248
Nibbāna II: Nothingness 253
Nibbāna III: The Secret of Happiness 257
Simplicity 261
Practices of Simplicity 266

Unitarian Universalist Spirituality

An Openness of Being 273
Unitarian Universalist Maturity 277

In the Buddha's Footsteps: Sujata 281
In the Buddha's Footsteps: Transformation 286
Bright Faith 289
Faith and the Art of Questioning 293
Embodied Faith 297
Relax 302
Unitarian Universalist Spirituality: Finding the Soul 307
Unitarian Universalist Spirituality: The Goodness in Everyone 312
Unitarian Universalist Spirituality: Radiant Heart 317
Unitarian Universalist Spirituality:
    From Interdependence to Oneness 322
Swimming in the Deep End:
    The Dark Side of Unitarian Universalism 327
Swimming in the Deep End: Merging with the River 332
Swimming in the Deep End: Beyond Self as We Know It 337
Unitarian Universalist Spirituality: Choosing Love 342

Indexes

Sermons by Title 347
Sermons by Date 349

Foreword

*So the end-point of the path is to get home again. This longing for
belonging, this homing instinct of the heart, is the path within every path.*
– Brother David Steindl-Rast

Home is messy.

In his poem, "The Death of the Hired Man," Robert Frost famously wrote: "Home is the place where, when you have to go there, they have to take you in."

In a good home, we aren't taken in begrudgingly, but openly and affectionately. Our foibles are seen clearly, and still we are embraced heartfully. Frost wrote: It is "something you somehow haven't to deserve." In an ideal home we aren't loved for what we *do* or even for what we *are*, but simply *because we are*.

This is a tall order. This side of enlightenment, none of us has our lives completely together. The folks in our circles of friends, work, community, congregations, and elsewhere are probably not interested in all the details of our love life, political frustrations, spiritual practices, emotional wounding, or peculiar enthusiasms. So in most places, we encapsulate parts of ourselves. It helps us get along.

Ideally, home is a place where, when we go there, we don't have to encapsulate. We can let down our guard and be ourselves in all our grace and awkwardness, perfections and incompleteness, moments of wisdom and moments of craziness.

Therefore, even an ideal home can be messy.

There is a kind of homesickness in all of us – a deep yearning to relax, be ourselves and have it work out. Deep down we long for others to see us as we are. Yet stripped of our defenses, most are afraid of what people will see if they see all we are.

So our lives are a messy mix of love and fear, courage and timidity, grace and awkwardness, impatience and procrastination, truth speaking and dissembling, minimizing and exaggerating — as we go to the store, hang out with friends, negotiate with co-workers, relate to our families, and try to find some way to help our planet and her creatures.

Many religions project this spiritual homesickness onto another realm — a heavenly afterlife where no one gets upset or has petty thoughts or embarrassing fantasies. It is an ideal place where God sees us and takes us in.

Unitarian Universalism has never taken much interest in dimensions we can only speculate about. It has always been more interested in the world we are living in now. It encourages us to love this world as it is and help it be more homelike for all her people and creatures.

In a larger sense, earth is a home we all share — we don't have the ability to live elsewhere yet. And with ever-faster technologies, we are living in each other's towns, neighborhoods, backyards, and homes.

Real love, embodied love, love grounded in this world is messy.

For the past 10 years the Unitarian Universalist Society of Sacramento has been my religious home. This is where I've spent most of my Sunday mornings – often in the pulpit.

If there is any common theme running through the 250 or so sermons I've pulled together over the decade it is this urge to return home – the pull to be at home with ourselves, our families, our communities, and our world.

Our world is not an ideal place. But it has great beauty. It is a place for us to savor that beauty and engage for wellbeing for all.

Each Sunday we take a slightly different look at love in the context of the messiness of it all. This exploration doesn't take us elsewhere. At its best it brings us here.

*We shall not cease from exploration
And the end of all our exploring
Will be to arrive where we started
And know the place for the first time.*
– T.S. Eliot

In Gratitude

As I approached the end of my tenth year in Sacramento, the Rev. Roger Jones suggested the congregation put together a volume of my sermons.

Linda Klein guided this project from inception to final printing. She was the first to reread the entire corpus of what I had written. Bless her heart. I'm grateful for her talented efforts.

Maxine Cornwell also read through a large percentage. Bless her as well. Linda and Maxine were unwilling to cut enough to make the project a manageable size. So we decided to limit the collection to those sermons with a more explicit spiritual focus.

Mike Malinowski did the layout. And along the way, many people read, selected, and edited. I'm grateful for the help of:

*John Abbott
JoAnn Anglin
Kathryn Canan
Maxine Cornwell
Carole Czujko
Lisa Derthick
Bonnie Galloway
Mary Howard
Eileen Karpeles
Linda Klein
Peter Kosar
Kris Malinowski
Mike Malinowski
Doris Simonis
Patty Taylor Gutermute
Chris Webb-Curtis
Margaret Wilcox*

And I'm grateful to all the members and friends of the congregation who listened to me. When my oldest son, Nathan, visited Sacramento for the first time, he came to a service. Afterward he said, "Dad, this is a sham. You love to talk about this stuff and now you've got a bunch of people paying you to do so."

Their deep and careful listening constantly encouraged me to go deeper. Without them these sermons never would have been written.

If there is a secret heroine in this collection, it is Erika, my wife and partner for over 40 years. She not only endured my angst in writing. She read most of sermons in their early stages. She made suggestions (mostly cuts) that saved me extra work and saved the congregation unneeded suffering.

Notes

The sermons are divided into several large sections. Within each section, the sermons are listed chronologically. The earlier sections have more of the earlier sermons. The later sections have more of the later sermons.

Some of the sermons are part of an obvious series. These are included in their original order. However, each was written to be freestanding with enough information to make sense (hopefully!) without having heard earlier sermons.

A few poems and stories appear in several different places in this collection. Rather than edit them out or make reference to their earlier use, we left them as is. This way each chapter can stand on its own. You can read them in any order. Or just the ones that intrigue you most.

All sermons were first delivered to the Unitarian Universalist Society of Sacramento on the date given on the first page. The one exception is "Unitarian Universalist Spirituality: Choosing Love," which was first delivered to the District Assembly of the Pacific Central District of the Unitarian Universalist Association.

Doug Kraft, July 2010

Many thanks to Michael Morrison for his thorough re-editing in 2018.

Doug Kraft, May 2018

Arriving

Getting Real

May 7, 2000

Late on Friday afternoon, October 15, 1982, my wife, Erika, and I went for our weekly visit to Bernie, our family doctor. Erika was in the eighth month of our second pregnancy. She had some water retention, her blood pressure was slightly elevated – not unusual for late in a pregnancy but still something to keep an eye on.

At the end of the examination, the doctor said he would like to have his obstetrician have a look at Erika. His secretary made an appointment for the following Monday morning. The doctor said, no, that was not soon enough. He wanted it that day. The secretary left and came back saying we should go directly to the obstetrician's office. His name was Dr. Serjie Bogojavlenski. Everyone called him Bogo.

When we arrived at Bogo's, the door was open and the lights dim. The waiting room was empty; the nurses and receptionist had gone home for the weekend. Across the waiting room and down a hallway was a table. Bogo sat on it with his hands holding the edge and his feet dangling in the air.

We greeted each other. As Erika and I walked toward him, he watched Erika keenly. When we were still 10 feet away, he said, "We're going to deliver the baby tonight. I'll give you an examination, but I can tell right now what the result will be. Let me show you what I mean."

He took us into an examination room. Erika's blood pressure was up even more. He had her sit on the edge of the examination table with her legs hanging. He tapped her knee with his rubber hammer. Rather than jerking a few inches as one would expect, her leg shot up as far as it could go.

"You're wired," he said. He explained that the condition is called "preeclampsia." In some women, blood leaks back across the placenta late in pregnancy. In rare cases, the mother has an allergic reaction to the baby's blood. *Eclampsia* is the Greek word for lightning, which describes how the condition strikes – very fast and potentially lethal. Once the baby is delivered, the problem no longer exists. Given that Erika was within a week or so of her due date, the risks in an early birth were negligible, especially compared to the risks of continued pregnancy.

We said we would go home, get a few things and come back to the hospital. He said, "No, I want you to go straight there. I'll call your doctor and meet you up there myself."

A half hour later we were getting Erika settled in the hospital. Her blood pressure had gone up more. Bogo tried several different medications to bring it down, but nothing helped. Erika was becoming glassy eyed. By 9:30 her blood pressure reached 270 over something. I understood why it was called "eclampsia." Bogo finally said, "Nurse, give her a shot of Valium. She's about to have a seizure."

The Valium worked very quickly. Her blood pressure dropped. Erika became coherent. The obstetrician's face relaxed.

"Okay," he said, "now we're going to give you Pitocin to try to induce labor. It isn't going to work. The drugs we are using to keep your blood pressure in control will stop the contractions. But it still makes sense to give it a try before we go to a cesarean section."

Bogo went home to supper, family, and bed. Our doctor, Bernie, stayed to monitor Erika's situation. By 1:00 o'clock in the morning it was clear that Erika would not go into labor. Bernie woke Bogo up and told him to come do a C-section.

I was glad that they allowed me into the operating room. Seeing my wife cut open was disorienting. I was surprised at all the layers they had to go through. Then they drew out a black, damp mass. It did not look like anything I could recognize. But I knew it was our child. My head began to spin. I have fainted about a dozen times in my life, so I recognized the symptoms. I looked around and found a stool to sit down.

Bogo brought the baby over to the nurse next to me so he could concentrate on sewing Erika up. I wanted to touch my child, but held off because I was feeling so dizzy. He was black and deep purple. As he started to breathe, his body flashed pink and then turned black again.

After several moments, his breathing was established and he was all pink.

Bernie came over to examine him. He pronounced him healthy and full-term. He was taken to the nursery as Erika was wheeled from the operating room.

I went up to meet my son. In the nursery, I could sit alone with him. When Nathan was born five years earlier, he spent ten days in intensive care. The IVs and monitors made it awkward to hold him. Now, I was grateful to be able to just hold this little being and look into his eyes. Erika and I had decided we had to meet him before we could settle on a name. I could tell he was Damon. I sat with him for an hour or more.

Erika came out from under the anesthesia. She felt pretty wretched and just wanted to sleep.

It was after six in the morning, so I decided to go home to Nathan and my mother-in-law and fill them in.

As I turned in the driveway, Nathan came running out of my mother-in-law's apartment carrying the doll we had given him. I told him the essentials: He had a brand new baby brother, it had been a tough delivery but everybody was all right, I had a birthday present for him, and we were going out to Bickford's Pancake House to celebrate.

By 9:30, I was back home. I wanted to get a few hours sleep before going back to the hospital. I sat in bed for a few minutes before lying down. Years later, I thought Damon might ask what it was like when we first met. I wanted to write down the experience while it was fresh. I closed my eyes and put myself back into the nursery when I first held him. I tried to remember as closely as I could what went through my mind as I looked into his eyes. This is what I wrote:

Welcome, little friend, little being entrusted to our care. I just keep thinking, "Welcome, little friend."

Where did you come from, you with the stars in your hair and the ocean depths in your eyes? Such tiny fingers. Such a large soul.

Wherever you came from, you are here now. This is the earth and I'll be your daddy this time. In the years ahead, we will laugh and cry and no doubt quarrel together. We will watch our lives unfold.

But somehow, at this moment, when your body is so soft and new to the world, we seem closer to who we truly are together. And the love in it nearly overwhelms me.

Do you understand this? Do you know what I'm thinking? Have we met before? This feels more like a reunion than a meeting of strangers.

How can such a little being affect me so, unless the essence is not what the doctors and nurses weigh and measure.

There is mystery here — something much bigger that I can capture. And I'm truly grateful for that.

Welcome, little friend.

What Are We Doing Here?

This is our first official meeting. I've met many of you, but today is the first I've stood before you to lead a worship service. This may not be as dramatic as meeting a newborn for the first time, but it is not without its newness and expectancy. As we look into each other's eyes, it is a good time to ask some basic questions like, "What are we doing here? On a beautiful fall day, why should we put on our good clothes and come sit in this room with each other? What is this church enterprise all about anyway?"

We know what the answer is supposed to be. We are here to find God, peace of mind, fulfillment, enlightenment, or love. We are doing a community spiritual thing.

These aren't bad answers. The problem is I don't know what these words mean to you. In fact, I'm not sure what they mean to me. "God" has been used for everything from an old man on an uncomfortable-looking stone chair in the clouds to the life force. "Love" has been used for everything from kindness to sexual desire to generosity. I don't find these words very satisfying. What is this spiritual game really all about?

These days, the phrase I like the most is "getting real." A church at its best is a bunch of people trying to help each other touch what is most real. I began with a description of Damon's birth because that moment of looking into his eyes is an example of what I mean by getting real. As I held Damon, my ideas about God, my definitions of love, my beliefs about the nature of spirituality, my thoughts about how to find peace, my theology of fulfillment ... none of them seemed particularly relevant. They would have been distractions from what was most real: the little body in my hands and those eyes gazing at me like brown pools of eternity. As far as I'm concerned, that's what spirituality is.

We find the transcendent, the sacred, and the holy when we set aside our ideas about the transcendent, the sacred, and the holy and just be with what's right here.

There is an old story about this in the book of Exodus:

Moses was having a tough time. After getting free of the Pharaoh, the people's spirits had been high; their cooperation had been good. But after trudging through the desert for month after month, the people began to grumble. They complained about the water. They fussed about the food. They bickered about each other. Some days Moses had to sit from dawn to dusk settling one dispute after another. Moses himself began to get peevish and short-tempered. Sometimes he sent his brother, Aaron, to deliver messages because he couldn't stand all the quarreling.

Moses was a smart man. He knew what was happening. He knew that to serve his people, he had to take care of himself. So he told the tribes, "You all hang out here for a while and behave yourselves. I'm going on retreat for a few days. I need a little inspiration, a little guidance. I'm going to climb that mountain over there – the one they call "Mount Sinai" – to commune with God."

Moses hiked and climbed and climbed and hiked. As he got away from the masses, he began to settle down inside. His worries began to drain away. The haze in his mind started to lift. As he looked at the plants and trees and birds, he once again could recognize their beauty. He could feel their living aura.

Finally, near the top of the mountain, the auras were so clear and strong that he saw a bush that seemed on fire. It burned without being consumed. He could again hear God speaking in his brain. In his excitement, he wanted to rush into that sacred presence. He'd been here before and yearned to return to that holy space.

But he heard a voice inside. He wasn't sure if he was talking to himself or if God was speaking out of the burning bush. The voice said, "Hold on there Moses. What do you think you are doing? You can't just rush into a holy space like you dash up to a fruit vender's stall. Pay attention to what you are doing. Prepare yourself." Then God told him what he had to do to enter into holy space.

Do you remember God's instructions to Moses?

He said, "Take off your shoes."

I think those are profound instructions. If we want to experience the divine, we have to walk barefoot with our skin in direct contact with the earth. If I'm standing in my Birkenstocks, I may think I'm standing on the ground. The sandals may be more comfortable than the gravel. But I can't feel the sand and pebbles and grass. I'm insulated from directly experiencing the land. I'm insulated from some of the aliveness we call divinity.

Of course, the real issue is not baring the soles of our feet. It is baring our inner souls from the ideas, wishes, beliefs, and desires that mitigate our experience each moment. Our leathery preconceptions insulate us from direct knowing. As our minds quiet, the world around us comes alive. As Elizabeth Barrett Browning put it:

Earth's crammed with heaven
And every common bush afire with God.
But only he who sees, takes off his shoes –
The rest sit round and pluck mulberries.

Every Day

Sometimes what is going on in the world is so powerful that it breaks through our distractions and runs over our defenses. There was nothing that could prepare me for watching my wife almost die, for seeing her cut open, for witnessing another body yanked unceremoniously from her innards, for looking into those eyes. My mind was blown, to use the vernacular. My ideas and coping strategies were inadequate to the moment. Yet my concern kept me engaged. There was nothing left for me to do but be present and be real. I could not have put up a pretense if I'd tried.

But mostly, our days are not filled with these kinds of crises. Mostly we are just brushing our teeth or opening the mail or looking through the kitchen cupboard or sitting in church. As we scrub our teeth, we may be thinking about a conversation with our boss. As we open the cupboard, we may not feel the handle or smell the aromas. We may be thinking, "I wish I'd bought those cookies yesterday." Our bodies and senses are in one place and our minds are in another.

It's no wonder we feel fragmented. It's no wonder we think reality is split into different arenas: physical, mental, emotional, spiritual, political, sacred, mundane, and so on. But reality is unified. It is our minds that are fragmented. It is our consciousness that is compartmentalized. It is our awareness that is scattered.

We project our inner feelings of disunity upon the world. We think the sacred is not part of our everyday life. So we go to church or meditation groups or libraries or workshops to try to find that aliveness. Mostly what we get is other people's ideas about reality when what we hunger for is a taste of what's right here. We just want to be real.

This Moment

So what about right now? Does this moment feel crammed with heaven and ablaze with divinity?

Maybe we need to take our shoes off. Maybe we need to open up a little more deeply and heartfully to this moment. I'd like to think that we are here to help each other to do that.

Can we do this right now?

For example, I can feel my hands pressing on the podium ... my belly rubbing against my shirt as I breathe ...

I hear the sounds from the street ...

A few thoughts and images flick through my mind ...

What do you experience? ...

This is your life. It is happening right now. Can you see what it is? ...

Can we just be? ... It's exquisite ... Just be.

Dying into Life

When we give up our dead we enter into a common sorrow that visits the proudest and humblest, that has entered into unnumbered hearts before us and will enter innumerable ones after us, a sorrow which should make the world one, and dissolve all other feelings into sympathy and love.

– William M. Salter

January 7, 2001

David used to lightly refer to himself as "cat man" meaning he could climb anywhere. He had been a contractor for years. He used to walk the ridges of the houses he was building before the roof was on.

Several years ago he fell. A lower spinal injury left him paralyzed from the waist down. The way he described it, he died. The person he knew himself to be – the agile, physically mobile person – ceased to exist. That person was no more. And born out of the accident was someone else with a different set of attributes, someone who had a different life to lead, someone he had to get to know and accept.

We die many times: crippling injuries, divorce, loss of a job, graduation (in which we die as a student), aging, moving to a new house, and so many others. These are just the obvious transitions. There are also subtler forms: A long held idea is discarded; feelings about yourself or a loved one change; new insight enters your life. We are constantly changing. Consider who you were 10 years ago: what you did, felt, and thought. That person is no more — he or she died. You are not the same person you were 10 years ago, 10 months ago, or even 10 days ago.

Physical death seems special because we have so little information about what it is like on the other side. When Nathan was born, I died as a childless person. That was probably the most significant transition in my life. But there were many people I could talk to who had gone through this transition and could give me clues as to what to expect and what to do. But who can tell us what to expect in bodily death? Our information is tenuous at best. This makes physical death seem like a bigger deal. But when you think about it, it is clear that we die all the time in many ways.

How do we face death? How do we grieve?

This week is the transition into the new year. Our custom is to set goals for the future and adopt a resolute attitude. But New Year's resolutions often fail because they try to move forward without dealing with the transition. We try to grab something new without first letting go of the old.

A friend who is a lot younger than I am said that she had reached the age where she can no longer eat what she pleases, not exercise, and not gain weight. If she wants to maintain her health, she may need to grieve the loss of her youthful metabolism. This grieving may be more important than resolving to follow the latest diet.

To move gracefully into the future, we often need to first grieve the past.

Death is the ultimate symbol of these transitions. Death is an integral part of life. *The attitude with which we face death and loss is a clear reflection of the attitude with which we face life.* Those who fear and resist death or loss – and most of us do to a degree – fear and resist life. Those who can give themselves to death can give themselves to life. Those who live completely – who die into life – fear neither life nor death.

Stages

Some of the pioneering work on the attitudes with which people face death was done by Elizabeth Kubler-Ross in the 1960s. In her now classic book, *On Death and Dying*, she delineates five stages which terminally ill patients often go through when they learn of their approaching death. With a little reflection, it is clear that these five stages apply not only to bodily death, but to all transitions. In fact, it is hard to think of any attitude toward anything that is not contained in one of her stages.

Because her work is so useful, I want to structure my thoughts around her five stages. I would like to share with you Kubler-Ross's description of each stage. As I do this I want to expand on how each reflects our attitude toward living in general. And finally, I will close with some general comments about embracing loss and giving ourselves to our dying, living, grieving, and birthing.

Denial

The first stage Kubler-Ross describes is denial. When patients first hear that they are terminally ill, their first response is often denial of one sort or another. They cannot or will not believe it. "The doctor must be wrong." "This couldn't happen to me."

When any organism experiences a lot of pain, it tends to go numb. When we experience a lot of emotional pain, we tend to deny it.

There are events or changes in our lives which we sense deep down, but we have not yet faced squarely. We all have our blind spots. Perhaps your job is not going right; feelings toward a loved one have shifted, or there are early signs of a disease.

Sometimes we have to work hard and stay busy to maintain our denial. If you have ever said, "I have to think about this in a positive way," you were probably trying to push some feelings aside. Denial is very human and very understandable. But if it persists, it can lead to an increasing sense of isolation from one's friends, one's family, and even one's self. Denial must be faced frankly and compassionately. It requires open eyes and an open heart.

Anger

Kubler-Ross's second stage is anger.

When patients are no longer able to completely deny the reality of their condition, their first acknowledgment of it may be accompanied by anger. They may think, "Why me? I don't deserve this!" The anger can be displaced onto family and doctors, making the person very difficult to be with.

Anger is a large topic we will return to in another sermon. Briefly, anger is a natural, biological response to hurt, threat, or to being stopped. It has little to do with thought, will, or intent. Loss can easily cause hurt, threat, or feelings of being stopped. Therefore, anger can be a normal, natural part of grieving.

The only danger with anger as it is related to grief is that if it is not acknowledged, surfaced, and allowed to run out, it can degenerate into bitterness. All of us have probably tasted bitterness at one time or another. And all of us probably know someone for whom some tragedy or unfair turn of events produced a bitterness which colors the rest of their living.

Regret

Bargaining is the third stage Kubler-Ross describes. But the feeling beneath it is regret.

When patients' anger is spent, they may not only acknowledge their condition, but also begin to accept it.

Regret is characteristic of this stage. I remember the contractor saying, "If only I had not climbed the building that day, how different my life might be." We all do this at times. "If only I had studied harder, I would have gotten into a better school." "If only I had not irritated my boss." "If only, if only, if only."

It may be true that if only something had been different then, everything would be different now. But this clinging to the past event – while it is certainly understandable – keeps one from fully accepting the present.

Depression

Kubler-Ross calls the fourth stage depression, but I think it encompasses two sub-stages: unworthiness and grief. The unworthiness is associated with a loss of self-esteem. Kubler-Ross gives examples of a woman who had a mastectomy, a man who could no longer hold his job, an opera singer who had to have part of her jaw removed. Something that they had valued about themselves was taken away, leaving them feeling less worthy.

I think we all know what that feels like. Who has never had his or her feelings of self-worth enmeshed in being physical, vital, or in doing a job well, or in being a perfect parent? Then, when you find yourself weak or unable to do the job or flawed as a parent, your self-esteem sags. Some people go through this depression quickly. For others, it becomes a way of life.

This feeling of unworthiness is also natural and human. It is not a problem as long as you hear it as a feeling and not an objective truth.

Grief

Kubler-Ross speaks of a second kind of depression which she calls "preparatory grief." This is quieter and cannot be lifted by reassurances. It is a feeling of emptiness which is a genetically programmed response. If we bond deeply, then when a bond is broken our heart feels empty or torn. It is difficult to stop this grieving, and it is best not to try, as it is a natural healing process. Saint Exupéry captured it beautifully in *Wind, Sand and Stars*:

> *Bit by bit . . . it comes over us that we shall never again hear the laughter of our friend, that this one garden is forever locked against us. And at that moment begins our true mourning, which, though it may not be rending, is yet a little bitter. For nothing, in truth, can replace that companion. Old friends cannot be created out of hand. Nothing can match the treasure of common memories, of trials endured together, of quarrels and reconciliations, and generous emotions. It is idle, having planted an acorn in the morning, to expect that afternoon to sit in the shade of the oak.*

I want to add another comment about this stage of grief.

When my father died, my first response was to take a day off, grab my journal, and go for a long hike. In some respects, I did not have a lot in common with my father. But we shared a love of the outdoors. This was my way of being with him. I hiked. I wrote. I sensed his presence. But I did not shed any tears.

I worried a little that I might be in some kind of denial since I was not crying. But I did think about him a lot and in some ways felt closer to him than I had in years.

A few months ago I ran across an article that said that 70% of the subjects in the early research on grief had been women. It turns out that many men and some women have a different pattern of grieving, similar to what I did. Rather than cry and share sad feelings, they engage in activities they might have had in common with the person. In men especially, there does not seem to be a strong correlation between tears and later emotional adjustment. Feeling what is going on inside is important, but how you express it is less important.

So don't let anyone tell you how to grieve. Not me, Elizabeth Kubler-Ross, or anyone. Each of us may grieve a little differently. Honor your process.

Acceptance

If patients have enough time, sometimes they reach the final stage of total acceptance. There is no more denial, anger, bargaining or depression. They just accepts what is.

The acceptance is not resignation. There is a qualitative shift here from trying to take from life to giving oneself to life or death.

I heard of a woman who asked her dying mother if she was afraid of death. The mother's response was, "I'm not afraid to die, but I do not know how." This answer shook up the younger woman who went to lie down on the couch and think about it. A little later she went back and said, "Mother, I think you have to give yourself to it." The older woman said nothing then, but later asked, "Fix me a cup of tea with lots of cream and sugar the way I like it because it will be my last cup of tea. I know now how to die." She drank the tea, set the cup down, let out a breath, and never took another. There was no holding back. Just total acceptance.

It is a quieter, openhearted acknowledgment. It is a sense of moving on without rushing ahead. It is just being with life as it is.

Strategy

These five stages – denial, anger, bargaining, depression, and acceptance – represent the phases terminally ill patients tend to go through when facing death (although they don't necessarily go through them in any neat progression). They also represent the attitudes we go through in facing the events in our lives. You may find yourself in different stages in relation to different events in your life. For example, in relationship to your divorce, you may be at the stage of anger, in relation to your aging you may be in denial, in relation to your finances you may be in depression, in relation to your child leaving home you may be in acceptance, in relationship to your weight you may be in the "if only's," and so on.

It can be helpful to look at the events in your life and see where you honestly stand in relationship to them.

Obviously, the most peace, vitality, and clarity come in the acceptance state.

An optimal strategy for living, then, would be to move yourself to acceptance in relation to all the events in your life.

But there is a subtlety here that needs to be watched. If, for example, you are at the stage of anger about a divorce, the way to move to acceptance is not to deny the anger. That moves you backward to denial. The way is to accept the anger, not by getting hysterical, but by opening to it, "Boy, am I furious." Or if you are depressed or grieving, you don't deny it. You accept it. "Wow, I haven't been this sad for a long time. Far out."

When an experience of anger or regret or depression comes at you, rather than punch back, you open to it. You accept it for what it is. You give yourself to it. You let it be.

To simplify this five-stage model, think of it as a continuum with denial on one end and acceptance on the other. If you are at one end, you are in complete denial. If you are mostly in denial but have just a little bit of acceptance, you feel angry. You don't want to accept it, but you have just a little. If you are half denying and half accepting, you are in the bargaining middle stage: if only … if only … if only. If you are mostly accepting but not totally, you feel pretty lousy: This is the depression. When you no longer deny it at all, you are in the stage of acceptance.

So no matter where you are, the way to move toward greater acceptance is to trust your process. Accept where you are for the moment — be it anger, depression, or whatever. This helps move you toward greater acceptance.

Getting Born

One final thought …

One difficulty many people have in facing death is that they don't feel they are fully born – they have not wholly become what they sense themselves to be.

Physical birth was given to us. We did not have a choice in the matter. But we are not truly alive if we are just vegetating. All traditions speak about a second birth or a rebirth. This is getting born into a deeper spiritual life.

Spiritual birth is not given to us. We have to choose it. We have to freely give ourselves to it.

The way to die, the way to live, the way to be born is to give oneself to the eternal moment, to whatever is happening right now – no resistance, no holding back. You do not give yourself to what you think should be but to how you are: happy, sad, elated, discouraged, bored, angry, tired, confused. However you are, you open to it.

What makes you choose life often is the challenge of facing death and loss. What makes one open to life is learning how to die not tomorrow, but right here and now.

The fullness of life and spirit is not something you can have or possess or write a book about or preach a sermon on. It is only something you can become by dying into life.

Lines in the Sand:
Creating a Self Through Boundaries

The ultimate metaphysical secret, if we dare state it so simply, is that there are no boundaries in the universe. Boundaries are illusions, products not of reality but of the way we map and edit reality. And while it is fine to map out the territory, it is fatal to confuse the two.

– Ken Wilber

January 27, 2002

Several Americans were traveling through the Soviet Union a number of years ago en route from Europe to India. As they approached Iran, the landscape was desolate and rocky, with little vegetation and no sign of human life. The dirt road brought them to a river that ran along the Soviet-Iranian border. The river was dry. Nevertheless, a huge steel bridge with a large gate spanned the dusty riverbed. Two soldiers stood on each side. The travelers told the sentries they wanted to cross. The guards cranked up a telephone to call their counterparts twenty yards away. Then the four soldiers marched up the bridge, put keys into the gate simultaneously, opened the locks, let the Americans pass through, closed and locked the gate, and marched back to their former positions.

Twenty minutes later, the bridge was far behind. The Iranian countryside was desolate and rocky, with little vegetation and no sign of human life.

We humans love to create boundaries. Some are more obvious than dry rivers; many are less. Viewing the earth from outer space, there are no boundaries – just land and water. Viewing the maps we make of the earth, there are boundaries galore. We divide land into nations, nations into states and provinces, states into cities and counties, towns into building lots, and buildings into rooms. When I was growing up, I shared a room with my brother. Actually, "shared" is a euphemism. A line down the middle separated my side from his, and woe to the person who put his foot on the wrong floorboard without permission. We love to create borders and are often willing to fight to protect "our space" from "trespassers."

Boundary drawing is not limited to imaginary lines in the dirt. We split time into years, months, weeks, days, and hours. We group body characteristics into races, education into grade levels, music into measures, hues into color groups, spiritual experience into realms, inner turmoil into psychiatric diagnoses. It is hard to imagine an area of human experience that has not been overlaid with fences.

These divisions serve a utilitarian purpose: They help us organize and communicate our experience. The problem is not that they are inaccurate. Night, of course, is different than day; the mountains are different from the plains; red is different from orange. The problem is that where we put the dividing line between night and day, hills and valleys, red and orange is arbitrary. Nature does not make the neat distinctions our language makes. If we take the borders too seriously, we begin to mistake the map for the territory.

The most fundamental boundary we draw is the one between what we think of as "me" and "not-me."

Moving away from the earth a few miles, it is clear that political demarcations are whims of the collective imagination. But gaining the perspective necessary to see that personal boundaries are whimsical is not so easy. Self-sense is deeply ingrained. So to begin this exploration of self as boundary, let's look more closely at how we do it.

Boundary

The process looks like this:

There is a wide array of phenomena that we experience: thoughts, feelings, visual impressions, sounds, ideas, words, … "the whole catastrophe," as Zorba the Greek might say. Out of this vast field, we draw a circle around certain phenomena. Everything inside the circle is called "me." Everything outside is called "not-me." "Self" is defined by this boundary or envelope.

For example, we can think of self as being defined by our skin. Everything inside is "me;" everything outside is "not-me." In this instance, self is equated with our biological organism, which is delimited by the surface of the body.

This may seem so obvious that we think, "What's the fuss? Why make this sound so esoteric? Of course, I am this organism."

But most of us really do not think of ourselves as a body. A body is something we have, not something we are. When you look at your hand, you are more likely to think, "This is my hand," than, "This is me." If your arm were cut off, it would be tragic. But you would still feel that your essence was intact. My mother had her stomach removed because of cancer. There was fear and grief. She lost a dear friend and lifelong companion. But she was still here even if her stomach was not.

Most people's sense of self rests not in their whole body but in their head somewhere behind their eyes. They see themselves as a brain moving around with a body dangling from it. The physical form tags along like a faithful dog. It is something to be trained and maintained, like a circus pony.

This second definition of self draws a circle around our mental and emotional processes. Everything inside it is essential to me. Everything outside is not me. Some things, like my body, live in close proximity. But they are still outside.

This second boundary line may seem closer to the way most people think. But very few people identify with all their mental processes. We repress thoughts and feelings. We identify with the ones we are conscious of, not the whole inner collage. We form a self-image. We think of ourselves as kind or generous or ill-tempered or anxious or some combination of feelings and inclinations. We draw a circle around a set of internal experiences and say everything inside this is me. "This is how I am." Emotions and impulses that lie outside this self-image are "not-me." The eminent psychiatrist Carl Jung called this our shadow. For example, anger is a part of all of us. But if we were never conscious of being angry, anger would be in our shadow. (Perhaps you have heard someone get very upset and the next day say, "I'm sorry. I wasn't myself." (If they weren't themselves, then who were they?) All of us have longings. But, if we cannot acknowledge them, they are relegated outside our self-sense to our shadow.

So now we have three different places to draw the boundaries. The first is the skin. The second is around mental phenomena. The third is around a self-image.

A fourth place to draw a circle is around things over which we have conscious control. For example, I might say, "*I* am chewing the food while *my* stomach digests it." I have a relatively large amount of conscious control over chewing, so I think of this as me. I have little control over digestion, so I think of it as mine – I own it, but it is not me. We would not be likely to say, "My mouth is chewing the food while I digest it."

Is the boundary placement beginning to sound a little arbitrary?

Let me suggest a fifth place. We have been drawing tighter and tighter boundaries. Let's draw a larger one. Perhaps you have walked through a dark room and gingerly felt for furniture you might bump into. Sometimes you can sense the furniture before you actually touch it. Or perhaps you have felt someone looking at you and turned around to find, sure enough, a man was staring at you from behind. We can sometimes feel things beyond the boundary of our skin. You can demonstrate this with a simple experiment. Shake your hands loosely but vigorously for a few minutes. This helps sensitize the fingers. Then, with your hands relaxed and palms facing each other, slowly move them towards each other. Many people will feel a tingle or pressure before their hands actually touch. This kind of sensing is subtle but is there in all of us and accessible to most of us.

So why not extend our boundaries a foot or two beyond our bodies to include this energy field? This might be a little confusing when we shake hands because both of us will be occupying some of the same physical space — your hand will be inside me, not just touching me. But a case could be made that who we are should encircle an aura around our bodies.

As long as we are drawing wider circles, we might include all of humanity or even the entire planet. The health or illness of any part of the earth has an increasingly demonstrable impact on our lives and vice versa. Our survival as individuals and as a species may be tied to our capacity to feel "self" as all of us.

We might debate long into the night which one of these seven circles makes for a better self-definition. Or we might come up with an eighth or ninth or twentieth way to delineate self. But in all cases, the process is the same. We draw a circle to include some phenomena and exclude others. We may differ in where we draw the boundary, but the fact of drawing some perimeter is common to both of us.

The point is that where we draw our bounds is ultimately arbitrary. How we answer the question "Who am I?" is capricious because in drawing the line, we are creating a self-concept, not discovering a pre-existing self. We may do this unconsciously, but it is something we are doing, not something we are revealing. If we create a self, we can just as easily destroy it or build a different one. Self is not based on any objective reality. To be sure, our self-sense may include things that are tangible. My arm is real. But why I should include my arm as who I am versus what I own, why it should be me or simply be mine, is an arbitrary decision. It is built out of whim and inclination.

Battle Lines

So what? Does self as boundary have any practical implications or is it just a philosophical curiosity?

Actually, it has a profound effect. It creates a great deal of unnecessary conflict and stress. When Robert Frost wrote, "Good fences make good neighbors," he was taking issue with the statement. Strong fences make enemies. As any military commander will tell you, any boundary line is a potential battle line. Look at Israel, Bosnia, Korea, the U.S. Congress. Anytime we make a strong separation, we encourage problems. Whether we draw lines in the sand to create separate nations, lines around ethnic identities, racial characteristics or political philosophies, we run the risk of civil wars, political gridlock, ethnic cleansing, and so forth.

To be sure, there are differences in the world. To deny this would be silly. There is a difference between the ocean and the land. The shoreline is where they meet. It does not have to be thought of as something to keep them apart. It can be a meeting place. There are differences between you and me. But these do not have to keep us apart. Our skin can be the place where we touch each other, not just a barrier.

In truth, if we looked deeply at what people actually thought about self-determination, children, human rights, desire for happiness, possibilities of divinity, caring for each other, and so forth, we would find differences in beliefs. But they are probably not as large as our labels imply. When we divide up into Catholics, Baptists, Buddhists, atheists or into Democrats, Republicans, socialists, anarchists, … we accentuate the differences and make it more difficult to appreciate common ground. Territorial ideas become battle cries more often than invocations to search for truth.

Self as boundary creates even deeper stress. We gather certain feelings and attitudes and say, "This is me." What do we do when we feel something that does not fit this self-image? We have a crisis. We have to keep feelings at bay. Perhaps we like to think of ourselves as composed in most situations. Then, when we feel disturbed, we have to project the upset onto those around us, suppress it, deny it, or struggle with it using some other psychological mechanism. Whatever the case, we drain energy and create internal conflict.

No Boundary

What can we do? One possibility, as I suggested earlier, is to push the boundaries out so they are more inclusive than exclusive. We could stretch our self-concept to include more people and life forms.

Another way to overcome the limitations of boundaries is to consider what it might be like to live without any sense of boundary, without a sense of self. As radical as this might sound conceptually, it is something we all experience. In moments of joy and ecstasy, in times of peak experience and mystical perception, we feel at one.

For example, I taught meditation for years. One evening, Jim showed up about 20 minutes late for class. He apologized. He said he had gone cross-country skiing. Dusk was his favorite time. While skiing by the river, he stopped for a few moments. Ducks flew down the waterway. He noticed his breath rising and falling, the ducks, the snow, the twilight. It was exquisite. He stood there for about twenty minutes feeling very alive and present with each breath and each moment.

Prior to the evening, Jim had been having difficulty understanding what meditation was about. So when he finished his story, I said, "You've got it. That was a no-boundary moment." As he stood by the river he experienced no self. That concept was not relevant. There were just the woods and the birds and his heartbeat. There was no need to group some phenomena into a package called "self." To be sure, we could imagine this scene and in our minds draw a circle around his body and say, "That is Jim," and draw a circle around the ducks and say, "Those are ducks. Those are not Jim." But why bother? It's totally unnecessary and distracts from the epiphany of the moment.

If I practice noticing these no-boundary moments when they arise spontaneously, then I may be able to do it more when things are not quite so delightful. I feel down and say, "Oh wow, I haven't been this depressed in a long time. Far out." Or deep unfamiliar yearning wells up and I say, "Fascinating. Look at what life is bringing me now." What comes through is what comes through.

If I cultivate no-boundary awareness, then I am more open and welcoming of experience, pleasant or unpleasant. If a moment of joy arises I do not say, "Ah, *my* joy." I just say, "Ah, joy." If pain arises, I don't say, "Oh, *my* pain." I just say, *"The* pain."

Nothing has changed. I have altered nothing. I still feel all that I feel. I act in ways that are appropriate to the experience. The only difference is that I am not trying to build a wall to keep out certain phenomena like anger, yearning, or pain. I am not in conflict with them. And this makes all the difference. It makes for a more peaceful and energized way of being.

To cultivate no-boundary awareness with other people is to be more expansive of heart. Someone comes up oozing racial bigotry, chattering incessantly, or emitting strong body odor. Maybe they have more money than I have, or less. Maybe they talk about Jesus more or less than I. I don't automatically draw a line and assume they are another species. I may look to see what parts of me are reflected in them and what parts of them are reflected in me.

All I have done is take away the make-believe packaging that creates the illusion of separation between us. I relax and let things be what they are. As I dissolve, nothing real changes. My body and mind do not evaporate. My decision-making ability remains intact. All that is lost is a sense of being separate or isolated. I see that we are all deeply interrelated and interconnected. There is nothing essential that keeps us apart.

Beyond the Storyline

May 20, 2001

It was early afternoon, the day after Christmas, a number of years ago. I was living in Massachusetts back then. My kids were younger.

That afternoon was my first day off in several weeks. The month had been crowded with the demands of the season, the demands of the church, the demands of my family. The baby was napping that afternoon, no other pressing obligations. I closed my eyes, asking for strength and guidance: what might most restore me? I realized that my mind was too jumbled and too out of practice at being still to hear any clear guidance. So much for being spiritual.

I opened my eyes and looked around. The new cordless telephone was next to me. Erika, my wife, had given it to me for Christmas. She wrote on the card, "For the illusion of freedom." Idly I wondered how far I could go out back and still receive calls. Thinking of nothing better to do, and using it as an excuse to get outside, I wrapped up warmly and took the receiver out the door.

When I was satisfied with the phone's performance, I snapped it securely in a large coat pocket and hopped over the back fence. I had no clear plan in mind, but the marsh behind the house was inviting.

Normally, walking was difficult in the wetland behind our property. But it had been so bitter cold that everything was frozen solid. I walked over the ice to places I had never been. There were tracks of birds and mice and even a rabbit. I pushed through brush, over a stream, across an open expanse of ice, through a flooded wood lot and eventually found myself standing at the foot of a hill. In the years I had lived in that small New England town, I had never been to the top. An open gate invited me up.

Every few minutes I turned to absorb the larger view. I was surprised at how far I had come. I could not find my house, but I saw the woods and fields and Spring Street beyond. There was the Dorland's barn looking a little weary and neglected, just as they often did. There was Lorraine Churchill's house. I could picture her smile, which was both regal and warm despite her arthritis. And the Cardins: I pictured the kids inside playing around their pregnant mom. Off to the right was the little road up to Tom Archer's house: I saw his congenial smile, his high blood pressure, his alcoholism. Further up the hill I saw the steeple of the church rise out of the trees. Beyond the steeple is the old orchard where we held services once a year. Beyond was the Carsons' and his ambition. And I could see where the road wound over the hill to the next village. I knew these people in so many ways. Each life had its own unique human qualities, its own projects and style and texture.

Near the crest of the hill, I finally spotted the roof of my house. Sometimes the things closest to us are the last to be discerned. I pictured my own life as I had imagined those of others. There was Doug carrying his Sears Roebuck attaché case to and from the church. I could see him visiting those homes, moving over the landscape, sitting in the church study. I sensed the qualities of his life – the worries, the pleasures, the responsibilities, the stresses, the quiet moments. That was the person we refer to as "Doug." But up here watching was … well, somebody or something different. All his affairs were down there. That person was a part of me, but only such a small part.

If only I could remember that …

Suddenly, I remembered that I had left the impression that I'd only be out five or 10 minutes. Judging by the sun, an hour or two had gone by. From the perspective of the hill top, I knew there was no sense in rushing. But it was time to start the return.

The next few days were working days – catching up on things set aside for Christmas, putting together the upcoming Sunday service, getting in touch with people, calls, office hours … Soon I was completely back into the role of Doug-the-minister.

Wednesday evening my family went to bed early. I received a Paul Winter album for Christmas. I put the record on the stereo and lay down on some blankets on the floor between the speakers.

The clear, warm, and welcoming sound of a soprano sax softly filled the room. It was accompanied by an Imperial Grand Bösendorfer – probably one of the finest pianos built. Its tone was crisp and full. The recording was made in the Cathedral of St. John the Divine. The organ was never overbearing, but provided a lush background over which the lilting saxophone moved.

As I closed my eyes, I felt surrounded by rich browns. As the music filled me, I was lifted through deep orange, bright yellow, and into a pale white sunlight. The name of the album was *Sun Singer*. The music invoked a sense of moving into a very broad and sun-filled spaciousness – like singing to the sun.

Something let go inside of me. That part of me that tried to be somebody – a good parent, a good spouse, a good minister – that part of me that strived to be competent, reliable, likable, worthy … just relaxed. The sound of the music, the expansiveness became everything. I became nothing. Dougness disappeared. Doug-the-minister, Doug-the-parent, Doug-the-spouse … all of them faded. I lost the feeling of being a distinct and separate entity. It felt full, poignant, and very loving.

Superficially, these two events were very different. One took place on a snowy hillside in the middle of the day. The other took place lying on the floor of my living room late at night.

But there was a similar quality to them. One way to describe that quality is to say I stepped out of the storyline of my life. On the hillside, it was as if I could see all the storyline spread out across the landscape of that little town. But I was not those happenings. I was the observer, not the doer. Lying on the floor surrounded by the organ and soprano sax music, I was not observing a vision of my daily routine. I just stepped out of the storyline completely. I ceased identifying with my history. My sense of even being a discrete individual faded into a warm spaciousness.

Scrim

This morning I would like to talk about moving our consciousness beyond our storylines and return to my favorite topic – spirituality or the depth dimension in human experience.

Spiritually, the key issue is not who we are. It is not our relationship to the rest of the cosmos. It is not our ultimate fate. All those are just fine. They are not a problem. Spiritually, the problem is who we *think* we are, what we *think* about our relationship to the cosmos, what we *believe* is our ultimate fate.

Spiritually, the main issue is seeing past our identifications.

In a previous sermon (*Light Beyond the Scrim*, p. 175), I introduced this idea with a metaphor. In theaters, a scrim is a flat curtain of very loose weave. Set designers paint background scenes on scrims. Because of the loose weave, scrims have a magical quality. When the light behind the scrim is dark and the light in front is bright, the curtain appears solid and opaque. What is painted on it can be seen as clearly as a mural on a cinderblock wall. But when you turn down the lights in front and turn up the lights behind, the audience can see right through the gossamer tapestry to the actors behind.

Skillful directors know how to use the lights to draw attention to the mural scrim or to draw it beyond the scrim.

We humans are often not as skillful at directing our attention. We too easily get caught on the flat surface of things and miss the depths beyond. We end up identifying with a small segment of our experience and miss the subtle spaciousness.

Part of the surface of our lives is the events of our days. Most of us identify altogether too much with their storylines. In our crowded, fast-paced lives we may move at such a speed that there is hardly time to notice much more than the happenings on our schedule. The light of our consciousness may never shift off the surface of the scrim. I hear people state this formally and with conviction: "You are your history." Or they may say it more romantically: "You are the collection of your past experiences."

It's just not true. There is so much more to us than the events in our lives. Working as a psychotherapist for many years, I am keenly aware of how powerful past conditioning can be. But to say that is all we are is to mistake the wrapper for the package, the scrim for the stage, the cloud for the sky in which it floats. We are the space within which we can experience the events of our life. We are the space, not the events.

So, in this sermon, I want to talk specifically about stepping out of our identities as doers, actors, and movers in our lives. I want to remind all of us that there is much beyond the story and outside the script.

Congregation

One of the best examples of this is what we have done this year as a congregation.

When I first met this congregation a year ago this month, you had a particular storyline. It worried you. Many people were apologetic and chagrined about some of the events here in the last few years. Former members had been removed. A show down with your last settled minister resulted in a negotiated resignation. Other individuals had stepped on people's toes.

There were some lovely, generous events as well. But you had several installments of Jerry Springer right here.

If I believed you were your history, I'd have been crazy to come here. But I don't think I'm crazy. I sensed something from the beginning that was different from the historical rendition. There was a heartfulness and caring.

I was faced with this contradiction: a storyline that did not match my felt sense of the congregation. It was even more of a dilemma because I had an invitation from another church that had a delightful storyline. I wondered what to do and where to put my faith.

I trusted my sense of the congregation more than the history I was told. And I'm delighted that I did. Many have said what a different atmosphere there is here from a few years ago. You give me credit for this shift. If what you needed was a minister who had faith in you, then I'll take some credit. But mostly the change was the natural heartfulness of the congregation coming to the surface. If my vision of you had been wrong, I would not have helped. If I had thought that underneath you were all pigmies with wings, all the faith in the world would not have caused you to shrink and sprout feathers. But what I sensed here was correct. Many of you knew this as well.

So it was easy to step out of that storyline. This place feels very different as a result.

I'm not suggesting that we should ignore history. It is informative. But it is not definitive. It can show us things to learn and watch for. But it is crazy to limit ourselves to a story we don't like.

Individual

But I want to talk about your individual lives and storylines and how to cultivate a sense of stepping out of them. If we can do it as a collective, it ought to be easier as individuals.

That afternoon on the hillside and the evening floating in the music are examples of stepping out of our stories. I imagine you can recall similar moments in your life.

Rather than talk about this more, maybe we should just do it together. I'd like to offer a guided meditation. Then I'll close with a few words about cultivating these experiences in our everyday lives.

Close your eyes, if you would.

Feel yourself sitting here breathing. Resting on the chair as your belly rises and falls with each inspiration and expiration. …

Let your mind drift back over your past week. Remember some of the things you did – the ordinary comings and goings and the unusual.

Stand back as if from a hillside and see yourself walking, driving, eating, dressing, brushing your teeth, talking to people, moving through the last few days.

Sense the quality of the thoughts you had, the texture of your moods, the worries, the pleasures. Observe from a distance. …

Then notice the observer, the one who is now recalling all these events and seeing them from afar. …

Let your attention shift from the storyline to a deeper sense of yourself. Notice the watcher, the witness of your life, the consciousness that attends to the experience. Feel the beingness beyond the surface, beyond the scrim, and beyond the events.

Feel the space.

When you are ready, you can open your eyes and come back here.

Every time I offer this guided imagery in a group, there are a number of people who find that the deeper sense of themselves is quite different from the events they live. Maybe they lead a busy life and notice a spaciousness deep inside to which they rarely attend. Or maybe their lives look depressed or discouraging but underneath are feelings of energy and vitality.

Prescription

It is helpful to detach from the surface of our lives and find our way to the hilltop, to get lost in the music, to drop out of the trance of ordinary consciousness and look around. If you want to cultivate this ability, here is a simple prescription.

Notice

First, notice the moments when you step out of yourself. We do this all the time, but are generally too busy to notice. So just be aware when it happens.

For example, I was bicycling down the American River bike path the other day. A half hour before, I had received a bunch of annoying emails. I did not answer them right away. As I rode along the river I was mentally conversing with these email messages – I was grousing, cajoling, explaining, arguing.

Suddenly a voice cut through all of it. "Shh. There are deer." Riding toward me was a 10 year old girl with an overgrown blue yamaka of a bike helmet strapped to the crown of her head, strawberry blond hair streaming around her face and an expression that was serious despite the missing front tooth.

I replied quietly, "Okay."

She was gone.

In that instant, I dropped my storyline. The email drama raging in my brain popped like a soap bubble. Suddenly I was just there, a little girl on a blue bicycle disappearing behind me, people up ahead, birds on the power lines, flowers scenting the air, river, and clouds. It was delightful.

When we are out of practice, it may take something dramatic to pull us out of our melodramas. You are sitting at the stop light having a mental exchange with your boss about a long standing trend. A car backfires and startles you into the moment. "Oh, how did I get here?"

But with practice, something as subtle as the movement of a curtain may bring us into the present. Perhaps you are walking down the street lost in tunnel vision and the sound of a bird on the roof top pulls you out of your mental cave.

Whatever the case, the most important thing is to notice these moments as they happen.

Lean

Second, if you want to cultivate spaciousness, then when these moments arise, lean into them. Hang out with them rather than rush back into your thought patterns. Take them as a moments of ordinary grace and savor them.

Repeat

Third, notice what tends to draw you out of your storyline, and do it more often. It might be a stroll by the river, a hike up a hill, folding laundry mindfully, lying in a hammock watching the evening sky. Whatever helps, do a little more of it.

Practice

And finally, if you really feel drawn to this, consider some more formal spiritual practices like meditation, chanting, or prayer. But that's another topic.

Lightness

In closing, let me emphasize that I'm not advocating repression, reframing your life, reinterpreting or doing anything to "improve" your thoughts. I am just suggesting that we take ourselves lightly. Look at your dramas with a sense of humor. Humor makes spiritual awakening easier. We are not our stories. We are not our histories.

Drop your story whenever you can. You don't need it.

Namasté.

Anger

The Buddhist's attitude is to take care of anger. We don't suppress it. We don't run away from it. We just breathe and hold our anger in our arms with utmost tenderness. Becoming angry at your anger only doubles it and makes you suffer more. If you leave it alone, it will be destructive. You will say and do angry things. Also, if you don't say or do angry things, it will still continue to destroy you inwardly. The Buddhist practice is to go back to breathing and to recognize your anger as anger. The important thing is to bring out the awareness of your anger in order to protect and sponsor it. Then the anger is no longer alone. It is with your mindfulness.

Anger is like a closed flower in the morning. As the sun shines on the flower, the flower will bloom, because the sunlight penetrates deeply into the flower. Mindfulness is like that. If you keep breathing and sponsoring your anger, mindfulness particles will infiltrate the anger. When sunshine penetrates a flower, the flower cannot resist. It has to open itself and show its heart to the sun. If you keep breathing on your anger, shining your compassion and understanding on it, your anger will soon crack, and you'll be able to look into its depths and see its roots.

– Thich Nhat Hanh

October 7, 2001

Meditation

Remember a time when you were mad about something. When was it? What were the issues? Who was involved? …

Now shift your attention away from the external circumstances. Remember how it felt. What was it like inside? Breathe into it as Thich Nhat Hanh suggested.

How did it feel in your body? What energies and sensations did you experience? …

Underneath anger, there is usually hurt. Were there ways you felt hurt, or sad, or misunderstood?

Breathe into the hurt. Give it space. …

Underneath hurt, there are almost always some feelings of loneliness, alienation, and disconnection. If we felt completely at one with all of life, how could we ever feel hurt or angry?

See if there is some feeling of aloneness, abandonment, or separation. Breathe into it. … Give it space. …

Dad

Twelve years ago in early January, I got a call from my father. He was living on the Gulf coast at the time and I was in Massachusetts. Typically I heard from him once every 12 to 18 months. He told me he would be vacationing in the Northeast the next summer. "Great," I said. "It will be good to see you." He said he'd call me when he knew specific dates.

In June, I still had not heard from him. I called his home in Texas, but got no answer. I called my sister in New Jersey. "Yes, he is sitting right here at my kitchen table with Lavern." (Lavern was his second wife). When he got on the phone he said, "We'll be up next weekend."

"Good," I said. "I'm working six days a week and most evenings. I can see you this weekend. If you tried to come any other time, I wouldn't be free."

On Wednesday, I got a call from Sturbridge Village: "We'll be there in a few hours."

I was furious. Shortly after he arrived I had to leave for my office in Peterborough, New Hampshire to see clients. We had just a few minutes to make arrangements. He said he would go up to see my brother Charlie (Charlie had no idea he was on the East Coast, but that's another story). Then he'd come back to Groton for supper. That way he could spend time with Erika and my boys even if I could not be there. I told him it was important to me that my kids know their grandfather. He assured us three times that he would be back.

He and Lavern left for Charlie's. I made arrangements to get some free time the next morning to be with him. Erika made a big supper and waited. And waited. And waited.

My father never showed up.

The next morning I called Charlie. "Oh yes, he was here. They said something about staying at the Henniker Inn up here."

I stormed off to work. I told Erika that if he did come back, tell him to stop by my office and have lunch with me.

He showed up at noon. When I got in the car, I wanted to rip his head off. "Where were you!"

"Oh" he said a little puzzled. "I guess we didn't make it." My anger evaporated.

There is a Chinese story about a man rowing across a river in a fog. His boat hits another boat. The man becomes furious and turns on the man in the other boat. Then he sees that the other boat is empty. It was just drifting. The man's anger evaporates.

When my father said, "I guess we didn't make it," I felt as if I was looking at an empty boat. He seemed like an Alzheimer's victim. He had no notion of what he had done. He was a frail, lost child in a burly body. I had been mad at someone but not the confused old man in the car.

Several years later my rage about my childhood emerged from beneath years of hurt and numbness. I smashed a pillow thousands upon thousands of times in therapy to try to release the pent-up tension. One afternoon as the tennis racket hit, the image in my mind suddenly shifted. I stopped seeing my father standing up to the blows or even cowering. He was dead. It was as if I had beaten him to death. My anger vanished. "This is not what I wanted," I thought. It was not a statement of guilt, just acknowledging reality. I didn't want to kill him. I wanted to reach his heart. To break through his armor would require enough force to kill him. "This is not what I want."

Simple

This sermon is the first in a series on anger and compassion. Today, I want to start by focusing on anger.

Displaced anger can be extremely destructive as we see in road rage, domestic abuse, gang violence, and the attack on the World Trade Center. However, in its healthy form, anger is a necessary force in the cycle of life. It can turn religion into spirituality, help nice intentions become passion, and clear impediments to creativity. Rather than suppress anger, we should practice it, let it flow through us until it finds its source, engages life and becomes a "yes!" If I had not been willing to go after my father when I got in the car, I would not have seen so clearly that he was but a frail, lost child in the body of an old man. If I had not been willing to let the rage rip through my arms in therapy as I beat a pillow, I would not have seen as clearly that what I really wanted was to touch his heart. Anger was the force that enlivened the numbness, pushed through my depression and confusion, and helped me see how much I loved him even though he had been far from the ideal parent.

Anger itself is a simple emotion. But how we respond to it can be quite complex. These examples are complicated. So let me step back and look at the role of anger in the cosmic scheme. Then I'd like to look at anger as a simple biological phenomenon that mirrors this spiritual force. And then I'll say a few things about ways it can go out of balance.

Brahma, Vishnu, Shiva

In Hinduism, divinity has three major personifications. There is Brahma the Creator, Vishnu the Sustainer, and Shiva the Destroyer. In Judeo-Christianity we also find these three personifications, though not quite so clearly separated. We have God the Creator of heaven and earth. We have God the loving Father and sustainer of life. And we have the wrathful Jehovah, the destroyer who flooded the earth in Noah's time, incinerated Sodom and Gomorrah, and so forth. We also find Jesus the Creator, the miracle worker and healer who raised Lazarus from the dead. We have Jesus the sustainer who, according to church doctrine, sacrificed his life so we might live in eternity. And we have Jesus the destroyer who threw the money changers out of the temple and condemned stupidity and self-indulgence.

We don't feel the same about these three aspects of sacred energy. We'd like to invite Brahma and Vishnu over for dinner. God the Father and Jesus the sustainer are welcome guests any time. But Shiva the destroyer and the wrathful Jehovah … we'd just as soon that they dropped in at the neighbor's, thank you. In fact, if they didn't ever show up on the street, that would be just fine.

Religious institutions, likewise, have not given these aspects of divinity equal treatment or equal air-time. If you want people to be docile and conform to your will, you don't encourage them to be angry, rebellious destroyers. Anger and sexuality are hard forces to control and direct. So the church has called them bad and sinful and tried to repress them.

But destruction is a necessary part of life's cycle. Imagine what it would be like if nothing ever died. You couldn't eat because eating kills and destroys food. There would be no room on the planet to roller skate, hike, or paint a picture because we'd be piled miles deep in people, woolly mammoths, pterodactyls, baboons, and all the other creatures who never died. The lawn would be too thick to walk through if it weren't over-crowded with 5,000-year-old oak trees, kelp, and herds of bison and bunny rabbits.

Without death and destruction, life is impossible. We need death.

These macrocosmic forces are reflected in our own microcosms. Since we are essentially in harmony with nature, we also embody Brahma, Vishnu, and Shiva. If you are open to yourself as you walk through your day, you will notice times when you feel your Brahma, your inspiration and creativity. Other times you may feel your Vishnu, the part of you that sustains, nurtures, and heals. Other times you feel your Shiva, your irritation, annoyance, frustration, and anger. To be fully alive, we have to be open to all of them.

In fact, these forces are so much a part of us that they are wired into our biology. So let's turn for a few minutes from spirituality to physiology to see how our genetic makeup expresses Shiva and Jehovah.

Triggers

The knee jerk and startle reflexes are wired into our bodies. Anger is a little more complicated, but I think it is also wired in. Like reflexes, it has triggers. Pause for a moment and think about what makes you mad. …

Anger has three kinds of triggers. The most obvious is threat. A lion steps in front of you. The energy rises in your body preparing you to kill it or run to keep it from killing you: fight or flight. After September 11 we may have felt threatened by terrorists – and angry. Anger is a natural reflex.

The threat doesn't have to be to your body. The boss makes a derogatory remark; someone shows excessive interest in your spouse; your child chases a ball into the street without looking; you contract a serious disease. All of these can be experienced as a threat and elicit the fight or flight response.

A second trigger is hurt. Stubbing your toe can hurt. It can also make you mad. Not having a phone call returned can hurt. It can also make you mad. Many felt hurt by the September 11 attacks. It left many angry as well.

In general, we humans have three responses to hurt. If it hurts a little, we feel hurt. If it hurts a lot, we feel anger. If the hurt is overwhelming, we feel shame. These are not rational responses. They are just ways our physiology responds to hurt.

To take it one step further, underneath anger there are almost invariably feelings of hurt. And underneath hurt, there are almost always feelings of separation, alienation, or disconnection. If you felt totally connected with life, what could possibly hurt you or make you angry?

So, anger is a force that rises up inside when we feel hurt or disconnected. It wants to break through some barriers so it can reconnect with life. This is what happened to me with my father. I loved him. I wanted him to feel my love and for me to feel his. But he was a little crazy and alcoholic. I would reach out to him, and he usually could not respond. The hands that reached out in love became fists of anger. I wanted to shake him and get his attention. When that failed, I dropped into a kind of despair. As the despair lifted, the anger reemerged. As the anger reached a fuller expression as in the two incidents I described, I realized that underneath I was not just angry. I was hurt. I wanted to be closer. As I saw that more clearly, I was freed up to look other places for the love that he was unable to give.

In the wake of the terrorists' attacks, wouldn't it be wonderful if the anger and hurt freed us up to feel more connected in a compassionate and realistic way with others who suffer around the world?

So these are two of the triggers for anger: threat and hurt. I think most of us understand these fairly clearly.

Movement

There is a third trigger, which I did not fully appreciate until a few years ago. And I think it is probably the most common trigger for anger. It is having your movement stopped.

Consider: you are driving down a narrow country road on your way to visit a friend. You come around a bend and find a tree has fallen blocking your way. You get out of the car and push the tree, but it's too heavy. You can't seem to budge it. You feel frustrated. You are not feeling threatened or hurt by the tree. You just want it out of your way. You were so looking forward to seeing your friend. The frustration turns to anger. It rises in your body, charging your shoulders and limbs. With one mighty shove, you dislodge the tree enough to slip past. A few minutes later, you are driving down the road again, the anger having subsided as you enjoy the day.

Life is about movement. When your emotions stop moving, you feel dead inside. When your body stops moving completely, you are placed in a coffin. The difference between life and death is movement.

Any time your movement is stopped, you are liable to feel hurt or angry. It does not take something as obvious as a tree across the road to feel stopped. I was a few minutes late leaving the house one morning. I rushed to the car, slid behind the steering wheel, went to put the key in the ignition, and realized I had the wrong keys. "Damn." There was no one to blame. No one had done anything wrong. Anger was not particularly rational. But my momentum had been stopped as I had to get out of the car and go back inside to get the right keys. The physiological response was anger.

Or to give another example, I was on my way to work on a sermon when Erika, my wife, asked me to call the doctor about an appointment for our son Damon. I felt annoyed. I could have said, "No, you do it," but she had done more of the family business and was late for work. I had time. Still, I felt ticked off for a moment because my juices were up for writing, and I felt I had to stop.

This can also be part of our anger at terrorists. Our movement through airports and daily life has been disrupted. That free and easy feeling of movement is stopped.

This trigger for anger is very important to understand: anytime your inward or outward movement is thwarted, you may feel angry. It's a physiological response, not a rational response. If you see this compassionately, then you are not as likely to blame those around you or blame yourself. Erika had done nothing wrong. It was a reasonable request. And there was nothing wrong with me for feeling angry. There was no need for blame or shame. There is nothing that needed to be rationalized, explained, or made meaningful. It was just a biological response to feeling stopped. We do not need to have a culprit to explain or justify anger. Anger is only anger. It is neither good nor bad. Shiva is Shiva.

Pathologies

If anger is such a great, wonderful, natural part of the life force, why do we have so much difficulty with it? One reason I've already suggested: It is hard to control. If you are a bishop or social engineer or politician, you might prefer people to be docile and compliant rather than little Shivas running amuck.

A second reason is that, like anything else, it can go out of balance. Anger is a powerful energy, so when it goes out of balance it can create powerful problems.

Let's look at a few.

Loss of Focus

A series of problems arise when anger loses its focus. Anger is a charge that wants to be directed at a specific object: the tree in the path, the boss who made the cutting remark, the father who was unresponsive, terrorist networks. But what if anger is unable to move the tree? What if you don't want to risk your job by yelling at the boss? What if bombing Afghanistan only makes the world more dangerous? What if your anger is not effective in creating the change you need?

The tension in your body may feel intolerable. So you swear at the tree or kick the dog when you get home from work. The yelling and kicking relieve some of the physical tension. You feel a little better. But it does nothing to resolve the situation. You can kick the dog every night until you kill it, and it does not change your boss one iota. You can get caught in an endless expression of anger that does no good because the anger has lost its focus. Bombing Kabul into cobblestones would only inflame an inflamed world.

To take this one step further, sometimes anger has no clear focus because it is not true anger. It is a disguise for another feeling. There was a woman in one of my groups who, as a child, had been shamed or shunned when she asked for love or support. So feelings of vulnerability left her anxious. However, she was not afraid of feeling angry. So she'd relieve her anxiety by getting mad at me. It was not a conscious decision. She'd just find herself feeling mad at me every time I noticed some of her softer spots. It took me a while to realize what was going on. When she started attacking me, what she really needed was support and reassurance.

So if you find yourself getting angry a lot without it going anywhere, you may want to stop and look inside yourself a little more deeply. This is what Thich Nhat Hanh calls "breathing mindfulness into the heart of your anger." Open your heart to your anger until you can see its roots. Ask yourself, "What else might I be angry about besides the dog or the tree?" If you find yourself over and over fighting with your spouse over money or who gets the good car today, ask yourself, "Is there something else that is bothering me? Is there something that makes me a little anxious that I'd rather not see?"

Rage and Fury

Another way that anger can go out of balance is that it can degenerate into rage or fury. Anger is hot. Rage is cold. Someone who is angry has fire in his or her eyes. Someone who is enraged has ice. Anger is engaged with a specific issue. Rage tends to be disengaged. Often someone who is enraged has eyes that glaze over. It can be very frightening to see because the person is out of contact. The terrorists are extra frightening because they've turned cold. The destructive aspects of the energy are still active, but the focus for the anger has been lost entirely.

The way to relieve rage is to heat it up. Its fire has to be found so it can turn back into anger, find its focus, and come to some kind of resolution. But rage and fury are such frightening, potentially destructive forces, that many people do not know how to work with them compassionately.

Depression

If the rage cools further, the person becomes more and more disengaged. He or she may sink into numbness or depression. The person becomes so cool that he or she feels little if anything. Much depression has suppressed anger at its roots. And if it doesn't, sometimes anger is one of the few energies with enough force to enliven a depressed system and get it going again.

One of the turning points in my depression years ago was when I started to get mad about how bad I felt. Logically it made no sense. But energetically, it made a lot of sense. As I could express that anger, it started to enliven me in other ways. As my anger emerged more fully, I could find the real focus for it.

Conclusion

If you can't say "no" forcefully, then you can't say "yes" meaningfully. If I ask to come into your house and you can't say "no" to me, then saying "yes" means little. It just means that I'm walking over you. But if you can say "no," then saying "yes, come in" means a lot.

So, listen to your anger. Listen deeply if need be. Find its source. Find its focus. Find out how it wants to flow. As anger becomes simpler, more focused, and engaged, the heart flows out behind it. The fist that was raised in a defiant "no" becomes an exuberant "yes." Once you can say "no" forcefully to what you don't want, you can say "yes" powerfully to what you do want. Anger is the destructive part of the Brahma, Vishnu, Shiva cycle. When it becomes fully engaged, anger can clear a deep connection with love and life.

Compassion and Anger

November 4, 2001

I went on my first 10-day meditation retreat twenty-five years ago.

At that time, I was the founder and director of a counseling center for street kids. Part of our program was a drop-in center. We did not open the center until 3:00 in the afternoon because we did not want to encourage the kids to skip school to be with us.

By 2:30 kids started gathering outside our door. They always wanted to come in early, but we were firm about the rules.

The first day back to work after my meditation retreat was typical. Kids gathered noisily. Theresa said she had an urgent message to get to her mother. Could she come in for just a moment to make the call? This seemed a reasonable exception so I allowed her in.

As she started to talk to her mom, I said, "I'll give you some privacy. Just let yourself out when you are done." I left the room.

Ten minutes later I came back. Theresa was yacking on the phone to a friend.

I was pretty mellow after 10 days of meditation. But I noticed a curious feeling of heat rising up from my belly. My face felt warm. I was fascinated to watch the sensations of anger welling up in my body.

At the same time I could see Theresa's life situation. Like many street kids, she came from a rough family. To survive, she had learned how to maneuver and manipulate. To cope she had grown a thick skin and bravado.

I knew that if I just told her quietly that she'd broken our agreement, it would have no effect. She was too tough. To get through to her required more force. The anger welling up in me might do the trick.

So I let the anger come into fruition and yelled at her.

It was a curious sensation. I was not identified with the anger. It was just passing through me like a big, warm shiver. What I actually felt was compassion for this young woman and her difficult life that taught her to be opportunistic.

She looked up at me with shy smile and a twinkle in her eye, as if she'd been seen for the first time in her life. Our eyes connected. There was a moment when we just hung out soul to soul. I wasn't a director and she a delinquent. We were just two beings who happened to be living human lives.

She laughed and said she was sorry – two things that were totally out of character. Then she got up. She usually walked with hard eyes and head erect. But her eyes were down and there was a warm smile on her face.

Common

This sermon is about anger and compassion. In a previous sermon, I spoke about anger, and in a subsequent sermon I will focus on compassion. But in this sermon, I want to look at compassion and anger together.

They seem to conflict with each other. But I want to suggest that they have much in common. And whether you feel aggressive or caring is less important than whether or not you can open your heart to the other person and see the light in their heart.

What are some things common to anger and compassion?

Share Opposites

First, they share an opposite. The inverse of anger is not love; it is indifference. The inverse of compassion is not anger; it is indifference. So anger and compassion are both the opposite of indifference or lack of concern.

Love and Anger in the Body

A second way they are similar is how they move through our bodies physically. I was a body-oriented psychotherapist for many years. Through my training and experience, I became familiar with both these pathways.

Anger usually starts at the base of the pelvis or in the belly. It rises up the back. You can see this in animals as they get their hackles up. It rises up through the shoulders and out the arms into fists or other aggressive gestures. It also rises up the neck into the head and out the eyes and teeth. You can see this as a person's face turns red, eyes become ablaze, and teeth snarl ready to "bite someone's head off."

Not all anger reaches this full expression, but the potential is there.

If you want to block your anger, you can tighten your shoulders, put your hands in your pockets, clamp your teeth shut, and divert your eyes. This is not very satisfying. It can lead to headaches, stiff necks, knotted shoulders, and even nearsightedness (as the eyes are pulled in). As uncomfortable as this is, we all do it sometimes.

Now consider how love moves through the body. It starts in the belly or heart. It rises up the front to the shoulders. From there it moves out the arms in gestures of longing or compassion. It also rises up the neck and flows out eyes that become moist and sparkly. It flows out the lips in a kiss or reaching.

The pathway is almost the same as anger. If the shoulders are knotted, the arms limp, the lips pulled back and the eyes dry, neither love nor anger can flow very easily. Conversely, when someone is expressing something passionately, it may be hard to tell if they are feeling anger or love because they are the same energetic pathways.

I have had clients come to me complaining about suppressed anger. As we enlivened the anger we often discovered pent-up passion and joy. At the outset it is difficult to distinguish between repressed anger and repressed love. They feel the same when they are held back. Freeing up the capacity for anger also frees up the capacity for love, joy, and compassion.

Suffering

A third factor that compassion and anger share is that they both are a response to suffering. Both have roots in suffering.

Let's look at compassion first in this regard.

Without suffering and an awareness of suffering, there is no compassion. Without suffering we can feel love, delight, warmth, and affection. But compassion is a caring reaction to the perception of hurt or the anticipation of hurt. One of the traditional descriptions of compassion is the quivering of the heart in response to suffering. It is an outflowing that wants to heal, soothe, or comfort or at least not let the wounded person be alone in his or her injury. I picture Mother Theresa and her instinct to engage and take in the lepers and outcasts on the streets of Calcutta.

Without suffering and awareness of suffering, there is no anger. In a previous sermon, I went into this in more detail. To summarize briefly, there are three things that can trigger anger.

One is hurt itself. You stub your toe and swear under your breath. Or you hear of a child or woman being abused or a minority being oppressed. You sense their injury and it makes you angry.

A second trigger for anger is threat of pain or suffering.

The third trigger for anger is the pain of frustration, of having your momentum stopped. You are in a hurry to get to work and hit five red lights in a row. You find yourself getting madder and madder.

These things do not always trigger anger. But they can. Underneath anger there is almost always some kind of hurt.

Different Focus

Obviously, anger and compassion are not identical. One of the ways they differ is the object of their focus.

Compassion starts with the perception of pain or the anticipation of suffering. It wants to reach out and care for the sufferer. Anger also starts with the perception of pain or the anticipation of suffering, but it wants to reach out and destroy the source of suffering.

For example, you see a woman in a grocery store yelling at her small child. You see the suffering and want to do something about it. Out of caring you may want to protect the child. Out of anger you may want to confront the mother. Depending on how you go about this, either response can be useful or just cause more problems.

Unity and Duality

Now we come to the core. What makes caring or anger helpful or problematic? Both can be twisted in many different directions. What determines whether they heal or damage does not have a lot to do with whether the urge feels caring or aggressive, soft or powerful. It has everything to do with whether they carry a sense of unity or duality, a sense of oneness or a sense of twoness.

For example, consider our war on terrorism. What concerns me is not that we might be angry at Osama Bin Laden, Al Quaida, or the Taliban. That seems pretty human in reaction to the death and destruction of September 11. What concerns me is our talk of good and evil, right and wrong, black and white. Our rhetoric divides the world into this great duality: you are with us or against us. It is this kind of thinking which encouraged those 19 men to commit crimes against humanity. I feel very uncomfortable with our promoting this kind of dualistic thinking.

Similarly, what concerns me about anger in my family or in my church is not people being upset with each other. That is inevitable from time to time. What concerns me is when I hear dualistic thinking: "he's just selfish" (as if I never am), "she's just incompetent" (as if I always know what I'm doing). In a dualistic response there is a sense of disjoining: "I'm here; she's there." Us and them. The person is an object, an "other."

In a unity or oneness response there is more of a sense of us being in this together. I may not feel *sympathetic*, but I can still be *empathetic*. I'm willing to see myself reflected in the person and the person in me. We may have our differences, but I have not lost touch with all we have in common.

This does not mean that we can't be forceful when appropriate.

My anger at Theresa was forceful. But I was open to her even as I was yelling. In fact, the strength of the anger made me real to her. It actually helped her see that I held her in my heart. For a moment, we joined. There were good boundaries in the psychological sense. And there was a free flow of love between us. It resulted in a breakthrough in our relationship.

Response to Suffering

Let's look more closely at this sense of duality or twoness. Where does it come from?

The natural, biological response to pain is to pull away. You touch a hot iron and your hand jerks away. You don't think about it – it's just a reflex. And a reflex that protects you from further injury.

If the injury is emotional rather than physical, we still have the same instinct. We pull away. Perhaps you had a very close friendship. Then the person said something thoughtless and insulting. You found yourself feeling a little cold toward her or him. You distanced yourself emotionally.

Wired into our animal nature is the instinct to pull away from physical and emotional pain. To be fully human, we have to acknowledge and embrace this aspect.

This pulling away is what creates the sense of separation and duality. It creates language like "good and bad," "righteousness and evil," "black and white."

Separation and Anger

The reason we usually think of anger as more damaging than caring is because it is most often accompanied by pulling away. Even if you attack a person, you emotionally distance them as you get in their face. You make the person into an object: a thing, something separate from you.

The separation can be more hurtful than the emotional charge. This is most obvious with our children.

When our children misbehave, we may get angry and scold them. As with Theresa, the forcefulness may be useful. But most of us are not at ease with anger. The sensation of anger is uncomfortable. We want to pull away. We distance ourselves and distance ourselves from our kids. This can be more painful than the anger itself.

One afternoon a number of years ago I was kicking in the attic of our old home. I was in therapy at the time, trying to loosen up some of the anger I'd held inside for years. One day I had a particularly glorious session lying on a mattress kicking and screaming.

When I got up, I felt energized. I felt good, having freed up some energy. I felt powerful.

As I came down the stairs, my son, Damon, greeted me at the door. He was four years old at the time. At first I pulled my power inside. I didn't want to scare him. Then I thought better of it. I bared my teeth, made my hands into claws, looked him straight in the eyes, and growled loudly.

He was startled and taken back. But he just looked at me looking at him. Then he bared his teeth, made his hands into claws, and growled back.

Then he wanted to know what I was doing upstairs. So we went up, and I showed him. He wanted to try it. So we took turns lying down, kicking and screaming while the other person beat one of my hand drums.

Don't assume that it is the bigness or power of your energy that scares your kids. More often it is the pulling away that hurts.

The same is true with adults. When a friend gets mad at you, would you rather he or she pull away and not tell you or be up front and direct? Most often we'd like to know. Yet, when we get angry, we may mistakenly think we are doing the person a favor by being silent.

In fact, one of our most potent means of punishment is social isolation, for example shunning in Mennonite communities.

Separation and Caring

What may not be as obvious is that distancing and duality can also creep into caring. In this case it is not true compassion but an imposter like pity.

Let me give an obvious example. Let's say you come across a homeless person. He is a little dirty and pungent. You feel bad for him. You'd like to help, but you instinctively pull away. So you try to help, but it's what I call "dirty diaper" caring. You keep him at arm's length and figuratively hold your nose. You quickly give him a few dollars or work at Loaves and Fishes. But you are really acting more out of pity than compassion.

Pity may be better than self-righteous rejection or indifference. But it is not compassion because of the distancing.

You aren't to be condemned – you may be doing the best you can. And it may be of some help. But it's not true compassion because of the tight heart.

Most of us don't really want another person's pity. Pity can hurt.

Compassion

Even though our biological instinct may be to separate ourselves from pain, we are also capable of a different response. Another part of our human-spiritual essence is the urge to reach out toward injury, to soothe or heal a wound. This is the true compassion that I want to speak about more in a subsequent sermon. The healthy human heart actually moves toward suffering in a caring way. We don't seek suffering, but neither do we turn away from it when it arises.

Sometimes this requires more courage than flying a plane into a building. Sometimes we struggle between the urge to close and protect our hearts from discomfort and the urge to open them no matter what. The spiritual task is to throw away the cloak of indifference and allow the suffering to touch us deeply. When we let suffering touch that deep stillness inside us, true compassion arises.

Summary

To summarize, anger can be accompanied by a sense of joining, in which case it feels more like passion. Or it can be accompanied by distancing, in which case it feels more like rage or fury or loneliness. Caring can be a joining, in which case it is compassion. Or it can be distancing, in which case it becomes pity or disgust. In both anger and caring, the issue is the quality of your heart or how much you can let the other in.

Kabir, the 16th century ecstatic poet, put it this way, "Never put a person out of your heart. Yell at them, scream at them, throw them out of the house. Do what you have to do. But don't put them out of your heart."

Compassion

November 11, 2001

In his book, *Who Dies?*,[1] Stephen Levine described a woman, Ann. She was camping on the Oregon coast with her husband and two kids. She was cooking supper by the tent while the two kids played in the surf nearby. The children were yelling and laughing and squealing.

Then the voices stopped. The parents looked up. They could see their son, but not their daughter. They ran down to the water. They searched and searched, but couldn't find her. They called the police for help, but she was gone.

Three days later Ann got a call from the coroner's office. A body had been found that might be her daughter. Could she come down and identify it?

At the morgue, the body was covered by a white sheet. The coroner took hold of one end of the sheet, then looked up at the woman. "I should warn you," he said. "This child was attacked by a shark."

Then he pulled back the sheet revealing the half eaten remains of her daughter.

The intensity of that moment was more than Ann would have thought she could survive. Her mind was blown. Her heart was ripped asunder.

Later, Ann said that she was confronted with not just the loss of her daughter. Flashing before her eyes was every moment she had ever turned from her child, not appreciated her, or been cold to anyone she loved.

Her life was permanently changed. It was as if her heart was torn open and she was never able to close it afterward. After surviving that moment, she no longer felt the need to protect her heart from anything. She had experienced the worst.

In the years that followed she lived with more presence, more patience, and more compassion.

There was a touch of grace in the moment. You could not find any teacher anywhere who could show the importance of love and compassion more than that moment. We'd never wish it on anyone. But you can see that there is grace in suffering when we are open to it.

Most of life's difficulties are not of this magnitude. The hurts and disappointments are usually milder. Usually we are not overwhelmed. We can shut them off if we want. We live in a society that encourages us to distance ourselves from suffering. But if we want more compassion in our lives, we must open as best we can to whatever suffering comes our way.

This morning I want to talk about cultivating compassion. This is the third sermon in this series on anger and compassion. Previously, I described how both anger and compassion arise out of suffering. Anger starts with the experience or anticipation of hurt and wants to reach out and destroy the source of hurt. Compassion starts with the experience or anticipation of hurt and wants to reach out and soothe the wound or the wounded.

What is important is not whether the urge to reach out is aggressive or caring, forceful or gentle, powerful or soft. What is most important is whether there is a sense of two-ness or oneness, a sense of separation or connection.

It's easy enough to feel a sense of oneness when life is great. It's difficult to maintain that when confronted with pain. The power of compassion comes from the ability to keep our hearts open even in the midst of hurt.

As you listened to Ann's story, you could probably feel some of the impact of her pain. If you let it in, you felt your compassion soften and open. If you could not, or chose not to, you probably felt a little cold.

---

[1] Stephen Levine, *Who Dies? An Investigation of Conscious Living and Conscious Dying.* (Anchor Book, Garden City, New York). 1982, pp. 86-87.

Suffering

To cultivate compassion, we open not only to suffering itself but to people who suffer. And since everyone suffers to one degree or another, this means seeing how everyone is worthy of compassion.

So, how do you see people? Charlie Brown once said, "I love humanity. It's people I can't stand." With some people it is easy to stay open to their hurt. With others, it's very difficult.

Let's skip over the easy ones and focus on the most difficult people. These are the ones whose suffering causes them to get angry at you or to assault you.

When the Chinese invaded Tibet, the soldiers destroyed temples and ancient manuscripts; they murdered monks, nuns, women, children, and old men. They jailed and tortured people and did many unspeakable things. The Dalai Lama barely escaped with his life.

When asked how he felt toward the Chinese invaders, the Dalai Lama responded, "When I think about those soldiers, I imagine what must be inside them in order to commit such terrible acts. They must be filled with coldness and bitterness. Such painful hearts. How could I feel anything but compassion for them?"

In the eyes of compassion, there is no such thing as a bad person. Just unconscious people. In Paul's first letter to the people at Corinth, he said, "We see in a mirror dimly." We don't see clearly. We have our blind spots. We are not fully conscious. Out of our blindness and distortion we may not act clearly. We may do terrible things. We all carry a bit of the Chinese soldier in us.

But at our core, there is no such thing as a bad person. We are all here on earth doing the best we can with the limitations of our understanding. Ultimately, everyone is worthy of compassion.

First Task

I have had some wonderful training in this over the years.

When I was a psychotherapist and new clients came to me, I knew my first task was to love them genuinely. Not in a sentimental, ignore-their-faults, spacey acceptance. But to be able to hold them in my heart in a real way.

Sometimes this was not all that easy. Sometimes the first work I did with them was aimed less at the problem they presented and more at helping me see through a mean or rough exterior. I knew that if I could not find a way to honestly care about them, I'd have to refer them to another therapist.

I always managed to do it. Sometimes, like with Theresa whom I mentioned in a previous sermon (p. 25), I had to be very forceful. But I never found a person in whom there was not something to love.

As a minister, I carry the same intention. I fail sometimes, but that is my failing, not a problem with the other person's essence. I still have not found a bad person.

You may remember Diogenes, the ancient Greek who went around with a lamp trying unsuccessfully to find an honest man. I've had a different kind of experience over the years. I feel that I've held up a lamp and looked into the eyes of many people. I have not been able to find any unworthy of respect.

There have been times when I began to doubt. There have been times when I wanted to say to someone, "Is it nature or nurture? Were you born a jerk or did you have to work hard to become one?" Occasionally I have even said something like that.

But more often, the power of grace saved me. Before the words came out of my mouth, the person would come to me and say, "Look. I have to talk to you about something. My mother is very sick, but she's not admitting it to me or even to herself. It is driving me nuts trying to figure out what to do."

One of the privileges of being a therapist and a minister is that people are a little more apt to share their vulnerability than if I were a pizza maker, telemarketer, or dentist. Many times, just when I was ready to nail someone, he or she would tell me this heartrending situation they carried silently.

My heart would melt. I'd see their jerky behavior in a whole new context. We'd talk about their mother, how they felt about it, how it was affecting them. Then I'd say, "The other day I saw you yell at Ralph. I couldn't understand why you did that. Now I see. You've been a little crazy worrying about your mother's condition."

"Yeah, you're right," he'd say. "I guess I was pretty hard on Ralph."

Then we could talk about his abusiveness and how to deal with it. I wouldn't get so sentimental that I'd condone destructive behavior. I'd confront him. But I wouldn't separate myself from him in the process. We'd be in it together.

I recognize that there is a bit of the Chinese soldier in me – a place that can get self-righteous, indignant, and justify my saying or doing hurtful things. But the Theresas and others have taught me that while there are actions to be condemned, there are no people to be condemned. That's why I'm a Universalist. It is just that with some people I have needed a little more patience to see below the surface.

Namasté

Years ago I fell into a practice of closing sermons with a word, "*namasté*." It is a Sanskrit word used in India as a word of greeting and parting. It translates roughly, "I honor the light within you." Rather than acknowledge the personality or shallow layers in a person, namasté invites you to look to that deeper essence. As a practice, you can say this silently as you meet or part from someone. It reminds you that there is a deeper essence that is worthy of love and invites you to look for that.

I close with that line from Kabir that I shared last week: "Never put a person out of your heart. Do what you have to do. Yell at them, scream at them, throw them out of the house. But never put them out of your heart."

If you truly want to deepen your compassion, then take this vow: "I'll do whatever I can not to put someone out of my heart."

"I'll cultivate the patience that allows me to see something of worth in each person."

That is the practice of namasté.

I honor the light within you. Namasté.

Spirituality of Despair

January 6, 2002

A few years ago Tom Toles created a cartoon for the *Buffalo News*. It depicted a lawyer's office. Several people sat expectantly as the lawyer read a will. The will went as follows:

Dear kids,

We, the generation in power since World War II, seem to have used up pretty much everything ourselves. We kind of drained all the resources out of our manufacturing industries, so there's not much left there. The beautiful old buildings that were built to last for centuries, we tore down and replaced with characterless but inexpensive structures, and you can have them. Except everything we built has a lifespan about the same as ours, so, like the interstate highway system we built, they're all falling apart now and you'll have to deal with that. We used up as much of our natural resources as we could, without providing for renewable ones, so you're probably only good until about a week from Thursday. We did build a generous Social Security and pension system, but that was just for us. In fact, the only really durable things we built were toxic dumps. You can have those. So think of your inheritance as a challenge. The challenge of starting from scratch. You can begin as soon as – oh, one last thing – as soon as you pay off the two trillion dollar debt we left you.

Signed, Your Parents[2]

Some people might consider this an optimistic assessment of what we are leaving behind. Consider:

• Every day, about 75 species become extinct. That's about 3 species during the service this morning. This is 100 to 1,000 times the normal rate of extinction. This die off rate is the highest in 65 million years, when the dinosaurs were lost. Some scientists believe it is the highest rate ever. We're leaving our kids shrinking biodiversity.

• Last October was the warmest October ever recorded worldwide. A massive piece of the Antarctic shelf broke off – the biggest ever seen. Each of the last six years has been warmer than the one before. Politicians argue about global warming, but the scientific community agrees it is real. We're leaving our kids a warming planet with unpredictable changes in climate.

• Holes in the ozone are growing and will continue to grow for quite a few years. Already, sheep are going blind in Australia from solar radiation coming through.

• Deforestation. Desertification. Population growth.

• And I have not even mentioned the nuclear bomb and other means of willful mass destruction. September 11 brought home how vulnerable we are to terrorists. Instruments to destroy us are increasingly available to small groups.

By many, many reasonable scenarios, we could be the last generation of humans. Not only are we leaving no inheritance for our kids, but it is also as if we have strapped them into the back seat of the car, released the hand brake and allowed the car to roll downhill toward a cliff.

Despair

What does it feel like to listen to me speak this way?

A month ago I was listening to our Forum speaker outline some of the dangers of current U.S. foreign policy. I found myself getting angrier and angrier with him. Then I realized that I actually agreed with him. But I didn't want to hear it.

So, maybe some of you listening to me are feeling annoyed: "Happy New Year to you, too! I came for uplift, not depression." Or maybe you feel angry with the agents of disaster: corporate polluters, ignorant politicians, and so on.

Or maybe as you listen you feel a sinking sensation in your belly. You feel your spirits sink into a lugubrious lump in your stomach.

---

[2] Thanks to Joanna Macy for this passage and many of the ideas expressed in this sermon. See Joanna Macy, *World as Lover: World as Self.* (Berkeley, California: Parallax Press, 1991).

Or maybe you find a kind of white noise in your mind: a mental numbing. Or maybe you find yourself deliberately trying to think about other things.

In short, you may feel one of the many manifestations of despair.

Take a breath. Whatever you may be feeling, let's just let out a collective sigh. Let your feelings be whatever they may be, and, at the same time, let your shoulders soften and breathe. It's okay.

Holding Energy

This morning I want to talk about holding the energy of despair. "Holding the energy" may be a new phrase to some of you. If you had some disturbing feelings arise around my opening remarks and were able to relax and just be with the disturbance, then you were holding the energy of these states. You weren't trying to push them away, make them more meaningful, or anything else. You were just open to them.

Holding the energy is easier with positive experiences. If you've just heard some exquisite music or had a bite of delicious pie, sometimes you savor it. You don't talk about it, try to analyze, or understand why it is so wonderful. For a few minutes you just let yourself be with the experience. "Ah."

Holding the energy is similar to savoring, but the experience may not be pleasant. You don't grab the experience and milk it for all it's worth. You don't obsess over it or punish yourself. You just relax and open to it. "Ah. Despair."

Last spring, I delivered a sermon called "A Teaspoon of Salt." The metaphor was of a spoon of salt. If you stir it into a glass of water, it makes the water so bitter you can hardly tolerate it. But if you stir it into a ten-gallon cistern, you hardly notice the salt.

Life has its bitterness, its hurts, grief, and despair. Holding the energy means expanding so you can be with the unpleasant in a relaxed and potentially creative frame of mind.

Touched with Despair

Holding the energy of despair is a very important skill to cultivate for a number of reasons.

First of all, we live in a world touched with despair. The first line of our covenant says we want "open minds, open hearts, and helping hands." You can't be open and helping in our world without experiencing some pain about it.

Over the years that I did psychotherapy, I worked with a number of suicidal clients. When someone is suicidal, it is difficult to evaluate precisely how great the risk. But even if I thought the potential was small, it weighed on me. The consequences of misjudging were so irreversible.

Similarly, we are bombarded with signals of planetary distress. It is difficult to know how great the risk truly is. But even if the likelihood of any disaster is small, the consequences are so great. The possibilities lurk on the edges of our awareness. They weigh on us, if only unconsciously.

Joanna Macy defines despair as "the loss of the assumption that the species will inevitably pull through." She goes on to say that despair "represents a genuine accession to the possibility that this planetary experiment will end, the curtain rung down, the show over."[3]

I actually remain optimistic about our possibilities, despite all I've said. I'll get to this some other Sunday. But I don't think any of us can say that "the species will *inevitably* pull through." This leaves us with some measure of despair.

Numb and Dumb

The second reason it is important to learn how to hold the energy of despair is that the alternative leaves us numb and dumb. The way our society encourages us to ignore despair leaves us exhausted and uncreative: numb and dumb.

Despair is not mentioned in polite society. It's death to a political career. It is taboo, the way grief once was. We live in the land of Norman Vincent Peale and Dale Carnegie. Unflagging optimism is the official religion. Despair is a sinful loss of faith in the power of positive thinking.

We also hate despair because it signifies a loss of control. During the Viet Nam war,

---
[3] Ibid., p. 17

Lyndon B. Johnson said, "Don't come to me with problems unless you have a solution." We want to be on top of things or at least have a quick fix.

But the issues we are trying to wrestle with are too large and complex for quick fixes or simple answers. You can't go out in the morning and say, "I'm going to fix global warming," and come back that night, dust off your hands and say, "I took care of that beast."

If we are to bring any intelligence and creativity to these large issues, we have to be able to tolerate the feelings they elicit in us. If we can't tolerate the feelings, they will drive us more or less mindlessly. We end up shutting down emotionally. The roses don't smell as good. The kids' laughter is less charming. The world turns a little grey. And we lose creative potential. We become numb and dumb.

Any suppressed feelings will find some other outlet. This may be why disaster movies are so popular. Earthquakes, rampaging sharks, asteroids and aliens from outer space, blazing skyscrapers with terrified people, and more draw huge crowds and profits. The despair buried in our psyches looks for some expression.

The same suppressed despair may also drive our frenetic lifestyles. We become too exhausted to feel anything and too busy to think about much beyond dinner and soccer practice.

Waiting

The third reason it is important to hold the energy of despair is that it brings us out of being numb and dumb. We fear that we will sink into a dark bottomless pit of dread. But the reality is that creativity and energy emerge.

Gandhi exemplified this. A group of Indian political activists went to him and asked if he would lead the campaign to rid India of British colonial rule. Gandhi said he would. The activists said, "Great. So, what do we do next?"

Gandhi said, "Well, I don't know. I'll have to meditate on it."

Gandhi retreated into an ashram. A few days later, the activists came to him. "So, Mahatma G., what's the plan?" Gandhi said, "I don't know. I haven't heard it."

They came back a week later. "I'm still meditating," he said. The activists started to go a little nuts.

Two weeks later, he still didn't have an idea.

Three weeks later, people began to seriously doubt his leadership. But he just sat for three months holding the energy of the situation, waiting patiently in the discomfort.

Then it came to him. He was going to illegally mine salt by scooping up the salt deposits on the beaches.

This morning is not the time to go into all the detail of the salt march. Suffice it to say England was one of the most powerful nations in the world at that time. His nonviolent campaign broke their hold and drove them out.

Today, we are in a comparable position. But rather than the British oppressively occupying India, we have humanity oppressively occupying the planet. And rather than one person going off to find a strategy to save us all, we need groups of people willing to sit with all of it.

And by "sit," I don't mean sit in a dumb stupor in front of the TV set. I'm sure Gandhi did not spend those three months playing pinochle and reading romance novels. We need to sit with an open mind and heart about the difficulties. We need to be willing to sit quietly and feel all these realities in our bodies and psyches. We need to be willing to share our responses with others. We need to be willing to not have the whole answer.

Out of this waiting can arise a new consciousness that may well be the saving grace of humanity. I'll come back to this in a moment.

Process

The fourth reason it is important to hold the energy of despair is that despair is truly not a single state. It is a process. It is similar to grief in many ways. We know grief is a multifaceted process that can have many expressions besides sadness. Grief can go through phases of denial, anger, regret, and depression before resolving into a peaceful and sometimes poignant acceptance of loss.

Despair is also a dynamic process that can take the form of denial, numbness, malaise, anger, irritability, frenetic pace, worry, fretfulness, helplessness, and hopelessness. And if we are not open to the despair, it stays locked in these uncomfortable forms: it drifts between denial, worry, hopelessness, and frenzy.

But if we are open to it, if we are patient and willing to feel and acknowledge what happens inside us, we move toward an acceptance which releases creativity and more energetic engagement.

There are two ways that despair is different from grief. First, grief is usually about a single person's loss. Collective despair is about the loss of large numbers of people if not the human race itself. This makes collective despair that much more powerful and overwhelming.

Second, grief is about a loss that *has already* occurred. Despair is about a loss that *might* occur in the future. Grief may resolve into acceptance of what has happened. Despair may move into an acceptance of what could happen. But since it has not happened yet, despair can move past acceptance to creative engagement.

When we make peace with our possible loss, the result is a newfound commitment and energy to do whatever is in our power to heal the problem.

Birthing a New Consciousness

And this brings us to the fifth reason it is so important to be able to hold the energy of despair. "Holding" does not mean "holding still." It means giving ourselves over to this process of despair: letting go and letting it work on us. The pain of despair turns out to be a kind of birthing pain for a new consciousness that could save us all. While grief resolves into a psychological understanding, despair resolves into a spiritual consciousness with new possibilities for all of us. And this "new" consciousness has been described by spiritual masters for centuries: compassion, selflessness, detachment, and creativity.

At the core of despair is compassion. The pain you feel is not for your life but for the lives of other, and indeed of future generations. This, by definition, is compassion: empathy for others.

At the core, collective despair identifies less with your separate organism and more with humanity or all of life. Your sense of identity shifts away from preoccupation with your particular life and toward a more selfless identification with all life.

At the core, despair teaches detachment. As the despair moves into phases of acceptance and creative engagement, you learn how to act with less assurance about the outcome. The planetary issues are so complex that you can't know the effect your actions have. You do what is in your power to do and then relax.

So, as the salt of despair spreads out into the larger container, it births a way of being that has more compassion, selflessness, detachment, and creativity.

Not Everyone

Not everyone can tolerate the dark aspects of despair. Not everyone can hold the energy of it. And that's okay. We just need a few more people doing it to help nudge the planet along.

So let me close with a few words from Christopher Reed. On the surface he's talking about ecology. But underneath you can feel this new-old consciousness emerging:

> *None of us can do everything alone. Focus on what you come into direct contact with: what you buy, what you eat, and what you throw away. Recycle everything you can – there's no such thing as trash. Live as simply as you can, and talk to people about what you know. Give what you can in time and money where you feel it will be most effective, without attachment to results. Write to whomever you can, in government and industry; tell them how you feel. Be kind. Live your life for the wellbeing of the planet and all the creatures in it.*
>
> *Do some reading from the literature, join a few groups. Breathe. Smile, you have saved the world, for the moment.*[4]

---

[4] From "Down to Earth," as printed in *Dharma Gaia*, Allan Hunt Badiner, editor (Berkeley, California Parallax Press, 1990).

Fire Unbound by Longing

I laugh when I hear the fish in the sea are thirsty.
— Kabir

October 6, 2002

Imagine a piece of key lime pie sitting in your refrigerator. Or if that is not your favorite, when I say "pie" substitute something else that you really love: Häagen-Dazs ice cream, a chocolate truffle, mint cookies, whatever.

It's been a long day. You're hungry. You've been thinking about that pie and looking forward to it. Now you are home and you really want it. You put your hand on the refrigerator handle and think, "On no, what if someone ate it!" You open the door: "Ahh, yes! There it is." Your desire is overwhelming. You hold the pie in your hand, so it won't get away as you look for a fork. You raise a piece to your mouth. You close your lips around it. Sweet sensations burst through your mouth. Your mind stops. Ahh! This is heaven. This is the peace that passes all understanding. This is nirvana.

If you are like me, that ecstasy lasts two or three seconds. The sensations fade ever so slightly. You think, "Boy, this is great. I want more." You stab for a second piece. The bliss of the second bite only lasts one second. By the third, the ecstasy is gone. But it is still pleasant as you gobble down the rest.

What causes that moment of ecstasy with the first bite? What creates that instant of total happiness?

Any fool will tell you, "I was happy because I got what I wanted. I was hankering for the pie all day. When I finally got it, it made me happy."

In our quest for happiness, we have built lifestyles, economic systems, and an entire culture around this philosophy: "Getting what I want makes me happy." We have become proficient at satisfying desires: pies, ice cream, hot tubs, designer clothes, luxury cars, evenings at the theater, varieties of chocolate, 300 cable TV channels, beds with personalized comfort settings, vacation packages, books, music, and on and on and on. Our technologies for producing comforts surpass anything the earth has ever seen. We are the Gods on Mount Olympus — the envy of the world.

But are we really happy? Most people spend more time earning money to buy the good life than they do enjoying it. Crime and violence abound. We worry about letting our kids roam free and unattended in the neighborhood. Teenage suicide. Alcoholism. Domestic violence. Some level of depression affects 75% of the population. Diffuse anxiety. You know the statistics.

I have traveled a little in India. I do not envy them their poverty. But I cannot say that they are less happy than we here in America with all our comforts.

So what's the matter up here on Mount Olympus? How come it doesn't feel like heaven? Maybe our analysis is wrong. Maybe the fool was foolish when he said, "Getting what I want makes me happy."

Let's take a closer look at this key lime pie. What's really going on?

Longing for the pie all day is not happiness. It is an experience of hunger or grasping. It is not pleasant. In fact, it is so unpleasant that we try to take our mind off the actual experience. Instead we fantasize what it might be like to have the pie: "Sweet anticipation" we call it. This takes our awareness off the unpleasantness of the moment. This is unfortunate because without awareness, there is no wisdom. Without wisdom there is no way to deal with the discomfort of the moment other than fantasy. So in America we have a whole entertainment industry – TV, movies, radio, books, magazines, and more – to keep us distracted.

So wanting the pie is not pleasant. But what about that first bite? Certainly that is genuine contentment.

I think it is. But if you look closely, you see that during those few seconds, the desire evaporates. You no longer want the pie, because now you have it. It is not having the pie that creates the happiness. It is the absence of desire that feels wonderful. Furthermore, the taste sensations are so strong that the mind stops thinking for a moment. We cannot think and experience in the same instant. So with strong sensations, the mind stills. There is no wanting. No holding. No grasping. Just blissful savoring.

We on Mount Olympus confuse having what we want with not wanting. Since we are deeply conditioned to believe that getting what we want brings happiness, we don't notice the absence of desire. As soon as the peace of the moment fades, we leap back into the desire, "Boy, I want another bite," and another and another.

Most of us are sophisticated enough to realize that material items don't give us the deepest wellbeing. So rather than just collect stuff, we collect experiences. We think that the road to happiness is collecting as many pleasant experiences as we can. So after tasting the pie, we have a glass of wine. Then watch a little TV or go to a good movie. Then, let's soak in the hot tub for a while. Then we'll listen to music, have sex, read a good book, go for a nice walk, take in a play. Yum, yum, yum. We leap from desire to desire and from comfort to comfort until we are exhausted, frantic, and dying from stress-induced diseases.

No Charge

Ascetics and some fundamentalists from many different religious persuasions have figured out that worldly comforts do not bring lasting happiness. So they push these things away. But many of these folks seem kind of grim. On the whole, they don't look that much happier either. So avoiding stuff does not seem to be the entire answer.

Let's look at that ecstatic moment a little more. Notice that the first bite has no charge. There is no positive charge in the sense of grasping. And there is no negative charge in the sense of pushing the experience away. You are just savoring. There is no charge to it at all. And it is lovely.

So surprisingly, the deepest happiness arises in moments that have no charge. It seems like a paradox. It is very difficult to find language to describe a moment that is both neutral and contented. But all the great spiritual traditions do their best.

Jesus said heaven is all around us if we can just open our eyes and ears and see it. Huh? How can it be all around us without it being obvious? It is perplexing. Heaven on earth is not obvious to most people because it has no charge.

In the East it is described as "empty" or "void." But it is an ecstatic void. It's all around us. We don't have to earn it, create it, or manufacture it. But it is ineffable, because it has no charge.

Imagine a class of two dozen kids. Twenty-three of them are laughing and joking or fighting and yelling. One is sitting quietly and contentedly. You probably won't even notice her because of the rowdiness all around.

That is what it is like with the moments of our lives. Most of them have a charge: we are working, pushing, trying to get finished, avoiding, holding on to what we love, fighting what we dislike. There are quiet moments of happiness sprinkled throughout. But we don't notice them because they do not attract our attention.

This morning I refer to this as "the mind like fire unbound by longing." The phrase is a translation of the term *nirvana*. Students of Buddhism tell us nirvana literally means "extinguish," as in extinguish a fire. It sounds as if nirvana means ceasing to exist, like a fire doused with water.

But a scholar, Thanissaro Bhikkhu, explains that the Buddha was referring to something more simple and ordinary. Ancients did not understand combustion the way we do. They had a different theory. In the Buddha's time fire was thought to permeate everything. It was the force of life itself. But it was normally invisible. However, if the fire became grasping it would burst into flame as it clung to a piece of wood or straw. When the fire extinguished, it simply let go. It did not cease to exist. It just spread out to become part of everything: "fire unbound by longing or grasping."

So nirvana is a state of nongrasping and non-pushing. It can be high energy or peaceful, but there is no longing in it.

Lao Tzu called it *Tao*. "The Tao that can be grasped is not the true Tao." It has no charge.

There is nothing to hold onto. Yet it is everywhere.

The ecstatic poet Kabir wrote, "I laugh when I hear the fish in the sea are thirsty." Tao is as present to us as water is to a fish.

So what I am suggesting is that nirvana, Tao, or heaven on earth is right here. They sound so esoteric, yet are quite accessible. And we do access them in those few seconds of the first bite of pie or the momentary absorption into a piece of music. But we slide right through them because there is nothing to hold onto. What we can hold onto – the pie or the music – is not it. "The Tao that can be grasped is not the true Tao."

Fools Rush In

This is probably the most audacious sermon I have ever tried to deliver. I'm trying to describe nirvana, heaven, and the Tao. Fools rush in where wiser folks remain silent. So let me rush ahead.

How can we experience more of this joy that Jesus, Buddha, Saint Francis of Assisi, Lao Tzu, Kabir, and others say surrounds and permeates life?

To go back to the classroom analogy, if we can quiet down the noisy kids, the quiet, contented ones will be easier to notice.

A Quaker elder once described meditation as settling a litter of puppies. One puppy sticks its head up to yap. So you stroke its head, and it settles back down. Another sticks its head up. You pat it until it lies back down. You keep doing this until they are all asleep.

Prayer, meditation, contemplation, and other spiritual disciplines help quiet the noisy puppies in the classroom enough to notice the subtle wellbeing.

Banana

For the last twenty-five years I have pursued some of these disciplines. There have been times when I've been able to spread an ecstatic moment over an hour or more.

I was on a ten-day retreat a number of years ago. It had been difficult. I had been agitated physically, mentally, and emotionally. I was discouraged. But seeing no alternative, I stayed with the practice as best as I could.

At 5:30 on the sixth morning I sat down on my meditation cushion. Surprisingly, my mind settled. Barely a whisper went through my mind. Twenty minutes later I thought, "This is great!" But the thought just evaporated into that unbound spaciousness. Thirty minutes later another thought arose. But it, too, disintegrated into a pervasive wellbeing. At 7 a.m. the gong announced breakfast. Everyone got up and went to the dining room.

I remained on my cushion, feeling content to just sit. About 10 minutes later, I shifted to a walking meditation. Rather than turning left to the dining room, I went right to go outside.

The sun was just rising. The sky was indigo. The air was crisp and fresh. The whole world was conspiring to keep me in bliss.

I went back inside. Still in a walking meditation I entered the dining room.

I noticed a banana peel on someone's plate. The food at the center was prepared to support the meditation – it was as undistracting as possible. I love bananas. Unfortunately, they usually ran out of them. I was at least 20 minutes late.

I looked across the dining hall. The serving tables were at the far end. I couldn't tell if there were any bananas left.

Outwardly I still walked with the serenity of an Appalachian mountain. But inside I was ducking and dodging and trying to cut ahead to get to the serving table as quickly as possible.

To this day I cannot remember what happened next. I remember looking across the room at all the people between the serving table and me. The next thing I remember is sitting at a table. A bowl of cereal was in front of me, a half a banana was in my hand, and a half a banana was in my mouth.

I thought, "I just traded enlightenment for a banana."

A few years later one of my teachers, Larry Rosenberg, described a similar experience. He had been meditating in his room. He had gone into a peaceful state that he had been trying to access all his life. Then the bell rang for dinner.

The next thing he remembers was standing in the dinner line with a plate in his hand.

My point is that, yes, these contemplative practices can help us learn to notice these elusive moments that are all around us. They can quiet the puppies enough so we can be with them a little longer. This can be very helpful because it grounds us in our true nature. It strengthens our faith in what is possible. And the states themselves are quite healing.

But …

Even if you meditate two hours a day, you still have twenty-two hours when you are doing something else: pushing, pulling, seeking what you want, avoiding what you don't want, distracting yourself. So if you spend 8% of your time letting go and 92% of your time holding on, what do you get? Holding on.

If we really want to be more conscious of that fire unbound by longing, we need to do something with the other 22 hours of the day when we are out interacting with people, raising our families, earning a living, and all the rest. Otherwise the momentum of our restlessness will overrun the quietness. We will be thirsty fish in the sea.

There is a set of ancient techniques that have been used in daily life for thousands of years to overcome the basic grasping habits of the mind. You will find these same techniques in all traditions: Christianity, Hinduism, Judaism, Confucianism, Buddhism, Islam, Taoism, Humanism, Native American spirituality – across the board.

And they work. They work by cultivating spaciousness, energy, stillness, and the absence of charge in how we interact with people and the world at large.

These techniques generally are called "virtue" or "moral character." They include kindness, generosity, gentle strength, forgiveness, patience, courage, compassion, and truthfulness.

The morality I'm speaking about has nothing to do with self-righteousness and everything to do with a mind like fire unbound by longing.

Next week I want to pick up at this point when I speak about morality and consciousness.

Negative Spaces

Let me close by suggesting that we just notice those quiet, joyful moments. Know that they are there all the time and watch for them. The classroom may be noisy. But, if you know there is a quiet child, you may be able to see her. Your mind may feel like a bunch of drunken monkeys stung by bees. But there is space between the monkeys, if you think to look for it.

I studied for three years with a wonderful sculptor named Alan. The first thing he taught me was to notice negative space. I remember carving a boxer out of a tree stump. Alan had me pay attention not just to the shape of the arm and head and body, but also to the shape of the space between the arms and the body and the head and the shoulders. These negative spaces are essential to pleasing art.

In great music, the sound is important. But as important are the rests, all the silent places between the sounds.

Life is filled with these spaces. Life is like Swiss cheese with mostly holes and little cheese. But we mostly look at the formed curd, not the spaces around it.

But once you know to look for these spaces, you begin to notice. No matter what else is going on, fire unbound by longing is there as well – maybe right next to the longing that so readily grabs our attention. Just notice those spaces.

My favorite part of the Sunday service is those few moments before the sermon. Years ago I decided to take a few moments when I step into the pulpit: settle my notes, sip some water if needed, gather myself, and just notice who is here.

As I did this, I found that we were all just here in a quiet space. People were waiting patiently for me to start. We were just here. Nothing going on. And it is exquisite.

I just love those moments.

Then I start talking and everything goes downhill from there.

If I have anything valuable to convey, the deeper message is not in the words. It is in the spaces between the words. In good living, fulfillment is in the spaces between the doing.

Sermons need words. Life needs doing. But the joy comes forth in the spaces in between.

The joy permeates everything, but becomes more noticeable in the spaces.

If you notice, you can even feel it now. …

And now…

Namasté.

Consciousness and Morality

October 13, 2002

A number of years ago Erika, my wife, and I went to visit her mother for a weekend. On Saturday afternoon Jenny came into the living room. Jenny was a beagle who had been part of the family for many years. Jenny's tail was between her legs. She crawled more than walked, her chin dragged the ground, and her eyes overflowed with guilt.

Erika's brother, Ben, went to see if she had knocked over the garbage, peed on the rug, or chewed on a shoe. He found nothing amiss. But Jenny was still whimpering. So he looked upstairs. He found nothing. He looked outside. He found nothing. After 30 or 45 minutes, he still had found no sign of a transgression. Jenny was lying on the floor with her legs up.

So out of great compassion, Ben leaned over and said, "Bad dog," as he swatted her lightly on the head. Jenny yelped and ran out of the room.

Two minutes later she bounced back in with her tail wagging and her eyes sparkling.

We never found out what she had done. But she was happy that the punishment had restored her to good graces within the family.

As children many of us were taught that morality is a kind of dog and master relationship. We humans are not dogs, but we are moral adolescents in this school called "earth." Morality is the school's code of conduct. And God is an infinitely perfect vice-principal in charge of discipline. If we hope to graduate, we have to stay reasonably within the rules and within the good graces of the divine authority.

If we break the rules, a wrathful Jehovah will lean over and smite us upon our heads. A more dignified God on High might merely scold us. The gentler Heavenly Father gives us a look of painful disappointment. But whatever the case, being immoral breaks our relationship with the divine. To restore it, we must confess, be absolved, do penitence, stay for detention, or something to get back in good graces.

Beyond the Vice-Principal

In this sermon, I want to speak about morality, consciousness, and grace. However, I will not be talking about an infinitely perfect vice-principal. That is a developmentally young understanding of God and morality even though many adults still subscribe to it.

A more sophisticated understanding sees moral behavior as inherently fulfilling.

To develop this theme I want to say three things: (1) There is a kind of grace – a subtle and profound sense of wellbeing – that is always available to us no matter who we are or what we do. It's here right now. (2) Our deepest human instinct is to treat each other with kindness, generosity, courage, compassion, patience and truthfulness. (3) When we treat each other this way, our minds and hearts settle and make it easier to notice this grace that's been here under our noses all along. To quote Donovan: "You can have it all if you let yourself be. Why? O, because."

In a previous sermon ("Fire Unbound by Longing," pp. 35-38), I lay out the background for this topic. Let me summarize the major points. The topic is subtle and elusive enough that it might be worthwhile to pick up a few essential elements from before.

Elusive, Ever-present Bliss

Heaven on earth, the Tao, and nirvana sound esoteric and as if they have nothing to do with the daily experience of ordinary souls like you or me. But, in fact, these states are quite accessible to all of us. And most of us do stumble into them, if only fleetingly.

For example, during the first few seconds of savoring your favorite dessert, during a moment of absorption into the Barber Adagio for Strings, during a moment of sexual ecstasy, during a moment of being overcome by the beauty of a sunset, we may experience something that is hard to put into words. The mind stops. There is no thinking, no grasping, and no aversion, just this ecstatic delight.

The next moment, confusion sets in. The few seconds of joy were so wonderful that we want to hold onto them or repeat them. But grasping that ecstasy is like grasping a soap bubble – it is beautiful to behold, but as soon as we try to grab it, it pops, leaving the sting of soap in our eye.

Bliss is elusive. We cannot hold or grasp it. What we can grasp is the dessert, the music, our sexual partner, or the view of the sunset. So we get more food, buy more CDs, seek more sex, or build a house on the mountaintop. These might be pleasant. But they don't have the wonderful delight of those first few seconds of savoring.

While we cannot hold this joy, all the mystical traditions say that it is always available to us. There is nothing we have to do first in order to experience it. It permeates all existence. Since it is always here, we cannot create it. Any pleasantness that we try to create will not be it because the deepest wellbeing cannot be created. It doesn't need to be created. It is always here.

No Charge

If this joy is always here, why don't we know it more?

Heaven on earth, the Tao, and nirvana have no charge. There is nothing about them that draws our attention. In a previous sermon, I used the analogy of a classroom of 23 rowdy kids and one kid who sits quietly and peacefully. She is always there, but you may not notice her in all the hubbub.

Consider another analogy from perceptual psychology. There are ganglia – bunches of nerves – in the back of the eye that respond only to visual contrast. So if we try to look at a completely blank wall, we'll find it hard to focus. The eye will look for edges or imperfections in the wall to focus on. There is nothing in blankness that draws our attention.

Similarly, this deep wellbeing, as wonderful as it is, paradoxically has nothing to draw our attention.

In Christianity, the language used for this is "grace." Divine grace is not something we can go out and find or buy or earn like a piece of pie or a CD. It's not a service God gives us when we are good. Grace surrounds us all the time. The only thing we can do is open up and receive it.

We can't storm the gates of heaven because there are no gates to keep us out. Whatever we try to enter will not be heaven. All we can do is learn to relax and notice this subtle joy that imbues every moment.

Cultivation

With this background, we can shift into the heart of the topic for this morning. If this deepest joy is always here and always elusive, how can we receive more of it? We can't grasp it. We can't earn it. Is there anything we can do to open ourselves to it?

The answer is "yes." The way to do this is to cultivate a mind that has as little tension as possible. Energy and excitement are fine. But tension, grasping, aversion, fear, striving, and so forth make it difficult to notice the elusive delight that surrounds us.

What is the greatest source of disturbance to the mind and heart? It is disturbance in our relationships. We are intensely relational creatures.

Relational

I was talking about this with my son, Nathan, a few years ago. He was taking a course from Brown University on the Anthropology of Religion. The question came up, "What is a human being apart from cultural context?" We all know that we are affected by our cultural surroundings, families, and relationships. What if we could strip off the effects of this conditioning? What if we could remove all the layers of learning and get down to the essence of pure human nature unaltered by what we learn from others? What would the pure human essence be?

Someone observed that Homo erectus, Australopithecus, and other pre-human ancestors lived in small hunting bands. They had communication, learning, and simple elements of culture. These pre-humans had brains half the size of ours.

Think about the implications: Half the evolution of the human brain took place in the context of culture and relationships. Evolutionary processes wired relationships into us. The organism we are today has no idea what it would be like to not have relationships. An infant cannot survive without interaction.

So the question, "What is a pure human without the effects of relationships?" is completely spurious. What is most profoundly human in us does not come into existence without culture. The notion of a completely independent being is a total fiction. Just as a single bee or ant cannot survive for long without the colony, we humans exist only because of a sea of interactions with other humans.

Because of this, there is little that gets to the average person more than the quality of his or her connections. Even when we are alone, most of our inner agitation has to do with relationships: unfinished conversations, old hurts, anticipated encounters, and so forth.

So almost all spiritual traditions say that if we want peace in the core of our being, we have to deal with relationships. The foundation of spirituality is how we treat one another. If we interact with harshness, anger, revenge, vindictiveness, cowardice, lying, and stealing, we'll carry a huge charge of tension, grasping, and aversion. The subtleness of Tao will be beyond us. The classroom will be just too noisy to notice the quiet one.

But if we cultivate patience, courage, kindness, truthfulness, generosity, compassion, and forgiveness, the mind tends to cool off. The tensions release. There is less grasping. It is easier to be receptive to the grace of wellbeing.

These latter qualities are generally lumped under the heading of "virtue" or "moral character."

Complexity of Lying

Let me share a few examples of what I mean.

A divorced friend of mine had a son who had been living with his father. As the son got into his adolescence, his grades began to drop, he started dabbling in drugs, and he lied about everything. Then he began to get into trouble with the law. It got so bad that plans were made to send him to a school for delinquent kids. She knew this would be disastrous.

So, she persuaded everyone to have him come live with her.

When he moved in she told him, "There is just one thing I ask of you. If you'll abide by this, I think we can work everything else out. You have to tell me the truth."

This broke open a long conversation about what it had been like for the boy to lie all the time. He said it made life extremely complicated. He had to remember which story and which version of each story he had told which people. It caused a lot of inner turmoil just keeping it all straight.

So the problem with lying is not that you'll displease a petty God. The problem is it creates a lot of charge inside: fear of getting caught, fear of the lies unraveling. The more charge, the more tension and the more difficult it is to notice joy and bliss that surround us.

The moral precept of speaking the truth is not a matter of technical truthfulness that can stand up in a court of law or survive the vice-principal's lie detector. It's a matter of cooling out the mind.

If you speak only the truth – no lies, no dissembling, no half-truths, no white lies, no misleading silences – then you have nothing to keep track of. You don't have to remember what you told anyone because you always speak the truth. If speaking the truth would violate a confidence, then you just say, "I can't tell you because that would violate a confidence."

The moment you walk away from a conversation, you can forget what you said. You don't have to keep it in your mind. That leaves more spaciousness inside and more room to notice that ease and wellbeing all around us.

Falling off the Cushion

Or consider another example.

There was a man in a meditation retreat a few years ago who could not stay on his cushion. Every time he tried to meditate he became so agitated that he literally fell off.

We later found out that the Canadian Mounted Police wanted him for larceny, embezzlement and kidnapping. Every time he closed his eyes he pictured the police bursting through the doors to get him. He wanted to develop a deeper sense of equanimity, but it was impossible because his unethical behavior was so disturbing to him.

Inherent

Similarly, if you look through your life at times when you were not kind, generous, truthful, patient, and the rest, I think you'll see that it left a little discomfort inside. It left a charge that lingers with you.

Notice that I am not saying that being good is a way of earning favors from God, as if there is some divine power scrutinizing our actions. And I am not even saying that moral behavior inherently feels good, like a drink of cool water when you are thirsty.

I'm saying that the joy and wellbeing are already all around us. There is nothing we have to do and nothing we can do to bring them to us because they are already here. All we can do is cool out inside so it becomes easier to receive that grace which is inherent in life.

In another sermon, I want to take this one step further. If morality is the foundation of spirituality, then generosity – generosity of spirit – is the foundation of morality. I will talk about "Freeing the Monkey," generosity, and ask you to consider some ways of cultivating more generosity among us.

Closing

To close, let me note from the pulpit that our country's leaders seem to be hell bent on raining fire down and smiting Iraq. To me it seems like using a rusty hunting knife to remove a tiny splinter: It may do the job but it creates more damage than it heals.

You may find this deeply disturbing. I certainly do. I find myself feeling disbelief, anger, frustration, and grief.

We are intensely relational creatures. When we quiet down inside enough to open up to those places of peace, we also feel what is going on around us. To intentionally harm someone is deeply disturbing. To stand by silently and do nothing while harm is coming to another is deeply disturbing. Our basic sense of morality says that we should not be visiting harm on others unless all other options have been thoroughly explored.

So this raises the age-old debate, "Are spirituality and religion about how we treat one another?" or "Is spirituality about developing some personal peace and fulfillment?"

The answer to both questions is "yes" because they are inseparable.

Relating to others in deeply ethical ways leads to peace and contentment. And the path to peace and contentment motivates us to relate more ethically to others. Caring for others out of a sense of self-denial doesn't work. Caring for yourself while ignoring others around you does not work either.

So take care of yourself by caring for others wisely. And care for others wisely for yourself.

Namasté.

Forgiving Ourselves

January 5, 2003

Jill and Brian were so happy about the pregnancy. Together they went to checkups and childbirth classes. At four months, they had painted and furnished the little room that would be a nursery. At five months, they had settled on a midwife. At six months, Jill left her elementary teaching position to rest and prepare for the birth. At seven months, Brian was okayed to take a month and a half of paternity leave when the baby arrived.

Jill was in labor a little longer than anticipated. But everything went well. They named the baby Sara Jeanne.

Unfortunately, Sara Jeanne cried a lot. They fed her, changed her diapers, and she cried. They snuggled her and sang to her and still she cried. The doctor and midwife diagnosed colic. They made suggestions, but nothing helped. The baby cried.

Jill and Brian's mood shifted from joy to worry to frantic concern to despair. Their dream of a baby was turning into a nightmare. And still, colicky Sara Jeanne cried.

Finally, Brian was so depressed and exhausted that he said to Jill, "I've had it. I can't take it any more. I'm going to close myself in the bedroom and sleep for a few hours. I don't know what you are going to do. But I'm going to sleep."

Jill went and lay down on the carpet in the middle of the living room with the crying baby on top of her. She felt like a complete failure. She was flunking the thing she cared most about and had a crying baby to prove it. Tears began to slide down her cheeks. She was too exhausted to help little Sara or resist her own feelings. She let down into deep sadness and sobbed uncontrollably.

The effect was miraculous. As Jill relaxed into the sadness in her body, the baby relaxed as well. As Jill started crying, the baby stopped crying and fell asleep. A few hours later when Brian woke, he found them both sleeping sweetly in the middle of the living room.

This is the first Sunday of the new year. The new year is usually represented by a newborn baby. I hope 2003 does not start colicky. The new year is also a time of New Year's resolutions. But I think forgiveness of past misdeeds is a far more effective way to change than steely determination to do better.

So this morning I want to talk about forgiveness. It can feel as miraculous as a colicky baby relaxing and falling asleep. It can be as restorative as a long overdue nap. It can feel as refreshing as a cloud of despair suddenly clearing.

Yet forgiveness is complicated. The term is used to refer to two different processes. One is forgiving ourselves for the bad things we have done to others and to ourselves. The other is forgiving those who have done bad things to us. Until we have let down enough to forgive ourselves, we will not have the depth to forgive others in a meaningful way. So I'll leave that topic for next week and focus this morning on forgiving ourselves.

Cycle

Forgiving ourselves is part of a cycle of guilt and forgiveness that can involve our whole body: hands, feet, head, gut, and heart. The cycle starts symbolically with our hands and feet. This is to say we do something we should not have done or walked away from something we should have done.

From there, it goes into our head: we have thoughts about what we did. We have judgments about our actions. Our thoughts might be skillful discernment or unskillful condemnation. But one way or another we evaluate our behavior.

From there, the cycle goes to our gut. We have feelings such as remorse, guilt, shame, or regret.

If the process leads to genuine forgiveness, sooner or later it moves into our heart. We hold our thoughts and feelings in our heart. We let them be whatever they are as we just observe. We are present. With time, there is a sense of release. This is the core of self-forgiveness.

From this core, the process flows back out to the gut and head: our mood shifts and our thoughts become less condemning and more understanding. And finally, the process might move out to the hands, as we do what we can to correct our misdeeds, or resolve to never do it again.

So this is the cycle: from the hands and feet to the head and gut to the heart and back out to the head and gut and hands. Let's talk through this process and look at each phase in more detail.

Hands and Feet

The cycle of guilt and forgiveness often starts with our hands and feet. It starts with something we have done or walked away from without doing. What is important is not some metaphysical or philosophical code of right and wrong. What is important is our own personal values. We have all done things large and small that conflict with our own values.

The old adage says, "It is the truth that makes us free." And the truth is that, intentionally or unintentionally and with malice or goodness in all our hearts, we have all done things we wish we hadn't.

Perhaps you fudged on your taxes. You said you *had* to work late when the truth was you *wanted* to work late. You stayed silent when you knew speaking up would get you in trouble. You "borrowed" something without asking first. You wished someone ill.

What are some of the bad things you or someone around you has done?

Notice that intentions count. There is a difference between intentionally and unintentionally doing wrong. Yet we can judge ourselves or feel guilt even when we do something unintentionally. Actions count as well as intentions.

Head

The cycle of guilt and forgiveness next moves to the head. We are reflective creatures. We have thoughts about what we did or didn't do. This discernment is important. It deepens our self-understanding and guides our future actions.

However, sometimes our minds get overly enthusiastic. Sometimes they move from discernment to judgment to condemnation. A dispassionate discerning becomes an emotional critiquing. "I did something bad" becomes a global "I am bad."

I suspect all of us are quite familiar with this judging mind. It is universal. In fact, it can be an object of meditation. You may be familiar with the practice of counting breaths. Similarly, you can also count judgments. You notice the thought, "I don't like that racket." Judgment one. "It's bad of me to judge like that." Judgment two. "I'm pretty good at this counting business." Judgment three. And so forth.

Through this practice you can become more conscious of judgments, appreciate how automatically a mind can append an opinion to any experience.

In general, it is usually more skillful to observe the mind's judging rather than try to curb it. First of all, sometimes the judgments are true and objective. They can be helpful. Secondly, even when the judgment is not objective, thoughts are only thoughts. Rather than make too big a deal of them, it is wiser to develop a sense of humor and just notice. Then the judgments lose their power to drive us into action. We are freer to choose to follow or ignore them.

Gut

From the head, the guilt-forgiveness cycle next moves to the gut. We see that we have done something to hurt someone and we feel remorse or guilt.

I am not of the school of thought that says we should never feel guilt. I do not believe that it is necessarily bad to feel bad. Not all guilt is an emotional disease. Sometimes it is a healthy response we can embrace. If someone is hurt by our doing something, it is natural for us to feel remorse. There are terms for people who never feel guilt. We call them sociopaths and psychopaths. So if you feel guilt, you can be thankful that you are not a sociopath.

However, sometimes we feel guilt without a precipitating action or thought. Sometimes the guilt-forgiveness cycle actually begins in the gut. I have Catholic friends who can feel guilty without doing anything bad. There is a story about a woman who gave her son two ties. The next time he visited her, he wore one. She greeted him with, "So, I see you didn't like the other tie." Some people feel guilty no matter what they do.

The old Catholic and Calvinist doctrine of original sin says that we are bad for being born – we are born in sin. Unitarians and Universalists rejected this idea – we are born pure and wholesome. But emotional conditioning can run deeper than beliefs.

Gut level guilt can also be the aftermath of emotional trauma. I had a client, Paul, who never had a best friend while growing up. His first real buddy was a guy he met in the army in Viet Nam. Late one morning, they hopped a ride on an American tank as they came back from patrol in the bush. After riding for fifteen minutes, they switched places. A few moments later, a Viet Cong rocket hit the tank were Paul had been sitting and where his buddy was now sitting. His buddy was blown to pieces, his head landing in Paul's lap. Paul spent three months in the hospital and many months beyond recovering from the physical wounds. But 20 years later, he still felt emotional wounds. He felt guilty for surviving when his best friend died. Objectively, Paul had done nothing wrong. But still he felt guilt and needed forgiveness.

Jill and Brian felt guilty about little Sara Jeanne. Their intentions were pure. Their actions were informed. But still, they felt so bad that they began to think they were bad. They needed self-forgiveness, though they had done nothing wrong.

Some people try to treat irrational guilt with rational thought. They would remind my Catholic friend, Paul, Jill, and Brian that they had done nothing wrong. Occasionally, this actually helps. But mostly it does not. If the guilt were rational, reason might have more effect. But often we can't be talked out of it. Or even worse, we feel guilty for feeling guilty. What we need is a deeper process of self-forgiveness.

Heart

The guilt-forgiveness cycle eventually enters the heart. Without the heart there is no healing. When I say "heart," I mean looking at our actions, thoughts, and feelings in an open, accepting way. We don't try to cover them, change them, or make them better or worse. We just see them as they are.

This is what Jill did in the middle of the living room.

Jill thought that if she were an adequate mother, she could comfort her daughter. She couldn't. In her fatigue and despair she felt she must be doing something bad. She had been so focused on taking care of her infant, that she was not even fully aware of the self-condemnation in her mind or the despair in her body. Most people are not adequately aware of their bodies.

It may sound strange to say that Jill lay down and opened her heart. After all, she didn't say, "I need to love myself more. I need more compassion and self acceptance." She did not have a moment of emotional or spiritual clarity. Rather, out of physical, emotional, and spiritual exhaustion, she gave in. She accepted that she thought she was a terrible mother. She had no energy left to resist her thought or despair. She had no energy left to *try* to do anything. She relaxed into her body and felt the grief in it. She sobbed deeply. The tension drained out of her.

This is the essence of giving in to the heart: letting ourselves be with whatever we experience in our bodies.

Meanwhile, the baby had been tense with colic and tense with over-eager parents. All that the baby really needed was for them to stop trying so hard and just be. She didn't need them to be anything particular, just to be who they were.

As Jill let down, Sara Jeanne could feel this. She was able to relax and fall asleep despite the colic.

This is what forgiveness is like. We accept what we've done, thought, and felt. We stop trying to change anything. We stop trying to have a better past and just accept things as they are. This doesn't mean that we feel better right away. Forgiveness sometimes takes time and patience.

But gradually, the heart is able to sort out our actions and intentions. Gradually, the heart can sort out the discernment from the condemnation. Gradually, the heart can sort out the irrational guilt from the natural remorse. This leads to the alchemy of release. We call this forgiveness.

Outflowing

The cycle of guilt and forgiveness does not always end the heart. It may flow back out to the gut and allow it to relax. It may flow out to the head where old habitual judging loses its power. And it may flow to the hands, which take corrective action if appropriate.

This outflowing of forgiveness helps you reflect objectively on past actions. You see why you acted the way you did. You see your weaknesses and know better how not to get caught by them in the future.

Thich Nhat Hanh is a monk from Viet Nam. He tells of an American soldier who became enraged at villagers who harbored Viet Cong who had killed his friends. So he made some cookies with explosives in them and left them along the road for children.

Many years later, the retired soldier carried a debilitating guilt at the harm he probably caused innocent children. Thich Nhat Hanh asked rhetorically if there was anything he could do to correct his past actions. The soldier said there was not: it was too long ago and too far away. Thich Nhat Hanh did not condemn him or try to talk him out of his remorse, but said he might use it more skillfully. Letting it destroy his life did nothing to help the children and compounded the tragedy. But he could use it to motivate himself to live more consciously and compassionately. There are plenty of sick, injured, and neglected children in the world. Maybe he could use his remorse to help some of them.

The man followed this advice. He will probably never be without the remorse. But as he engaged to do some good in the world, the cloud that had covered his heart for decades began to dissipate. Helping others was part of this man's self-forgiveness.

You may not have done something as extreme as making exploding cookies. But we have all done things to injure others. Remorse teaches us by focusing our attention. Is there something you can do to correct the wrong? If so, it is wise to do it. If not, let it become an intention to not repeat the harmful action. We come out humbler and wiser and more conscious.

New Year's Resolution

I raise the topic of self-forgiveness today because this is the first Sunday of 2003. It is a time of New Year's resolutions. Resolutions are intentions to behave differently.

As we've seen, intentions are part of the cycle of guilt and forgiveness. But they are only about 5% of the process. They are just the tail end. Most New Year's resolutions are feeble and ineffective because they are the tail trying to wag the dog. They don't do 95% of the work. They rely on will power rather than going through the whole process of self-forgiveness.

So, if you make a New Year's resolution to keep better control of your temper or to manage your money better or to get more exercise or spend more time with your family, you might want to pause and reflect on what motivated you to make that resolution in the first place.

Consider your hands and feet: what have you done or not done in the past that relates to this resolution? Consider your head: what thoughts and judgments do you have about those actions? Consider your gut: how do you feel about all this? Remember your heart: take it all into your heart and sit patiently with an open awareness.

Rather than make New Year's resolutions, we might start with old year forgiveness. Resolve that comes out of the heart of forgiveness is vastly more powerful than resolve that comes out of will power.

Forgiveness Meditation

Let's close with some words from Jack Kornfield. These mediations can be repeated as often as you need. You might want to close your eyes now and follow along. Say to yourself:

> *There are many ways that I have hurt and harmed others, have betrayed or abandoned them, caused them suffering, knowingly or unknowingly, out of my pain, fear, anger, and confusion.*
>
> *Let yourself remember and visualize the ways you have hurt others. See the pain you have*

caused out of your own fear and confusion. Feel your own sorrow and regret. Sense that finally you can release this burden and ask for forgiveness. Take as much time as you need to picture each memory that still burdens your heart. And then as each person comes to mind, gently say:

I ask for your forgiveness, I ask for your forgiveness …

Just as I have caused suffering to others, there are many ways that I have hurt and harmed myself. I have betrayed or abandoned myself many times in thought, word, or deed, knowingly or unknowingly.

Feel your own precious body and life. Let yourself see the ways you have hurt or harmed yourself. Picture them, remember them. Feel the sorrow you have carried from this and sense that you can release these burdens. Extend forgiveness for each act of harm, one by one. Repeat to yourself:

For the ways I have hurt myself through action or inaction, out of fear, pain, and confusion, I now extend full and heartful forgiveness. I forgive myself, I forgive myself.[5]

Closing Words

The person whose love you need most is your own. To love yourself does not mean that all the things you did or didn't do are okay. It just means that you forgive yourself. Forgiveness performs an alchemy whereby remorse is transmuted into wisdom.

May it be so.

---

[5] Jack Kornfield, *The Art of Forgiveness, Lovingkindness, and Peace.* (Bantam Books, 2002). pp. 49-50.

Forgiving Others

January 12, 2003

Ashrams provide a simplified life. You don't have to put a lot of energy into daily decisions because a schedule makes most of these for you. You don't have to put energy into worldly distractions because most of those are removed. Your energies are freed up to focus on spiritual matters.

Several decades ago, Ram Dass observed that prisons simplify a person's life. The prisoner doesn't have to put energy into daily decisions because most are made for him. He doesn't have to put energy into worldly distractions because most are removed.

What if a prisoner wanted to use this simplification to look inward and cultivate spiritual freedom rather than just sit around and wait for external freedom?

Ram Dass started the Prison Ashram Project. For inmates who genuinely wanted to use their incarceration for spiritual practice, the Project provided literature, letters, face-to-face counseling, and support for turning their prison cell into an ashram cell.

When I first heard Ram Dass describe this project, he concluded, "If all the prisoners think they are in an ashram, the only people left in prison are the guards."

This morning I want to talk about forgiveness as a kind of key that can let us out of an internal prison.

All of us have done bad things. Last week I spoke about forgiving ourselves for the harm we have caused others and ourselves.

Just as we have all done bad things, others have done bad things to us. We have all been injured emotionally and physically by other people's malice or confusion. If we can't forgive them, then we are like guards locked inside our own prisons.

But forgiving others is not always easy. So let's address a few different questions: (1) What is the relationship between forgiveness and spiritual freedom? (2) What is the difference between forgiving and condoning? (3) And finally, what can we do to cultivate forgiveness?

Freedom and Forgiveness

Let me start with spiritual freedom and forgiveness.

The essence of spiritual maturity is an inner consciousness, which is often called "freedom" or "liberation." Our hearts and minds become unfettered and spacious. In theistic traditions, this is achieved by surrender to God. We let go of our self-centeredness and egocentrism and expand into a will larger than our own.

In non-theistic traditions, we let go into a less-defined spaciousness. The emphasis is more on the release itself and less on what we are released into. Rather then surrender to God, we surrender into love, emptiness, or nirvana. Actually "surrender into nirvana" is redundant because nirvana literally means "unclinging." It's like saying we "uncling into unclinging."

The opposite of being with God or nirvana is grasping, holding and attachment. We all have places where we grasp, hold, or attach. One of the times we do this is when we are injured. If you break your arm, the muscles around the break freeze and hold the bones in place. When hurt emotionally, our minds and hearts tend to tighten, grasp, and hold.

Spiritual maturation is about moving from a state of holding and grasping to a state of release and freedom. Forgiving others is a very potent practice that supports this maturation.

For example, let's say someone insults you. It hurts. You hold this against them. If the person cares about you, your grudge may cause them pain. Both of you are in prison. You are the jailer. The key to freedom is forgiveness. You hold this key in your hands (or heart). But both of you are in prison if you don't use that key.

On the other hand, maybe the person feels remorse, but doesn't cling to guilt. They are sorry, but aren't weighed down by shame. At the same time you harbor resentment. They are free but you are still in prison. Or maybe they don't know you felt insulted. Or maybe they know but don't really care. Your bitterness may or may not confine them. But it definitely confines you. It keeps your heart dense, heavy, and enclosed.

Sometime we don't think we are holding grudges. We say we are just interested in justice, fairness, or accountability. "An eye for an eye, a tooth for a tooth." "She made her bed, let her lie in it." We can come up with religious or philosophical justifications to not forgive. Our prisons become elaborate – plate glass, steel bars, electric locks, and alligators in the moat. And we are prison guards wearing clerical collars and balls and chains.

Conversely, when we forgive, we let go of these complicated thoughts and feelings. Our internal life becomes simpler and less burdened. We are liberated.

Forgiving versus Condoning

This brings us to the second question: Forgiveness is wonderful in theory, but aren't some acts unforgivable?

There are people who have been raped. There are people who have had a friend or relative injured or killed by malicious acts. There are people who have been robbed by someone unrepentant. How can we forgive such action?

The answer lies in the difference between forgiving and forgetting. There is an old phrase, "forgive and forget." It is an oxymoron. Forgiving is not the same as forgetting and forgetting is not forgiving. Let's say I tell someone something in confidence, and she lets it slip out. I feel betrayed. She says, "Forgive me." If I say, "Forget it," I have not necessarily forgiven her. I've just said, "Let's pretend it never happened and speak no more about it." I might even say, "Forget it," because I don't want to forgive. I'm holding offense.

On the other hand, if I genuinely say, "I forgive you," I am acknowledging that the injury happened. I am not saying I am forgetting it. I might be more careful about what I tell her in the future. But I am saying that I am not holding ill will. I have released it.

When I was working as a psychotherapist, I worked with a number of incest survivors: women who as children had been raped repeatedly by their father or another relative.

When they learned that I was a minister as well as a therapist, they invariably asked, "Do I have to forgive him?"

My short answer was, "Absolutely not." I answered this way because they were usually asking, "Do I have to forget what he did to me? Do I have to pretend it never happened?" Many had already spent years trying unsuccessfully to forget it and pretend it didn't happen.

After we had talked about the difference between forgiving and forgetting, I could give my long answer: "You don't have to forgive him ever. However, if you work on the issues deeply enough, one day you may find that you have forgiven him."

Think about some of the worst things people have done to you …

Forgiving is not forgetting. It is not saying that what they did was okay. It wasn't. Forgiving is not condoning.

You can forgive and still confront the person. You can forgive and still hold people accountable. You can forgive and still remain vigilant to prevent it from ever happening again.

However, forgiving does not require that you confront the person. It doesn't require you to act as if it didn't happen. It doesn't even require you to ever see the person again.

Forgiveness is just a release. Jack Kornfield wrote, "Forgiveness is giving up the hope of ever having a better past."

Wherever there is lack of forgiveness there is holding onto the past. There is a measure of resentment or bitterness that weighs on the heart. Letting go of the hope of changing the past lets go of that weight and allows you to settle into the present. You don't have to forget. You just accept that it was what it was.

Cultivating Forgiveness

This brings me to the third question: how to cultivate forgiveness. Sometimes you'd like to forgive someone but can't find it in your heart. You'd like to be free of that bitterness, but can't force yourself. What can you do?

First of all, I would commend you for your wisdom. Forgiveness cannot be forced. The pretense of forgiveness can be manufactured. But real forgiveness is not an act of will or intention.

Once, a farmer was so eager to help his crops grow that he went out into the fields every night and pulled on the young shoots. Forgiveness can't be forced. It can be cultivated like anything organic. But force doesn't help.

The seed wants to grow into a sprout. The sprout wants to grow into a mature plant. The human heart wants to forgive. Its natural state is open and caring. But buried under rocks, deprived of rain and sunlight, planted in infertile soil, it has difficulty doing what is natural. So there are things we can do to cultivate forgiveness. But even in the best conditions, it takes time and patience. It doesn't help to pull the shoots.

So, if you find yourself unable to forgive, rather than try to force it, you may want to see if there are things you can do to cultivate it. Last week in talking about self-forgiveness, I spoke about the hands, head, gut, and heart: that is actions, thoughts, emotions, and compassion. These same areas apply to forgiving others. The heart can take care of itself. That leaves the hands, the head, and the gut or actions, thoughts, and feelings. We can look in these areas to see if they are providing a good environment for forgiveness to take root and grow.

Hands

If you cannot forgive someone, the first thing you might want to ask yourself is, "Is there something I need to do about this?"

For example, if someone makes a joke at your expense in public or borrows something without returning it, you may find you can't forgive them. You have a lingering resentment you can't shake. This resentment serves a purpose. It helps you guard against letting it happen again.

If the person expresses regret or asks for forgiveness, it is easier to believe it won't happen again. It is easier to let down your guard and forgive.

If they don't express regret, then you may want to be more proactive. You may want to confront them, hold them accountable, remove yourself from the situation, or take some other steps to reduce the likelihood that you'll get hurt or taken advantage of again. Once you've done this, it is easier to let go of the situation, easier to release the bitterness, and easier for forgiveness to grow.

Head

Sometimes there is nothing you can do. You still feel unforgiving. You may want to look into the head. What are your thoughts about this person? Have you demonized them? Do you see them as something other than fully human?

If a tree falls down on your house, you probably don't go out in the yard and shake your finger at it. "What are you doing falling on my house? Don't you see what a mess this is making for me? Get off of there right now or I will never forgive you."

Somehow with acts of nature, we are more accepting. We may not like them, but we don't get into blame and demonizing.

But if people do not behave the way we think they should, there is hell to pay.

And yet, if we really understand the pain and suffering someone has gone through, I don't think we blame them in the same way. We see that they were acting in a way congruent to their inner and outer circumstances.

It can be helpful to develop an empathetic understanding of why the person did what they did. What are their injuries and hurts? Most predators were once victims themselves. This doesn't make their actions okay. But it does mean they are only human.

Gut

Perhaps there is nothing for you to do. Perhaps you have a sympathetic understanding of a person's psychology. And still you don't find forgiveness in your heart. In this case, it can be helpful to look into your gut. The most persistent blocks to forgiveness are often in our feelings. Anger, grief. and fear may cloud or encase the heart. These deep feelings may require sensitive, heartful. and courageous attention.

Betsy was an ex-prostitute who came to me for help. When she was little, her father and brother had both raped her repeatedly over a number of years. She remembered a woodshed where they took her. She tried to fight them off, but she was too weak and they were too strong.

Twenty-five years later, her father was dead and her brother was no longer in her life. But I could see in her body that she was still fighting them. There was a kind of bracing, rigidity, and coldness.

When the time was right, I said to her gently, "They got to you. They really got to you. You were too little to stop them. But now they are gone. It need not ever happen again. It is safe to feel it now. But they got to you."

Her eyes closed, as if she were immersed in the memory. Her body went rigid, as if she were little trying to resist them. Suddenly she began screaming, "I'm not a dirty person. I'm not a dirty person." Her life as a little girl and her life as a prostitute flashed before my eyes as she kept screaming, "I'm not a dirty person." Tears streamed down my face.

Then she collapsed into heartbreaking sobs. They had broken her heart in a deep and violent way. At last she could let herself feel the depth of that.

In the weeks and months that followed, the rigidity in her body began to soften. There was more color in her skin and softness in her eyes. She was beginning to reclaim the life force that had been taken from her as a small child. That force had been walled off in her heart.

She never forgave her father or brother in the sense of saying that what they did was okay. It just wasn't. But she did forgive them in the sense of being able to let go of hoping to have a better childhood. It was what it was.

This freed her up to look more heartfully at what she wanted to do with the remainder of her life. She didn't have to fight them any more. She forgave them in the sense of releasing the hold they had over her.

All of us have been injured. For some the wounds had more to do with abandonment than abuse. Some of you may have had traumas as powerful as Betsy's. Many have not. But the process is still the same, if subtler. If you find it difficult to forgive, see if there is some hurt, grief, or anger that needs to be embraced more fully.

To the extent you can find the support and courage to let those feelings surface, you clear away the rocks and stones that keep forgiveness from taking root. The tears of your grief moisten the heart and moisten the soil.

Meditation

I opened with the image of a guard locked in his own prison by unforgiveness. It would be a mistake to think the guard can just decide to walk out of jail.

The most common mistake people make about forgiveness is to think it is an act of will, to think they can decide to forgive someone. But in reality, it is something that happens when the conditions are right. We can cultivate forgiveness, but not create it.

It is like love. You cannot create love. You can only clear away blocks to it. But it must emerge on its own, if it is to be genuine.

So if someone asks you if you can forgive them, the most honest thing you can do is look inside and see if there is forgiveness there. You might respond, "Yes, I have forgiven you." Or "No, I really haven't forgiven you." Or maybe even, "I'd like to forgive you, but I'm not there yet."

With this in mind, I offer a closing meditation. This is not a one-shot meditation, but one that you can come back to again and again to help cultivate forgiveness.

There are many ways we have been injured, insulted, slighted, violated or forgotten. Knowingly or unknowingly, we have been abandoned, abused or both. Through thoughts, words, and deeds we've been hurt or betrayed.

Let yourself remember ways this is true. You don't have to forget what happened. See the images.

Is there is a place in you that genuinely would like to be free of this burden? If so, gently consider if there is something you need to say or do. No matter how big or small, is there something to be done? …

See if there is some way you demonize the person. Is there some way you can understand more sympathetically their human nature? Who are they? What forces drive them? …

What are the feelings left in your body and soul? Hurt, anger, fear, tension, vigilance? Don't turn from these. Touch them gently. Hold them in your heart. …

Your awareness is like sunlight and rain that can soak into dark, dry places. Let your awareness settle in gently. Be patient. Forgiveness will grow in time.[6]

Closing

The stupid neither forgive nor forget, the naïve forgive and forget, the wise forgive, but do not forget. (Thomas Szasz)

May forgiveness help us live more fully in the presence of what is.

---

[6] Adapted from Jack Kornfield, *The Art of Forgiveness, Lovingkindness, and Peace.* (Bantam Books, 2002). p 49-50.

Of Sisyphus and Groundhogs

February 2, 2003

Happy Groundhog Day! According to folklore, if the groundhog sees his shadow today, we will have six more weeks of winter. Devorah, our student intern, tells me that Groundhog Day began as a pagan festival. It is midway between the winter solstice and the spring equinox. It is the true dead of winter. The holiday celebrations have thoroughly faded, and spring is not yet on the horizon. In colder climates, it is a time of ice, snow, frozen mud, and cars that won't start in the morning. Even in California, we have rain, fog, and overcast skies.

It's a time when we can identify with Sisyphus' dreary life, rolling a boulder up the hill each day only to have it roll back down. So this morning, I'd like to talk about Sisyphus, groundhogs, and those times when life feels like a struggle and a burden.

Groundhog Day

In 1993, Columbia Pictures released a movie about Sisyphus. It was called *Groundhog Day*. The main character is a weatherman named Phil Connors. Phil is a self-centered, prima donna jerk played by Bill Murray. As weatherman, Phil must cover the Groundhog Day festival in nearby Punxsutawney, Pennsylvania. Rita and Larry, Phil's producer and cameraman, go with him. Rita and Larry are charmed by the folksy scene. Phil thinks it is beneath his dignity and potential. He finds the festival as much fun as rolling a stone up a hill.

Phil covers the story with his characteristic sarcasm and insults and leaves town as quickly as he can. Unfortunately, a blizzard closes the highways. They must return to Punxsutawney for a second night.

When Phil awakens the next morning, it isn't February 3rd. It is February 2nd. It is Groundhog Day all over.

No one else knows the day is repeating. Phil wonders if he's having a massive case of *déjà vu*. But the third morning is also Groundhog Day. The same music is on the radio; the same obnoxious insurance salesman corners him; the same homeless man stands on the corner; the same puddle awaits his foot. The only thing different is Phil: he remembers the previous days and can respond differently.

Ten Groundhog Days later, he is sitting at a bar in a bowling alley with two drunks moaning, "I remember a day in the Virgin Islands. I met a beautiful woman. We ate lobster, drank piña coladas, and made love. Why can't I repeat that day over and over?" Phil is caught in his own personal version of hell.

Sisyphus

The parallel to the ancient Greek myth is more than superficial. Sisyphus is not a weatherman. He is the king of Corinth. But he is a self-centered, egotistical jerk who robs people for his own pleasure. In some traditions he is evil. In others he's just fun loving and irreverent. I could see Bill Murray playing Sisyphus.

In the ultimate prank, Sisyphus captures Thanos, the god of death, and puts him in chains. With death out of circulation, humans become immortal. This is too much for the gods to stand.

They free Thanos and take Sisyphus into the underworld where he has to roll a stone up a mountain. It takes all day to get it to the top. But just as he reaches the peak, the boulder rolls back down. The next day, Sisyphus must start all over again. Like Phil Connors, he must repeat the same tortuous day over and over and over and over.

A few years ago I was sitting beside a lake in Canada reading a book that mentioned Sisyphus. And I got to thinking: "What is it with Sisyphus anyway?"

Think about it. Is he a terminal optimist? After 10 years, does he wake up in the morning and think, "Oh goody! Today I'll push that ole boulder up that ole hill. It'll be a lot of work. But what a rush when I get it up there!"

That kind of endless optimism hardly qualifies as hell on earth. To be sure, there is that moment of disappointment when the boulder rolls back down. But disappointment is not hell.

Tree House

For example, I remember the first tree house I ever built. My friend Phillip Black and I spent the whole day on the project. There was an old, faded red fence behind his house. We got permission to tear it down and use the boards. The boards were punky with dry rot, so they'd be easy to nail.

We carried the boards two blocks to my house and nailed the boards to the tree to make a platform. I understood the engineering principle that triangles are stronger than squares. So we used a diagonal brace to hold up the cantilevered side of the platform.

When we were done, we stood back. It looked great.

Forty-five years later I still have a vivid picture in my mind of the next few minutes. As I watched, Phillip climbed out onto the platform. It sagged a little. I looked at the diagonal brace. The nails holding the brace to the tree did not move. But the boards were so soft that they just pushed through the nail, like a loaf of bread being pushed through a bread slicer. In slow motion, the brace slid down the tree, the platform tilted and Phillip came tumbling down.

That was disappointment. I know what disappointment feels like. We all know disappointment.

But unlike Sisyphus, we learned something. We did not go out the next day, find some more dry-rotted boards and repeat the whole failure.

No. The next day Phillip and I rode down to a construction site. We stole a few planks, suspended them between our bikes and rode home. The boards were harder to nail because they were solid. But once up, they stayed there. When we were done, tree house number two was strong enough to hold both of us at the same time.

Brain Damaged

So, what's with Sisyphus? I can understand his disappointment the first day. Maybe the next day he tries again. That failure would be a bigger disappointment. Maybe he tries the third day. But how many days before he gets it: no matter what he does, the boulder always rolls back down. It's hard to imagine that on day 453 he gets up and thinks, "Boy, today's going to be the day!"

Maybe the boulder rolled over his head. Maybe he was brain damaged and had no memory.

We had a brain-damaged cat once. Fritzie was very sweet. But she persevered. For example, if a door was closed, both of our cats learned to hook their claws on the door and pull. If the door wasn't latched, it would open. If the door was latched, it wouldn't. If the door was latched, our other cat, Molly, would scratch at it a few times, let out a yowl and go do something else. But not Fritzie. If it didn't open, she'd think, "Oh, I'll just try it again." If that didn't work, she'd think, "Well, maybe this time." She would go for hours without any sign of frustration: "Maybe this time." Scratch. "Maybe this time." Scratch. "I bet this time." Scratch.

It was an endless, repeating, futile task. But she was quite content. If she did this in the middle of the night when I was trying to sleep, it was torture for me. But she was fine.

No Consequences

So, back to Sisyphus: if he were oblivious to his foreordained failure, it would not be endless torture. If he weren't oblivious, he would stop. Wouldn't he?

The myth of Sisyphus ends with this question unanswered. But the movie *Groundhog Day* carries on. As each day repeats itself, Phil Connors gets more and more depressed until he realizes, "If tomorrow never comes, I can do whatever I want. There are no consequences."

He drives a car over a mailbox. "I've always wanted to do that." He drives down the railroad track with the police chasing him. He laughs as he forces the police car into another mailbox. When the policeman walks over to his car, he asks for two burgers, French fries, a chocolate milkshake, and an order of flapjacks. At the end of the day, he's thrown in jail.

But the next morning Groundhog Day starts fresh. He can get away with anything!

For the next several scores of Groundhog Days, he goes on a hedonist spree: robbing money, buying big cars, eating sweets and cholesterol, smoking: "Eat, drink, and be merry for tomorrow never comes."

No Exit

I wonder what it would be like to have Bill Murray play Sisyphus. Knowing full well what was to happen at the top of the hill, he might push the boulder in a direction that caused mischief, learn to run backward down the boulder as it rolled down the hill or go swimming rather than push it at all. That makes more sense than Sisyphus just doing the same thing knowing the outcome.

Back in *Groundhog Day*, Phil walks up to the most beautiful woman he sees. He asks her name, the name of her high school, and the name of her twelfth grade English teacher. The next day he walks up to her and says, "Nancy. Nancy Taylor. Don't tell me you don't remember me. I'm Phil. Phil Connors. I sat behind you in Mrs. Walsh's class at Lincoln High School!"

"Well, gosh," she says with a blank expression. "It's been a long time. So how are you?"

Over the next several days he learns enough about her to seduce her. But in the moment of seduction, he calls her "Rita" not "Nancy."

Beneath his ego and bravado, he realizes he is drawn to his producer, Rita. So he tries the same approach with Rita. Each day he gets a little more information from Rita about her ideal lover. He molds himself into her ideal. She is surprised that the prima donna knows French poetry and prays for world peace. She is taken by him. But she is sensitive and ultimately sees through his changes as just a seductive act. He tries hundreds of times, but she always sees through him and slaps him for trying to take advantage of her.

Phil slides into a deep depression. He kidnaps the groundhog from the festival and drives off a cliff. The next day starts over. He steps in front of a truck. He leaps off a church steeple. He kills himself every way he can imagine. And the next day he wakes up.

He is really caught in an existential hell. There is no exit. This is eternal torture worthy of Sisyphus. This is the dark night of the soul.

As he becomes keenly aware of his suffering, he begins to notice the suffering in others. He can't do anything for himself. So he tries little things to help others. He feeds a homeless man. He catches a kid falling out of tree. He repairs a flat tire for some ladies. He learns the Heimlich maneuver to help a choking man.

Rita notices his egotism dissolving. She falls in love with the man beneath his old pretense. He is no longer interested in sexual conquest, but loves her presence. When he falls asleep that night, she is still with him.

When he wakes the next morning, she is still there. It is February 3rd. The curse is broken. Or maybe it wasn't a curse. Maybe it was fierce grace that had finished its work. Whatever the case, Sisyphus is free.

Suffering and Struggle

I share these stories with you because I wanted to say a few words about suffering and struggle. In Sisyphus, the suffering and struggle is gross and obvious: carrying a boulder up a mountain. In the movie, the struggle is psychological, but only a little bit subtler. Phil must carry a boulder-sized ego up the mountain every day.

What makes Sisyphus' task a living hell? Was it disappointment? We already looked at this issue. If he didn't remember his disappointment, it wouldn't be torture. If he did remember, he wouldn't repeat it.

Was it a living hell because of the routine? It is a pointless, futile, monotonous repetition. We can all identify with that.

However, if we examine our own lives, it is clear that we all have pointless routines.

For example, our bodies are boulders we must carry around. Each morning we have to get it out of bed, take it to the bathroom, wash it, dress it, feed it, brush its teeth, comb its hair, take it through the day. We have to feed it a few more times before we bring it home, undress it and put it to bed. The next day, it starts all over again.

And if we give it good food, rest, exercise and care, what does it do? It gets old, falls apart, and dies.

That is about as pointless a routine as there is. And it goes on our entire life!

All of us suffer in this routine from time to time. Some people suffer often. But for most of us most of the time, it's not a problem. We don't even think much about it. It's not a big deal.

So endless, pointless routines cannot be the source of struggle and suffering; otherwise every moment of every day would feel like torture.

Maybe the suffering of struggle is the result of effort. Sisyphus had the huge boulder. Phil Connors had that huge ego to lug around.

But effort doesn't really explain it. Erika, my wife, showed me a chart the other day that puts karate right up there with swimming for the number of calories burned in an hour. I love to work up a good sweat. People here ski, hike, take walks, do aerobics, travel on vacation, do nights at the theater. We put effort into many physical, mental, emotional, and spiritual endeavors. We enjoy it.

Attachment

I believe that the suffering of struggle comes from attachment to the results of our efforts.

The gods must have messed with Sisyphus' head. They took all his egotism and self-centeredness and attached it to an impossible task: getting that boulder to stay on the mountaintop. If he were not attached to this result, his labors would not be hell.

In Phil's case, at first the attachment was to ego gratification. He wanted to be admired. He wanted money, power, big cars, chocolate cheesecake, alcohol, and beautiful women. As his egotism wore out, he attached to nobler desires. He found an old man dying in an alley and spent many days trying to save him, but couldn't. The attachment to results kept pulling him back into the same day, over and over and over and over.

We can get attached to anything. We can get attached to money, power, sex, cars. We can get attached to psychological health, stopping the war, or ending world hunger. And we can get attached to enlightenment.

Desire itself is not a problem. Desires arise in us unbidden. Effort is not a problem in and of itself. Some efforts are wholesome. But attachment to getting results leads to suffering. Whenever attachments dissolve, there is wellbeing.

There are two different kinds of paths to happiness. One is the so-called positive path. You seek the positives you want: security, health, prestige, inner peace, world peace. A consumption-driven economy likes this approach, because it can fan desires and attach them to toothpaste, big cars, DVD players, books, opera tickets, and so forth.

The other approach is the so-called negative path. Rather than grasp for happiness, you look at the nature of the suffering itself. The Buddha never said, "I teach happiness." He said, "I teach the end of suffering." This path explores the nature of suffering.

When we see deeply how much suffering comes out of this grasping, holding quality of mind, then it starts to relax all by itself. For Phil Connors, it took three or four hundred repetitions of the same day to see how futile and painful his attachments were. His egotism gradually wore away.

If Sisyphus is still suffering rolling that stone up the hill, it could only be because he's got a bigger ego that takes longer to wear out.

Once that grasping relaxes, our true nature begins to surface. Deep in the human soul is a simple urge to be of some use to others.

Like Phil, as our attachments wear away, we become more generous and helpful. This generous heart is not a means to achieve happiness. It is not something we do to gain something – that's just attachment. Generosity and love are an end in and of themselves. It's our natural state.

Like any good teaching story, the myth and the movie can be interpreted in other ways. So I'll leave it to you to talk over with friends or just consider in your own reflections. Ask yourself:

What if you had to repeat today forever? What if this were it? What if you could change your response in any way you wanted, but tomorrow never came?

What are the subtle and not so subtle boulders you carry through this day? What are your attachments and struggles?

Imagine that no matter what you do, this day will simply present itself again and again. What do you want to do with this day?

Happy Groundhog Day.

Remorse and Guilt

October 12, 2003

Desperado

Bruce Zeeman pulled me aside on the fifth grade playground. He showed me his wallet. I was impressed because I had no wallet in the fifth grade: I had no need. His was filled with green and grey paper money. We both grinned. He pulled out a five. "Want it?" he asked.

My allowance was 50¢ a week. "Wow," I said, "Yeah!"

He handed me the bill as the recess bell rang. We hurried in without talking.

Three days later, Bruce, Ricky Levi, and I met by the same bush on the playground. Bruce handed Ricky a $10 bill and me a few singles.

"Where did you get them?" I whispered.

"My mother."

"What if she misses them?" I asked.

"She won't. She's got lots of dollar bills. She won't notice a few gone."

I was excited by this unprecedented wealth.

That Saturday, Bruce and I rode our bicycles over to Ricky's house. Bruce brought a few cigarettes as well as more money. We bought matches, lighter fluid and candy bars before riding down to the bayou. There we made paper boats, soaked them in lighter fluid, shoved them into the bayou, and set them on fire as we puffed and choked on contraband Lucky Strikes. Boy, we were wild and tough!

In the following weeks, the money flowed in a few dollars at a time. Bruce split it between the three of us. Bruce and Ricky bought pistols that used CO2 cartridges to shoot BBs, pellets, and darts. I was reluctant to spend that much money. I bought a hunting knife instead.

After that, Bruce and Ricky took a larger portion of the stolen cash. They spent theirs right away. I pretended to spend mine, but secretly hid it under the mattress of my bed.

After a month, the life of a desperado left me jittery. I wanted to tell my mom. But doing so would bring Bruce and Ricky down with me. My 11-year old sense of honor-among-thieves wouldn't let me rat on the only friends I had.

So I continued to take my portion of cash, continued to pretend to enjoy it, and continued to hide most of it in my bed.

To prove I wasn't a wimp, I carved models of naked women out of balsa wood, painted them with flesh colored model airplane paint and showed them to Bruce and Ricky.

Two months and a hundred dollars later, my mom came up to my room one afternoon. She had just gotten a call from Bruce's mother. She said we were going over to Bruce's house, as were Ricky and his parents.

I took the cash and hunting knife from under the mattress and gave them to her.

I remember sitting in the Zeeman's living room trying to disappear into the cracks between the cushions of the chair. We gave the details of our crime spree. Mrs. Zeeman said she had almost fired their maid for suspicion of thievery. An image flashed in my mind of the black woman who supported her family on meager wages. My stomach tightened into nausea as I thought, "Thank God we were caught."

Bruce, Ricky, and I were forbidden from seeing each other. My mother returned the cash I had. We calculated how much I had spent and she gave Mrs. Zeeman that amount.

On the way home, my mother told me I would repay her by doing extra chores. She put a chart in the kitchen. Every hour I worked I could cross off 25¢. I would be grounded until the debt was repaid. It took me about three months.

Meanwhile, Ricky was grounded for three weeks. Bruce was grounded for a week. I felt sorry for Bruce. A week at home was hardly enough to cleanse his soul of the tarnish it had accumulated. I feared he would go through life damaged because his parents didn't honor him enough to give him adequate means of redeeming himself.

I have only one regret from my quarter year of labor and home incarceration. Two weeks into my sentence, *X the Unknown* and *The Blob* were released as a double feature at the movie theater. I remember standing in the front yard watching my older brother and his friend Jess ride their bicycles down the street on the way to the movies.

That afternoon, he cheerfully informed me that *X the Unknown* and *The Blob* were the best shows ever made. Ever. He and Jess saw them both two more times.

To this day I have never seen *X the Unknown* or *The Blob*.

Missing those movies was the worst part of my rehabilitation. The best part was sleeping at night. I was not back in good graces yet, but I had a path to redemption. Knowing that, I slept better than I had in months.

We Break Promises

The October theme of the month in our Religious Education program is "We make promises." In our east wing this month, the children and youth are exploring promises and the kinds they want to make about how to treat each other.

This year, we intend to bring the children's theme of the month into the adult part of at least one of our services. Hopefully, this will encourage conversations across the generations about important topics.

The aspect of this theme I want to address this morning is not about making promises. It is about breaking promises.

From the perspective of spiritual depth and consciousness, making promises is not nearly as interesting as what happens when we break our promises. One of the results of breaking a promise is remorse and guilt. My escapade with Bruce and Ricky was one of the most intense stretches in my life of continuous remorse and guilt. But I have had others.

How many of you have felt remorse or guilt in the last year?

How many of you have felt remorse or guilt in the last month?

Promises

This morning I want to say a few things about the kinds of promises we make, about the significant differences between remorse and guilt and how we can make friends with them and use them wisely.

Explicit or Implicit

As a place to start, let's look at different kinds of promises. Some are explicit and specific: "I'll return your book tomorrow." "I'll be home by 9:00." "I'll mow the lawn on Saturday." You don't have to say "I promise" or "I swear." The statement is clear.

Sometimes we make these promises too casually. "I'll get the project done by next week," may have been your intention. But if you'd thought it through, you'd have realized that was not practical. The project was too big. So explicit, specific promises have their pitfalls. But for the most part, we can figure out what to do with them: we honor them. If we break them, we do what we can to fix the situation.

The opposite of explicit, specific promises are implicit, general promises. These are tricky. They are more like general guidelines. Every Sunday morning we promise to "travel together with open minds, open hearts and helping hands … caring and laughter" as we "pledge our time, talents, and support" to each other. A month ago I spoke about our first Unitarian Universalist principle where we promise to "affirm and promote the inherent worth and dignity of every person."

Our covenant and marriage vows are spoken out loud. But for the most part, general promises are implicit and unspoken: "I promise to be honest and fair." "I promise to be generous." "I promise to speak out against injustice." "I promise to be a positive influence in the world."

Motivation

Another way to think about promises is the motivation behind them. Some are ego motivated. Some are spiritually motivated.

An ego-motivated promise is one that boosts the ego. "I will always speak the truth because I'm such a good guy." "I'll be honest because more people will respect me." "I'll be generous because that will make people want to be generous to me." "I'll avoid conflict so people will like me." "I'll get offended easily so people won't push me around." "I'll be a good boy."

A spiritually based promise is one that grows out of a deeper wisdom. "I will always speak the truth because lying troubles my heart." "I will be generous because it helps me feel more spacious." Spiritually motivated promises usually hold up better under social pressure than do ego-based promises.

Instinctual

There are also certain promises that we are born with. These are wired-in instincts. They are general and implicit. And they can be quite powerful.

For example, when my children were born, I realized to what extremes I would go to protect them: I might actually kill someone if I thought that was the only way to protect their lives. As a lifelong pacifist, it was a shock to see that inside me.

Self-protection is an instinct. So are love and generosity. Humans cannot survive by themselves. The instinct to care for each other is strong. In Buddhism, the foundational precepts are generosity followed closely by compassion. In Christianity, the foundational principles are love – love of God and love of your neighbor – followed closely by charity. Love and generosity are at the core of most of the world's great religious traditions because they are wired into our deepest nature.

You might prefer to call these "instincts" rather than "promises" because they are so general and often unspoken. But, to go against them has the same effect as breaking a promise, so I'd prefer to think of them as instinctual promises.

Situation Ethics

Now, we come to the interesting part. There are so many promises we make, principals we adopt, and instincts that guide us, that it is inevitable that we will break them over and over.

Situation Ethics states the problem formally: If you have one promise to live by, you simply follow it. Let's say your one rule is to always speak the truth. Someone says, "What happened to my cake?" You say, "I ate it." You speak the truth. It is easy. Someone says, "Aren't you glad we are together?" You speak the truth, "No. Your breath is terrible." As long as you have only one rule, you follow it and are at peace.

But, Situation Ethics notes that a problem arises if you have two rules. "I will always speak the truth," and "I won't hurt people." There will be times when these two conflict. Therefore, I need a third rule to decide how to resolve the conflict. My third rule is, "I will speak the truth unless it hurts someone's feelings." So I don't tell Jack his breath smells like a garbage truck. But now I have three rules. There are times when those three will conflict, so I need more to sort those out. And so it goes.

This was my problem in the fifth grade. One implicit promise I had made was not to steal. But I had had a lonely year, and I implicitly promised myself I'd do what I could to make friends and have fun. When Bruce offered me money, he was offering friendship and excitement. This conflicted with my promise not to steal, so I made a third rule. "As long as Bruce takes the money and gives it to me, I won't actually be stealing. I am just accepting a gift."

Then, after the initial excitement wore off, I became uncomfortable. I decided being honest was more important. But I also had an implicit promise of loyalty to friends. For three months I decided that loyalty was more important than honesty or peace of mind.

We may think we have matured beyond these childhood dilemmas. But we have to deal with them in our kids and we have to deal with our adult versions of these same issues. Many people have made an implicit promise to avoid conflict. What happens when this conflicts with being honest? Many people have made an implicit promise to not let injustice befall them or their friends. What happens when this conflicts with the promise you've made to slow down a little and simplify your life? Fighting injustice can be wearing and complicated. Many of us have made a promise to be honest in our dealings. What happens when that trip you took is both business and pleasure? Is that a legitimate tax deduction? All of us pledge our time, talent, and support to this congregation. How do you decide where the balance is between supporting this congregation and supporting your family and other causes?

Remorse and Guilt

We live in a web of promises, some of which conflict. What happens when we break a promise? We experience remorse, guilt, or numbness.

I want to make a distinction between guilt and remorse. Guilt arises from breaking an ego-based promise. You tend to think you are a bad person. Your self-image slips. You feel small or "less than."

Remorse arises from breaking a non-ego-based promise. Remorse is less a judgment about your worth and more a feeling of regret or grief. It may have a spiritual dimension. If you lie to someone, it is disturbing on some deep level. Maybe you hadn't even intended to lie – the person misinterpreted your remark. You don't think you are a bad person because someone did not understand you. But you may feel remorse anyway because you don't like to mislead people.

Consider another example: you are driving attentively through your neighborhood at about 20 miles per hour. A child darts from behind a parked car. Your car crushes her foot.

At first you may feel guilt: "How could I have done something so terrible? I must be a bad person." But after you've had time to think and reflect you come to a genuine conclusion that there was nothing you could have done. It was truly not your fault. The guilt lifts. But you still feel a deep remorse for having been part of such suffering.

I worry about our soldiers in Iraq. They may feel they are morally principled in standing up for freedom and protecting the world. But in the process, they may pull a trigger and put a bullet through another human. Even if they feel morally justified, killing is still counter to our deepest nature. It can leave them with numbness or remorse in their souls.

If Mrs. Zeaman had fired her maid, that would have left remorse in me that I might still be carrying to this day.

The Dalai Lama said that to live in this world is to cause suffering. You can't drive your car, purchase clothes, or buy food without indirectly contributing to suffering somewhere in the world. Therefore, to be alive, fully alive, is to carry some level of remorse, even if we are relatively free of guilt.

So What?

So what do we do with guilt and remorse? They can be overwhelming and incapacitating. They can also be guides that help us live more consciously and joyfully in the world. How can we use these states wisely? Let me suggest three strategies.

Mindful of Promises

First, be mindful of what is going on inside you when you make a promise, when you state you will do or be something.

Is it a specific promise that will be over and done? "I'll be home at 5:30." Or is it a general promise with a lifetime commitment? "I'll never be late again."

Is your promise really an intention? Would it be better to say, "I intend to be home by 5:30" rather than "I will be home by 5:30."

What motivates your promise? Is it ego-motivated? Are you making a commitment because it makes you look good or feel good? In my experience, making ego-motivated promises is like eating too many cookies: They taste good in the moment but feel bad later.

Over the years, I find I make fewer and fewer promises because most of them are ego-motivated or intentions confused as promises.

Make Friends

Second, be mindful of the signals your body gives you that you are breaking a promise.

I was talking with colleagues the other day when I noticed a catch in my breathing. I paused to check out what I was feeling. It was guilt. Then I realized my comments reflected poorly on another colleague. Long ago I had made a general promise to myself that I would not gossip: I would not speak negatively about someone who was not present unless I had spoken to the person first about my critique. So when I felt that catching in my breath, I knew I had to go and speak directly to this person about my concern.

I could have figured all this out using logic. But it would have taken a lot longer. And given a busy life, I may not have gotten around to it.

However, our bodies can be very wise when we listen to them. They can point things out to us very swiftly.

We live in a culture that labels any feelings less than "I'm having a great day" as pathological. Remorse and guilt are feelings we think we should not have. If we were upstanding folks we'd never do anything to feel these "negative" states.

There are so many promises: explicit and implicit, conscious and unconscious, ego motivated, instinctually motivated, and spiritually motivated. The web is so complex and self-contradicting that we are going to break our promises again and again. All of us should feel remorse if not guilt from time to time. I'm not saying it's a good thing that we break our promises and feel bad. I'm just saying it is reality. Therefore it is helpful to be adept at recognizing our body signals.

The alternative to feeling remorse is feeling numb. Numbness is pathological. Numbness can make us moral jerks.

So it is helpful to become sensitive to the body signals. Sometimes there is a catching in the breath. Often there is a sinking feeling in the heart and belly. Sometimes the shoulders curve forward as if to protect a wounded heart. Sometimes the body tenses as our thoughts speed up anxiously.

Each of us is different and these signs can mean different things to different folks. But it is useful to get in touch with them and how remorse and grief express themselves in you. Make friends with them rather than push them away.

Distinguish Remorse and Guilt

Third, be mindful of the difference between remorse and guilt. Superficially they are similar. But underneath they are very different phenomena.

A few years ago I introduced the old Buddhist metaphor of a teaspoon of salt. If you stir it in a glass of water, the water becomes so bitter you cannot drink it. However, if you stir it in a five-gallon cistern, you barely notice it.

When we break our promises, we get a teaspoon of salt. Guilt is like stirring it in a glass of water. We feel small. We shrink inside. We feel "less than." Our self-esteem slips, and our capacities are reduced. Life tastes bitter.

Remorse is like stirring that same amount of salt into a cistern. You may still taste the salt, but you don't shrink. Remorse is expansive. Your capacity for compassion and empathy increases. You become more connected with the world. Maybe your heart is heavy with grief or regret, but you don't see yourself as a bad person. You may feel compassion or empathy, but not as if you are a bad girl or boy.

Guilt is a waste of time and energy. We all feel it at times. We all have to cope with it. We all have to heal from it. But if you've done something to harm others, beating yourself up doesn't help them, and it doesn't help you become a better person.

Remorse, on the other hand, connects you with others and lets you see them and yourself clearly and deeply. It can guide you in how to help others and help yourself.

Our capacity for remorse also increases our capacity for love, joy, and connection.

Fallow Time

January 4, 2004

Spring is pale green. Rains melt snow in open fields and swell streams and rivers. Pale green shoots break through in forests and meadows.

Summer is deep green. Chlorophyll darkens the grasses and leaves. Nature is prolific in the warm nights and long days.

Fall is golden. Fields and groves turn yellow, red, and brown. Nature yields her abundance. Animals store food or fat for the cold months to come.

Winter is white. The fields lie fallow under a blanket of snow. Like God's seventh day, nature rests.

Our lives, too, follow this cycle: spring is for new beginnings, summer is for tending the crops, fall is for laying in provisions, and winter is for rest.

Yeah, right. How many of us actually follow this cycle? A more common cycle for us is: spring is for spring fever, summer is for travel, fall is for new beginnings, and winter is for ski trips and post-holiday depression.

There is not much time in this cycle for lying fallow, hibernation, rest, or rejuvenation.

Generations

Yet fallow time is bred into us. Our prehuman ancestors had no choice but to honor the cycle of the seasons. If they didn't gather food while it was abundant and rest when it was not, they died.

Then, for tens of thousands of generations, our human ancestors were hunters and gatherers, farmers and shepherds. They knew that the earth was unyielding and dormant during the winter months. Mother Nature and the gods did not reward hard work this time of year. Better make hay while the sun shines. Then, after the harvest and harvest festivities, people lived quieter lives. They hung out with family and friends through the long winter's evenings. It was a time of story telling, mending garments, renewing ties, and quiet reflection.

We lived in these cycles for so many thousands of generations that it became bred into us. It became part of our genes.

Then, about 10 generations ago, something hit us: the Industrial Revolution. Suddenly, our livelihood was no longer tied to the seasons. We could build machines, manufacture textiles, or program computers when the ground was frozen.

The new technologies promised we could transcend the limitations of Mother Nature and the gods. By being productive even when the earth was not, we could raise our standard of living. We were lured by the promise of a better life. But in a way, we sold our souls. When we don't pause and reflect, we lose touch with our souls. We lose touch with our depths, our meaning. We fall out of harmony not only with the world around us but with our own essence as well.

Nevertheless, there remains deep within our genes the knowledge that we need the down time. We may not have to follow the cycle of the seasons. But our spiritual and emotional health requires quiet as much as our physical health requires sleep.

New Year

This morning is the first Sunday of the new year. Recent tradition says its time to take stock of our lives for a few moments and resolve to diet and exercise for a few months until our wills weaken. It gives us something to fill the fallow season.

This morning is also the second Sunday of winter. I want to suggest a different approach to the New Year: going back to an even older tradition, the one that says winter is for lying fallow. I want to talk about the value of being unproductive.

This will not be a "how to" sermon. I will not speak about how to create fallow time, how to meditate, walk in the woods, set aside Sabbath time, pursue hobbies, hang out, or rest.

We already know how to do these.

The problem for most of us – and I include myself in this – is not that we don't know how to take time off. It is that we have lost touch with the motivation and intention. We've lost touch with that wisdom within us.

In the recent congregational survey, the most checked issue facing our lives was "I am too busy and stressed by my work, avocation, and regular activities." And the younger you are, the more likely this is your major issue.

We know we need some quiet space. We feel the urge within us. Yet, in our fast-paced, 24/7 world, there is little support for being unproductive. We think we have to get everything done on the schedule first. Then we'll take a power nap. But everything rarely gets done.

So this morning, I want to give voice to that part of us that already knows what we need to do. I want to help us line up our intentions more consciously.

To do this, I'll say a little more about what fallow time is. And then I'll speak about its importance for kids and its importance for cultivating wisdom and compassion in grown-ups.

Negative Space

What is fallow time?

Decades ago, I studied sculpture for three years with a New York artist named Allan. Among other things, he taught me about negative space. If I was carving a figure out of stone or wood, the positive space was the shape of the arms, head, and torso. The negative space was the emptiness between the arm and torso and between the head and torso. Without negative space, you couldn't see the statue: it would be an undifferentiated mass. But more than this, Allan said to me, "Most people don't consciously note the quality of the negative spaces. But their shape and form affect the aesthetics as much as the shape and form of the wood or stone itself."

Fallow time refers to the negative spaces in our lives. It can be formal meditation or informal strolls in the neighborhood. It can be resting with a novel or sitting in a hot tub. It can be children playing without adult structure. It probably isn't watching TV.

Like winter and negative space, fallow time can feel a little sparse. Watching TV may be useful for unwinding. But it is probably not true fallow time because it is not sparse enough. Our consciousness is filled with sounds and images from the screen. We are attending to something "out there" rather than being with ourselves "in here."

In the dead of winter, producing crops is a waste of energy. Fallow time is any time we are not trying to produce. We are more concerned with enjoying the moment than producing something for tomorrow. We are *being* rather than *doing*.

We need fallow time in our daily, weekly, and yearly cycles. Without some negative space, we feel so busy we can't see our lives: it becomes an undifferentiated mass. We need a certain quantity and quality of negative space. It makes the difference between so-so art and good art. This makes the difference between a humdrum life and a rich and satisfying life.

Kids

Fallow time is also developmentally crucial. So let's focus on kids, particularly middle-class Americans kids.

Children are usually treated differently in the third world. In many countries, children are not loved for being productive. They aren't praised for doing well in baseball, arithmetic, or farming. Instead, kids are loved for being what they are: kids. They may have chores but no one follows them around building up their self-esteem for doing such a good job of picking up the eggs.

In our society, particularly in the middle and upper classes, emphasis on performance begins with parents applauding their infants for walking the first time and continues through gaining admission to a good college. There is less and less time for random play and hanging out.

To give some hard data, consider the 2002 General Society Survey conducted by the National Opinion Research Center at the University of Chicago. It found that 41% of poor and working class families in this country socialized with extended family one or more times each *week*. On the other hand, half of middle-class families socialized with relatives once a *month* or less. In other words, poorer families spend several evenings a *week* in multigenerational gatherings while middle-class families spend a handful of times a *year*.[7]

In middle-class homes, the schedule is the organizing force: soccer, homework, music lessons, scouts, and so on. It is difficult for the nuclear family, much less the extended family, to get together for a meal. The University of Michigan Survey Research Center found that in the last two decades, children lost 12 hours per week of free time and half of their unstructured outdoor time.[8]

I don't want to romanticize the life of the working poor, but let's not romanticize the life of middle-class kids who have hardly any fallow time.

Middle-class kids are deprived of the pleasure (and yes, sometimes the burden) of spending time with extended family. They don't share meals, rides, and companionship with cousins. They aren't routinely disciplined by aunts, uncles, grandparents, and other adults.

And since visits are rare, they are more stressful: kids get directives about how to dress and how to behave, what to do and what not to do. These directives allow less freedom for kids to be kids.

I grew up in a more relaxed time. I ran and played in the neighborhood on my own most afternoons. I had a few activities scheduled once or twice a week. But mostly I was on my own.

But still I have a voice in my head that says, "Doug, you'll be loved more if you produce more." It's hard for me to imagine what it is like for kids today.

This is one of the reasons I love intergenerational events in our church. At the tree trimming party, the kids tend to run in a pack. It looks so natural and healthy. At the all-church campout one June, I watched a little girl who was being gruff with her peers. No one wanted to play with her. She was very unhappy.

Two older girls noticed this and casually invited her to join them in some fantasies they were playing. The younger child melted in the attention of older girls. They had a wonderful time together.

This natural wisdom and compassion does not arise in scheduled, adult-directed, structured activities. These arise in fallow time when kids can just be who they are and figure out through their own instincts how to relate.

Adults

Fallow time is just as important in cultivating wisdom and compassion in grown-ups. So let me shift from children to adults.

Angela Arien is an anthropologist who has a succinct way of describing the process of insight. It goes like this:

Insight arises all the time. It leads to action. Action creates satisfaction. Satisfaction resolves in a pause. Out of the pause, new insight arises. The cycle is insight, action, satisfaction, pause, insight.

It sounds like the cycle of the seasons: Insight is like spring where a new understanding springs forth. Action is like summer activity. Satisfaction is like the fall when we harvest the rewards of wise action. Pause is like winter and lying fallow. It is a time of germination and rejuvenation out of which new insight eventually springs forth.

Now, let's go through this cycle more slowly. Insight just means you recognize something to be true: "We are out of butter." "I'll get a snack sooner if I wake mommy from her nap." "Big cars have more steel and provide more protection in crashes." "I'd be happier if I could just get this right." Insights can be as profound as the meaning of your life or as shallow as realizing you need a new light bulb in the refrigerator. They can contain great wisdom or great inanity.

These insights can give rise to actions: you buy some butter, you wake mommy, you buy a big car, you try a little a harder

If the actions are based on wise insights, they will probably give satisfaction. You feel good. When you feel good, you relax. You pause. And in that quiet, you may see something else.

---

[7] As quoted by Daniel Weintraub in a *Sacramento Bee* editorial, December 23, 2003
[8] David Whitford, "What Family Time?", *UU World*, December 2003, p. 31

Angela Arien asks, "What happens when this cycle is speeded up or slowed down?"

If you speed up the cycle, the first things to get shortened are the satisfaction and the pause.

For example, I worked for Digital Equipment Corporation a number of years ago. I remember my first software release. We started the cycle collecting information about what the software product needed: collecting insights. This led to a product design. We all then dug in and went to work to build it: the action phase. As is common in the software industry, the work took longer than we expected, so the final phase of the release had us all working long days and weeks. Finally, at 10:30 one Thursday morning, we got it out the door. We all cheered and decided to go have a big lunch together to celebrate: the satisfaction. Just before we left for lunch, an email came around from our manager saying, "Congratulations, good work, wonderful product, go out and enjoy yourself and be back in an hour and a half because we are already behind schedule on the next release."

The satisfaction and pause got greatly curtailed. Consequently, the same problems kept showing up in release after release. We never learned much from our successes or failures because there was not time to enjoy our success or pause and reflect on the process.

So, when the pause gets shortened, the insights that arise will have less depth, wisdom or compassion. And they will tend to be more ego-centered.

On the other hand, when we take time to enjoy the fruits of our labor and to genuinely pause, the insights are deeper and less ego-centered. And the deeper insights lead to wiser actions. For example, the insight "I'll get a snack sooner if I wake mommy" upon reflection yields to a deeper insight: "If I wake mommy she'll be grumpy and we'll all be less happy. So maybe I'll let her sleep." The insight "big cars are safer in crashes" upon reflection yields to a less ego-centered insight: "Big cars cause more damage to small cars and encourage a kind of automotive arms race. And they are harder on the environment. So we'll all be better off and I'll be more at ease if I get something small and environmentally friendly." The insight "I'll be happier if I try harder" yields to the deeper recognition: "My perfectionism is making me miserable. Maybe I'd be happier if I were more accepting."

We live in an economy that encourages us to go faster and faster, to take less and less fallow time. We live in a political climate of fear and sound bites that does little to encourage us to stop and reflect. This means that our insights and actions will be less informed by wisdom and compassion. It also means we can be more easily manipulated by politicians and media (and ministers and friends).

Closing

So feel that which pulls us into greater and greater activity. And feel that which pulls us toward fallow time. As we feel both of these more deeply, it becomes easier to find a wise and harmonious balance. It becomes easier to move from acting to rest to acting to rest in a life affirming cycle with insight and satisfaction woven in between.

If being idle sounds depressing or anxiety provoking, if it brings up an inner monster that whispers "don't be a lazy good-for-nothing," pat the monster on the head and say, "there, there, it's okay." Lying fallow is as natural as breathing in and breathing out. It is the way we deepen and rejuvenate.

Whether we are trying to raise happier children, create a more enriched life for ourselves, or create a better world for all of us, one of the most important things we can do, one of the most radical things we can do, one of the most subversive things we can do, one of the most creative things we can do is pause. Give ourselves regular fallow periods. Let ourselves have times of being unproductive and useless. It can save our souls. This is to say, it can put us in deeper touch with our own souls, the soul of the community, and the soul of our mother earth.

Blessed be.

Wise Speech

May 2, 2004

The old Buddhist master sat before the assembled yogis. "Tonight I would like to speak to you about wise speech," he began. "According to the Buddha, wise speech is truthful, gentle, helpful, spoken from a kind heart, and timely." Then he spoke at great length about the harm that can come from words that are mean spirited, harsh, or careless.

A young yogi raised his hand and said, "Venerable sir, I do not understand how this can be. A stone can bruise. Theft can deprive. Brawling can cause bleeding. But words are just sounds. They have no substance. I must disagree with you when you suggest they are so powerful."

The old man replied, "If you weren't such an idiot, you'd understand. So sit down, shut up, and stop interrupting with your ignorance."

The young man dropped to his cushion and the master continued his dharma talk.

Fifteen minutes later the young yogi jumped to his feet without raising his hand and yelled, "You are a fraud! You cannot possibly be the great teacher you pretend to be." His face was red, his eyes were bulging, his fists were clenched, his body shook.

The old man turned to the yogi and said, "You seem perturbed. Your gentle disposition is shattered. What happened to you?"

"You hurled insults I did not deserve. No man of wisdom could speak so harshly. You are a fraud."

The old man responded, "Ah. I see. It was my words that had such a transforming effect upon you. It seems you have changed your philosophy. It seems you and I agree that speech can be quite powerful."

The young man's face went blank. His angry flush subsided. A shy smile formed at the corners of his mouth. He bowed slightly, "You are certainly a wise teacher. I shall never forget this lesson. Speech can be very powerful."

Speech is not only powerful, but we are bombarded with more and more every day: billboards, magazines, telephones, TV, advertising, radios, cell phones, email, chat lines, satellite communication. Our technology amplifies speech, but our wisdom for using it atrophies.

This morning I'd like to talk about wise speech and its companion practice of deep listening. They bring the healing power of speech into the world, into the lives of people around us and at the same time cultivate our own wisdom and peace.

Samma Vaca

Wise speech and deep listening have to do with being truthful, gentle, helpful, kindhearted, and timely. But before we go into specifics, let me give a little background.

"Wise speech" is a translation of the Buddhist term *sammā vācā*. In the late 1800s when the Jesuits landed in Ceylon, they came upon some ancient Buddhist texts, which they tried to translate into English. They rendered *sammā vācā* as "right speech." It sounded familiar to the Christian ear: as in right and wrong, good and bad, should and shouldn't.

Christian morality is based on obedience: obedience to God's law and God's will. Even non-theists in the West tend to base morality on obedience to higher moral principles as if they were a higher reality.
Buddhism is non-theistic. It does not base morality on obedience but on *sammādhānam"* which means "harmony," "coordination," or "generosity." Buddhist morality is based on living in harmony, living in coordination with life, and living generously.

Notice *sammā vācā* and *sammādhānam* have the same root: *sammā*. So "right speech" remains the popular translation. But a more accurate rendering is "wise speech" or "skillful speech" or "speech that promotes harmony."

I share this scholarly tidbit with you because Unitarian Universalism has its roots in Judeo-

Christianity. We tend to think of morality as adherence to ethical principles as if they come from a higher realm of truth. At the same time, Unitarian Universalist theists and non-theists alike emphasize the importance of this world and living peacefully and fairly in it. So the Buddhist approach to morality is helpful to us UUs.

The Buddhist approach also recommends a parallel practice of deep listening. When your speech is not truthful, gentle, helpful, kind, and timely, it does not mean you have broken God's law, fallen out of divine favor, sinned, or become a bad person. It only means you have spoken unwisely or unskillfully. Rather than harshly beating yourself up, it is time for the practice of deep listening.

Deep listening is contemplating what is going on inside you and the person with whom you are speaking. You attend in a way that is honest, gentle, supportive, kind, and timely. This may or may not solve your immediate situation. But over time, the practice makes you wiser, more alive, and more effective.

Truthful

With this background, let's look at wise speech in real life.

First, skillful speech is always truthful. Lying creates discord. Love does not exist without truth. All religions speak about the importance of speaking truthfully. And I think all of us understand this as well.

However, there is more to aligning with truth than not saying falsehoods. We all know how lawyers, politicians, and advertisers can stay within a narrowly defined version of the truth and still be deceptive. And in our own lives, we run into problems all the time.

Fat

For example, consider the question, "Does this dress make me look fat?" If it does, you may feel the little white lie coming on.

If you take truth seriously, you know it is time for deep listening.

As you look inside, perhaps you noticed a pull toward truth and a pull toward a nice relationship. (We often confuse being nice with being loving and supportive.) Or maybe you feel the desire to avoid conflict: the truth can be upsetting.

At the same time you listen deeply to what might be going on in the woman asking the question. Is she concerned about her weight? Is she afraid she is unattractive or unlikable?

Or maybe she really does not want an answer. You could say truthfully, gently, kindly and helpfully, "The dress looks great." You didn't answer the surface question, but you answered the underlying question. And she's fine.

Or maybe she really does want an answer, but you feel resentful for being put on the spot. You are tempted to say, "It makes you look like a tugboat." But that is not gentle, helpful, or kindhearted. You listen more deeply and say, "It doesn't make you look fatter or thinner. I feel nervous responding to your question."

Deep and sensitive listening does not guarantee that you'll come up with a clever answer or that there is one best answer. But you may be able to find ways to speak that are truthful, gentle, helpful, kindhearted, and timely.

Of course, if you only have a few seconds to respond, you won't be able to do all this introspection. You do the best you can in the moment. But afterward, take some time to do deep listening. And each time you explore this way, you become wiser and more adept in the next tough situation.

Kinds of Falsehoods

There are lots of ways to deviate from the truth besides blatant lying. For example, exaggeration is a form of lying: "He's perfect." "She never listens to me." "I always have to do it all myself."

Another kind of lying is passing on information that you are not absolutely sure is true. This is gossiping or spreading rumors. If you find yourself doing this, listen deeply. What is motivating you? Are you looking for excitement? A sense of importance? Demonstrating that you are in the know? Relieving tension? Be gentle with yourself, but look honestly.

Another form of lying is the so-called "forked tongue": you say one thing to one person and something different to another person. To a co-worker you say, "That was a wonderful presentation." To another co-worker you say, "I wish he'd learn how to get to the point more quickly."

Anytime I say different things to different folks, an alarm goes off in my head. I know I'm off balance. It's time for deep listening. Why did I tell him it was wonderful? Was I doing some legalistic dissembling: I thought it was wonderful *for him*. But I left off the last two words. I thought I was being gentle, helpful, and kindhearted. But then why did I say something negative behind his back? What am I scared of?

Asking these questions in a gentle, friendly way can lead to wiser speech and deeper understanding in the future.

Gentle

Wise speech adheres to truth. Wise speech is also gentle. It is not harsh or abusive. Abusive language is a form of lying.

We live in an increasingly crass culture where the importance of gentleness may seem lost. But many years ago while running a counseling center for street kids, I learned how important gentleness is.

One afternoon Tina, Louise, Betsy, Danny, and I were sitting around the linoleum table in the drop-in center. Danny had his boot up on the edge of the table.

Louise said, "Danny, your boots are gross. Why do you wear them?"

Danny said, "Because I want to, you toad." (He used a more colorful word.)

Louise said, "Come on, Danny, I was only asking."

Danny mimicked, "'I was only asking.'"

"Okay, okay," Louise said, "I'm sorry."

"Yeah, you are one of the sorriest people I know."

I injected, "Come on Danny, she apologized."

But Danny was on a rip. "The button is missing on her shirt. Her shoes are falling apart. She probably hasn't washed her hair or taken a bath in a month."

I tried to intervene, but nothing slowed him. Finally in frustration I said, "Danny, stop being such a jerk."

Suddenly you could hear a pin drop. Tina and Louise looked at me with their mouths half open. Danny turned and looked out the window. I could see in the corners of his eyes that he was hurt.

I was flabbergasted. The word I used really was "jerk." It was nothing compared to the profanity flying from their mouths.

Then in a flash I got it. These kids were verbally abused by their parents, their teachers, the police, and their peers. They appeared unfazed by language that would make a sailor blush. But they trusted I was the one adult in their lives who listened carefully and spoke respectfully. I could be tough. I had to be tough. But I was respectful.

With that one relatively mild word, "jerk," I had betrayed that trust. And this wild, swaggering, drug abusing, delinquent kid was hurt.

I apologized and made a lame excuse about needing to get his attention. Inwardly, I vowed to remember this lesson and not be fooled by appearances.

It didn't take a lot of deep listening to realize why I had called him a jerk: I was frustrated. So I learned to be straight with the kids about what I was feeling.

I'd say, "I'm getting really frustrated and wish you would stop." That would usually get their attention. Or if I thought they were baiting me, I'd say, "I think you're trying to make me angry and it's working."

If you doubt the effect of harsh language, remember a time someone said something crass to you and you outwardly appeared unfazed, but lay awake later that night fuming about it.

Useful

Wise speech is truthful, gentle, and useful. It is helpful and beneficial.

A number of years ago I went through a period where, before speaking, I asked if what I was going to say was more useful than silence. I found that most of my speech didn't pass that simple test.

Small talk can ease tension or strengthen bonds in a community. But much idle chatter doesn't even do this. Deep listening often reveals other motives and ways to be more effective.

Friendly Heart

Speaking from a kind or friendly heart is an important check against emotionally dumping.

For example, you are annoyed at someone's bossiness. It doesn't take a lot of deep listening to see that he wants to be in control of situations. He is a control freak. This analysis may be truthful, but it is not friendly or kindhearted. So listen more deeply. Why would someone be controlling? Probably because they are scared. If they weren't scared or insecure, they would have no need to control. As you sense their fear, you may find a more friendly or empathetic way to deal with them effectively. Your wisdom grows.

Timely

Speaking in a timely manner is a way to avoid all kinds of mischief. For example, your husband promised to mow the lawn this weekend, but got sidetracked by other projects and forgot. Monday morning, as he leaves for work you say, "You forgot to mow the lawn again." Your comment may be truthful and gentle. You may even convince yourself it is useful and kindhearted. But the lack of timeliness reveals something else.

Deep listening may show fear, resentment, or frustration you aren't being straight about. Or it may show that you simply have bad timing.

Closing

So these are five ways of describing wise speech: truthful, gentle, useful, kindhearted and timely. When your speech doesn't fit these criteria, it does not call for harsh judgment. You look at it honestly, gently, helpfully, and kindly. This cultivates wisdom. And it helps even when you don't have the opportunity to speak.

A few weeks ago, my son Nathan and I rode bikes 20 miles up to Folsom Dam. On the way back, I told Nathan to go on ahead. I was tired and wanted to take my time.

I rode along slowly, watching the birds, spacing out, enjoying sore legs and the late afternoon sun. I heard a voice behind me: "coming through." I had been drifting across the bikeway so I swerved back into the right lane. A guy in yellow spandex said, "Stay in one lane, damn it!" as he sped past at 20 miles an hour.

As he zipped around the curve in front of me I felt a flush of anger. Fifteen minutes later I was still making up conversations in my head: giving him a piece of my mind for being rude, harsh, and condemning.

Finally I recognized the rants in my head were not wise speech: they weren't gentle, helpful, kindhearted, or timely. I also wasn't letting it go.

I know the guidelines are not about right and wrong, good or bad. So I didn't judge myself. But I knew this was a good time for deep listening.

I recognized that my anger covered embarrassment. I didn't want to admit it but his critique was accurate: I had been wandering around lanes. When I was gentle and honest with myself about that, some of my anger subsided. And I imagined the guy in spandex leading a hurried, harried life. He must have been stressed or scared by my swerve to be so harsh. As I imagined what I could say to him that would be skillful, that would be honest, gentle, useful, kindhearted, and timely, my agitation and sense of separation diminished. I felt more at ease and harmonious.

So wise speech ultimately is about our own consciousness. It is a way of putting us in touch with the wisdom within us that gets lost in the rush of the day. It slows us down and connects us with life in a way that is truthful, harmonious, and vibrant. This brings our inherent wisdom, compassion, and courage to the surface.

Namasté.

Little Mind, Big Mind

We participate in our natural spaciousness so seldom that we have come to believe we are whatever arises in the mind.

– Stephen Levine

June 5, 2005

I stared at the dark ceiling. I rolled onto my stomach. I rolled onto my side. I rolled onto my back again and closed my eyes to meditate. My eyes popped open. I stared at the ceiling.

Church issues called for attention. I was leaving on a minister's retreat the next day and I hadn't worked out the parts of the retreat I was leading. And being away for a few days put more time pressure on all the other issues.

Ordinarily, these would not keep me awake. But my son Damon was home for a few weeks. Between the time I got back from the retreat and the time he went back to college, I had no time to hang out with him.

People visited Henry David Thoreau when he lived in a cabin on Walden Pond. If they wanted to talk about the market price of beans or local politics, Henry David was content to sit inside with his visitor. But if they wanted to talk about the nature of life, he took the chairs outside. Important discussions about big issues need more space.

I had some bigger issues to explore with Damon. Grabbing a few hours here or there did not give us the space to settle into them.

Staring at the ceiling I thought, "I can skip the retreat to get more time. But I'd be letting colleagues down. I could cancel church meetings. But I'd be letting people down who had shifted their schedules to accommodate me. I could forget about quality time with Damon. That feels bad."

My mind spun around and around this circle of thoughts like a dog exhausting himself chasing his tail. "Maybe this obsessive thinking is part of post-concussion syndrome." That thought didn't get me anywhere. I rolled over again.

Finally I fell asleep for a few hours.

First thing in the morning I called a few colleagues. "I'm not coming to the retreat," I said. "I need to spend some time with my son." They said, "We'll miss you, but we can cover for you. Family comes first. Do what you need to do with our blessing."

An hour later, Damon and I were heading down Interstate 80 toward Point Reyes for the day. As we drove, Damon told me about the courses he had taken last semester and the things he was thinking about. He told me about a new girlfriend I had not heard about before. I reflected on my life at his age and my memories of him as a baby. We even imagined different futures for Damon without me getting into a parental, "What are you going to do with your life, young man?" We listened to the News from Lake Woebegone from my iPod. We waxed philosophical and told inane jokes.

Near the coast we turned north toward Elk Reserve and Tomales Point. The road ended at Pierce Point Ranch, a dairy farm built in the late 1800s. We walked amongst the old buildings, through a grove of huge bishop pines sculpted by winds from the sea and out onto the grassy hills with cliffs dropping to the ocean.

We still talked. But there were longer pauses as we looked at flowers, smelled the salt air, listened to the surf a half-mile away, and scanned the ocean for signs of whales.

After a while, Damon walked ahead.

As I came up a rise, I could see Lawson's Landing a few miles across the water. There was Sand Point and Tomales Bluff. Many miles to the south, past Elephant Rock and several beaches I could see the cliffs around Point Reyes itself. Off to the east was Sacramento. I couldn't see the city, of course. But I knew about where it was. It took up about one degree of the horizon. Around the other 359 degrees were hills and shoreline and the expanse of sea itself. And the sky was huge. My worries and concerns and delights and ambitions were still with me, floating in the background, like that one-degree speck on the horizon. All around me was a bigger sense of life and all its textures.

A half mile ahead I could see Damon walking his own path, literally and figuratively.

When I came up the next rise, Damon was gazing out to sea. We were still several miles from Tomales point itself. Neither of us spoke for a long while.

"Wanna head back?" Damon asked.

"Sure," I whispered. We had come far enough. Time to return.

On the way back, we spoke of simpler things: the way the elk looked at us as they munched, the flight of a raptor amongst the cliffs below, where to stop for food, whether to pick up a movie before we got home.

Damon and I didn't solve any problems or unearth any insights that day. We did connect more in a father-son kind of way. Still, the issues in his life were the same. The issues in mine were unchanged. But I could see them in a larger context – like waves and tides that come and go, ebb and flow. My mind was more expansive, my heart more trusting of the flux of life itself.

I slept very well that night.

Little Mind, Big Mind

This morning I want to talk about little mind and big mind. Little mind is the ordinary consciousness most of us spend most of our days in. Big mind is a wiser, deeper, and higher form of consciousness. If you sense my consciousness lying in bed that night and my consciousness walking the wind swept bluffs, you have a feel for the difference between little mind and big mind.

Summer with its ease of being outdoors and more relaxed pace is more conducive to big mind. So this morning seemed a good time to talk about big mind: what it is, why it is important, and how to cultivate it.

What

It is difficult to define exactly what big mind is, because defining is a small mind activity. So I offer an analogy.

Spider

Close your eyes, if you like, and imagine being very close to a very large spider with hairy legs, alien head, and grotesque mandibles: good material for a low-grade horror movie. Feel your consciousness.

Now imagine moving back enough to see the spider and the leaf it is standing on.

Move back a little further so you see the spider, leaf, and bush that holds them all. To the right is a large web covered with dew lit up by the morning sun.

Move back several feet and take in the field that contains the bush: birds and bugs and grasses and the little ecosystem.

Move back further. See the spider and web and bush and field and hilltop and oceans and mountains in the distance. Feel your consciousness now.

Nothing essential has changed. You can still see the spider doing its spider thing. But now you see it in the context of all the processes of life. What has changed is you: you've shifted from little mind toward big mind.

Examples

As I said, big mind is both rare and difficult to define. But we've all experienced the difference between little and big mind.

If you've ever lain awake at night with your mind going over and over a conundrum, you know what it feels like to be trapped in little mind.

If you've ever stood on an ocean cliff or mountaintop and said to yourself, "I'm not going to think about my problems. I'll set them aside and look at the beauty around me instead," you know another, more pleasant experience of little mind.

But if you've ever walked by the surf not trying to block anything out, if you've relaxed and let your worries and dreams wash over you like waves slipping over rocks and at the same time noticed the ocean and sky and a larger sense of life in all its flux and textures and depth, then you've tasted big mind.

If you've ever tried to do a big holiday grocery shopping with a grumpy two-year-old in tow, you know how pressed and compressed little mind can feel. If you've ever looked in on your sleeping child and felt the fatigue in your body and love in your heart, you know how sweet big mind can be.

If you've ever been caught in a spiral of pessimism, you know how obsessive little mind sometimes is. If you've ever taken a course on the power of positive thinking, you know how dogmatic little mind can be. If you've ever caught yourself in the midst of a familiar habit pattern and laughed at yourself, "Wow, there I go again. Far out," you know how relaxed and wise big mind can be.

Why

Why is big mind important?

Little mind is small and tight and narrow. It is concerned with the content of your life – usually one or two fragments at a time. It sees the tree but not the forest. If it is looking at a spider close up, life feels terrible. If it is looking at a flower, life is beautiful. If it is wrestling with bills, life is annoying. If it is thinking about a lover, it is enchanted. Little mind gets jerked around by the content of it experiences.

Big mind is concerned with the context of your life more than the content. It sees the trees and the forest and the hills and the mountains around them. It sees the spider stinging a cricket in its web. It sees a butterfly in the meadow. It is less horrified by one or seduced by the other. And it senses the flow of love and life that holds them all.

Big mind is more than a shift in perspective. It is a shift in modalities. Little mind uses one faculty: usually the intellect or the emotions.

Big mind uses multiple faculties at once: the intellect, emotions, body, sensory perception, compassion, intuition, direct knowing, and more. And big mind does all these with a wide-open embrace that is relaxed, clear, mindful, heartful, and intuitive all at once.

Who Are You?

By focusing on one or two fragments of your experience, little mind confuses who we are with our experience. Little mind says we are our history or our memories or thoughts. "I think, therefore I am." We are our feelings, our personality, our body, our aspirations, or the sum total of all we have experienced.

In contrast, by taking in the content and the context through multiple modalities, big mind says we are none of these fragments. We are the space within which we experience the content of life. We are not the clouds; we are the sky. We are the spacious awareness that can see it all at the same time.

Little mind gets bounced around by the content of our lives. We are scared by spiders and soothed by flowers, disturbed by an unfair reprimand and delighted by praise, content when we have political leaders we like and anxious when we don't. We feel sunny in good weather and cloudy when it rains.

On the other hand, big mind finds peace and contentment even in the midst of loss, failure, and pain. It feels those things without being thrown by them. It knows that all things pass. It is less buffeted by the winds of fate. It is a source of stability, grace, wisdom, compassion, love, joy, and contentment.

Big mind is an evolutionary leap in how we think and perceive. It combines and integrates a wide range of faculties. It is a higher form of consciousness, if you will.

Cultivating

How do we find big mind?

Searching for big mind is like a fish in the sea searching for water. Big mind is not a big fish amongst all the other critters in the ocean. It's the ocean itself. Big mind is everywhere. It permeates everything. It is part of everything.

But invoking it takes a certain kind of letting go and letting be, a certain spaciousness of heart, an openness to what is. Traditional consciousness disciplines like meditation and contemplative prayer can be invaluable tools. And there are many, many less formal approaches.

Welcoming

For example, our approach is cultivating a welcoming attitude toward whatever life brings. If we are busy judging events as good or bad, right or wrong, something to be held or pushed away or ignored, we are investing in the content of our lives. We are less apt to notice the broader context. On the other hand, if we are more relaxed and accepting of whatever comes along, it is easier to sense the larger flow. We *respond* to the *big picture* rather than *react* to the *details*.

Years ago I heard a story about this.

There was a monk living in the hills outside a fishing village. A young woman in the village became pregnant. When her child was born the villagers demanded to know who the father was. The father was a young fisherman. But the woman didn't want to get her lover into trouble. So she said, "The father is the monk who lives by himself up in the hills."

The villagers picked up the baby and marched out of town to the monk's cottage. They rapped on the door. The door opened and the monk bowed in greeting.

They were not in the mood for pleasantries. They got right to the point: "This is your baby and your responsibility." They handed him the infant. He held it, bowed and said, "Ah so." They turned and stormed back down the hill.

Fifteen years flowed by. The woman became deathly ill. She didn't want to die with this terrible lie on her conscience. She confessed, "The monk was not the father of my child."

A few hours later, a delegation of villagers knocked gently on the monk's door. The monk opened the door and smiled in greeting. Behind him was a young man with sparkly eyes.

With hat in hand the leader of the delegation said, "There has been a terrible mistake. We are so sorry. The child we left with you is not yours or your responsibility. We've come to relieve you of this burden."

The monk bowed and said, "Ah so."

Ah So

The story is a little outlandish. But it touched something in me. "Ah" is the sound of release. "So" is the sound of just looking at what is with soft, open eyes. I imagine the monk living in big mind. For me, "ah so" became an invitation to remember all those qualities: expansiveness, presence, ease, clarity, kindness, joy, love.

I'd be driving through town late for an appointment, caught behind a slow driver. Sitting at a red light, my frustration rising, I'd remember the story and say "ah so" to the streetlight and remember big mind. I'd either be late or I wouldn't. Nothing I could do would change that now: "Ah so." I'd feel my irritation: "Ah so." Something inside me would relax. I'd find myself smiling at this cute little drama.

One evening I went into the upstairs bathroom of our old house to find our cat, Billy, curled up on the floor. He'd been a family member for fifteen years. His kidneys were failing. I sat next to him and put him on my lap. He was too weak to move. I patted him softly. He purred deeply. I stroking him for fifteen minutes as his purring grew weaker and weaker. It stopped. His breathing stopped. Tears ran down my cheeks. "Ah so." I felt the sweetness and richness of it all: the blessing of this little life. I was very sad and very okay. "Ah so."

Maybe you are having difficulty with a relationship: a parent, a child, a partner. You lie awake at night tossing and turning as you go through a repetitive cycle of thoughts. Nothing settles it. "Ah so" can be a reminder of a larger context: all relationships struggle at times. This too shall pass. "Ah so" can be a reminder of all your faculties: thinking, feeling, perceiving, intuiting, knowing, imagining. Rather than focusing just on the content of your thought, you feel the textures of your thoughts, the sensations in your body, the sounds of the night. "Ah so" reminds you of big mind. No need to grasp or push away any of it. You let it all wash over you and let the flow take you deeper and higher.

Or maybe you are having an ordinary, mundane day: no particular problems or special delights. Just routine. Your mind is running in its familiar groove. "Ah so." Ordinariness is a part of life. "Ah so." Your mind and heart expand into this simple moment with birds and cars in the background, people sitting around you. Lights buzzing. Just this moment. Big mind is here. Spread out into it. Let yourself be.

Meditation

In fact, let's try it now. Close your eyes if that will help, and just be present.

There are worries and delights in your life, hurts and hopes. No need to push them away or grasp hold of them. No need to ignore or fix. Let them be.

Feel the sensations in your body, the color of your mood, the texture of your thoughts, the movement in your heart. Hold nothing. Push nothing away. Let everything be just as it is.

Invite yourself into big mind. Spread out into it. Imagine your body feeling soft and light, expanding out into the room.

Just let things be as they are for now. Float in the space of big mind.

You are not the clouds. You are the sky.

Be like the sky.

Sengstan, the third Zen Patriarch, once wrote:

The Way is perfect like vast space where nothing is lacking and nothing is in excess. Indeed, it is due to our choosing to accept or reject that we do not see the true nature of things. Live neither in the entanglements of outer things, nor in the inner feelings of emptiness. Be serene in the oneness of things.

Song: Sweet Quiet

Sweet quiet, boundless sea, where joy and grief are the same; Endless sky, pale breeze of dawn breathe your light into me.

Closing

As big mind gets more and more expansive, it sees life in broader and broader context. As it incorporates more and more ways of seeing, feeling, sensing, and knowing, it becomes difficult to describe this way of being in words that little mind can grasp.

Mystics use words like "God" and "God consciousness" to describe the broadest, ultimate context with its widest spectrum of modalities. For little mind, God is a big fish. For big mind, God is the ocean. For small mind, God is a thing: perhaps the ultimate thing but still a mysterious object. For big mind, God consciousness is all the ways of experiencing all things. For little mind, God is a being. For big mind, God is beingness.

If God language helps you see the ebb and flow of life, great. Use it: ah so.

If God language doesn't help you in this way, that's okay. Ah so.

Big mind is an evolution in consciousness from a small, reactive mind to a spacious, wise, and loving consciousness. Big mind brings greater and more lasting happiness because it is not dependent on things being one way or another. It makes us more effective in our lives and in the world. It brings more depth, love, and wisdom.

I bow to the big mind that is all of us.

Ah so.

Loving Your Consciousness

August 28, 2005

Imagine a cavern: a vast cavern with many chambers and vaults, nooks and crannies. It contains everything in your life or that ever could be in your life. The cavern contains your car, iPod, MasterCard, the orange you are having for lunch. Under that rock is the quarter you lost last week and some old toenail clippings. Sitting over there are Aunt Mirabel and Uncle Joe. Around the bend is the cast you'll wear next year when you break your arm.

The cavern contains not only physical objects but mental and emotional objects as well. Your love of your kids, grief over your father's death, plans for next summer, and idle meanderings are all objects in the cavern. Down that hole is your fear of snakes. Up near the ceiling is this afternoon's daydream.

In this cavern there is only one flashlight. You can only see objects illuminated by the flashlight. It doesn't matter that an object is in the cavern. If it is not illuminated, it is not part of your experience.

The flashlight has a very good battery that will last lifetimes. And it has many filters over the lens.

The light can shine intensely on a single object allowing you to see lots of details (distorted by the lens' filters). Or the light can wave around on several objects in which case you see less detail. However, there is only one light.

Fierce and Kind

This morning I want to talk about a way of knowing your depths which is dead honest, fierce and fearless. And at the same time, it is kind and heartful.

In Buddhism this is called *bodhicitta*. Bodhi means seeing clearly. *Citta* means heart. Heartful seeing is said to be the essence of the enlightened mind. In Christianity it's called the "heart of Christ" or the "mind of God." In Islam, Allah is said to be totally fierce and totally loving.

This morning I'm simply calling it "loving your consciousness." By "loving" I don't mean romanticizing or holding on. I mean the opposite: seeing clearly and letting go.

To love something means that we see it openly for what it is. And it means welcoming it. To love your partner doesn't mean you agree with him, accept, or even like everything about him. It means only that you see him clearly and hold him in your heart.

So this morning I want to talk about bringing this fierce and kind abiding to the depths of your consciousness.

Objects

As a place to start, I should describe what I mean by consciousness. I'm concerned with three different aspects. We do not have a good, shared vocabulary of consciousness. So rather than try to define them, I'll use this cavern image as a metaphor.

As you travel through life exploring this cavern, there are four factors that affect your experience.

The first and most obvious is the objects in the cave.

Most people spend most of their lives attending to the objects: physical items, sensations, feelings and thoughts. Most people prefer some objects to others – they explore some parts of the cavern more than others. Some people are more interested in material stuff, some more in ideas, some more in feelings.

Consciousness is not about physical, mental or emotional objects. These are not our depths. So let's move on.

Filters

The next most obvious factor that affects our experience is the filters on the flashlight. They color our experience. They are part of our consciousness. So let's explore them.

Filters are anything so close to us that they color how we see things. Our perception can be distorted by our physiological states, emotions, personality, cultural background, beliefs, worldview, political leanings, or anything we closely identify with. Let's consider just a few.

Our consciousness can be distorted by physiological states like fatigue, intoxication, and even hunger. If I'm hungry when I go to the grocery store, everything looks so attractive that I buy twice as much as I need. On the other hand, if I'm feeling a little nauseous, everything looks so unattractive that I come home with one carrot and a roll of paper towels to hold me for the week. The groceries in the market are the same in each instance. My physiological state colors my perception of them.

Our consciousness can be distorted by emotions like fear, anger, pride, and so forth. For example, after telling a story on Sunday morning, the congregation is dead silent. You can hear a pin drop. No one stirs. If I'm feeling confident, I might think, "Wow. They were really moved. I'll let it sink in while I savor this moment." On the other hand, if I'm feeling nervous and worried I may think, "Uh oh. That went over like a lead balloon. I'm in trouble now." And I rush ahead.

The silence, stillness, and expressions on your faces are the same. But my emotional states dramatically affect my perception of you.

Personality and disposition can also filter and distort. Let's say you walk into a party of strangers. If you are extroverted by nature, you see a lot of interesting people to get to know. If you are shy, you see people who don't like you and would prefer you leave.

Cultural background can dramatically color experience. Someone walks up and in a flat tone says, "Hi, how ya doing?" Depending on where you grew up, you may see the person as superficial, as friendly, as cool and filled with bravado, or as incredibly rude for making an intimate inquiry in a public place. The person's appearance, words, gestures, and vocal tones may be the same. But depending on the cultural cues familiar to you, you may interpret the person very differently.

Beliefs, worldview, and political leanings can be powerful filters as well. Imagine being in a casual group at work during a lunch break. Someone says, "George Bush" or "Bill Clinton" or "Iraq." You can feel all the filters being activated as people's subtle body language says,
"Ooo" or "Agh!" or "Yes!" or "Ugh." If you were clairvoyant, you'd see tinted glass roll down in front of each person. On the glass would be movie images projected from their beliefs.

When Dennis Warren was here a few weeks ago, he mentioned research that shows many people stop listening in political discussions because their consciousness becomes preoccupied with their own ideas.

Loving Your Filters

The phrase "the world is an illusion" doesn't mean the world is a mental fabrication. It means our perception of it is deeply distorted. How can we get free of distortion?

You can't get rid of your physiology, emotions, personality, preferences, beliefs, and ideas. Sometimes you can change them, to be sure. But then you'll just have different filters. No matter what we do, we all have a body, feelings, character structure, personal history, and points of view. These come with being human.

It is not reasonable to try to get rid of them. However, it is possible to take them off the flashlight lens. This is doable. This changes them from being a filter on the lens (a part of your consciousness) to being another object in the cavern. They will still be around. They may stay very near you. But they won't color everything you see. They become an *object of consciousness* rather than a *filter in consciousness*.

How do we do this?

Loving your consciousness, in part, means loving your filters and distortions. This requires being fierce and fearless with yourself. Be a warrior. Be dispassionate. Look at your personality, feeling, beliefs, conditioning, and all the rest as unflinchingly as you can. See them as they are.

This is easier to do if you are kind, gentle, and compassionate at the same time. Beating yourself up for imperfections is unnecessary and unhelpful. So welcome your filters without grasping hold of them or pushing them away.

For example, when you are hungry in the grocery store, heartfully embrace your hunger. See it and feel it. Then, your hunger and the cantaloupe will both be objects in the cavern. You can stand in the fruit section and see "cantaloupe," "hunger," and "strawberries" right next to each other. You don't see the cantaloupe through your hunger. Your decision to buy or not has a chance of being based on something more than a momentary craving.

Or consider that silent moment in the church service. Whether I'm nervous or confident, I see the feeling as clearly and heartfully as I can rather than celebrate, indulge, or squash it. It becomes less of a mood that filters all my perceptions. It comes off the flashlight and into the cavern.

Some of you are familiar with the phrase "deep listening." This is what I'm talking about. You see your moods and preoccupations deeply and heartfully so you can set them aside and listen deeply to the person before you rather than project your inclinations and beliefs onto them.

As you relate fiercely and lovingly to your filters, they come off the lens of the light and become objects in the cavern. Your consciousness becomes clearer, more penetrating and more heartful.

That Which Directs the Light

So far we have looked at the objects in the cavern and the filters on the light. What else affects our experience?

The next factor is "that which directs the light." Remember, in a cavern the light must shine on an object before it becomes visible. What is it that directs your attention to one thing or another?

This is more mysterious than the filters because people pay less attention to it. Most people assume they control their attention. After all, you are the one choosing to listen to me or think about something more interesting or watch that attractive person across the room.

But do you really think you have control of your attention? I challenge you to not be aware of the buzzing of the lights above us right now.

How many of you were aware of them a few moments ago? How many notice them now? Are you in control?

Try not to think about a blue horse. Blue horses don't even exist in the natural world. But I bet most of you have some blue horse image in your mind right now.

How many of you have ever tried to meditate? You put attention on the breath or a mantra or some single object and say to your attention, "Stay." But the mind is like a frisky puppy. In a few moments it is off chasing some thought or fantasy. We have a little influence over our attention, but we are not in control. The mind has a mind of its own.

To be sure, something directs our attention. Something pulls it hither and yon. We don't have a good, shared language to name what it is. But we can sense its qualities.

Inner Voice

Most people experience an internal voice that comments, advises, and directs them. Walking down the hall of the office, it may go something like this:

"Oh, there's Henry. Last time I saw him he was obnoxious. I'll look down, so he won't notice me."

"There's a cigarette in wastebasket. I hate smoking in here. I bet it was Joe."

"My foot hurts. Did I cut it?"

"There's Alice. I need to talk to her. But if I stop, I'll be late for the meeting. I'll see if I can find her later. I hope I'm not making a mistake. "

"Oh! I haven't even thought about what I'm going to say at this meeting. I'll sound foolish. Maybe I can start with … "

Most of us go around with an internal commentary that critiques, warns, editorializes, and so on. It directs our attention.

Loving your consciousness means noticing the quality of this internal voice: the tone, not the content. The content goes by with blinding speed. We can't remember it all. But you can notice the qualities of the voice speaking in your mind. Is the inner voice sad, excited, expository, scolding, tense, relaxed, demeaning, protective, soothing, affirming? The attitude of that voice causes you to notice some things and ignore others. It directs and colors your consciousness and experience.

It is not helpful to try to control, change, or manipulate the tone. Just look at it heartfully, honestly, clearly, fiercely, kindly.

After a while — it may take some practice and patience — the tone of voice becomes an object or set of objects in the cavern. You can see beyond the direction of the flashlight beam.

Next time you are walking or driving by yourself, pay attention to the tone of your thoughts. Be clear and kind with yourself: *bodhicitta*, heartful awareness. With a little patience, this practice can lead to an enormous sense of freedom. Try it.

The Light

So, we've looked at the objects in the cavern, the filters on the lens and that which directs the light. What's left?

What's left is the subtlest, most stable, most mysterious, and most essential element.

It is the light itself. It is "that which knows." Behind everything else is the actual knowing faculty. But what is it that knows? What is this light?

This is one of life's most intimate and pervasive mysteries. It has been called "pure consciousness" because it is consciousness without filters and without direction. It's been called "soul," "spirit," and "essence" because it is so deep and basic. Sometimes it is called "God" or "divine spark" because it is more than what we think of as mere human.

Big Mind

How many of you have actually been in a sizable cavern?

I was 9 or 10 the first time I went into a large cavern. I was in a group of 10 or 15 people. A quarter of a mile beneath the earth, our guide turned off all the lights. It was total darkness. I could put my palm against my nose and still not be able to see it.

Then he turned on his flashlight. It was a big four-cell light that puts out an intense beam. And it was amazingly unhelpful. I could see the end of the stalactite that it illuminated. But nothing else. As he moved the light around, all I could see were the tiniest segments of the cavern. It was difficult to get a sense of the place from that narrow beam.

Then he turned off the big flashlight and lit one puny candle. It was dimmer than the flashlight, to be sure. But it sent out a soft glow in all directions and lit up the entire chamber.

As my eyes adjusted, I could see the people around me, the shape of the chamber. It was easy to move around and even see a lot of detail.

I'm sure Wal-Mart can make more money selling big flashlights than puny candles. But the candles are more useful.

Last June I spoke about little mind and big mind. Little mind is like the flashlight: it is intense, focused, sees detail, draws attention to itself but has no sense of context or perspective.

Big mind is like the candle: soft, laid back, panoramic, receptive, and doesn't draw attention to itself. Big mind is a taste of that light of pure consciousness. It is like a candle that illuminates in all directions. It is pure and fearless and loving and clear.

Closing

To summarize, consciousness is the most intimate, familiar and pervasive aspect of our existence. It influences everything we do, everything we think, everything we say, and everything we experience. It affects how we eat, who we like to talk to, how we make love, who we prefer to make love with, where we go on vacation, who we vote for, and what we think about in quiet moments.

The most effective way to cultivate a light, buoyant consciousness is to love it. Loving your consciousness is one of the most effective tools for increasing our wisdom, happiness, and effectiveness in the world whether we are talking about the world of intimate relationships, families, communities, socio-political realms, or the larger ecosystem.

So I invite you to be fierce and gentle with yourself. You've got the ability to see yourself clearly. You've insight into your hang-ups, your fears, your preferences, your disposition, your moods, your talents, your inclinations. You've got the ability to see the filters on your lens and that which directs the light.

Be fierce and clear. But be loving and respectful as well. We all have unpleasant things in our consciousness — coveting, vengefulness, greed, petty grudges, and so forth. There is no need to add self-judgment to these. Be as clear, fearless, relaxed, and compassionate as you can.

In doing this, you cultivate qualities that resonate with that mysterious light of pure consciousness. In traditional religious language, you cultivate the qualities of God or Goddess or Jesus or Mohammed or Buddha.

Cultivating clearness, fearlessness, compassion, ease, welcoming, openness, and so on does not turn you into a God, Jesus, or Buddha. But it increases the odds that you will have moments of directly experiencing that light of pure consciousness that is clear, fearless, loving, and expansive. It's always been there. It helps you know it and have faith in it.

It increases your wisdom, insight, wellbeing and effectiveness in life.

Meditation

Let's try it now.

Take a moment to stretch. Then close your eyes. Let your body relax.

Picture the candle flame right in the center of your heart. It is soft and warm. It is relaxed as it sends out an even glow in all directions.

Let your awareness be like this candle: soft and radiant and multi-dimensional.

As it glows, it gets stronger and brighter, clearer and more intense. It becomes fierce and steady even as it remains kind and loving.

Let your awareness be like this light: fierce, steady, and kind.

If thoughts or feelings or memories or images come up, that's okay. Let them be objects in the cavern.

You be the light. Be fierce. Be kind. Be open. Be relaxed. Be receptive and expansive.

Big mind. Bodhicitta. The heart of Christ. Heartful awareness.

Being Who We Are: Playing Golf in Calcutta

September 25, 2005

After the British were comfortably in control of India, they looked around for entertainment. They decided that India needed golf — a game that stressed skill and control more than chance. So they built a golf course in Calcutta.

But they hadn't counted on monkeys. India has lots of monkeys. The creatures were fascinated by the little, white balls popping around the tidy, green lawns. They chased them, carried them, and threw them around.

The British exclaimed, "This will never do!" and built a high fence around the course to keep the animals out. The monkeys were delighted. Now they had wonderful structures to climb as well as the little white balls to toss around. There were more monkeys than ever.

So the British trapped the monkeys and carried them far away into the jungle. But the amusement park was so fascinating that for every monkey they carted off, there were two more to take its place.

Next the British tried to lure the monkeys away. But to the monkeys, nothing was more enticing than humans in white shorts jumping up and down and yelling every time they picked up a little white ball.

Finally, the British came up with a solution: they changed one rule of the game and posted it at the entry to the golf course. It read, "You must play the ball wherever the monkey leaves it."

Monkeys

This morning I want to talk about living contentedly with monkeys.

Make no mistake: there are monkeys in our lives. They may not have curly tails and swing through the trees, but mischief and chaos love to play with us. There are monkeys who crash your computer after you spent three hours on that spreadsheet. There are monkeys who spill coffee on your shirt as you walk into the job interview. There are monkeys who start a fight amongst the kids just as you try to leave for the gym. There are monkeys driving down our highways.

Some monkeys live outside us raining on our picnic, breaking the car at the most inconvenient time, or emailing lots of spam.

Other monkeys live inside us. I had a client once who was a chronic liar. He did not set out to deceive people. But he'd find himself in the middle of a conversation making things up. It was an unconscious habit that made a mess of his life.

Maybe you resolve to eat healthily, exercise more, and watch TV less. Then you find yourself lying on the couch in front of the TV eating corn chips. You want to spend more time with the family, but you find yourself working late or surfing the Internet.

We all have our quirks and habits, our conditioning and personality.

In Western culture and particularly in America, we think we should be in control of our lives. We should be masters of our fate. No one thinks monkeys are in their destiny. If things don't go the way we think they should, we feel guilty or look for someone to sue: shame or blame.

So this morning I want to talk about playing the ball where the monkey leaves it and finding contentment in our lives just as they are. I want to talk about being who we are without shame or blame.

I'll start with the traditional concept of original sin. Few of us here accept this old church teaching intellectually. But it is deep in the cultural psyche. The way we raise children and the way we were raised as children leaves us with the psychological equivalent of original sin. Shame and blame permeate the American landscape. Once we've explored these we can come back to the comparing mind and finding contentment.

Original Sin

Our great, great, great, great, great, great, great, great, great grandparents, Adam and Eve, lived an idyllic life according to the traditional church. It was a life we can all envy. They walked in a paradise with God: the climate was mild, food was plentiful, creatures were friendly, their moods were innocent. There was only one requirement. They weren't supposed to be curious. God commanded: "Don't eat of the tree of knowledge for it will destroy your innocence and cause you to die."

As we all know, Adam and Eve couldn't restrain themselves. There was a monkey in the Garden of Eden. In the text, the monkey is called a serpent. In Eden snakes had arms and legs and a long skinny tail. Eve blamed the serpent. Adam blamed Eve. God blamed everyone and tossed them out of paradise to suffer and die.

Eating the forbidden fruit was the "original sin." It was our first sin, our first transgression. And yes, it is consider "our" sin. Like bloodguilt, we inherited the shame of that disobedience. Never mind that you and I were not around back then to say, "eat" or "don't eat." We carry the stain of that mischief. We are bad. This is why there are monkeys tossing our golf balls into the creek. It's our fault.

There may not be anyone here who takes this story literally. Yet, many of us live with a vague sense of original sin, a vague sense that something is wrong with my life: I should be richer, smarter, thinner, something.

Not Loved for Being

To see where this guilt might come from, let's get an outside perspective on child rearing in modern America.

A man I study with describes visiting remote villages in northern Laos and on the high plains of Tibet. Here there is no electricity or running water, no TVs or radios. Once every few weeks a newspaper gets into town. Maybe one or two people can read it. There is one old watch in town. That is the only machine or appliance.

Village life proceeds as it has since long before there were all the gadgets and gizmos we take for granted. If you want to talk to a friend in the next village, it takes a half a day to walk over there. If you want to eat supper, it takes considerable time and preparation. The pace of life is slow. And life expectancy is shorter. More children die young.

The most striking thing about these villages is that the kids are loved for simply being. They don't have to do anything to be cherished. They are loved simply because they are there.

Now, contrast this with child rearing in our society.

We applaud kids for learning to walk, for speaking their first words, for drinking out of a cup, for using the toilet. These are things they do for which we express approval. As they grow up, we give them praise for making good grades, for being great athletes or musicians, for expressing intelligent thoughts. We reward the winners and everyone else is ignored as if they had failed. When a reporter interviews an Olympic silver medalist, the first question is likely to be, "How are you handling your disappointment?" The assumption is either you win or you are a failure.

Many see the destructiveness of this trend and try to make children feel better by saying, "Everyone is a winner." Think about this statement. A child knows to win means to come in first. Secretly he worries, "What if someone notices that only one person came in first and it wasn't me? Will they still love me?"

There are parents (I imagine all of you here) who genuinely love their kids for simply being. But the cultural backdrop of our children's lives is filled with striving to win. It's hard to shelter them from it. And it's hard not to get unconsciously drawn into it ourselves.

My point is that most of us walk around with a vague sense of not being enough. We all are not the winner. We all are not above average. When we are loved for what we do rather than for who we are, it leaves a feeling that we are not enough: if we don't perform adequately, we will be less than lovable.

Variations

There are many subtleties and variations on how this manifests in our lives. Portia Nelson's "Autobiography in Five Short Chapters" illustrates some of this variety:

CHAPTER ONE
I walk down the street.
    There is a deep hole in the sidewalk.
    I fall in
    I am lost … I am helpless
        It isn't my fault.
It takes forever to find a way out.

CHAPTER TWO
I walk down the same street.
    There is a deep hole in the sidewalk.
    I pretend I don't see it.
    I fall in again.
    I can't believe I am in the same place.
        But it isn't my fault.
It still takes a long time to get out.

CHAPTER THREE
I walk down the same street.
    There is a deep hole in the sidewalk.
    I see it is there.
    I still fall in … it's a habit … but,
        my eyes are open.
    I know where I am.
It is my fault.
 I get out immediately.

CHAPTER FOUR
I walk down the same street.
    There is a deep hole in the sidewalk.
    I walk around it.

CHAPTER FIVE
I walk down another street.[9]

How many of you can relate to this story?

---

[9] Portia Nelson, *There's a Hole in My Sidewalk: The Romance of Self-Discovery.* (Hillsboro, Oregon: Beyond Words, 1993), pp. 2-3.

We all have holes in our lives: old habits and new circumstances that appear in our path. Portia Nelson struggles with whose fault it is that she lands in the hole — again and again. Do you know that feeling?

Shame and blame are different aspects of finding fault. Fault projected onto others becomes blame or self-righteousness. Fault turned inward becomes guilt or shame.

They stem from the same feeling: something is wrong. They can be so painful that we disguise them behind other feelings like helplessness, surprise, defensiveness, feeling stuck, denial, pretending not to see, anger, anxiety, depression, irritability, working too hard, boredom, and above all else striving. We are a country of strivers.

We Unitarian Universalists preach about universal love. And we may believe it sincerely. But we also like to strive for perfection. This can leave a residual sense of not being enough as we are.

This morning I'm referring to this whole menagerie of feelings, habits, conditioning, and circumstances as a pack of monkeys.

This is how life is. You may think there should not be holes in your sidewalk, but there they are. You may think you should not fall into them, but there you are. You may think you are above anger, confusion, denial, blaming, guilt, and all the rest, but there they are.

In her autobiography, Portia Nelson begins to accept them. With acceptance, her "eyes are opened." She sees life more clearly. This doesn't get rid of the holes in the sidewalk or the monkeys in her mind, but it helps her deal with them realistically and effectively. For the first time she is able to "get out immediately." This is what it means to play the ball where it lands and just get on with it.

Contentment

How do we develop this wisdom and clarity?

If the root of discontent is not being loved enough, then the root of contentment is loving ourselves as we are and accepting our lives as they are.

Monkeys are curious, playful creatures. It is not that hard to enjoy them and their antics.

Remember that client of mine who was a chronic liar? I knew we were making progress when he came in one afternoon and reported a phone conversation. He had been talking to a friend when he drifted off into a pointless fabrication. Right in the middle he caught himself and laughed out loud, "There I go again."

Rather than kill, avoid, pretend, blame, or chastise his inner monkey, he embraced it with humor – not easy to do, to be sure. But he accepted his monkey and began to play with it rather than try to fence it out or send it to the jungle. As he relaxed and became more self-accepting, the habit of lying began to subside.

Let me give another example.

The other day my wife bought a new faucet for the kitchen sink. I took out the old and secured the new. Then I tried to connect the faucet to the water supply. The tubes were not long enough. I looked at my watch, paced back and forth, grabbed my car keys, sped off to the hardware store, bought longer tubes, sped home, connected up one end and discovered the fittings on the faucet and the water supply were different sizes. I looked at my watch, paced back and forth, grabbed my car keys, sped off to the hardware store, spent a half hour with two clerks figuring out a combination of fittings that would work, brought them home, connected up one end, and then discovered a little package in the corner of the faucet box. Everything I needed had been there without any trips to the hardware store.

I was frustrated about the wasted time. I swore under my breath and decided I was an idiot. I felt ashamed of my incompetence and imperfect attention. I was a little dark cloud brooding around the house.

The next day I went back to working on this sermon. I began to see the faucets, connectors, adaptors, and my various moods and responses as monkeys making mischief in my life. With acceptance, my mood lightened up. Now I can laugh at the whole episode.

I invite you to look at the struggles in your life and see if you can spot the monkeys.

Monkeys are voices that say you should be more attentive, smarter, richer, more easy going, more disciplined, weigh less, exercise more, be more artistic, more knowledgeable, wiser, … something. Monkeys are the voices that say my boss should be nicer, my partner should be alive, my illness doesn't belong here. These are all monkeys on the golf course.

Things break in this world. This is how life is. We are imperfect creatures. It doesn't have to be a problem. There is nothing wrong fundamentally. The sooner we stop blaming the monkeys or blaming ourselves for having a life where fate is mischievous, the richer and more rewarding our life is. The less concerned we are with why the ball is where it is, the quicker we can just get on with the game. The more we can transmute shame and blame into acceptance and love, the easier it is to get on with being who we are and living the life we have.

Closing

Before we close, I want to come back to the issue of contentment. I've been talking about comparing our situation to some ideal, to some thought about what is best or worst. But the mind also has a tendency to compare our situation to someone else's. The mind likes to compare our good or ill fortune to others.

For example, my meditation teacher, John Travis, was telling me about another teacher, Guy Armstrong, with whom I might take a course. John told me that Guy had been a monk in Southeast Asia for a while. Then he came back to the Pacific Northwest in this country. He got connected with Microsoft during the early years of the company. He worked for them for five or six years and made several million dollars. Then he retired from the computer industry and devoted his life to the dharma — that is, to Buddhist teaching.

I thought, "Boy, I wish I had that kind of money in my bank account."

John must have seen the envy on my face. He shrugged and said, "It's just his karma. It was his karma to have that kind of money. But it's not part of yours or mine. Each person's path is different."

I thought, "Oh, right." My envy evaporated. The monkeys left my ball in a different place on the golf course. Who is to say his is better or worse. But even if it is, all I can do is play the ball where it landed for me. That's fine.

The wiser question to ask ourselves is not "Am I the best I can be?" "Am I doing all that I can imagine?" or "Is my life better or worse than someone else's?"

The problem is that no matter how wonderful you are or how good your life is, the mind can always imagine better. The mind can always find someone who seems to be in better shape (which can lead to envy) or worse shape (which can lead to a sense of entitlement).

There is something noble and inspiring about reaching higher. But we have gone way out of balance into striving and comparing.

The wiser question is not "Am I the best I can be?" or "Am I as good as him?" The wiser question is "Is this good enough?" If not, then there may be something to deal with. But if it is enough, maybe you can relax on a deeper level.

Maybe I don't have to be the best plumber, the most astute observer, the smartest home repair guy. Maybe it is enough that I eventually got the thing to work. Can I be content with that? Maybe I don't have to have a million dollars. Maybe a place to sleep, food to eat, and satisfying work to do is enough.

You do not have to be your ideal body weight, the most attentive parent, the number one in your field, the most creative musician or painter. It is enough to be who you are, monkeys and all.

Monkeys are pretty smart. When they are hated and shunned, they can become clever demons. But when they are treated with love and respect, they are fun and playful.

So love your monkeys. Live the life you've got. Be who you are. In reality there is not much choice because you are who you are complete with monkeys and potholes.

So play the ball where the monkey leaves it. Be who you are. This makes life a whole lot easier.

Deep Listening

I found that the chief difficulty for most people was to realize that they really heard new things, that is things that they had never heard before. They kept translating what they heard into their habitual language. They had ceased to hope and believe there might be anything new.

– P. D. Ouspensky

October 16, 2005

If you could speak to Osama bin Laden, what would you say to him? Think about it.

Shortly after the World Trade Center destruction, Thich Nhat Hanh was asked this question. Thich Nhat Hanh is a Vietnamese monk who has worked for years to reduce violence in the world. Martin Luther King once nominated him for the Nobel Peace Prize. This is what he said:

If I were given the opportunity to be face-to-face with Osama bin Laden, the first thing I would do is listen. I would try to understand why he had acted in that cruel way. I would try to understand all of the suffering that had led him to violence. It might not be easy to listen in that way, so I would have to remain calm and lucid. I would need several friends with me who are strong in the practice of deep listening, listening without reacting, without judging and blaming. In this way, an atmosphere of support would be created for this person and those connected so that they could share completely, trust that they are really being heard.

After listening for some time, we might need to take a break to allow what has been said to enter into our consciousness. Only when we felt calm and lucid would we respond. We would respond point by point to what had been said. We would respond gently but firmly in such a way to help them to discover their own misunderstandings so that they will stop violent acts from their own will."

Thich Nhat Hanh alludes to a process called "deep listening." We can't listen if we are busy venting our fear, sadness, or anger. We can't listen if we are busy judging or blaming. Deep listening acknowledges our emotions and thoughts. But it sets those aside so that we become more calm, lucid, and open. Sometimes it is an end in and of itself that helps the person we are listening to hear their own depths more clearly. Other times, as in Thich Nhat Hanh's imagined conversation, it is the prerequisite for a meaningful dialog, for communication that enables us to touch each other where we truly live.

Spiritual Context

There is a deep, natural wisdom and compassion available to us all the time. Some people imagine it comes from deep inside: our Buddha nature, the God within, our core essence. Some people imagine it comes from outside: an external God or divine source that can flow through us.

These are just models. The important fact is tremendous wisdom and compassion and healing are available.

This sounds wonderful, doesn't it? But there is a catch. The nature of deep wisdom is that it is quiet. In the Old Testament, 1 Kings 19 uses a wonderful metaphor: "… a great and powerful wind tore the mountains apart and shattered the rocks, … but God was not in the wind. After the wind there was an earthquake, but God was not in the earthquake. After the earthquake came a fire, but God was not in the fire. And after the fire came a gentle breeze. When Elijah heard it, he pulled his cloak over his face and went out and stood at the mouth of the cave. Then a voice said to him, 'What are you doing here, Elijah?'" God was in the gentle breeze.

Our thoughts, emotions, and the urge to express ourselves are the winds, earthquakes, and fires. Compassion is not an emotion. It is a heartful connection. It arises from a place that is quieter than emotion. Wisdom is not thought. It is a direct perception that is quieter than thinking. Wisdom and compassion are the gentle breeze. The Quakers call it the "still small voice within."

Before we can hear that soft whisper, we have to settle some of our emotional reactivity and mental activity. Let's look at each.

Reactivity

The first impediment to heartful listening is emotional agitation. If I am busy venting anger, sadness, fear, or other feelings, I won't be able to listen well. I may not even want to listen. But if I do, I'm more likely to hear my commotion than the other person.

I assume most of us understand this. So let's go to the second impediment, which is not understood as well.

Mental Constructs

The second impediment to deep listening is mental construction. There is a natural world around us. But the mind, in its enthusiasm to help, paints the natural world with signs, labels, stories, and mental constructs that obscure clear perception.

For example, consider the object in front of us that we light at the beginning of each service. We call it a "chalice." This seems obvious. No mental imagining here. We can see it, touch it. It seems like a totally real chalice.

However, the chaliceness is a construct that comes out of our mind, not out of the natural world. If we took out the flame and filled it with water and placed it outside, we might call it a birdbath. The natural object would remain the same but the chalice would be gone and replaced by a birdbath. Or if we put dirt and flowers into it, we could call it a flowerpot: we'd paint a different construct onto it. Or we might wash it up and use it as a small, elegant chafing dish. Or we could turn it over and use it as a little stool.

The point is that there is a natural reality: an object that any healthy human from any culture or any intelligent species from another planet could see. And then we paint a construct on top if of it ("chaliceness", "birdbathness", "flowerpotness", etc.).

Different people may paint the object differently. If you see it as a practical footstool and use it as such, and I see it as a sacred religious object that embodies all I hold dear, I might launch a holy war against you because my mental construct is right and your mental construct is sacrilegious.

Deep listening separates the natural object from the mental constructs.

The chalice-birdbath-footstool is a simple object. Human behavior is intricate. What occurs naturally in human interaction is small compared to the constructs we paint on top.

For example, I once mentioned my early martial arts training. In class, sensei typically showed us a movement, like a straight punch, and asked us to practice it as he walked around and made corrections.

He might walk up to Bob who was working out next to me and say, "Keep your elbow closer to your body and don't rotate your fist until the last few inches."

Then he'd look at me for a moment and move on without saying a thing.

Bob would think, "Sensei doesn't like me. He's always picking on me in class. He likes Doug. He leaves him alone."

Meanwhile I would think, "Sensei likes Bob and gives him extra attention. He doesn't like me and doesn't want to waste his time on me."

Bob and I would see the same actions and hear the same words but paint different dramas on top of them.

Deep listening separates what actually occurs from our storylines.

Consider self-esteem, worth, purpose, or self-image. In these elaborate constructs the paint is so thick and gooey it's hard to see anything natural beneath it.

Several years ago a group of American meditation teachers and psychologists were in Dharamasala, the Dalai Lama's home in exile in northern India. They managed to get an audience with the Dalai Lama.

During the conversation, one of the teachers asked, "Do you have any suggestion for working with people with low self-esteem?"

The Dalai Lama asked, "What is low self-esteem?"

"When someone has a bad opinion of themselves."

"Why would someone have a bad opinion of themselves?"

"Perhaps because they have been mistreated a lot."

The Dalai Lama said, "If someone has been mistreated, I can see that they might feel sad or angry or lonely or upset. But why would they think they were a bad person?"

The conversation went back and forth for almost an hour. The Dalai Lama, as sophisticated as he was about consciousness and feelings, had difficulty grasping low self-esteem. It was completely foreign.

From his perspective, feelings arise because of causes. He could understand how someone would feel hurt, angry, envious, confused, upset, and so on. But why a person would clump these feelings together into a mental construct called "low self-esteem" boggled him.

Self-esteem is a constructed reality that the Dalai Lama had not heard of before. Yet in the West, we paint it everywhere.

The point is that there is a difference between natural and constructed reality. Natural reality refers to experiences that can arise in any healthy human no matter what his or her cultural or personal background (hurt, fear, anger, love, caring, wisdom, and so on). Constructed reality refers to things that are created by the human mind (for example self image, life purpose, philosophy, language, religious beliefs, and so on.)

It's not that the constructs are necessarily wrong. It's just that we can get so caught up in our mental paintings that we miss the natural reality below it. We get so caught up in our stories that we don't notice our natural depths. We are so convinced that sensei doesn't like me or that my self-esteem is bad that we miss the quieter truth.

Deep listening tries to sift through to the deeper, natural truth.

Deep Listening Examples

Let me give you a few examples.

In karate class, Bob and I got to talking and realized our opposing views of sensei's actions. I knew they couldn't both be right. I also know I felt ignored as a child, and I'm sensitive to feelings of abandonment. Perhaps my emotional stir was being painted on his behavior.

So I switched into deep listening. Next time sensei came around, I let my feelings slide off to one side and observed him closely. His face had the usual karate deadpan. But I noticed the hint of a smile in the corner of his eyes as he looked at me and passed on. And I saw the same smile when he was working with Bob.

I was startled. My whole mental construction collapsed. He actually cared about all his black belt students and took a quiet pride in us all. Both Bob and I had been wrong. He took satisfaction in both of us.

Or let me give you another example. Several years ago during a particularly low moment, I said to my therapist, "I hate myself." She didn't respond right away, but looked at me quietly for several long moments. She was doing deep listening: letting go of all her ideas and feelings and sensing what was happening deep inside me.

Then she said, "I don't think you hate yourself. You hate how you feel."

Something flashed inside me. I felt the wisdom and compassion of that observation. The problem wasn't low esteem. I simply felt bad a lot. It was healing to be seen so clearly.

Deep Listening Practice

And what about you? All of us have probably done some form of deep listening at some time.

Maybe a friend or child comes to you with a difficult situation. You want to help. You feel the urge to advise, analyze, or reframe. But you sense that that won't be enough. Something more is needed. But you don't know what.

Wisdom begins with not knowing. So you set aside your urge to fix. You let go of all that attractive advice. You move into "don't know mind."

From this quiet openness, you listen: not just to the words but to the whole being. You imagine being her: feeling her feelings, looking at the world through her personality. You note her mental constructs, interpretations, and storyline. But you don't stop there. What's going on beneath these? Is she lonely, sad, frightened, worried?

You go deeper. You feel her heart, her core energy, who she is beneath it all, her beingness. You receive her totality as fully as you can.

Even though you may not be speaking, the quality of your listening encourages her to touch her own heart and deeper wisdom. Out of that emptiness, insights arise – maybe in her, maybe in you, maybe in both of you. You share these gently.

Deep listening is also valuable in a conflict between friends or children or relatives or congregants. You have them sit down with you. You don't offer solutions, fixes, or even any ideas of what they should do. You give up your preconceptions. You empty yourself and listen openly and carefully.

You invite them to take turns listening deeply to each other. If one person seems to not hear the other, you reflect what you hear and ask if that is correct. Otherwise you just listen.

It is amazing how often seemingly impossible situations evaporate with this kind of steady, loving presence. Just like a chalice evaporating into a birdbath, entire situations can shift. I see it happen all the time.

Deep listening is also helpful when people are angry with you. This is more challenging. It helps to center and ground yourself: perhaps breathing deep into your belly or feeling your connection to the earth.

Then you go blank inside. You drop all your ideas. You drop your defenses as much as possible and listen heartfully to the story they are telling ("You did such and such"). You also listen to their feelings. You notice the mental constructs and the energy beneath.

If you agree with any parts of their accusation, you can acknowledge that. But at first you don't give rejoinders. You reflect back as deeply and honestly your heart sense of what is going on inside them: "You seem to feel betrayed." "It sounds like I hurt you."

You don't always get it right. But the intention to hear them fully helps establish trust. Then, when they know you know their experience, you can offer what it looks like from your perspective.

The important thing is to empathize with them first. If you can't hold people in your heart, then you don't know what's inside them.

As Thich Nhat Hanh suggests, deep listening is appropriate in almost all levels of social life. Think how much saner our politics would be if people did a little more listening and a little less characterizing people they don't know; if we did a little more sensing what is going on and a little less ideologically driven interpretation; if we did more seeing and a little less painting events with our favorite political stance.

Time and Commitment

The drawback to deep listening is time and commitment. It requires patience. Patience is the seed of grace.

In this congregation we say we value the goodness in everyone. But the wisdom and compassion that comprise that goodness are not terribly accessible on the run. They are not captured in noisy thoughts. They are a gentle breeze, not a firestorm.

So if we value seeing the goodness in others, deep listening is a way of putting our time and commitment where our values are. It is a practice that brings our abstract values into the natural world.

In a society that is too fast-paced, too stressed, too motivated by ideas rather than wisdom, and too driven by emotion rather than compassion, deep listening can be very healing. But it does require time, commitment, and patience.

It can transform you as a listener as much as the listener. You begin to see someone like them looking out through a different personality and different life story.

You both become the listener. You both become heard. The separation between listener and listenee, between self and other is just an idea that evaporates in the gentle breeze.

Self as Trance

October 28, 2005

When I was in college, a fellow psychology major undertook an experiment. Every time his roommate moved his hand toward his ear, he smiled. He never told his roommate his scheme. The smiles were never broad or obvious – just a subtle show of approval. Within two weeks, his roommate developed a habit of pulling on his earlobe.

Several years ago, a psychology class at Harvard University conducted an experiment on its professor. It was one of those large lecture classes with three or four hundred students. When the professor was out of the room for a few minutes, they agreed that every time he walked to the right side of the stage, they would be very attentive and take lots of notes. When he walked to the left side, they would drift off, gaze out the window or look bored. Very quickly the professor was glued to the right side of the stage.

We like to think of ourselves as free and independent, governed mostly by our own volition. But in reality we are social creatures, strongly influenced by those around us. The more we deny this, the more powerful these forces become.

Each of these two examples involves one behavior, subtle reinforcers, and a short time. Consider the impact of targeting many behaviors and attitudes, using obvious as well as subtle reinforcers, and continuing the process for years. We would expect large changes in people's actions, underlying attitudes, feelings, and even thought processes. We might expect changes in who they think they are.

Spiritually, the issue is never who we are. It is who we *think* we are. I'd like to look at some of the subtle but powerful forces that shape our sense of self and can shape it falsely. These forces point to the need to set aside our thoughts and self-image and look with fresh eyes at what is real.

Hypnosis

The ease with which we can be influenced has long been demonstrated by hypnosis. Formal hypnotic induction is an unremarkable procedure that can produce remarkable results. If I were to hypnotize you, there are basically two things I would do. First, I would ask you to fix your gaze on a single object, such as the chalice flame. After a while, I would suggest that your eyes were getting heavy and your vision was getting distorted. This is a predictable result of staring fixedly at one point, but you might take it as a sign that the hypnotic suggestion was working. Second, as you stared at the flame, I would say, "Think about what it is like to relax. Allow yourself to relax. You are becoming relaxed. You are feeling sleepy." Interspersed with these would be reassurances that hypnosis is easy and normal, that since you are allowing me to hypnotize you, you must be willing and so forth.

After 10 to 20 minutes, you might go into a light hypnotic trance. In such a state I could suggest that your arms had gotten very heavy. You would be unable to lift them.

If you had a talent for hypnotic states, you could go into a deeper trance in which more fundamental perceptual distortions would be possible. For example, if there were three glasses on the table, and I suggested there were two, you would swear there were only two. This is called a negative hallucination – not perceiving something that is present. I might say, "Someone wants to talk to you on the intercom." You would listen and respond to questions from the intercom despite the fact that it was turned off. This is called a positive hallucination – perceiving something that is not there.

Another well-known hypnotic phenomenon is post-hypnotic suggestion. For example, I could tell you that after coming out of the trance, every time I use the word "button" you will walk to the window. If you were responsive to hypnosis, I could bring you out of the trance and weave the word "button" into our conversation. Each time, you would get up and walk to the window.

A fascinating aspect of this phenomenon is that people responding to post-hypnotic suggestion make up explanations for their behavior: "I'd like a breath of air," "I hear someone calling me," or "I love the way the sky looks this time of day." They are unaware of why they are doing what they are doing and spontaneously come up with reasonable though spurious rationales. They construct a reality.

There are limits to hypnotic suggestion. It is difficult or impossible to get somebody to do something that clashes with strongly held values. Still, it is amazing how drastically our thoughts and perceptions can be altered by such an innocent-looking procedure.

Child Rearing

Child rearing uses all the techniques of hypnotic induction and many more. We do not tell our children that their eyes are getting tired as they stare at a flame, but we do tell them over and over what they might experience as they grow. When these predictions come true, the child magically believes that what we say must be true. And we suggest to them over and over who they are, what they can do, what is "normal," and how to get along. Good parents tell their children they are wonderful, capable and talented. Other parents tell their kids they are no good and will come to nothing. But even the most *laissez-faire* parents give signals more obvious than the quiet smile given to the roommate as his hand moved toward his ear or the look of attention as the professor moved to the right side of the stage.

Child rearing uses all the techniques of hypnotic induction and uses them in ways that are hundreds of times more powerful. Unlike formal hypnosis, child rearing is not confined to 10 to 20 minutes but extends over 10 to 20 years – and the most impressionable years at that. While the hypnotic subject usually has no special relationship to the hypnotist, the child is very dependent on his or her parents. Children usually want to please their parents. While formal hypnosis is voluntary, a child does not have the option of choosing parents. While formal hypnosis does not use reinforcers, child rearing applies positive reinforcements like touching, holding, stroking, and praising, and negative ones like disapproval, guilt and, sometimes, physical punishment.

The most reasonable conclusion is that we are in a kind of hypnotic state and responding to post-hypnotic suggestions. Charles Tart[10], an expert on hypnosis, has come to exactly this conclusion. He calls our normal state the "consensus trance" or the "sleep of everyday life." Spiritual teachers from many traditions say we walk around half asleep in a trance of inner words.

Identity States

When we look inside ourselves, we do not see trances. We see more or less familiar patterns of thoughts, feelings and images. We identify with these patterns, calling them our own. They define who we think we are: "I am a person who takes comfort in rubbing my ear, likes to stand on the right side of the room, sleeps with open windows, keeps two glasses of water on the table, believes God is an abstract creative principle, and prides himself on being a free and independent thinker." These patterns are part of the trance. Self-identity or personality is a very complex and intricate hypnotic state. It gives us a sense of self. Self is this familiar trance state.

It is easy to see how these identity states form. For example, when I was a child, I had to remember many things: put my bicycle in the garage, not on the driveway; pick up my marbles from the front porch; wash my hands before coming to the table; wait to start eating until everyone was there (which meant waiting for my father, since he always wanted to be last); clean up my room Saturday mornings; express feelings as long as they were not too wild or strong; play roughly only outdoors; brush my teeth; and so on.

The list was endless, but the mind is efficient. When I did what I was supposed to, I was told I was a "good kid." All these behaviors were lumped together under that label. When I came in for supper, I did not have to think, "Wipe my feet. Don't slam the door. Wash my hands. …" I merely remembered, "I'm a good kid," and everything fell into place without much effort.

"Good kid" is an example of an identity state. It included behaviors, attitudes, thoughts,

---

[10] Charles Tart, *Waking Up: Overcoming the Obstacles to Human Potential.* (Boston: New Science Library, Shambhala, 1987).

feelings, and images that defined a way that I saw myself. All the conditioning and hypnotic induction you and I receive is not experienced as individual suggestions, but as a configuration. It becomes a self-identity. Good parents try to foster positive self-images. They do this by helping their children create positive identity states.

Whether your current state is "good kid" or "talented musician" or "no-good bum" or something else, it radically affects your perception of yourself and your world. For example, I know a man who is very short. All through his childhood and adolescence when much of his self-image was forming, he was tall for his age. It wasn't until mid-adolescence that he stopped growing and other people passed him in height. Today, despite his diminutive stature, he still thinks of himself as a tall person. Other examples of the power of identity states are found in people with poor self-images who, despite years of successful careers and social lives, are still haunted by feelings of being a failure. Unexamined, identity states are powerful and persistent.

No matter how benign our parents' intent, the suggestions, the approval and disapproval, and the experiences provided as we grew up left a profound impact on us – so profound that most people's perception of the world has more to do with their conditioning than their actual surroundings. Most people's normal waking consciousness is fuzzy and bears a closer resemblance to a trance than to being fully alert. We are crippled by our self-images. Our actual power and beauty are vast. Our self-images are relatively abysmal. Self-sense is part of the confining shell.

Continued Induction

Trance induction extends beyond childhood through advertising, television, political slogans, and social conversations.

It also continues through mind chatter. Our minds are rarely quiet. If we sit back and observe, we see an almost endless parade of internal commentary. Mostly we are telling ourselves who we are: what we like, what we don't like, our opinion of this, our fear of that, how we can explain something else. It is as if the mind believes that if it were to stop defining itself, it might disappear. In a sense, that is true. Artists and meditators find that, as the mind slows down, self-identity fades. The constancy of the internal monologue keeps forming and shaping our self-identity. It has an effect similar to that of a hypnotist speaking softly and continuously. We have become our own hypnotist!

A second way we self-induce identity is seeking experiences that reinforce the states. For example, someone may have an identity that says the world is hostile and people will not like him. He carries anger inside. From the outside, he looks as if he has a chip on his shoulder: he is quick to take offense and frowns a lot. Such an attitude can be irritating and aggravating to those around him. It provokes their anger and dislike, thus confirming what the identity state believed in the first place. This process is called a "self-fulfilling prophecy."

Not only do we draw self-validating experiences, but we reinterpret what we experience to fit our self-image. This is to say, we construct our own reality.

A woman stood beside one of Picasso's paintings and said rather disdainfully, "That is not a cow!" Picasso, who was standing nearby, replied, "Madam, you are correct. *That* is not a cow. That is a *picture* of a cow!" In our minds we create pictures of the world around us. We do this so automatically and so habitually that, like the woman, we forget that the picture is *a picture* and not *the reality*.

Identity trance states are very intricate mental constructs painted on top of natural reality.

Reality Flux

So what? What difference does this make in everyday life? Why am I talking about this? Before I answer this, let me reflect further on Picasso's painting.

Picasso's picture of a cow is essentially the same today as it was when he painted it. The real cow aged and died a long time ago. Reality is fluid. It changes, evolves, and shifts constantly. What is inside is always in flux. However, mental constructs can be static. Trance states can remain unchanging for a lifetime.

For example, let's say a loved one dies. You think, "I'm sad and alone in the world." If you pay attention only to this thought, you may become entranced into thinking "I'm a lonely person."

However, if you pay attention to your actual experience, you notice a flux of feelings and energies. You feel intense sadness, then numbness, then anger that the person died. This flows into melancholy. Next you feel hungry and wonder what's for lunch. Sadness arises and flows into love for the person followed by enjoying the song of a bird outside the window followed by interest in the daily news. Sometimes the flux is dramatic, sometimes subtle, but it's never static.

If you pay attention to the self-image trance, you are an orphan. If you pay attention to fluid reality, there are fluxes of possibilities. You are not the same person you were last year or yesterday.

Take another example: you have an argument. If all you pay attention to are your thoughts, you notice, "He's a jerk. This is impossible. We are irreconcilable." Those thoughts can remain unchanging for a long time, like an enchanted curse on the relationship.

However, if you let go of the thoughts and look at what naturally arises inside you, you will see a changing stream: anger, determination, sadness, humor, empathy, concern, annoyance, fear, and so on. Always shifting.

This brings us to the most essential point of all I've tried to convey. It comes down to this:

Wisdom, compassion, and the deepest healing arise out of the flux of natural reality. Thoughts, constructs, and self-identity can be helpful up to a point. But clear seeing and open hearts arise out of a place that is quieter, deeper, and more fluid than thought, trance, or identity.

This is why Jesus kept saying, "You've got eyes, open them! You've got ears, listen!" This is why the Buddha said, "Wake up!" See what is right here. Divinity – the deepest wisdom, compassion, and healing – arises naturally when we pay attention.

The trick is to drop the mental constructs, break out of the trance state, forget who you think you are, and contact the fluid reality.

Fortunately, trances are never complete. They are never 100%. We always have the capacity to wake up and see what's truly going on.

Remember the guy who was hypnotized into thinking there were two glasses on the table when there were really three? He was so confident in his opinion that he didn't look closely. He would swear there were two. But if he really observed the table, if he set aside his beliefs about what was there and looked with fresh eyes, the third glass slowly would appear.

Most of us go through life only glancing at what is around us. It seems more efficient to look at our internal pictures of the world than look at the reality of the world. Our perception is dulled.

But we always have the option of setting aside our beliefs and looking with fresh eyes. The capacity to see is still there. We simply need to learn (or relearn) how to perceive.

Awareness is the key.

We have the capacity to wake up. We have the capacity to see the fluid truth if we are willing to use it. This often means setting aside ideas and notions we take for granted, like selfhood, so we can look with fresh eyes.

Henry David Thoreau wrote:

We must learn to reawaken and keep ourselves awake, not by mechanical means, but by an infinite expression of the dawn.

Presence

Sànùk: Fun

June 11, 2006

I walked past the ornate temple entryway of Wat Phra Doi Suthep. I passed the row of huge bells. As I came around back, I noticed a group of five teenagers. They were laughing and joking and carrying on. Each had a long pole with a crosspiece at the end. A large, square rag was attached to the crosspiece. With a flick of the pole, the rag wound around the crosspiece, turning it into a large mop. With a different flick, the rag unwound and could be hosed and cleaned.

Wat Phra Doi Suthep is perched on the side of a large mountain range. The temple is surrounded by a marble terrace with a breathtaking view of Chiang Mai, a city in northern Thailand. Every day, hundreds and hundreds of people take buses or taxis from the city up the mountain to worship, make offerings, ask advice, listen to monks chant, ring the bells, gawk at the gold Buddhas, photograph the valley, or just hang out in the mountain air.

Those five teenagers were supposed to keep the marble terrace sparkling for the visitors, but they didn't seem to take their work seriously. I couldn't understand their language, but from their laughter, gestures, and loud voices, I surmised they were goofing off.

I sat on a marble bench beneath a tree of magenta flowers. I could see the entire Chiang Mai Valley, and I could surreptitiously observe these teenagers.

I was surprised! The kids wound the rags into mops, pushed them across the marble for 50 or 60 feet, ran to a hose, cleaned the rag, rewound it, and wiped another 50-foot swath. They worked hard and efficiently. The way they joked and carried on would be a sure sign of laziness in America. But here it was a sign of something else. It was a sign of what the Thai call *sànùk*.

I spent the month of March in Wat Chom Tong about 30 miles south of Chiang Mai. Midafternoons, I often took a 20-minute break from my meditation regimen to stretch my legs and walk along the rice fields.

Typically, it was 90° with 90% humidity. The workers in the fields sloshed through mud to their ankles and water to their calves. It was backbreaking labor. Not speaking Thai, I couldn't understand what they called out to each other, but by their tone and gestures, it seemed like jokes and amusing stories.

They were a sign of sànùk.

The wats where I stayed charged nothing for food, clothing, shelter, meditation instruction or anything else I needed. Nevertheless, I wanted to make a donation. On one occasion, I made out several traveler's checks to a wat. Later, I found out they could not cash them. They returned them to me.

One afternoon, I went into a bank to see if they could cash these checks that had already been signed and made out to someone else. The clerk made phone call after phone call up through the bank hierarchy and eventually through the American Express hierarchy. After a half hour, she found a way to cash them for me. All the while she was wrestling with these bureaucracies, her boss was watching from several desks away. Their exchanges were polite, professional, and often playful.

Even in the bank there was sànùk.

Fun

Sànùk is a Thai word that translates roughly as "fun." Something with sànùk is enjoyable, pleasant, or playful.

For the Thai, sànùk is not a conscious philosophy or belief. It is an unconscious frame of reference that says anything worthwhile has fun or playfulness in it. The Thai understand that valuable endeavors may require effort, discipline, hard work, sacrifice, and even pain. Nevertheless, anything worthwhile will also have some element of play in it.

Sànùk is not something you bring to a task. It is not grafted onto an onerous job. It is not making lemonade out of lemons. It is already inherent in anything that is wholesome. It is there to be noticed or discovered.

To call something "mai sànùk" or "not fun" is to condemn it. Someone who sticks with a task that is never enjoyable must be mentally or spiritually imbalanced. The person must be arrogant or misguided. The gods don't intend us to stick with something that is never fun.

Saving Face

Sànùk is light and embracing. It is fun but never makes fun of. American television sitcoms that find humor in people being embarrassed would not be considered fun by the Thai.

Saving face is very important to the Thai, but it is not something you do for yourself. It is something you do for others. If I tripped in a group of Thais, no one would think of saying, "Stumbling over your own toes, are you?" They would be more likely to say, "Oh, you are always doing things to amuse us," as if the stumble had been intentional. They would reflexively look for ways to ease my embarrassment so I could save face.

In Thailand, to intentionally embarrass someone or purposely make them uncomfortable is a sign of immaturity. To angrily confront someone is barbarous. Civilized people find gentle ways to work out their differences. From this perspective, many Westerners are crude and rude. But the Thai are too polite to say it or even think about it much.

To summarize, sànùk is a point of view that expects anything that is sacred or valuable to have a measure of fun in it. And the enjoyment will be embracing of everyone involved. It will feel harmonious.

The teenagers mopping the marble terrace were working very hard, and they embraced sànùk as they worked. The rice field workers knew what it was like to toil for long hours in the hot sun. This did not prevent them from enjoying themselves anyway. The bank clerk knew how to persist with frustrating bureaucracies. She also knew how to find some pleasure in the process.

Questions

I have read enough about sànùk and face saving in Thailand to know that I was not imagining these things. They are real phenomena, not just my projections.

However, I only spent two months in Southeast Asia. I was in silent meditation for seven of those weeks. I am not an expert on Thai culture. I'm sure I missed many nuances and don't appreciate the dark side of sànùk.

That's okay. This morning, I'm not really interested in Thai culture. I'm interested in American culture. I'm less interested in how the Thai live and more interested in how you and I live.

I invite you to reflect on a few questions.

How would your life be different if fun were an element of everything you do? What if your religion or philosophy of life required you to abandon anything that consistently lacked pleasure? Clearly, many very worthwhile things require effort, discipline, sacrifice, and sometimes pain. But what if the gods or the universe want you to look for moments of enjoyment in everything you do? If you can't find any, what if this is a message from a divine source saying, "Drop it, you fool!"

America

In America, we have a frame of reference that is the opposite of sànùk and the opposite of helping others save face. It is called the "Puritan ethic."

Puritanism sees some people as good and some as bad. To demonstrate your closeness to God, you stand up to bad people. Sometimes, you call them out even if it embarrasses them. Good people show others their sinful ways. It's the noble thing to do. Civility is less important than righteousness.

The Puritan ethic says that anything worthwhile must be a burden to bear: "Take up your cross and follow me." If something is worthwhile, you must suffer for it. If you are having a lot of fun, you must be goofing off. You are irresponsible. God intends us to work hard and to suffer in this life.

The Puritan ethic is alive and well in America. Last year, a study by the Families and Work Institute found that one-third of Americans are chronically overworked. One-third! Half report feeling overwhelmed on the job sometime in the previous month.

In Sweden, the average worker took 44 days off in 2004. Eastern Europeans took only half as many: 22 days off. In America, only 14% took two weeks or more vacation. Fourteen percent! One-third took less than one week of vacation.

Limiting vacation time is rationalized as a way of increasing worker productivity. However, overwork increases depression and stress and decreases energy and efficiency. Even if limiting vacation did increase productivity, who says the meaning of life is to be a producing unit?

Many of us act as if this is what we believe. The phrase "supporting my family" usually means "producing money for them," rather than "spending time with them." Many feel we have to work hard to earn fun. We feel guilty just enjoying ourselves. One-third of Americans did not even take all the vacation they had coming. We are more Puritan than the Puritans!

Europeans look at us and wonder if we are crazy or just crazed.

The majority of Americans probably reject Puritanism and the Puritan ethic as a conscious set of beliefs or philosophy, but it is so deeply engrained in American psyches, institutions, and habits that secular Puritanism is an unconscious frame of reference. The Thai say, "No fun, no value." We say, "No pain, no gain." "Suffering builds character." "Anything worthwhile must hurt." "I'll be home as soon as my desk is cleared." "I can't afford the time to rest," and so on.

Play

Philosophically, many of us believe that the purpose of life is happiness, wellbeing, and fulfillment. Yet, to use fun and play as guiding principles seems a bit trivial. It lacks gravitas.

Let's look a little closer at how fun relates to real spirituality.

Higher consciousness is spacious, compassionate, and embracing. It is light and gentle. Play, imagination, creativity, and fun bring out this higher nature. They show spiritual maturity.

As we move up the evolutionary ladder, we find more and more of these qualities. Why do people have more cats and dogs as pets than cockroaches and alligators? Cats and dogs are more evolved and have more capacity for fun, play, and relationship.

Our nearest animal cousins, chimps and monkeys, have a tremendous capacity for fun and mischief.

Fun and enjoyment bring out our higher qualities. Without them, we live reflexive lives like cockroaches and alligators. Our behavior is driven more by physical survival.

In fact, I'd suggest that play may be an instinct as basic to humans as sexuality. The Victorians tried to repress sexuality, but they couldn't. Repression just caused the sexual drive to be expressed in twisted and imbalanced ways. It split it off from everyday, acceptable life.

Likewise, our repression of fun and play with overwork and over commitment doesn't stop our desire for fun and play. But it is more likely to come out in imbalanced ways: violence, abuse, ridicule, franticness, and so on. And it is more likely to be split off from our normal working days, rather than be integrated into it.

Subversion

I considered starting a national campaign for fun and play. It would be quite subversive, to be sure. What if we got more fun and enjoyment out of our everyday lives, including our work? It would undermine the current political climate that depends on fear, rather than fun, to drive people's votes. It would undermine the entertainment industry that wants us to buy fun from them. It would undermine the advertising industry because disgruntled people are more vulnerable to ads. It might even undermine our consumption-driven economy, as people became less motivated to buy stuff as a substitute for fun. The economy would be unhappy. But the people would be happier.

However, the more I thought about it, the more a national campaign seemed like it would not be fun for me.

Therefore, I'll leave it on a personal level. That may be more effective subversion anyway.

Summary

Let me summarize the questions I'm posing and then open it up to your questions and reflections:

How would it change your life to sincerely believe that fun is an inherent part of anything worthwhile? Effort, discipline, and hard work may be necessary at times, but what if you didn't separate work from play? What if you knew that enjoyment should be a part of everything you do?

When things aren't fun, how can you tell when you need to examine your own attitudes? It's been said that angels can fly because they take themselves lightly. Do you sometimes ascribe too much importance to yourself and make it difficult to see inherent sànùk, inherent fun? If so, how can you lighten up and let go? What helps you discover the fun around you?

On the other hand, when something isn't enjoyable, how do you know when you have no business being involved any longer? When should you just say: "Enough. The gods must not want me here."

How do kindness and civility relate to good fun? How can you help those around you save face, feel more relaxed, and have more fun?

How much of your vacation are you taking this year? What are your plans for fun and play this summer?

That's enough questions from me. What are your thoughts?

Closing

Without fun, we get stressed. When stressed, we regress. Our intelligence drops. We focus on the immediate and have difficulty seeing the long view. We become more concerned with surviving through the day than thriving into the future.

Trashing the planet, starting wars, and oppressing people are shortsighted. I would argue that if we were more relaxed, if we had more fun, we'd change our ways. We'd know that polluting, warring, and oppressing are not fun and just plain stupid in the long run.

Our capacity to enjoy ourselves in a way that embraces all people may be essential to building a healthy world for ourselves and our children.

Conflict and Ill Will

*If we have love, no disagreement can do us any harm;
but if we have not love, no agreement can do us any good.*
– Hosea Ballou

September 10, 2006

Highway 1

The Northern California coast features high bluffs, surf crashing on the rocks, grassland, and wooded areas. There are birds, seals, otters, and occasionally whales. Highway 1 follows the contour of the coast, rather than slicing hills and filling ravines. North of the Russian River, there are 30 miles of road that never straighten long enough to pass a car in your lane.

My wife, Erika, and I are not the only people in California who know the coast is gorgeous. On a Sunday afternoon in midsummer, we were joined by sedans, station wagons, vans, sports cars, trucks, SUVs, bicycles, motorcycles, and boats of all sizes being pulled by vehicles of all sizes. Fortunately, there were lots of turnouts. We didn't get caught behind slow drivers for more than a few minutes before they'd pull off and let everyone pass.

Then we got behind a small, top-heavy camper truck that waddled along. I waited patiently for the next turn out. The truck didn't pull over. I waited impatiently for the next turn out. The truck drove past. The road in front of him was clear for a mile, and the road behind us was packed for a mile. "What's the matter with this guy?" I pictured the driver wearing a torn leather jacket, drinking beer, and listening to loud rock as he ambled along with rude indifference.

We came upon a sign: "Slower traffic use turnout." I thought, "Now he'll get the hint." He didn't.

I imagined telling this guy what I thought of his driving. In my fantasy, he swung his fist at me. I considered which martial arts move I'd use to wrench his arm and throw him to the ground.

At a hairpin turn, I glimpsed him. He was an old man in a light blue windbreaker and fishing hat. He was gripping the steering wheel, his attention riveted to the road ahead. "Poor guy," I thought. He looked more like a doting grandfather than a Hell's Angel.

We crawled along. Then in the mirror, I saw a sports car speeding up the left lane. "Who does he think he is trying to get ahead of the rest of us?" I grumbled.

The road curved up a blind incline. A truck appeared coming toward us in the left lane. The sports car nudged over to cut in front of me.

An image appeared in my mind: I was driving along pretending to be oblivious to the sports car like the old man was oblivious to us. The sports car was stuck in the lane where he didn't belong. The truck smashed into him. The words "that'll teach him" arose in my mind.

Meanwhile, I put on the brakes to let him in. But I was taken aback by how easily this malicious fantasy arose in me. I'm a lifelong pacifist. I registered as a conscientious objector during the Viet Nam War. I oppose the death penalty. I'm clergy. I don't kill ants in my house. Yet, I easily imagined condemning someone to death for trying to pass me on the highway.

I glanced over at Erika. She hadn't noticed my thoughts. Whew. I drove on in silence.

Meditation

Do you ever have thoughts of ill will like these? Not conscious plans or premeditated plots, but maybe little images that come up when someone cuts in line or gives you a rude gesture? Do you ever get frustrated and think, "I wish someone would wop him up the side of the head?" Have you ever secretly wished a political figure (I won't name names) would just fall out of a helicopter?

I invite you to close your eyes and recall the ways you may have experienced ill will recently.

Remember as clearly as you can.

How did it feel? Did you have any thoughts and rationalizations for that touch of malice?

Hold them all in your heart. Don't try to condemn, ignore, or change any of them. Just hold them in kind awareness.

May we bring fierce clarity and fierce compassion to our darkness.

Blessed be.

Ill Will

I want to talk about ill will. The potential for malice lies deep inside all of us. It can seep up into our consciousness. If we don't relate to it skillfully, it can distort our thoughts, speech, and actions.

Unitarian Universalism is about engaging the real world. In the real world, ill will arises inside and around us. Learning to relate to ill will in a way that is mature and spiritually grounded is essential to living in the real world in a way that is mature and spiritually grounded.

Conflict is a very large topic. I want to focus on the central problem. It is not conflict per se. It is ill will.

For example, in the conflict in the Middle East various groups want to live in the same area. Present this conflict to a fourth grader, and she'll come up with three or four ways to manage it peacefully. The problem in the Middle East is not conflicting interests. It is the massive amount of ill will that makes the situation intractable.

Consider terrorism. The problem is not conflicts of religion or ideology or even resources. We teach our children the value of sharing. A third grader can figure out a solution. The problem of terrorism is ill will and related demonization on all sides – all sides.

Consider this congregation. We value different beliefs, ideas, and aspirations. As long as we have trust and good will, these are no problem. But if trust and good will break down, we are in deep trouble. As that great 19th century Universalist Minister, Hosea Ballou, put it, "If we have love, no disagreement can do us any harm; but if we have not love, no agreement can do us any good."

I want to focus on ill will in our own lives: why it is so destructive, where it comes from, and how to work with it in a life affirming way.

The Problem

What is the trouble with ill will? We intuitively sense a problem. But how does it wreak so much havoc? What is the "illness" of ill will?

Ill will makes us dumb and numb. Ill will is a cloud that covers the heart and mind. It shuts down our caring and empathy. It blinds us to the otherwise obvious fact of our interdependence. It makes us stupid and cold hearted: dumb and numb.

How does it accomplish all this?

Have you ever looked at somebody who is filled with ill will? Seen the expression on their face? Did you think, "Boy, I wish I could feel more of that?"

No, of course not! People with a little ill will look unhappy. People filled with malice look tortured. But when we are filled with ill will, we don't notice the state we are in.

Ill will makes us dumb and numb by blunting our capacity for self-reflection. It turns our attention away from what is going on inside and toward what is going on outside: who frightened us, hurt us, or insulted us.

Without knowing our own hearts, there is no wisdom. Ill will diverts us from the only source of healing and inspiration possible: that which comes through the human heart, and that which comes through a clear, receptive mind. This is why it can be so destructive.

This is very important. So let me see if I can say the same thing differently.

I suspect ill will does not originate in the neocortex, the most advanced area of our brain. It probably doesn't even come out of the limbic system below the neocortex, an area of the brain that has to do with feelings and emotions. Ill will is colder than emotion.

I suspect ill will starts deep down in the R-Complex, our so called "reptile brain" that is similar to the highest part of the brains of reptiles. This area controls impulse, ritual behavior, and territoriality. It is alive and well and on display in many corporations, bureaucracies, and political bodies in the form of turf wars, backbiting, ritualized adherence to meaningless procedures, cold-blooded me-first attitudes, and indifference. I suspect, we all could tell a story of dealing with a large bureaucracy that felt cold and reptilian.

Reptiles do not understand the interdependent web. They only understand their own narrow interest at the moment and how to fight for it.

Ill will energizes us to destroy a competitor, fight off an attacker, or run like crazy to save ourselves: fight or flight. When we were puny, and mightier creatures ruled the world, it kept us alive. But now that we are the most powerful creatures on the planet, it can destroy us.

Our higher capacities for love, generosity, kindness, empathy, and rationality can override these ancient instincts. But the old potentials remain in us. When the reptile complex gets hold of our senses, it distorts our rationality. We become less civilized. We become "cold blooded." We start thinking, "me first," "us and them," "good and evil." Our IQ drops. We demonize others.

When I imagined the driver of the wobbly truck to be a low-life, I was demonizing him, seeing him as a lesser human. When I fantasized the sports car driver being hit by a truck, to me he wasn't a fellow human. Primitive reptile impulses were coloring my feelings and dulling my thoughts. They arise so easily.

Working with Ill Will

If we don't want malice seeping into our consciousness and messing up our lives, what can we do?

There are four general strategies: condemning, ignoring, indulging, and embracing. Let's look at each.

Condemning

The first strategy is condemning: "I shouldn't have ill will." "You shouldn't have malice — shame on you for thinking those thoughts and feeling those feelings."

This strategy directs ill will toward ill will. It's about as effective as putting out a fire by dousing it with gasoline.

So please, don't beat yourselves up for having ill will. The potential for malice is wired deeply in us. It's part of our neural anatomy. This side of enlightenment, we'll feel it from time to time. Condemning just doesn't help.

Ignoring

If condemning doesn't help, maybe ignoring it will. This is popular with many Unitarian Universalists: "Since I believe in the inherent worth of every person, I don't have to deal with ill will." "I'm better than that." "I've transcended my lower nature." "I'm too mature for that." "I've risen above such petty feelings."

Yeah, right.

If we lived in some fairy tale heaven, ignoring our ill will might even work. If this life were nice and easy, our meanness might not be stimulated.

But our world is stressful. Different people who are driving at different speeds down the same road is a good metaphor for the real world. And not all those unconscious drivers are doting grandfathers. Some are starting wars, killing, destroying the environment, giving our money to the wealthy, threatening our jobs, our comfort, our families, and our safety.

There is a lot to stimulate anger and fear: fight or flight. Our deeply wired instinct for ill will is easily triggered. Ignoring doesn't help. Ignoring just makes us ignorant.

This summer, Erika and I took out most of the grass in our backyard and planted things that take less water. But of course, the old Bermuda grass keeps poking through. Its roots are very deep. Cutting the grass off at the surface is akin to pruning. The grass loves it. For every shoot cut, it sends up two more.

Ignoring ill will is like that. On the surface, it may be cut out of our awareness. But beneath the surface of our consciousness, it proliferates until it bursts through.

Indulging

If condemning and ignoring don't work, how about indulging ill will? How about fanning it a little? You may think, "Why would we indulge ill will?" There are many reasons.

We might indulge it because we think it will make us stronger. Ill will can energize. If we feel weak and vulnerable, we may like the sense of power malice gives us.

Or, we might hold onto ill will to penalize someone. We may think letting it go is the same as saying that the harm someone caused is okay.

To the distorted mind, holding onto ill intent punishes the person.

Another reason we may fan malice is camaraderie. We can join together in grousing about the boss, or neighbor, or world problems. For centuries, politicians have known that they can enhance their power by focusing people's attention on real or imagined threats: "Mongol hordes," "barbarians," infidel," "heathens," "niggers," "blue bellies," "Japs," "Krauts," "communists," and more recently, "liberals," "homosexuals," "terrorists," and "illegal immigrants." Or, if you have different political leanings, you can demonize "conservatives," "homophobes," or "the religious right."

Using ill will and demonization to draw us together is stupid. It may serve the selfish interest of a few, but it is harmful to the greater good. For example, we have an immigration problem in this country. Mobilizing the military against poor folks trying to feed their families is like buying a gun because we are out of milk: the response is not in the same universe as the problem. It wastes time, energy, focus, and resources in the process.

But as I said, ill will makes us dumb and numb. If we fan ill will, we can expect unintelligent, cold-hearted, reptilian reactions.

Embracing

If condemning, ignoring, and indulging don't work, the only option left is embracing ill will. You embrace it with as much good will as you can honestly muster.

Remember, ill will gets its power by taking your attention off what is going on inside you and fixing it on the person out there. So, the antidote is to bring your attention from the person there back to yourself. You notice the state you are in: anger, ill will, fear, aggression, and so on. There is no need to be critical. You just see your internal states with friendly good will.

When I clearly saw the ill will I had toward the sports car driver, my focus came back to myself. I saw how ugly it felt. Like letting go of a hot stone, I just let it go. Well, I let go of a lot of it anyway.

At the same time that you bring some attention back to yourself, you let go of who you thought the person was. You accept that your perception may be distorted by the reptile brain's penchant for demonizing. You look at the person with fresh eyes, with "don't know mind." You try to empathize with them or put yourself in their situation.

When I saw that the driver of the wobbly truck was really a nervous old man, my image of him as a lowlife dissipated. I felt concern for him.

This process is simple in theory. But if we have spent a lot of time or energy in bad mouthing or "bad thinking" someone, it may not be so easy to embrace ill will with good will. Ill will can be very tenacious. It requires discipline.

Also, malice has a way of disguising itself. If it were a frothing monster rearing up inside, it would be easy to see. But it dresses up in garbs that look very reasonable.

For example, one disguise is calling someone "impossible." "That person is impossible to deal with."

The year I arrived in Sacramento, many people came to me with a problem they were having with someone in the congregation. I'd listen and then say, "You must talk with him."

"Oh, I can't do that," they'd say. "He is impossible," or "She is unreasonable, stubborn, and hopeless."

I'd respond, "You have no choice. We are a religious community. We talk to each other."

Then the person would say, "But he scares me." Or, "I don't know how to talk to her." Or, "I get so upset that talking doesn't work."

I'd think, "Good. This is progress." Out loud I'd say, "So the problem isn't just that so-and-so is stubborn or unreasonable. Some of the problem is your difficulty. So let's see what we can do about that."

I was amazed at how often the person would then go and talk with so-and-so, even if it was difficult. I admired the courage. And it worked.

The thought, "He or she is impossible and unreasonable" is a telltale sign of ill will. Demonization begins with seeing fellow humans as "them" or "those people," and not as "us."

Other signs of ill will include a lack of empathy, me-first-you-second thinking, language of good and evil, and of course, those fleeting fantasies of wrenching someone's arm or seeing them smash into a truck.

Practice

I invite you to explore ill will as it arises in you in various nuances, flavors, and disguises. Notice what is going on any time you use the word "them." Experiment with the meditation we did earlier: when ill will arises, don't condemn it, ignore it, or indulge it. Embrace it with the opposites: goodwill, openness, curiosity, love, and courage. See if you can let go of who you thought the "impossible" person was and empathize with them.

This makes you stronger, wiser, and more compassionate because you are engaging your higher capacities and probably more of the neocortex.

Closing

Next, I want to talk about bringing good will into the larger world that sometimes directs ill will at us. There is so much name-calling, appeal to me-first thinking, demonization, and language of evil in our culture. If we want a kinder world, it behooves us to cultivate kindness, goodwill, and generosity. It behooves us to practice in small ways in our own lives. This generates the models, images, and practical skills that are the building blocks for a more peaceful world. They may not solve all the world's problems, but they are the essential building blocks of solutions.

To link this personal work with the work of becoming a more effective force for healing in the world, I'll close with a passage from Alexander Solzhenitsyn's *The Gulag Archipelago*:

If only it were so simple. If only there were evil people somewhere insidiously committing evil deeds and it were necessary only to separate them from the rest of us and destroy them. But the line dividing good from evil cuts through the heart of every human being. And who is willing to destroy a piece of his or her own heart?

When conflict arises and stimulates ill will, may we have the wisdom to look patiently into our own divided hearts until we rediscover our wholeness.

Conflict and Goodwill

If only it were so simple. If only there were evil people somewhere insidiously committing evil deeds and it were necessary only to separate them from the rest of us and destroy them. But the line dividing good from evil cuts through the heart of every human being. And who is willing to destroy a piece of his or her own heart?

— Alexander Solzhenitsyn

September 17, 2006

Yaksha

Once upon at time, the king and his prince left for several days of travel. While they were gone, a tiny *yaksha* — a little woodland creature — wandered into the throne room. Seeing the throne empty, he climbed up to take a nap.

A few nobles saw him and said, "Hey you, you can't sleep on the king's throne."

The yaksha swelled and stared at them without moving.

A few more people came into the throne room and said, "Get out of here you insolent little beast."

The yaksha grew bigger and glared without budging.

The guards tried to drag him away, but the yaksha had grown heavier than the guards could lift. Soldiers threw stones and spears, but its skin had grown thick as armor. Lances and arrows bounced off causing collateral damage.

When the king returned, a hideous ogre overshadowed his throne spreading terror about the palace. The king's advisors said, "You must launch a war on this terror!"

The king shook his head "no."

From a safe distance, he bowed to the yaksha and said, "It is so good to see you again. I hope you are doing well."

The yaksha looked at him with a mixture of malice and confusion. His breathing slowed. He shrank a little.

"I am so sorry you were treated poorly. What can I do to make you comfortable?" the king said.

The yaksha shrank a little more. The anger in his eyes softened.

"Let me bring you some food and fine clothes."

The yaksha continued to shrink until it was a tired little creature that leaned over on the throne cushion and fell asleep.

The king wrapped a blanket around its shoulders. When they looked in a few hours later, the throne was empty except for the small blanket.

In the weeks and months that followed, the yaksha could be seen from time to time ambling through the palace halls, running on the grounds, or playing tricks like tapping a guard on the back of the knee and hiding. But most often, he was curled up by the throne as the king absently scratched its ears.

"How could that little creature cause so much destruction?" the prince asked.

"Only with a lot of help from us," the king replied. "His monster nature feeds on anger, hatred, and ill will. Without these, he is just a mischievous woodland creature."[11]

Ill Will

This is the second of a series on conflict. Previously, I suggested that we are all yakshas: we all have dual potentials. The potential for malice lies deep inside all of us. It is an ancient instinct wired into our neural anatomy. We also have the potential for love, loyalty, caring, generosity, and kindness.

The question is "which potential do we want to feed?" Condemning ourselves for malicious thoughts just adds ill will to ill will. Ignoring this potential doesn't work either: in a stressful world, ill will gets stimulated whether we ignore it or not. The only strategy left is caring for it: embracing it with kindness gradually softens and dissolves ill will.

---

[11] I first heard this story from John Travis. The yaksha appears in many Eastern mythologies.

However, the ill will that we are most concerned about is probably not the *potential within* us but the *actual* ill will directed *at* us. There are monstrous yakshas out there. The malice in their eyes is frightening. We see overt ill will in war, crime, and terrorism. We see covert ill will in environmental destruction, policies that favor the rich over the poor, lack of health care, and so on.

I want to shift our focus from the potential ill will within us to the actual goodwill we can bring to the larger world. I want to suggest that the interdependent web is a meta-yaksha. The economic system, political system, social system, natural world, weather system – the whole kit-and-caboodle — is a gigantic yaksha with the potential to harm us or to treat us with generosity and kindness. As in the story, what we bring to this yaksha affects what it gives back to us.

Realism

I am advocating kindness, generosity, and goodwill as a foundation of community, national and global policy. In today's political climate, this sounds flaky: "There are bad people out there." "Not all yakshas are so easily tamed." "We have to be tough and realistic."

So, let's be tough and realistic.

Most of us, regardless of our politics or theology, would like to live in a world where good and virtuous people are safe from harm. I certainly want this.

Let's be realistic: it ain't gonna happen. There have been bad things happening to good people since there were people walking on the good earth. Who has never been hurt, lonely, treated unfairly, gotten sick, and suffered? Who thinks they can avoid sickness and suffering in the future? No governmental system, social configuration, or utopian formulation can protect us from all harm. There is no almighty God to protect us from hurt, disease, and death if we are just virtuous enough.

This is because sickness, harm, and suffering are part of the interdependent web. They are part of the meta-yaksha. There is also a lot of love and kindness. But suffering is part of the fabric of this realm.

This is good news. If bad things happen to you it is not always your fault. You aren't that important. Sometimes, it is just the way things are. Sometimes, bad things happen to good people.

This is also good news because we can lay down the burden of striving for a perfect world and embark on the venture of making the world a little better. Rather than work for a kind world, we move toward a kinder world. Rather than try to rid the world of all selfishness, we move in the direction of generosity. Rather than a fair world, we move toward fairness. Rather than rid the world of malice and ill will, we put goodwill into it.

Ecology

Ecology is a metaphor for how this works. If we put poisons into the air, we don't know if they will blow back in our faces and poison us. No one can predict the winds with 100% accuracy. Maybe we'll get away with it. Maybe we won't. But there is a good chance some will blow back on us. And there is an even greater certainty that someone will be poisoned.

If we heat up the atmosphere, we will have bigger storms. Heat is energy. The more energy in the weather system, the more energy we'll have in storms. We'll have more category 3, 4, and 5 hurricanes. We'll have more floods and droughts and more climatic variation. Will you or I be directly affected by these storms? Who can predict? Maybe we'll be lucky — maybe not. But the odds are greater that we'll be hit by a storm because there are more of them. And we can be confident that more people will be hit by weather disaster.

Think of international conflict as a weather system. Each time we use military force, we put more heat and violence into the global atmosphere. The heat we pour into Iraq radicalizes people into hating us. We put more hatred into the system. Will this directly impact you or me? It's hard to know, but we have increased the odds that we will be directly impacted. We can be confident that more people will be impacted, and that we will be indirectly impacted.

In this interdependent web, there is no individual salvation. We are all in this together. We all have the capacity for good and ill. And the interrelated system has the capacity for good and ill.

How do we realistically cope with individual destructive potential, and at the same time, feed the gentle and not the monstrous aspect of the yakshas?

Previously, I spoke about keeping the heart open while maintaining good boundaries. Next, I want to speak about how, in the face of conflict, we can keep goodwill flowing, and at the same time, maintain good boundaries. I address this in the next sermon, "Conflict and Community" (p. 110).

I want to share some examples of what can happen when we bring good will to the larger world.

September 11

In the first few days after September 11, there was a tremendous outpouring of goodwill. People around the world held America in their hearts and sent aid. People in America poured out selflessness and goodwill. Firemen and police knowingly risked their lives and died in the World Trade Center because of a deep and gritty compassion to help others. My youngest brother, Roger, was in the towers when they were hit. He got out fine, but his first reaction was not to run for the stairs. His first reaction was to search his floor to make sure that there was no one too hurt to get to safety. He was just one ordinary guy there on a carpentry job. There are thousands of similar stories of ordinary compassion and heroism.

How do we honor those who died helping others? I don't think it's by bombing people in far off lands. Those who rushed in to help were not motivated by anger, ill will, or the desire to destroy.

What if, in the days and weeks following September 11, the leaders of America had pointed to the goodwill that was flowing around the world? What if they had acted with wisdom and humility? What if they had tempered the reflex to lash out? What if they had responded with sorrow and goodwill rather than anger and violence? What if they had held up the truly spiritual values manifested by so many people?

The world would have become more united in goodwill. Respect for the courage and heart of the American people would have grown. The terrorists would have stood out in sharp contrast. They would have been more isolated, found fewer refuges, less support, fewer new recruits, and more defectors in their ranks. With widespread support, tracking down the criminals who blew up the Trade Center would have become a police action.

Instead, our administration and its supporters quickly focused on fear and self-righteousness. They even turned back some aid from well-wishers around the world saying, "We can take care of our own," as if we weren't all in this together. They escalated into a so-called "war on terrorism" that continues to feed the monstrous aspects of yakshas.

Last year, 40 times more people died in car accidents than in terrorist acts. If we really wanted to preserve life, we'd focus more on traffic accidents. But the war on terror is not about preserving life. It is about preserving an ideology based on ill will that says, "There are bad people out there we must destroy."

By fanning the urge for revenge, escalating the rhetoric, promoting illogical policies like "preemptive war," defending torture, and in other ways pumping more heat and violence into the political ecosystem, we have made the world hotter and more dangerous.

Last week, a comprehensive U.S. intelligence report confirmed this: the "war on terror" has increased war and terror.

The tragedy of September 11, 2001 could have tilted the world toward unity, rather than toward the medieval ethic of us and them. We don't need to be naïve about those who might wish us ill. But we do need to set an example. As the most powerful nation in the world (for the moment), we need to set an example of what it means to respond with courage and compassion, not violence and ill will.

It's not too late to do so.

Exporting Goodwill

What would the exporting of goodwill to the larger world look like in other areas? Let's imagine some possibilities.

What if we dedicated a mere 5% of our economy to helping people in the world who do not have the resources we have here in

America? Many call this a "World Marshall Plan." What if we encouraged other industrial nations to join us in this generosity? What if, in a generation, America had a reputation not as the world's largest exporter of arms and corporate domination, but as an exporter of tangible help for the poorest in the world? Our need for military protection would drop tremendously, making it possible to dedicate even more than 5% and still have money left over. We'd be exporting tangible goodwill. And we'd reap benefits from what we'd sown.

What if we developed a Gross National Happiness index? We have a Gross National Product index that measures material production. There are countries like Bhutan who have a Gross National Happiness index that measures things like health care, employment, access to education, and other indices of happiness. Any measures would be imperfect, but they would help orient national policy away from material competition and toward physical, emotional, and spiritual wellbeing. We'd focus less on personal gain and more on goodness.

What if we required our larger corporations to justify their existence based on their generosity, kindness, and goodwill? This is being called a "Corporate Responsibility Amendment" to the Constitution. Face it: large corporations are a major force in the world. In America, we issue charters that allow them to do business here as legal entities. What if those charters expired every 10 years? In order to renew them, they'd have to present evidence to a jury of ordinary people demonstrating what they had done in the last 10 years to promote generosity, kindness, and wellbeing.

These are only three seed ideas that are being developed around the country today. As a religious community, we may not have the resources to develop the finer points of policies, but we do have a responsibility to examine public policy from the perspective of real moral values. We have a responsibility to raise questions. We have the responsibility to insert these values and questions into the public dialogue.

Redemptive Goodwill

One of the theological beliefs propagated in the world today is that violence can redeem violence. People look at the number of violent yakshas in the world and proclaim that more violence is the way to protect ourselves. Great teachers from Lao Tzu to Jesus to Gandhi to Mother Theresa to Martin Luther King have spoken eloquently about how this stance is impotent.

When we Unitarian Universalists put our faith in inherent goodness, we aren't saying that by sitting around passively, goodness and kindness will automatically predominate in the world. We see the capacity for torture, cruelty, and indifference.

What we are saying is that if we bring anger to anger, fear to our fear, answer violence with violence, respond to insult with insult, name calling with name-calling, we just get a world that is filled with more and more anger, fear, violence, insults, and name-calling. This is not complicated.

Our faith encourages a different strategy: bring love to violence, generosity to selfishness, kindness to insults, and goodwill to the frightening yakshas.

Goodwill is the only way to redeem violence. Compassion, kindness, and generosity will not protect us from all harm. But in the long run, they move us toward peace and fairness for all. It is the most effective way to come together, deepen our lives, and be a force for healing the world.

Conflict and Community

Conflict is inevitable in any community.

The health of any congregation or any community is not measured by the presence or absence of conflict but by our willingness to effectively, responsibly, and compassionately address interpersonal tensions when they arise.

Unitarian Universalism seeks to engage in the world. Thus, our intent is to attend to and learn from conflict, rather than just seek relief. In this way, our religion can transform our lives rather than merely comfort us.

Our approach is not based on good or bad, blame or guilt, winning or losing, offenders or victims. Rather, it is based on addressing the suffering of all concerned. Hurt, anger, fear, sadness, and doubt are taken seriously. We value gatherings that allow everyone to speak honestly, safely, and completely about their experiences and feelings. Thus, we value dialogue over silence, reconciliation over estrangement, forgiveness over resentment, confession over accusation, and reparation over punishment.

October 22, 2006

The Reverend Bob Hadley was my nearest colleague in the Unitarian Universalist Church of Littleton, Massachusetts. Bob had a passion for prison chaplaincy. He volunteered half a day or more each week at the maximum-security prison in Concord, Massachusetts.

He used to say, "Eighty-five percent of the inmates are not that different from you and me. Given different families or different circumstances, they would be leading lives just like you and me. With a little help, they'd be fine."

Then, with wide eyes and tense jaw, he'd continue: "But the other 10 to 15% are scary! I believe in the worth and dignity of every person. But I'm glad those people are locked up. I don't know how they got the way they are: bad genes, bad karma, bad families, bad social environment, bad planet alignment. Whatever it was, we are not going to be safe with them walking the streets of our communities."

Ill Will and Goodness

I want to talk to you about conflict and community. This is third in a series of talks on conflict. First, I spoke on the inner dimensions: the potential for ill will that is wired deeply into all of us — not just psychopathic criminals — but all of us (pp. 101-105).

Next, I spoke about the global dimensions: goodwill as an antidote to ill will and making compassion, kindness, and goodwill the foundation of our national and international policies (pp. 106-109).

Now, I want to talk about the middle ground between the inner and the global. How do we reconcile malice and inherent goodness? Ill will can take hold of the senses of some people: the dairy truck driver who murdered those Amish girls, people who fly passenger planes into skyscrapers. How do we reconcile the reality of dangerous people with the reality that goodwill is the only thing that can move us toward a kinder world?

In our everyday lives, we encounter people who don't respect personal boundaries, who purposely shade the truth, whose fear, greed, or ambition overrides concern for the common good.

How do we cope with the intractable conflicts in our everyday life and affirm our Unitarian Universalist values of the worth, dignity, and goodness of everybody?

Warm Heart and Cool Head

I offer an approach to conflict that can transform our view of ourselves, others, and the world.

This approach encourages us to let go of traditional views of conflict. We let go of good and bad, right and wrong, blame and guilt, offender and victim, who did what to whom, and even justice and injustice as abstract principles. Instead, we attend to the suffering of all people concerned. First and foremost we ask, "What can we do to lessen everyone's suffering in the present and future?"

This strategy requires both a warm heart and a cool head. In the first talk in this series on conflict, I talked about the reptile portion of our brains that can make us dumb and numb: hotheaded and coldhearted. The approach I'm suggesting is the opposite: a warm heart and a cool head, compassion and dispassion, heartful and clearheaded, openhearted with good boundaries.

For example, there are people we humbly want to isolate from society. I agree with Bob Hadley. Having faith in worth, dignity, and goodness doesn't mean being stupid or fuzzy headed. It does mean distinguishing between those who have made a mistake and need some help, and that tiny sliver of the population that must be isolated. When we do restrain someone, it means being as firm as we have to be and as kind as we can.

This requires discerning the difference between safety and punishment or revenge. Our judicial system has gotten hotheaded and coldhearted. It has far too much fear and ill will. We all too readily lock people up or put them to death. In California, we have built a new prison every year for 10 years. They haven't made us safer. They punish, but they don't make us safer. We don't have to judge the worth and dignity of others in order to protect ourselves.

Bringing more love and kindness to the world doesn't require sticking our hands in a fan. It does require us to look for kind and intelligent ways to deal with the conflict.

This requires a cool head and a warm heart, and it requires us first and foremost to consider the suffering of all involved.

Inevitability

This orientation is not easy. Therefore, I have summarized it in the four paragraphs included at the beginning of this talk. The core of this approach is in the final paragraph. I have included the first three to set the stage.

Let's unpack this conflict statement. The first paragraph reads:

Conflict is inevitable in any community.

Let me illustrate:

A year ago last spring, I went down to the Unitarian Universalist Community Church in South Sacramento for one of Reverend Melora Crooker's last services. The worship leader opened with a canned statement about including people of different sexual orientations. Despite the mumbled delivery, a shiver ran down my spine. I was reminded of the power of words coming from the pulpit, even if they are words with which we all agree.

In this congregation, our style is not formulaic statements. So, at the next religious services committee meeting, I encouraged the worship leaders to write their own statement of inclusion for the opening welcome.

I also spoke to members of our congregation who are gay, lesbian, bisexual, or transgender. I wanted to know how the statements sounded to them.

One of our worship leaders used the phrase "sexual preference." This inadvertently implied that sexual orientation is a matter of choice, which it rarely is. Someone else spoke generally about including everyone. People in oppressed groups have heard "inclusion" and "welcome" all their lives in places that did not include or welcome them. To feel included, their identity had to be named.

However, if we name one identity, it sounds like others are excluded. So, do we open with, "We welcome you regardless of your sexual orientation, gender identity, economic class, racial genes, mental abilities, hearing acuity, dress preference, country of origin, whether you are atheist, pagan, theist, Christian, Zoroastrian, recovering alcoholic or gambling addict, lover of dogs or cats, even if you don't like chocolate … "? It sounds like a Garrison Keillor parody.

The conversations about opening statements were amicable at first. After a while, some of the worship leaders felt their hard efforts were not appreciated, and those who had been the focus of societal prejudice felt they weren't being taken seriously. Those who wanted poetry were at odds with those who wanted clarity. Motives were questioned. Feelings were hurt. Everyone had started with good will and generous intent, but we were in conflict.

At this point, I flew to India to begin my sabbatical.

Addressing Conflict

The second paragraph of the conflict statement reads:

The health of our congregation or any community is not measured by the presence or absence of conflict but by our willingness to effectively, responsibly, and compassionately address interpersonal tensions when they arise.

Conflict is inevitable because human experience varies. Conflict is not necessarily a sign of ill will, bad faith, egotism, hot heads, or cold hearts. It can be a sign of different points of view.

It is as if the entire truth is as vast as the sky. Each of us views the sky through a single straw. One person sees a bird in flight; another, a distant mountain; a third, clear blue; a fourth, rain clouds. These different views seem to conflict like the blind men and the elephant.

If we think of a healthy community as one with an absence of conflict, then we may think we have to eliminate conflict. We can hold an instant run-off vote where everyone rank orders their preference for bird, mountain, blueness, or cloud. The view that wins becomes official, and the others are banned. We end up with a harmonious but narrow view of reality.

In this congregation, we value breadth, we value differences. Just look at all our banners. This means we should value conflict. Conflict can be a sign that we are letting our individual differences show. We are better off if we don't try to resolve differences but seek to understand and clarify the tensions. The tensions themselves are not bad. Tension is just a sign that something needs attention.

The third paragraph of the conflict statement puts it this way:

Unitarian Universalism seeks to engage in the world. Thus, our intent is to attend to and learn from conflict rather than just seek relief. In this way, our religion can transform our lives rather than merely comfort us.

While I was traveling about India and Nepal, emails about the opening statement flew around the congregation like a fire accelerant. Finally, several people said, "Hey, wait a minute. This isn't working. Let's get together face-to-face and see if we can understand what is going on."

By the time I got back in January, the worship leaders, Interweave folks, and anyone else interested had been invited to a meeting. I sat in to listen.

I did offer one observation. Across the denomination and beyond, people who have done meaningful anti-oppression work have found it painful. It calls into question deep assumptions we carry unconsciously. Someone looking through a different straw may see something we miss completely. It can be humbling. And it can hurt.

The fact that this conflict had been painful might not be a sign that we are doing anything wrong. It might be a sign that we are doing things right. It might be a sign that we are more interested in doing meaningful work than in avoiding pain. We were not looking for comfort for comfort's sake. You can't have breakthroughs without breakage.

Suffering of All

Now, we have come to the core of using conflict as a tool for transformation. It means attending to the suffering — not avoiding it — but attending to it. The fourth paragraph begins:

Our approach is not based on good or bad, blame or guilt, winning or losing, offenders or victims. Rather, it is based on addressing the suffering of all concerned.

This is the crucial shift in focus. If we can deal with the suffering of all people, the tension dissolves. Issues of good or bad or even offender or victim get in the way of seeing the suffering.

The paragraph goes on:

Hurt, anger, fear, sadness, and doubt are taken seriously. We value gatherings that allow everyone to speak honestly, safely, and completely about their experiences and feelings. Thus, we value dialogue over silence, reconciliation over estrangement, forgiveness over resentment, confession over accusation, and reparation over punishment.

At the religious services meeting, we went around the room and gave everyone a chance to speak. For the first round, we did not say what others had done or propose solutions. We avoided ideas of good or bad, blame or guilt, or who did what to whom. For the first round, we just listened to what each person's experience had been.

By the time everyone had spoken, we had an empathetic understanding of where each person was coming from. We had a glimpse through each other's straws. We understood with warm hearts and cool heads what the other people's suffering might have been. Perspectives had been enlarged.

This is how transformation begins.

By the end of the meeting, we had not solved the conflict. But we had a strategy to manage it and a better appreciation of the subtleties of the issues.

Today, the welcome statement is still a work in progress. There is still a conflict between the urges for poetry and clarity, for succinctness and thoroughness, for having it long enough so guests will understand and short enough so longtime members aren't bored, for the different meanings words have for different people, and so on.

I don't think we are ever going to get a statement that resolves all these differences, but if we, as Unitarian Universalists, truly value differences, we are better off listening with warm hearts and cool heads to all the concerns, rather than pushing for artificial conformity.

Other Conflicts

I use the struggle over the welcoming statement as a concrete example of the inevitability of conflict in any meaningful community. A spiritual approach to conflict values learning and transformation over the comfort of superficial harmony.

I'm sure we can think of other conflicts in our families, schools, jobs, and the larger world. Some we've handled very well, others not so well.

I invite you to reflect on the ongoing conflicts in your life. What is your suffering? What is the suffering of the other people? Are you willing to let go of assigning blame and guilt, offender and victim, so that you can more clearly see the suffering?

I find this very difficult. If someone speaks to me harshly, I may want to blame him or her. I may secretly treasure my status as a victim. Considering suffering first and foremost is not easy, but it gives an enriching approach to conflict and community.

Summary

To summarize: There are two common approaches to conflict. One is romanticized liberalism as in: "We all have goodness and worth, so let's just be nice and everything will be fine."

Actually, in my experience, 95% of conflicts arise out of misunderstanding, miscommunication, or people getting lost in fear, anger, or confusion. A little time, goodwill, and careful listening may not resolve the conflict, but it can dissolve the tension. This allows for more creative thinking.

However, it doesn't work in all situations.

The second common approach to conflict is cynical conservatism as in: "There are terrorists, psychopathic criminals, and unsavory characters running around. We must be tough." We don't want to sit by idly as someone abuses a child. We don't want to let a serial killer run loose. We may not want to support a policy of "preemptive war." There are times when we need to stand firm and be fierce.

If we hold onto either extreme, we'll get stuck. We combine these two approaches by, first and foremost, considering the suffering of everyone. This requires a warm heart and a cool head, keeping your heart open and keeping good boundaries, and speaking the truth in love.

We could explore this strategy in other situations, from suspension of habeas corpus to North Korea to Iraq to oil depletion to marriage equality. Can you imagine if all our leaders looked at suffering with warm hearts and cool heads? It wouldn't solve our problems immediately, but it would set us on a healing course.

Therefore, when we practice this in our own personal lives, we are strengthening a skill we can bring to the larger world. We are developing a healing presence as we engage with family, neighborhood, or the global community.

Discontentment

November 5, 2006

Robert docked his boat in a tiny Mexican village as Manuel, a local fisherman, unloaded his catch. Robert complimented Manuel on the quality of his fish, and asked, "How long did it take you?"

"Oh, not long," Manuel answered.

"Then, why didn't you stay out longer and catch more?"

Manuel shrugged. "This is enough to take care of my family."

Robert looked puzzled. "But what do you do with the rest of your time?"

"I sleep late, fish a little, play with my children, and take a siesta with my wife. In the evenings, I go into the village to see my friends, have a few drinks, play guitar, sing a few songs, ... "

Robert interrupted, "I have an MBA from Harvard, and I can help you! You can start by fishing longer every day. Then you can sell the extra fish and buy a bigger boat."

"What would I do with a bigger boat?" Manuel asked.

"With the extra money the larger boat will bring, you can buy a second one and a third one until you have an entire fleet of trawlers. Then, instead of selling your fish to a middleman, you can sell directly to the processing plants and maybe even open your own plant. Then, you can leave this little village and move to Mexico City, Los Angeles, or even New York! From there, you can direct your huge enterprise."

"How long would that take?"

"Perhaps 25 years," replied Robert.

"And what would happen after that?" Manuel asked.

"Afterwards? That's when it gets really interesting," Robert enthused. "When your business gets really big, you can sell stocks and make millions!"

"Millions? Really? And then what?"

"After that, you'll be able to retire, live in a tiny village near the coast, sleep late, play with your children, catch a few fish, take a siesta with your wife, and spend your evenings drinking and enjoying your friends."[12]

A Kind of Unhappiness

I want to talk about discontentment. Another time, I'll talk about contentment. If we can deal with our discontent, contentment is easier.

Discontentment is unhappiness with how things are or how we imagine them to be. When we are in conflict, the suffering may be obvious. However, when we are discontented, the unhappiness can be quieter and more subtle.

We might be discontented with a relationship: we aren't fighting, but it just isn't satisfying. Or, we might be discontented about something we don't have: a boat, a Harvard degree, a bigger salary, more naps, longer vacations. Or, we might be discontented about something we have but don't want: illness, long workdays, bills, project deadlines.

Discontentment can be a response to almost anything.

The deepest discontent arises not out of external circumstances but out of who we are or who we think we are. We Unitarian Universalists speak about the worth, dignity, and goodness of every person. Spiritual discontentment arises out of not knowing how to fully embrace our own goodness.

Societal Dimensions

Here in America, were masters of discontent. We have the discontent of fear: terrorist alerts, crime statics, and politics of fear. We have the discontent of speed: the natural pace for many of us may be closer to the Mexican fisherman's than our daily routine. We have the discontentment of complexity: deep down many long for simpler lives.

---

[12] Adapted from Courtney Carver www.bemorewithless.com/the-story-of-the-mexican-fisherman/

The parable suggests the biggest societal source of discontent is a consumer-oriented economy. To be efficient consuming units, we must be discontent: not happy and not too upset or worried, but quietly ill at ease.

We saw this right after the September 11 attacks. We didn't consume as much. We were stunned. Rushing to the mall seemed gross in the face of what had happened. As a result, the economy sagged. President Bush went on television and encouraged people to go to the malls. We could thumb our noses at the terrorists by going out and buying: "Don't let them stop our way of life." Consumption was equated with patriotism.

Sixty percent of the American economy is, in fact, fueled by consumer purchases. The advertising industry tries to fine-tune our dis-ease. Then, it offers a product to ease the discontentment. Robert advertised to Manuel on how to find the good life.

Even if we are able to shield out 95% of advertising hype (which is optimistic), it can still get to us. We are left with a vague sense of emptiness, of not having enough or not being enough.

Advertising is better at creating discontent than resolving our dis-ease. It creates a spiritual sickness: an imbalance from not seeing ourselves clearly.

Chökyi Nyima

During my sabbatical, I wanted to get outside these cultural forces as much as possible. I went to India, Nepal, and Thailand. Let me tell you a story:

Last December, my wife, Erika, and I spent a few nights on the fifth floor of a little hotel in Tamel, the old city section of Katmandu. We arose one morning to climb into a mini-bus with the small group we had been traveling with. We had been granted an interview with Tulku Chökyi Nyima Rinpoche.

We drove to the Boudhanath Stupa in Northern Katmandu. We walked around the huge stupa and four blocks up a narrow alley to the Ka-Nying Shedrub Ling Monastery.

We climbed narrow stairs to the top floor and sat down in a stark white marble waiting area.

I knew little about Chökyi Nyima except that he was a Tulku, someone Tibetans recognize as a reincarnated spiritual master. Most Tulkus are exquisitely and lovingly trained from an early age. Later, I learned that the Dalai Lama had personally asked Chökyi Nyima to teach Westerners about Tibetan spirituality.

After a half hour, our group was invited into the audience chamber. Large windows showed Katmandu spread about below in one direction and the Himalayas rising out of sight in the other direction.

On a bench covered with bright Tibetan cloth, an impish little man sat next to a bowl of cornflakes. He chatted animatedly. He was surrounded by an aura of vast, alive space.

Protocol invited us to come forward and bow. Each of us had a traditional gift of a white scarf. He accepted each, gave it a blessing, and then gave it back.

As he placed the scarf over my neck, he said to everyone, "This is Einstein." I assumed he was referring to my wire-rim glasses and tufts of hair sticking out from the side of my head, like Einstein.

In another setting, I might have been offended. But his laugh was infectious, intimate, and embracing. I smiled and pulled my hair so it stood out further.

Someone in our group said, "Actually, he's a minister. He's clergy."

"Ah," he said, "a Christian. I like talking with people of other religions."

I could have explained how, in the history of Protestantism, we were the left wing of the Reformation. In America, we split away from the Orthodox Congregational Church in the early 1800s. We do not tell people what to believe. Since we don't require people to accept Jesus as the divine Son of God, the World Council of Churches does not see us as Christian.

Somehow, at the foot of the Himalayas in Northern Katmandu, high up in the audience chamber of a laughing Tulku, none of that seemed particularly relevant.

When introductions were done, he sat still for a few minutes looking at us. Then he said four words: "You have good hearts."

I've heard those words before. I've spoken them. I believe them, pretty much. But there was something about his depth of contentment, vitality of spirit, and clearness that made the words resonate deeply.

"I really do have a good heart," I realized. I looked around the room. "Yes, we do have good hearts."

He went on, "Trust your hearts. Enjoy your hearts. Being happy is good."

He spoke for a while in this vein.

Then he invited: "Imagine a Tibetan gun. It would have beautiful carvings, ribbons, bells, cloth, and incense swinging from the barrel. The barrels might not be that straight. And since Tibet has little metal, Tibetan gunsmiths might make wooden barrels.

"Tibetans probably wouldn't have bullets. They are way too complicated. So, when the enemy attacked, we'd all be pouring gunpowder down the barrel, pushing it down with a stick. We'd turn to the enemy and say, 'Wait a minute. Stop running. We have to load our guns before we can shoot you. It'll only take a minute.'"

He mimicked trying to get gunpowder into a wooden gun and light it with a match.

When our laughter finally subsided, he looked down, shook his head, and said, "We Tibetans don't do guns very well. We don't know much about technology. We are better at wisdom.

"Each country should do what it is good at. If you want a good watch, the Swiss make the best. I saw them in Geneva. If you want cheese, ah, the French. If you want chocolate, the Dutch. If you want a radio, the Japanese are good. If you want technology, the Americans are very clever. But they're not so good at wisdom. Tibetans are better at wisdom.

People should do what they are good at."

After 20 minutes, he asked if we had questions. He had seen much of the world, so someone asked what wisdom he might have for President Bush.

Chökyi Nyima looked down. His face clouded. "I have never met President Bush. I don't think he would listen to me."

Then he looked up, "But if he did, I'd say he should listen to people more. He says, 'Either you are with me or you are against me.' But good people have different ideas about things. There are a lot of people who disagree with him who aren't against him. If he listened more, he'd know that there are fewer bad people in the world than he thinks. He'd be happier. We'd all be happier."

Later, someone asked about guilt.

"We Tibetans don't do guilt very well. That's more Christian. Let's ask Einstein."

I was flattered and embarrassed. There were people in the room from all over the world. I felt like a novice being asked by Yoda to converse publicly with a Jedi Master.

I mumbled something about the difference between remorse and guilt: "To feel remorse about something you've done wrong can be useful to help you live better. But to feel guilty in the sense of thinking you are a bad person . . . I don't think that ever helps."

Chökyi Nyima nodded.

Then he looked up and smiled, "People should do what their hearts enjoy. Contented people make the world better for others as well as themselves. Trust your good heart."

We had been with him for an hour and a half. It was time to go.

The Ills of the World

Chökyi Nyima had every right to feel discontent. He, his father, the Dalai Lama, and so many others had fled the Chinese invasion of Tibet. They lived in exile. He traveled the world in support of many causes. Meanwhile, the Chinese trashed his culture.

Yet, he showed no hint of discontent. He felt sad about his homeland, but he was content, spacious, buoyant, funny, and engaged.

We Unitarian Universalists feel the ills of the world as well: Environmental havoc, war proliferation, obscenely uneven wealth distribution, the struggle to maintain a good educational system for our children, skyrocketing health care cost, starvation, disease. But, unlike Chökyi Nyima, we often feel discontent.

There is nothing wrong with feeling discontent with some of the conditions of the world. But I am concerned about our discontent with ourselves: not trusting the goodness of our hearts to know what our minds don't grasp.

Perhaps we feel discontentment because we do guilt so well. We may not all be Christian in the narrowest sense: we may not accept Jesus as our personal savior, but our historical tradition includes Catholics and Calvinists and Puritans who did guilt very well. We are good at it.

Unlike Chökyi Nyima, we still live in our homeland. We have not been physically exiled. We can't say, "Don't blame me. I'm not even living there any more." We do live here.

Whether we blame some of the ills of the world on America or not, we still have that American sense that "We should be wise enough to make the world better. Our role is to fix things. And if we don't, there is something wrong with us."

Many of us personalize this: "If I can't stop the war, save the environment and feed the poor, there is something wrong with me. I'm not doing enough. I'm not engaging enough. I'm not caring enough. There's something not good enough about me." We do guilt very well. We do discontent well.

Humility

Chökyi Nyima would advise humbly trusting our hearts. Humility is important both nationally and personally.

Less than a third of Americans own passports. Most haven't been out of the country. Most haven't seen how others live or what they are good at. Who are we to say how the world should be, when we barely know what it is?

As we walked back to the market around the Boudhanath Stupa, I remember reflecting on our fast-paced, commercial-driven, fear-infused culture. I thought, "Most people like American ideals of freedom and democracy. It's our commercialism they reject. We should be humbler about pushing our system on the rest of the world without knowing more about what others do. Just because we make better guns doesn't mean we have more wisdom about when and how to use them."

Many of you probably agree with this general sentiment. Yet, when it comes to applying it to ourselves, it can be difficult to trust that if we are humble and aware, we will know what is ours to do and what not to do.

In fact, some of us feel guilty if we start to feel a little contentment. We mistake contentment for complacency. We confuse discontentment with worldly awareness. We think discontentment will make us more effective in the good struggle.

Grumpy people make very poor change agents. Nobody wants to listen to them.

When we are happy, content, rested, and feel drawn to engage the world, we become almost irresistible change agents. Like Chökyi Nyima, we can laugh and respond with great energy.

Cultivating a deep contentment based on trusting the goodness of our hearts deepens our lives and makes us a more effective force for healing in the world.

Closing

As we approach the most commercial time of the year, I invite you to reflect on the discontent in your life. If you feel manipulated by commercialism, don't put yourself down. See if you can relax, and see the discontentment for what it is.

If you feel discontent about the state of the world, don't be afraid to feel that as well. It's not personal. You are resonating with some of the pain in the world. If we embrace it, it brings us together. That's where the power to change comes from: feeling our connection to each other and the larger world enlivens and empowers.

Many of us think, "I'm unhappy because of the state of my life," or "I'm discontent because of the state of the world." There may be some truth to this. But it is also true that if we were more content, we'd cause fewer messes in our lives and fewer messes in the world. As a nation, we'd be less like soldier termites devouring the planet and starting wars. And as individuals, we'd be kinder and gentler and know when and how to rest and when and how to engage.

I'll leave you with a Unitarian Universalist kōan: "How can I engage in the world as it is and be content at the same time?"

"How can I be in my life as it is and be content?"

Contentment

November 12, 2006

I came home from high school one afternoon to find my father had come home early. He was a physically powerful man with tightly held emotions and somewhat rigid thinking.

Yet, that afternoon he was sprawled on the living room floor. His eyes were closed. His stereo was cranked up. Beethoven's Ninth symphony shook the house. There was a hint of a smile at the corners of his mouth. It was good to see him so content.

One August, I sat in the backyard of our New England home making plans for the upcoming church year. It was the start of my third year serving the First Parish Church Unitarian in Groton, Massachusetts. As I reflected on my congregation, I thought, "I could spend the rest of my life as a small town country preacher, and die a happy man."

It wasn't that Groton and I were an ideal match. They were more traditional and theistic. I was more folksy and up-and-coming-Buddhist. But that didn't matter. I liked the people. I enjoyed the work. It was good enough. I was content.

On a hot day, I hiked toward Round Top Mountain in the high Sierra's. The last few miles of trail faded into loose rock on the steep slopes in the thin air.

When I scrambled onto the summit, I felt my accomplishment. As I gazed around the mountains, that satisfaction mellowed into quiet. I sat for the longest time taking in the sky and the peaks and valleys far below. I wasn't thinking about anything. I had nothing I wanted to do. I was content.

Then thunder cracked behind me. I turned to see a dark cloud drifting my way. I was no longer content. I wanted out of there. Yet on the return hike, the sweetness of contentment lingered.

I want to talk about contentment. It is a kind of happiness that can arise out of how things are. Previously, I have described discontentment as a kind of unhappiness with how things seem to be. Contentment is the opposite. The deepest contentment is happiness with who we are. It is a wellbeing that emerges out of our core.

Our consumer-oriented, fast-paced, fear-driven, overly complex, advertising-haunted society offers little support for contentment. If, on a job application at a large corporation, you list one of your qualifications as being a contented person, they might be disinclined to hire you. They figure you will work harder if you are discontent, dissatisfied, and ambitious. Contentment is not valued in the mainstream culture.

Nevertheless, it is a natural and deeply human experience we all have had in various degrees. I want to talk about three ways to cultivate contentment: changing our environment, releasing the tensions, and abiding patiently or observing with a lightness of mind. As we explore these, we'll also explore what contentment is and why it is so important.

Changing the Environment

The most obvious strategy for cultivating contentment is changing your environment. What creates contentment may be different for each of us. So, you can recall when you felt content and create similar situations.

If you enjoy hiking and camping, spend time in the wilds. If camping reminds you of swatting bugs, sleeping on rocks, and eating food that is both burnt and raw, you may be content to spend less time in the wilds. You may need a few more amenities around you.

Over the years, I've used my father's technique of lying on a padded floor as music fills every corner. But Beethoven doesn't do it for me. Yet, Palestrina, Vaughn Williams, the Barber Adagio, the sound track from "Dances with Wolves," Paul Winter, the acoustical guitar of Bill Frisell, and others sweep through me, relaxing jangled nerves and smoothing me out.

Contentment-evoking situations can be as simple as singing a child to sleep, relaxing on the patio after a full week, finishing a house project, taking a nap, or going for a jog.

Some people feel guilty about pursuing contentment when there are so many unhappy people in the world. Remember that your misery doesn't help anybody. It's okay to be happy. It's okay to note contented situations and use that knowledge to guide you.

However, there are limitations to this strategy.

Spending a month in Bali may be ideal for you, but you may have neither the time nor the finances. Getting rid of that irritating person in the office might be wonderful, but you have no choice. You have to work with him. Being free of grumpy children or incorrigible parents may be conducive to contentment, but you are stuck with them.

We have limited control over the world around us. The advertising industry would like us to think we have total control. If we just buy this car, anti-toenail fungus pill, Carnival vacation package, weight-loss program, or weight-gain food, we'll be happy. But it is not true. If we try changing the environment too much, we risk becoming addictive, narcissist control freaks: not content.

While it is wise to do what is reasonable to put ourselves in situations that evoke contentment, at some point, we may want to consider other strategies.

Letting Go

The second strategy is to look inside, see where you are holding, and let go. There is an inverse relationship between tension and contentment.

As you press the gas pedal to the floor and race down the drag strip, you may be thrilled. But you are not content. Bungee jumping, playing one-upmanship with your boss, engaging in contact sports, cheering your basketball team, or watching a suspense movie can be thrilling, exciting, pleasurable, satisfying, and even healing. But they are not contentment.

Contentment is a particular kind of happiness that arises when there is a lack of tension inside. If you want contentment, it is helpful to release physical, emotional, or mental strains.

A Presbyterian minister once heard clanking in his basement. He thought, "It sounds like my furnace is breaking."

He opened the basement door, turned on the light, and started down the stairs. Towards the bottom, he tripped and landed flat on the hard floor. He got up, checked himself for bruises, dusted himself off, and said, "Whew. I'm glad I'm done with that."

I can imagine having a very different response to falling down the stairs.

Discontentment and contentment are not inherent in anything or any situation. They are responses to situations. Discontent is not inherent in falling down the stairs. Contentment is not inherent to Beethoven, Palestrina, or Jerry Garcia. One person responds to camping with bliss, another with misery.

This second strategy involves shifting focus from the external environment to the internal. Rather than manipulate what's around you, you let go of the holding inside you.

People who have a strong belief in God, fate, or destiny may find it easier to be content. Like the Presbyterian minister, whatever happens can be seen as God's will or fate. They surrender to it. The car breaks down: "God's will. Nothing to get uptight about."

If you don't believe in a benevolent God or fate directing your life, it may help to frame this differently.

For example, in Sanskrit the word "*nirvana*" means "extinguish," as in a fire going out. In the Buddha's time, the fire element or heat was thought to be part of everything. Some things had more fire than others. A flame arises when fire clings to wood or a candle. When the flame is extinguished, the fire doesn't disappear. It merely ceases to cling. It disperses and becomes part of everything again.

To enter nirvana means to let go: let go of things, let go of ideas and opinions, even let go of a sense of a separate self. You are extinguished and become part of everything.

The essence of most spiritual paths is this deep release. Different traditions use different words for this process. In the monotheistic religions like Judaism, Christianity, and Islam, the language is "surrendering to God's will." In other traditions, the language is "letting go" or "the freedom of release." It is a similar process, just a different concept of why it works.

To practice contentment in our everyday life, we can do this in smaller steps.

For example, I was in a training group for several years with a woman who left me uptight. I was in knots around her. I didn't understand what was happening until I looked inside for the source of tension. Then I realized what I had to do to release it. In the group I told her, "I don't like you, and I want you to like me."

I was embarrassed to admit this neurotic tension. Yet, when I did, it began to let go. Very quickly, I was free of it. I cared much less about how she felt about me, and it was easier to feel kindness for her.

Another example: if someone accuses me of doing something wrong, I may feel defensive and want to save face. Yet, as that tension unsettles me, I become more interested in releasing it than in looking good. Therefore, if there is any truth to the accusation, I just say, "Yes, you're right. I'm sorry. Let's see if I can make amends." I'd rather be humble and content than right and uptight. Usually.

The practice of surrender or letting go can be quite effective in cultivating contentment, but it has limitations.

In some situations, it may not be wise to say, "I don't like you. I want you to like me." That could be too hurtful or confusing and create more difficulty. Sometimes, naming it heartfully and silently to yourself can be enough to release it. But sometimes it isn't. The tightness holds.

Sometimes, the stress is due to an ongoing situation: the nagging boss, the degrading environment, the ill parent. If so, you might ask yourself, "Is there anything more I can do today?" If you've done everything you can for now, maybe you can let go for today.

Sometimes, nothing works. We say to ourselves, "Let go, let go, let go!", and we can't. We push it under, condemn ourselves, or become tense about being tense: a special kind of misery.

We need another strategy.

Abiding Patiently

The third strategy is abiding patiently or just observing the tension without trying to release it. The key to this strategy is the quality of mind with which you observe.

When the human potential sage, Jean Houston, was growing up, she lived on the Upper East Side of New York City. Sometimes, she had difficulty getting going in the early hours of the day.

One morning, she ran down the sidewalk trying to get to her school bus before it left her behind. She whipped around a corner and ran smack into an elderly gentleman, knocking them both off their feet.

"I'm sorry, I'm sorry," she said, as she reached out to help the gentleman.

As he got to his feet, he said, "Young lady, are you going to be in such a hurry all your life?"

Still out of breath from running, she panted, "I don't know, sir. I guess maybe I will."

His eyes sparkled as he said, "Well then, bon voyage!"

This sparkly "bon voyage" hints at contentment on the run or contentment in the midst of discontent. The quality of awareness is key.

In Buddhism, the term "*chanda*" points to this quality. "Chanda" is often translated as "zeal" or "effort" as in "practice with great effort." A more careful translation is "joyful enthusiasm" or "smiling mind."

You don't try to change anything outside you or inside you. Instead, observe whatever is going on with patient abiding, joyful enthusiasm, delightful curiosity, quiet embrace, or "a smiling mind."

Previously, I described the Tibetan Tulku, Chökyi Nyima Rinpoche. He displayed a lot of delightful interest. It can be very energetic, as in a Sufi mystic, or very quiet, as in a good Christian monk's kind interest.

Thus, you look inside with joyful interest: "Look how depressed I am. Far out." Or with a smiling mind you notice, "Wow, look at this anger." "Hmm, I'm really holding onto this one." Or with patient abiding you see, "What a rush I'm in. Ah so." Whatever is going on, you bring to it a gentle interest or joyful awareness.

The limitation of this strategy is that it is foreign to a popular culture that is more into control than awareness. It is not an easy practice. However, it has no other limits. You can learn to be content no matter what is going on by abiding patiently with a smiling mind.

So What

So what? Why is contentment important?

Some people think, "I work better under pressure. I'm more creative when demands are on me. Tension can be a good thing."

Scientific studies disagree. People who say they produce better under pressure actually produce better work when they are not under pressure. When they are relaxed, they are more creative and efficient.

Maybe they don't do anything when they are relaxed. If producing something is better than nothing, they produce better under stress.

Many are stressed enough that when they truly relax, they fall asleep mentally if not physically. Our minds, bodies, and souls need rest. We are truly at our best when we are both rested and relaxed.

Whatever the case, these studies are just the tip of the iceberg.

When the mind relaxes, there is a kind of intelligence that becomes available. There is a wisdom and clarity and vigor that simply cannot be found when the heart is tense or distracted.

Contentment is a doorway into this consciousness. It is a doorway to another universe. This realm has been called grace, the divine, emptiness, nirvana, the Beloved, Shakti, sacred understanding, and on and on. There are as many labels as there are people who have genuinely touched this space and tried to articulate it.

When we aren't content, we respond more from the surface of our lives: our personality, conditioning, and adaptations. When we are content, we respond more from the core, and we sometimes respond from something that is beyond our normal understanding of what we are.

What this other realm is will be a topic for another time.

Practice

I invite you to explore all three of these strategies for cultivating contentment. Ask yourself, "What stands between where I am right now and complete wellbeing?" Make a list. The longer your list, the more discontented you are.

Then take a few items on your list and use the first strategy: "Is there anything I can reasonably do to change my circumstances?" If so, by all means, do it.

Practice the second strategy as well: "Can I let go of any tension I have around this?" "Even if you situation is not the best, is it good enough that I can surrender a bit?"

Also, practice the third strategy of abiding patiently. See if you can smile gently at whatever is going on inside you. Use a steady, joyful awareness.

I'm an advocate of practical religion. Think of contentment not as something we gain, but something we practice. Practice whatever helps.

Contentment tends to strengthen itself. As we feel more of it by whatever means, it develops confidence in what is possible. That confidence helps us relax and find more contentment. This, in turn, opens a creative intelligence that is the true source of wisdom.

In a word: "Enjoy!"

Bon voyage!

Bad Reality, Good Reality

November 19, 2006

Bad Reality

I visited California for the first time the summer I graduated from high school. I was living in New Jersey and had never been to the Pacific coast. I took a bus west from New York City to San Francisco and north from San Francisco to the town of Philo.

How many of you know Philo?

That's what I thought. I had never heard of Philo either. Philo is a tiny town just north of Boonville. How many of you know Boonville?

That's what I thought. I had never heard of Boonville either.

I did know that a mile from Philo was a place called "Clearwater Ranch." Clearwater Ranch was a home for children with emotional or mental problems. I was to be a summer counselor at Clearwater Ranch.

One of the children was a boy named Sean. Sean had no real friends because he had autism. He didn't know how to relate to people. That is what autism does.

Sean was smart. Both of his parents were university professors, and Sean was very smart in his own way.

For example, Sean used to sit on a 20-foot rope swing outside his cabin and count. He might count by 1's: 1, 2, 3, 4, 5, 6, 7, 8, 9 … Or, he might count by 3's: 3, 6, 9, 12, 15, 18, 21, 24 … Or, he might count by 37's: 37, 74, 111, 148, 185 … In fact, he could count as fast by 113's as I could count by 1. I don't know how he did it, but he could just whip out numbers by 23's or 77's or 213's or anything.

One day, I found Sean spinning slowly on the swing as he grinned and counted: 0, 0, 0, 0, 0, 0, 0, 0, 0 … He was counting by 0.

He was very smart in his own way.

The thing Sean said that I remember the most was not about zeros.

Clearwater Ranch owned a beat up Jeep. Sometimes, we got to ride in the Jeep on the old lumber roads in the hills behind the ranch. One day, Chuck was driving the Jeep, Sean was riding "shotgun" in the other front seat, and I was in the back with Martin, another kid who lived at Clearwater.

As we drove up the dirt road, a branch hit Sean in the face.

Sean said, "Bad reality."

We laughed. A minute later, the Jeep hit a bump and all of us said, "Bad reality." Sean grinned.

That was forty years ago. To this day, when life does something I don't like, I think, "Bad reality." It became a phrase my family used when life seemed to be without grace.

What are some of the bad realities in your life? Things like too much homework or parents in a bad mood. Sometimes, we think, "If I were God and I were running the world, I wouldn't have rain during rush hour, cavities, braces, pimples, politicians with bad ideas, or people who don't listen to each other."

Do you know what I mean?

What are some of the bad realities in your life? What are some of the branches that hit you in the face?

Good Realities

I think you've got the idea.

For me, bad realities are things that we did not earn. They are no one's fault. They just happen. Sometimes, bad realities just happen.

Sometimes, good realities just happen. Sometimes, life gives us things that we didn't earn or do anything to deserve. They just happen.

I have two different words for these good realities: miracles and grace.

Miracles

When I was going to Starr King School for the Ministry, my wife, Erika, and I had little money. She sold pots and pans in the basement of a department store to earn a little money as I studied to become a minister.

We ate a lot of Swedish rye bread that year because rye flower and yeast were cheap. We could buy them and make our own bread. We ate a lot of beans because they were cheap protein.

As Thanksgiving passed and Christmas approached, we were depressed. Her family was in Wisconsin. Mine was all over the country from New Jersey to Arizona. We had no car. We had no money to travel. We were going to be stuck in a dark basement apartment that Christmas.

Then a check came in the mail from my grandmother. I had not spoken or written to her since we arrived in California. Yet, here was a check with enough money for bus tickets to Arizona to spend the holidays with my brother. It was a miracle.

I know some of you think miracles are things we can't explain. I can explain how we got that check. My mother spoke to my grandmother, and my grandmother wanted to give Erika and me some money. But the fact that I can explain it doesn't mean it was less of a miracle in my mind.

I think of miracles as good surprises that life sends us. We don't earn miracles. If you study hard for a test and do well, that is not a miracle. It is an accomplishment. But if you didn't study and got a good grade, that's a miracle. You didn't earn it. You didn't expect it. You were surprised, and it happened.

Grace

Miracles are one kind of good reality. They are easy to notice.

Grace is another kind of good reality that is not as easy to see. Grace is a low-key miracle. It's not a big surprise, but it is a good reality we did not do anything to earn and is there for us to enjoy anyway.

Nice weather in Sacramento is not a surprise. It is not something we did anything to earn, but we can enjoy it anyway. It is a free gift from life. Because we've come to expect good weather here in California, it does not seem miraculous, but it is grace.

Sometimes, it is easier to notice the bad realities than the good realities. When the weather is not to our liking, we notice. When it is to our liking, we take it for granted. Or, when we are sick, we notice our health. But when we aren't sick, we don't pay much attention to it.

Imagine you are the child of a rich Roman Emperor 2,000 years ago. You have servants and all the good things of ancient Rome.

Now, suddenly you are transported to a 21st century America home. Here you can look out the window at a storm while eating an apple, reading a book, and wearing a T-shirt. These are things the wealthiest Roman could not imagine possible even for their gods.

Yet we think nothing of them because we take for granted glass that keeps out the cold and lets in the view. The Romans didn't have window glass. We take for granted central heating, insulated homes, food from all over the world at all times of year. We have electricity. We talk to each other on little machines called phones. We keep up with the rest of the world with our magic picture boxes called TVs. We can make pictures and sounds move on the picture boxes by pushing little bumps called "game controller buttons."

Even without our gadgets, we are surrounded by grace. Have you every gotten a cut on your hand and studied it for a few minutes each day? Without your doing a thing, your body fixes itself. That is grace. That is miraculous.

We are surrounded by miracles and grace and good realities that we did not earn or do anything to earn: bodies that grow, cats that purr, sunshine, a path by the river, parents who listen, school vacations, religious traditions of freedom and tolerance, pets that adore us.

The Grace We Bring

Let's take this further:

When my grandmother sent me a check, she was an agent of grace. Each of us is a miracle. Each of us is grace. Each of us brings gifts we share without asking for anything in return. Yes, I know, there are things we do for which we'd like something back, but we also bring gifts for which we didn't want anything in return.

I stand up here and look around at all of you. You listen so heartfully. I don't think you are trying to do anything good for me. You are just being you, bringing your interest and intention. That is such grace for me: just your presence. We are grace for each other by coming with our intentions.

The graces we offer the world are the things that we take for granted about ourselves. Sometimes, you help and want something back. Sometimes, you just help because, well, because it's just what you do. You don't think about it. Sometimes, someone speaks to you about a problem and you think, "I haven't a clue how to help them. I wish I could do something." Just caring enough to listen can be grace.

The good realities and grace you bring might be musical passion, quiet respect, enthusiasm, passion for justice, curiosity, caring about a friend, quiet reflection, thoughtfulness, a good joke, patting the cat. We may feel shy about acknowledging them because it sounds like bragging, but it is important to be truthful. So let's name them.

Name the grace that you bring or the grace of someone you know. Name the gift. Name the grace. Name the good reality that comes through them or comes through you.

Generosity I

February 4, 2007

The narrow streets of the Old City of Katmandu were packed with people, vendor carts, and animals, but mostly, lots of people in T-shirts or Tibetan fabric, in jeans or monk robes, and everything in between.

It was our second to the last day in Asia. As I walked up the street, I thought, "I'm going to miss this place." The coins in my pocket thumped against my leg. "Maybe I'll just give all these coins away at once."

Then thoughts sputtered through me like: "What if I want some cloth, or a statue, or a snack, or a souvenir?" and "I'm only supposed to give beggars a few rupees at a time."

Nevertheless, I scanned the crowds to see whom I might give the coins to. After a few blocks, we came to an intersection where five streets came together. In the middle, a man stood with his palm out. I'd seen him several times before. He was skinny. His clothes were ragged and dingy. One leg was missing below the knee. A stick propped under his arm kept him upright. The fingers on his hand were stubs – I assumed he had lost them to leprosy. His face was sullen as people brushed passed him.

I pulled all the coins from my pocket. Holding them with both hands, I carefully deposited a pile on his palm. He looked at me sourly. He looked down at the coins. His mouth dropped open a little revealing three teeth. He looked back up at me with widening eyes.

I placed my palms together, bowed slightly, and left before he had a chance to say anything.

I floated into the crowds with his three teeth and astonished eyes in my mind and a glow in my heart. You could have whacked me with a two-by-four, and I would have just smiled. I was so happy. I couldn't get the grin off my face.

If I had kept the coins and bought something nice for myself, that would have been pleasant. That would have been good, and I would have soon forgotten.

Instead, here we are over a year later, and when I think of the look on his face, a glow lights up inside me. Giving away those rupees has given me more happiness than anything I could have done for myself.

Reflection

I want to talk about the power of generosity.

As a place to begin, I invite you to reflect on what generosity feels like in your life. You can close your eyes if you like:

Recall some time when you've been generous. Maybe you gladly gave a few dollars to a homeless person. Maybe you kindly yielded in traffic. Maybe you were pleased to give a significant amount of money to an organization you believed in. Maybe you soothed the fears of a child or gave time to a friend. Maybe you nursed someone with a disease. …

It may be something you did recently or years ago, and yet the memory still smiles inside you.

Remember what generosity feels like and sit with that for a few moments. …

Simple Glow

That simple glow can connect us with the depths of our heart. It can connect us with the divine. It can enlighten our lives. It can bring us home.

If skillfully cultivated, it can awaken us out of the cultural trance that drones, "Happiness comes from getting the most for yourself." This hypnotic suggestion comes through advertising, politics, and blatant greed touted as "realism." As a path to happiness, it is a dead end. It is a lie. It contains bits of truth: taking responsibility for our happiness is wise; self-care and self-love are essential; respecting our limitations is sensible. However, the way these are packaged together as, "He who gets the most toys wins" is delusional.

On the streets of Katmandu when the natural instinct to give came up, I could feel my cultural conditioning as sputtering thoughts: "What about me?" "Hold those rupees." "Keep them for yourself."

The simple little glow of generosity, if skillfully cultivated, can cut through this conditioning. It can awaken us out of this stupor. It can transform our lives individually, and as more and more people trust that glow, it can reorganize our society. It can truly deepen our lives and bring healing to our world.

Transformation

Let's look at generosity in our personal lives. At another time, we'll come back to this topic and explore how it can restructure society (see pp. 130-134).

For now, we'll look at the practice of generosity as a tool for personal transformation.

Transformation is not a process of getting something. It is a process of letting go. We let go of a limiting self-image and discover something different about ourselves. Maybe we let go of our self-image of shyness and discover we can motivate people in large crowds – we feel transformed. Or, we let go of thinking we are a spiritual klutz and find we can tap a source of deep insight– we feel transformed. Or, we let go of moroseness and discover a font of joy inside.

The practice of generosity is similar. We take some large or small piece of ourselves — something we've invested in — and release it. We literally give it away for someone else's benefit.

Practicing generosity is like practicing transformation in tangible steps. When done artfully even in small ways, we get that little glow inside. It is a glow of release and inner freedom.

To explore this, let's back up and look more closely at several aspects of generosity: giving, joy, release, and gratitude.

Giving

The most obvious ingredient of generosity is giving. We might give money, food, or time. We might spontaneously reach out to catch someone who has stumbled. We might listen to a friend's struggles. We might spend an evening serving St. John's Shelter. Generosity doesn't exist without tangible deeds.

I could have walked passed the Katmandu beggar and felt great empathy, kindness, and compassion. I could have quietly and sincerely wished him well. He probably would not have noticed, and I would have soon forgotten.

We can sit here and feel gratitude and warmth toward all. That is lovely and helpful, but if these sentiments are not accompanied by acts of giving money, time, kind words, or some deeds, it doesn't have that same depth or transformative potential.

Beyond Expectation

Generous giving is usually beyond what is expected. We probably would not consider paying our taxes an act of generosity because most of us pay the minimum we can get away with. Generosity goes beyond the minimum.

When I worked as a psychotherapist, clients gave me a fee, and I gave them time and counsel. As long as I stayed within the allotted time and they within the agreed costs, this was a business deal. This is not bad. It was done with heart, but it wasn't true generosity.

In fact, one of the reasons I came back into the ministry was to be in an environment based on generosity rather than quid pro quo business. The congregation – all of you – gives me a salary. I give my time without measuring fee for service hours.

The less we operate out of expectation and the more out of going beyond the minimum, the more potential there is for that glow of generosity.

Giving Ourselves

In generous giving, the gift carries a piece of us. Let's say, I have a shirt I never wear and, rather than throw it out, I give it to Goodwill. I can feel good about helping someone, but it is not generous giving because I was going to toss it out anyway. It required nothing of me.

Generosity requires something of us. Therefore, it can feel like a stretch.

A number of you helped in the New Orleans area after Katrina. You were giving pieces of your time. Caring for an ailing parent is usually giving a piece of oneself. The Peace Corps, AmeriCorps, and marching in demonstrations are this kind of giving. Raising children definitely devotes large pieces of oneself to someone else.

For many, the pledge we give to our church is a generous stretch. For others, it is more like a fee for service. All our donations are helpful. We can feel good about them, whether they are a stretch or not. But we'll know inside ourselves whether our donation is a cover charge or the stretch of generosity.

Therefore, the first essential ingredient of generosity is tangible giving that goes beyond the minimum and includes an investment of ourselves.

Joy

The second ingredient is joy. Generosity has both an outward action – giving – and an inward feeling or consciousness – joy, delight, happiness. Without both, it is not generosity by my understanding.

There are many ways to give. I can give out of anger ("I'll give her a piece of my mind."). I can give begrudgingly ("Okay, if you must. I'll let you have it."). I can give out of revenge ("I'll give the jerk just what he deserves"). I can give out of fear ("Please put the gun down. I'll give you my wallet."). I can give out of ego ("I'll work hard so everyone will think I'm a good guy."). I can give out of power ("I'll give so I can control what they do."). I can give out of guilt, social pressure, obligation, pride, and so on.

There are many ways of giving, and many of them can be a benefit to us and to those around us. But without joy or happiness, giving is not really generosity.

Release

The joy in generosity comes from letting go, from release. We live in a culture that emphasizes accumulation and consumption — a consumer economy. The core of generosity is the opposite: letting go. Rather than grasping and holding, we are releasing.

Grasping is inherently uncomfortable: it has tension, tightness, sometimes fear. Release is inherently comforting: ease, relaxing, freedom.

Conceptually, this is easy. In practice, it can be difficult. Because we are giving ourselves, generosity is sometimes a strain.

If our giving is so little that it doesn't mean much to us, then there is no release because we haven't given anything of ourselves.

However, if we empty our bank account, in our gut we may wish we hadn't. Outwardly, we gave a lot, but inwardly, we are still holding on. This is not skillful – we've overextended. There is no release. There is no joy. There is holding and worry.

This is a problem. When we give beyond expectations and give of ourselves, it can ignite that light of generosity inside us, and it can ignite fear, strain, worry, resentment, regret, anger, upset, and so on.

How we negotiate this letting go without falling back into fear, worry, regret, or grasping is unique to each of us. It's what makes generosity an art more than a science.

We can control the physical act of giving: whether to give, how much, when, and so on, but we can't control our feelings. Genuine feelings arise on their own or not at all. We can't create them directly using will power.

There are things we can do indirectly to cultivate feelings. This is the art of generosity.

Receiver's Response

One thing we can do to enhance joy is to be mindful of the receiver's response. This response is not essential to generosity, but it can affect the experience.

Consider: I give 20 dollars to someone down on their luck. They buy liquor and get drunk. Even though my intent was generous, I probably won't feel that inner glow. Rather than relieve suffering, I have contributed to it. On the other hand, if the person uses the money to buy some food for his child, the glow inside me is enhanced: I've helped several people.

There is a mystical aspect of generosity: someone else's wellbeing impacts ours. Call it empathy, compassion, or connection. It is a tangible experience of our bond. In generous giving, we strengthen that tie. The natural heart tends to feel joy in seeing others' joy. We tend to feel good when we've done good for others.

Seeing the Katmandu leper's sour expression crumble into the precursor of a smile just delighted me.

To help make that connection to the other person, the Buddha recommended that we use both hands when we give. In Southeast Asia – particularly away from Western influence – this is practiced literally.

I landed in Thailand a year ago today. Tired, hungry, jet-lagged, and culturally disoriented, I wandered the streets of Chiang Mai into a little café. I ordered some vegetables, rice, and yogurt.

When I was done, I handed the café owner a 100 baht note. He received the money and gave me change using both hands and a tiny bow as he said, "kaup koon," which I thought meant "thank you." I was so touched that I turned to him to receive the change with both hands, and said "mai bpen rai," which I hoped meant "you're welcome."

Using both hands felt sweet and personal and honoring of the humanity of both of us. I was a stranger who was welcomed.

Giving with one hand can be casual. Maybe we are looking sideways at our wallet or watch with one hand as we hand over the money. Our attention is split. But with both hands, our attention is fully on the giving. Our body is physically focused directly toward the person. We can't help but take them in.

In our more technologically complex culture, it may not be practical to personally go around and with both hands give our donation to NPR, Greenpeace, the Sierra Club, the Animal Rescue League, or even the Unitarian Universalist Society of Sacramento.

Nevertheless, there is still part of us that wants to know the effect our gift has had. One of the problems with giving a lot of small donations to Peace Action, public radio, the symphony, the UU Service Committee, and on and on is that we don't get a sense of whether our gift had a significant impact: did it make any difference?

To cultivate generosity, some people recommend that we not give so many small gifts to so many places, but pick a few favorites and give more significant amounts so that we can know it had an impact and feel the inner reward.

It's something to think about.

The other important symbolic aspect of two-handed giving is mindfulness: giving with full attention so that we can know if we are giving out of joy or guilt, resentment or delight. If we are in a painful state, it is easier to release it if we are fully aware of it. If we are in a wholesome state, we can savor it. We get more benefit if we are fully aware of it.

Gratitude

Another way to cultivate generosity is to cultivate gratitude. Generosity is closely tied to gratitude. The more grateful we are for the generosity around us, the easier it is for generosity to flow naturally through us gratefully.

Helen Bradfield once showed me a responsive reading used in this congregation shortly after the building was opened.

The worship leader said something like: "We looked for a piece of land to build this building."

The congregation responded, "And we scrimped and saved and scrimped and saved and worked and scrimped and saved."

Then the worship leader said, "And we had raffles and fund raisers and bake sales and pledge drives."

And the congregation responded, "And we scrimped and saved and worked and scrimped and saved."

The worship leader said, "And we made cardboard forms and poured concrete to make these walls."

"And we scrimped and saved and worked and scrimped and saved."

It went on for pages naming the people and things that went into this building. I could feel the sacrifice, the effort, the stretching: how people poured themselves into the project. I could feel the joy in it: the sheer delight despite the challenge, or because of it.

How many of you were around here at that time?

If the rest of you talk with those who were here, you'll experience how that generosity is still glowing inside them.

This congregation has not undergone such a major stretch since then. Maybe it's time. After 45 years, maybe it's time. Don't be surprised in the next year or so if …

Fields of Generosity

The point is that, as we sit here in this building, we are sitting in a field of generosity. We live in many fields of generosity, both large and small.

On a large scale, we would not be here were it not for the generosity of the earth. We are so well-suited to life here: it is part of us. The more we recognize the generosity of nature, the kinder and more generous we are in return.

We drink from wells we did not dig and harvest from trees we did not plant.

The roots of this congregation go back five generations to 1868. We would not be here were it not for all those who put so much of themselves into this place.

Again, we drink from wells we did not dig and harvest from trees we did not plant.

We would not be here were it not for the generosity of all of you here today. You are part of this field of generosity.

What are some of the other ways you see generosity around you in this congregation or in other parts of your life?

The glow of generosity is also all around us, and it's alive and well in all our hearts. We are truly blessed.

This little light of mine, I'm gonna let it shine. Let it shine, let it shine, let it shine. ...

Generosity II

*Your rulers are ... companions of thieves; they all love bribes and chase after gifts.
They do not defend the cause of the fatherless; the widow's case does not come before them.*
— Isaiah 1:23

February 18, 2007

The words painted on the window were in both Thai and English: "Free Internet Access." Underneath, in smaller lettering, it said: "Donations accepted as you are comfortable." It didn't say, "Donations accepted unless you are a schnook," or even, "Donations accepted to feed our starving orphans." It merely reassured: "Donations accepted as you are comfortable."

The internet café was in Wat Phra Doi Suthep high in the mountains west of the city of Chiang Mai in Northern Thailand. I had been living there 10 days. I was training in meditation with a monk named Phranoah Yuttadhammo. Phranoah was starting another meditation center at Wat Sopfang in a bamboo forest in the far north of Thailand. He had invited me to come with him. I wanted to let my family know where I was going. The Internet was the easiest way to do this.

As I walked into the Internet café, the monk in charge smiled broadly and gestured for me to sit down as he booted up a computer. I suddenly realized I had no money on me to make a donation. But the monk didn't understand English and seemed so happy to have me there that I sat down anyway.

When I was done with my emails, I stood up. The monk waved to me from the other side of the room. He smiled, bowed, and returned his attention to whatever he was doing. There was not the slightest hint of solicitation. The sign on the window was true: donations were not expected and were accepted only as I was comfortable making them.

A wat is a bit like a monastery in that monks and nuns live there under simple and austere moral vows. Unlike monasteries, wats are not isolated. They are embedded in the surrounding community. They offer chanting, meditation, counsel, and rites of passage. Some offer libraries, medical help, schools, food, and much more, including Internet access and even a radio station. Literally hundreds of people visit Wat Phra Doi Suthep every day. Even in the rural Wat Sopfang, the villagers regularly stop in to pay their respects to the old senior monk, ask advice, or just hang out.

From the beginning, Phranoah knew that I was a serious meditation student. He wanted me to study with Ajaan Tong Sirimangalo, Northern Thailand's most revered meditation master. Ajaan Tong does not speak English and rarely works with Westerners. However, after training with Phranoah for three weeks, I was considered his student first and a Westerner second.

Under these circumstances, Phranoah personally took me to Wat Chom Tong, made the introductions, set me up to study under Ajaan Tong, and stayed to do the Thai-English translations during interviews.

Besides the meditation instruction and daily interviews, I was given a private *kuti* or meditation hut, food, clothing, and blankets. When I was in a phase they call "determination," I would spend up to three days meditating without sleeping or leaving my kuti. During this time, the kitchen help brought food to my kuti. A sweet Burmese nun, Mai Chi Chai, would leave me fruit juice and soy milk with sesame. Had I gotten sick, I would have gotten the best doctors. When I traveled, they paid the bus fares or hired a van.

For all this, I was never asked for a single baht. Like the Internet café, I knew donations were accepted as I was comfortable, but it was made clear that they weren't expected. Generosity is just what they do.

The generosity I received was not special. Many Westerners and Easterners flowed through the wats. Some stayed a few days. Some hung around for months or even years. If they weren't in meditation training, they helped out as they were comfortable. They were integrated into wat life, but always on a basis of generosity rather than payment or expectation.

The generosity that touched me the most was the treatment of the indigenous people. These so-called "hill people" were having such a hard time financially that some would bring their kids to the wats. The kids were taken in, fed, housed, clothed, *and educated*. Every morning, I'd hear them coming from their dorm area on their way to classes. The kids stayed a few months or a few decades. When they left, they were better able to support themselves and their families because of the education. The monks and nuns were helping to lift them out of poverty.

Money

All the wats' services require a lot of money. Yet, they receive no government subsidies. There are no faith-based initiatives. They don't write grants. They don't have stewardship drives or pledge campaigns. They don't even pass the basket at the evening chants. They don't do solicitation of any kind.

Their only support is the generosity of the surrounding communities. People give food directly to monks on their morning alms rounds. People place donations in discreet donation boxes or find the wat offices to write a check. That's it.

After living in the wats for almost two months, I began to see them not only as spiritual and social institutions. They were also significant economic engines in Thai society. People entrust them with their wealth. It flows in from the surrounding communities on the wings of generosity, and then flows back out to the communities.

Haggling for a Shirt

Generosity as a driving force was not confined to wat life.

The last week I was in Thailand, I left the wats to take a room in Chiang Mai and do a little sight-seeing. Late one afternoon, I wandered into a seamstress' shop looking for a shirt. I found one I liked. The proprietress and I haggled over the price. After agreeing on a fair amount, I found I didn't have as many bahts on me as I had thought. I apologized, and said I would walk over to the bank, cash a traveler's check, and come back in a few minutes.

The woman who had haggled so fiercely smiled and said I should take the shirt for what I had. Since I liked it, she wanted me to have it.

Thailand has a market economy. Bargaining in the markets and shops is part of the economic system and social fabric. When that was done, they found generosity more satisfying than getting the best deal for themselves.

Phenomena of Generosity

I want to continue our exploration of the phenomena of generosity. Previously, I talked about the glow we feel when we are truly generous, and how that can be a catalyst for personal transformation. The Thai people have a palpable sweetness and kindness that comes, in part, from that glow of generosity.

I want to talk about generosity as a catalyst for societal transformation. Whether we are talking about the environment, the war, health care, wealth distribution, crime, education, water rights, or other concerns, even the smallest overall increase in generosity would help.

In Thailand, I saw some of the ways that generosity can manifest on a societal level. Thailand is not utopia: it is a Third World country with many problems. Without competition and driving individualism, there are fewer people with extraordinary wealth, but there are fewer people in extraordinary poverty. Also, there is much less crime.

The Unitarian Universalist Society of Sacramento

I would like our congregation to operate financially more like a wat and less like a typical church. I would like us to operate more out of unsolicited "donations as you are comfortable" and less out of financial reports, stewardship drives, and passing the plate. After all, like wats, we are a religious and spiritual community embedded in a larger community. Like wats, we are completely dependent on generosity for our existence. Like wats, we promote the health and wellbeing of the larger world.

However, wats are embedded in Thai society where generosity and kindness are organizing forces. We are embedded in American society where individualism and competition are organizing forces.

For us to function, we have to dance delicately between the generosity and service we value and the consumer economy in which we are situated. If we emphasize our financial realties too much, we sound like a moneymaking corporation. If we emphasize it too little, people think we are sweet but probably don't need financial support.

So, we try as best as we can to be wise and discerning and we run stewardship drives. One year we emphasize generosity. Another, our financial need. Another, the value of our presence. Another, a specific program. Another, long-term plans. Some years, we do it with fanfare. Other years, we are low-key. There is no ideal strategy because we are sifting and winnowing through a clash between our values and the "me-first" of the larger culture.

How to Pull It Off?

Let's look at the larger culture. How do the Thai pull it off? How do they seem to get along as well as they do without going through all our machinations? Where does Thai society get its glow of generosity?

Religious Tradition

The most obvious answer is their religious tradition. Ninety-five percent of Thai people self identify as Buddhist. The foundation of Buddhism is generosity.

Our predominant religious roots are the Judeo-Christian tradition founded on loving a God who sometimes can be fierce and demanding.

Generosity is also central to the monotheistic traditions, though the language is different. The Old Testament stresses hospitality: care for the stranger, the widow, the sick, the outcast, the poor, the oppressed. The New Testament has stories like the Good Samaritan and the prodigal son. It has the Golden Rule, "Love your neighbor as thyself," and "How you treat the least amongst you shows how you love God."

Most mainline Christians are inspired by the "social gospel:" Jesus' generous treatment of the poor and disempowered.

Differences in religious traditions don't explain the Thai emphasis on generosity and ours on competition.

Genes

Perhaps the difference is in our genes. The Thai descended from millennia of refined civilization. We descended from Norsemen and rugged pioneers going it alone. Maybe we're just more selfish by nature.

This doesn't hold up either. The core American psyche is quite generous. Consider the outpouring after September 11: in the midst of fear and tragedy, the impulse of most people was to help others. Consider the aftermath of Katrina: the horror and shame so many felt that our government, acting on all our behalves, responded so ungenerously until goaded into doing more.

Consider a poll done just a few weeks ago by Harris and the *Wall Street Journal*. They asked people how much they admired the 60 highest-profile companies in the world. Who do you think came out on top?

It was Microsoft. This puzzled me because I don't admire their products or business plan. The reason Microsoft got the highest ratings had nothing to do with their products. It was because of the highly visible philanthropy of the Bill and Melinda Gates Foundation. We admire generosity.

Who would you guess was at the bottom of the list?

Halliburton. It was least admired because of war profiteering and self-interest.

Despite all the destructive things we have done as a country, I still see the American spirit as very generous. Sometimes, we are not very wise, but we are generous in our collective intent.

Practice

If it is not our religious-cultural history and not our intent, why do the Thai operate out of generosity more successfully than we? How do they pull it off?

To cut to the chase, I think the essential difference between Thai and American society is that they teach, encourage, and practice generosity from a very young age. They give to the monks. They give to each other. Those who have more give to those who have less.

Consider: a third of the young adults ordain as monks for one to three years. As monks, they practice simple living. They own little more than a robe and a begging bowl. They live under strict moral precepts. Then, after a few years, they go back to civilian life.

Monks are deeply respected in Thailand. All these young people, at an impressionable age, get all this admiration and deference for living very simply and generously. This affects how they live for the rest of their lives.

In this country, we flood youth and young adults with advertising about cars, clothes, iPods, electronics, CDs, and money. We teach people to live complicated, self-centered lives.

In this country, we do have the Peace Corps, AmeriCorps, City Year, and other voluntary services that people can join for a while. What if we said, "Support our Volunteers" with as much enthusiasm, respect, and money as we say "Support our Troops"? What if we gave more support to service that didn't involve learning to kill other people? The generosity inherent in our traditions and inherent in the American spirit might rise and flourish.

Muscle

Think of generosity as a muscle. We all have muscles. We all have generosity. If we don't exercise, our muscles get weak and ineffective. If we don't exercise our generosity, we don't feel that inner glow that gives us faith in bigheartedness.

If we practice regularly, it gets stronger, and we feel healthier and more human. The glow lightens our spirit and the spirits of those around us.

In the end, the greater generosity of the Thai culture is not a big mystery. It's straightforward: they start practicing when they are very young. We need to practice more and support each other in the practice. We need to share our stories of generosity, so others can enjoy the glow as well.

Butterfly

What does this have to do with societal transformation? The butterfly is the quintessential metaphor for transformation.

A caterpillar is an ugly little bug with no eyes or ears or awareness of anything around it except what it touches. All it is interested in is eating and growing.

When the caterpillar reaches a certain bloated state, it slows down and draws into itself to form a chrysalis or cocoon. Inside the chrysalis, its immune system attacks the caterpillar, breaking down the tissue. It reduces the organs into a creamy mass of organic material.

Then tiny structures called "organizer cells" float into the mush and start organizing the material into tiny objects that biologists call "imaginal buds." The imaginal buds start forming into eyes, legs, wings, and other structures that eventually become the butterfly.

Essentially, the old organs of the caterpillar break down into an organic slush, and the imaginal buds use this to create the different organs of the butterfly.

Joanna Macy, David Korten, and other writers note the poetic parallels between this process and humans living on the earth. Collectively, we seem like bloated caterpillars with voracious appetites, unable to see beyond the next quarterly report. Twisted corporate policies, misguided political ideology, money in politics, the breakdown of the social safety net, runaway greed, the mess in Iraq … Sometimes, it seems like our society is breaking down into mush.

Many of you are working on voter reform, caring for the homeless, environmental protection, rebuilding the education system, taking on the industrial war machine, and much more. You are working to make the world better for all of us. Done skillfully, this puts organizer cells and imaginal buds into the societal mush.

Another imaginal bud we need to keep putting into our culture is generosity.

Practicing generosity, sharing our stories, sharing the glow is not a grand design, it's not a gigantic cookie cutter, it's not a detailed blueprint of enlightened society.

As we share stories and work with each other in new ways, we become imaginal buds. We can't predict exactly what effects we are going to have. We aren't in control of societal evolution in that sense, but imaginal buds reorganize things in ways that are aligned with our deeper values. They catalyze from the bottom up, rather than the top down.

Imaginal Buds

Let me close with a story of how easily imaginal buds can operate.

After church two weeks ago, a member of the congregation told me about going for a walk a few days earlier. It was cold, so she grabbed an old coat on the way out.

Walking up the street, she noticed a woman sleeping on the ground between houses. On her way back, the homeless woman was still there, but she was sitting up awake.

On impulse, our member walked over to her, took off her old coat and offered it to the woman. The homeless woman was speechless. Her eyes were wide and watery with gratitude.

As our member told me this story, I could see the quiet ecstasy in her. I could feel her glow of generosity, and I thought to myself, "I want more of that for me."

Simply sharing our stories and joy stimulates the urge in us to realign around generosity.

I encourage you to continue to do what you feel truly drawn to do to serve our world on whatever level. When you don't know what to do or when things feels a little mushy, remember you can't go wrong with generosity.

We are inherently generous people. Outwardly, we may look a little grubby and a little caterpillar-y at times. Often we don't look like butterflies at all.

However, the potential is there. The genetic material – the organizer cells – is there. The impulse and the movement toward generosity are in all of us.

May we trust the generosity in us. May we share our stories of generosity. May we be imaginal buds and inspirational buds for those around us.

May it be so.

Cultivating Happiness

June 10, 2007

I was walking down Willowdale Road towards my house in a small New England town. A map drawn in 1850 labeled this area "Pollywog Hollow." I was feeling a little "pollywog hollow-ish" myself that afternoon – vaguely unhappy without being able to put my finger on why.

Then I remembered a trick I had discovered years earlier. I called it "flipping a switch." I wasn't quite sure how I did it, but I just flipped something inside me.

So, as I walked past the Squanacook Radiator Shop, I flipped that switch. A soft buoyancy rose up through me. The thoughts chugging through my brain lightened. I began to smile despite myself.

"Why don't I do this more often?" I mused.

After a few minutes, the mild elation began to subside. In 10 minutes, I was back to my baseline depression, except for a faint afterglow deep inside.

I tried describing this experience to any number of consciousness experts – therapists and spiritual teachers. They responded with blank stares. I decided there must be something peculiar about me. I stopped talking about it.

Then one day I tried flipping the switch while meditating. The familiar buoyancy welled up in me. I smiled for quite a while. Yet, when I asked meditation teachers about it, I got those blank stares. "Don't get distracted," they advised. "Just go back to the breath." But every once in a while I'd flip the switch anyway and go for a little ride.

One June, I was in a retreat with a teacher named Larry Rosenberg. Larry gave a series of talks on the Anapanasati Sutta – the Teaching on the Full Awareness of Breathing. In the sutta, the Buddha described stages of breath awareness. Then, he went on to describe a deeper state called "*pīti*." Larry said "pīti" means "joy" or "rapture" and described some of the sensations.

As a recovering depressive, I didn't relate to joy or rapture. That was for advanced meditators, not me. I only half listened.

Then, I realized that Larry's description sounded vaguely like what I experienced when I flipped the switch.

I became attentive.

After pīti, Larry said, "The next stage is called '*sukha*' which means happiness. Imagine walking through the desert. You are very thirsty. You come to a cool spring and lean down to take a drink. The feeling the moment before you drink the water is pīti or joy. The moment after you take the drink, 'ahhh!' is sukha or happiness."

The metaphor was intriguing, but again, as a lifelong depressive, I didn't get along with happiness either.

After the dharma talk, I went up to Larry. "I may know what you are talking about. But I'm not certain."

"Tell me what you experience," he said.

"I sometimes call it a 'high energy calm,'" I said. "Energy wells up inside. It's like excitement, except it is relaxed and large and smooth. It makes me smile."

Larry was looking down and listening. He nodded, "That's pīti."

"And after a while," I went on, "if I just let go into the sensation, the energy cools out. Everything gets very quiet and serene."

"That's sukha," Larry said.

I said, "I've struggled with depression all my life. Words like 'joy,' 'rapture,' and 'happiness' are foreign to me."

He looked up at me. There was a soft smile in his eyes. He placed his hand on my shoulder and patted. "I give you permission to be a happy person."

That evening, I learned that flipping a switch had other names: pīti, sukha, rapture, joy, happiness. It was part of the normal field of consciousness that had been mapped out in detail for thousands of years.

However, I still didn't know what these states were or exactly what I did to elicit them.

In the years that followed, I couldn't find teachers who knew much more about them, so I stumbled along in my own fashion.

Then, a few months ago, I met a Western monk who had trained in Southeast Asia for 25 years. He described my experience in minute detail. He knew exactly what I was doing when I flipped that switch. He related it to the original teachings of the Buddha that had been overlooked or poorly translated. He said it was the secret to real happiness.

I'd like to share with you the secret of happiness. It's not "The Secret" of the best selling book by that name. In some ways, it's the opposite. Think of this as the real secret for cultivating real happiness.

The fact that it took me all these years to figure this out doesn't mean that the secret is hidden, esoteric, complex, or moneymaking, or that I'm a spiritual adept. If anything, it shows that I'm a slow learner who does things the hard way and doesn't recognize the obvious until I've ruled out every other possibility.

I believe the secret of cultivating real happiness is being fully present and letting go at the same time. It's that simple. Not always easy, but very simple.

What I was calling "flipping a switch" was being completely present and relaxing my mind deeply at the same time. When I did that, a wave of happiness came through me. It was physical, mental, and emotional, as well as spiritual.

Try it now: Humbly, be present with whatever is going on inside and around you. Be present with all of it, and at the same time, let go inside. Particularly, let the mind relax as if the brain was a muscle you could release.

I'd like to explore this process.

I want to come back to the theme of everyday spiritual practices. In some ways, the practice of happiness is the ultimate everyday practice.

Chocolate

As a frame of reference, let's look at an experience of happiness.

Let's say chocolate makes you happy, but you haven't had any for some time. You think about it. Your mind reaches out for it. You want some. There is tightness in this yearning. It is not a happy feeling.

Then you decide, "Okay, it's been long enough. I'm going to give myself a treat. I'm getting some premium chocolate."

With that anticipation, the tightness of wanting relaxes a little. You feel happier.

Now, you hold a chocolate bar. "It's right here in my hand!" You smile as you unwrap it. You are excited but relaxed. It is high-energy happiness similar to what the Buddha called "$p\bar{\imath}ti$," rapture, or joy.

You take a bite. "Ahhh!" The taste is strong enough to bring you fully present. You stop thinking so you can savor the flavor. You no longer want chocolate because you have it. Your mind releases. You are so happy. This is similar to sukha or happiness.

If you are like most people, you don't actually pay attention to your inner states. You just know that you are happy, and that it has something to do with chocolate.

"This is great," you think. "Chocolate makes me so happy. More chocolate can make me more happy. I want more." Your mind revs up, wanting more. You focus less on the present moment and more on the next bite in the next moment. You tighten up. Rapture, joy, and happiness subside.

You take another bite. "Ahhh." Your mind/body lets go again. "Heaven. This is so good."

After the second bite, the mind starts up a little more quickly. By the third or fourth bite, the mind hardly relaxes at all. You just gobble down the last half with diminished pleasure.

Note: as the mind lets go, happiness increases. As the mind tightens, happiness subsides.

Confusion

In our consumer society, we confuse the inner state of happiness with the external stimulus. Americans are not addicted to happiness. We are addicted to stimulation. In our quest, we have developed voracious appetites, devouring the planet. But it comes with less and less satisfaction.

The generation coming up is particularly prone to this because misguided parenting tried to give them everything they wanted. After the T-ball game, everybody got a trophy, as if a trophy is what makes you happy. A child made a mediocre effort, got mediocre grades, and was told, "Oh, that's wonderful," as if praise and affirmation was the key to happiness. It's not. Happiness arises from relaxing inside, particularly relaxing the mind.

We have become masters at demanding that we get more and more of what we want, or else we'll sue for damages. More and more people feel their lives are somehow empty and devoid of meaning. Teenage suicide rates are up. Addictions are epidemic. We've forgotten how to savor the little pleasures. We've forgotten how to relax and humbly be content with whatever is here without wanting something more or getting rid of what we don't want. That grabbing and pushing creates tightness which destroys happiness.

Varieties

Let's come back to the actual experience of real happiness. There are many varieties.

For example, there are high-energy states like rapture, ecstasy, excitement, joy, enthusiasm, rush, thrill, and romance. There are more modest energy states like buoyant heart, enjoying the day, feeling good. And there are low-energy states like equanimity, wellbeing, inner peace, and ease.

They all require the ability to let the mind relax into the moment, and different energy states present different challenges.

For example, high-energy states can be overwhelming. We tighten up. I love to quote Rollo May: "Anxiety is excitement without oxygen." Too much excitement and we brace ourselves. Excitement turns to anxiousness, thrill turns to fear, joy become tension, enthusiasm becomes franticness.

If we can let go, these high-energy states reverse: demons become angels, anxiety becomes excitement, fear comes thrill, tension releases into joy, franticness opens into enthusiasm.

Low-energy states present a different problem. They have so little charge that they can pass by unnoticed. Equanimity has little for the mind to focus on. If we think happiness comes from stimulation, we start grasping for something more entertaining than inner peace.

We have a word for grasping for stimulation: *boredom*. Next time your child says, "Dad, I'm bored," notice her tension and grasping. Tell her, "Mellow out. Relax, and you'll be fine." Most likely, she'll hear your wisdom and say, "Dad, you don't understand me." She wasn't seeking happiness. She was seeking stimulation.

Life is always changing. If we can let go and be present in a variety of energy states, then we have flexible happiness.

Presence

There is a caveat. Sometimes, life hurts. This is normal. To cultivate real happiness in the real world, we can't avoid or push away hurt or unpleasantness. Instead, be present and let go.

Wrathful Entities

In the Nepal Valley, statues of demons, dragons, and wrathful deities surround the temples. In Christianity, gargoyles sit on the eaves of Cathedrals scrutinizing those who would approach, and seraphim with flaming swords block the gates of Eden. They guard the entry to the sanctuary of happiness, if you will.

In Nepal, the temples have very low doorways. If you walk straight in, you whack your head. To enter, you have to lower your head and bow before these wrathful entities.

Life's normal hurts and disappointments can feel like unwelcome demons. If we fight them, push them aside or ignore them, we create more tension in the long run. This blocks the deeper, more spacious forms of happiness. On the other hand, if we bow to them, befriend them, and let their energy run through us, we can walk into the inner temple.

Path Through the Field

What I called "flipping a switch" was doing just that. I'd say to myself, "Here I am walking down the road by Squannacook Radiator feeling down," and I'd try to be fully with it. Not analyzing, but just being present to the whole situation. Even depression has some deep inner holding. I'd relax, and a whoosh of mild elation would pour down through me. It was like being touched by the divine. In Christianity, it's sometimes called, "surrendering to God" or "giving it all to God."

What was confusing was that I didn't appreciate the strength of habit. Just because I felt happy didn't mean that my old habits of mind and heart would suddenly stop. The internal tightness would return. My attention would wander off again.

Happiness is not something we find like a pot of gold at the end of the rainbow. It's not a place we get to. Happiness is a way of traveling. It's a way of relating to the angels and demons and everything else that travel with us. In this congregation, we call it traveling with open minds, open hearts, and helping hands.

Imagine walking through a field every day. You wear a path through that field. It becomes easier and easier to just follow that trail. It's a habit.

Then you find a different way through the field. There is more sunlight, a better view, a pleasanter walk, but the grass is thick, and it takes more effort. It's so easy to fall back into the old familiar path, even if it's not as nice.

So the practice – the discipline of happiness, if you will – is coming present and letting go. Coming present and letting go. Humbly being with what is and offering it to God. Coming present and letting go, over and over again. Gradually, it becomes a different set of habits. You wear a different path through the field. When you think of how many times you've walked that old course, you appreciate that forming a new one takes some time.

Every time you walk that way, happiness comes as high-energy joy, or medium-energy "feeling good," or low-energy peace. Sometimes, wellbeing comes immediately. Sometimes, not for a while. Sometimes, it hangs around. Sometimes, it fades quickly. Sometimes, unhappy feelings come up. We treat them all the same: be present, open, relax. Imagine the brain is a muscle that you can just relax.

We can do it every day. There is not a situation where we can't do this. Maybe we remember it once a day or maybe a thousand times a day.

Each time we do it, it wears that new path a little deeper. Gradually, it becomes less of a practice we have to remember and more of just a way we live.

Namasté.

Seeing Simplicity

August 26, 2007

Burning Bodies

The body was wrapped tightly in muslin and covered with cloth. Mourners carried this human cocoon through the winding streets and laid it on the ground next to the Ganges River. After negotiations with the ghat workers, wood was piled three feet high and stuffed with dried grass. The family laid the body on the pyre. One of the men used a long reed to pick a coal from the fire in the nearby Shiva temple. He carried it around the pyre three times and set it ablaze.

The decorative cloth gave scant hints of gender and wealth. But there was little else to distinguish the body from any other. As the flesh dried out and incinerated, there were no clues to gender, status, age — how the person had died, how he or she had lived, earned a living, or whom he or she had loved — the heartbreaks and accomplishments of a lifetime.

Within an hour, the soft tissue was gone – nothing left but blackened bones. Within two hours there was nothing but ashes and a few charred bone fragments. All were swept into a straw basket and tossed in the Ganges.

I stood entranced at the burning ghat for several hours. Every 10 or 15 minutes another shrouded body arrived. Sometimes there were 6 or 7 burning at the same time. The elements were simple: a body, cloth, wood, grass, fire, river, sky.

It was both simple and mysterious, ordinary and touching. If my body were wrapped in cloth and placed on a pyre, it would be indistinguishable from all the others. Despite the time, love, worry, striving, ease and efforts of a lifetime, within a few hours it would be grey ashes.

As I was preparing to leave the ghat, I turned to an Indian gentleman next to me: "How long has the fire in the Shiva temple been burning?"

"About 5,000 years," he said. "We never let it go out."

Varanasi is the oldest continually inhabited city in the world. It was a contemporary of the Sumerian civilization. For over 20,000 generations, bodies have been brought to this spot on the banks of the Ganges – 100, 200, 300, sometimes 400 bodies a day, all wrapped in anonymous shrouds, all set aflame with a coal from the same Shiva fire, all reduced to forensically identical ash.

It offered a different perspective on life. Balancing my checkbook, catching the latest political news, figuring out how to get a bite to eat before the next meeting, writing a next sermon — most of the complexities of life faded into the background in the face of 20,000 generations of indistinguishable ash. Knowing that it would take only a few hours to lovingly burn this body to dust made life less pretentious.

Two Jeeps

Erika, my wife, and I were staying in a hotel on the Ganges about a quarter of a mile from the burning ghat. The hotel wasn't 5,000 years old. But the streets around it may have been. They twisted and turned, rose and fell, widened to 15 feet and narrowed to 4. It was difficult getting a bicycle through this rabbit warren. A car was impossible.

We were traveling with 15 people. After five days in Varanasi, we were preparing to leave for Sarnath and the Deer Park where the Buddha delivered his first sermon. Sarnath was only 15 kilometers from Varanasi. But first we had to get out of the old city with all our packs and gear. The nearest road that could handle a motorized vehicle was over half a mile away.

So, we hired a boat to ferry us down river a mile and arranged for three large cars to meet us. We got down the river okay. But when we met our drivers, rather than large cars they had little jeeps. We looked at the jeeps. There was one passenger seat in the front and two in the back of each. We looked at all of us and our stuff. You know that the law of physics precludes two objects from occupying the same space at the same time? We had a physics problem. Panic percolated through our group.

The Indian drivers looked at the jeeps, looked at our belongings, looked at our dismay, smiled, and said, "No problem."

Perhaps the time in the burning ghat helped me relax. Perhaps it was just spending time in India. But I smiled along with them.

In America, we like to think we are in charge of our lives. If things don't go the way we like, either it's our fault and we should feel guilty, or it's someone else's fault and we should retain a lawyer. Things get complex very quickly here.

In India, conditions are more overtly chaotic. Fate and the gods pay no attention to our plans. Indians I met were less burdened by the illusion of being in charge of their lives.

So when surprise happened, they were less likely to ask, "What's wrong?" and worry about things they could do nothing about. This simpler outlook freed up creativity for things they might be able to do something about.

When the driver said, "no problem," he meant,

"It is not a problem that you asked for large vehicles and we brought small ones because we can't get large vehicles this close to the old city. We can do nothing about that, so that is no problem.

"It is not a problem that you had asked for three vehicles and we brought two because only two were available. We can't change that, so that's no problem.

"It is not a problem that you would have liked to know earlier what to expect because, well, that is in the past that we can't change in the present: no problem.

"The only real problem is how to get you and your things into little jeeps. But we know how to do this: no problem."

And he was right. Check the photograph. You'll see five of us riding in one of the jeeps. The hands of a sixth person stick up on the left. Two more people are in the back behind me. And the driver is outside the camera angle. Nine in that jeep with backpacks tied on the roof: no problem.

Simplicity

Sometimes life appears as complex as getting 15 Westerners and their stuff from Varanasi to Sarnath. Sometimes life seems logistically impossible.

This time of year we may feel the pressure of complexity as summer's relative leisure gives way to the fall's rush. And each year life seems more complex. Large corporations are taking control of more resources – everything from oil, to water, to health care, to job security. Those of us on the middle and lower rungs of the economic ladder find fewer resources left for us. We have to scramble harder to care for our families and ourselves. This causes more stress and complexity.

Nevertheless, some of the problems in our lives might be less complex than we think. So, I'd like to talk about seeing simplicity in the complicated. I'd like to talk about relaxing the mind and heart so that we can see more clearly. With a little tranquility, we see what truly needs our attention and what is really no problem.

Simplistic

When someone says to me, "No problem, just relax," normally I don't smile. Normally my first response is an urge to throttle them: "What do you mean 'No problem'? Are you blind? If you knew what was going on, you'd be uptight too! Do you think I wake up in the morning and think, 'I'm relaxed. So let me see what can make me tense'?"

So let me begin by saying, "Yes, I know life is sometimes complicated, at least on the surface."

I'm advocating simple seeing, not simplistic thinking. Seeing simply and thinking simplistically may sound similar, but they are polar opposites.

Simple seeing is about seeing – perception. Simplistic thinking is about ideas and beliefs – thought. Perception and thought are different

140

universes. We get into trouble when we confuse our thoughts about reality with reality itself.

For example, consider this belief: "People are inherently good. Therefore if I'm nice enough, I'll never get hurt." There is some truth in this, but it is simplistic in that it ignores the reality that good people sometimes hurt other good people.

"God will provide and give me what I want." It is a pleasant thought that simplistically ignores the reality that we don't always get what we want.

"Saddam Hussein is bad. We are good. Therefore invading Iraq is good." This kind of simplistic thinking spawned catastrophe.

"The wealthy handle money with more success than the non-wealthy. So if we give more money to the wealthy through tax breaks, the economy will be better for all." This simplistic proposition won votes even as it wreaked havoc on the economy.

Fundamentalist religions, political ideologues, and superstitions use ideas and beliefs to obscure reality. They encourage us to focus on an idea about life rather than see life on its own terms.

But life is not impressed with our opinions. Life is what life is. It doesn't care what *we* think. When we fight reality, we lose. When we don't see reality as it is, our lives become more complex than they need be.

Simplistic thinking puts dust in our eyes. Simple seeing washes away ideas and beliefs so we can see more clearly. We see the complexity. And in looking with clear and patient eyes, we may begin to see some natural simplicity beneath the complexity. Getting to Sarnath was not that complicated. As Lao Tzu put it, the mark of wisdom is the ability to "see the simplicity in the complicated."

Strategies

We Unitarian Universalist love our ideas and beliefs. How do we let go of our complex thinking and cultivate simple perception?

There are lots of practices. The most obvious is to slow down and take a little more time. But first I want to speak about two practices I've found helpful: befriending death and mellowing about our likes and dislikes.

Contemplating Death

First, befriending death.

Standing in the burning ghat was a contemplation of death not as an abstract idea but as a simple, tangible phenomenon. Watching the bodies disintegrate showed how easily and simply my body could be reduced to ashes.

Knowing that bodies had been cremated this way at this place for thousands of years helped me see my life as a hiccup in eternity: not that special, just a simple life.

Participating in memorial services can do the same thing. As sad or difficult as they are at times, being closer to the reality of someone's death keeps me closer to my own death. It puts life in a simpler perspective.

The writer Carlos Castaneda called this "keeping death as an advisor." We can die at any moment. He suggested imagining death sitting on our right shoulder, looking at what we are doing and advising us: "You could die today. Is getting a plasma TV how you want to spend it?" "Your children could die tomorrow. What's most important?"

Contemplating death and seeing the insignificance of our lives can help the mind and heart relax into a larger vision and see more clearly. But they can also cause them to contract: "I'm going to die. There is so much I want to get done. Life seems so futile in its brevity. I don't want to die. I want my life to be more important."

As the mind-heart tighten, life seems more complicated. As they relax, we see the simplicity beneath the complicated.

Mellow Likes and Dislikes

So let's look at another practice that centers on the tightness itself. We could call this practice "Mellowing about our likes and dislikes."

Likes and dislikes are the root of much tension. *And they are the roots of much thinking.* This practice involves letting our preferences be without fussing about them.

Let me back up and explain what I mean.

In life, things happen that feel good: ice cream, cool breeze on a hot day, an unexpected bonus, the smile of a child, and more. And things happen that don't feel good: headaches, disappointments, stubbed toes, flat tires, unenlightened politicians, and so on.

Sometimes we feel good, sometimes not. If we left it there, life would be simple. But we usually aren't so relaxed about feeling good or bad.

The mind clings to likes and pushes away dislikes. This grasping and pushing are always accompanied by thinking. The mind makes plans, creates rationales, obsesses, turns that whole thing into a problem, and more. This is very important to notice: *thinking always has some tightness.*

For example, in our journey from Varanasi to Sarnath, we didn't like seeing just two little jeeps. It was uncomfortable. Distress rippled through our little group.

In response to distress, minds started churning: "How could they bring only two cars?" "What were they thinking?" "How could this happen?" "Why didn't they tell us about this?" "Are we being hoodwinked?" "Can we get back to the hotel?" "Is there a bus line nearby?"

When the drivers said "no problem," it was a kind way of saying: "Never mind what you want or don't want, what you think should or shouldn't happen, what you like and dislike. We have no control over them in this moment. So relax, they are not a problem.

"In this moment, we have only one real problem: how to get you and your things to Sarnath in time for your supper and rest using two jeeps. We are Indian. We have been putting lots of things into small places all our lives. We are good at this. Trust us. No problem."

And they were right.

Meditation

So, let's bring this back to your life. Let's shift into contemplation. But first, I invite you to think of some problem you have: a situation at home, with friends, at work, in the congregation, in the larger world … Notice how you feel.

Is it possible to relax in the face of these problems and feelings? It is not always easy. It requires looking clearly at what is going on and being mellow at the same time. And it involves relaxing so you can see more clearly. It's not always easy, but it is a skill that can be cultivated.

To do this, we let reality be as it is. If we are comfortable or uncomfortable, we let that be as well. We don't fight reality or fight our reactions to it. All we do is relax the mind and heart. We don't force the thinking to stop. We just let our minds relax.

If you like, you can close your eyes and try it now.

First, recall some time when you've felt love or contentment. … Recall what love, kindness, or ease feel like. … We've all known these. However imperfectly, remember what they feel like. …

Now, recall a problem you have. Notice how you feel inside about this problem. Don't judge the problem or yourself. Don't try to fix the problem or fix yourself. Don't try to control anything. Don't fight reality. Part of reality is how you feel. So just see what goes on inside: sadness, worry, frustration, tension, concern, whatever. Just let them be there as they are. …

Now relax your mind and heart. One way to do this is to smile softly. Let the problem and what you feel just be there as you relax and smile into it. …

Now repeat the cycle in your own rhythm: (1) Touch some of those wholesome states of love, kindness, ease, equanimity, compassion, joy. Feel them, however imperfectly. (2) Let your problem be there. Don't try to analyze or think. Release the thoughts. Just feel how it feels. (3) Relax any tension you have around it. Smile gently. …

This is a practice. So, we practice it over and over, even as we walk around.

In touching love, kindness, and ease, we become more receptive to the divine. We begin to see our former problem through God's eyes. If you aren't comfortable with God language, think of it as looking at our issues from a more enlightened and wholesome state.

However we frame it, we are relaxing around our discomfort. As we do so, thinking softens. And perception gets clearer. Some complexity starts to fall away. Things over which we have no control don't disturb us as much. It is just what is. And we may see more clearly some things that we do need to attend to.

Whatever the case, we see more of the simplicity in the complicated.

Our Divine Vulnerabilities I

September 16, 2007

Zeus, the king of the gods, had a fond eye for beautiful woman. And there was none more beautiful than the mortal Alcmene. And she was lonely because her husband was away at war. So Zeus disguised himself as her husband. Fooled by this deception, she took him into her bed.

She became pregnant and gave birth to a boy she named "Hercules." Hercules was thus half god and half mortal.

The gods would not accept Hercules into Olympus because of his mortal half. So Hercules was raised by Alcmene in the world of humans.

When Hercules was old enough to venture out on his own, he came to a crossroads. In one direction the road was wide and beautiful. In the other, it was narrow and difficult. He sat down to consider which road to take.

Unbeknownst to him, up ahead, the wider road became thin and ugly and the narrow road grew wide and beautiful.

As he reflected, two women came up the road. The first wore beautiful clothes and jewelry. She said, "Hercules you are the strongest man in the world. Take what you will in this world and live a life full of pleasure."

Hercules asked, "What is your name?"

She replied, "My name is Happiness, yet my enemies call me Evil."

The second woman was dressed in poor clothes, though her face shone softly with humility and respect. She said, "The gods gave you strength to help the weak. Use your strength for the good of all."

Hercules asked, "What is your name?"

She replied, "My name is Virtue. I have no enemies."

The woman named Happiness walked down the wide path. The woman named Virtue walked down the narrow path.

Hercules chose to follow the path of Virtue.

Indeed Hercules did use his strength to help others. When a rogue lion terrorized the people, he fashioned a club from the branch of a wild olive tree. With one blow he killed the beast. When an army threatened Thebes, he single-handedly defeated the intruders.

He became widely loved and respected for his virtue, compassion, generous spirit, and physical strength. The king of Thebes was so grateful that he offered his daughter to be Hercules' wife. The two fell in love, married, and had three children. His life seemed ideal.

But he wasn't beloved by everyone. Hera, Zeus's wife, was jealous of her husband's philandering. She focused her anger on Hercules. She plotted many ways to do him in, but she always failed.

However, when Hercules married and had three sons, Hera saw another way to get revenge. She cast a spell that made him unable to distinguish good from bad, right from wrong. Under this spell of ignorance, he became angry and killed his wife and children.

The people were horrified and turned against him.

So Hera lifted the spell and allowed Hercules to understand what he had done. His heart was shattered. He fell into inconsolable grief. He stopped eating. He didn't bathe. His clothes became rags. He wandered aimlessly. He became demented with guilt.

However, there was a spark in him that was not totally subdued. Eventually, he sought help from the priestess oracle at the temple of Delphi.

She told him about the spell Hera had put on him. This relieved some, but not all, of the burden on his heart. To redeem himself, he must do penance. She said his penance was to submit himself to do the bidding of Eurystheus, the king of Mycenae.

The relationship between Eurystheus and Hercules is a tale unto itself. Briefly it goes like this: Years earlier, the throne of Mycenae should have gone to Hercules. But in her plotting, Hera had tricked Zeus into promising it to

Eurystheus. After that, Eurystheus and Hercules had become mortal enemies.

So when the Delphi oracle told Hercules to submit to Eurystheus, she was saying he had to submit to his greatest enemy and greatest fear.

Eurystheus was suspicious of Hercules. Under Hera's influence, he suspected Hercules was plotting to get his throne back. So when Hercules said, "I will do whatever you ask of me," Eurystheus gave him 10 tasks. Each was so difficult it would probably kill Hercules.

The 10 tasks became 12, the famous twelve labors of Hercules. Each is a story in itself. But suffice it to say that over the next twelve years, he fulfilled all twelve obligations.

As the people learned of Hera's role in his crime and as they learned of his success with the twelve labors, their fondness and respect for him returned. Through his penance, his mental balance was restored.

After that, Hercules joined the Argonauts in the search for the Golden Fleece, had many other adventures, married again, and lived a long, full live. When he died, the gods finally accepted him into Mount Olympus.

He is a god who truly knows what it is like to be human.

Divine Vulnerabilities

The story of Hercules is the story of you and me on the path from birth to enlightenment, from humble beginnings to realizing our full potential. The tale illustrates some of the essential elements of the spiritual path we are all on.

So, for three sermons on divine vulnerabilities, I'd like to reflect on the story of Hercules.

To start this series, I want to propose that, like Hercules, we all have divine gifts; we all have vulnerabilities, and our gifts and vulnerabilities are intimately tied together. One way to bring our gifts to the surface is to open our minds and hearts to our vulnerabilities, just as Hercules submitted to his greatest enemy, Eurystheus. If we are skillful, our weakness can become a doorway to our divine gifts.

Dual Nature

But before we dive into this, let me set the stage: We humans seem to have a dual nature. We have a capacity to act with love, compassion, and selfless generosity. And we have a capacity to act with greed, pettiness, and selfish cruelty. One day we have exalted spirits and the next day we are mean-spirited.

This dual nature is portrayed in the New Testament when the very human and innocent Mary is impregnated by the Holy Spirit. She gives birth to Jesus. His mother was human, his father divine. He has a dual nature: human and divine.

In the Greek story, the mortal and innocent Alcmene is impregnated by Zeus, king of the gods. She gives birth to Hercules. He has a dual nature: mortal and immortal.

The stories are similar with some differences. In the Greek story, Zeus's motive is clearly lust. In the Biblical story, the Holy Spirit's motives are not mentioned.

In the Biblical story, Jesus has all the divine qualities. Like the Buddha, he is perfect. In the Greek story, Hercules has some divine qualities, but he isn't perfect. He has great strength, but not much subtlety. He has heart, but not much serenity. He has virtue, but not much wisdom.

For me, it is easier to identify with the flawed Hercules than a perfected Jesus or Buddha. Like Hercules, each of us is vulnerable. Our gifts and vulnerability probably are the same as his. But we have both.

Gifts

So let's look more closely at these gifts and vulnerabilities. The fact that we have strengths and weaknesses is not news. However, I want to refine this insight in two ways.

First, we all have divine as well as "ordinary" gifts. Ordinary gifts are talents for things like music, writing, cooking, fixing machines, debugging computers, or painting pictures.

Divine gifts, on the other hand, are ways we connect with the divine or the mystical core of life. They are ways we touch a source of wellbeing that is undisturbed by the surface of life. They are ways we are already enlightened.

All of us have one or two divine gifts. They may be so close to us that we don't recognize them. They may have been so ignored in our childhood that they don't seem real. They may be so denied that we have become cynical about them. But they are there.

Let me give some examples.

Some of you have the gift of oneness. You feel how everything is a part of everything else. Maybe the only place where this surfaces is in your love of nature. When you are in the wilderness or a field, something deep inside you relaxes. It is as if your armor – the ways you contain yourself – begins to melt. You feel more a part of everything.

Some of you have Hercules' gift of compassion. You are drawn to serve those who are suffering or oppressed. You are not trying to relieve guilt or to be a do-gooder. You just find that you feel more alive and whole when your heart pours itself into service.

Some of you have the gift of serenity. You are not as drawn to action because you see the perfection in everything as it is already or as it is unfolding. Your capacity to look at suffering and remain calm is a gift of peace to yourself. And it gives comfort and serenity to those around you. They feel calmed and healed by your presence.

Some of you have the gift of lawfulness. Instinctively, you know there is an order to the universe behind the surface complexity. You are drawn to discover these laws and express them to others so they might stop hurting others so unconsciously.

Some of you have the gift of joy. Some have the gift of faith. Some, the gift of selfless generosity. Some, the gift of innocence and openness. And so forth.

There are probably 10 to 15 relatively distinct divine gifts. Each is related to all the others. So all of us know all of them a little. We can relate to each. But I suggest that each of us has one or two of these gifts in great abundance. Our gifts may not be the same as Hercules's, but we have one or two that really shine while others are dimmer in the background.

Vulnerabilities

If this were all there was to the story, we'd be living in a heavenly realm. Life would be sweet, wonderful, blissful, clear, and delightful in our various ways. Like Hercules, we'd be loved and respected by all. We'd have a partner if we wanted, a family if we wanted. Life would be groovy.

But alas, life is more interesting than this. There is a dark side to each gift. We all have a dark side. Like Hercules, we are gifted and cursed. We all have flaws, weaknesses and blind spots.

Just as there is a difference between ordinary and divine gifts, there is a difference between ordinary and divine vulnerabilities. These divine vulnerabilities are related to our divine sensitivities.

Let me explain. There are many obstacles on the road of life: detours, barricades, washed out bridges, potholes, fallen trees, and more. Life can impinge on us in different ways: insults, thoughtless people, stubbed toes, blocked opportunities, disappointments, and more.

When different people run into the same obstacles, they may have very different responses.

To recognize our divine vulnerabilities, we need to recognize which obstacles get to us most deeply and recognize our most common response to those obstacles.

For example, social rejection rolls off one person like water off a duck's back while another gets soaked through until he is drowning. Under pressure, one person is serene, another frantic, another lethargic, another worries about safety. When blocked, one person feels oppressed, another invigorated, another abandoned, and another resentful. Some people are more prone to melancholy, others to worry. Some jump the gun again and again while others can't get off the dime.

Have you ever been in difficulty and heard a little detached voice in the back of your mind wondering, "How'd I get here, again? Why does this keep happening to me? I know this pothole so well. How'd I fall into it again?"

You were probably caught in one of your deepest vulnerabilities. Divine vulnerabilities are the ways we get thrown off balance, over and over.

If you take only one thing away from this sermon, I hope it is the willingness to explore the possibility that our deepest gifts may be tied to our deepest vulnerabilities. Our greatest strength may give rise to our greatest weakness.

For example, if you have the gift of oneness, when thrown off balance, you are more vulnerable than others to feeling isolated, alone, separated from the goodness of life. Because your sensitivity to feeling interconnected is so strong, when it is cut off, you more easily feel cut off from all of life.

If you have the gift of serenity, when thrown off balance, you may feel jumpy or moody. Your mind may race.

If you have a gift of compassion and you run into a roadblock, you may feel frustrated, angry or irritable. "Passion" makes up 70% of the word "compassion." Because of the strength of your compassion, when it is thwarted, it can flare outwardly into anger or inwardly into seething or grumbling.

Hercules's greatest gifts were virtue and compassion. When Hera blinded him to his virtue, his compassion went into passionate rage.

Next Time

In the next two sermons, we'll look more closely at the curse of Hera – the blindness or ignorance cast upon us – and how it causes us to hurt ourselves and those around us. And we will look at what happens when the curse of Hera lifts and we see the pain we've caused. This is a crucial moment. It is a time when we need the support of others. The deeper spiritual path is much more difficult if we try to go it alone.

That's a preview of the next sermon.

Three Questions

This morning I am emphasizing our divine gifts and vulnerabilities and the intimate tie between them. I have been painting in broad brushstrokes. In fact, the ties can be subtle, complex, and nuanced. If we had time we could explore in detail one or two gifts and the vulnerabilities they create.

But this morning, I'd rather ground this in your life. What are your particular gifts and vulnerabilities?

One way to explore this is through three essential spiritual questions. We'll start with two of them in this sermon and get to the third later.

I had difficulty finding a way to frame these questions that might appeal equally to all of you. Depending on your gifts and vulnerabilities, some metaphors resonate deeply inside you while others feel dissonant.

So I'll word them several ways and invite you to find the language that is most helpful for you.

Contemplation

The questions can be used as a contemplation. For example, when you are relatively mellow, sit back and look at yourself with detachment. Then bring up the first question:

What are my strengths? What special gifts do I carry? How does the divine manifest in me? What is my beauty?

Use whatever language resonates for you. Don't try to analyze yourself. Just see what comes to you.

And then, after a while, shift to the second question:

How do I hide my gifts? What blindness and vulnerability hide the light in me? How is my beauty obscured?

Notice this question doesn't ask, "What's wrong with me? What are my faults? How do I keep shooting myself in the foot?" It does ask you to obsess on your weakness. It encourages you to see your vulnerabilities clearly and see their relationship to your divine gifts.

Friends

Another way to explore your gifts and vulnerabilities is with trusted friends. We all have the curse of Hera. We all have blind spots. Sometimes those who love us are able to see things in us we miss.

So ask friends to reflect back to you:

What are the strengths, gifts and beauty you see in me? How do these manifest?

Then ask:

What are the ways I hide my beauty and gifts?

Then see how openly you can listen.

Congregation

In a congregation that supports one another's deepening, one of the most important things we can do for each other is reflect the particular spiritual strengths and vulnerabilities we see in one another.

If people don't ask us overtly, we can still use the questions to frame how we see each other. They can be held in the back of our minds as we talk during the social hour or at work or even passing someone on the street:

What is the beauty in this person?

How do they hide their gifts?

I encourage you to hold these questions as you reflect on yourself and the people around you. They can help us open our minds and hearts to our greatest fears. If we do this skillfully, our difficulties become doorways. They become the path, which at first seems narrow and restrictive but eventually becomes wide and beautiful and leads us to our divinity.

Our Divine Vulnerabilities II

September 30, 2007

Wrist-Rocket

When I was 10 years old I got a Wrist-Rocket! A Wrist-Rocket is a souped-up slingshot. For elastic, rather than using a dinky little rubber band, it uses surgical tubing. And the handle has a brace that goes over your wrist and forearm to help you steady the weapon as you pull hard on the surgical tubing. My big brother told me that pebbles were wimpy. I should shoot nails rather than little stones.

So one afternoon after school, I went out into my backyard with my brand new Wrist-Rocket and a can of rusty nails. I put a bent nail in the weapon and looked around for something interesting to shoot at.

There were three Chinese tallow trees in the backyard. There were three or four pigeons on the branches.

I quietly turned to face the birds. I slowly pulled back on the surgical elastic. I held the Wrist-Rocket steady as I calculated the trajectory. I released the nail.

"Thup!" A mass of feathers and blood fell from the tree. "Whump." A warm carcass lay on the grass. The nail had turned it inside out.

I looked around to see if there were witnesses. No one. I quickly hid the carcass behind the garage, found a shovel and buried the evidence.

I never told anyone about the killing. Not my brother. Not my friends. No one. And I never used the Wrist-Rocket again.

BB Pistol

Several years later, I was an aspiring juvenile delinquent. My friend Bruce was taking $20 bills from his mother's purse and sharing them with me and our friend Ricky. We bought cigarettes, hunting knives and other contraband. We did not buy Wrist-Rockets – they had gone out of style – but we did buy pistols that used CO2 cartridges to shoot BBs and darts. We went down to the bayou to practice being tough, choke on cigarettes, and shoot at paper boats in the water.

One day two kids appeared on the opposite bank. One of them called us names, threatened and taunted. I was silent. My jaws and lips grew tighter and tighter until I pointed a pistol at him and pulled the trigger.

He grabbed his upper arm as he twisted back. His eyes grew wide. His hard voice became whiney: "You're really in trouble now. I'm going to tell. I'm going to call the cops."

He was more surprised than hurt. It was only a BB from a distance. But I pictured what could have happened had I hit him in the eye. My stomach fell.

We scurried away. I never went back to that part of the bayou. I never shot the pistol again.

Mom

Many decades later, my wife and four-year-old son Nathan and I were living in the small town of Groton, Massachusetts. My mother moved to town from New York City so she could be closer to us and be a part of the congregation I served. She found an apartment several blocks from us and stopped by several times a week.

One afternoon when I was alone with Nathan, I saw my mother walking up the street. I was behind in preparing the service for the coming Sunday. "This is my chance," I thought. "I'll get mom to watch Nathan so I can go write."

When she walked in the back door, there was a sad look in her eyes, as if she needed to talk. I pretended not to notice. "Hi, mom! Good to see you. So glad you came by. Can you play with Nathan for awhile so I can go work on my sermon?"

She was my mother: I knew the tone of voice that would make her feel compelled to oblige me. And she did.

She died four or five years later. She was a writer who left a stack of journals to my sister, Stephanie. Stephanie divided the journals between herself and her four brothers. I got the ones from her Groton years.

Looking through them one day, I came across an entry. "I was feeling lonely and confused and went over to Doug's this afternoon. As usual, he was too busy to talk with me. He shoved Nathan on me and ran off to his study. Nathan is a joy. But this afternoon I really needed to talk to an adult. Or if not, at least be alone."

Hurting Others

We all intentionally do things that hurt others. Sometimes our tools are as gross as a flying nail. More often they are as subtle as asking for a favor in a way that takes advantage of someone's weakness. Rarely are they documented with a journal entry. Still, we carry them quietly in the back of our hearts as secrets we try to forget.

Let's pause for a moment to remember some of the suffering we have knowingly caused. Maybe you turned away someone you could have easily helped. Or you slighted someone. Maybe you wanted the person to hurt. Or maybe you didn't, but you knew your actions would hurt, did it anyway, and pretended you didn't know. …

Let's pause and reflect for a few moments on what was going on inside. …

Hercules

In a previous sermon (pp. 143-147), I began painting a picture of the spiritual journey, this path from birth to enlightenment, from naïve innocence to realization of our full potential. We looked at two elements of this journey: our individual, divine gifts and their related vulnerabilities. In this sermon, I'd like to add two more elements to the picture. One is the blindness that allows us to intentionally hurt ourselves and others. The second is our capacity to wake up out of this trancelike fog and see with dismay the harm we've caused.

The story of Hercules dramatizes these dynamics.

You may recall that, at one point, Hercules was living an idyllic life. Because of his virtue and compassion, he used his strength to help the weak. He was widely loved and respected. He had a wife, Megara, and three sons. Life was good.

Then Hera, the queen of the gods, put a curse on him. It was a subtle spell. She didn't take away any of his gifts. She didn't change his essence in the least. She merely put a fog over his mind so that he could no longer distinguish good from bad, right from wrong.

Under this spell, he killed his wife and sons. With his strength, it was easy. With his ignorance, he saw nothing wrong.

The people saw what was wrong. They were mortified and turned against him.

At this point, Hera lifted the curse. He was able to see right and wrong and the significance of what he had done. His heart was shattered. His mind fragmented. He became demented with guilt and grief. He wandered aimlessly, his clothes and spirit in tatters.

Finally, he reached out for help and found it with the Oracle of Delphi. With her help, he began his recovery.

Adam and Eve

This part of the story has elements similar to Adam and Eve in the Garden of Eden. They lived under the curse of Hera. Life seemed sweet and delightful in the Garden. But, like Hercules under the spell, they didn't know right from wrong, good from bad. For a long time they didn't eat from the Tree of Knowledge of Good and Evil.

When they did eat the fruit, the first thing they felt was guilt and shame. Curious response: what had they done to feel guilty about? The Bible hints that they were ashamed of their nakedness. But we are told they were shaped in the image of God. Why should looking like God feel shameful?

Perhaps, like Hercules, they had done some terrible things. But they were oblivious to the implications until they ate of the fruit of awareness of good and evil. They were immediately thrown from the Garden of Innocence and into the real world where we live to this day.

Fog

What are these stories about? What is this curse of Hera, this particular kind of blindness to right and wrong, this capacity to hurt someone and pretend we didn't notice?

I am not talking about times we hurt people when that truly is not our intent. Perhaps two friends are having birthday parties at the same time. We can't be both places. We are open about our dilemma. But each insists her party is more important.

There is a story of a man whose mother gave him two ties. The next time he saw her he was wearing one of them. She said, "So, you didn't like the other tie!"

At times we hurt people when that is not our intent. This is not what I'm talking about.

When I released the nail at the bird, a part of me knew what I was doing. But I was in a fog of excitement about the Wrist-Rocket. I was thrilled. I was entranced. When I actually hit a bird, Hera's trance lifted. I was horrified at the murder I'd just committed.

By the bayou, I was blinded by anger and self-righteousness ("He's got no right to say that. I'll teach him a lesson"). Anger and self-importance clouded my mind and suspended my morality until I pulled the trigger and saw the guy flinch.

When my mother came up the driveway that afternoon, stress and fear of making a fool of myself in the pulpit hindered my seeing her clearly and allowed me to ignore her need.

These are real life examples of the real curse of Hera. We humans seem susceptible to it. It is a kind of static in the brain or fog in the mind that covers clear seeing.

How the fog manifests in each of us is different. Two weeks ago I spoke about our divine gifts, things like joy, serenity, seeing the oneness of life, seeing the perfection of things as they are unfolding, compassion, lawfulness, and so on. Each of us has one or two of these divine gifts in great abundance, whether we know it or not.

Different divine gifts create different vulnerabilities. Different vulnerabilities have different kinds of blindness.

We all have a divine gift, and our gifts vary. We all have vulnerabilities, and our vulnerabilities vary. We all are susceptible to mind fog, and how we experience the fog varies.

Sometimes it manifests as thrill, excitement, being carried away or distraction. Sometimes as temper, fear, ego, attachment to our ideas, strong beliefs or strong feelings. Sometimes we want someone to hurt. Sometimes that is not our conscious intent, but we know we are being hurtful and fake ignorance. Sometimes we are just selfish. Sometimes we try so hard to be generous and nice that we get befuddled. It manifests in many different ways.

Seeing

This morning I am advocating opening our eyes and looking skillfully at those times we have hurt others. I'm advocating looking skillfully at our state of mind and heart at those times to see our form of ignorance.

This is not Spirituality 101. This is advanced work. And it is not easy. So it is very important that we approach this work skillfully.

By skillful looking, I mean cultivating a dual vision. First, we see our spiritual strengths. We stand in our particular divine gifts. We see the ways the divine manifests in us. We embrace our beauty and light. From that place we turn and look at the harm we've done and the nature of our blindness – the particular trance we fell into.

Seeing both our beauty and the hurt may create dissonance: "How can I be a good person and do these bad things?" "How can I have inherent worth and dignity and harbor ignoble motives?" "How can I be gifted and blinded?" This paradox can be destabilizing.

There are a number of unskillful ways to manage this dissonance. One is to discount our beauty, gifts, and divine light. Perhaps we go into a Calvinist self-loathing. "I'm a bad person." "I'm worthless." "There is little redeemable in me." This is what happened to Hercules for a time: His heart collapsed.

At the other extreme, we can ignore the harm we've done. We try to blind ourselves and return to the Garden of Innocence. We cling narcissistically to the Light. This is religion as a bonbon. This is not religion but a let's-all-just-feel-good workshop. It is religion as cotton candy: It tastes good but doesn't nourish. And if we eat too much, it will rot our teeth. We may begin to think, "I'm a good person. If someone is hurt by my actions, it is their fault, not mine." We march off to war thinking that we are good; therefore, whatever we do must be good.

Another unskillful strategy is to muddle in the middle. We lop off both ends: "Yes, I have gifts, but they aren't *that* wonderful. And I have hurt others, but there is no need to look at that *too* much." Probably most of us prefer this muddle strategy.

The dual vision is none of these. We open our minds and hearts to our divine gifts and to the harm we've perpetrated. We fully embrace both even if they contradict.

Out of this ferment, many things can happen. Seeing the hurt can open our hearts. Our compassion deepens. Our empathy grows. Our humility becomes more enlightened.

Seeing our gifts and strengths helps us see things we may want to do to make amends. We see the fog that caused us to harm and forgive ourselves for our temporary ignorance.

Feeling the dissonance may destabilize us in a good way. It may be hard to imagine how someone could be as gifted as we are and still fall into a fog and hurt someone. It is hard to imagine. Nevertheless, here we are – someone who is real but beyond what we previously imagined. Our sense of self is rattled and transformed in a good way.

Whatever the case, out of this ferment, we emerge from the Garden of Eden, emerge from the curse of Hera, emerge from the fog.

This is the beginning of the true spiritual path. It is not Calvinist esteem bashing, religion as bonbons, or muddle in the middle. It is the beginning of true awakening, if you will. As the fog lifts, we see what our next steps might be on this journey.

We'll pick up at this point in a subsequent sermon.

Many Levels

But for now, let's stay with the paradox of embracing our divine gifts and falling into a trance that allows us to harm. Embracing this paradox is important for individual transformation.

It is also important for community transformation. As a congregation, what are our gifts and blindness? We'll come back to this in another sermon and when we look at us as a sacred community.

It is also important that we do this as a nation. Can we see the harm we Americans have brought to the world without falling into "ain't we awful"? Can we embrace the gifts of the American spirit without blinding ourselves into thinking we can do no wrong? As the political season heats up, we'll come back to this and look at some key issues. We'll imagine the stories that can help us as a nation embrace our gifts and deal with the harm we've caused. We'll look at how we can grow from an immature democracy based on individual freedom to a mature democracy based on collective responsibility.

But all of these wider, collective considerations begin with our ability to do this in our own lives.

Closing Contemplation

Take a moment to stretch or move around a little if that will help. Then settle in. Close your eyes. Let you body and mind relax. Then ask softly:

What is the beauty in me? What are my strengths and divine gifts? How do I most easily connect with the highest in life? …

After a while, shift to the question:

What harm have I caused? How have I hurt people? What was the fog in me, the blindness, that allowed this to happen? …

Then shift back to the first:

What is the beauty in me? …

At your own pace, move back and forth between these until you can fully embrace both at the same time: your form of grace and your form of blindness.

Our Divine Vulnerabilities III

October 14, 2007

Rodrigo Mendoza was a Portuguese soldier turned slave trader operating in Paraguay in the mid 18th century. He captured local Guaraní Indians and sold them legally to the Portuguese and illegally to the Spanish.

Father Gabriel was a Jesuit priest setting up missions in the same region. By the standards of the day, these missions were utopian communities with schools, hospitals, short workdays, fair wealth distribution, music, art, and 100% literacy. They also protected the Guaraní from the slave traders.

Rodrigo and Gabriel are fictitious characters in the movie *The Mission*. But the setting for the movie is historically accurate, including the tension between the capitalist slave traders and the independent Jesuit communities.

In the movie, Rodrigo, the slave trader, is very close to his brother, Felipe. Then Rodrigo's wife and Felipe fall in love. Rodrigo is angry and hurt and wants to get away from both of them. But Felipe insists they talk. The talk erupts into a scuffle. In the scuffle, Rodrigo jabs a knife into Felipe's belly and kills him.

Seeing his brother's blood on his hands, Rodrigo snaps out of his fog of rage and betrayal. His love for his brother is stronger than his love for his wife. He is horrified at what he's done.

Rodrigo leaves his wife, his home, his business, everything, and submits himself to his old adversaries, the Jesuits. They give him a small room. He closes himself in, stops eating, and waits bitterly for death and damnation.

Father Gabriel is assigned to redeem Rodrigo. Rodrigo is contemptuous of the priest and yells to be left alone to die in his own misery. So Gabriel calls him a coward — resignation is the easy way out while penance would take more guts.

Goaded by this tough love, Rodrigo takes the penance to spite the priest and prove he is unredeemable.

For penance, Rodrigo is told to take the knife he used to kill his brother, the guns and swords he used on Guaraní Indians, all the helmets, breastplates, and armor and bind them in a net and tie the net to his body. Everywhere Rodrigo goes, he must drag the tools of his violence.

For months and months he drags the weaponry through the streets, up the river, up mountains where he slips and gets bruised, up waterfalls where he gets battered. He is dogged and bitter and taciturn.

One afternoon by the river, another priest approaches Father Gabriel. "The brothers have been talking. We feel Rodrigo has suffered enough. His penance is sufficient. You should absolve him."

Gabriel responds, "We are a Jesuit order, not a democracy. His penance will not be put to a vote." Then he explains, "Rodrigo does not believe he has done enough penance. Until he does, I don't believe he has done enough penance."

I saw that movie 20 years ago. That line sticks with me: "Until Rodrigo feels he has done enough penance, he has not done enough penance."

I had always thought of penance as a cross between punishment and superstition: I do something bad. A priest gives me a task as punishment. Doing this task magically takes the badness out of me.

As a religious liberal and spiritual progressive, I'm more interested in the quality of a person's mind and heart than external actions. Intentions are more important than deeds. Using external actions for spiritual development seemed mechanistic, superficial, and naïve.

But watching Rodrigo's story, it was clear there are times when outward deeds can heal our inner states. Sometimes we may need to do something over and over, not to punish ourselves or appease a petty God. We need to do something to restore our confidence in who we truly are.

So the question I want to explore with you in this sermon is: "What do we need to do next to help restore our confidence in our original magnificence?" "What can we do that will deepen our faith in the light within us?"

Ingredients

This is the third sermon in a series on our divine vulnerabilities. We have been exploring the spiritual path, this journey from birth to enlightenment, from naïve innocence to embracing our full potential.

On this journey, the issue is never changing our essence. The issue is never who we truly are. The issue is changing who we think we are. It is strengthening our confidence – our faith – in our core nature.

In this series we've reflected on the four ingredients of this journey.

The first ingredient is our divine gifts. There are many divine gifts. Each of us has one or two. These are unique ways that each of us easily connects with the depths and richness of life.

The second ingredient is our vulnerability. We humans have soft underbellies that we expose to the world when we stand up. Our greatest vulnerabilities – the ones that catch us again and again – are often tied to our greatest gifts.

The third ingredient is a mind fog that allows us to hurt others. We've been calling this the curse of Hera. In the myth of Hercules, Hera, the Queen of the gods, casts a spell on Hercules. She put a fog in his mind that blinded him to the difference between right and wrong. Under this curse, he killed his wife and three children.

In the second sermon in this series, we explored the many different forms this mind fog can take: excitement, fear, attachment, ego, anger, hurt, confusion, aversion, and so forth.

The fourth and final ingredient of the spiritual journey is the capacity to wake up out of this trancelike fog and see the harm we've done. In the Hercules story, Hera literally lifts the curse, and he feels the enormity of what he's done.

Rodrigo sees Felipe's blood on his hands and wakes out of the trance of jealousy. He sees what he's done.

Previously, I told you about a Wrist-Rocket, a kind of souped-up slingshot I got when I was ten. I was so blinded by my excitement that I shot a nail through a bird. Then the fog lifted, and I was horrified at my callous slaughter.

Mess

So now we have looked at all four essential ingredients of a human being: the gifts, the vulnerability, the fog that allows us to harm, and the capacity to see it all.

But it feels like a mess. We have these divine gifts. But we stumble and get hurt over and over. How can someone who is supposed to be so gifted have all these lowly problems? Confidence in our gifts wanes. We may not even believe in them.

Then, on top of this, we see the hurt we've caused. Maybe we haven't literally killed. But we have all done things that violate our deepest sense of what's right. We have all gone into states where we went against our core values. We have all hurt others when we should have known better.

Seeing what we've done feels like a curse. It hurts. It undermines our confidence. But notice, in the Hercules story, the capacity to see clearly is the lifting of the curse. This capacity to wake up is actually a gift. It is grace — fierce grace perhaps — but something that can heal us.

Hercules had killed his children – probably the worst thing a soul can do. He eventually heals. It takes 12 years and the famous 12 labors of Hercules, but he heals. The message is: No matter what we've done, we, too, can heal.

So the question before us is, "Given these four elements – our gifts, vulnerabilities, the fog that allows us to harm, and the ability to see it all – what do we do now?" The risk is resignation – maybe not as dramatic as Rodrigo locking himself in a room and starving himself. The risk is settling for humdrum, where our greatest inspiration is trying to pay the bills and get through another day. The question is, "What can we do to embody our divine gifts?"

Pain of Awakening

Before looking at next steps it might be helpful to consider two things: the role of pain in the spiritual journey and the role of community in our individual journeys.

In general, pain is the soul's way of bringing our attention to that which needs attention. Pain is neither good nor bad, moral nor immoral, a sign of godliness or ungodliness. Pain is just pain. It's a signal.

Yet understandably, many people have difficulty with pain. They try to push it away or hold onto it or both.

Rodrigo did both. He was convinced he'd burn in hell for his crime. Dragging the armor around for months softened him a little. But a tight fist of bitterness and self-hatred still surrounded his heart.

If you hold your fist tightly for a little while, it starts to ache. If you hold it for a long while, the ache goes away – your hand goes numb. Now, if you try to relax your fist, it really hurts. The temptation is to tighten and numb it.

This is what it means to try to get rid of pain — we numb it or look away — while we actually hold tightly. But pain is just a signal to pay attention so that we might release it and regain some freedom.

Help of Community

Because of pain, difficulty, confusion, and loss of confidence, the support of a community can be extremely helpful.

Hercules

We saw this already with Hercules. Like Rodrigo, when Hercules saw the implications of killing his family, he fell into a pit of grief and guilt. He could not get out of it by himself. Eventually he reached out to a religious community at the temple of Delphi. They helped him see the nature of the curse that had been placed on him. And they told him what he had to do to heal: Submit himself to his old enemy Eurystheus, who gave him 12 dangerous tasks – the famous labors of Hercules.

Rodrigo

Rodrigo Mendoza's story is more illuminating:

After many months, he was dragging the armor up the riverside one day when he encountered a group of Guaraní Indians. They recognized him as the soldier who had killed or enslaved so many of their people. One of them jumped on his back, yanked his head back, and held a knife to his throat.

Rodrigo didn't resist. He was completely passive. If anything, he had a look in his eyes that said, "Go ahead and slit my throat and put me out of my misery."

The Guaraní were puzzled. This wasn't the fierce mercenary they had known. Something was different. So rather than slit his throat, the man slit the rope that bound Rodrigo to the weapons.

This act of mercy was more than Rodrigo could comprehend. He cracked. He began to cry, perhaps for the first time in his life.

The Indians laughed. They patted him on the head and stroked his arms and laughed. Eventually, they took him into their village.

This was not Rodrigo's redemption or enlightenment. There was more he needed to do. But it was a turning point. From this community he experienced a mercy he couldn't imagine. But he could feel it. This encouraged him to bring forth those qualities from himself.

He began to live with and help the Guaraní. His healing changed from the gut wrenching, bitter pain of dragging around the armor of his crimes to the bitter sweetness of knowing the people he had once oppressed to an outflowing of love. Pain is the soul's way of bringing our attention to that which needs attention. Pain was no longer necessary for Rodrigo to see what he needed to see. So it released. The fist around his heart began to relax.

But regaining confidence in his heart first required help from others.

We all have blind spots. Sometimes we need others to reflect back to us what we may not see. Then we can act to embody those qualities ourselves.

Next Step

Now we come to the final question: the essence of it all. What is our next step?

Sometimes our next steps are easy. But sometimes we have to face pain, make amends, or ask for forgiveness so we can forgive ourselves. Sometimes we have to change our behavior to reflect a deeper essence.

For example, a Hindu man came to Gandhi during a time of sectarian violence in India. The man confessed to killing a Muslim out of hatred. Now his eyes were opened, and he saw how wrong this was. He feared for his soul. He asked Gandhi to absolve him.

Gandhi told him his next step. He must find a Muslim orphan – a child whose parents had been killed. He must take this child into his home and raise him as a Muslim. This course of action would cleanse his soul.

Most of the things we've done out of blindness have not been so harmful as killing. Yet outward actions can still be helpful.

For example, let's say our divine gift is selflessness. But out of hurt and blindness we've become stingy. We've developed tightfisted habits. Our next steps may be to practice giving a little more. When generosity flows naturally, it feels wonderful. As the fist relaxes, confidence in selflessness increases and the joy of giving fills us. But at first, relaxing that fist – giving a little more – may be painful.

Often our next steps don't involve forgiveness or correcting a mistake or difficulty. Those steps may be just changing a habit, developing a spiritual practice, getting involved in service, simplifying our life, and so on.

Whatever your specific next step, the general strategy is first to open up to all four essential ingredients: our gifts, vulnerabilities, fog, and awareness of the hurt we've caused. And then we ask, "What can I do to help bring forth my beauty, strength, and light?

Three Questions

I don't know specifically what your next steps are. They are different for each of us. But you know. You may not know you know. But deep inside you have that wisdom.

One way to access this wisdom is through three essential questions. We started this sermon series asking ourselves two of them. They were:

What is my beauty? What are the divine gifts I carry?

And:

How do I hide my beauty and strength? Where are my vulnerabilities and blindness?

Now we can add the third question:

Given the gifts I may have lost confidence in, given my vulnerabilities, given the mental fog that allows me to harm others, what is my next step?

Or more simply:

Given the ways I hid my beauty and strengths, what can I do to bring them forth?

We can reflect on these questions for ourselves. We can also reflect on them for others. As we interact with people, hold them in our hearts:

What is the beauty in this person?

How does he hide his gifts?

How can she bring forth her strength?

We can also hold them for ourselves as a congregation that can grow and mature spiritually:

Collectively, what are our beauty and gifts?

Collectively, how do we hide our gifts and strengths? What are our vulnerabilities and blind spots?

Collectively, what can we do to reveal our gifts and beauty?

Closing

Often we carry the burden of armor we no longer need. May we lay down our burdens. May we have faith in our hearts and wisdom. May we have confidence in our true nature.

Experiments in Truth

April 27, 2008

My father came home from his classes at MIT to find a note from my mother on the kitchen table: "Gone to the hospital to have a baby. Come on over when you get a chance." He hurried across the Charles River to Boston Lying-In Hospital. Later that day, I was born. It was April 27, 1948.

I'm 60 years old today. Amazing. I don't feel much different than I did yesterday when I was still in my 50s. Some body parts don't work as well as they used to. And I am more content than in earlier years. But I basically don't feel different and don't know quite how to relate to being 60.

I don't actually remember my mother's note or my father crossing the Charles. But I do remember other things about my birth – I just had a different vantage on events. You may raise an eyebrow and think, "No one remembers his or her birth. Doug must be deluded." No doubt I am. No doubt all of us are deluded, at least a little.

Gandhi titled his autobiography, "Experiments in Truth." I've always been drawn to explore the truth of human potential. I've not limited myself to conventional venues. Many of my experiments have come to naught. I won't trouble you with these. But some of them have touched me deeply even if they were a little weird.

So this morning I'd like to talk about my birth, the birth and death of the universe, everyday psychic sensitivities, and a few other things that may raise an eyebrow. But what the heck, it is my birthday, a day when custom asks you to indulge me, listen politely, and pretend to be interested.

Birth Memory

One afternoon a quarter of a century after April of 1948, I was lying on a mattress on the floor of the basement office of a psychotherapist named Steve, in Cambridge, Massachusetts. I had been yelling and screaming. Now I was spent. My eyes were closed, and I was curled up in a ball.

Vaguely, I felt enveloped in something soft. It was cold and clammy rather than warm and womblike. Then something dull and grey grabbed the sides of my head. It pulled. I resisted: "I'm not ready. I need more time. I'm not ready. It's too soon. I'm not ready." But the pull was overwhelming.

Next, in my mind's eye, I saw the blurred image of a man. He was wearing a white coat. He had red, curly hair, freckles, and a smile. But his eyes were distant. He looked at me without making eye contact, like I was an object or thing of no particular concern to him.

There were other people in a grey haze. Visually, I couldn't make them out. And emotionally, I couldn't feel them. Psychically the room was empty. Nobody was present, just bodies moving around.

"Hmm. This isn't right," I thought. "There's nobody here. There must be some mistake. I don't belong here."

It was as if I had been zipping through the cosmos. As I passed Jupiter, I was supposed to turn left. But I accidentally turned right and ended up in the wrong body, the wrong family, the wrong life, and the wrong world.

"What am I doing here? How long will I be stuck before I can get back on track?"

Gradually this scene faded, and I found my awareness back in Steve's office.

Steve and I talked about the images. Knowing how subtle and fluid the mind is, we didn't take them literally. They were metaphors for things I'd felt throughout my life.

For example, I recognized that feeling of being a stranger in a strange land. I grew up in a schizoid family – not much feeling tone. In the birth images, I was not upset or depressed. I just knew something was amiss.

I also recognized the feeling: "I'm not ready: I need more time." How often I had been thrown into situations I didn't think I could handle. And yet, when I looked back, I saw I was ready. I just didn't know it at the time. Over and over the power of grace dragged me down the road toward the light with me kicking and screaming the whole way. I always seemed to learn things the hard way.

The therapy hour ended, and I left.

My mother and I never talked about my birth. So a week later, I told her about the session. She was silent.

Then she said that in those years she was disconnected from her body and her sexuality. It made sense that her womb felt energetically cold and clammy.

She said I had a forceps delivery – I had not suspected that before.

She said her regular doctor had been on vacation. The backup doctor came in that day, did the delivery, and left. He seemed more interested in his golf game than the delivery. So he gave her scopolamine, induced labor, dragged me into this world, and left. We never saw him again.

And she said he had worn a white coat and had red curly hair, freckles, a forced smile, and distant eyes.

There is nothing in medical science to explain how I could remember those events. And yet the details are so specific and accurate.

After 60 years of my experiments, I suspect we all have the ability to know things we can't explain, remember things without knowing how, and perceive things through senses we don't understand.

Our scientific maps of ourselves and the world are limited. All maps are limited. We are all vast, multidimensional, complex beings who don't fit completely on any map. Conventional reality is a dull trance that does none of us justice.

This brings us to a story about science and the conventional map of the universe.

Big Bang

Some 14 billion years prior to April 27th, 1948, our universe was born with a big bang that sent matter flying in all directions. All matter exerts gravity on all the other matter. So gravity is pulling the universe back towards its center: I'm not the only one who resists going into a bigger life. However, the force of the initial big bang was so powerful, that the universe is still expanding despite 14 billion years of gravitational resistance.

There are two main theories about the end of the universe. One says that the gravitational pull of everything on everything else will eventually stop this expansion and reverse it — all matter will be pulled back to one central point. This contraction will crush and melt every particle back into an incredibly hot cosmic mash. This is called the hot death theory.

The other theory of the end of the universe says that the outward expansion is too great. Gravity will never overcome it. All the galaxies and stars and planets will continue to spread out and cool off forever. This is called the cold death theory.

If we want to know which end game to bet on, we only need two pieces of information: how much matter and hence how much gravity is in the universe, and the speed of the expansion. If we measure these precisely enough, we can calculate: Will we implode in a hot death or fizzle into a cold death? Will the universe go out with a bang or a whimper?

Our scientific instruments have not been precise enough to take these measurements. But with the Hubble telescope circling in orbit around the earth, we can now make these calculations.

Do you know which theory to bet on?

Neither. Our science is incomplete and woefully ignorant. It turns out that the expansion of the universe is not slowing at all. Despite the collective gravitational pull, the galaxies are actually flying apart faster and faster. The expansion is accelerating. The birthing continues to this day!

There is no force in the universe known to humans that can explain how or why universal expansion is accelerating. Physicists describe only four forces: strong atomic force, weak atomic force, electromagnetism, and gravity. That's it. That's all we know. None of these explains why the galaxies are flying apart at a faster and faster rate.

There is a fifth force. For now, it's called "dark energy" because we don't know what else to call it. We know zilch about it. You and I and every atom and star in the universe are affected by it. But we haven't a clue how it operates. We can see some of its effects. But we don't know what it is.

A lot of us fall back on science to inform us about the nature of the universe and what is real. It's important to understand how profoundly ignorant we are. This is not a cause for despair. Life goes on despite our ignorance. But it is a cause for profound humility. Our beliefs about life are not informed by much true understanding. There are elementary forces at play in all of our lives that we haven't a clue about.

Love and Hate

Dark energy may seem abstract or cosmic or "over there." So let's consider at a different force that is up close and personal, that we can't explain, and yet affects everything we do.

There is an easy way to demonstrate this in a group. Have a volunteer come forward, stand facing away from the group, and hold up one arm. Press down on the arm to get a measure of the person's strength.

Then instruct the group that when you hold up one finger they should project love toward the person. When you hold up two fingers, they should project anger or hatred.

Then alternate holding up one or two fingers in a way that the group can see your gesture but the person with their arm out cannot. Each time, test the person's strength.

In variably, the person is dramatically weaker when anger or hatred is projected onto them than when they are surrounded in love or kindness.

I've altered the procedure in a number of ways to account for other contributing factors. But always the results are the same: love strengths us; hatred weakens us. This is true of both the senders and the receivers.

Just as there is little on scientific maps to explain dark energy, there is little in our scientific understanding to explain how mood and intention can have such a profound and immediate effect upon us. But there it is: life is a lot more interesting than we grasp.

Love and Wisdom

I have another story to share:

Years ago in my exploration, I had a psychic reading from a channel. She went into a light trance as her "teachers" spoke to me through her. They began by telling me about one of my past lives that informs my current life.

I'd like you to tell you the story. Don't worry about psychic phenomena, channeling, or past lives. I'm not asking you believe or disbelieve in any of that without doing your own experiments. I have little faith in blind faith. But I would like you to hear the story even if it is just a story.

The teachers said that I was born female more often than male. And in many lives, I had abusive families – so often that abuse seemed familiar and normal to me. I had come to believe that I was bad and deserved whatever I got.

Then, in one lifetime, something shifted. On a soul level – or deep in the unconscious – I no longer believed I was bad or deserved bad treatment. It wasn't an angry or even conscious realization. But on a soul level, I knew I had to leave the abuse.

Consciously, I still thought I was an awful person. So I planted a thought in my mind: I was so awful that I didn't deserve this family. My presence spoiled their lives. I should leave them because I wasn't good enough.

I snuck out of the house, left, and never returned.

If I had stayed any longer, the escalating violence would have killed me. So unconsciously my actions were wise, loving, and life-affirming. But consciously, the only way I could get myself to act on that love and wisdom was to tell myself I was terrible.

The story hints that there may be a measure of love and wisdom in everything even if on the surface it is covered by negation and denial. Sometimes we do the right thing for the wrong reasons. Sometimes we do the wrong thing for the right reasons. But there is a seed of love and wisdom to be found in everything.

The channeled teachers finished the story, saying in lifetime after lifetime since, I have never turned back. I kept moving toward love and wisdom even when it was confusing. I was more interested in doing what was practical to find that glimmer than doing what seemed logical.

In my current lifetime, this faith showed up in many places. When a suicidal person came to me, my first question was, "What in you needs to die? The impulse to kill yourself may have some love and wisdom in it. But you may be interpreting it too literally. If we can figure out what in your life needs to die, maybe your body won't have to go."

This willingness to do whatever is practical to find love and wisdom also manifested in my own battle to overcome depression, in my work with street kids, in my draw to the ministry, meditation practices and so forth.

That was the first 15 minutes of the reading. The entire reading took five hours. Recovering from the reading took six months.

It felt the opposite of my birth experience. In the delivery room, nobody was there. Nobody saw me.

In that reading, I felt seen as never before. I have no memories of those past lives. I don't know if there is any literal truth to them. But the patterns, instincts, feelings and tendencies they described are me. Whatever was speaking that day saw me more deeply than I'd ever seen myself.

In the years that followed, that psychic became a good friend. She could turn her VCR on and off with intention. She could break crystals. She lived off the conventional scientific map. If you met her in the grocery store, she blended in just fine.

She and I knew the abilities she had are in every one of us. There are lots of psychic quacks, to be sure. There are plenty of deluded people. Nevertheless, genuine abilities are latent in all of us. If we are willing to poke around, experiment intelligently, make mistakes, and risk being foolish, we just might stumble into genuine capacities.

Questions

So I have a few questions for you to contemplate and discuss with friends and members of this community:

Have you ever known things you can't explain knowing?

Have you ever done something that seemed wrong at the time but later on turned out to be wise?

Have you ever seen the light in a person when they couldn't?

Has someone ever seen a light in you that you didn't believe was there until they pointed it out?

Conclusions

To summarize, I offer three things for you to consider:

First, reality is more complex, subtle, and far out than the human mind can grasp. There are basic forces we hardly recognize and certainly don't understand. No one has a full map of reality. When it comes to understanding life, we are out of our league.

Second, we are all strangers in a strange land. None of us really fits the conventional image of a human. Like the universe itself, we are vast, complex, multidimensional beings. All of us are far out. What the world recognizes is a tiny, distorted fragment of our true nature. What each of us recognizes in ourselves is but a tiny, distorted fragment.

The discrepancies between what the normative world embraces and who we are are part of life's humor and beauty. There is much to learn and delight in when we trust that there is more to us than we know.

Third, there is a glimmer of wisdom and love in every person, every action, and every thing. Some things on balance may be wrong, but there is still a glimmer in everything. We won't always find it in conventional reality. But it's here. Our lives are enriched by the patience to search for it.

If we don't have the time or energy to search, then humility is a good fallback — accepting that there is wisdom and love even if we can't see them at the moment.

Conduct your own experiments in truth. Risk being kooky. It's okay. What the heck? Keep an eye out and a heart open for that measure of love and wisdom. Doing so might transform your life. It is transforming mine. I'm still being born.

Ethical Lapses

February 22, 2009

Let's begin with a little test of your perceptual judgment. I invite you to look at the values statement in your order of service. You'll notice that it has three lines. The test is to discern which line is the longest.

Now imagine you are sitting up front and this morning is your first visit with us. (For some, it is. Welcome!)

You think, "This is pretty silly. The second line obviously has more letters, more words and more length. What's the big deal?"

I ask a person in the first row on the opposite side of the room, "Which line is longest?"

"Line 1 is," he says.

You smile and think, "He must not have been paying attention."

The second person says, "Line 1."

The third person says, "One."

You start to feel a little agitated. What's going on? They're all giving the wrong answer.

The fourth person says, "Line 1."

Everyone is straight-faced and serious. "Maybe I didn't understand the instructions," you think.

The fifth says, "One."

"Excuse me, Reverend," you say. "Did you ask which line of the values statement is longest?"

"Yes," I say. "I'll get to you in a moment."

As we go around and everyone says "Line 1 is longest." You feel confused and edgy. You wonder if you missed something. You're unclear about how to respond.

Then you notice that everyone is silent. They're waiting for your response. What do you say?

Dr. Solomon Asch of Harvard conducted a similar experiment many years ago. He didn't have the benefit of our values statement. Instead he used large cards with different length lines. The first 14 people were confederates secretly working with Dr. Asch. They all gave the same wrong answer. The 15th person was the real test subject and faced a dilemma: Do I conform and lie or non-conform and say the truth?

The test subjects conformed 37% of the time. They conformed one time or more 75% of the time. Three quarters lied at least once!

Lapses, Traps, and Delusions

This morning I'd like to talk about ethical lapses, ethical traps, and ethical delusions.

We all have a strong ethical core, or a strong conscience. An ethical lapse is acting counter to this inner moral compass. Lying, for example, is an ethical lapse.

Ethical traps are forces that pull us into ethical lapses. Conformity is one such force. We are social creatures. Babies will die without minimal social interaction. Adults can feel quite uncomfortable when they are shunned or don't feel part of a group. Conformity pulled 75% of the people to lie at least once in the line length experiment. It was an ethical trap causing an ethical lapse.

Ethical lapses are disturbing. We can get agitated and upset. This is a good thing. Our moral compass is signaling: "Off course! Correction needed! Off course!"

The discomfort can be so painful that we may be tempted to kill the messenger rather than heed the message. We numb out or unwittingly distort our thinking: "I must not have understood the instructions" is an ethical delusion.

This sermon is in response to a request to speak about ends not justifying means. The claim that the end does justify the means is another example of an ethical trap. Take torture for example. The rationale for torture is that we want information. But under threat of pain, most people will say anything. Torture gets information. But the information is notoriously unreliable.

So the claim that the end (getting information) justifies the means (torture) is a delusion and an ethical trap that creates ethical lapses.

Severity

How we measure the severity of an ethical lapse gets to the core of the nature of ethics. Some lapses are minor – like lying about line length. Others are severe – like torture.

The best measure of severity is how much damage it does. The foundation of ethical behavior is empathy. Ethics is essentially about relationships – how we interact with people and the world.

Humans along with other mammals and birds have young who cannot survive without care and nurturing. So we are genetically wired with caring instincts. In response to suffering, we want to help if we can.

Most reptiles don't care for their young. They don't have the same caring gene. This is why reptilian behavior can seem immoral by human standards.

The biological foundations of morals and ethics are these caring instincts. Therefore, the severity of an ethical lapse is the amount of harm it causes or caring it avoids.

In the early 1960s, Stanley Milgram studied severe ethical lapses. His research was very revealing. So let's take a look at it.

Stanley Milgram

Imagine you are living in New Haven, Connecticut in the early '60s. You see an ad in the paper asking for volunteers for scientific research at Yale University. The ad says you'll be paid $4.50 an hour for participating. (That was more money 50 years ago than it is today.)

So you decide to give it a whirl.

When you meet Dr. Milgram, he is wearing a white lab coat, carrying a clipboard, and looking serious. He introduces another volunteer, Mr. McCourt. Mr. McCourt is a soft-spoken young man with an Irish accent, lively smile, and firm handshake.

Dr. Milgram explains that he is studying the relationship between punishment and learning. After giving some details of his study, he says that one of you will play the role of teacher, the other of student. He asks you to draw a piece of paper out of a hat. Yours says, "teacher." Mr. McCourt tells you his says, "student."

Dr. Milgram leads you both into an adjoining room. Mr. McCourt is strapped into a chair. "It is important that he doesn't move and disconnect the electrodes," Dr. Milgram explains. As electrodes are pasted to Mr. McCourt's body, he looks tense. "This isn't dangerous?" he asks. "I have a heart condition."

Dr. Milgram shakes his head "No. The shocks can be extremely painful. But they cause no permanent tissue damage."

You are then led into an adjoining room and asked to sit in front of a shock generator with a row of 30 levers. They are labeled with voltages: 15 volts at one end up to 450 volts at the other end. The levers are also labeled with words: "slight shock" at one end and "Danger: severe shock" near the other end. The last two levers are labeled "XXX."

Dr. Milgram attaches an electrode to your wrist, "I'd like you to experience a shock of 45 volts so you get an idea of what it is like for the student." Dr. Milgram presses the third lever on the instrument panel. You jump forward and yelp! It hurts!

Dr. Milgram then explains that you are to give Mr. McCourt a memory test. "If he gives a wrong answer, give him a shock. Each time he gets a wrong answer, increase the voltage to the next level."

You begin the memory test by reading a list of paired words into an intercom. Then, you go back and recite one word of each pair. Mr. McCourt's job is to give you the other word in the original pair.

At first, Mr. McCourt gets them right. But as you continue, he starts to make mistakes.

When you get to 75 volts, Mr. Court groans loudly over the intercom. At 120 volts he shouts that the shocks are painful. At 150 volts he cries out "Stop! Release me! I refuse to continue!"

You stop and push your chair away from the generator. Your palms a sweaty. You jiggle a leg rapidly. You turn to Dr. Milgram and say, "I don't like this. I'm not sure I want to go on. I'll hurt his heart."

Dr. Milgram looks you straight in the eyes and says, "It is absolutely essential that you continue. You have no choice. You must go on."

As you go higher and higher, the screams get louder and then fall silent. Dr. Milgram encourages you to continue, saying, "I take full responsibility."

As it turned out, Mr. McCourt was not a volunteer. He was a hired actor. The hat drawing to assign roles was rigged. And there was no electric shock actually given.

But in exit interviews, the test subjects had not suspected a ruse. They believed they were delivering shock.

In the original study, only one volunteer – a Holocaust survivor – refused to participate. All the rest gave shocks of 300 volts or more. And 65% went all the way to 450 volts.

They were not placid torturers. One volunteer was described as "a mature and initially poised businessman [who entered] the laboratory smiling and confident. Within 20 minutes he was reduced to a twitching, stuttering wreck, rapidly approaching nervous collapse. He constantly pulled on his ear lobe and twisted his hands. At one point, he pushed his fist into his forehead and muttered, 'Oh God, let's stop it.' And yet he continued to respond to every word of the experimenter, and obeyed to the end."

Stanley Milgram was interested in an ethical trap called "obedience to authority." In the wake of World War II and the revelations of what people in Nazi Germany had done in the name of following orders, he was interested in how far people would go.

Dr. Milgram and others were dismayed at the high level of obedience. And the study has been repeated using people from all walks of life, in different countries, and over 25 years with remarkably similar results. These studies reflect normative human behavior, not personal or cultural deviations.

If subjects in a one-time experiment with a professor they will never see again cannot resist the impulse to obey, think how much harder it is for a corporate or government worker whose job and family's welfare are at stake.

When we hear about Enron executives going along with unethical schemes or soldiers at Abu Ghraib torturing prisoners, it is tempting to think that they are aberrations. But they are normal folks.

Our military, for example, carefully screens its interrogators. They don't want sociopaths who won't follow orders. They want good, stable people like you and me. They train them, to be sure. But torturers start off like most of us here.

We are more ethically pliable than we like to imagine. And faced with ethical traps and delusions, most of us can be pulled into moderate and severe ethical lapses

Variety of Traps

So far, we have looked at three ethical traps: conformity, ends justifying means, and obedience. Let's look at a few more common ones.

Minimizing

During his last press conference in office, a reporter asked President Bush to name some mistakes he'd made during his eight years. Mr. Bush responded in part, "Well, not finding weapons of mass destruction in Iraq was a disappointment."

This was a curious statement.

If I want to go for a hike, and it's raining or go skiing and there is no snow, that's disappointing. But bad weather is not a *mistake* I made.

Saying he was disappointed was not admitting to a mistake as much as wishing the weather had been nicer for his war.

But his choice of the word "disappointment" is curious in a more fundamental way. As one news analyst put it, "A flat tire is a disappointment. Totaling the car is a disaster." Given the thousands of lives lost, billions of dollars spent, corruption tolerated, and America prestige undermined, I'd rather hear him say, "O boy, I really screwed up big time on that one."

President Bush's comment illustrates one of the most common ethical traps — minimizing.

Saying, "It's not a big deal" or "It's not so bad" downplays the damage of a moral lapse and makes it easier to brush it aside rather than learn from it.

Self-Righteousness

And my response to Mr. Bush illustrates another ethical delusion. Self-righteousness or any strong feeling can override our ethical perception. I can get so mad that I start to think, "I'm not like him. I'm a better person than that. I never do those things."

In fact, I minimize at times. I suspect most of us do. I don't have as much power as a major politician, so my acts of good and ill don't get magnified as much. But that doesn't mean that he and I are a different species. All of us are vulnerable to the ethical distortions of strong feelings.

Self-Enhancement

This brings us to a related trap: self-enhancement. I ask you, "Are you more ethical than the average person?"

If I went around the room and got your frank answers, I'll bet 80 to 90% of you would say your morals are higher than average.

Surveys show that most people perceive themselves as better than average in originality, friendliness, reliability, tolerance, intelligence, honesty, ability to get along, concern about social issues, and personal ethics. In fact, 90% of us rate ourselves better than three-quarters of the population.[13] The vast majority of us think we are better than the vast majority.

Garrison Keillor famously describes his mythical Lake Woebegone as a place where "all the women are strong; all the men are good looking, and all the children are above average." We chuckle, knowing we think this way though it is statistically impossible.

Thinking we are above average is an ethical *delusion* for some of us. It is also an ethical *trap* in that it encourages ethical lapses.

Again, President Bush illustrates this. He says that he is so confident that he is right that he doesn't second-guess himself. Yet he presided over one of the most corrupt and damaging presidencies I know.

People highly confident of their ethical standards are less self-reflective in morally grey situations. This makes them more vulnerable to the distorting effects of ethical traps. Research bears this out: The higher a person's opinion of their moral rectitude, the higher the chances of ethical lapses.

So, I ask again, raise your hand if you believe you are more ethical than the average person. …

Other Traps and Delusions

I have mentioned six ethical traps: conformity, ends justify means, obedience to authority, minimizing, self-righteousness, and self-enhancement. In their book, *The Ethical Executive*, two Stanford social psychologists, Robert Hoyk and Paul Hersey, list 45 such traps. They include things like:

Time Pressure

It takes time to figure out morally difficult situations. When pressed for time, we are more prone to ethical lapses. Good ethics takes time and reflection.

Renaming

Renaming is a delusion where we choose a different word to obscure a problem. For example, in war "killing innocent people" has been renamed "collateral damage."

In the transcript of a conversation, one Enron executives said, "It's all how well you can weave these lies together, Shari."

Shari responded, "Greg, I feel like I'm being corrupted."

Greg said, "No, this is marketing."

Shari replies, "O.K."

Renaming "lies" as "marketing" didn't change the lie, it just made it sound acceptable.

Others

Other traps include deflecting, small steps, self-interest, "everybody does it," "we won't get caught," "it won't hurt them that much," "Don't make waves," "it's not my fault," and more.

---

[13] Robert Hoyk and Paul Hersey, *The Ethical Executive*. [Stanford University Press, 2008] p. 46.

So What?

If we want to live in a more ethical world, there are many things we can do. I'll mention three.

Self-Knowledge

First, self-knowledge, self-awareness, and self-reflection are powerful antidotes.

Ask yourself with fierce honesty, "Where do I get caught most easily?

The more aware we are of ethical traps and our particular vulnerabilities, the less likely they will catch us unaware and pull us in.

Remember: Modest opinion of our moral strength makes us less likely to be taken in. The issue is not low self-esteem. Low self-esteem doesn't make us moral. Rather, humble awareness makes us less vulnerable.

Also, attend to the unsettled feeling that can be a sign of an ethical lapse or delusion. It is saying, "It is time to slow down and pay attention lest you get pulled into something you'll later regret."

Emphasize Relieving Suffering

Second, if we want to live in a more ethical world, put less emphasis on ethics and morals and more on caring, suffering, and relieving suffering.

The foundation of ethics is empathy. It is not philosophy or theology. It is gut level connection.

Emphasis on ethics and morals tends to put us in our heads and involves us in thinking about good and bad, right and wrong, black and white. Our minds are much more gullible than we imagine. Think of all the crusades, wars, and jihads started in the name of morality.

It is not difficult to go to war or hit a person in the name of right and wrong. It is difficult to do so in the name of caring and relieving suffering.

In some of the variations of Milgram's study, the volunteer "teacher" administering the electric shock was put right next to the "student" where they could touch. Under these conditions, twice as many "teachers" refused to go the whole distance.

The closer we are to suffering, the more our empathetic core is strengthened.

Share Misgivings

And finally, if we want to live in a more ethical world, share our misgivings.

Recall the conformity experiment where all the confederates gave the same wrong answer. If only one confederate gives a *different wrong* answer, conformity drops to 9%. One dissenting voice, one break from the crowd even in the wrong direction, gives tremendous courage to others to listen to their moral compass.

Closing

May we be humbly aware of our vulnerability.

May we be less judgmental of others' morals.

May we be steadfast in relieving suffering.

May we have courage to share misgivings.

May we come together, deepen our lives and be a force for healing in the world.

Killing a Friend

November 1, 2009

When I was in the third grade I was given my very first pet to care for and befriend. She was a cat. I named her Suzie.

A year later, Suzie disappeared to deliver her first litter. She returned daily for food. But I had no idea where the kittens were until they began to hop out from under the house and into the strawberry beds.

The next year, when she had a litter, I crawled under the house and brought her milk and canned food.

She had her third litter right in my closet. I loved having them run around my room.

When she gave birth the fourth time, she actually let me watch. She purred and convulsed as she pushed the globs from her and licked them to life.

Somehow in those days, we had no trouble finding homes for all those kittens. And when we didn't have kittens, she slept on my bed with me.

One afternoon, I came through the chain-linked backyard gate as my father backed our white Chevy station wagon down the driveway. I walked around the corner just in time to see Suzie go under the wheel.

She didn't let out a sound. But my father stopped the car. He must have felt an unnatural bump. Or maybe I yelled.

Suzie lay on her side with her back toward me and her head in a faded oil stain. There was an unnatural bend in her back. She thrashed so violently that she flew completely into the air.

I thought, "We have to get her to the vet." Then I realized, "She's not going to live that long. I've got to stop the pain."

My father must have had a similar thought. He said, "I'll get a knife for her throat," as he rushed into the house.

I pictured my Suzie lying still on the driveway surrounded by red. I shuddered inside.

I looked around quickly. The kitchen wastebasket sat by the back door after being emptied into the garbage can and washed out. The yellow plastic was stained grey from years of use. I grabbed the garden hose and filled it three-quarters of the way.

I put one hand under Suzie's shoulder. She let out a quick cry. It was the only sound she had made since being run over. But she didn't look at me. Her eyes were out of focus. Her head turned in a strange direction. I placed my thumb loosely around her neck to steady her. I put my other hand under her hip and lifted as gently as I could.

Tenderly I lowered her headfirst into the wastebasket. Suddenly her motions became coordinated and purposeful as she tried to back out of the water. I closed my hand around her head and held it at the bottom. She struggled. Then went limp.

I didn't move for a few moments. Then I slowly removed my arms. A bubble came out of her mouth and broke the surface.

My father appeared on the back steps with a carving knife in his hand. He looked at the wastebasket with the wet tail and feet sticking out. He looked at me. Neither of us said a word.

I got up and walked away.

I went into backyard for a few minutes, then walked across the patio and around behind the screen porch. It was secluded there. A brick wall, vines, and bushes blocked all outside view. I stood there. No thoughts went through my mind. I just stood, fingering the edges of the leaves on the bush and staring absently at the sky. It was overcast.

A quarter hour later, I walked back into the yard and across the patio. As I opened the gate, I noticed a red streak on my arm. I looked more closely at both my forearms. A dozen claw marks ran from my wrists to my elbows.

I showed the cuts to my mother. Her eyes flicked from my arms to my face to my arms to my face. She said something about me being brave and asked what I felt. I shrugged silently and went up to my room.

My father never spoke to me about it. In all our remaining years, he never raised the topic. And neither did I.

Thirty years later I described the incident in a writing exercise. There was a lot I couldn't recall. I wasn't certain of the year or the season or Suzie's age. I didn't remember what I was doing in the backyard that brought me through the gate at that moment. I had no idea what I did the remainder of the day.

But I remembered her death vividly.

I showed the sketch to a writing companion. She was so taken by the story that she couldn't give me a literary critique. "Do you know what you want to do with it?" she asked. "If you want to make it into a short story, you have to get more of what you felt into it."

I said, "I don't remember feeling anything. To this day I've never cried about it." My voice shuddered a little.

"Then you could use it to introduce an article on post traumatic stress."

I had not thought of that label. But it fit. However, an article sounded too dry to appeal to either of us.

We ended our conversation not knowing what to do with the piece. But I was strangely pleased that it had such an impact on her.

In the days that followed, I felt compelled to tell the story to other people. I didn't know why. My voice remained flat and emotionless, though sometimes my eyes watered.

I did send it to a few magazines. An editor from *Psychology Today* sent me a handwritten note. She said she had passed it around the office and they all had a good cry. But she was returning it to me because they couldn't figure out how to use it.

Then one morning while meditating, I realized I was telling the story to see if the violence and horror registered on people's faces. Maybe they could feel what I couldn't.

I burst into tears. I cried for Suzie. I cried for the boy who had to kill a friend. I cried for the man who couldn't find his grief.

Some years later, my father died. I don't remember the year or the season or his age without looking it up. He had been living on the Gulf Coast. I was in the Northeast. I didn't travel the thousand miles to his memorial. It didn't seem relevant to me.

Perhaps if we'd talked about Suzie's death and similar topics, I'd have felt more connection with him.

I've been with people who died gracefully after many long years. I've been with people who died painfully after what seemed like too few years. I've known people who took their own lives. And a few times, like with Suzie, I've had a hand in killing a friend.

But lest we get too caught up in the length of a life or the method of death, let's remember the more basic truth: we and all our loved ones, one way or another, will die.

It's good to talk about this more than I have all these years.

Last month as I was planning to tell you about Suzie, it occurred to me that perhaps my father didn't talk about Suzie because he felt guilty about running over her. My father was not the kind of man who shared his feelings. His inner life was a mystery to me.

But that insight about his guilt seems so basic. So obvious. Yet it took me 50 years to come to it.

Perhaps if I'd talked about death more, I would have realized long ago. And maybe I would have gone to his memorial.

It is good to talk about death. It can show us how to live by reminding us of what we love.

Joy, Enjoying, and Being In Joy

June 6, 2010

In the late 1990s, a midterm chemistry examination at Washington University contained a bonus question: "Is hell exothermic (meaning it gives off heat) or endothermic (meaning it absorbs heat)?" One student answered this way:

First, we need to know how the mass of hell is changing in time. So we need to know the rate at which souls are moving into hell and the rate at which they are leaving. I think that we can safely assume that once a soul gets to hell, it will not leave.

As for how many souls are entering hell, let's look at the different religions that exist in the world today. Most state that if you are not a member of their religion, you will go to hell. Since there is more than one of these religions and since people do not belong to more than one religion, we can project that all souls go to hell. With birth and death rates as they are, we can expect the number of souls in hell to increase exponentially.

Now, we look at the rate of change of the volume in hell because Boyle's Law states that in order for the temperature and pressure in hell to stay the same, the volume of hell has to expand proportionately as souls are added.

This gives two possibilities:

1. If hell is expanding at a slower rate than the rate at which souls enter hell, then the temperature and pressure in hell will increase until all hell breaks loose.

2. If hell is expanding at a rate faster than the increase of souls in hell, then the temperature and pressure will drop until hell freezes over.

So which is it?

If we accept the postulate given to me by Teresa Banyan during my Freshman year that, "it will be a cold day in hell before I sleep with you," and take into account the fact that I slept with her last night, then number 2 must be true.

Thus I am sure that hell is exothermic and has already frozen over.

The corollary of this theory is that since hell has frozen over, it follows that it is not accepting any more souls and is, therefore, extinct, leaving only heaven — thereby proving the existence of a divine being which explains why, last night, Teresa kept shouting "Oh my God!"

The student received the only A+.

As Universalists, we are confident that hell froze over a long time ago. We're delighted to hear that someone else has converted to our faith. And we're delighted to hear a rigorous scientific proof confirming our faith.

So it is with regret that I inform you this story is fake. The essay was originally written by Paul Darwin Foote in 1920. Dr. Foote was a well-established scientist and expert in high-energy physics, not some cheeky sophomore trying to impress his professor.

In the late 1990s, someone added the chemistry exam and Theresa Banyan and sent it out on the Internet. The story is fraudulent.

But who cares? It's a great story anyway.

This morning I'd like to talk about joy.

During the summer we give ourselves more permission to relax, let down and enjoy – to be "in joy" as it were. So as we move toward the easy-going months, I'd like to say a little about what joy is, why it is important, and how it can be cultivated.

What Is Joy

First, what is joy?

The best way to describe joy is to point to it, and let it describe itself. If you enjoyed the ruminations on Universalist theology – or remember the afterglow of any good story – you know what joy is.

Joy is a light, expansive state of consciousness infused with wellbeing.

Many birds eat more calories than they need each day. This extra energy helps them stay warm if the night is unusually cold. But in the morning, excess weight interferes with flying. So they burn off the extra stored energy by singing vigorously.

Joy is like this. It releases unneeded energy and lightens our spirits.

Just as there are many kinds of songs, there are many kinds of joy. Some are high-energy. Some are mellow.

High Energy

For an example of joy from the high-energy end of the spectrum, imagine a football player running downfield with the ball. He's focused and determined as he dodges tackles. Then he crosses the goal line. He releases the tension and explodes into joy. Pent up fans likewise leap with ecstatic release.

People can get addicted to competition, not because of the tension but because of the joy of releasing the tension.

Humor

Humor works the same way. But it is mellower in that the gathering and releasing of tension is more mental and emotional than physical.

For example, consider a few passages purportedly gathered from student writers learning the art of simile and metaphor:

Her vocabulary was as bad as, like, whatever.

John and Mary had never met. They were like two hummingbirds who had also never met.

He was as tall as a six-foot-three-inch tree.

As we listen, we may tighten as we grasp for deeper significance. When we see the image is meaningless, we let go and experience the rush of uplift.

A similar tension and release can be created by incongruities – joining two things that don't belong together:

- *He was deeply in love. When she spoke, he thought he heard bells, as if she were a garbage truck backing up.*
- *Her hair glistened in the rain like nose hair after a sneeze.*

Something that might otherwise be painful can feel quite joyous if we truly release:

- *He was as lame as a duck. Not the metaphorical lame duck either, but a real duck that was actually lame – maybe from stepping on a land mine or something.*
- *It hurt the way your tongue hurts after you accidentally staple it to the wall.*

Of course, analyzing humor or joy can take them away because analyzing is trying to grasp something. Humor and joy are releases:

He fell for her like his heart was a mob informant and she was the East River.

She had a deep, throaty, genuine laugh, like that sound a dog makes just before it throws up.

I'd love to read these to you all morning. But maybe this is enough to make the point that joy comes from release of tightness.

Long Held Release

Mellower forms of joy don't intentionally build up a charge. They release an existing one.

For example, imagine a difficult situation in our extended family or our job. It's been a source of awkwardness for months – maybe years.

Finally we get all the people in the same room at the same time and have a clear, open discussion. The conversation is edgy at first. But gradually a solution is hammered out.

Later that day or evening, it sinks in that the problem is over. We're free of this chronic stress. We may not burst into laughter. But we settle into a deep glow of relief that is joyful in its own way.

This kind of joy can also arise in religious conversion – people feel as if they are laying their burden down or resting in God's hands. "Glory, glory, hallelujah, when I lay my burden down."

All-Pervasive Joy

The deepest, most transformative joy could be called "all-pervasive" because it doesn't focus on a specific punch line, action, thought, or situation.

Imagine sitting by a lake in the early evening. We hear loons and peepers and crickets calling into the night air. We feel serene and peaceful.

This joy is not high-energy laughter or even the sigh of deep satisfaction. It is more profound: a subtle release that spreads out and pervades everything.

The Trappist monk Thomas Merton described it:

There is in all things an inexhaustible sweetness and purity, a silence that is a fountain of action and joy. It rises up in wordless gentleness and flows out to me from unseen roots of all created being.

In all-pervasive joy we relax from trying to get anywhere, do anything, or be anybody. We relax into a natural spaciousness. It reveals something about our core nature. It shows us we aren't quite what we thought we were.

We'll come back to this in a few minutes.

Why?

For now, let's shift from the flavors of joy to why we'd want it.

When we are in joy, we don't care where it came from as long as it causes no harm. Like enjoying the story about exothermic hell or the student writing, it needs no external validation, supporting facts, or proof of pedigree. Its value is self-evident.

However, when joy eludes us – when we are grumpy, anxious, morose, worried, or angry – the value of joy may elude us as well. When our mood is dark or frightened, joy may seem frivolous, naïve, or even irresponsible: "There is so much pain and injustice in the world. How dare you feel joy!"

So let's ask the question straight on: Why is joy important?

The answers are as varied as there are ways to approach life. What is important to us?

Do we want less burden and stress and more happiness? Joy is an obvious ticket.

Do we want good health? The biochemical side effects of joy are medically quite beneficial.

Do we want better family life? Families that share any form of joy get along better.

Do we want closeness to God? Grim determination and sanctimonious holiness cloud the soul. Joy brightens and lightens consciousness so we can see the divine clearly.

Do we want inner peace? Joy is the beginning of a meditative path that leads successively to happiness, peacefulness, spaciousness, stillness, and eventually nirvana.

In Buddhism, all-pervasive joy is an enlightenment factor.

Do we want more justice and fairness in the world? Joy makes us more effective. Protesters filled with joy draw more people to their cause than those who are merely upset. A potential political opponent is more easily persuaded with joy than critique.

Do we want a healthier ecosystem? The more joy we have, the less need we feel for distractions and the smaller our appetite for consumables.

Do we want to be miserable? Then it is important to know how to cultivate joy so we know what to avoid that could spoil our misery.

Cultivation

So, whatever our motives, let's turn to the final question: how do we cultivate joy? There are two kinds of strategies: systematic and unsystematic.

Let's look at each.

Cultivate Systematically

Though joy is difficult to contain, it can be cultivated more or less systematically. Some spiritual traditions note that in our core, all of us would like to be of help or benefit to others. They use this deeply human instinct to focus our distractible minds by sending positive thoughts and feelings to others.

After doing this a while, joy, ease, or uplift arise in us. Then the trick is to let go of the words or thoughts and focus on the feeling – the consciousness itself. As we relax into it, it gradually shifts from easy-to-notice but short-lived energetic joy toward subtler, longer-lasting peace and all-pervasive joy.

I've described this process in relation to meditation, and we've practiced it here on second Saturday mornings. But I would say that the same process is followed in many Western prayer disciplines. Monastic contemplative prayer begins with fairly thick language. The novice monk is told to pray using lots of Biblical words he's memorized.

As we know, our minds can be very distractible and drift off into many different kinds of thought. So the novice uses lots of words that grab his attention from his habitual pattern of thought and focus it outside his ego and usual preoccupations.

When his prayer begins to feel uplifted, he's instructed to use simpler, lighter prayers. As the joy deepens and becomes more peaceful, he's told to shift to a simple phrase or two. Then to a single word like "God" or "love" or "peace." He prays by repeating these over and over.

Then as his consciousness gets quieter, he drops into silence – verbally and mentally. He is left with all-pervasive joy. Prayer traditions call this "divine illumination" or "nearness of the Holy."

Cultivate Unsystematically

For those not drawn to systematic approaches, fortunately joy is so deeply human and has so many varieties that it can be cultivated informally.

Doing What Triggers Joy

One way to do this is to trigger joy in ourselves. We can recall things that help us move from grumpiness to laughter, from humdrum to happiness.

Let's hear from you. Will you call out some things that help you feel high-energy joy or peaceful wellbeing?[14]

…

One unsystematic way to cultivate joy is to do more of these things that trigger joy in us.

Leaning Into Joy

An even more direct way is to simply lean into joy. Since joy is an inner state more than an outward doing, we can simply remember what it feels like and invoke that feeling. Joy doesn't want to be forced. But we can remember what it feels like and "lean" in that direction.

If you like, do it now: remember how joy feels in the body and drift that direction. …

If this feels good do it any time or place you think of it.

Untangling

Another way to cultivate joy is to release feelings that block it. Anger, melancholy, fear, stress and other dense emotions can obstruct the light flow of joy. Pushing these aside usually doesn't work – pushing creates more tension and opacity.

Nevertheless, these denser states may need to be untangled a bit before they release. The details of untangling are a topic for another time. For this sermon, suffice it to say that as they untangle, they become absorbed into a natural state of joy. Fear may become excitement and aliveness. Anger may become passion and joie de vivre. Sadness can become poignancy and sweetness.

Home

Before closing, let's note that it is difficult to feel joy if we are too self-conscious or too self-involved. Conversely, with joy we are less preoccupied with our needs and desires. Joy lifts us beyond egotism. When we are in joy, we care less what others think of us.

In this way, cultivating joy is not so much a journey to a strange new land as it is a return home. Whether we think of it as returning to God, connecting with our true self, or being one with the universe, it feels like a homecoming. If we've been away for a while, coming home feels unusual. Yet deeply familiar.

This is why we cannot grasp joy. Grasping is holding while joy is releasing. Grasping stretches us beyond ourselves while joy settles into what we've always been but may have forgotten.

William Blake wrote:

He who binds to himself a joy
Does the winged life destroy;
But he who kisses the joy as it flies
Lives in eternity's sun rise.

Like a bird singing to the dawn, when we are in joy, we trust what we are enough to let go of what weighs us down.

So let's close by singing to that dawn. This is a prayer inviting us to lean into all-pervasive joy: what Thomas Merton called "inexhaustible sweetness … [that] rises up in wordless gentleness and flows. …"

---

[14] Or if you are reading this, quickly make a list of things that help you feel joy or wellbeing.

Like any contemplative prayer, it repeats and invites us to settle.

We'll start with a few quiet moments.

Close your eyes, if you like. Take a deep breath. Then release the breathing into naturalness. And let go of everything but a smile – the deep relaxed natural smile of home. ... Trust that whatever arises is just as it should be. It's okay. ...

Song: Sweet Quiet

*Sweet quiet Boundless sea,
Where joy and grief are the same,
Endless sky, pale breeze of dawn,
Breathe your light into me*

Everyday Practices

Light Beyond the Scrim

September 24, 2000

In January a few years ago, my son Nathan and I flew into New Delhi, India. We did not expect Delhi to welcome us with open arms. It didn't. It kept chewing our spirits and spitting them out in our hands. It wasn't us personally. It was just what Delhi is: people everywhere, street vendors, hawkers, beggars, lepers, cons, rickshaw drivers wanting to take us where they wanted, men urinating by the road, children playing cricket in the dirt, indifferent officials. There were crowded alleys festooned with shops, eggs sold on the street, everything sold on the street, the sweet milk tea called chai, seersucker pants, and beautiful saris. We had to deal with garbage, contaminated food, bottled water, no hot water, no soap, no toilet paper, power outages, jerry-rigged wiring, haggling, commissions, traffic jams, Hindi, cows, dogs, rickshaws, rupees, and fumes so thick our mucus turned black.

Despite the grime and rawness, people smiled more than at home. Away from the tourist areas, children ran up to us, delighted to be able to shake hands with tall foreigners. There were always people wanting to help us. Our first day, as we wandered with dazed eyes and conspicuous packs, a man in a baby blue and pink jacket befriended us, found us a cheap hotel, argued with the manager for a cheaper rate, and found a shop where Nathan could get new glasses. For two days he was our guide. When I tried to tip him he was completely uninterested. Yet he was delighted to have one of my business cards – something with personal rather than monetary value. I never got his name.

Nathan and I walked through a twisting kaleidoscope of sights, textures, moods, and smells. "I don't think we're in Kansas anymore," I kept saying to myself. One evening I looked at the sky and thought, "It looks just like the moon back home!" I was surprised to see something familiar in this alien landscape.

Yet, we were determined to meet the culture, meet the people, make a go of it. We went out each morning rested and hopeful. We crawled back each afternoon and lay panting on the bed, our minds blown and spirits frayed. Somehow we were able to laugh at how green we were.

Our second day in the cacophony, we decided to find a quiet spot to sit, watch the crowds, and gather our scattered senses. Connaught Place is in the center of New Delhi. It is a round park the size of a large city block. We haggled for a few oranges and peanuts and then pushed through the crowds into this little oasis. Scattered groups were sitting and lying in the grass. We picked a quiet place by a tree and settled down.

"Hallo." A man squatted beside us with his shoe repair box. "How are you?"

"Fine," I lied.

"Good. Very good. What country from?"

"U. S. A."

"Amereeca. Ah. Nice place. Very nice place." He smiled and gazed quietly across the park. "You like India?"

"Yes." I didn't want to be insulting. We were trying hard to like it. "It's crowded. But we like it here."

"Thank you," he said graciously.

By this time, several others had squatted around us. I did not see vendors converging on others in the park. Were we that obvious? Casually, the conversation shifted to, "Your shoes are dirty."

"No, thank you."

"Five rupees and I make them clean."

"No. I'm not interested."

"Two rupees, then." He picked at Nathan's ragged sneakers as if to say, "My, my. These are a mess. But I'm an expert. I can help you out."

"No."

"You don't pay. I fix them. If you like, you pay one rupee. If not, pay nothing."

"No! I'm really not interested!"

"No problem. It's okay. You be in India how long?"

And so it went. We talked about family, kids. The vendors described their work in the park as a job. They would be insulted to be called beggars. "You go to an office to go to work. I go to the park. This is my office. I work here 12 years." "I don't want to pressure you," they said. "Yeah, right," I thought. The talk always came back to the shoes or dirty ears or whatever services they offered.

We felt like flowers around bees as the friendly hawkers tried to get their proboscis into our pockets. If we got too uptight or angry, they'd say, "Relax. It's okay. You're frightened. Maybe tomorrow I do your shoes." I did not like the fact that my mood was so transparent.

It was a delicate balance: being firm without being rude or insulting. But after a while, we began to enjoy the dance. Nathan, particularly, was delighted. We began to sense the person behind the sales pitch. They'd talk about family, what different parts of India were like, where they lived. We were getting little glimpses into these people. That was what we came for.

Just when we thought we'd seen it all, a kid sat down about 10 feet away. He opened a dirty, plastic bag and drew out an instrument – some kind of flute stuck into a gourd. He played a few notes. A cobra stuck its head up. He stroked its chin, played a few notes, batted it on the head to make its hood flare more, stroked its chin. Occasionally it hissed and lunged at him, always missing. He'd bat its head and stroke its chin to bring it upright, then play a few more notes.

When the shoe, ear, and massage people left, he moved over to us. "Would you like to touch my snakes?"

"No, thank you."

"It's okay. The poison was taken out."

"No, thank you. I really do not want to touch your snakes." Part of it was the snakes, but mostly it was knowing that he might ask to be paid.

"Would you like to play the flute?"

"No, thanks."

"Would you like to buy the flute?"

Nathan laughed. "No. Really."

And so it went. As soon as one group of vendors left, another would quickly gather. At one point a man settled in next to me. He had grey hair, a dusty turban, and torn pants. He was thin and gentle. He said he had studied yoga, reflexology, and massage. He spoke casually of the importance of the heart, seeing the God in each person, valuing people over things. I couldn't tell how much he was speaking from his heart and how much from a sales pitch. But his grey eyes were soft and sincere. There was no obvious masking. Something about him touched me.

Rubbing my palm he said, "Your neck is tight. You have tension in your back, particularly your lower back." He was right. He wanted to work those areas.

"No, thank you."

"No, no. It's okay. You don't need to pay. I like my work. I just show you. If you like my work, maybe tomorrow when you come back you won't be so afraid and you can hire me then. I just want you to feel good about my work. That's all."

Eventually he worked my arms, shoulder, and back. I stopped him from doing my legs. He kept insisting it would cost nothing. I was too uptight to relax, so I couldn't really take advantage of the massage.

When he was done, I felt like I had to give him something. When I pulled out a 50 rupee note, he said his work was very hard. He usually got more than ear cleaners (100 rupees). I gave him 100 – about $3.50.

Nathan and I had been in the park two hours at that point. So much for a quiet rest by ourselves. We left.

I have thought about the masseur since then. Was he conning me? A cynic would say, "Yes." He had a way of presenting his product which worked with me. But does that mean it was a con? If I can say he conned me, then I can be the victim, he the perpetrator. It puts a gulf between us: good guy, bad guy, me and him, self and other. There is something temporarily satisfying about believing in that separation. But I can't believe it was all con.

I can see myself in him. His eyes were full of contact. I don't think you can fake eyes that much. I believe there was as much sincerity in him as there would be in me, if I were in his situation. Am I capable of conning? You bet. That very day I bought a shirt for 250 rupees. The stall keeper first offered it to me for 450 rupees. I was very interested in it, would not have minded paying 450 – about $13 for a beautiful wool shirt. But I walked away as if I was not interested. He kept dropping the price the further away I walked. I know I can fake my intentions.

To put it in perspective, a railroad clerk makes about 1,000 rupees a month – $35. If the guy in the park can make 100 rupees a day, that's pretty good by Indian standards. One rich westerner a day and he is making a darn good living.

So what would I do if I were in his circumstances? Let's say I was born in Delhi to a poor family. I never had the material advantages of growing up in America. What if I nonetheless still held the same values and beliefs that I do today: the importance of spirit, helping others, integrating body and spirit, seeing the oneness behind it all? What would my life be like? How would I support myself? How could I get by without compromising my values too much?

I could have been a masseur in the park. I'd have to develop sharper negotiating skills. I'd have to make peace with being a little more aggressive. But I could do that. I can see myself in that man's sandals. "There but for the grace of God go I." "There but for the whim of fate go I."

It's a good feeling.

Scrim

This morning I want to talk about a topic that I will no doubt return to many times. I want to talk about a very curious phenomenon, what we call a separate self.

That afternoon in the park exemplifies how connected we truly are. If an American living in a colonial house in New England can see himself in the eyes of a street vendor in a third world country, then we all must be connected together. We all breathe the same air. We all feel love, anger, dreams, and disappointments. We are all just different expressions of a oneness called "life."

This idea that we are all connected, that there is no "them," only "us," that there is a oneness about life, is not the majority view in this country. We grew up on images of the rugged individual, the master of his own fate. We tell our children they are unique and special. We put great stock in cultivating self-esteem based on individual accomplishment. We glorify the separate self and cringe at communalism. We are a narcissistic society where our ultimate concern is "How am I doing?" One could argue that we have made a religion of selfhood.

So let's look at this self that is so important to us.

Self is like a scrim. A scrim is a flat curtain of very loose weave used in theater. Set designers paint background scenes on them.

Scrims create a magical illusion. When the light shines on the front of the scrim and it is dark behind, the curtain appears as opaque as a wall mural. However, when the lights in front are dark and the lights behind are bright, the audience can see right through it.

For example, I saw a play a few years ago that used a scrim across the entire stage. The early part of the play took place on a city street. So a mural of a row of townhouses was painted on the scrim. All of the action took place in front of it.

However, as the play progressed, some action moved inside the houses. When the lights on the scrim were darkened and the lights behind were raised, we could see tables, chairs, furniture and actors "inside" the house. We could see and hear action behind the scrim almost as clearly as if it was not there.

Self is like a scrim. When we feel dark inside, when we feel angry or discouraged or depressed, self seems opaque and real. "This is who I am and it's awful!"

However, when we are filled with light, when we are filled with love and joy, self becomes gossamer. This is what began to happen to me with the masseur in the park: I could see him in me and me in him. The veil separating us seemed less substantial.

We all know these kinds of experiences. Perhaps when you fell in love, you felt deeply connected with your lover and all of life. Or walking on a misty beach, your stresses did not exactly vanish, but they faded into the sound of the surf and smell of the salt air. Or standing in a starry field on a summer evening, you felt yourself expand out as you became part of the night sky.

These are everyday mystical experiences. These are moments when the veil lifts, when your attention shifts from the scrim of self to the oneness beyond.

As a culture, we do little to acknowledge, much less cultivate, this spiritual consciousness. Because we ignore these innate spiritual capacities, they often atrophy.

So I encourage you to feel your connection with others. Even as you sit here, be aware of those around you. They breathe the same air. They have love and fear and aspirations and disappointments and dreams. You can sense these if only vaguely because you have felt love and fear and disappointment and dreams.

If we all did this for a few minutes every day, it might come home that we aren't that separate.

Implications

This is important not just for your own wellbeing. It is also vital to our survival as a species. I don't think I'm exaggerating. We either evolve or we extinguish ourselves.

We are in big trouble down here on planet earth at the beginning of the 21st century. We are pumping carbon dioxide into the air at unprecedented rates. Sheep in Australia are going blind because of solar radiation coming through holes in the ozone. Despite the collapse of the Soviet Union, we still have more nuclear weapons than needed for even the most outrageous theory of deterrence. The forests are being destroyed. Teenage suicide is epidemic. We use economic arguments as an excuse for greed and wanton disregard for the effects we are having on the environment and each other. An impartial observer from another planet would conclude, no doubt, that we are crazy. It's hard to know if an alien would consider us an intelligent species.

But listen to the nature of these issues. They are not technical in nature. They all stem from how we see and treat each other. We are not faced with a moon-sized comet or invaders from another galaxy. We are faced with ourselves.

For example, every day 50,000 people starve to death – that's about 35 people a minute. Yet according to a recent Presidential commission, every day and a half, the world spends enough money on weapons of war to solve world hunger for a year. If we gave the military one weekend off per year, we could solve world hunger.

Perhaps for the first time in human history, our difficulties are our own doing and the solutions are truly in our own hands. Our problems are not in the realm of science and technology. Our problems are in the realm of psychology and consciousness. There are no external forces stopping us, only internal. All we need is the awareness, courage, and political will to do what is well within our power.

Seeing ourselves as separate, disconnected individuals may have helped us survive on the prehistoric savanna when our technological prowess was puny. Today, this same separate consciousness – the mind of a ten-year-old — is about as useful as an appendix — an inflamed appendix, at that.

Your wellbeing and my wellbeing have always been connected, if only subtly. Today, your survival and mine are connected – and the ties are less and less subtle.

It is time we walk out of the jungle mentality and look at each other through the eyes of love. This is the gift of human consciousness – the capacity for compassion and idealism, the ability to see the light beyond the scrim. Don't let this gift atrophy. Honor it. Use it. Cultivate it. Support it in each other. Find yourself in the eyes of a stranger.

It is time we walk out of the jungle mentality and look at each other through the eyes of love. In those eyes, there is only one of us.

Love-Truth

October 15, 2000

Our faith and covenant do not call us to save the world. They call us to be a force for love-truth in the world.

Mr. Hayasi had lived on an island in Puget Sound since his father immigrated to this country from Japan many years earlier. He was a modestly successful farmer – able to support his wife, two daughters, son, and aging mother. He retained some of the old world customs, but had worked hard to adopt the practices of his new homeland. He was on friendly terms with his neighbors and was regarded as an honest man whose word could be trusted.

With the bombing of Pearl Harbor in December of 1941, public suspicion of Japanese-Americans began to grow into hysteria. In March of 1942, Lieutenant General John L. DeWitt, head of the Western Defense Command, issued the first evacuation order, giving all persons of Japanese ancestry one week to leave Bainbridge Island.

The next morning, Mr. Harrington, Mr. James, and Mr. McClellon knocked on Mr. Hayasi's door. They wished to speak to Mr. Hayasi in private. The three men were elders of the local Methodist church. They offered to buy Mr. Hayasi's farm for a dollar. They promised to hold it for him and return it to him after the war.

Mr. Hayasi consented. Within a few months, he and his family had been "evacuated" to one of the internment camps. Mr. Harrington's son moved into the abandoned farm to care for the property.

When the war was over, news of Mr. Hayasi's return spread through the small community. The elders moved the young Harrington out of the home and presented Mr. Hayasi with the deed to the property, which they sold to him for one dollar.

I heard this from Rebecca Parker, the President of Starr King School for the Ministry, our Unitarian Universalist theological school in Berkeley that I attended. I have mangled a few of the details, I'm sure. But the story is true. Rev. Parker was the minister to that parish early in her career. She had officiated at Mr. Harrington's funeral.

At the end of the service, the elderly Mr. Hayasi rose. He stood stiffly in formal attire and recited his story. He concluded by saying Mr. Harrington was a just and compassionate man.

Our faith and covenant do not call us to save the world. They call us to be a force for love-truth in the world.

Ignorance Seeds Violence

I wanted to share Mr. Hayasi's story because it illustrates two closely related points. First, ignorance is the seed of violence. General DeWitt did not know Mr. Hayasi or his family. He probably did not want to know these people – such knowledge might have interfered with his ability to do his job. General DeWitt was not an evil man. But his ignorance allowed him to promote violence against Mr. Hayasi's family.

If ignorance is the seed of violence, then knowledge and awareness are the seeds of nonviolence. The Methodist elders knew Mr. Hayasi personally. This knowing encouraged them – perhaps even compelled them – to do what was in their power to care for Mr. Hayasi and his family.

Love-Truth

Mr. Hayasi's story illustrates a second related point. In the abstract we can talk about justice, integrity, and truth as if they exist in isolation. But down here on earth with real, live, flesh and blood people, justice does not exist without compassion, integrity does not exist without acceptance, and truth does not exist outside of love. They all refer to different aspects of one unified quality.

We do not have a single word in our language that adequately captures this unified quality. Gandhi called it "*satyagraha*," which is usually translated as "nonviolence." But "nonviolence" says what satyagraha isn't – it is not violent. It does not say what it is. A better translation might be "the power of love-truth" or "the force of love-truth."

In Mr. Hayasi's story you can feel the power of love-truth when it is a unified quality.

When we separate love from truth, we run into problems. I'm sure General DeWitt thought of himself as a just and fair man trying to protect his nation. When we try to pursue justice as a depersonalized abstraction, we get things like internment camps.

It could be argued that a modern parallel to internment camps is our growing prison system. With the invention of mandatory sentencing, judges are not allowed to take personal circumstances into account when sentencing. Our legislatures (and the public hysteria behind them) fear that a judge's personal knowledge of the offenders distorts her reasoning. They want the judges to be General DeWitts, who judge without knowing the person.

In California's "three strikes and you're out" laws, stealing a bicycle can be one "strike" leading to a mandatory life sentence. The other day Eric Ross told me of a fellow who had 18 months left on a jail sentence when he momentarily picked up a small amount of drugs. Because of this, he is now in prison for life.

Without a personal context, mandatory sentencing is inherently violent.

Pursuing truth and justice without love and compassion results in less compassion and less justice.

On the other hand, if we pursue love and compassion as an abstraction that exists outside of truth and justice, we have a different problem.

You may remember, years ago three white Miami police officers shot a black youth. The police were absolved of serious wrongdoing. The officials knew the officers were in a tense situation. Under pressure, there is not always time to carefully consider all the options and possibilities. Maybe the officers overreacted a little. But we must make allowances for human frailty and not punish them for trying to do their job. This was the argument for love, compassion, and acceptance as an abstract quality.

Miami blew up. People's basic sense of justice, fair play and accountability was so deeply offended that they couldn't stand it. There were days of riots and burning.

In more recent years, we have seen similar episodes in New York, Los Angeles and other cities.

Compassion and acceptance without justice and integrity become offensive or even outrageous.

Covenant

A short while ago we recited our covenant. The second line says, "We value justice, compassion, integrity and acceptance." The phrase arose late one Saturday evening after a day-long workshop, after a year-long process of discussion and synthesis. Your covenant leaders were exhausted. Nevertheless, there is poetry and symmetry in the phrase. I hear in it a cogent statement about the importance of love-truth. This phrase reflects a firm sentiment in the congregation. So this morning I want to explore a little of what this phrase means to me. I hear in it a forceful statement about the importance of love-truth.

Inward and Outward

On the cover of the order of service is a visual aid to a quick analysis of the phrase. Love and truth both have an inward and an outward aspect. The inward dimension is how we see and relate to ourselves and those closest to us. The outward dimension is how we relate to the other people and society at large. If we consider the inward and outward aspects of love and truth, we end up with the four key words in the second line of our covenant: justice, compassion, integrity and acceptance.

The outward aspect of truth is justice, accountability and doing what is fair and equitable.

The outward aspect of love is compassion, kindness and caring for others.

The inward aspect of truth is integrity, honesty, being clear with yourself about who and what you are, not fooling yourself, rationalizing or distorting.

The inward aspect of love is acceptance and nonjudgmentally acknowledging who and what we find ourselves to be today.

These four words have other connotations. But taken as one phrase, I am struck by how succinctly they lay out love-truth with its inward and outward aspects.

The implications of this are vast and far reaching. I could speak for a year of Sundays on what this means for everything from homophobia to ecology to the Middle East to how we raise our children to the relationship between consciousness and social action. Indeed, in the next year or so, I expect we will address these topics and more. As we do so, it will be important to look at each from the perspective of love-truth, both its inward and outward aspects.

Informed

But for this morning, in the midst of the latest Mideast bloodshed and following last month's general election with its gazillion ballot measures, I want to emphasize the importance of staying informed. I have a tremendous faith in human nature. When we know what is going on, we know what is just and compassionate. The issue of justice and compassion is staying informed.

Let me give a few examples.

Rick Caughey has been working with some Zapatistas, members of a revolutionary group of Mayan Indians in southern Mexico and Guatemala. They have a number of problems. One is being gouged by large coffee companies. These multinational corporations hold off purchasing coffee beans from the peasants until they are desperate and will sell their crop for much less than it is worth. A few organizations buy the coffee at a fair market price. This so-called "fair trade" coffee is a little more expensive, but it does not exploit these people.

So we are going to shift to fair trade coffee in this church. It is not difficult to know the right thing to do. The difficulty is to be informed.

I was down at Loaves and Fishes learning what I could about the homeless situation in Sacramento. I found out that rain ponchos are very helpful to homeless people. They can wear them, use them to cover a few belongings, sleep on them, and more. With the rainy season approaching, programs that serve the homeless can't get too many rain ponchos.

I mentioned this fact in passing to a member of this church. The next day she walked in with a poncho to be given away.

Knowledge and awareness are the seeds of compassion and spontaneous acts of kindness.

Difficulty of Staying Informed

I am mindful of the difficulty of staying knowledgeable and aware. You won't find information about coffee beans or rain ponchos in the daily media. I do not consider the daily news media an adequate source of useful information.

I first came to this conclusion years ago when I was at the University of Wisconsin in the late 1960s. The campus erupted over the Viet Nam war. I was on the streets. I was on the student strike committee. Many evenings we ate dinner with the smell of tear gas floating in the back door. And I watched the national coverage of these events. What I saw on TV bore little resemblance to what was actually going on.

Several other times over the years, I have been close to stories that reached the national media. There was always a great disparity between what I actually saw happening and what was reported.

I began to realize that most of my information about what is going on in the world comes through that same media. I began to wonder if I had any idea what is really going on in Jerusalem, South Africa, the Balkans, or any place else in the world.

So if we want to stay informed, we have to find other sources: periodicals, people, first hand contact and media that take a longer view and offer a more sensitive analysis than daily sound bites can manage.

We are blessed in this congregation with our Sunday morning Forum. With minimal resources, we bring in speakers and programs that are informative, reflective, controversial at times, and enriching.

Time

The biggest problem with staying informed is time. Between jobs and kids and hassling traffic to get to the grocery store and committee meetings and soccer practice and on and on, where do you find the time? The daily media is not reliable; so turning on the radio as you drive around probably gives you more stress than useful information. So where do we find the time to seek out alternative sources of information, to personally visit programs, to sit and reflect on how we might be more helpful? It is overwhelming.

The temptation is to collapse in despair, cynicism, or quasi-intentional isolation. The temptation is to retreat into suburbs or behind gated communities and turn on the TV. But remember Mr. Hayasi. Ignorance is the seed of violence. The root of the word "ignorance" is "ignore" – quasi-intentional turning away. If we don't stay informed, we sow seeds of violence. This is just how it is.

Personally I wrestle with these issues a lot. I'm sure most of you struggle with them as well. How do you stay informed and keep your life in balance in other ways? I don't have an easy answer. I'd love to hear how you deal with this.

Love the World

Part of the answer is in the last two words of that second line of our covenant: integrity and acceptance. We must be informed not only in the outward sense of knowing the world, but in the inward sense of knowing ourselves. We must be aware of our limitations.

The sea of suffering in the world is vast. If we try to know everything and save everyone, our arrogance will exhaust us and soon be replaced by bitterness, cynicism, or despondency. Integrity and acceptance imply humility. We engage in the world at a pace we can sustain without wearing ourselves ragged. We take care of ourselves and take time to rest and reflect. We search deep in our hearts so that we will act out of love, not frustration, guilt, or self-righteousness.

Our faith and covenant do not call us to save the world. They call us to be a force for love-truth in the world.

This distinction is subtle and profound. It is captured in the phrase "It is better to light a candle than to curse the darkness." We are not called upon to save the world. We are called upon to love the world.

We value justice, compassion, integrity, and acceptance: love-truth.

Our faith calls upon us to love each other and love the world. Nothing more. Nothing less.

Loving Kindness

February 11, 2001

"May we be free of fear and danger.

"May we have joy.

"May we delight in a healthy body.

"May we have ease and wellbeing as we walk through our day."

It is late Monday morning in early February several years ago. It is the third day of an intensive meditation retreat. For three days I have been repeating and refining these four phrases. Sitting, walking, eating, moving through the meditation center – silently I've kept the phrases going. I've had lapses. At times it was so difficult remembering the next phrase that I thought, "This must be what Alzheimer's feels like." But this morning, the phrases have been coming with relative ease. Still, there is little feeling and lots of mind chatter between and during them. Things like, "It's still not going very well." "Maybe there is a better way to do this." "I wonder if I can keep from daydreaming until lunch time."

Earlier this morning Joseph, one of the teachers[15], suggested a trick. He said it was too much to expect the mind to stay concentrated for long. Instead, focus on the start of a phrase, hold attention through the phrase, then let it go. Then start again with the next phrase.

I try this. After 15 or 20 minutes it starts to work. Everything but the phrases quiets. Between each is just a touch of the meaning of the phrase, a sense of the person I'm focusing on, and empty space. Nothing extraneous. A soft, joyous feeling rises out of the stillness and spreads through me.

After 10 minutes I think, "This feels wonderful. Oh, I just wavered." I go back to the phrases. Fifteen minutes later a momentary thought comes in: "This is great." It is like sticking my head up out of the stream to look around. I just go back in.

The bell rings.

Going back to the meditation hall I notice how soft and open my heart feels. I don't have to pry it open. It is not a gigantic task I have been failing. As I quiet, my heart opens itself. Actually, it has never really been closed. How could it? It was just surrounded by fret and fear. My task is simpler: concentrate and let the agitation quiet. As I patiently return to the phrases, I begin to feel the heart's natural openness. There is a gentle confidence. I am suffused with warmth and ease and wellbeing. My breath shudders. A tear runs down my cheek.

Song: Breathe in Courage

Breathe in courage, let it be;
Behind it all your love is whole;
It's the patient heart that heals the soul.

Frame of Reference

This is Valentine's Sunday. I would like to talk about an ancient practice which is designed to open the heart, which is what Valentine's Day is all about. Mostly I want to share with you my early experiences with this practice. But first, I thought I'd give you a frame of reference for understanding the practice.

In our core, we all have a desire to be happy in the deepest sense. It is a simple wish and a profound one. It may be covered over, twisted, distorted, disguised, or temporarily forgotten. But it remains in all of us.

How can we fulfill this? Traditional Western psychology starts with the past. How did we get sidetracked? What childhood forces thwarted us? Buddhist psychology also places importance on self-understanding. But it starts in a different place. It starts in the present. This moment. What are we experiencing right now?

At any given moment, we might be experiencing many different states: anger, fear, restlessness, agitation, love, compassion, rapture, confusion, sloth, tranquility, and so on. Some of these are "wholesome states": they feel good and contribute to a sense of wellbeing. Others feel bad. It makes sense to try to cultivate

---

[15] Joseph Goldstein. The other two teachers at this retreat were Sharon Salzberg and Sylvia Boorstein.

the states that feel good. The Buddha taught a number of practices that encourage these states of mind-heart. *Mettā* meditation is concerned with four states that are considered particularly wholesome: mettā, compassion, sympathetic joy and equanimity.

"Mettā" is a Pāli word usually translated as "loving kindness." It actually has two root meanings. One is friendship. It connotes a feeling of kinship with all life. The other root meaning is gentleness. One classical image is of a gentle rain: it falls softly on everything. Mettā makes no distinction of worth about its recipients. It is unconditional. The Buddhist texts describe mettā as the feeling a mother has toward her child. It is the heart's response to seeing the goodness in another person.

Mettā has two "near enemies," that is, states that superficially resemble it but are really quite different. One is attachment, as in "I love you, I need you" or "I love it, I want it." Mettā does not want anything back. The feeling is of loving kindness flowing out with no desire for anything in return. The other state confused with mettā is sentimentality. Sentimentality is like a faded Hallmark card: it blurs the reality. It overlooks the harsher elements. It may refuse to see the faults in a person. Mettā is not like that. It sees everything very clearly. It does not romanticize. Yet it still wishes the being well.

Mettā is a "near friend" to compassion. Compassion is said to be the quivering in the heart in response to suffering. So that, while mettā is the heart's response to seeing the good in someone, compassion is the heart's response to seeing pain or hurt. Compassion can be confused with pity, sorrow or excessive grief. But in pity and grief, there is a collapse of energy back into oneself. In compassion, there is no collapse but a sense of reaching out to help relieve the suffering. Mettā and compassion are closely related. Yet they are quite distinct.

Mettā is where the practice starts because it is the easiest to get a good feeling. If you focus on the suffering in people before the mind is steady and open, it is easy to collapse into feeling bad yourself. So compassion is traditionally left for a later stage of practice.

The practice starts by sending mettā to people. So, who do you start with? The Buddha said that if you wanted to find who was most deserving and most in need of your love, you could search the whole world and not find anyone more deserving and needing than yourself. So the practice begins here. As it gains in strength, it expands to include more and more people.

It is not possible to force yourself to feel mettā when you don't. Someone asked about sending love to someone you feel angry toward. The teacher said that this is like pouring molasses into a cesspool. That's not mettā. Mettā may require discipline, but it is not forced or faked.

The practice begins by creating phrases that can resonate with the place of mettā inside you. "May I be happy." "May I be peaceful." "May I have ease and wellbeing." The phrases should be ones that feel natural and easy for you. They may be different for each person. You repeat them over and over. Sometimes the repetition feels dry. This is no cause for alarm. Focusing on the phrases tends to quiet the mind and as this happens, the heart feels its own openness. Patience is very important. The practice will develop. Confidence takes a while to grow.

The phrases are intentions. They are not mantras. Mantras may have no meaning associated with them. They can be mindless and still work. The meaning behind the mettā phrase is an important focus for the practice. Also, the phrases are not affirmations. A sentence in the form "I am happy" is an affirmation. As powerful as affirmations can be, they are not always true – sometimes I'm happy and sometimes I'm not. I feel a tension when saying something that is not true. The phrases point to intentions that can always be true. Whether I am happy or not, I may always have the wish to be happy. In fact, when I'm unhappy, the wish may be even stronger. This gives them power. Buddhism is unwavering in its commitment to truth. No "fake it 'til you make it" shenanigans.

Song: Listen Gently

Listen gently, open a little more;
Peace is already here.
No need to seek, no need to shun
Joy or pain or fear.

Country Road

It is late Tuesday afternoon, the fourth day. I am walking down a country road near the meditation center. The sky is overcast. The scene is tranquil and snow covered. Very pleasant. But I am feeling a bit heavy of spirit. Quiet sobs well up occasionally. They have been for several days – sometimes with feelings associated with them, but mostly with no particular emotion.

I stand on the edge of a field. I feel quiet grieving. There is no one around, so I do little to try to stop or control the energy. I walk a little further. "May I be free of fear. May I have joy. May I delight in my body. May I have ease through the day." I sit on a stone fence and cry more deeply. I am not even sure what I am crying about. It is hard to keep the phrases going. The sadness and grieving grows. A small part of me worries that I am letting unwholesome feelings distract me from the practice. If I stop to think about it, I do not subscribe to this notion. But the conditioning is deep to avoid unpleasantness. The night before, Sylvia, another of the teachers, had given a talk on hindrances: things like neediness, anger, excessive grief. These states do arise. They are part of our condition. But they are not really a problem if we don't worry about them. Her words come to me now. "No need to fret. It is only neediness. No need to identify with them. They are only mind states. Not to worry."

Joseph said the same thing more succinctly: "Happiness does not come from accumulating pleasant experiences." If we believe it does, then we do not open to unpleasant experience. We try to close our hearts and compassion cannot arise. However, if we can just see things as they are, then when mettā meets suffering, compassion arises. I feel encouraged just to let my feelings be what they are. The crying goes deeper.

After a few minutes I wonder if I can just let the energy go through me and keep the practice going. I try to say the phrases inside. But they seem heavy, clumsy, and out of sync with me. I gently try to reach to the core of the intentions of the phrases. They all grow out of that simple place inside that just wants to be happy.

Now the grieving fully erupts. All my life, that is all I have really ever wanted. I just want to be happy. I do practices, I do therapy, I try to help people, I try to help me. I try to please, appease, be courageous, be whatever. At the center it all comes out of a place that just wants to be happy. I feel like a little boy walking from parent to parent with my heart in my hands, trying to share it, just wanting to feel loved and good inside. No one really sees me. No one tries to help me. I don't know how to do it. I've failed. In the past, I tried explaining things to people. If they understood, maybe I could share my heart. They didn't. I collapsed into trying to get some validation. Eventually, anger, despair, and hopelessness settled in. I kept trying to explain, but no longer remembered my motives. I was lost. But underneath all these layers, I just wanted to be happy.

Tears run down my face as I look toward the sky. My fists are clenched. My yearning is powerful. "I want to be happy. I want to be free of fear! I want to have joy and energy! I want ease. I want to be free!"

I walk on another quarter mile or so. The energy softens a little. I sense that what I really want is not as ponderous and heavy as "I WANT TO BE HAPPY!" What I really want is gentler. The tone of "May I be free of fear," is closer. But the phrases are far too complex. I strip them down.

By the time I get back to the meditation center, it is dark. My heart seems lush and moist and not as heavy. I am back to quiet sobs every now and then. But there is more room inside for me. And my phrases are simpler. "May I be free. May I have joy. May I delight. May I have ease." Not as impressive, but they feel better. More akin to that gentle part of me that just says, "May I have joy and ease."

Tea and a Chickadee

After breakfast the next morning, I sit sipping tea looking out the window at the trees. I have been doing the phrase for several hours now. I feel teary and soft and sad and good. I have looked to meditation practice as something to pull me out of my muck. I have seen it as something outside to save me. Yet when I am most upset and unhappy, if I can find enough gentleness to keep looking deeper inside, I sense a simple desire to be happy in the fullest sense. That is all the phrases are about. I've been doing this practice to get away from me. And here it is pointing right to my center. I'm beginning to get it: the meditation is inside me. It feels like a personal gift from the Buddha. He taught this practice 2,500 years ago and it reflects what I want. "May I be free. May I have joy. May I delight. May I have ease."

Maybe it is okay to just say these to myself. So often I've been told it is better to love others: "Don't be so self absorbed." But, I am not bad for wanting to be happy. I may never want to wish these for anyone else.

The phrases become very deep and resonant. It feels as if there is a larger presence saying them and reassuring me that it is okay to love myself. It is as if the Buddha is out there saying to me, "May you be free. May you have joy. ..." My sense of ease and wellbeing spread out. I cry gently. I feel wonderful.

The chickadees fly onto the branches. They are all frisky with the morning. As they sit for a moment, they fluff up against the cold. My eyes rest on one: little black head and beak sticks out of a fluffy body. "May you be free. May you have joy. May you delight. May you have ease." A moment before, I thought I'd never want to say it to anyone but me. Now it flows freely to him. It feels just the same.

Song: Open Heart

> When I open up my heart
> And I forget my name
> I see God shining in your eyes
> And know we are the same.

Pathos and Joy

I wake early the last morning. Rather than try to go back to sleep, I go down to the defunct bowling alley in the basement where I like to do walking meditation. The phrase "May you be free" does not come so easily. There is a question of "Free from what? You must be trapped." I don't want to worry about being caught. I just want joy, delight, and ease.

I drop the first line and say to myself, to the chickadee, and finally to the two of us together, "May we be joyful. May we delight. May we have ease." The sobbing comes and goes. Thoughts drift in and out from time to time. My mind is not as one-pointed as it had been. I think, "Here I am, 5:30 in the morning, walking up and down a bowling alley sobbing quietly as I say to a chickadee, 'May you be joyful'. This would look bizarre to Denise. And it feels wonderful."

After breakfast I come to the final sitting with no expectations. I would like a dramatic, deep, wonderful experience to end with. But I don't think it will happen. I had to get packed and clean my room between breakfast and the sitting so I could leave promptly at 10:00. The busyness and thoughts of departing leave little possibility for states of absorption or the like.

I relax into the phrases. I send mettā to me and the chickadee. It feels very loving. Joseph says, "Let the mettā come easy. Don't try. Let your intuition guide you."

For the last few days, we have been invited to send mettā to large categories of being. I feel draw to the last three traditional categories: beings in the higher realms, beings in the middle or human realm, and beings in the lower of animal realm.

To wish joy, delight, and ease to higher beings sounds presumptuous. And it feels wonderful. The deep resonance of the few days before returns. I have faint images of Buddhas and guides and spacious beings just saying with me, "May you be joyful. May you delight. May you have ease." To send mettā to them is to acknowledge the kinship I have with them. There is an abundant flow of love and wellbeing from them back to me as we just share mettā.

To the human realm, I can no longer say "you." I use "we." "May we be joyful." I have distinct flashes of a starving child, a dear friend, my father, my son. "May you delight." Flashes of a woman in birth, Saddam Hussein, an unnamed man. "May you have ease." My wife, a man in a supermarket, someone swimming. The flashes are gentle and not distracting. There is a sense of the pathos and joy and love and texture and desire and rising and falling of the human condition. I don't feel any different toward my dearest friend or darkest political bad man. We are all just part of this realm, doing what we can based on our understanding. All of us just want to be happy. It is so moving to see it all in the same mettā.

I send mettā to the animal realm. An image of a cricket comes back again and again as does my chickadee. Tears flow out as I say to the horse down the road, "May you have joy." Worms and birds and all of them. All held in the same kind of gentle loving kindness as the chickadee. How would you hold a creature as fragile as a bird? Too loose and you'd drop it. Too tight and you'd crush it. A gentle, cradling flow of loving tenderness is what the practice is all about. "May all beings be happy."

The bell rings. The retreat is over.

Song: May We Be Free

May we be free.
May we have joy.
May we delight.
May we have ease.

Traffic Jam

That evening I take my wife and youngest son to the airport. As I drive home in rush hour traffic, I keep saying to the people around me, "May you be joyous. May you be happy. May you have ease." There is a story of a man releasing a charging elephant at the Buddha. The Buddha sent it mettā and the elephant stopped and bowed down to him. I have no illusions about having such strength of spirit as to stop a charging elephant or to perceptibly affect the mood of any commuter. The strength of my mettā is more like a single drop of cold water on a hot griddle. But it feels a world better to be sending love than frustration, well-wishing than anger. The practice really works.

One of the central insights of Buddhism is that our happiness is completely within our own control. We can be affected by what happens around us, but ultimately wellbeing arises out of what we do internally and externally. The practices of mettā or compassion or awareness are not easy. It can be extraordinarily painful to face the truth of what we find inside us. But with right effort, the barest of skillful practice and patience, we can truly cultivate our own happiness. The happiness and love radiate and can make it easier for others to find their own. But it does not force someone to be happy. That is in his or her power. We can inspire, but cannot force.

I have been cynical about the possibility of me being truly happy. It has not stopped me from trying. But my early years were so painful that I collapsed into a kind of despair of my own capacity to have joy or ease. They seemed beyond my experience. So, if I felt the pain of being angry and frustrated in a traffic jam, that seemed just like what my life has always been, more or less.

And yet, as I send mettā to surrounding motorists, I feel better. What a lovely toy. If I want to feel better, I can do something that helps. The results are not always immediate, as seven days of sitting demonstrated. It can bring pain for a time. It is a practice, not something you buy at a department store and save in the cabinet. I have to keep cultivating happiness. And it can be cultivated. It does work. It is so simple. Sending kindness feels better than ill will. So send kindness. I am astounded at something so simple, so obvious, so touching.

I send mettā to myself. A car swerves in front of me. I send it to the driver. It's natural. Sending mettā to myself does not make me selfish. Sending it to myself helps mettā spring up spontaneously with others. I do not want even to separate myself from them. I am no better or worse. Just another human being doing what I can to be content. We are all in the same traffic. We are all on this world, in this realm together. This is us. There are no them. "May we be joyful. May we delight. May we have ease."

Taking Refuge

February 24, 2002

Twenty-five years ago I began training in a Theravadan Buddhist practice called "Vipassanā" or "Insight Meditation." The retreat opened by taking refuge in the Buddha, the dharma and the saṅgha. I didn't quite understand what those terms meant. I was vaguely uncomfortable with the process and was glad to get on to the "real" meditation training.

Over the years since, I have come to appreciate these three refuges. I find them a valuable support not only for meditation but for general living. And they resonate with Unitarian Universalist principles. This morning I want to share with you something of the enthusiasm I have developed for them.

As a place to begin, will you join me in a song that paraphrases taking refuge in the Buddha and the Dharma.

Song: It's in Everyone (Pomeranz)

It's in every one of us to be wise
Find your heart
open up both your eyes.
We can all know everything
without ever knowing why
It's in every one of us by and by.

Outta Here

The phrase "taking refuge" does not fit comfortably on the English tongue. We don't use the phrase often. A few years ago, some researchers studied phrases used most often in Hollywood movies. They did not record one instance of "taking refuge." Probably it did not even occur to them to look for it.

The most common phrase they found was, "Let's get outta here." Doesn't that sound American? It was the pioneer solution to difficulty: "Let's move west. Let's get outta here." Today we see it in the politics of saying "no": no taxes, no incumbents, less government, "I don't like him."

We've become experts of what we don't like. "Let's get outta here." But we don't seem to know as much about what we do want. This criticism has been leveled at Unitarian Universalists. We seem to know more about what we don't believe than what we do believe.

"Getting outta here" is the opposite spirit of taking refuge. Getting out is escape. Taking refuge is going into a place of shelter, comfort, or restoration. Getting out is a call to action. Taking refuge is a call to rest and being.

Though we don't use the phrase "taking refuge" in our speech, we do it in our action. For example, when my kids were younger, I was often tired from the week on Friday evenings. I wanted to spend time with my family, but didn't have much energy to put into it. So we often went to the movies. It is a place where I could relax from the strain of doing anything meaningful. It was comforting and enjoyable. It was a refuge.

I used to take refuge in Hostess Snowballs. For those unfamiliar with this treat, it is a near-cousin to the Twinkie. It is made of devil's food cake, marshmallow, coconut, and enough preservative so that it can sit on the shelf unchanging for weeks. When I was a kid, they came two to a package: one white, the other bright pink. I loved them. When I ate one, it felt like a special treat and I felt special to have it. They gave me great pleasure. I took refuge in Hostess Snowballs.

I maintained my love of them into adulthood. By the time I got married, I was well aware that Snowballs were not a politically correct food. So I bought them secretly. Somehow Erika could tell when I'd had one. Perhaps it was the gleam in my eye. Probably it was the pink in my beard.

My point is that we can take refuge in almost anything. Some people take refuge in their work or staying busy, others in weekends or vacations. Some people look for security in money, in conservative political beliefs, in liberal ideals. Some turn to religion for comfort and inspiration. Some turn to gardening, aerobics or meditation.

It seems to be a natural human instinct. When we are tired, frightened, lonely, or stressed, we look for something to give us comfort, strength, or rejuvenation.

I can take refuge in eating a lot. My taste buds get pleasure. I get temporary relief from my craving. But my stuffed belly is really not comfortable, the logy feeling in my mind isn't great and the long-term health effects are bad. Taking refuge in overeating is not particularly skillful, though most of us do it from time to time.

I can take refuge in getting back at someone who has done me wrong. I may get some satisfaction: "sweet revenge" we call it. I get some relief from my anger and indignation. But in the long run I may quietly regret hurting the person and he may decide to get back at me for getting back at him. Revenge is not an intelligent refuge.

So the question is not "Do I seek refuge?" We do it all the time. The question is, "What do I seek refuge in? Are my refuges effective and useful?"

I'm sure you can think of many refuges that are better than the ones I have mentioned. The front of our hymnal contains seven Unitarian Universalist principals that are our official refuge. The Buddhist tradition speaks of three that are particularly sustaining: the Buddha, the dharma, and the saṅgha.

Taking Refuge in the Buddha

The first refuge is in the Buddha. When I first heard this over two decades ago, I thought, "Oh no, this sounds like a cult. Get me outta here." But taking refuge in the Buddha does not mean accepting Buddha as your savior as a Southern Baptist turns to Jesus.

Shortly after his enlightenment, Siddhartha Gautama was walking down a road. A group of yogis saw him and were taken by the compassion and clarity he emanated. They could feel by his presence that he had accomplished something remarkable. They asked, "Who are you? What has happened to you?"

He replied, "I woke up." The Sanskrit root "*budh*" means "to wake up." He described himself as "Buddha" or "one who has awakened." The name stuck. He became known as "The Buddha."

But he insisted that anyone could do what he'd done. Enlightenment is inherent in all of us. It is our natural state. It is who we are. We just have to uncover it, to realize it.

So taking refuge in the Buddha means taking refuge in our own Buddha nature, in the aliveness and clarity that are our essence. A Christian might call it taking refuge in the Christ within. Quakers call it the God within or the Light within. We have all the resources we need: "It's in every one of us to be wise."

Taking refuge in your Buddha nature is reverse Calvinism. Calvin saw human nature as essentially depraved. He said our only hope was intervention by external divine powers. "Amazing Grace, how sweet the sound, that saved a wretch like me." Calvin said we are all wretches. Siddhartha Gautama said we are all Buddhas. We may not feel it. We may not realize it. But we can rely on it. We can take refuge in it.

Zen Buddhists are perhaps the most fierce in their insistence that we are enlightened. In my first interview with the Korean Zen Master, Seung Sahn, he said to me, "There it is!" meaning a moment in which I was fully enlightened. I could feel the clarity, the sweetness, the spaciousness. He was right! I was enlightened! Then he said, "You've lost it." He was right again. My everyday mind had closed in and covered that wonderful aliveness.

I realized that all of us must have many such moments of complete clarity. But we are so caught up in self-images, storylines, and personal histories that say we are relatively wretched that we do not even notice these moments.

Seung Sahn's gift to me was his capacity to recognize a moment in me and help me know that it was true.

Song: How Could Anyone (Libby Roderick)

How could anyone ever tell you
That you're anything less than beautiful?
How could anyone ever tell you
That you're less than whole?
How could anyone fail to notice
That your loving is a miracle.
How deeply I'm connected to your soul.

Why Do Anything?

Well, if we are already enlightened, if we already embody Christ, then what's the fuss? Why meditate? Why work on ourselves? Why engage in spiritual practices? Why not just sit back, put our feet up and enjoy the ride?

If we knew our true nature through and through, we would just savor life. But we don't really get it. There was an episode of the original *Star Trek* series that illustrated our predicament.

The series featured Captain Kirk, a human, and his first officer Mr. Spock, who was half human and half Vulcan. Vulcans were devoted to logic. They used mental discipline to augment their intellect and suppress their emotions.

In one episode, Kirk and Spock got caught in an alien force field. It formed an energy barrier around them. When they were relaxed, the field grew weak and transparent. If they pushed against it, it got a little stronger. If they threw themselves against it, it became dense and powerful. The more they fought it, the stronger it got. Finally they realized that their prison was only as strong as their effort to be free of it. If they just saw that they were free, they could move out without effort. If there was any doubt in their mind – if there was even a flicker of concern – that was enough to feed the force field.

Kirk couldn't get out. He intellectually understood that they were free. But he still desired to get away from the alien apparatus. He thought he would be a little freer if he could "get outta here." That hedging was enough to keep him trapped. Spock, with his greater internal discipline, could see that they were free and harbor no doubts. He simply walked out.

This is a wonderful allegory for our situation. We are free, we are enlightened, we have Buddha natures, God dwells within us — use whatever metaphor you like.

The only place we can experience this wellbeing is in the moment, since the present is the only place we can actually experience anything. But if we think we would be freer, happier, or more peaceful in a future moment after doing some more "spiritual growth," then we feel less free, happy, or peaceful in this moment. We are trying to get outta here. We feel enchained relative to what we think we could be. Like Kirk, we are trapped by the belief that we are trapped.

It is a ghastly, wonderful paradox. Before we can feel liberated, we have to feel liberated. In order to be free, we have to know that we are already free.

Woody Allen once said, "I don't believe in heaven, but I'm going to take a change of underwear just in case." We say, "Ah yes, I know I'm a Buddha, but I need to change myself a little just in case."

Since we equivocate, we need help. We don't need help changing anything essential. That is not the problem. But we do need help in seeing the essentials more clearly. This brings us to the second refuge.

Taking Refuge in the Dharma

The second refuge is the dharma. *"Dharma"* means "law." Taking refuge in the dharma means taking refuge in the truth of how things are. We may not always see clearly. We may not know the truth. But we can take refuge in knowing that whatever the truth is, it will serve our highest best interest. It is a kind of reverse paranoia – the universe is not out to get us, it is out to support us.

Buddhists don't see truth as something obscure or hidden. It is not a relic buried in the wilderness waiting for us to dig it out. It is not an old tome lost in the dust of an ancient library.

Truth is out in the open. It is before us all the time. The Buddha said our problem is ignorance. In his language the word does not have the negative connotations English gives it. The root word is "ignore." The truth is before our eyes and we ignore it. Jesus said this when he exclaimed, "For he who has ears, let him hear." "Find your heart, open up both your eyes."

The problem in finding it is not the nature of truth, but the nature of the mind trying to see it. We are blinded by opinions, stances, desires, and other forms of confusion. Therefore, our task is to learn to see more clearly and simply. Taking refuge in the dharma implies a commitment to being as mindful as we can. We are humble enough to keep looking with fresh eyes.

For example, many people seem to think that happiness comes from collecting pleasant experiences. But, as we know, the barest objective observation reveals that nothing lasts. Pleasantness comes and goes. Unpleasantness comes and goes. Health waxes and wanes, spiritual communities change, relationships shift. Most people are like Kirk – they understand this without really getting it.

As our minds get clearer and less cluttered, impermanence becomes more obvious. We stop holding on to good times or pushing away difficulty. Grasping and shoving seem pointless. Nothing lasts. As we hold on or push away less, our lives lighten up. There is more ease and wellbeing.

Dharma specifically does not refer to a set of beliefs about the truth. It is not a Contract with America. It is not a liberal manifesto. It is not a New Age metaphysic. It is not a belief in impermanence, reincarnation, the 10 Commandments, or Unitarian Universalist principles. Taking refuge in the dharma is not accepting Buddhist doctrine the way a good Catholic accepts the teachings of the Holy Church.

And dharma specifically does not refer to a set of wants. We don't take refuge in what we want to be true. When I was working as a therapist, at times a client would tell me, "I don't want to look at those feelings; let's not go there." If I knew she or he was deeply committed to growth, I would say, "What you want is not relevant. The only thing that is important is what is true." Wants do not liberate us. It's the truth that makes us free.

Song: Listen Gently (Kraft)

Listen gently, open a little more
Peace is already here.
No need to seek, no need to shun
Joy or pain or fear.

Bad News

Truth is not always easy to take. An old spiritual joke says, "Self-knowledge is bad news." As our minds get clearer and more penetrating, we see all the little things we've been trying to ignore. Perhaps we see how we converse a little longer with someone we find sexually attractive or how we cut short someone who has nothing we want. We see our little coveting, greed, spitefulness, petty gripes, selfishness, and all the rest. Our egos can take quite a pounding.

As an abstract principle, we may understand spiritual work destroys inflated egos. We support this 100%. But we'd like our egos to get destroyed without getting bruised or shaken. It doesn't work that way. Our self-esteem can get battered. Spiritual work can be quite discouraging. We can become harsh with ourselves or disheartened. For this reason, we need the third refuge, the saṅgha.

Taking Refuge in the Saṅgha

"Saṅgha" literally means "gathering of monks on the path." A looser translation is "those who are consciously working on their spirituality." For all his emphasis on self-reliance, the Buddha said one of the greatest assets for spiritual work is the company of like-minded people. Similarly, Unitarian Universalists place great importance on working out our own religion, yet we enjoy coming together in churches and fellowships.

We are social creatures. We naturally want to be in a group that is small enough to appreciate our individuality (not a large herd that reduces us to being a head of cattle) yet large enough to give us some sense of belonging. This support from each other helps soften the sting of seeing our shortcomings and gives us the strength to keep looking deeper.

On intensive meditation retreats, I don't speak to or have eye contact with other people. Yet, sitting on my cushion, I know that the woman meditating next to me is doing her own difficult inner work. This is a tremendous support for me even if I don't know her name or the flavor of her issues.

We need our meditation groups, our Ministry Circles, our friends, our churches, our spiritual communities, our clans and tribes, our religious societies. Deep spiritual work is very difficult to do alone.

This does not mean that we will always find the support that would serve us best. It just means that the need for support is part of our genetic heritage. Life is easier if we acknowledge this and deal with it intelligently. We are a gregarious species.

Unitarian Universalism

These are the three refuges that I have come to appreciate so deeply: the Buddha, the dharma, and the saṅgha. I take refuge in the light within. I take refuge in the truth of how things are. I take refuge in the community of seekers. I take refuge in the light, the truth, the community.

This may sound a bit like Unitarian Universalism.

Unitarian Universalists "affirm and promote the inherent worth and dignity of every person." Buddhists take refuge in our Buddha nature. We "affirm and promote a free and responsible search for truth and meaning [and] the right of conscience …" Buddhists take refuge in the dharma. We "affirm and promote the goal of world community … [and] respect the interdependent web of all existence …" Buddhists take refuge in the saṅgha. It sounds like we are observing the same human nature and drawing similar conclusions. If Unitarian Universalism lasts 2,500 years, maybe we will develop more poetic metaphors. Rather than listing principles, maybe we will just say, "I take refuge in the light, the truth, and the community."

Meditation

So let's close with a short meditation. You've been sitting still for a while, so stretch and wiggle if you need.

Then close your eyes. And repeat these three phrases: "I take refuge in the light within. I take refuge in the truth of how things are. I take refuge in the community of seekers." Or more simply: "I take refuge in the light, the truth, the community." Then just sit with them openly and see what they evoke in you.

Song: It's in Everyone (Pomeranz)

It's in every one of us to be wise
Find your heart
open up both your eyes.
We can all know everything
without ever knowing why
It's in every one of us by and by.

Closing

Since we take refuge often, we might as well do it consciously. Where do you turn when you need sustenance and support? How much do you trust your Buddha nature to guide you? How much are you willing to look openly at the truth of where you do turn? How effective or ineffective is your refuge taking? What support is available from fellow seekers?

Joseph Goldstein perhaps summed up the three refuges when he wrote, "Be gentle with yourself. You are the truth unfolding." I like to think this is the core of our faith.

Namasté.

Resting in the Tempest

June 1, 2003

I sat across from John. I'd been seeing him once or twice a month since attending one of his meditation retreats last summer.

"How have you been?" he asked.

I reflected a minute. "I am running down a snowy mountain. There is an avalanche 20 yards behind me. At the moment I'm keeping ahead of it. So I'm doing fine. But if I stop to catch my breath, I'll be snowed under."

The glint in his eye was both sympathetic and mischievous. "You believe that in order to connect spiritually, you have to be still and quiet. It's just not true. You can be at peace as you run down the mountain in front of an avalanche. And Doug, you know how to do it when you remember that you know how."

I felt the room tilt slightly. I knew he was right. A buoyancy filled me as I connected.

John went on, "There will always be avalanches. Life is filled with tempests and tornadoes. None of these have to prevent you from connecting with that spiritual source."

I felt the corners of my mouth smile uncontrollably. "Maybe I should put less energy into fixing my foibles and more into enjoying them."

Peace While Running

This morning, I would like to speak about finding peace while running down the mountain in front of an avalanche. Many of us believe that spiritual awakening happens while sitting with our legs in a pretzel or drifting blissfully through a meadow. Since these make up so little of our daily life, we wonder if spirituality is really available as we change the diapers, drive to the grocery store, march in a demonstration, or confront our boss.

This morning I want to say, "Yes, it is always available." But there is a subtle art to noticing what is before our noses. The avalanche metaphor gives a clue to this art. But before I go into it, let me share a second metaphor. It comes from a poem by Donald C. Babcock that appeared in *The New Yorker* magazine on October 4, 1947. I hope a few of you remember it. I've read it here once or twice before.

Now we are ready to look at something pretty special.
It is a duck riding the ocean a hundred feet beyond the surf.
No, it isn't a gull.
A gull always has a raucous touch about him.
This is some sort of duck, and he cuddles in the swells.
He isn't cold, and he is thinking things over.
There is a big heaving in the Atlantic,
And he is part of it.
He looks a bit like a mandarin, or the Lord Buddha meditating under the Bo tree,
But he has hardly enough above the eyes to be a philosopher.
He has poise, however, which is what philosophers must have.
He can rest while the Atlantic heaves, because he rests in the Atlantic.
Probably he doesn't know how large the ocean is.
And neither do you.
But he realizes it.
And what does he do, I ask you? He sits down in it.
He reposes in the immediate as if it were infinity – which it is.
That is religion, and the duck has it.
He has made himself part of the boundless,
By easing himself into it just where it touches him.
I like the little duck.
He doesn't know much.
But he has religion.[16]

Duck

There are several things I love about this poem. First of all, it's about a duck, not a mandarin, Buddha, Christ or saint. It's not even about a swan, nightingale, or great blue heron. It's just a duck.

I have as much aspiration to holydom as anyone I know. Years ago Ram Dass commented about his IRS income tax forms. In the box for

---

[16] This is one of my favorite poems of all times. I referred to it many times over the years. You can find comments on it on pp. 253, 302, and 332.

occupation, he wrote "holy man." I'd like to write "holy man" as my occupation. But I don't easily identify with yogis, gurus, and holy folks. They can do all kinds of things I can't do. I find it easier to identify with a duck. If a duck can do something, I figure there's a chance I can too.

Heaving

Another thing I love about the poem is that the Atlantic heaves. Ain't that the truth? Too often we picture inner peace as a calm sunset, the water like a mirror. Or we imagine the serenity of a great snowy mountain covered with evergreens, the only movement a great bird sliding through a blue sky.

I have had calm moments in my life. I'm sure you have too. But for every minute of stillness, there seem to be 10 of waves swelling up from below or avalanches coming down on my head. And I suspect the same is true for most of you.

World

So let's look at this for a moment. Where do the heaves and the avalanches come from?

For some of you, the major tempests come from the larger world. Just when we recovered from the deficits of the Reagan years and got a little surplus in the national economy, we get a feeding frenzy of greedy policies that plunge us into record debt. Just when we get safely beyond the tensions of the Cold War, we get terrorist attacks and a petulant President willing to break international law and plunge us into a war that sows alienation in our allies and hatred in others. Just when our faith in scientific medicine gets stronger, we get a continuing epidemic of AIDS and fear of SARS.

As far back in history as we can see, there is greed, war, and plagues. It is a safe bet that they will continue into the future. It's how the world is: the Atlantic heaves and avalanches happen.

Community

What is true in the larger world is also true in our more immediate communities.

I have served churches for 30 years. I've never known a church to be a placid ocean or serene mountain for more than a few weeks. Just when everything seems fine, the furnace dies, the budget falls apart, I say something stupid and offensive in the newsletter, an elder commits suicide, a Sunday speaker has a heart attack, a pillar of the church is transferred across the country, a key staff person leaves.

These things have been happening in churches and communities for centuries and will probably continue. The Atlantic heaves. Avalanches happen.

Family

What is true in our communities is also true in our families. Just when we get the kids' lives moving in the right direction, the carpool schedule finely tuned, and even a little time for ourselves, our daughter leaps off the bed and cuts her head open, our son throws a rock through the window at school, our job is reorganized into oblivion, the transmission falls out of the car on the eve of vacation, our well-behaved son hints at unsafe sex and drug use.

Even in the most wholesome families, it's normal that the Atlantic heaves and avalanches happen.

Personal

What is true in our families is also true in our inner lives. Just when our life seems to be running smoothly, we find we're not feeling so well, a suspicious growth appears on our foot, self-recrimination creeps into our thoughts, our partner becomes distant, or 15 extra pounds settle into our thighs or midsection.

In our inner most lives, the Atlantic heaves and avalanches happen. It's been going on all our lives and will probably continue.

Good News

This may sound bleak. But it is good news. If we feel things like this in our life, it means we are in touch with the real world. Inner liberation is based on truth, not fantasy. The truth makes us free when we've developed a little poise and the art of being present.

This brings us to my favorite part of the poem.

The duck doesn't fly above the waters. He doesn't try to deny waves or rise above it all. He doesn't fly into a spiritual fantasy. If the only way we know how to handle storms is to fly above them, we'll soon drop from exhaustion.

The duck also doesn't plunge into the ocean. He doesn't wallow. He doesn't dive hysterically into a sea of despair.

The duck also does not try to control or change the waves. He doesn't wag a finger (or wingtip) at the heaving and say, "You shouldn't be so rough, you naughty waves."

And what does he do, I ask you. He sits down in it. He reposes in the immediate as if it were infinity – which it is. …
He has made himself part of the boundless
By easing himself into it just where it touches him.

The thought that the world or our lives should be different is probably the greatest source of needless suffering. The attempt to rise above, deny, indulge, or control creates what Jean Houston calls "schlock suffering." This is the pain that comes from trying to avoid the inevitable. There is enough unavoidable suffering in the world without adding schlock suffering.

Acceptance is magic. True acceptance is a middle path. It falls between the extremes of denial (trying to rise above the waves or have a tea ceremony in a snow slide) and self-indulgence (sinking into a watery despair). Acceptance falls between the extremes of control (trying to stop the waves or the avalanche) and resignation (floating upside down in the water or letting an avalanche bury us when we could get out of the way). Acceptance falls between activity and passivity.

Acceptance is about opening our eyes and hearts and being present to what is. We are responsive without being reactive. We are relaxed without being passive.

I think most of us can understand these concepts in the abstract. Applying them to real life is the challenge. So let's explore it with some specificity.

Think for a moment about what distresses you most. What catches you? What throws you off balance?

World

For some of us, the condition of the world is a source of turmoil. This year the greatest stress for me in the international scene has been this war on Iraq. I believe that this so-called preemptive strike on a sovereign nation against the will of the international community has encouraged terrorism, distrust, and violence and made the world less safe for our children. I'd rather not think about this. But denial doesn't make the world any better. Life is what it is. How do I repose in this immediacy?

I can breathe, soften, open up, and relax a little. "Yes, the world may be more edgy, unfair, and dangerous. I hope I'm wrong. But things are what they are." I just open my eyes and be with it as it is. I don't get lost in passive despair of frantic activism. Rather, I settle into the waves. For me it is a steady, long-term engagement. I don't try to save the world. Instead I try to be a force for love and truth in the world: no more, no less.

Community and Family

Another source of upheaval is our more immediate communities and families.

My dear friend Emily had two boys who were in their 20s when my boys were seven and twelve. I was talking with her once about how hard it was to deal with all the family issues – scouts, medical problems, school, soccer practices, and so on – and still find time to meditate or tend to my inner life. I had a wife and partner to help. Emily had been a single parent most of her life. Yet she had poise, depth, and clarity.

"How did you stay balanced?" I asked her.

"Oh," she said, "It was easier when my kids were younger. In those days no one had invented personal needs."

One of the greatest sources of suffering in our culture is the commercially driven belief that we should be able to do it all: raise a family, help the kids with homework, drive them to ballet, advance our career, go to school, renovate the house, and set aside time every day for yoga. It is insane the amount most of us try to do.

There is nothing inherently more spiritual about meditating in a cave, raising children consciously, or pursuing a career with heart and integrity. Each one of them can be a valid spiritual path. But doing them all is a spiritual stock-car race that is bound to leave us battered and bruised.

If you think that giving time to your children pulls you off the spiritual path, then you don't understand the nature of spiritual practice. It is about being present and open and as real as you can. It can be done sitting in the waves or running joyfully through the snow.

Personal

Another source of difficulty for us is our own personal emotional stuff.

The first year I was in Sacramento, I was without my family. They stayed back East so Damon could finish his senior year in the high school he loved. I enjoyed the freedom to just plunge into the church.

But Friday evenings, I was sometimes swept with waves of loneliness. Sometimes I even panicked, "What's the matter with me that it feels so bad. We decided to do this. It's temporary. Come on Doug, pull out of it."

Telling myself to pull out of it or rise above it, just made it worse – schlock suffering. Then I'd remember my Buddhist training. Buddhism teaches that there is something inherently unsatisfying about the world. The fact that I felt sad or lonely did not mean anything was wrong. It's just how it was.

So I'd open up to explore this feeling. I'd be with it – with a touch of curiosity. I'd explore the texture. I'd sit down in it.

There was a kind of poignancy and richness to it. There was love woven through it. It wasn't so bad when I just sat down in it.

Everything We Need

Many spiritual traditions say that each moment contains all we need to be totally happy, fulfilled, peaceful and enlightened. Some moments may contain things we don't want or not contain things we do want. But it's the difference between wants and needs. Each moment has everything we need if we can open up fully enough.

Some traditions go a step further and say that God or Life or the Universe actually gives us what we need. That might be true. But I'm less certain. It seems arrogant to assume that I am so important in the vastness of the universe that some higher power is organizing things for my benefit. Just because I am the center of my life does not mean that I'm the center of the universe.

But I do believe there is a natural harmony in all life if we learn how to cuddle in the swells. Even in loneliness. Even in carpool schedules. Even in wartime. Even in avalanches. We find harmony when we realize that this moment actually lacks nothing essential. Even when there is a big heaving in the Atlantic, we are just part of it. I don't have to change what is happening or what I'm feeling. We can rest while the Atlantic heaves by resting in the Atlantic. We can be at peace running down the mountain by not fighting it.

That is religion, and the duck has it.
He has made himself part of the boundless
by easing himself into it just where it touches him.
I like the little duck.
He doesn't know much.
But he has religion.

Mindfulness I: Wat Life

May 7, 2006

Bonnng … Bonnng … Bonnng. Bong. Bong. Bong, bong, bong, bongbongbong. As the cadence of the gong picks up, several dozen dogs near and far join in with yips, barks and outright howls. My eyes open. "Ah. It must be 4:00 a.m."

I'm lying on my side, looking across a dark floor. In the dim light from the windows I can make out cement walls.

My ribs feel bruised. They are an inch from the parquet floor. A cotton blanket and thin foam pad serve as a mattress.

I roll slowly onto my back. As the pressure and numbness come off my ribs, the pain grows intense. Then it fades.

I stare at the ceiling fan. This is a luxurious *kuti* (meditation hut) compared to the thatched hut I had been in a month earlier. It is 12-feet square, with a fan, screens on the windows and a sort of bathroom in the corner with a hose for a cold shower.

I close my eyes. I am in no hurry to get up.

By 4:30 I am up and dressed in my novice white pants and shirt. After turning the fan off I hear chanting in the distance. There is an outdoor screened area on the opposite side of the meditation hall from my kuti, about 75 yards away. The monks have started their morning chants.

I wander out of my kuti, around the backside of the meditation hall, and sit on the back steps. There are monks' rooms upstairs above the meditation hall. A monk with a tattooed shoulder descends past me. "You can join us," he says pointing to the rows of monks 15 yards away. "Or, if you like, you can meditate upstairs. It's okay," he reassures me.

"*Khòwp khun, kháp*," I say to him in Thai: "Thank you kindly." But I remain where I am. I don't intend to stay long.

By 4:45 I am back in my kuti. I know the exact configuration of zaphu and pillows that is most comfortable. I sit up straight with legs folded and hands on a small pillow on my lap. Then I relax.

I notice my abdomen rise and fall with the breath. I widen my attention to take in my whole body sitting there. Then I narrow my focus to a specific spot on my body: a so-called "touching point." In the last five weeks I've learned all 28 touching points.

With each shift of attention, I use a soft mental label: "rising" and "falling" for the breath, "sitting" for the whole body sitting and "touching" for each touching point. The labels help focus the mind and keep me honest and objective. "Rising, falling, sitting, touching, rising, falling, sitting, touching."

A dog barks. Like a rubber ball on an elastic band, my attention is yanked off the breath and lands on the sharp sound. I stay with it. "Hearing. Hearing. Hearing." I know this dog. He hangs out about 50 feet from my kuti. He believes his job is to watch for terrorists. The dog is very suspicious, so there are lots of barks.

I'm tempted to picture the dog, think about what he is doing, etc. But these are just mental constructs – thoughts. What I directly know is hearing. So I label the actual experience. "Hearing, hearing, hearing."

At the same time I notice a feeling. I don't like the dog barking and grabbing my attention. I label, "disliking, disliking."

The dog stops barking. But my aversion hangs around. I'm tempted to push the uncomfortable feeling aside and go back to the breath. But the meditation instructions are to stay with a phenomenon until it fades or a significant amount of time has gone by. So I stay with it. "Disliking. Aversion. Disliking."

In a few minutes the disliking fades. I look for it, but it is gone. So I go back to "rising, falling, sitting, touching."

The dog barks again. "Hearing. Disliking. Disliking."

This time the aversion fades more quickly. Short barking spells recur again and again. I just notice hearing and disliking as they arise.

In about 10 minutes, the hearing continues to arise, but the disliking doesn't come up anymore. In about half an hour, even the hearing fades into the background. The barking is just part of the sounds of life around me: birds, crickets, barking, rustling wind. It no longer pulls my attention away from the breathing. Rising, falling, sitting, touching are stronger than the sounds.

The dog is no longer disturbing. We call this "serenity." I can notice the bark with greater clarity and precision than when I was averse to it. But it doesn't perturb me. I'm a bit more serene.

Rising, falling, sitting, touching. Rising, falling, sitting, touching.

A thought flickers through my mind. It is 5:30 in the morning. Thailand is 15 hours ahead of California. Back home it is yesterday afternoon at 2:30. Erika is at work dealing with her programs and organizational changes.

I am no longer labeling "rising, falling, sitting, touching." I am not even aware of my breathing or my body. I'm just thinking about Erika.

The meditation instructions are not to suppress or ignore anything, but, so much as possible, be mindful of whatever is going on. What is going on now is I am sitting in a kuti in a wat in Chom Tong in northern Thailand thinking about my wife. The content of my thoughts is not important. We love our thoughts and their content. But from the perspective of spiritual training, the fact that I am thinking is more important than what I am thinking about. So I label the process: "Thinking, thinking, thinking." This loosens the grip of the thoughts so I notice them more clearly: thinking, thinking.

Usually, it only takes a few labels before the thoughts dissolve on their own. The thinking just stops, often in mid-sentence. But this morning, the thinking fades slowly and reluctantly. There is more going on than just an idle thought. I'm missing Erika. I feel lonely. So I label: "Missing her. Lonely. Lonely."

The temptation is to think about the feelings. But thoughts can go on forever. And what is driving my consciousness isn't a thought. It is a feeling. I've learned a trick in relating to feelings. They have body sensations with them. So I scan my body. I notice heaviness in my chest and fuzziness in my head. I label these: "Heavy heart. Fuzzy. Heavy heart." These feelings are uncomfortable. I don't like them. So I label that as well. "Heavy heart. Disliking. Lonely. Disliking."

The sensations are actually quite manageable. My heart softens and expands. The disliking fades. A quiet aching remains for a while. "Aching. Poignancy. Aching."

Bonnng … Bonnng … Bonnng. Bong. Bong. Bong, bong, bong, bongbongbong. It is 6:00 a.m.: time for breakfast.

Not all sittings go this smoothly. Sometimes I get lost in thoughts or explanations for a long time. Sometimes my body aches too much to sit still. But generally, the sittings in the cool of the morning are easier.

Breakfast

I weave through the rows of kutis to the kitchen and dining area. Wat Phra Chom Tong has over 200 kutis. They also have dorm-like rooms for children and high school kids.

The kitchen has two serving areas: one vegetarian, the other not.

The Thai make no distinction as to what kind of food is appropriate for different times of day. The morning meal is usually rice or noodles in a broth with tropical vegetables. Bowls are set out. The serving size is ample for the average Thai. But for a *farang* – a Westerner – with a body twice that of the average Thai, the serving is a bit meager.

I bring my bowl next door to a screened dining area. This morning, judging by the discrete logos on their white shirts, there are at least three groups of bleary-eyed teenagers from different high schools. They've come to spend a week in meditation training as part of their education. There are also several families including kids, adolescents, parents, and grandparents who have come to "meditation camp" for a few days' holiday. And there are nuns and other solo meditators like myself. The monks have a separate dining area.

As I sit down a group of eight seven-year-old kids gather round another table. They wear shorts and T-shirts with comic book heroes. These "monklets" (as I think of them) are in training. In a few days they will be bald and robed. They are very sincere and at the same time still very much kids. A nun starts a blessing which they pick up: *"Pañisankha yoniso pindapatam patisevami …"* It asks that food be used to sustain the body and mindfulness and not to feed bad habits. Most people recite the blessing quietly before eating in silence.

After breakfast, I wash my bowl and silverware in the back with soap and cold water. I rinse them in sinks filled with cold water and set them in a rack to dry. The U.S. Health Department would shut this place down in an instant. But this is Southeast Asia, not America.

Late Morning

After breakfast I go back to my kuti, brush my teeth, take my vitamins and supplements, straighten things up, sweep out the kuti. It barely needs straightening and sweeping. But there is very little entertainment here, so I am quite thorough. People in the kutis around me spend a half hour sweeping the leaves around their kuti. This seems excessive to me. But I understand the drive to find something to do.

By 7:00 a.m. there is nothing left to do but meditate. I am supposed to alternate between an hour of sitting meditation and an hour of walking meditation. I stand with my back against one wall: "Standing, standing, standing." I lift my heel and label "heel lifting," lift the foot, "lifting" and continue with "moving," "lowering," "touching," "pressing." Then the other foot: "heel lifting, lifting, moving, lowering, touching, pressing."

In the walking meditation, my attention stays on the foot. If thoughts or feelings arise, I note them briefly, and go back to the feet. The walking emphasizes *samādhi* or concentration: keeping the mind focused on a single object. Sitting meditation emphasizes mindfulness: being aware of whatever arises without holding to a single object.

I have a timer that lets me know when an hour has passed. Thus I alternate between walking and sitting meditation until the gong rings at 11:00 a.m.. Time for lunch.

Lunch

Lunch is more elaborate. Food is set out in large pans. We serve ourselves as much as we want.

I'm not fond of spicy food. Thais are very fond of spicy food. I can't tell if a food is spicy or not until I get to the dining area and try it. So I take more food than I need, knowing I won't eat all of the spicy dishes.

Afternoon

Afternoons are a challenge: sometimes a dread. No food is served between noon and dawn the next morning. There is no meal to break up the afternoon. And while mornings are cool to mild, the afternoons can reach 90° in my kuti with humidity around 90%. I bought a second fan in the hardware store across the street from the Wat so I can sit and walk in front of two fans. Still, in the heat, my mind can go to mush. In the afternoon I'm more likely to use labels like "drowsy," "fuzzy headed," "hot," "uncomfortable." As days went by, these feelings became less distracting. Like the dog barking, I could notice them but not be thrown off as much.

All that I experience is not uncomfortable or neutral. Far from it. There are times I smile uncontrollably. There are long stretches of delight, joy, happiness, or deep, deep stillness. I cry a lot in short spurts. Sometimes out of sadness. Sometimes out of joy. But most often out of release that feels sad and joyful, both and neither.

My teacher says the amount of joy I experience is unusual, a sign of having done a lot of good things in the past: a karmic return. These waves of energy are a good thing. They can be healing. But they can also be a problem if I get attached. So he encourages me to stay very mindful of any liking I have.

Noting "delight," "joy," and "happiness" causes them to grow stronger. Relaxing into them causes a shift toward deep, serene stillness. But, if I notice how much I like them and label "liking," "liking," "liking," they fade within a few minutes.

All things pass inevitably. The challenge is not to hold onto the positive or push away the uncomfortable. This allows for an even deeper source of happiness to emerge: a source that is not dependent on particular feelings or body states. This is a source that can be present when we feel either joy or agony.

Evening

Between 5:00 and 6:00 p.m. I go to "report" my meditation experience of the last 24 hours to Ajhan Tong. He is in his 80s. He is northern Thailand's most venerated meditation master. People come from long distances to meet him. He doesn't speak English and usually is not available to foreigners. However, I trained for three weeks with another monk who then brought me to Ajhan Tong and does the translation.

The interview is formal with kneeling, bowing, careful politeness, and deference. And in the midst of this formality, he might pick his ears or take a cell phone call. Sometimes I wait as long as two hours to get in to see him as *farang* – Westerners – are always last.

At first I found this disconcerting. He was my only support and guidance. In desperation, I pressed him, even if I broke the social formulas. He was unflappable and never offended. In fact, when I push him, he becomes sweet and deeply penetrating. By the time I left I saw why he is so venerated.

After reporting he adjusts my meditation instructions. I leave.

Now, it is cool enough to take a cold shower, do laundry if need be, and other small chores. Then I settle in for a few hours of meditation before going to bed between 9:30 and 11:00 depending on my level of energy and back pain.

A few hours later at 4:00 a.m., the gong sounds and the daily cycle starts again. I spent seven weeks in this kind of schedule.

Richness

Many of you have asked what I gained in Thailand. There were days when every hour could fill a sermon. And the topics ran from the personal to the political. For example, these monasteries have an understanding of mindfulness that is more precise, elegant, and practical than anything I've come across before. I'll share a little about this next Sunday.

On the other end of the spectrum, America is organized around consumption and being the best. Thailand is organized around generosity and kindness. Unpacking the implications is more than I can manage in a handful of sermons. So I ask for patience. Stories will be trickling out of me for a while.

This morning, I do want to thank you for granting me the sabbatical time to visit India, Nepal, and Thailand over these last six months. And I do want to offer something that might be useful.

Liking and Disliking

So let me pull one thread out of my experience and invite you to reflect on it in your own life. Consider this a quick introduction to Thai wisdom.

There is probably nothing inside us that causes more upset, more disruption of clarity, more derailing of wellbeing, more spiritual dis-ease, and more suffering than liking and disliking. Grasping, wanting, holding, yearning, pushing away, aversion, rejecting, and liking and disliking in any variation are inherently uncomfortable.

And if we try to ignore them, they implant deep inside us and grow like weeds. They grow into mental habits and recurring thoughts. They grow into agitation, stress, and fatigue. They sprout behaviors and addictions. And collectively, we end up stomping around the globe trashing the environment, starting wars, and exploiting people when we know better.

If our liking and disliking could be uprooted we'd live more harmoniously with other people and the environment. Our lives would become serene and joyful. Our mood would be serene. Our hearts would be luminous. In fact, the technical definition of nirvana is the absence of clinging, that is, the absence of liking and disliking. If we could get rid of them, we'd be in heaven.

But good luck. We can't control them. We have a little control over how we act, but no control over the states themselves. They arise on their own. The dog barks and aversion just appears. I think about my family far away and loneliness and disliking come up. A wave of joy spreads through me and I love it. We can't control this any more than we can control the weather.

We'd like to. We have lists of what is politically correct and incorrect to think and feel.

However, ultimately we are not in control. A car swerves in front of us: anger and aversion emerge. We see a fruit tart: hunger springs forth. Attempting to control our liking and disliking is itself a form of liking and disliking. It strengthens them.

So, what can we do?

The way to uproot liking and disliking is to cultivate mindfulness of the states themselves. As you attend to the actual experience, it tends to change or fade all by itself.

For example, someone lets the door slam in your face. Intense disliking emerges in you. You didn't create the disliking. You don't control it. It just comes up.

But, if you notice, "Ah, yes, upset. Disliking. Aversion. Ah so. I recognize these," and stay with the actual experience, it passes. It arises on its own. If you don't hold it or push it away, it fades on its own sooner or later. Conversely, if you hold it, push it away, or try to ignore it, it turns into a healthy weed sprouting thoughts, feelings, behaviors, and sometimes addictions.

But please don't take my word for it. Don't even take your own word for it. Try it out. Cultivate mindfulness and see. Cultivate awareness of holding and pushing away as they arise. Don't worry about the object of wanting or aversion: the guy who slammed the door in your face, the fruit tart on the table, the attractive person in the next row. Just notice the feeling itself. Scan your body to see what sensations you find.

Really stay with it as long as it lasts. Hold it in your heart. Be patient and attentive. See what you discover.

We'll pick up from this point next week.

As a closing thought: when meditation masters from Southeast Asia are invited to America to teach, they are blown away by the amount of self-criticism and self-hatred in Americans. So bring a lot of heart to your awareness. Try not to be critical or judgmental of your experience. If you are not observing yourself with the eyes of kindness, you are not truly mindful because kindness is essential to mindfulness.

As one meditation teacher, Joseph Goldstein, put it, "Be gentle with yourself. You are the truth unfolding."

Mindfulness II: Transformation

May 14, 2006

You can search long and hard for animals on the African savanna and find few. Naturalist photographers use a more effective strategy. Rather than search for animals, they search for a watering hole, settle in, and wait for the animals to come to them. All animals come for water sooner or later.

Gil Fronsdale, a meditation teacher in Palo Alto, suggests that mindfulness works the same way. To untangle your problems or deepen your spirituality, you don't have to search the wilds or your psyche or spirit. Just cultivate mindfulness. Then all that you need will come to you: it will appear and make itself known.

To be sure, mindfulness will not satisfy all your spiritual curiosity. For example, it won't tell you what is going to happen when you die. Will you reincarnate, go to a heavenly realm, disappear into oblivion, or something else? Mindfulness won't tell you because these are speculative questions. No one really knows the answer though some people are very impressed with their opinions. When you die, you'll know. Until then all you can do is guess.

However, if you want to know how to live a happy, fulfilling life you don't need answers to speculative questions. You need answers to the practical ones like, "How do I slow down?" or "How can I improve this relationship?" or "What will help me feel more wellbeing?" or "What's my next step?"

Mindfulness can help all these. It is a deceptively simple tool.

I have touched this topic before. But after meditating in Thailand for nearly two months, I want to distinguish between superficial mindfulness and transformational mindfulness. One just skims the surface. The other brings forth wisdom.

So this morning I want to describe transformational mindfulness, give a few examples, and (relate these to the purpose of religion and spirituality. And we'll leave time at the end for your reflections and questions.

Transformation

The word "mindfulness" came into popular culture from Buddhism. It is a translation of the Pāli word, "*sati*." In the West we distinguish between mind and heart. Buddhism does not. "Sati" can also be translated as "heartfulness." To be mindful is to take something to heart. Today is Mother's Day. Think of mindfulness as how a mother watches her small child. One teacher translated it as "calm abiding." You look at something with a steady, spacious heart.

Or think of mindfulness as photographing animals in the wild. First you must be patient. You wait quietly to see what comes along. If a wildebeest shows up, you don't say, "Oh, there's a wildebeest," snap a picture, and go back to reading a book or listening to your MP3 player. You don't assume that just because you recognize something that you know it deeply. And you don't critique the beast: "It shouldn't hold its head that way." "Why doesn't it move the other foot first?" "It shouldn't be so tense." You curiously watch for nuance and subtlety.

And you keep observing until the animal is gone. This is very important. Conceptually we know that everything changes. But for the cultivation of practical wisdom, it's important to observe the disappearance. If you don't, your mindfulness is superficial. By staying with an experience until it fades, impermanence becomes a living, breathing, immediate reality.

Let's look at a couple of examples to see how this works.

Back Pain

I have not fully recovered from my bike accident of two years ago. I'm still in physical therapy for a frozen shoulder and for muscles and tendons in my back that don't work properly.

So, on my seven-week retreat, I had back pain. As my back got sore, my first inclination was to ignore it. Who wants to look at something that hurts? If I didn't pay attention to it, maybe I could get through the next sitting or walking period before it became too painful. So I put more energy into watching the breath, daydreaming, or anything but the pain.

Sound familiar? How many of us first respond to a problem by pretending it isn't there? "Maybe it'll go away by itself if I just don't give it any attention."

As I ignored the pain, the muscles in my back tightened up. This is a biological reflex to pain: it stabilizes and numbs an injured area.

So, in the short run, looking elsewhere – ignoring my back – felt better. You may have noticed this in your life. If you ignore a problem, in the short run it does feel better than dwelling on it.

But the long run is different. Those tight back muscles fatigued and started to ache themselves. So now I had the original soreness and the area around it sore as well. The pain spread! If I continued to ignore it, it just got worse and worse until it was unbearable and impossible to ignore.

So, in the short run, inattention felt better. In the long run it felt worse.

On retreat, the only tool I was supposed to use was mindfulness. Soft, receptive attention caused the tightness to relax, the numbness to dissipate, and the hurt to intensify. It felt like a knife was sticking in it. It took a lot of faith to stay with it.

However, I was not adding tension or fatigue to the pain. As I tolerated it and let the muscles relax anyway, the throbbing gradually dissipated. Sometimes it took five, ten, or thirty minutes. But if I stayed with it, eventually it began to subside.

So mindfulness caused more hurt in the short run but less in the long run. What had been intolerable became easier and sometimes even disappeared.

Acceptance in and of itself is quite healing. We've all probably experienced that in other areas of our lives.

There are limits to the healing power of mindfulness, to be sure. It should be used compassionately and intelligently. There are times when I still had to shift my posture. But when I was mindful, I was able to be more discerning about this as well.

Principle: Short and Long Run

The basic principle is: lack of mindfulness feels better in the short run and worse in the long run. Mindfulness feels worse in the short run and better in the long run.

If this principle applied only to back pain, it wouldn't be worth spending sermon time on it. But it is a metaphor.

For example, if we listen closely to many people's speech, we can hear a subtext, "Do you like me? Do you like me?" Maybe you notice it quietly in yourself. We are social creatures and like to be liked.

In order to be liked more, we can modify our behavior and present ourselves as smart or clever or caring or attentive or tough or whatever we think gets appreciation. If it works, it feels good in the short run. We get positive regard and emotional strokes.

But, like fighting back pain, in the long run it's tiring. It's self-defeating. In the long run we don't know if people like us for who we are or for who we're pretending to be. People might like an image we project but we don't know if the real us is likable. This leaves us secretly lonelier. It intensifies the drive to get people to like us.

On the other hand, if rather than act in what we think are pleasing ways, we just become more mindful, then what?

Beneath wanting to be liked is loneliness or isolation or sadness. We had numbed that feeling in an effort to get people to like us. As we relax, we become aware of the underlying sadness. As with back pain, mindfulness at first feels worse.

Mindfulness of feelings takes some finesse. It's important to feel the feelings on their own terms. If we just think about being lonely or sad, we translate the feelings into thoughts. Our minds might produce thousands of lonely, sad scenarios. "I'm going to be alone for ever." "I'm completely unacceptable." These are just speculations, delusions. They don't help.

So it is important to know feelings where they live. They live in the body. All feelings have a body component. There are sensations somewhere. If we aren't used to attending to these, it may take a little time and patience to find them. But they are there.

Maybe we notice tightness in the chest, a slight burning around the eyes, or a constriction of the breathing.

As we bring mindfulness to these sensations, the mental stories, fantasies, and images slack off. The sensations of sadness, grief, or loneliness grow. They are not comfortable. But usually, they are manageable. It's okay to be with them. They aren't completely overwhelming. We can be with them.

And then, after a while, the sensations begin to shift. Our thoughts about loneliness can go unchanged forever. But the actual experience is alive and evolves with attention. With time and loving attention, it begins to dissipate. Like the animals by the pond, eventually they leave.

The secret is that, in being mindful of loneliness or sadness, we are with ourselves in a heartful way. Leaving aloneness alone makes us feel more alone. Ignoring our sadness makes us sadder. We become alienated from ourselves. But with mindfulness, at least we have our own good attention, our own company. We've got at least one person's kindness. And as I've said before, the person whose love we need the most is our own.

And since we are letting ourselves be ourselves, we start to relax. We don't get so worn out.

Mindfulness can be uncomfortable in the short run, but in the long run it helps us relax and be ourselves. If we happen to connect with another person, it is authentic. And if we don't connect with someone, we still have a much greater sense of inner freedom. How we act is less driven by fear of what others may think and more by what emerges from us.

Summary

Again, the principle is: turning away from what is uncomfortable feels good in the short run but makes life more painful, complex, stressful, and unmanageable in the long run.

Being heartfully aware of what is uncomfortable feels worse in the short run. But in the long run, it brings the possibility of deep healing and a greater sense of freedom. It lets us relax and get to know who we are a little better.

Physical pain or getting people to like you may not be concerns for you. But we all have our issues. What is it that gets to you? Where do you get thrown off balance: work related issues; family or friendship issues; stress; addictive habits? We've all got something.

I invite you to take whatever gets to you and bring more mindfulness to it. I'm not talking about a superficial, glance-as-you-go, "yeah, I got it" mindfulness. I'm advocating transformational mindfulness. Profound mindfulness takes some time. It is patient, steady, calm, kind, and curious. And it doesn't try to change anything. If you stay mindful of difficulty long enough, it will change organically on its own. If it doesn't, you aren't seeing deeply enough. So open up more, be curious, receptive and heartful.

With patience, transformational mindfulness can help untangle seemingly impossible situations.

Eccentric

Why am I making such a big deal of this?

If we do experience God as an active force in our life, how do we know the divine guidance that is available to us? If we don't think in terms of God, the basic question is still, how do we know the fullness of our being? Mindfulness goes to the core purpose of religion and spirituality of any persuasion. That purpose is not to make us into a better Christian or Jew or Muslim or Buddhist or humanist or pagan or atheist or Unitarian Universalist.

About 30 years ago Sheldon Kopp wrote a book called *If You Meet Buddha on the Road, Kill Him*. This is an old Zen saying: if you see some image of perfection to emulate, get rid of it. In other words, if we think the purpose of religion or spirituality is to tell us who we should be, then religion and spirituality have failed us miserably. They may make us miserable as well.

The purpose of religion, spirituality, and my sermons (if they are successful) is to inspire us to look more deeply for divinity within; to look with greater curiosity to discover who we *really* are, both within ourselves and within the social-political community of which we are a living part.

The Buddhist suttas contain a story about an *arahant*, a fully enlightened monk. A group of monks came to a river one day. This arahant lifted up his robes and pranced on his toes across the water. The other monks thought this was undignified for an exalted being. So they complained to the Buddha. The Buddha said, "Oh don't worry about it. In many previous lives he was a monkey. It is in his nature to be like that."

A friend of mine once drove the Korean Zen master, Seung Sahn, from Logan airport north of Boston down to a Zen center in Providence, Rhode Island. As they drove through downtown Boston, every time she stopped at a stoplight he hopped out of the car, ran around it, and hopped back in. He was a character. In my interviews with him he was remarkably clear. And he was totally eccentric.

There is no mold that fits all evolved beings. As they get clearer and clearer, they become more and more who they are in their own unique ways.

The same holds for us. Mindfulness is the most powerful tool we have for transformation. It allows the divine to manifest more clearly in us. It doesn't get us out of this world or out of ourselves. It pulls us more fully into both. It doesn't transform us into a Christ or a Mother Theresa or a Gandhi or a Buddha on the road. It transforms us into something closer to our true nature. It only transforms us into who we really are. And that is unique for each of us.

Religion, spirituality, and our life are so much more interesting if we aren't trying to make ourselves into someone we aren't. It is so much more interesting if we assume we don't really know who we are in all facets and develop a tender, kind, loving and fierce curiosity about who we are.

True mindfulness takes a lot of heart. As the fox in Antoine de Saint-Exupéry's *The Little Prince* said, "It is only with the heart that one sees rightly." True mindfulness is kind and heart-based. Americans have a lot of fear and self-criticism buried in them. Sometimes this is covered over by a layer of narcissism. But we have harsh voices deep inside. So mindfulness takes a lot of courage and heart to penetrate all of these. But in the end it allows us to emerge as the unique being that we are. Not Buddha. Not Christ. Not even a Unitarian Universalist. Just who we are. That is enough. That is all we have.

A famous Thai meditation master, Achaan Chaa, once said:

> *Try to be mindful and let things take their natural course. Then your mind will become quieter and quieter in any surroundings. It will become still like a clear forest pool. Then all kinds of wonderful and rare animals will come to drink at the pool. You will see clearly the nature of all things in the world.*

Spiritual Eyes

November 26, 2006

I pulled my bike off the American River bike path. My mind was cluttered. My mood was vaguely disgruntled. Despite riding for 40 minutes, I was brooding over the past week's stresses more than taking in the woods and fields around me. Three guys in multicolored spandex blurred past. Two talked loudly into cell phones. Annoyance rose in me like a swelling darkness.

At that moment, a little girl appeared on the path. Her bicycle was outfitted with training wheels and bright pink ribbons streaming from the handlebars. Sandy red hair flowed from the helmet perched on the back of her head. Her eyes were wide and her mouth grinned as she whispered loudly, "There's a deer!" and peddled by without slowing.

I looked up. A deer considered me, saw nothing interesting, and returned to munching the grass.

Despite my rising tide of grumpiness, I found myself smiling: not at the deer or even the little girl per se. It was the sense of mystery in her eyes. Her loud sotto voce. She had seen something magical – something sacred – and she wanted me to have the same experience.

And I did.

I imagined looking through her eyes. The little girl was an up-and-coming angel who had sprinkled me with fairy dust of awe and wonder. The guys with cell phones became festive splashes of boyish enthusiasm racing into the distance. The deer, the girl, the guys, and I were intertwining threads of light. The trees, fields, river, clouds, asphalt path, deer, other humans, and I all came from the same earth. We are all related to each other. We all belonged here.

And it was good.

An old man on an ancient green Schwinn bicycle peddled by. I smiled broadly, my heart spread out to the trees. Then I felt a little self-conscious, grinning away beside the path. I climbed on my bike and started pumping slowly. My smile turned shy. But it hung around for a few more miles.

Spirituality as a Quality

My friends, December is about to descend. December offers a cacophony of qualities: goodwill and greed, peace and profit, hope and hype, love and lavishness, bright lights and dark days, joy to the world and make haste while the sales last.

Some of us view the month with a swelling, dark annoyance or rising tide of grumpiness. Others of us view it with sense of magic and sacredness. Most of us have some mixture of these qualities. Perhaps you are asking yourself, "So, how am I going to handle Christmas this year?"

Traditionally ministers are supposed to offer wise and pithy advice as to how to negotiate the season for spiritual, not material profit.

This morning I will attempt to fulfill my sacred responsibilities. To wit, I would like to explore a way of looking at spirituality as a quality that can be cultivated. This will lead to the importance of informal everyday spiritual practice. And this will lead to a specific practice called "Spiritual Eyes." This is the practice the little girl with pink bicycle streamers inspired in me. It is appropriate to the season.

Quality

Let me begin with the question, "What is spirituality?"

It's been said that spirituality is a verb, not a noun. It is something we do, not something we are or something we hold. This morning, I'm suggesting that it is not even a verb. It is an adjective or adverb. This is to say, it is a *quality* we experience in something or a *way* of doing things. It is not a *thing* or *doing* in and of itself. It is a characteristic of experience or a characteristic of how we act.

As an analogy, consider the color red. It is easy to think about red in the abstract. You can picture redness in your mind. But in fact, it does not exist by itself. It is a quality of a red car, red teapot, red shirt, poinsettia, sunset, fire engine, or stop sign. If we take the object away, if we remove the car, teapot, poinsettia, or whatever, there is no red.

I'm not saying red does not exist. I'm just saying it has no existence apart from other objects. It's a qualifier, not an object.

Or consider wetness. It is a quality of some objects: water, puddles, streams, rainy days, baths, fruit juice, and others. But if we take those objects away, there is no wetness. Wetness does not exist apart from wet objects.

Similarly, spirituality is a quality, not a thing in and of itself.

I have ridden my bike past that same bend in the path many times without feeling magic or awe. I've stopped and gazed at the animals and people and felt no luminosity. If spirituality were a thing or a doing, I'd just have to go there, do that thing or hold that substance and I'd feel spiritual. But usually I don't.

I suspect all of us have had spiritual experiences in ordinary situations. Maybe, sitting outside on a lunch break, we were taken by the beauty of the day. Or while walking in the woods, watching children on a swing set, lying under the stars, or being enveloped in music, the ordinary seemed sacred and the sacred seemed ordinary. Spirituality was all around us.

We've probably also been to those same places and done some of those same things and felt distracted, isolated, numb, or uninspired. The ordinary seemed ordinary and the sacred seemed nonexistent.

In fact, if we examine the most powerful spiritual experience in our lives, it had a setting, a time, a history, other things happening around it. Whatever we were doing – whether it was walking, praying to God, or dancing a sacred dance – it could be done without that spiritual quality. Walking, praying, dancing can be experienced as simple, ordinary, nonspiritual things. The spirituality of that event was a quality of that particular incident.

So spirituality is not about a place, a thing, or a doing. It is not a noun or a verb. It is a qualifier.

Unitarian Universalism as a Quality

By the way, Unitarian Universalism implies that spirituality is a quality more than a thing. If spirit is a thing with an independent existence, then what we believe about it may be our ticket to salvation. But if it is a way of being, then what we believe may not be as important as how we relate to others and ourselves.

If we come at life with fear, anger, greed, and hatred, then the quality of bitterness flavors our days. If we come at life with love, courage and compassion, then the quality of sweetness and ease flavor our days.

So the question becomes, how do we cultivate these qualities?

Practice

I am a great fan of formal spiritual practice. I used to fast for a day and a half each week. I do at least one week-long meditation retreat each year. I sit in formal meditation for an hour most days. There is a Catholic monastery up the road where you can enter into a life of intensive prayer for a few days or a few weeks. There are Sufi retreats where you can spend a weekend in sacred dance.

But one drawback of formal practice is it makes spirituality seem separate from ordinary life. Spirit seems like a special place to go, a special substance we gain or a special action we do. It makes spirituality seem like a thing or an action: a noun or a verb if you will. We go to that special place or do special actions to get this spiritual stuff.

So whether we pursue formal disciplines or not, at some point we want to look at our everyday life. We do a lot of ordinary things – work, eat, raise kids, talk to family, vote, think, and so on. The quality with which we do those is the seedbed for spirituality.

Spiritual qualities can be part of just about anything, including driving the car, taking out the trash, buying groceries, or tending the garden. And these qualities can be absent from anything including prayer, meditation, and church.

Everyday Practice

This sermon is the first in a series on everyday spiritual practices. Once a month or so I'll come back to something we can do in daily life that helps us perceive in a spiritual way.

Some of the practices I'd like to talk about include patience, seeing through the eyes of kindness, forgiveness, apologizing (the other side of forgiveness), generosity, courage, commitment to speak the truth in love, renunciation and simplicity, service as a practice, and more.

Spiritual Everywhere

But for this morning, I invite you to consider how it would affect your day to see spirituality as a quality that is potentially embedded in everything.

It has been said often enough that God is omnipresent: the divine is everywhere. But if we think of God, divinity, or spirituality as a separate entity, this is confusing. How can God be everywhere in a world where children are raped? How can goodness be a part of everyone when ordinary people can be trained to be sadistic torturers (consider Abu Ghraib)? Where is the spiritual in corporations that operate as sociopaths (looking out for their proverbial bottom line with scant concern for who is hurt)?

But if we see spirituality as a quality, like color or wetness, the confusion disappears. Just because a car can be red doesn't mean it is. Just because the patio can be wet doesn't mean it is. Just because we all have the potential for kindness and generosity doesn't mean that we manifest these. They are qualities to be cultivated.

Our Unitarian Universalist principles begin with the phrase "we affirm and promote" the inherent worth and dignity of every person." Our intent is to both affirm (that is see) and promote (cultivate) these qualities.

What would it mean to see the sacred as possible in everything?

Spiritual Eyes

"Spiritual eyes" is a practice that helps us see the sacred potential in everything. It helps bring this quality into the world and deepen our own lives, even while holiday music plays in the elevator.

The practice is simple: you just shift how you look at the world around you. The little girl on the bicycle triggered it in me. Nothing around me changed. My consciousness just flipped into a different mode.

That's all there is to it.

But let me elaborate anyway.

We can look at the world through the eyes of cynicism and pick out all the hypocrisy. There are so many ways people say one thing and do something else.

We can look at the world through the eyes of want and see all the good things other people have that we want but don't have.

We can look at the world through the eyes of annoyance and pick out all the stupid, irritating things people do.

We can look at the world through the eyes of fear and see threats and potential threats that abound.

On the other end of the spectrum, Carmen Bernos DeGasztold prayed for "such philosophic thoughts that I can rejoice everywhere I go in the lovable oddity of things." We can look at the world through the eyes of "lovable oddity."

Or we can look at the world through the eyes of play, seeing the little girl or little boy that is inside all the people around us: the sales clerk, man walking his dog, the person sitting in front of us.

We can look through the eyes of awe seeing how incredible people and nature are.

And we can look at the world through spiritual eyes seeing the wonder, connection, goodness, and delight that is all around.

There is nothing you have to do first. Spiritual eyes is not a multistage path with successive levels. There is nothing to do first. You just do it.

In fact, try it now. Just look around, if you dare, as if through the eyes of wonder and awe. "Wow, look what's here!"

Now, I know that our minds have a kind of inertia. Old habitual ways of seeing can hold on strongly. Sometimes the shift is not as easy as I make it sound.

But I am a Taurus. Taurus's are known more for their stubbornness than agility. If I can do it, anybody can. Don't assume that just because it sounds simple that it is impossible.

Tips

However, if you aren't smiling and delighted, there are a few tips that can help.

Remember, it won't damage you. The practice does not ask you to renounce your political beliefs, your identity as a privileged or oppressed person, or your social critique. You can take back all your old ways of thinking and seeing in a moment. The practice merely invites curiosity: imagine seeing the world through sacred eyes for a few minutes. Then you can go back to your old ways.

Remember, it might not enlighten you. If you want the effect to last, it probably won't. Don't expect permanent change. It could happen. But old habits may reassert themselves. It's okay.

Recall moments when you felt delight. Perhaps as a child. Perhaps more recently when excitement or playfulness bubbled up. Perhaps you were meditating or listening to music or watching a humming bird or whatever.

Use that memory trace to help flip you back into the consciousness that you experienced before.

When I think of that little girl whispering, "It's a deer!" it is easier to flip into spiritual eyes consciousness.

Draw on some of your spiritual super heroes. Imagine you are Jesus or Buddha or Mother Goddess or Black Elk or a good witch or Gandhi. Look at the world through the eyes of Zorba the Greek or St. Francis or Pema Chödrön.

Practice thinking impossible thoughts. I believe it was the Red Queen in Lewis Carrol's *Through the Looking-Glass* who advised that we should always have three impossible thoughts before breakfast. This helps loosen up our consciousness. Picture chocolate floating in the air, a cow bathing in the kitchen sink, Donald Rumsfeld playing with flowers in a crib.

If you want to take this a step further, every day do at least one thing out of character. If you are neat, leave dirty dishes in the sink one day. If you are always in a rush, take a few moments to do nothing. Just break a pattern. Squeeze the toothpaste from the middle. It doesn't have to be a big deal.

This loosens us up and makes it easier to flip consciousness.

Set up reminders. For example, every time you stop at a stoplight, just make the flip for a moment. Or every time you sit down.

Talk with an understanding friend about what happened when you tried on your spiritual eyes for a moment. Just describing it helps remind you to do it again.

Closing

Angels fly by taking themselves lightly.

Sometimes we take the conflicts of the season way too personally. Humans have felt ambivalence about December since long before the name "December" was invented.

On the one hand, the days grow short; it is a time of foreboding. On the other, the crops are in; time to relax and enjoy the bounty of the harvest. On the other hand, winter is about to set in; we must be vigilant. On the other hand, for the Christian the messiah about to be born; it is a time to rejoice. On the other hand, birth can be precarious; Advent is a time to quietly attend one's moral bearing. On the other hand, for the modern political citizen the election is done; time to celebrate the new congress about to be born. On the other hand, those fallen from power cause mischief during the lame-duck session; it is time to be wary. On the other hand…

The ambiguity of the season is as old as humanity. We needn't take it so personally.

The practice of spiritual eyes does not address our personal psychology. It doesn't try to rearrange the furniture in our basement. It just suggests that our childhood wounds, cultural background, and biological predisposition may not be as monolithic as we think.

We don't have to rearrange the furniture in our soul. Just step outside and get a breath of fresh air.

When we go back inside, all our grumpiness may reassert itself. But it won't be quite as opaque. We'll have poked a hole in the wall. We may remember the delight and wonder that are possible.

So open your eyes, gaze around with wonder, let a smile brush your face, and whisper loudly, "It's a reindeer!" Or "Wow, look at this!" "Oooo!"

Religious Experience

Deep Connection

August 24, 2008

How many of you have been to the peak of Round Top? How many of you have heard of it?

To get to Round Top, you need good footgear, sunscreen, water, a little food, and some warm clothes even if it's hot here in the valley. From Sacramento, head east on Highway 50, southeast on the Emigrant Trail, then east on 88. A mile before Carson Pass, there is a parking lot on the right side of the road.

A trail out of the parking lot heads south, winding up and down, back and forth. Stay to the left of any forks. The trail curves east and rises to tiny Frog Lake. From the lake, go south into an alpine meadow. In a few miles you'll arrive at beautiful Lake Winnemucca. On the opposite side is Round Top. But you can't reach it from there because the peak is straight up over a thousand feet.

To get to the peak, head west away from it. After a few miles you come to a smaller lake. There is a bit of a ravine back on the east side of this lake. Follow it until it disappears.

At this point, the trail fades, along with all vegetation. There is only loose rock. You'll see Round Top Peak a half mile ahead.

The first time I climbed it, it looked easiest to go around to the south side. But the slope got steeper and slipperier and dropped to the creek in the dim distance. So I backtracked to the northwest side and picked my way to the summit.

The view from the top is breathtaking – literally. It is over 10,000 feet above sea level. If you aren't used to thin air, you get winded very quickly. And it is 1,000 feet straight down the north face to Lake Winnemucca and over 2,000 down the south face to Summit City Creek. Vertigo comes easily.

But the view is spectacular. Round Top is the highest elevation in the area. You can see Nevada to the east and the central valley to the west. In every direction there are lakes and mountaintops and meadows and forest and scraggy outcroppings. The cool air swooshes through the rocks. You can see and hear birds far below. Sometimes you look down onto the tops of clouds.

Sitting up there I feel how small we humans are compared to the immensity of space – and how little power we have. One time I watched a storm at eye level coming straight at me – I hurried down. But no matter how vast and impersonal the power of nature, we are a part of it – a tiny part to be sure. Earth is our home, and it's beautiful. I'm grateful to be here.

Three Descriptions

This isn't what I want to talk about here. I don't want to talk about Round Top. I want to talk about religious experience. And Round Top is as good a metaphor as any.

I described Round Top in three different ways. The three were woven together in my narrative, so let's pull them apart.

The first description was not of Round Top at all. It was a set of instructions about how to get there: what to bring and where to turn at various landmarks. Sunscreen and turning right at Lake Winnemucca don't give the flavor of standing on the peak. But if you want the actual experience, a map is more helpful than poetry. If all you know is that Round Top is in the high Sierras, you could wander for years and not find it.

The second description was of the nitty-gritty body sensations and sensory experiences: vertigo, shortness of breath, meadows, panoramic view, sounds of birds, chill in the air, and so forth.

The last description was the most abstract and conceptual: how small we humans are, the immensity of space and the forces around us, we are part of it all, this is home. This description is a set of beliefs.

Religious Discourse

Most religious discussions begin and end with beliefs: broad concepts, faith statements, and theologies. If these concepts are not grounded in concrete experience, they are just head-trips. Ungrounded mind-trips get us into mischief: "my God's better than your God," "my politics are better," "this little piece of earth I call 'my country' is better than yours," "you should do what I think," and off we go to war or self-justified stealing in the name of economics, incarcerating people we don't like, or whatever.

Our world is in turmoil. Religious ideology too often gets thrown in the pot turning a simmer into a rolling boil. Unitarian Universalists and other religious liberals often avoid religious language as a way to avoid this unpleasantness. But if we want to be a force for healing in the world, we must find effective ways to engage in religious discussions with people we don't agree with.

The best way to do that is to distinguish between beliefs, direct experience, and practices. They are different realms.

For example, imagine two people camping in the high Sierras. In the middle of the night they look out at the sky strewn with stars and galaxies and planets. They are bedazzled and humbled by the beauty and vastness. One concludes there must be a God that created all this. The other concludes it is vaster than any definition of God.

They have similar experiences and are touched by similar awe but have very different concepts and beliefs. Experience and beliefs are different realms.

On the other hand, two people sit side by side in the same church. They both believe in a Biblical God. For one, that belief calls her to cleanse the community of those who don't follow God's laws as best she understands them. For the other, that belief calls him to be more loving of the great variety of all God's children and to serve those in the greatest need.

Their concepts and beliefs are similar. Their experiences and actions are different. Beliefs, experiences, and actions are different realms.

Or consider: Christian prayer used to leave me cold. Then I read a little book on contemplative prayer by a Trappist monk, Thomas Merton. He detailed the specific prayer training given to monastics for centuries. I tried them out and found them powerful.

I still don't believe Jesus Christ is my Lord and Savior or that God spoke through the Bible in a unique way. But people who believe these things have developed practices I find moving. Beliefs and practices are different realms.

I am not the least bit interested in convincing you to believe or not believe anything. I don't care what you believe. I'm not even interested in what I believe. My beliefs have changed so much over the years that I don't take them seriously.

But I am very interested in what we can experience. I am very interested in the pathways that cultivate those experiences. And I am very interested in how these experiences change who we are in the world.

So in religious discourse it is important to distinguish beliefs, experience, and practice.

If you believe in God, and the person next to you believes in atheism, and you strike up a conversation about religion that is confined to the tiny box of concepts and beliefs, you'll probably feel frustrated.

But if you both step outside that box and openly ask, "What experiences and practices led you to your belief?" the discussion can be enriching.

Sharing experiences and practices leads to understanding and finding common ground. Arguing beliefs leads to bigger military budgets.

Definition

I offer a definition of religion not based on beliefs, but based on experience: religion is the experience of deep connection. If an experience deepens or widens or enriches our connection with life, I'd call it authentically religious. If not, it is something else. The specific practices, the nitty-gritty experiences, and the concepts may vary from person to person. But whatever gives your fullest connection with life is what I am calling your religion or your spirituality.

Sometimes we feel connection with the familiar part of life called "me," "my soul," or "my essence." Sometimes we feel that connection with that part of life called "not me," other people, other creatures, or nature itself. As experiences deepen, the distinction seems arbitrary. When we connect deeply with ourselves, we feel connected to all of life. When we connect deeply with life, we feel more attuned to ourselves.

Some of you are thinking, "I'm not a religious person. I don't have spiritual experiences. This doesn't apply to me." I'm not letting you off the hook. All of us have humdrum, boring experiences. And all of us have moving, touching experiences. Whatever connects us most deeply with life functions as our religion. That is our spirituality.

Saying, "I'm not spiritual," sometimes means "Another person's experiences are more powerful than mine."

Comparing our experience to someone else's is a loser of a strategy. One person may have a deep feeling of connection but have a humble temperament. They perceive and express their life in modest terms.

Another person has a relatively shallow experience, but has a flamboyant nature and expresses himself with breathless excitement: "I saw a dead flower on the sidewalk. Wow!"

Maybe they had a deep experience. Maybe not. We cannot tell the depth by how they express themselves. Comparing our experience to another's is not helpful.

This definition says compare your experience to your own experience. Whatever connects you most with life *is* your spirituality. We are *all* spiritual beings. Period.

Examples

Here are a few examples of spiritual experiences in my life:

- Holding my son in my hands hours after my wife almost died giving him birth

- Feeling my mind stop in deep meditation and being tearfully overwhelmed with joy

- Being on the streets with thousands of people coming together to express our yearnings about our country's war policies

- Praying during a high fever and being suddenly filled with ecstasy as the fever disappeared

- Getting lost in the Navajo Mountains as a teenager, lying down and watching the stars turn slowly through the night as I waited for dawn

- Listening to spacious music like Vaughn William's "Lark Ascending" or Paul Winter's "Sun Singer"

- Channeling a guiding spirit

- Petting my purring cat as he died in my lap

What are examples from your life? Would you be willing to share them?

Your Experience

I invite you to think about some experiences that have connected you more deeply with life. Ask each other, "When have you felt more deeply connected with life in you or around you?"

Use whatever concepts, beliefs, or language you feel most comfortable with. And be sure to include the nitty-gritty experience and the path that led up to it.

Series

This sermon is the first in a series on religious and spiritual experience. In it I'd like to explore many of the major beliefs, experiences, and practices that find their way into religious discussions. In each topic, I want to be sure we look at all three areas: not just beliefs and ideas, not just nitty-gritty direct experience, and not just practices – but all three and how they interact. I expect – and actually hope – that some of these topics will touch on your skepticism and push at fondly held ideas.

Fog

But before getting into specific topics I want to suggest there is something even more important than beliefs, experience, or maps. It is time and effort. Let me illustrate:

I flew to Seattle in January a few years ago. On the way home I gazed out the airplane window. The whole Sacramento valley was fogged in from the coastal range to the Sierras and from north of Redding to as far south as the eye could see. The fog was only 20- or 30-feet thick. Above it, the sky was clear, the Sierras were snow capped and gorgeous, the panorama was inspiring.

I imagined what it might be like to live our whole lives on the valley floor beneath such a fog. We're smart enough to conceive of dimensions beyond our fog – we call them "sky." With no direct experience of sky, some of us figure it is white. Others are sure it is blue. Others do laboratory experiments on light refraction and conclude, "No, the sky is indigo."

We casually argue about the nature of sky, write books, preach sermons, and discuss ideas on talk shows. Some even imagine something beyond the sky that is black and filled with points of lights. They are dismissed as laughable fools.

Then wind blows all the fog away from one person for a few moments. She sees the sky. It is blue! She no longer believes the sky is blue. She knows it is. When we experience something directly, faith and beliefs become irrelevant. We just know.

In the middle of the night, someone else gets lost and ends up on Sutter Butte above the fog. The sky is actually black and filled with points of light!

Someone else happens into a clear patch of sky at dusk. The sky is orange!

When some say the sky is orange, the blue-sky people feel the truth they've experienced is being negated. When someone says the sky is black with stars, the indigo-people feel the sacred is being sullied.

Casual arguments turn passionate. Armies are raised to defend reality from the deluded.

Most of us live most of our lives in a fog. We are too busy or stressed to notice beyond the twenty-foot visibility.

To be sure, we all have glimpses of the sky from time to time. I had a client once with breast cancer. The disease cleared the fog from her mind-heart. She became clearer, softer, kinder to her family, more open to the world around her, radiant. Then the cancer went into remission and she reverted to her old cranky self.

Most people are not curious enough to give their glimpses of sky more than a casual nod or quick snapshot for their memory scrapbook before slipping back into the fog of old mind habits.

So What?

Cultivating direct experience is crucial to authentic religion. But this is only the beginning of the journey. Experience must be repeated so we know the sky's many different states. Reality is far more complex and wonderful than one color of the rainbow! There are joy and peace, strength and humility, flow and stillness, gratitude and courage, and more. Ongoing spiritual practices allow us to taste this broader reality in different flavors and know many are real.

To sustain authentic religion we must put in the effort to explore, to go off the socially well-worn path, to break our own mental habits. We need the inspiration to put in the time to cultivate a variety of experiences.

Frankly, you can't get to Round Top on your lunch break. It takes time and effort. Maps and preparation help. But time and effort are essential.

It is difficult to sustain the energy and motivation by ourselves. As a religious community, one of the best things we can do for ourselves and the larger world is to share our experiences and practices. In doing so, we inspire and encourage each other on our spiritual treks. So do it for ourselves and do it for our community.

Sharing and sensitive listening brings us together, deepens our lives, and creates a healing force in the world.

Contemplation

I invite you close your eyes. ... Let your breathing relax. ... Then ask yourself, "When have I felt a little closer or deeper or fuller connection with life?" ... Remember what that felt like. ... Give yourself to the feeling. ... Don't worry about your beliefs about it. Just give yourself to the experience. ...

Now ask yourself: What practices help cultivate this experience? What can I do to deepen this direct contact with larger life? ...

May we share our experiences with others to strengthen our community.

May we listen to other's experiences and practices and be inspired.

Closing Words

Beliefs are cheap. Experience costs time and effort.

It is difficult to cultivate deep and continuing religious experience without support and encouragement.

May we share our experiences sensitively.

May we listen openheartedly.

May we encourage and support one another for our sakes and for the sake of those around us.

May it be so.

God and the Power of Surrender

September 14, 2008

I drove into Sacramento on Thursday afternoon a few years ago. Kate Rhode, the interim minister in our sister congregation, was with me. We were returning from the Fall Unitarian Universalist ministers' retreat north of Sebastopol.

I left Kate at her home in south Sacramento, turned on my cell phone and checked my voice mail.

A message from Lambda – the Gay and Lesbian Community Center on L Street – invited me to speak at a press conference. A recent court ruling had gone against same sex marriage. They knew me from speaking at earlier rallies and needed clergy. The press conference would be at 5:00 at the Lambda Center.

I looked at my watch: 3:40. I'd have to speed home, change clothes, and dash downtown during rush hour.

What to do?

Religious voices on marriage equality are very helpful. Yet, I had been away since Monday morning. There were four other pressing messages. I was behind on the upcoming Sunday service. I hadn't seen my family for days. I was tired.

I thought, "I'll go home, unpack, and check the other calls. By then it will be too late to get to L Street by 5:00. I'll call the Center, apologize for not being there, and explain that I had been out of town."

I settled on this course and started home.

But I felt agitated. My strategy involved dissembling. I thought, "Maybe I should be direct and tell them I believe strongly in marriage equality, but I was too tired because I had been on retreat." I didn't like how that sounded.

Maybe I should just go to the press conference. Fighting for social justice means doing things at inconvenient times. That's part of being committed.

Or did I have an overinflated opinion of myself and my role.

And what were my motives anyway: being a good boy, helping others, avoiding embarrassment, making the world better, getting time for myself?

By the time I got home I had a dozen voices whispering in my head.

I sat down, closed my eyes, and said, "Shut up. Enough."

I took a deep breath to let my mind relax. Then I said, "I can't figure out what to do. What is truly in the highest good here? You tell me."

I didn't know or particularly care who the "you" was. I directed my attention outside my personal drama as if there was a loving force wiser than me listening.

From a deep, quiet place arose a sense. It wasn't a thought – just a clarity: "Go to the press conference."

As soon as I put that sense into words, the voices started arguing: "What about family? What about rest? What about doing too much? What about justice? What about gays and lesbians? What about my sacred commitment as a minister? What about the overdue order of service for Sunday? What about over functioning? What about…?"

But for a moment there had been that quiet clarity: "Go to the press conference." It came from a place stiller and more connected to a larger sense of life than those nagging voices.

I got to L Street a few minutes before 5:00. A group was standing on the front steps of the Center. A few reporters and cameras faced them from the sidewalk. I slipped on my clerical stole, nodded to the woman in charge of the press conference, and stood to the side to see if I was needed after all.

The speakers emphasized that marriage and civil union do not carry the same respect in the general community. That is true enough, but they left the impression that marriage and civil unions were otherwise equal. And though they were articulate and impassioned, their arguments were long and complex. Reporters have tight deadlines and little airtime. They need sound bites.

So when the others were done, I asked if I could share a few thoughts. I said to the camera, "Civil union is a second class marriage at best. Marriage has 10 times more privileges, from tax exemptions to hospital visitation to pension sharing to child custody.

"We should stand on the side of love. When people love each other and are dedicated to each other's wellbeing, that is sacred intention. All relationships are hard work at times. They need and deserve all the support and encouragement we can give them. Strong, stable, well-supported families make our society stronger and more stable.

"Marriage equality is in our enlightened self-interest. It makes our communities stronger, more loving, more humane, and more decent.

"Civil marriage is a civil right."

"I know some people of sincere faith don't recognize same-gender marriage. I don't want to force a clergy to perform a wedding that violates his or her convictions. By the same token, I don't want to be denied the ability to bless and confer full marriage rights to anyone based on gender. If various clergy disagree, let us work it out or go our separate ways. The state has no business taking sides in a religious issue.

"Civil marriage is a civil right."

"Marriage equality will be with us soon because it is the American thing to do, it is the fair thing to do, it is the civilized thing to do, it is the decent thing to do.

"Period."

As I walked back to my car, I felt both energized and peaceful.

In the struggle for marriage equality, one press conference is not a big deal. But I had done what was in my power. Something had nudged me to step out of my personal concerns and into larger concerns and out of larger concerns into the life that is all of us.

As I walked up the street, I was more aware of trees moving in the wind, people on sidewalks, cars in the streets, and the city moving around me. I felt more connected to the flow of life.

The whispering thoughts were quiet. I could feel that deep, still place inside and around me.

Religious Experience

That afternoon was a religious experience. I call it "religious" not because I said self-righteous words or stood up for somebody or acted from a set of values. That would be moral, political, philosophical, or psychological experience. I call it "religious" because of that subtle and deep sense of connection with life.

Most people define religion by beliefs. I define religion as the experience of deep connection. If something deepens, widens, or strengthens our connection with life, however modestly, it is authentically religious.

This is the second sermon in a series on religious experience. In the first, ("Deep Connection" pp. 213-217), I encouraged you to reflect upon and share times you've felt part of a larger flow of life. And I made a distinction between belief, experience and practice. Now I'd like to focus on a particular kind of connection: the power of surrender.

To do this let's look at surrender through these three distinct lenses: belief, experience, and practice. We'll start with belief.

Belief

What do you believe was going on when I was deciding what to do that afternoon? Was God speaking to me? Or was I sorting through a guilty conscience? Was I listening to something "out there"? Or did I just quiet my emotions enough to connect to what is "in here"?

If you believe in God, my experience illustrates one way the divine works in our lives. If you don't believe in God, my experience illustrates tapping internal forces.

But what you or I believe does not change the actual experience one iota. Experience and belief are different realms.

Life is more complex than the human mind can grasp or formulate into beliefs. For humans, there will always be unknowns and mysteries.

So I don't care what we believe about God, or if we believe in any God. I do care about how we relate to life's mysteries. Do we relate with our congregation's values of openness, curiosity, love, and courage? Without openness we fall into self-absorption, rigidity, or isolation. Curiosity takes us beyond passivity to active questioning. Love engages our hearts. And courage allows us to venture beyond our comfort zone.

If you believe in God and your belief is an emotionally cogent, gut-level way of relating to the mystery with openness, curiosity, love, and courage, then it helps you surrender into life. Your belief supports authentic religion.

On the other hand, if you believe in God and your belief prompts you to say, "I don't question. I have confidence in my faith," that is sweet. But it is immature. It shuts down that open curiosity and loving courage. Blind faith is a disability. Blind faith is dysfunctional faith.

If you don't believe in God and your nonbelief fills you with wonder and inquisitiveness, it will draw you deeply into life. That is authentic religion.

On the other hand, if you don't believe in God and hold so strongly to your nonbelief that you assume anyone using the word "God" is confused, that is sad. You've lost some openness, curiosity, love, and courage. You're nonbelief is stifling.

So beliefs are not a big deal. They are just thoughts. What is important is how we give ourselves to life. So let's look at the experience of surrender.

Experience

There are at least three different kinds of surrender: intentional, desperate, and accidental.

The most common *image* of spiritual surrender is intentional, like a saint praying quietly, "Not my will but Thine, O Lord. I commend myself to do your bidding."

But a more common *experience* of surrender grows less out of piety and more out of desperation. That Thursday afternoon I was desperate: "I can't figure this out. You tell me."

Have you ever felt that? "My life is a mess. Tell me what to do." It's not clear exactly who we are talking to. But God or guiding forces are implied.

However, the most common experience of surrender is accidental. In this, God is not even implied. We just surrender without thinking about it.

Perhaps we are trying to figure out what to do with a problem child, a frustrating partner, or a work situation. We think about it, analyze it, ponder it, read books about it, agonize over it. Nothing helps.

Then someone walks into the room and changes the topic. Or it's time to go to Family Promise or St. John's Shelter and focus on someone else. Or maybe we say, "I can't think about this any longer. It's driving me crazy. I'm going to the movies." Or maybe we just fall asleep. But one way or another we let go.

Later on, we are out for a walk or listening to the radio or taking a shower – we aren't thinking about the issue – and out of nowhere an answer pops into our mind. "Where'd that come from?" we think.

Sometimes it's not a specific answer as much as a shift in perspective. Maybe we are walking along obsessing about a problem. We are emotionally all cramped up. Then we see children playing on a swing set freely and joyfully. They are fun to watch. Their mood resonates in our body and heart. Suddenly our problem doesn't feel like such a big deal any more.

In each of these examples, there is a point where we surrender. It might be intentional, desperate or inadvertent. And out of the surrender comes guidance, insight, or a shift in perspective. We are left a little more in contact with life beyond ourselves.

If you want more of that sense of connection, intentionally cultivating the power of surrender is one way to do that. So let's turn from the experience to the practice.

Practice

The art of surrender is in blending two different qualities: intention and relaxation. Each of the three kinds of experience has these two qualities. On the one hand there is focus, deliberate reaching out or effort to solve a problem. On the other there is letting go, letting be, relaxing and trusting the flow of life.

A metaphor might help.

The human brain has up to 100 billion neurons. Each neuron can have one or thousands of dendrites connecting it to other neurons. This vast neural network can design rocket ships, make love, paint flowers, play a violin concerto, and contemplate the meaning of life. But how much does any single neuron know about rocket ships, love, flowers, violins, or life? Probably very little.

We humans are like neurons. We are capable of connecting with other humans, other life, non-life, and other dimensions in a variety of ways. But how much do any of us really know about the interdependent web and what it can do? Probably very little.

We can pull our dendrites in and isolate ourselves. Or we can relax and let our various senses and intuitive facilities expand outward and connect with the web in many, many ways.

The difference between cutting ourselves off and cultivating lots of connections can be huge. A fully expanded human consciousness may be a thousand times wiser than an isolated, self-absorbed consciousness. But even in our most inspired way of being, we are still just one neuron, one human, one being. We can allow ourselves to be a flowing part of it all. But what we'll actually know is a fraction of the mystery.

The practice of surrender is the discipline of reaching beyond what we know as an isolated being to what we can know as a multidimensional connected being. We may have different ideas, names, or beliefs about that greater something. But *what's important is not the strength of our belief but the sincerity of our intention. It's not the eloquence of our words but the stillness of our listening. It's not the strength of our conviction but the fullness of our surrender.*

Don't confuse military surrender with spiritual surrender. In combat, surrender means giving up, collapsing, failing, shrinking, or pulling into oneself in defeat.

Spiritual surrender is the opposite. It is expanding outward. It is reaching out and asking or connecting openly with heartful curiosity and courage to stretch beyond the familiar.

To be sure, sometimes our ego can feel defeated. We may have to relinquish attachments, agendas, or points of view. This can hurt. Relaxing a tight fist can ache for a time.

But spiritual surrender reaches beyond the smallness of our individuality into a larger sense of connection. When we don't resist it, it feels loving and embracing. When we genuinely surrender, it *is* loving and embracing.

Closing Prayer

Close your eyes and surrender.

If there is some issue or concern that is in your mind or heart, let it be there. Let it come forward.

Silently put it into words that reach out. "Help me know what to do?" "Show me what I'm not seeing clearly." "Guide me through these waters." "What is the next step?" See what words feel natural to you. Open and lovingly reach out. ...

If you don't have a specific concern, reach out in a general way. "How can I feel most fulfilled today?" "How can I be this afternoon that promotes the highest good?" "What moves me in the direction of peace and vitality?" Use your own language. ...

Some people find it conducive to let their hands rest in their laps. Other find it helpful to raise the hands or arms to feel the sense of reaching out.

Whatever the case, as you reach out, relax. ... Open. ... Let your heart be large. ... Flow beyond yourself. ... Expand. ...

If some insight or guidance or sense of where to move next arises, don't dismiss it. No matter how subtle it is, notice it gently.

No need to grasp hold of it either. ... Just relax and let it be there. ...

Later on you can sort it out and decide if you trust it and want to follow it or not. Don't worry about that now. In this moment, just let it arise.

And if nothing arises, that's just fine. Let patience grow. You don't have to solve anything this morning. Just connect more deeply. That's plenty. ...

Reach out. ... Relax. ... Open. ... Let the heart be large... Expand... Connect... Allow love to draw you outward.

Atheism and the Wisdom of Uncertainty

September 28, 2008

"The soul enters the human body at the moment of conception." Is this a statement of deep faith? Or deep foolishness?

Regardless of how you feel about abortion, how could anyone know the soul enters the body at conception or at birth or at some other time? How could anyone know for sure the nature of soul or if it exists?

Anyone convinced they know the answer to these questions has confused conviction with certainty. He's confused being emphatic with knowing truth.

We aren't born knowing about soul or God. We aren't born knowing about self or world. In fact, we can't even distinguish between self and other.

As infants, we perceive colors, shapes, textures, sounds, flavors, smells, heat, cold, and so forth. Our movements are reflexive and sensory driven. We experience an undifferentiated sea of sensations and movements that are not organized into subjects or objects.

The Swiss psychologist Jean Piaget studied the development of human intelligence using thousands of sensitive observations of children from birth through adolescence. His seminal research mapped how human cognition unfolds from this undifferentiated mass to multifaceted, abstract thinking. It takes years. With full rational processing, adolescents can speculate about various theories of God, soul, existence, and life meaning.

Piaget once wrote that knowing begins at the contact between the organism and the environment. It begins at the surface of the body with sensory sensations. From this we extrapolate outward and develop a model of what is "out there" causing these sensations. And we extrapolate inward and develop a model of who we are "in here" having these experiences. But our knowledge of what is out there and in here are just educated guesses. The only thing we can be completely confident in is what we actually experience. What causes those experiences and who we are that have those experiences is conjecture.

The further we move away from direct experience, the more conjecture. The most conjecture is involved in the most abstract questions: "What is the ultimate nature of reality?" "What is the ultimate nature of life?" "Is there a God?" "Is there a soul that enters the body at some time?"

Religious Experience

This is the third sermon in a series on religious experience.

Most people define religion as a set of beliefs about ultimate reality. This is to say, most people define religion as assertions about that which we know the least – that which we have the greatest uncertainty about and the greatest possibility of getting wrong.

In this series we are trying to lay the foundation for an authentic religion based more upon what we actually know – that is what we actually experience – and less on speculation, beliefs, theological theories, or ideas.

Specifically, we are defining religion as the experience of deep connection to life. By this I mean facing life's unknowns in ways that are relaxed, inquisitive, heartful, and adventurous. Our congregation's values statement uses the words openness, curiosity, love, and courage. They point to the same qualities.

Our strategy has been to look at various areas of religious life through three different lenses: belief, experience, and practices that cultivate the experience.

Next, I'd like to look at atheism and the wisdom of uncertainty. I'd like to look at atheism as a religious experience and uncertainty as the foundation of wisdom. To do this, I'd like to explore atheism through these three lenses: belief, experience, and practice. Let's begin with belief.

Belief

Atheism is defined as the belief that God does not exist. But there are many beliefs about God. So there are many forms of atheism depending on which Gods it doesn't believe in.

Flatland

For example, one extreme is "flat land materialism." This says that reality is not multidimensional: it is a flat land. Things that truly exist can be verified scientifically. If it can't be verified, it is fantasy. And since God is impossible to verify with strict scientific procedures, it is a fantasy.

There are Unitarian Universalist atheists who subscribe to this view.

Watchmaker

On the other extreme is Deism. Deists say God created the universe and the natural laws that govern it. He is a cosmic watchmaker who made everything, wound it up, and then let it go. Now he rests on a cosmic beach. He's uninvolved. We are on our own.

When I was in theological school I took a course from the Jesuits called "A Christian Theology of God." They talked about a school of philosophy that says if there is no difference between believing and not believing something, they are functionally equivalent. Saying "God exists but is not involved" is functionally the same as saying "He doesn't exist." There is no way to distinguish between the two. So from their perspective, Deism is a form of atheism.

There are Unitarian Universalists who are Deists. In fact, if you look up deism online in Wikipedia, it says, "there are currently no established deistic religions, with the possible exception of Unitarian Universalism and Confucianism."

No Prime Mover

Between these two extremes there are many flavors of atheism. Some can deepen our connection with life. Let's consider two.

The thirteenth century Dominican theologian, Thomas Aquinas, took the Greek idea of a Prime Mover and popularized it as a proof of the existence of God. His reasoning went like this:

Everything is caused by something. For example, you pick up an apple because you are hungry. You are hungry because you haven't eaten for a while. You haven't eaten for a while because you slept all night. You slept because your body requires rest. Your body requires daily rest because of your genetics. Your genetics are the result of millions of years of evolution. Evolution is the result of self-replicating molecules. And so on. Everything has a cause.

Plato, Aristotle, and Thomas Aquinas argued that if we follow this causal chain back and back and back, eventually we come to the Primal Cause that started it all. This Prime Mover is defined as God. God's the one who started all this going in the first place.

This is an intellectually coherent and persuasive argument for the existence of God.

However, an atheist might object by saying there is a hidden assumption. It assumes the universe is hierarchical. Thomas Aquinas was a Catholic priest, so we can forgive his blindness. But perhaps the universe is an interdependent network rather than a vertical hierarchy.

Most things actually have multiple causes or multiple influences. And each of these has multiple causes. If we could trace these back through the network of relationships, we find that everything is directly or indirectly related to everything else. There is no one single Unmoved Mover but a vast net of interdependence.

If there is a God, It is not a single entity. God is all that there is – the network and everything in it. But this description is so far from the usual description of God that it is less confusing to start by saying, "There is no God."

God as Irrelevant

This brings us to another line of reflection that says God is irrelevant: God is a man-made concept that does nothing to answer our ultimate questions. This reasoning goes like this:

It is human nature to question. The big questions are, "Why do I exist?" "Why is there anything?" "What's the meaning of life?"

One answer is, "God did it. She or He made us and everything and that gives us meaning."

Think about that answer for a moment. … Does it really answer the questions? … Or does it just beg further questions: Why did God do it? Who or what made God? Why does God exist? What is the meaning of God?

The answer, "God did it," implies that there is God in one place making our universe in another place. So there must be a larger field that includes God and our universe. Why does this hyper-universe exist? Who or what made it? What is its meaning?

And whatever made this hyper-universe must exist in an even larger, hyper-hyper-universe. What's that all about?

We are caught in an infinite loop of speculation that goes nowhere and answers nothing. Saying God is the answer to our deepest questions simply dodges the questions. Therefore God is irrelevant.

Not a Proof

None of this actually proves God does not exist. We may say confidently that many images of God may be appropriate for children but not for thoughtful adults. We may say that many adult images of God are human constructs imposed on reality rather than direct perceptions of reality. This does not disprove all theories of God, but it does suggest that we look more closely at the experiences that give rise to our beliefs.

Experience

So let's shift from beliefs to experience. What are the experiences that give rise to atheist beliefs? I'll mention four different kinds.

One is intellectual: similar to what I've been sharing. We think things through and reach a gut-level feeling that God makes no sense and colors our perceptions.

Emotional

A second kind of experience is more purely emotional. Perhaps we grew up with images of God being vengeful, petty, threatening to send us to hell for thought crimes. We note damage people have done in the name of God: crusades, inquisitions, jihads, torture, murder, restrictive definitions of marriage, theft, and so much more. We get turned off to God and God language. We reject them.

This kind of emotional contraction deserves empathy. But it says nothing persuasive about larger reality. I don't like forest fires, car accidents, dishonest politicians, or market crashes. But just because I don't like them doesn't mean they don't exist.

Model Breakdown

However, there is a third kind of experience that is more potent. It is the breakdown of our models of life.

The human mind loves to create models of life. Jean Piaget exquisitely describes the cognitive structures that arise spontaneously in any healthy human. We use these to construct theories of the world and ourselves. If we hold them lightly, they are useful in helping us navigate our lives.

If our view of life includes God, we call ourselves theists. If not, we call ourselves atheists or agnostics. I know atheists who cling to their atheism more fiercely than fundamentalists cling to God. It's the functional equivalent of a religion. It imposes shape and meaning. A model is still a model, not reality.

The 16th century Carmelite friar, St. John of the Cross, wrote about the breakdown of all models and meaning. He had a strong faith in God, but his thinking can include atheism. It goes like this:

As we mature, we experience things that do not fit our understanding. Our childhood image of a bearded man on a throne in the clouds no longer feels credible. Or God as protector breaks down in the face of tragedy. Or atheism breaks down when we experience deep, inexplicable, loving connection.

St. John of the Cross used the phrase "dark night of the soul" to refer to these times when our old theories wear out. It is humbling, to say the least. But it is also a fertile time. If we can stay relaxed, inquisitive, heartful and adventurous, wisdom arises out of this darkness.

With this emerging wisdom we develop new models – perhaps they include God, perhaps not. They are just models. If we continue to grow, eventually they too will break down.

So one potent experience that gives rise to atheism is this breakdown of our old understandings.

Uncertainty

There is a fourth kind of experience that is even more potent. It is the direct experience of unknowing and insignificance. It is the experience of the void.

Have you ever looked out an airplane window at 25,000 or 30,000 feet and tried to find a single person on the ground? Perhaps you see trucks or cars. But from that altitude, people are too tiny to be discerned by the naked eye.

We are tiny specks on the vastness of the earth. And the earth is a speck of dust in the vastness of our galaxy. And there are over 100 billion galaxies in the known universe.

The profundity of our insignificance can be overwhelming. The mind-heart may shy away from feeling this directly.

Similarly, what we understand of life's complexity is tiny. The profundity of our ignorance can be unnerving. We look into the void and see a void.

Practice

These experiences suggest two kinds of practices. So let's shift from experience to practices.

Atheist spiritual discipline may sound like an oxymoron. But the practices are not about cultivating particular beliefs or non-beliefs. They are about allowing old worn-out beliefs to collapse as we hang out gracefully with uncertainty and feel our way more fully into life.

Contradictions

One practice is holding contradictory understandings.

I used to train psychotherapists. I suggested to them, "Get comfortable with several psychological theories that contradict each other. No person ever conforms to a theory. We humans are vastly more interesting and complex than any theory. So if we want to see our clients clearly, it helps to have ideas that contradict each other. It keeps us more receptive and less likely to miss something important because it doesn't fit our theory."

The same applies to spirituality. It deepens our connection to life to hold several beliefs that conflict with each other. This keeps us receptive.

For example, if you believe in God, imagine life without God. Ask yourself, "Can I find a sympathetic model of the cosmos that does not include my sense of God? What would that be like?"

If you don't believe in God, ask yourself, "What images of God do I feel sympathetic to? Can I imagine a cosmos that includes God?"

I'm not asking you to change your beliefs, just to stretch beyond them. We know the universe is more far out than our understandings. So reach out quietly and heartfully and taste a different understanding.

Holding contradictory beliefs won't deepen our connection to a set of beliefs. But it can deepen our connection to the flux and flow of life itself.

Beyond All Models

A fiercer practice is to try to go beyond all beliefs. Stretch beyond our understanding. And at the same time remain heartfully connected to the flow of life. Remain relaxed, inquisitive, heartful, and adventurous.

The most succinct statement I know of this kind of practice comes from St. John of the Cross. He said, "God, please remove from me all images of God."

He knew that any model of God could not be ultimately true. He tried to reach beyond it.

Try it yourself for a few moments: "God, please remove from me all images of god." Regardless of your beliefs, just play with it sincerely. If you have negative conditioning around the word "God," substitute a functional equivalent:

"Universe, please remove from me all theories of the universe."

"Life, please remove from me all ideas about life."

"What is, please remove from me all images of what is."

"Divine, please help me reach beyond the divine."

St. John of the Cross's prayer is a paradox. It gives the prayer a playful touch. At the same time he is sincerely reaching out to engage the ultimate – not just with cold, dry intellect but fervently with love and courage to reach beyond the familiar.

It is these attitudes – playful sincerity and humble courage – that cultivate wise contact with life.

Uncertainty and Wisdom

These attitudes – playful sincerity and humble courage – may be helpful in all aspects of life, not just ultimate questions. We face uncertainty every day. How do we deal with a child's fears? A partner's stubbornness? Inner turmoil? A shaky economy? The war? A letter to a failing parent? We face uncertainty all the time.

When we don't know what to do, the natural urge is to get on top of the problem and solve it! Cleverness comes from figuring things out. Wisdom doesn't come from cleverness or figuring things out. Wisdom is perception. Rather than conquer a problem, wisdom tries to see into the heart of a situation. It waits patiently for an answer to arise. If no answer arises, it just connects more mindfully to what is.

When not knowing unnerves us, rather than turn toward convictions we can turn toward each other. Rather than make pronouncements, we can share our uncertainty with one another.

This is why we need strong communities, particularly religious communities like ours that don't claim to have found the truth: communities that value nuance over simplicity, seeing clearly over gaining control, the quality of a decision over decisiveness, humility over conviction, and wisdom over cleverness.

It takes courage to face confusion and say, "I don't know." But foolishness begins with conviction about things we don't know. Wisdom begins with embracing uncertainty. Then it relaxes, opens our minds with curiosity, and opens our hearts with love so we can step forward with courage and connect deeply with the mystery of what is.

May it be so.

Paradise and the Struggle for Harmony

October 19, 2008

A window in my home study looks out on our backyard. Below the window, a profusion of lavender attracts dozens of hummingbirds. It also attracts hundreds of bees. On spring mornings I can hear the ominous drone of wings through the open window. When I go outside, the bees are more interested in the flowers than me. If I give them the least amount of space, we all live together quite easily.

Above the window an arbor is covered with wisteria. The vine grows so fast that I have to cut it back every week or two, but the dense green shade is worth the effort. A bird feeder attracts yellow finches and other small birds. They are lovely when they aren't pecking each other on the head.

The birds create a mess. They hop under the bushes and flap their wings to blow the mulch all over the patio. This helps them find insects in the ground. I don't mind cleaning up after them – it's a fair trade for keeping the bug population down.

Our big black-and-white cat, Sylvie, likes the birds too.

When we lived in New England, Sylvie used to chase German Shepherds and Labradors out of our front yard and hunt rabbits. Sylvie was a fierce hunter outside the house.

But inside was different. In the winter when snow drove the voles into our home, they would crawl into his food dish, eat, and poop. I thought it would be the height of embarrassment for a cat to have little rodents pooping in his food. But Sylvie merely sat in the kitchen and watched them attentively – almost affectionately.

Sylvie thinks creatures outside the house are predators or prey. But inside the house, everyone is family. To him, sharing food with a hungry rodent was elementary civility.

Ten years later in California, Sylvie is an old man. He loves the backyard. He sees it as an extension of home. So the birds and squirrels that come into it are family.

He rubs his back on the concrete patio with his belly to the sky as he watches the birds hop all around him picking up stray seeds. He smiles at them through squinted eyes or dozes in the sun. It's not exactly a lion lying down with lambs, but it contributes to the feeling of living in paradise.

On the other side of the house, four camellia bushes grow outside our bedroom window. They produce brilliant pink flowers. But the different bushes bloom at different times. We have flowers seven or eight months of the year.

Last spring a scrub jay built a nest in the camellias about three feet from where we rest our heads at night. We looked out the window one morning to see the mother sitting on eggs. A week later, tiny birds peeped in the nest. Then small birds were being fed. Then larger birds wobbled around the branches. Then one morning they had flown on.

We live in paradise. I can imagine more dramatic or spectacular views out a window. But as a humble paradise, I can't imagine anything more convincing than wild birds growing up a few inches from my pillow.

I woke up in the middle of the night a few weeks ago. There was sound in the camellias. I knew the bird nest was long empty. Besides, the noise sounded like a bigger animal than birds.

Perhaps a squirrel? But squirrels are hyperactive – they either sit very still and twitch or run as fast as they can. The movement of this sound was slow and deliberate.

Perhaps a raccoon? But it didn't sound large enough to be a raccoon.

By then I was fully awake and wondering. I sat up looked out into the night. A shadow moved slowly down the bushes from the eves. It was five or six inches long and a few inches wide.

There are rats in paradise!

Our property is adjacent to the greenway along the American River. The greenway has lots of deer. In the evening, we hear coyotes laughing. One day I came home to find a wild turkey in our front yard. And there are smaller creatures as well: otters, squirrels, and rats. They are all a part of the ecosystem.

A few years ago I told you about shining a flashlight between the refrigerator and the cupboards at 1:00 in the morning. Three little pink noses pointed up at me. They were surrounded by whiskers, tiny ears, and shiny eyes. They looked cute and innocent. Sylvie thought so too. To Sylvie, they were family, just like the voles and the birds.

But holes in the cereal boxes, poop on the pots and pans, and nibbles in the fruit on the counter didn't feel like paradise to me. Maybe in another lifetime when I'm more enlightened, I'll be able to share a pantry with rats – but not this lifetime.

A few months after telling you about the rats in our kitchen, I found a hole under the eaves. Two sections of the roof came together leaving an opening wide enough for three squirrels to walk in shoulder to shoulder.

I put some hardware cloth – a heavy wire mesh – over the opening. And lo and behold, we no longer have squirrels in the attic or rats in the kitchen. The squirrels and birds and rats still crawl over the house and scratch in the rain gutters and climb in the bushes. But since they can't get inside the house any more, we peacefully coexist. It is possible to live harmoniously in paradise with rats.

In this fourth sermon in a series on religious experience, I would like to talk about paradise and this struggle for harmony. Let's move into this topic by talking about beliefs about paradise and harmony.

Where Is Paradise?

All religions talk about living in greater happiness. It may be called heaven, paradise, nirvāna, or peace. As the spiritual says, "There is more love somewhere. There is more peace, more joy, more harmony somewhere." The question is, "Where do we find it?"

Classical conservatism – religious, social, and political conservatism – sees paradise in the past. It was in the Garden of Eden until we fell from grace and got thrown out into this world of pain. It was in a past Golden Age. It was in the "good ole days." Happiness is found in tradition and returning to traditional values.

On the other hand, classical liberalism sees paradise and harmony in the future: "onward and upward forever." Progress evolves us toward a better day to come. Depending on our theology, this golden age to be may be found in an improving world or a heavenly afterlife. It is something we work toward or look forward to.

This morning I ask you to consider a third possibility: maybe the world we live in right now is the paradise promised by mystics and sages. It is right under our noses in the lavender, camellias, bees, birds, and yes, even the rats.

It does not surprise me to find this view in eastern mysticism and new age "be here now," but I was surprised to find it in ancient Christianity. So let me elaborate on this.

Ancient Christianity

When we walk into Christian churches today, the most prominent symbol is a cross, perhaps with a dead Jesus hanging from it. The cross depicts pain, suffering, and death. It says we will be redeemed by this destruction. Jesus died for our sins so if we accept his death and resurrection, we'll be saved – not in this life but in the next. That's where heaven is found: not in this world but in the next.

Rebecca Parker and Rita Nakashima Brock spent over five years tracing the origins of the cross and its symbolism. Their book is called, *Saving Paradise: How Christianity Traded Love of This World for Crucifixion and Empire.*[17]

They traveled all over Europe exploring ancient churches and catacombs and texts. In the chambers of worship they found images of Jesus' life and living presence. Murals depicted the rivers of Eden, forests, meadows, flowers, deer, sheep, and lions lying down with lambs. There were angels and saints helping people.

As they imagined ancients worshipping in these spaces, it was clear that murals depicted heaven on earth.

---

[17] Boston: Beacon Press. 2008.

In the first thousand years of Christianity, they could not find one cross or depiction of Jesus' death. In fact, the earliest crucifix they could find was made in Germany in 1025.

The early Christians saw this earth as a heaven. When Jesus said, "I will live with you in paradise this day," he was not referring to an afterlife. He was referring to this life, as it is, right here and right now. He was saying that this world is a paradise given to us by God.

But just because it was given to us doesn't mean we actually live in it. Jesus said, "to enter heaven you have to enter into yourself." To enter paradise, we have to enter into a sacred relationship with the world and her creatures.

If this world is paradise, when we see something we like, the way to deepen our connection with paradise is not to try to collect, accumulate, take control, or keep if for ourselves. To enter paradise, enjoy, savor, and cultivate gratitude for the gifts around you.

The early Christian communities shared wealth rather than accumulated individual fortunes. They cultivated the joy of sharing over the tight-heartedness of hording.

If this world is paradise, then when we see the sick, injured or oppressed, the way to deepen our connection with life is not to pass them by. Like the Good Samaritan helping the injured, how we treat the least amongst us is how we connect to the most sacred.

The early Christians built hospitals and infirmaries and cared for the sick, the abandoned, and the orphaned. They were more concerned with cultivating compassion than privilege.

If this world is paradise, then when we see people hurting others or doing things we don't like, the way to deepen our connection with Spirit is to treat everyone as part of our family. We don't always passively indulge our crazy uncle. We may put limits on him. But we don't kill him or send him to Siberia. He is still welcome at the table.

The early Christians were pacifists. They saw the discipline of love as higher than the discipline of fighting.

So the way to enter paradise was to cultivate heavenly relational qualities: generosity, compassion, and love.

From Love to Death

This early version of Christianity was widespread over Europe until Charlemagne in the ninth century. He wanted to unite Europe under him. He needed soldiers to expand his empire. Since he was a self-identified Christian, he wanted Christian soldiers.

But good Christians were pacifists – you don't kill someone in God's paradise. Pacifists didn't make the most effective army. If he wanted Christian soldiers, he needed a different kind of Christianity.

So he threw his support behind marginalized theologians who claimed that Jesus' death through crucifixion was a sign that God thought death and suffering could be a good thing. After all, he let his own son be killed.

So killing non-Christians was a way to convince them to accept Christ. In fact, it was their fault that we had to kill them. If God didn't want them dead, he'd stop us. We were just doing God's work. This provided a rational for Christians to kill.

But there was another problem for soldiers: even a good Christian doing God's work in battle sometimes got killed. How could a good person get killed doing God's work in paradise?

So these theologians said that, since this world contains bad people we have to kill, it couldn't be the real paradise after all. The real heaven is in the afterlife.

The vast majority of Christians at that time saw these theologians as ninth century Lee Atwaters and Karl Roves. They saw them as laughable at best and abominations at worst. They were horrified that someone would actually kill in the name of God.

Nevertheless, they received the support of the state and all its resources. It became the official state religion and was propagated by the empire. Think of it as a virus that got into the body of Christianity. We can still see signs of Charlemagne in the crosses in most churches.

Belief and Practice

Where does this leave us with paradise and the struggle for harmony?

We've looked at a *belief* that this world is paradise – not a perfect place and not a place where we don't have to struggle at times, but a paradise nonetheless.

We've looked at some of the *practices* this belief can generate. To enter paradise is to enter into relationships with the world that are kind, generous, caring, humble, and selfless.

So what is the *experience* of paradise in this world like? How does it deepen our connection to life?

Experience

Sharon Saltzberg, the Buddhist teacher, suggests a thought experiment that gets at the experience:

Imagine aliens coming down and sealing off our campus. All of us are going to be with one another on these four acres forever.

How does that affect our relationships?

We're still going to like some people more and some people less. We'll still get angry and irritated at times. But we'd probably struggle more to cultivate empathy and understanding. It would be in our enlightened self-interest to do so given that we're going to be together forever.

That's the experience of heaven on earth. It connects us more deeply with life.

Conclusions

Before closing, let me acknowledge explicitly that paradise and the struggle for harmony may feel like an awkward topic to us Unitarian Universalists for two reasons.

First, paradise and heaven are associated with Christian concepts of other realms and the future – paradise is a place we may go when we leave this world. Unitarian Universalism focuses more on this world, the present, and how we live here and now.

So it may come as a surprise that our UU focus is in sympathy with the most ancient, orthodox Christianity. To be sure, they spoke of Christ as a living presence in the here and now while we may feel ambiguous about that language. But what that presence meant for them – kindness, generosity, service, justice, and more – are things we value as well.

There may be more harmony between true orthodox Christianity and us than we think.

The second reason my title may feel awkward is that the phrase "struggle for harmony" sounds like an oxymoron. We think of harmony as effortless perfection rather than struggle.

But I would suggest that harmony in this world is not about perfection. It is about relatedness. It is about how we relate to ourselves and the world around us.

The road to perfection is the road to perdition. The road to perdition starts with ideas about perfection. It starts with some religious, political or economic ideology and tries to impose it on reality that never conforms to our ideas.

For example, if my idea of perfection does not include rats, then I may convince myself they don't belong here and God wants me to kill them off. After the rats, who's next? Bees? Wolves? Before long we are sending indigenous people to reservations, cleansing ethnic minorities, and so forth.

If my idea of perfection includes unlimited energy use, then I tend to see oil and the environment as mere commodities I can exploit to achieve my ideal – I mean "God's ideal." This too easily slides into environmental destruction, wars, and more.

The road to perfection is the road to perdition – hell on earth.

On the other hand, the road to harmony starts with savoring the world – with loving it for what it is – and coming into a balanced relationship with it and her people and creatures.

This does require struggle. It does require effort to cultivate gratitude as an antidote to greed, compassion as an antidote to dislike, and courage as an antidote to fear and joy as an antidote to discouragement.

May we love this world fiercely.

Namasté.

The Pursuit of Happiness

November 16, 2008

Sam died. He'd lived self-indulgently and wanted to indulge life longer. But lying in the hospital bed growing weak, he closed his eyes and died.

Then he opened his eyes. He was standing in a meadow. The air was fresh. The sky was iridescent. There was a faint sheen on everything.

"This must be heaven," he thought. "Maybe I lived better than I thought. Or maybe God is kinder than I imagined."

Wandering around the gently rolling meadows, he thought, "I wish there were some place I could sit back and take all this in."

Coming up the next rise he noticed a house with a wide, inviting veranda. He nestled into a big chair and put his feet up on the railing. He gazed at the fields and forests and a sea in the distance. "A perfect view," he mused.

Inside the house he found carpets, couches, large windows, and soothing décor. "Just what I always dreamed of. If there was only some music, it would be perfect." Then he noticed a stereo. He pressed a button on the remote and his favorite music filled the room.

He closed his eyes and fell asleep.

He awoke hungry. In the kitchen he found fresh fruit, garlic bread, chocolates, ice cream, and more. "All my favorite foods are right here," he mumbled through a full mouth.

After several days, he began to feel lonely. "If only I could share this with someone," he wished absently.

He heard a knock. When he opened the front door there was a woman. She was strong, smart, sexy, and instinctively attuned to him – his ideal partner. She moved in.

And so he settled into the most comfortable existence imaginable. Everything he wanted materialized.

Nevertheless, as weeks stretched into months he felt dull and edgy. Nothing pushed him to look deeper. Nothing encouraged him to search his heart. He felt both sated and unhappy, both fuzzy and heavy. Vaguely he thought, "I need a challenge."

Just then a pool table materialized in the next room. Excitedly he picked up a cue stick, eyed the table, and took an energetic shot. The balls bounced around the table. A ball went in the side pocket. A second slipped into the corner. And another and another until only the cue ball was left rolling to a stop. One shot had sunk everything!

"Ahhhh!" He ran out of the house yelling.

He found the man in charge. The man bowed. "Are you okay? You seem agitated. Is there anything wrong? How can I help?"

"I don't mean to be ungrateful," Sam said. "But I think I'd like to transfer to hell."

The man looked at him blankly. Then a smile slowly spread across his face. He bowed to Sam and said, "Where do you think you are?"

Pursuit of Happiness

This morning I would like to talk about the pursuit of happiness. The long campaign in pursuit of the White House is over. But as the campaign ends, we are beginning what could be a long and deep recession. We could be entering tough economic times.

Right now is a good time to pause, step back, and reflect on where happiness truly comes from. We all want the freedom to pursue happiness. It might be helpful to reflect on where to pursue.

I suggest three ingredients of happiness: faith, diligence, and mindfulness. Let's reflect on each of these.

Faith

By "faith" I mean faith in ourselves, confidence in our essential nature. I don't mean blind faith in some happiness-giver out there. I do mean trust that contentment can be found in what we have right now.

All religions speak about at least two different kinds of paths to happiness, though they use different words for it: God, heaven, paradise, harmony, the divine, nirvana, contentment, peace, and more.

One kind of path is the small-hearted, small-minded, external path of accumulation. It seeks symbols rather than happiness itself. It confuses the pursuit of happiness with the pursuit of wealth, power and prestige. Like Sam, it confuses fulfilling desires with fulfillment itself.

The second is the big-hearted, big-minded inner path. It recognizes that desires can be infinite. Quenching desires can be like quenching thirst by drinking salt water. Yes, we have material bodies and material needs for food, clothing, shelter, health care, companionship, and so on. But our true needs are modest. Beyond that, happiness is found inside. It doesn't come from accumulating stuff out there but from cultivating qualities in here like gratitude, compassion, generosity, and kindness.

Years ago I found the story of the man mistaking hell for heaven in a book called *Who Dies?* by Stephen Levine.[18] Listening to it we may feel the pull of each of these two paths.

The wisdom of the inner path is obvious – the endless pursuit of stuff doesn't result in meaningful happiness. It can lead to a subtle hell on earth.

And yet, we may also hear a voice inside saying, "Yes. But wouldn't it be nice to live in the beautiful home with that wonderful view. Wouldn't it be nice to snap my fingers anytime and have someone massage my shoulders, have a delicious meal appear, or have any other desire satisfied so gracefully? Can I just try it for a while?"

We can feel the pull of both paths because both are embodied in our physical-psycho-spiritual being. Recognizing the sweet pull of the external path and how it fails helps strengthen faith in looking within.

The World

Working wisely with both pulls is important not only for our individual psychological and spiritual health. It is also important for our collective health as a nation and a world.

During the last few decades, the predominant economic and political views in this country have been small-hearted and small-minded. So called "bleeding heart liberalism" has been despised by some as if empathy and caring for those in need and other inner qualities are an expression of weakness and naiveté: "It's a dog eat dog world so let's promote unbridled competition rather than coddle the weak. God favors the strong."

Throughout history, those in power have favored policies that don't restrict their power. The mantras of free market capitalism and freedom to do what we want are a disguise for unrestrained pursuit of money, power, and prestige. Charlemagne would be proud.

America is an experiment in putting government, economy, and society in the hands of we the people. This means setting up policies and regulations to make sure everyone is playing fairly by the same rules.

The mantras of privatization and deregulation have meant we the people have less oversight or even knowledge of what is going on. Those with the strongest drive for money, power, and prestige have been relatively free to do what they want.

And this is what we've seen: a smaller and smaller group of people has drained resources from the general welfare for their own personal welfare. The commonwealth – environment, transportation systems, health care, education, and services – has been degraded. The disparity between the super-rich and the middle class has become obscene. And now the financial system itself is devastated. Like Sam, we see that the results of unrestrained pursuit of desire are not pretty.

We the people – all of us – will be paying for this for years. We can clean up the economic wreckage. We can clean up the aftermath of two wars.

But it will take time and effort. It won't always be easy.

Diligence

This brings us to the second ingredient of happiness: diligence. Just because that deep

---

[18] Adapted from Stephen Levine, *Who Dies? An Investigation of Conscious Living and Conscious Dying*. Anchor Books, New York. 1982, p. 47-48.

connection with life and happiness is available all the time doesn't mean it comes without effort.

The South Vietnamese monk Thich Nhat Hahn wrote: "You can buy the conditions of happiness, but you can't buy happiness itself."[19] It must be cultivated diligently.

For example, let's say making music makes you happy. You can buy expensive instruments, hire gifted teachers, rent a practice studio, and so on. Those are conditions of musical happiness. But the happiness itself arises when you cultivate your talent through practice.

Erika, my wife, ran a community music school when we lived in Massachusetts. She had as many as 75 faculty members. Over the years, Russian and east European musicians joined her faculty. Some of them were exquisitely trained. They had grown up with old pianos in poor repair. They had worked hard to learn how to pull beautiful music out of anything.

Also on her faculty were American musicians. Some had studied in elite conservatories and owned beautiful instruments.

When Russian and American teachers were in a studio with a mediocre instrument, the Russian was in heaven and the American was in hell. The Russian could draw beauty out of a few strings and a keyboard. The American felt frustrated and blocked.

The point is: if we have enough money we may be able buy the conditions of happiness, but not the happiness itself. The more faith we have in the happiness inside us and the more diligently we cultivate that happiness, the fewer external conditions we require.

Mindfulness

The third ingredient of happiness is mindfulness. It is not enough to just believe happiness is inside us and to practice diligently. We need to experience it directly. Mindfulness is the ability to look deeply into the nature of things and experience fully.

When we look deeply into happiness, we see different flavors. Some are strong but leave a bad after taste. Others are subtle but long-lasting.

Excitement

For example, consider excitement. Getting a new car, a new iPod, a raise in salary, or a new jacket can feel delightful. But the rush doesn't last. For most people, the excitement of a raise lasts a week or so. Then they adjust to it and the good feeling fades.

There is nothing wrong with enjoying nice things. In fact, if we look deeply into delight, it melts into a deeper ease and contentment.

The problem with excitement is it draws our attention outward rather than inward. As it fades, rather than mellow into contentment, we may look outside for something else to rekindle the rush. We can get caught in an endless pattern of consumption. When we do this as a nation, we can end up in the economic mess we are in today. Or like Sam, we end up in a vague ennui – a meaninglessness one writer called "existential flu."

Distraction

Another flavor of happiness is distraction. During tough times we may feel stress, worry, or sadness. We may look for something to numb us or divert our attention from this discomfort.

Like excitement, distractions require energy and don't last. As they fade, the unhappiness comes back even stronger. Like an ignored child, it nags for attention.

There is nothing wrong with diversion as long as we are mindful. But when the distractions weaken, the temptation is to escalate and look for bigger distractions. Distraction is the opposite of mindfulness.

Contentment

Another flavor of happiness is contentment.

Contentment is hard to see. It has very little charge. Excitement has a positive charge and is easy to see. Worry, fear, and sadness have a negative charge and are easy to see.

But peace and wellbeing have very little charge. They are neutral. They are with us all the time – every moment. They are part of our core being. But they are difficult to see because they don't draw attention to themselves.

---

[19] *The Art of Power*. HarperOne, 2008, p. 81

And when we do notice them, we may be tempted to hold onto them. This is like grasping smoke: it slips away.

But with mindfulness, rather than grasping, we open up with big heart and big mind. And when contentment fades, we mindfully let it go and open up with big mind and heart to the next moment.

Deeper happiness is not a thing to hold. It is a way to open deeply and mindfully to anything that comes along. It is not a feeling as much as a way of relating to what is inside and around us.

Like the early Christians who saw this earth as paradise: the way to enter heaven or happiness is not grasping stuff already here. It is entering into a sacred relationship with the world, relationships based on generosity, caring for the oppressed, and taking care of one another.

Practice

Don't take their word for it. Don't take my word for any of this. Try it out. In fact, let's try it out right now.

If you like, close your eyes, ... take a few deep breaths ... and reflect on those times you felt the most happiness, contentment, or wellbeing. What was going on in your life?...

Remember what it felt like ... Go ahead and feel it right now...

The fact that you can even touch that deep happiness now says that it is available all the time, beneath our excitement, beyond our distractions, quietly sitting right there in the center of our being...

It's here right now. It's subtle and easy to miss. But it requires nothing more than learning to notice it. ...

What helps you notice this quiet place? This contentment? Peace? Wellbeing ...

See what's true for you. ... See what helps you touch your own happiness. ... Remember what this is.

If you like, open your eyes and come back into the room.

Summary

To summarize, during tough economic times we can feel stress, fear, or worry. The risk is that we'll regress. The brain's reptile-complex with its fight or flight impulse gets stimulated. Then, like Sam, we're vulnerable to the illusion that happiness comes from the shopping mall. The reptile-complex is not very smart.

On the other hand, sobering times can encourage us to pause, reflect, and look deeply at what's going on. We engage the higher mind and bigger heart. They are smarter as well as more compassionate.

We see that the happiness we yearned for has been with us all along. It was deep inside us. What we needed wasn't more stuff but subtler qualities like faith in our underlying being, diligence to cultivate our inner lives, and mindfulness to see deeply.

And we begin to know that happiness is more powerful than money, power, or prestige. Happy people are difficult to manipulate.

Reflect on this: Who would you rather have solving our collective problems? People who are angry, scared, or worried? Or people who feel content and are only motivated to serve?

Individually or collectively, the greatest power is not fulfilling desires. It is happiness itself. When we are filled with quiet happiness, our minds clear. We see more of the complexities and interconnections. Our problem solving capacities increase. We become smarter. We are less vulnerable to external manipulation.

We become a compelling force for healing in our own lives and in the world.

May it be so.

Namasté

Peaceful Heart

December 7, 2008

Sunday morning, December 7, 1941: The Imperial Japanese Navy sends 353 planes in two waves over the United States Naval Base at Pearl Harbor. In 90 minutes they sink or damage 8 U.S. battleships, 3 cruisers, 3 destroyers, 1 minelayer and 188 aircraft. They kill 2,400 people and wound another 1,300.

Japan wanted a peaceful world organized around what they saw to be a more enlightened society – their own. Japan saw the United States as a threat. They suspected we would soon enter the war against them. Neutralizing the U.S. Navy would also give Japan access to much needed oil and other natural resources in the Pacific. So they launched a preemptive strike.

The Japanese attack was a brilliant tactical success. And it was a colossal strategic failure. It galvanized this country into a determined foe.

Two-thirds of a century later, our "preemptive war" on Iraq was a stunning tactical success. But in the so-called war on terror, it has been a colossal strategic failure creating more foes.

This morning I do not want to glorify our role in World War II or vilify our role in Iraq. You know the pros and cons as well as I. And you know my strong pacifist leanings.

This morning I would like to look deeper than good and bad, right and wrong, just and unjust. I would ask, "Why do we humans keep doing this?" "What are the causes of war inside us?"

This morning I want to talk on a personal level. I think the season encourages us to do this. Advent is a time of quiet reflection. Christmas is a promise of peace and goodwill. The solstice marks a time when nature herself goes dormant and looks inward.

When we look inward, I think we see the root cause of all war is the hardening of our hearts. Whether we are talking about war in our families, in our communities, amongst the nations, or between ideological groups, war starts with the hardening of the heart. Therefore true peace – not a tactical cease-fire, but transformative peace – comes from the courage to find the softness inside us that is deeper than the hardness.

Individuals

To explore this proposition, I begin with the words of Henry Wadsworth Longfellow that have been set in a Christmas carol:

I heard the bells on Christmas day
Their old familiar carols play,
And wild and sweet the words repeat
Of peace on earth, good will to men.[20]

The message of joy, peace, and good will touches a poignant sentiment deep in all sentient creatures.

War and peace do not start in an oil field or epithet or war slogan. Arrows don't leap off the ground and fly through the air on their own. War and peace start in the heart of individual humans. And deep in our hearts we all want peace. It is just that our ways of getting it are not always wise or skillful.

Consider: We're driving along enjoying Christmas music on the radio. An SUV cuts us off. Reflexively we blow the horn. The other driver rolls down his window and calls out. We can't hear him – the windows are shut and the radio is playing. But judging by his furrowed brow and colorful gestures we surmise he's not yelling "peace on earth, goodwill to you."

We roll down the window and retort, "Learn to drive, you jerk!" We swerve around him and speed away as the radio sings, "Joy to the world, the Lord has come." We punch the radio off and mutter dark words about the crassness of the season.

What happened?

We were enjoying a peaceful moment and wanted it to continue. Getting cut off caused fear or anger and disrupted the inner calm. Yelling was an attempt to discharge the upset and restore justice so we could have peace of

---

[20] Composed in 1863

mind and heart. We wanted peace but our method of obtaining it was dubious.

Or consider: It's been a tiring day. We look forward to getting home and letting down.

But when we walk into the house, the kids are running around fueled by holiday excitement and sugar. "Quiet down!" we yell. "Pick up your toys and give me a little peace and quiet!"

Their faces collapse and they mope off to their rooms. We feel more guilt than peace.

Again, we wanted peace but our strategy was not effective.

Or maybe we don't actually yell at them. We try to act calm. But despite ourselves, our voice is taut and our words have a snippy edge. Our unspoken tension is obvious. The seeds of war are in us.

Hardening of the Heart

In each of these scenarios the urge for peace turned into the seeds of war when the heart hardened. What we call "hardening" is a shift in consciousness and probably a shift in brain function from the cerebral cortex to the reptile complex. So let's look at this more closely.

Imagine a peaceful consciousness. It is relaxed, tender, clear, and spreads out through the heavens enveloping everything. It knows our lives intermingle. We are one. A familiar carol by Phillip Brooks beings:

> *O little town of Bethlehem,*
> *How still we see thee lie.*
> *Above the deep and dreamless sleep*
> *the silent stars go by*

Then an SUV cuts us off or we walk into domestic chaos. It is jarring, like getting kicked in the belly. It hurts. Reflexively we move to protect that soft place. Our shoulders may pull in, hands tighten, jaw stiffens and eyes harden. Our spacious mood shrinks into anger, fear, irritation, or distress. Our consciousness becomes thick and heavy. In short, we create a physical, emotional, and mental flack jacket around that tender peacefulness.

Sometimes these shifts are subtle. But at the very least there is a contraction around the heart. We can feel it if we look.

We might not notice these inner changes because our attention is focused outward on the driver or the kids or whatever is seen to be a threat.

If we want to be instruments of peace in the world or peace in our lives, it is important to know when the heart tightens. Usually, it is not something we do intentionally. It just happens. But we can notice it if we are willing.

Hardening of the Mind

If we don't notice this hardening of the heart, then the mind starts to harden as well. It loses its suppleness. We begin thinking in terms of black and white, us and them, who's a threat and who isn't.

One definition of fundamentalism is rigid thinking. Rigidity can arise in conservatives and liberals, religious and irreligious, politicians and parents. It provides the rationale for ethnic prejudice, scapegoating, epithets, slavery, shipping indigenous people off to reservations, attacking Pearl Harbor, interning Japanese-Americans, invading Iraq in the name of self-defense, and terrorizing in the name of freedom. Longfellow's poem continues:

> *And in despair I bowed my head,*
> *"There is no peace on earth," I said,*
> *For hate is strong and mocks the song*
> *Of peace on earth good will to men.*

Peace

Wars – personal or national – start with hardening to protect that soft place deep inside the heart. Therefore, peace starts by touching that soft spot behind the hardness – finding the tenderness we are protecting. Sometimes this is all we need to do. We reconnect with the spacious heart and the road to peace opens up. The hard heart is like an igloo – a wall of ice that insulates inner warmth. If we touch that inner glow, it starts to flow out and melt the ice. A carol based on a poem by Christina Rossetti suggests:

> *In the bleak midwinter,*
> *In this world of pain*
> *When the heart is open,*
> *Love is born again.*

However, sometimes touching that softness or melting that ice is not so easy. Our feelings may be too strong, the ice may be too thick and hard.

What can we do?

Patience

If we can't connect with that soft warmth inside, the next thing to do is probably nothing. Pause. Wait a while. An old prayer says, "God give me patience and I want it right now." Rather than speak or act immediately, we can practice patience.

Emotions are like waves: they naturally swell and then subside. If we take a breather, the hardness may ebb on its own.

Traditionally Advent is a time for quiet reflection, like Mary waiting quietly for the birth. It is easier to find the peaceful heart when we aren't rushing around, multiprocessing, problem solving, and juggling hectic schedules.

It is helpful to create quiet times to sit, reflect, do something soothing, or do nothing at all. The more often we feel the heart's spaciousness in gentle times, the easier it is to do so in stressful times.

Enter the Hardness

However, sometimes patience is not enough. The tightness is too strong. The ice is too thick. We are too identified with the fear or anger or judgments.

In this case we may need to deal directly with the tightness itself. Listen to it. Feel it. Loosen it up and give it expression. That is to say: vent.

When I was a body-oriented psychotherapist, I had a client whom I'll call Jane. Jane was very bright. She had a healthy family life and a successful career. But there was coldness about her. She understood she had old anger and fear. But she couldn't actually feel them.

So we decided to train her to throw a tantrum. She lay down on her back on a mattress in my office. I had her roll her head from side to side as she said, "No, no, no!" This helped loosen her neck and voice. Then I had her hit the mattress with her fists to loosen her arms and torso. Then I had her kick to loosen her lower body.

At first she did these exercises mechanically. Then one December day, she flew into a full-blown tantrum about Christmas, her husband, her parents, and more. She screamed and flailed. I made sure she didn't slide off the mattress and hurt herself.

Then, as she flailed, she suddenly stopped, sat up with a glowing grin, and said, "I haven't had so much fun since I was a little girl!" She immediately dropped back into the tantrum.

What she meant by "fun" was it felt so good to release that numbness around her heart. Tightness, fear, and anger are uncomfortable. We naturally want to discharge them to get rid of them. This is why we feel the urge to yell at a rude driver or noisy kids. It is a fundamentally healthy impulse to express these feelings.

However, since our heart and its wisdom are not fully engaged, it is important to release the feelings in a protective setting. We didn't want Jane to throw dishes around her house, slap her husband, and yell at her daughter. That wouldn't be safe. But my office was safe and protected.

As Jane got better and better at throwing tantrums in my office, a huge, powerful, glowing heart began to emerge in the rest of her life.

Jane's release was more dramatic than most. But the point is that even powerful feelings can be released safely.

Wise and Safe

So, when you feel like yelling at the clerk in the department store, don't. Practice patience. When you get back to your car, if you still feel stressed, roll up the windows, turn on some music, and yell. If someone walks by your car they'll just think you are singing out of tune. It's safe.

When you feel like venting at the kid, don't. Instead, go into the next room and vent into a pillow over your mouth. Or find a sympathetic friend with whom you can kvetch.

There are thousands of wise and safe ways to loosen up: hitting pillows, stomping around an empty house, screaming under water, exercising, getting the support of a friend, and more. Experiment. Be creative, have fun and be safe. The carol "O Little Town of Bethlehem" reminds us:

*Yet in thy dark street shineth
The ever-lasting light.
The hopes and fears of all the years
Are met in thee tonight.*

The dark and the light, the hopes and the fears sometimes get intertwined and stuck together.

Genuine spirituality is about connecting deeply with life and its movement. It's not about being a manikin. If we want to be a force for peace in the world, it is important to get the non-peaceful energies moving and out of our system in a safe way. It is sacred work. Difficult sometimes. Not very pretty sometimes. But it is sacred. It helps us become instruments of peace.

Relation

One caveat: Sometimes we get angry with our kids or family or people we care about not because we want to hurt them but because we want to get through to them. We don't want to destroy them, just connect with them.

Going off by ourselves and venting doesn't help the connection. It doesn't hurt. It may help us find our wisdom and clarity. But it may still be important to come back, look them in the eyes and say, "I'm so angry with you [or frightened or whatever]. I want to tell you about it. And I want to hear what you have to say."

We aren't venting any longer. We are being honest and open about our upset *and* we are connecting with them. Both are important. They can make a strong relationship even stronger.

Empathy

So these are some tools I've found helpful: connecting with that softness, patience, venting safely, and reconnecting. Another tool is empathy.

As I said earlier, if the heart stays hard, the mind starts to harden as well. We may think, "He's a jerk," "She's a control freak." "He's a conservative and out of touch." "She's a liberal and lives in a fantasy." Our thinking has become rigid, black-and-white, overly generalized.

Rigid thinking can be loosened with empathy. We put ourselves in the other person's shoes. We imagine looking at the world through their eyes. We try to feel what it might feel like to be them.

It is easier to recognize rigid thinking in others than in ourselves. So if you see it in a friend, say, "Hmm. I wonder what's going on inside the person you're mad at. I wonder what they're feeling and thinking."

Social Justice Work

Empathy is very important in social justice work. If we don't like what a leader or a group of people are doing in the public arena, seeing them in black-and-white terms is the road to war. Empathizing with their hopes and fears is the road to peace. We don't have to agree with them, just empathize

Publically venting frustration at political leaders isn't wise. It's emotionally understandable. But it doesn't make the world more peaceful.

Publically, we can give voice to yearnings, fears, hopes, anger, and dreams in ways that genuinely try to connect without demonizing. If we can empathize with people we don't agree with we'll be more effective in communicating our concerns.

The world is too precarious for us to vent in destructive ways. So vent in a protected setting. Connect in a public setting.

Closing

If we want to be a force for peace, it helps to monitor our own hearts. Notice the ways it opens and closes in various situations and around various people as we go through the season and beyond.

This is a fierce practice. We may notice subtle hurts, fears, grudges, and unkind thoughts. It helps if we are kind to ourselves. It doesn't help to judge ourselves when the heart closes. But we can be both honest and kind.

If we can lovingly open to our hardness, it becomes easier to open to our softness.

We will be bringing more peace into the world and our lives. We become instruments of peace. As Phillip Brooks put it:

*How silently, how silently,
the wonder is made known,
when God imparts to human hearts
the gift that is our own.
No ear may hear it coming,*

but in this worldly din,
when souls are truly humble, then
the dear babe rests within.

Namasté.

Joy and Formless Wellbeing

December 14, 2008

December is a season of contradictions.

In preindustrial ages, the harvest was in: ah, time to relax and celebrate. And the winter was upon us: yikes, time to hurry up and batten down before the harsh weather descended.

Perhaps relax and hurry got bred into us. In the postindustrial age the Christmas season is a time of quiet anticipation and impatient preparation, delight and dread, joy and seasonal affective disorder, generosity and pushing to get to the front of the line, Handel's "Messiah" and Randy Brooks' "Grandma Got Run Over by a Reindeer."

In this year's postelection season many feel the mix of hope that Obama brings a change in policy and temperament to the Presidency and fear about the worsening economy.

How do we cope with all the conflicting moods and customs and possibilities?

Traditionally, Advent recommends slowing down. On the last few Sundays Roger and I spoke about different flavors of Advent practices: waiting, mindfulness, patience, empathy, monitoring our hearts, and touching the softness beneath our hardness.

This morning I would like to talk about a complementary practice: joy.

The high energy of the season is not necessarily a bad thing. It can go out of balance in all kinds of crazy ways – commercialism, short tempers, stress, hectic schedules. But high energy is not necessarily a problem.

So this morning I'd like to talk about riding the energy of the season –enjoying the rush, as it were.

This sermon continues a series on religious experience. In it we distinguish between religious beliefs, religious experiences, and religious practices.

Most people define religion as a set of beliefs about the cosmos or stances toward life. But the cosmos is more complex than any beliefs. And life is more fluid than any stance we take toward it. Religions based on beliefs or stances fail sooner or later.

So in this series we define religion as the experience of deep connection to life.

Joy cannot be confined to a set of beliefs. Joy is not a stance. And joy does connect us more fully with life.

So this morning I want to talk about joy as a simple movement of the mind and heart that can be cultivated. It is not a mysterious gift of whimsical gods. And it can't be controlled through force of will. But joy is a natural flow in all of us that we can surrender into even in times as contradictory as the holidays.

Experience

Let's begin with the actual experience of joy.

Bill Storm and Danielle Gouldeman invited me to officiate at their marriage three weeks ago. Both have children from previous marriages. Their kids are very important to them, so we included them in the ceremony.

Just before the ceremony was to begin, I checked with Danielle to make sure she was ready. Her eight-year-old daughter, Emma, was walking back and forth in the hall.

Danielle said, "Emma 's nervous."

I looked at Emma. As she walked, she raised her arms high. With each step she floated up onto her toes. When she looked over her shoulder at me, her brown eyes were large and shiny. Her face glowed.

"She's not nervous," I said to Danielle. "You're the one who's nervous. She's excited. She's over-flowing with delight. She's having trouble staying on the ground."

Danielle smiled and said, "Yes. She's been so happy about this wedding."

Emma was the personification of joy. Joy is a sense of wellbeing that flows up through us and carries us beyond our normal boundaries.

Joy can animate our bodies like a child rising up on her toes or a dervish whirling. Or it can flow through us with little outward movement.

I came home once to find my father spread out on the living room floor with Beethoven booming from the stereo and shaking the house. My father was usually a tightly controlled, scary man. But when he listened to Beethoven, bliss flowed through him even though he wasn't moving a muscle.

Another quality of joy is it pulls us into the present.

Years ago I drove into the Zen Center in Providence, Rhode Island for a retreat with the Korean Zen Master, Seung Sahn. After registering, I parked my car in a nearby field.

As I walked back to the center I saw a little man scrubbing a pot on the steps behind the kitchen. He was so totally present with that pot that I could feel the joy emanating from him even from fifty yards away. I had never met Seung Sahn or seen his picture. But I thought, "That must be him." It was.

Another quality of joy is it transcends thought.

A traditional image of joy is found in the Gospel of Luke. In chapter 2, angels told the shepherds to look for Jesus in Bethlehem. "They hurried to the village and found Mary and Joseph and the baby, lying in the manger. … All who heard the shepherds' story were astonished. … The shepherds went back to their flocks glorifying and praising God." (Luke 2:16,18,20) One translation says the shepherds "let loose, glorifying and praising."

As I imagine the shepherds letting loose, singing and praising, I don't see them marching in cadence, "1-2-3, hip, hip, hurray, yea God!" I don't imagine them arguing, "Are we praising a three-part Trinitarian God or a one–part Unitarian God?" "Are we singing to God out there or God in here?" "Does this God intervene in life or watch impassively?"

They were astonished by what they experienced. Their minds were blown. They were ecstatic.

Joy is not about concepts, ideas or theologies. It transcends these. It is purer, simpler, and more expansive than the intellect can analyze or contain.

So, joy is a high-energy sense of wellbeing that flows through us. It may relax our body into movement or relax it into stillness, but it relaxes. It also relaxes the mind. Thinking tends to fade as we're pulled into the present.

Taking a Break from Joy

This means that if you have too much joy or want to take a break from it, there are things you can do like:

Tighten

Tighten up your body, preferably to the point of numbness. When you move, move stiffly. When you don't move, be wooden. This obstructs the free flow of wellbeing.

Control Freak

Cultivate your inner control freak. Think about all the things that can go wrong if you don't keep a firm grip on yourself –ways you can stumble, forget, or get into trouble. Joy takes you beyond yourself. So clamping down on yourself clamps down on joy.

Misery of Hurry

Turn the joy of movement into the misery of hurry. When you're out shopping or strolling by the river, think about all the things you have to get to. Life is short and there is so much to get done. Joy can only arise in the present. So rather than enjoy where you are, hurry to the next task.

Think

Think, think, think, think – think about everything from cynical abstract questions to the meaning of shopping malls and streetlights. Joy takes us beyond thought, concepts, and ideas. So clutter your head with ideas and endless speculation. If the Inn at Bethlehem is filled with thoughts, there will be no room for joy to enter.

Other

There are many other techniques we all can think of.

Benefits

Of course, most of us don't actually want to reduce joy in our lives. But we've been trained and conditioned to do so many things that can suck joy out of us. Therefore, it might be helpful to remind ourselves of some of the values of joy. Let me mention a few:

Feeling Good

Joy feels good.

Balance

Joy is the perfect antidote for boredom, dullness, lethargy, and grumpiness. It brings us back into balance.

Peace

Joy is a road to peace on earth. Joyful people pick fewer fights and pull fewer triggers. They are more committed to finding peaceful solutions. Spreading joy reduces the chance of war.

Environment

Joyful people place less strain on the environment. They have less drive to consume resources they don't really need.

Enlightenment

Joy is a part of higher states of consciousness all the way up to and including enlightenment and merging with the divine. Higher states have other qualities like calmness, clarity, and luminosity. But these are subtle and not as easy to see. Joy is easy to see. So joy is a toe in the door to these higher states. In January I'll describe a road map that starts with joy and leads to nirvana.

Practices

We've looked at the experience of joy and some of the values of joy. Let's look at some practical ways to cultivate joy during the holidays and beyond. I'll mention four this morning. You probably have others that work for you. That's great.

The four I offer can be summarized with four words: body, present, relax, and smile.

Body

First, be in your body.

Higher states of awareness envelop both the inner and the outer worlds equally. In this culture, we emphasize the outer world. This throws us out of balance. We even treat our bodies as a thing "out there" to be fed, exercised, dressed, cleaned, and managed.

The more awareness you have of your body, the easier it is for joy to arise.

Even when you're stressed, lonely, worried, or rushing through traffic, it is helpful to be aware of the body. Don't try to change anything. Just lovingly notice what's going on.

How is your body right now? Don't think about it. Just feel it on its own terms. As you listen to the rest of the service, keep half your awareness in your body and see the effect it has.

Present

Being in your body also helps ground you in the present, the only place where joy exists.

Have you ever noticed that we can't actually think about the present moment? Thoughts that seem to be about the present are really about a moment ago. The closest we come is thinking about what happened a half second ago or what may happen a half second from now. We can't think about the present. We can only perceive it.

Don't get me wrong. Thinking is magnificent and useful. It helps us plan, organize, figure out how to get through traffic, negotiate the relatives, or decide what to do with our lives.

Thoughtfulness is good. And it is wise to review our plans from time to time. And it may even be helpful to re-review.

But sitting in traffic going over and over how we wish we'd taken another route or how that meeting might have gone differently or obsessing over a mental shopping list. I'm not convinced that is really useful or wise.

So, if you find yourself in not-useful thought, anticipation, or worry, just be present. Get curious about this moment. Whether you are walking through Walgreens, sitting in traffic, or hiking in the mountains, see what's going on around you in a deeper way. Notice.

Relax

Excessive thinking is a sign of stress. It disguises tension in the body or mind. So be aware of that tightness and invite it to relax.

You can relax while napping. And you can also relax while rushing from one end of the mall to the other or from the grocery store to school to home.

You can relax even while excited. Emma is an example of this. I love to quote Rollo May on this: "Anxiety is excitement without oxygen." If you are anxious and relax and breathe into it, it becomes excitement. And if you give the excitement space to move, it becomes joy.

Many of you have trained in the martial arts? What is the secret of speed in the martial arts? It is relaxing. When we are tight, it is hard to move swiftly. But when we are loose, it's possible to move very quickly.

The same is true of music — you can play faster when the hands are loose.

So if you are in a hurry, know that tightening up doesn't help you get there any faster. Relax. Enjoy the rush.

Smile

Once you're in your body, in the present and relaxed, then smile and joy will surely follow.

My friend, Emily, was in the Peace Corp in Africa many years ago. When she came upon a local person she knew, his expression would be blank – a deadpan. As he recognized her, a smile would start from his toes and spread slowly up through him until it lifted the corners of their eyes and mouth.

When I say, "smile," I don't mean commanding your face to smile like the poor clerk behind the fast food counter. Simply invite wellbeing to rise softly through you.

And if a smile won't arise, laugh at yourself for being so serious. It's been said that the angels can fly because they take themselves lightly.

And don't worry: smiling won't make you stupid. By lightening and brightening the mind and heart, it actually makes you wiser. And it resonates with the wellbeing that is already deep inside. It helps you connect with that intimate joy.

Formless

Before closing, I want to mention one more aspect of joy: it is formless. This is the bad news. Since joy has no form, we can't hold onto it.

If we try to hold onto joy, we'll end up grasping some object that we think brings us joy.

Perhaps I enjoy a flower. "It gives me joy," I tell myself. Rather than attend to both the outer world and the inner world – the flower and the joy – I focus just on the flower. I hold it. And I hold on and hold on. Eventually the joy leaves. I'm left with a dead plant.

When we try to hold onto joy, it can create a counterfeit joy: a mild hysteria that is no fun at all.

Joy itself is formless. This is the bad news. And it is also the good news. It means that joy can arise anywhere, any time, any place, in any person, for any reason, or for no reason at all. It can arise while resting or while moving. It can arise at work, at home, at church, or in the grocery store. It can arise when we are feeling delight or dread, high spirited or grumpy, listening to "The Messiah" or "Grandma Got Run Over by a Reindeer." It doesn't come from a formula.

When you come into your body, come into the present, relax, and smile, then joys starts to seep into your being.

So when you enjoy something, enjoy it with relaxed abandonment. When you don't enjoy something, enjoy it with a sense of humor: "Boy, that one really got to me!" Laugh kindly at yourself.

Let yourself be surprised.

Enjoy.

Forgiveness

January 4, 2009

Geraldine lived in one of the rough neighborhoods in Washington, D.C. Derek, her only son, was 13. Derek's father had disappeared many years earlier.

Samuel lived in the same neighborhood but knew neither Geraldine nor Derek. To gain membership in a street gang, Samuel had to demonstrate his toughness. So, he got a gun.

One afternoon, he was in a vacant lot when he saw a few of the gang members. This was his chance to prove himself. He pulled out the gun. "Hey, punk," he called to a strange kid walking by. It was Derek. As Derek turned, Samuel pulled the trigger.

Derek was pronounced dead at the hospital.

Samuel was caught. Geraldine sat in the back of the courtroom through all the proceedings, her face stoical.

Samuel was convicted and sentenced to juvenile hall. As he was being led out of court, Geraldine stood and pointed at him: "You killed my Derek." Her voice was low but carried through the courtroom. "And I'm going to kill you!"

Before the bailiff could reach her, she had turned and walked silently out of the chambers.

She went back to work the next day. She had to. Life goes on. But with Derek's room empty, the apartment felt cold and lifeless.

Six weeks later, she went to juvenile hall to meet Samuel up close. He walked in with an awkward swagger, but his eyes were unsteady. He slouched in a chair facing her.

She said nothing – just looked at him.

Finally, he looked away at the wall. "Sorry," he said. "It wasn't personal."

"It wasn't personal!" she exclaimed. "Derek liked applesauce with cinnamon. He liked to read stories. He put cheerios on the windowsill for birds. He was a person. It was very personal."

Samuel twitched nervously, but he didn't try to leave.

She went on to tell him more about Derek: his likes, his dreams, his quirks.

Then she asked, "What's it like here?"

"I can't get cigarettes – no money," he shrugged a little, "but I get three meals a day."

Samuel didn't volunteer information, but he responded obediently to her questions.

She found out that his mother was strung out on drugs or dead. He didn't know for sure. He had no father. No friends. No one had visited him since his arrest. Nobody.

She rose to leave. Then she turned back to him, opened her purse, took out a few dollars, and said, "Here, this is for cigarettes."

She left.

She began to visit him regularly, sometimes bringing small gifts like a pair of gloves to keep him warm in the drafty facility.

Years went by.

As his release date drew near, she asked, "What are your plans when you get out?"

"Don't have none," he said.

"Where will you stay?"

"Don't know. I'll find something, I suppose."

"I've got an empty room," she said. "Why don't you come stay with me?"

And so, Samuel moved into Derek's bedroom. Geraldine found him a job. Without realizing it, he began to call her "mom."

Then one afternoon when he came home, she said, "Come sit down. I want to talk with you."

"Sure," he said. "What's up?"

"Remember the trial? Remember how I told that boy I was going to kill him?"

"Remember," he shuddered, "how could I forget? Your words went through me like steel."

"I meant what I said. I killed that boy. He no longer exists. I got rid of him forever, and in his place is you. Now, I have another son."

I found this story, in a book called *After the Ecstasy, the Laundry*, by Jack Kornfield.[21] On a train from Washington to Philadelphia, Jack found himself sitting next to an African-American man who ran a rehabilitation program for juvenile offenders. Most of the youths were gang members who had committed homicide. He told Jack this story. I added names and a few details to ease the telling, but it's a true story.

A pivotal moment in the story was when Geraldine gave Samuel money for cigarettes. I don't think she was trying to get him to smoke himself to death, but the story I have is three tellings away from the actual events. It doesn't say if she was already plotting to transform him – kill him with kindness as they say, or if it was simply a spontaneous gesture.

Losing one's child may be the most painful experience a human can endure. Thinking about the person who killed a loved one is conducive to self-righteousness and demonizing.

At that moment, Derek's death and Samuel's role in it receded into the past. They weren't forgotten, but they were a little in the background. In the foreground was a young man about the same age as her son – a boy who was confused and struggling awkwardly with his life.

Geraldine opened to that present moment and responded.

That is the essence of forgiveness: nothing more, nothing less. It is giving up trying to change the past and responding heartfully to the present.

I would like to talk about forgiveness. I know it is the first Sunday of a New Year – I'm supposed to talk about buckling down on those New Year's resolutions to lose weight, exercise, meditate, be patient, whatever. However, we all know resolve is a clumsy tool for self-improvement. Will power requires constant vigilance. Eventually, we tire, and our New Year's resolve retires. As they say, "Habit is stronger than will."

Rather than look at past failings and resolve to do different in the future, it is wiser to forgive ourselves in the present.

This is my annual New Year's sermon on forgiveness. It is part of a series of sermons on religious experience. In this series, we look deeper than beliefs and ideas about religion to the actual experiences that connect us more deeply with life. I'd like to explore forgiveness not as a moral commandment but as an experience that connects us more fully and mysteriously with life itself.

The essence of forgiveness is giving up trying to change the past. The experience of real forgiveness is an expansiveness or sense of freedom that comes with release from trying to change the impossible. As much as we might like to go back and change the past, we relax into the truth that the past is, indeed, beyond our reach.

Conversely, lack of forgiveness leaves us frozen. Life is always in flux. To engage deeply with life, we immerse ourselves in that fluidity. Lack of forgiveness takes us out of life's flow by fixating on something in the past.

There are three kinds of situations where we can get stuck in lack of forgiveness: someone hurts us, we hurt someone, and we hurt ourselves. Whatever the situation, something hardens or tightens up inside and won't let go.

Let's look at how forgiveness helps in each of these three situations.

Someone Hurts Us

The first situation arises after someone hurts us. Sometimes, we accept this and move on with relative ease. Other times, we get stuck in resentment, grudges, hurt, fear, or lingering judgments. Think about times you've felt this. Perhaps, you even tried to forgive, but deep down you couldn't let go. There is a lump in your heart.

What can you do?

Not Okayness

First, distinguish between forgiveness and approval. One thing that can create that unmoving lump is the thought that what the person did was not okay. But saying, "I forgive you," is not the same as saying, "What you did was okay."

Samuel killed Derek. Samuel was mixed up. Even if we empathize with his confusion, the killing was not okay. It was wrong.

---

[21] Bantam Books, 2000. pp. 235-236

All of us have been hurt, neglected, abused, or put down in ways that are wrong.

However, at its deepest level, forgiveness is giving up trying to change the past. It's not approval or disapproval of the past. Forgiveness merely says, "What happened is over. I can't change it now. It is time to embrace what I feel now and let the present unfold as it will."

Not Naïveté

Another thing that can create that lump is fear that the hurt is not over – fear that it will continue or repeat. It would be much harder to forgive Samuel if he was still roaming the streets ready to shoot people to prove his toughness.

If someone is stealing things from your desk or keeps hurtfully blowing you off, it may be hard to forgive them because it may happen again.

In this case, it is helpful to distinguish between forgiveness and naïveté. To say, "I forgive you" is not the same as saying, "I know you'll never do it again." That may be dumb.

Forgiveness is wise in letting the past be in the past. In the present, you may be wise to protect yourself or restrain the person or prevent the hurt from recurring.

This is why it is easier to forgive someone if they show genuine signs of remorse, regret, or self-improvement. If not, you may want to be more attentive, confront the person, hold them accountable, or avoid that relative who often turns abusive.

Just because you forgive someone doesn't mean you become passive. You can open your heart and still keep good boundaries. Taking appropriate action may help you to be able to forgive.

Whatever the case, forgiveness does not require naïveté.

We Hurt Someone

A different kind of situation where we can get frozen in lack of forgiveness is when we have hurt someone or done something wrong. All of us have done things that are not okay. We may feel guilty. So think about guilt in your life. Forgiveness is giving up trying to change the past. Guilt is a fixation on the past that leaves us stuck.

If this is the case, there are a few things you can do to loosen up that lump of guilt.

Amends

First, make amends: apologize, make restitution, do anything reasonable to alleviate the hurt or correct the mistake. If you don't do this because of pride or fear or ego then, bless your heart, you should feel guilty. You are passively prolonging the hurt.

Wisdom

Second, reflect on how you came to do something you regret. Learn from your experience. Wisdom and self-knowledge grows out of such reflection.

Remorse

Third, if you've made amends and gained some insight and still feel stuck on the past, you may need to look deeper. There may be something you are missing.

In these reflections, it is helpful to distinguish between guilt and remorse. Both refer to lingering bad feelings, but guilt says you are a *bad* person who has done something bad. Remorse says you are a *good* person who has done something bad.

We are all inherently good, and we all do bad things. Wisdom and depth come from reflecting on this paradox.

For example, when I was 10 I wanted to play king of the mountain with my friend, Lindsey. He didn't want to play, but I insisted. For our mountain, we used a picnic table in his back yard. I talked him into climbing up on it. Then, to start the game, I pushed him. He fell and broke his arm.

I felt so terrible that I ran home.

Later, I genuinely apologized. It was all I could do. Lindsey didn't hold a grudge, but his father was mad at me for years.

In my own ten-year-old way, I did reflect on what I'd done. I saw that I had acted out of enthusiasm, not meanness, and I saw that I had been insensitive to Lindsey's wishes. This taught me something, changed me a little, and helped me grow.

My guilt feelings subsided, but my remorse lasted for years. In fact, to this day I regret breaking his arm. However, I'm not stuck on it or see myself as being a bad person.

Remorse embraces the past without getting stuck. Remorse is a healthy response to doing something wrong. Guilt is not. Remorse helps us become humbler and wiser.

We Hurt Ourselves

The third area where forgiveness is helpful is when we have hurt ourselves – we are both the perpetrator and the victim, the harmer and the harmed. Everything I've said about the other two arenas can be helpful here: apologizing heartfully to oneself, making amends, reflecting on how you came to hurt yourself, separating remorse and guilt, and so forth.

This arena can be both subtle and pervasive. For millions of years, we evolved in small hunting and gathering bands. The shift to agricultural, city, industrial, and post-industrial cultures happened in only a few thousand years. This is not long enough for our biology to adapt.

Hunters and gatherers worked three or four hours a day. How many hours do you work? They lived close to nature. Education was an organic part of tribal life. There was no processed food. Exercise was part of living. There were difficulties, to be sure, but it is natural. We are biologically wired to live this way.

A large part of our difficulty adapting to 21st century life is that it makes unnatural demands on us. When we have difficulty adjusting, rather than making New Year's resolutions to "do better," we are wiser to reflect on why we did what we did and forgive ourselves. This allows us to be in the present and cope with more clarity and kindness.

Joy

Next in the series (pp. 248-252), I'll take this one step further:

There is a natural joy – a brightness and lightness of being – that is part of our natural selves. I will talk about a road map that goes from this joy all the way to nirvana, enlightenment, or merging with the divine.

Joy is where this path to nirvana begins.

If this joy – this lightness and brightness – is elusive, the most effective medicine is not self-indulgence, tough spiritual discipline, or greater resolve. It is forgiving ourselves for having a mind that gets stressed, a heart that gets pulled in many directions, habits that aren't always fulfilling, eating patterns that aren't optimal, or whatever disturbs.

The road to the joy that leads to enlightenment begins with self-forgiveness.

Summary

To summarize, let's go back to another pivotal moment in Geraldine's story: the moment she decided to visit Samuel in juvenile prison.

The version of the story I have is not explicit about what she was feeling or intending, but I can imagine her sitting in that empty apartment with her grief, anger, and despair like an immovable lump in her heart. She doesn't know what to do next. She's frozen.

A subtle force in her wants to be alive and loving and whole. It says, "To get moving, you have to look into that young man's eyes for Derek's sake and for your own." She confronts Samuel not to vent her feelings, but to see who it was who could do something so monstrous. Who was he really? She wants to see the raw truth.

If she had seen a hopelessly damaged psychopath, she might have felt pity for his miserable existence. She could have forgiven him and left, never to return.

However, she saw a lost young man who had done some terrible things and who was struggling to say he was sorry. She saw redeemable good in him.

Forgiveness is not about right and wrong, okay and not okay. It's not moralistic. It's not about being passive or naïve. In essence, it's about seeing the truth and acting from it. Truth without love is not truthful. Love without truth is not loving.

All of us have done bad things. All of us have goodness at our core. All of us struggle awkwardly to resolve this paradox. All of us deserve forgiveness. All of us would be wise to find ways to forgive ourselves. All of us have the ability to live enlightened lives. Regardless of what you've done in the past, you have the ability to live lives of depth and service from this moment on.

May it be so.

Nibbana I: Unbound by Longing

January 11, 2009

The story is told of a yogi with amazing physical abilities. He bragged he could hold his breath for four weeks with no harm to his person. The king was astonished: "If you can hold your breath for a month, I will give you 20 of my finest horses."

"Very well," said the yogi. "Place me in a stone box and bury me. Come back and dig me up in a month, and you'll see that I'm fine."

Two weeks after burying the yogi, an army overran the kingdom and overthrew the king. In the chaos, the buried yogi was forgotten.

Several months later, some people remembered and quickly dug him up.

They opened the stone box. He slowly came out of his trance. Then he sat up, opened his eyes, looked around, and said, "Where are my horses?"

Road Map

Just because a state is interesting, impressive, or requires great discipline does not mean it is useful or wise.

There are many, many states of consciousness. Some are familiar: greed, generosity, love, hate, fear, joy, and so forth. Others are not so familiar: telepathy, holy illumination, enlightenment, realization, and so on. Some sound downright esoteric: *rigpa*, *satori*, the realm of infinite space, the realm of nothingness, the realm of neither-perception-nor-non-perception.

If we were to draw a map of all possible physical, mental, and spiritual abilities and states of consciousness, it would indeed be a very large map filled with metaphorical mountains, valleys, forests, deserts, oceans, ponds, villages, castles, and cities in great variety. If we want to expand our consciousness and develop all our potential abilities, it will take eons. Frankly, most states are relatively useless. Like holding ones breath for a long time, they do nothing to alleviate unhealthy desires, enhance wellbeing, serve others, or deepen our connection with life.

Siddhartha Gautama was a very bright man. Not only did he become a living Buddha, but he laid out a road map of consciousness that went from familiar, easy-to-enter states up to the highest, deepest fulfillment possible.

He was also a practical man. His road map includes only eight stages called "*jhānas*." These are not ideas or concepts but tangible states that we can experience directly. The states link together in a natural progression that lead to nirvana, enlightenment, merging with the divine (choose your metaphor). It leads from simple joy to the deepest happiness and wisdom.

Stabilize

Tsoknyi Rinpoche is a widely respected Tibetan Buddhist teacher even though he's relatively young (in his 40s) and has a playful sense of humor. Last spring when he was in California, he met with a group of senior, Western dharma teachers. They asked him about differences between his Tibetan and Western students. He said, "Westerners come to realization much more quickly than Tibetans."

This was a surprise. Considering the depth of spiritual tradition in Tibet and its reputation for producing teachers of the caliber of the Dalai Lama, it was perplexing.

Tsoknyi said he found Western students to be intelligent and inquisitive. When given teachings, they "get it" relatively quickly.

"However," he said, "Westerners don't stabilize in these realizations. They go home and say, 'Did I really experience that? I wonder. Oh well, I wonder what's on TV.'"

Tibetans are slower to "get it," but once they realize something, it sticks. They don't lose it.

Access

In the last few years, I've come to understand and experience more of Buddha's road map. I've seen how states that sound esoteric are easier to access than they sound. As I listen to you talk about your experiences, it's clear many of you, too, have greater access to these states than you suspect, though you use a great variety of words to describe them.

I'd like to sketch out this path with its eight jhānas or eight stages. I've been reluctant to talk about them for fear of sounding weird or irrelevant. My hope is that you will recognize things that you have experienced but didn't realize their value, and you will be encouraged to discover that the deepest source of happiness, peace, and effectiveness may be much closer than you think. You may still have some hard work to do – we all do, but you might appreciate your own accomplishments.

I'd like to talk about the first three stages. At a later time, I'll talk about the middle stages, beingness, and nothingness (pp. 253-256). After that, I'll talk about the end point of the path and the secret of happiness (pp. 257-260).

Nibbāna

Before we delve into the first stages, it might be helpful to have a conceptual overview of the whole road map.

First, where are we going? In his native tongue, the Buddha called the end point "*nibbāna*." The more scholarly Sanskrit equivalent is "nirvana."

If you ask most people what nirvana is they will probably either say, "a rock band" or "some mystical state I don't understand."

The word "nibbāna" or "nirvana" literally means "extinguish." To reach enlightenment is to become extinguished. This doesn't sound appealing: "If I get rid of myself in order to find happiness, who will be around to enjoy it? Am I supposed to do all this intense work only to vaporize?"

However, "extinguish" is only a metaphor. For us, when a flame is extinguished, it is gone. The understanding of fire in the Buddha's time was different from modern science.

In the Buddha's time, fire was thought to be part of everything. Some things have a lot of heat – like burning coals. And some things have little heat – like ice, but everything has some fire element.

A flame is created when fire clings. When the grasping relaxes, the flame extinguishes. The heat element is still present; it just disperses. Nothing is lost. It just no longer holds.

So nibbāna is a metaphor for lack of grasping. As we travel this road to nibbāna, the mind remains clear and attentive. With each stage, it becomes more and more relaxed. Grasping – even very subtle grasping – dissipates more with each jhāna. One monk, Thanissaro Bhikkhu, calls nibbāna, "fire unbound by longing."[22]

Overview

Now, let get a bird's eye view of the whole path.

It starts with joy. Joy is a bright and light state of delight that has quite a bit of energy.

As you relax into joy, the energy starts to dissipate into a broader and deeper happiness.

As you relax into happiness, a subtler and more pervasive peacefulness arises – this is the third jhāna: equanimity.

As you keep relaxing, body feeling starts to disappear from awareness – this is the fourth jhāna: equanimity without body.

As you surrender into this deep equanimity while staying mindful, a feeling of great spaciousness arises. The fifth jhāna is called the realm of infinite space.

As you surrender into spaciousness, you notice gaps between thoughts. A thought arises and passes. Then, there is a moment of full consciousness with no thought at all. The sixth jhāna is called the realm of infinite consciousness.

If you allow your awareness to go into the gaps between thoughts, gross thinking relaxes completely. There are still subtle pulls and tugs and movements in the mind, but nothing forms into thought. This seventh jhāna is called the realm of nothingness.

At this point, there still may be an experience and someone observing the experience – you. There is a subtle tension holding together this sense of an observing self. As you relax this tension, the observer dissipates. There is just a flow of experience with no separate observer or observed.

---

[22] Thanissaro Bhikkhu. *The Mind Like Fire Unbound*, (Barre, Massachusetts: Dhamma Dana Publications). 1993

You may also notice that perception, itself, entails a subtle tightness. As you relax this tightness, perception and memory start to fade as you enter the eight jhāna, the realm of neither-perception-nor-non-perception. It is also called "tranquility."

As you release the last subtle bits of tension, you enter nibbāna. There is still being. There is clear awareness, but there is no separate you. It has dispersed into an impersonal knowing and being. At least, this is what I'm told.

First Jhāna

Now, let's go back and look at the first few stages more closely. There are three words that are helpful in describing the first jhānas. In *Pāli*, the language the Buddha spoke, they are: *pīti*, *sukha*, and *upekkhā*. Pīti means "joy," sukha means "happiness," and upekkhā means "equanimity."

One way to experience these is to savor a bite of good chocolate. As it touches your tongue, there is a blast of joy. "Yum!" The energy of joy subsides into a quieter, broader happiness. "… ah …" This happiness mellows into contentment or equanimity. Then, the mind wanders off to think about the next bite or something else. The experience is gone.

These states may arise around a good-hearted joke. You laugh out loud and feel energetic pīti. The laughing subsides into sukha. This subsides into a generalized upekkhā.

You may experience these states while watching small children play. Perhaps the blast of pīti – the energetic joy – does not come up. As you watch the children laughing, you relax directly into sukha – happiness, and as you savor the experience, the sweet, broad wellbeing of upekkhā arises.

The trick is paying attention to the inner states as you move through this cycle. If you are talking with a friend or reading the paper or contemplating a problem as you pop the chocolate into your mouth, there may be a second of pīti – delight – with the first taste. As the energy subsides, rather than notice happiness and equanimity, your attention goes back to your friend or paper or problem. Happiness and equanimity are polite – they don't demand attention the way joy does.

The first jhāna is awareness of this cycle from pīti to sukha to upekkhā – joy to happiness to equanimity. Like that bite of chocolate, it can pass very quickly – maybe just a few seconds. That's okay. To just be aware of each state as they blend from one to the next is the first stage of the Buddha's path.

Cultivation

To cultivate this cycle, you can eat a lot of chocolate, tell a lot of jokes, or watch a lot of children. However, there are limitations to this strategy – particularly if you are trying to watch your weight. Your attention is constantly focused outward, and you may miss the internal states all together. Or, you may confuse the internal states with the external stimulation.

A different strategy is to send joy, happiness, kindness, or well-wishing to others. This is the strategy the Buddha often recommended, and, of course, sending love is central to Christianity, Judaism, and Islam. Saint Francis of Assisi called it "being an instrument of peace."

If you like, try it now. Relax with an attentive mind. … Close your eyes. … Take a breath. …

Think of somebody you feel very good about – a kind aunt, a helpful teacher, a dear friend, a grandchild. … Silently say to them, "May you be happy." "May you be healthy." "May you find fulfillment." Any positive state is fine. … Send them kindness or ease or some quality you'd love them to have. …

You may notice a little feeling of lightness or delight that comes up in you. If so, notice it. That's pīti – a gentle joy.

Or, it may not arise. That's okay. Be patient. Don't judge yourself. If you do judge yourself anyway, forgive yourself. Smile. Be light.

Pīti – joy – is a quality of heart we've all felt. If we relax, we can access it again, if only for a moment.

You can open your eyes or just continue, as you like. …

You can walk through your day sending joy and kindness to those around you. Don't be pushy or showy. Just broadcast it gently.

If you try this, let me reassure you that you will get distracted a lot. However, if you remember to do it only for one minute for every hour, that's still more than twenty minutes a day. That is a toe in the door – the beginning of this path.

Of course, it is easier to relax into these states if you are sitting quietly. This is called "sitting meditation."

Second Jhāna

Whether your practice is formal sitting or informal walking around, if you keep relaxing into these states, they last longer and grow stronger. Rather then cycling through in a moment, each phase lingers and intensifies.

Conversely, if you try to hold onto the states, they'll fade quickly.

Malvina Reynolds sang, "Love is something if you give it away, you end up having more." She warns, "It's just like a magic penny, hold on tight and you won't have any."

So relax.

Before I had any idea of what I was doing or had any knowledge of the Buddha's road map, I found myself at times sitting in retreat smiling uncontrollably. I called it a "high-energy calm." It spread throughout my body and mind for longer and longer stretches. I was trying to be a serious meditator, and all I could do was grin.

I complained to a teacher. I confessed it felt like a non-climactic, non-genitally focused orgasm. It was distracting me from paying attention to my breath.

He put his hand on my shoulder and said, "Relax. Enjoy. Let the feeling be the focus of meditation rather than the breath. It will pass eventually. Meanwhile, don't fight it. It is too strong. It can be very healing. Trust it."

The second jhāna or second stage of the Buddha's path is similar to the first in that it has this cycle of pīti to sukha to upekkhā – joy to happiness to equanimity. However, there are two differences.

One, the states are deeper and more stable. They last longer. Two, you develop more confidence or faith in the process and in your essential being.

The confidence arises because you aren't trying to hold onto these wonderful states. If you grasp, they vanish. But the more heartfully you broadcast them to others, the stronger they become in you.

So where do these states come from? They aren't coming from out there. They simply arise on their own as you send loving kindness. They must arise out of your essence or some essence you partake of.

As you feel this, confidence grows.

Third Jhāna

As faith in these states gets stronger and stronger, joy and happiness arise less and less. You settle straight into equanimity – peaceful wellbeing. This is the third jhāna: upekkhā.

At this point, the practice shifts from sending out joy and happiness to one person to broadcasting peace and equanimity in all directions to everyone.

Inner Distractions

It is important to note that there may still be lots of thoughts, feelings, and sensations. Joy, happiness, and now equanimity are not pure and pristine. They co-exist with other stuff going through the mind and heart. That is fine. Don't let this discourage you.

It is not until the seventh jhāna – quite a bit further down the road – that even coarse thinking subsides. Meanwhile, as long as there is any pīti, sukha, or upekkhā just rest in them, even if there are other thoughts or images floating through your mind. When you get completely distracted, don't worry about that, either. Just notice where you attention has gone. Let things be as they are. Relax, smile, and send out loving kindness or well-wishing again.

Rūpa

These first three stages are called rūpa jhānas. "Rūpa" means "body." Body sensation and body awareness accompany these jhānas. The remaining stages are *arūpa* jhānas. The body relaxes so deeply that body sensations fade. These are very interesting. We'll pick up here at another time.

Summary

As Tsoknyi Rinpoche says, these states are quite accessible. The trick is not in accessing them – we do this all the time. The trick is to stabilize them, and the trick to stabilizing them is no trick at all. It is practice.

The more often you consciously touch joy, happiness, and peace, the easier it is to do so next time. So practice. Spend some time daily sending out kindness. As you grocery shop, drive through traffic, read a story to your child, go through your workday, send out goodwill.

Don't worry about how often you forget. That's all we've been doing all our lives anyway. Nothing new. Nothing to worry about. When you remember, relax and send out delight, ease, comfort, uplift, or any positive state, even if just for a moment.

Practice stabilizes.

In the popular culture, "relax" often means "distraction." To relax, we have a meal, watch a movie, read a book, or daydream. However, relaxation on this path is the opposite of distraction. You pay more and more attention even as you release tension.

Non-Self

I leave you with a paradox.

If you want to bring more joy, happiness, peace, or healing to the world, cultivate these qualities in yourself. If you don't, what you have to offer will be relatively superficial. To cultivate these states, pay attention to what is going on inside you.

Yet, if you try to grasp these states for yourself, they will remain elusive. If, once they arise, you try to hold onto them, they will fade quickly.

However, if you send them out to others, they strengthen.

In Judaism, Christianity, and Islam this is called "selflessness." In Buddhism, it's called "anattā" or "non-self." There is no real distinction between self and other. To care for yourself, care for others. To care for others, care for yourself.

The Zen master, Dogen, put it this way:
To study the way is to study the self.
To study the self is to lose the self.
To lose the self is to be enlightened by all things.
To be enlightened by all things is to remove the barrier between self and other.

Nibbāna II: Nothingness

January 25, 2009

Two weeks ago we began exploring a road map of consciousness discovered by the Buddha. It begins with joy and traverses an inner landscape to something called *"nibbāna."* The Sanskrit equivalent is "nirvana" or enlightenment. This roadway has eight stages called *"jhānas."*

Two weeks ago we explored the first three stages. This morning I'd like to explore four more.

But in case what I said two weeks ago didn't make sense or you weren't here, I want to catch you up. The third jhāna or the third stage is equanimity. This is where we left off. So I'd like to share a poem about equanimity.

It is one of my all-time favorite poems: I like to recite it for you at least once a year. It was written by Donald C. Babcock and first appeared in the *New Yorker* magazine in October of 1947.

Now we are ready to look at something pretty special.
It is a duck riding the ocean a hundred feet beyond the surf.
No, it isn't a gull.
A gull always has a raucous touch about him.
This is some sort of duck, and he cuddles in the swells.
He isn't cold, and he is thinking things over.
There is a big heaving in the Atlantic,
And he is part of it.
He looks a bit like a mandarin, or the Lord Buddha meditating under the Bo tree,
But he has hardly enough above the eyes to be a philosopher.
He has poise, however, which is what philosophers must have.
He can rest while the Atlantic heaves, because he rests in the Atlantic.
Probably he doesn't know how large the ocean is.
And neither do you.
But he realizes it.
And what does he do, I ask you? He sits down in it.
He reposes in the immediate as if it were infinity –
which it is.
That is religion, and the duck has it.
He has made himself part of the boundless,
By easing himself into it just where it touches him.
I like the little duck.
He doesn't know much.
But he has religion.[23]

Life's ocean is filled with waves. Sometimes they rock us gently; sometimes they knock us not so gently. Calm waters are rare and don't last long.

If we want peace in our lives, calming the waters is not an effective strategy. Try driving to the ocean, wading out waist deep, and stopping those waves. It is futile. It is beyond our power.

To get stability, some people try holding onto a boulder. But getting drenched in the crashing surf as we hold on is stoic misery more than ease and wellbeing.

To get peace, some people try to fly above the waves. This can give inspiration and perspective. But it is tiring and unsustainable. Eventually we run out of energy and come down into the turbulence.

So, if we want sustainable ease, the best strategy is to learn to rest in the waves themselves. It's not easy. But it is possible. It is very possible.

We don't have to understand where the waves come from, why they change, or the dimensions of the ocean. We just have to learn to sit down in it: to "rest in the immediate as if it were infinity – which it is."

Meditation

One practice that helps you sit down in it is loving-kindness. You connect with life around you by sending out kindness, happiness, ease, good health, or other positive states. You can use short phrases to focus your intentions: "May you be happy." "May you delight." "May you have ease." You broadcast this gently in all directions.

We did a version of this last week.

---

[23] This favorite poem of mine also appears on pp. 193, 302, and 332.

And of course, as you send this out, your attention will wander. When you notice you've wandered, don't worry about it. Distractions are just waves – not a problem. Recognize them. And relax.

Shall we do this a little now to help settle into equanimity?

You can close your eyes if that is more comfortable for you. ... Relax with an attentive mind. Let your breathing relax. ...

Ease, equanimity, peace, wellbeing. ... These are qualities you've felt. Relax into one of them now.

Imagine broadcasting it in all direction: "May you be happy." "May you be healthy." "May you find fulfillment" ... Send kindness or ease or any positive quality. Indiscriminate love sent in all directions. ...

If your attention wanders, don't worry. Distractions are just waves in the ocean. No big deal. Just part of what is. See what drew your attention. Recognize it. Let it be. Sit down in the wave. Be a duck. ...

Relax. Soften. Smile and return to the phrases: "May you be free. May you know love. May you have ease." ...

You can open your eyes or just continue, as you like.

The duck is calm and peaceful even in the waves because he rests in the ocean. He rests in a larger beingness.

This is where we ended two weeks ago. It's called "the third jhāna," "equanimity" or "being a duck."

Let's continue from here.

Fourth Jhana

As you relax more deeply, you may move into the fourth jhāna.

This stage is called "*arūpa upekkhā*." "Upekkhā" means equanimity. "Rūpa" means "body." And "a-" means "without." So "arūpa upekkhā" means "equanimity without body."

Sounds pretty strange, doesn't it? Especially in English it sounds esoteric. But I suspect most of you have experienced arūpa upekkhā.

Have you ever laid quietly in a hot bath or a hot tub without jets? The heat relaxes your body and takes the edge off your mind. If you stay mindful as you float in the hot water you may notice, "I can't feel my arm. Uh oh. It's nerve dead." So you wiggle your fingers. They work just fine. Sensation comes back into your arm immediately.

So you relax into the heat again. In a few minutes sensation is missing in both arms. This time, you aren't so alarmed. But just in case, you wiggle again. Sure enough full sensation comes back at once.

So now, you make a game of it: how long can you stay so relaxed that there is no sensation?

How many of you have ever done that?

If you can sit on a chair or cushion in equanimity for 10 or 15 minutes with your mind and body so relaxed that sensations fade, that is the forth jhāna.

If, as you relax, your mind goes dull or drifts off into fantasy, that is called "day dreaming." But if your awareness stays present and peaceful even as your body seems to fade, that is arūpa upekkhā – equanimity without body. It is considered an advanced stage of meditation.

Light

A common side effect of the fourth jhāna is luminosity. It is not uncommon for a subjective bright light to emerge. It is not intense like a blazing sun; but softer and cooler, like a full moon on a clear night. In some traditions, the luminosity is called a "*nimitta.*'

People who have a near-death experience often describe moving toward a light that feels like a loving presence. Depending on their belief systems, they may call it "God," "angels," "guiding spirits," "light," etc. Many report it changes how they see their life. I wonder – and this is speculation on my part – if that "white light of death" is the same phenomenon as a nimitta. I wonder if people who relax into death go into the fourth jhāna.

The forth jhāna can be deeply healing and starts to shift how you see your life, just like a near death experience can.

It can also be more subtle than this.

Fifth Jhana

It can be tempting to try to hold onto the equanimity. But if instead, you send it out in all directions, eventually a feeling of spaciousness arises. You may suddenly feel suspended in the vastness of space –some people get a sense of vertigo. Or it may come on more gradually and gently.

When I was five and six years old, I used to lay on the lawn and gaze at the blue sky. If I relaxed enough, the sky would start to move away into infinity. It was a very pleasant feeling.

"Hey, Ricky," I'd say to my big brother. "Ever see this neat thing in the sky."

He'd look at his nutty little brother. "Get up," he'd say. "I'm the cowboy now. You are the Indian. Let's play."

I complied. He still thinks I'm his nutty little brother.

Looking back, I realize this was the fifth jhāna or stage. Traditionally it's called "the realm of infinite space." But it's not "spacey" as in fuzzyheaded. It can be quite clear. It's an expansive feeling available to children and adults alike.

Sixth Jhāna

As you relax into this spaciousness, you may witness thoughts themselves. Normally, thoughts are seductive – they draw you right in and carry you away. We get involved in their content and story. But instead, you sit back and observe. You are in the audience watching thoughts walk across the stage. You aren't on the stage. You are the observer. It's like sitting on a bank watching thought bubbles float down the stream of consciousness. You aren't the thought bubbles. You are an observer.

The trick is to not get into the thought content. But instead just notice the process – the texture, feel and movement of thought. As you do this, you notice that each thought has some tension compared to the space around it. As you relax that clinging, the thought loses its cohesion and dissipates. There is a moment of no thought – no actor on the stage, no bubbles on the river. Then another thought arises. You see its texture without getting drawn into the subject of the thought. You relax. It dissolves.

In the space between thoughts, you don't fall asleep. Your consciousness is clear and spacious.

The sixth jhāna is called "the realm of infinite consciousness." In English, it sounds grandiose. But it is merely a time when there are gaps in thinking rather than a cluttered stream.

Seventh Jhāna

Gradually there are fewer thought bubbles on the river and longer gaps between them. Rather than watch for the next bubble, you pay more attention to the space between them. Thoughts stop altogether.

The seventh jhāna is called "the realm of nothingness." The label is confusing because there is a lot going on. It is just that there are no thoughts.

In normal, everyday consciousness, everything we experience gets shrink-wrapped by a thought. So experience without thought sounds strange. But it's not.

Imagine holding an ice cube in your hand. It's cold. You think, "This is cold." But you were aware of cold before the thought shrink-wrapped around it.

Or imagine hearing a soft bell: "binnnnnng" You're aware of the sound before you think, "What a pleasant bell."

In the seventh stage cognizance or knowing is very strong. Your awareness is clear. You notice cold and sounds and many subtle sensations. But the mind is so relaxed and spacious that thoughts don't come up and cling to each experience. You know without thinking about it. Awareness is free of thought.

This pure awareness is conducive to insight and wisdom.

Blank

Robert M. Pirsig in his book *Zen and the Art of Motorcycle Maintenance* writes about traveling across country on a motorcycle that needed regular repairs. He does the work himself. But there are times when he can't figure out what the problem is. He finds himself staring blankly at his bike.

When I read the book years ago, cars were simpler and I did my own car repairs. So I knew what he was talking about. At times my car baffled me. I'd stare at the engine for a long while. If someone walked in, they'd think I was figuring something out. But in truth, I had no idea what to do and no idea what to think. I was blank.

Do you know that place?

Pirsig points out that this blank, focused attention devoid of thought can be creative and insightful. With patience, it can get you beyond the limitations of your habitual thought patterns. Out of the mental emptiness and clarity may arise a whole new way of seeing the situation.

There is intelligence inherent in this state of awareness. There is a knowingness that goes beyond personal knowing. There is beingness that is more spacious than personal being. There is awareness that is broader than personal awareness. And yes there is love that is larger than personal love.

In that blankness with its clarity, you may sense these, though words are inadequate.

Sharing

As you move down this path toward greater freedom, love, and wisdom, thinking fades. It becomes difficult to verbalize. But I suspect many of you – maybe most of you – have felt things as distinct as the feeling of cold, sound of "bing," or taste of chocolate. But when you try to describe them, words seem clumsy.

It is helpful, encouraging, and supportive to share these subtle experiences as best we can.

Words are metaphors that point toward something hard to name. The word-pointers you use may be different than the ones I use. But yours may be more helpful to some people than mine.

Self Sense

I leave you with one last contemplative inquiry. We've been talking or listening or daydreaming this morning. Who is it that experiences these words, sounds, and thoughts? Where is the self that experiences?

Most people experience self-sense in their head behind the eyes somewhere. From here you look out through your eyes, listen through your ears, guide movements of your body, and so on.

Can you locate that sensation called "me"?

What is that sensation like?

Do you notice some tension or subtle holding in that sense of self?

What happens if you relax that tension?

In *Pāli*, the language the Buddha spoke, "*bana*" means "bind" or "hold together." "Ni-" is a negation. So "nibbāna" means "unbind" or "release" or "relax." What happens when you release the binding in that sense of self?

I invite you for the next week or so to explore this. Find that sense of self and see what happens if you let it soften. This is where we'll pick up next time.

Nibbāna III: The Secret of Happiness

February 15, 2009

Spirituality does not create purity, but it can reveal it. Purity is our true nature.

The secret of happiness, according of the Buddha, is in our true nature – who we really are. He taught a style of meditation that quiets the mind and opens the heart, so that we might experience it fully. The end point of this meditation is a relaxed knowingness he called "*nibbāna*" (or "nirvana" in Sanskrit).

Previously, I shared a metaphor of this quality of mind and heart. It was a duck cuddling in the swells. "He can rest while the Atlantic heaves because he rests in the Atlantic. … He has made himself part of the boundless by easing himself into it just where it touches him." (From a poem by Donald C. Babcock.)

This is the third and final sermon in a series on nibbāna. It is part of a larger series on religious experience. We've been looking at various religious concepts and the experiences that give rise to these ideas. The experience, itself, is more valuable than ideas about it.

We've been approaching the experience of nibbāna by looking at a path that begins with joy and leads through eight phases or "jhānas" to this quality of mind and heart the Buddha called "fire unbound by longing."

So far, we've looked at the first seven of these jhānas or stages. Now we come to the eighth and nibbāna itself.

I would like to do three things. First, share my own experiences that come as close to nibbāna as I know. Two, reflect on a few of the implications this has for how we regard ourselves and live our lives. Third, explore your reflections and questions.

First, the experiences.

Experience

In the West, nirvana is often viewed as so exoteric, abstract, and unattainable that we shouldn't waste our time on it. The Thai Forest tradition has a different view. Ajahn Chaa, a famous Thai master, once said, "During the first year of practice, most monks have an enlightenment experience. It is good to get it over with. Then they can get on with the real work."

In the Thai Forest tradition, nibbāna is a technical problem. They have a twelve-step program (or ten-step) to solve it. Their style of communal living is closer to the style the Buddha recommended than in any other extant communities in the world today.

Ajahn Tong is Northern Thailand's most revered living meditation master. He doesn't speak English or work with Westerners. Through diligent search and good fortune, I connected with one of his top students, a young monk named, Phra Noah Yuttadhammo. He offered to train me. He said that after three weeks, I would be considered one of his students primarily and a Westerner incidentally. Under these conditions, Ajahn Tong would give me his advanced instructions.

At least, that was what I hoped.

Ajahn Tong

In February of 2006, without knowing quite what I was getting myself into, I took a China Air flight from San Francisco to Chiang Mai in Northern Thailand. It was part of the sabbatical you gave me.

After three weeks of training, Phra Noah drove with me several hours to Wat Chom Tong, introduced me to Ajahn Tong, and remained for over a month to do the Thai-English translation. I am very grateful to him and Ajahn Tong.

The training with Ajahn Tong was structured in ten-day cycles. Each cycle ended with a phase called "determination." For several days, I remained in my *kuti* (meditation hut) meditating around the clock without sleep. Meals were brought to me, and I was given a little sign for my door (pictured here) that said I was in

determination.

During the first days of determination, I was to keep track of the number of times I experienced something called "ceasing and arising." These were moments of losing contact with the conventional world (ceasing) and quickly reconnecting (arising). Subjectively, it felt like blacking out for a fraction of a second.

After the first day of determination, I was to time the length of an experience called "peaceful cessation." This was a longer period of losing touch with my normal self and the normal world – a longer period of blacking out.

I had seen people doing these practices. It looked to me like they were nodding off. Sitting still while sleep deprived, what could be more natural than blacking out into sleep?

"Peaceful cessation?" I thought. "Yeah, right. Give me a break. This is hokey." I didn't want to have anything to do with it. "Get me outta here."

However, Wat Chom Tong is a long way from Sacramento. Having invested all that time and energy to fly to the other side of the planet to hang out with a Buddhist superstar, I thought I should at least give it a try – give it as sincere an effort as I could muster.

Peaceful Cessation

During the first day of meditation without sleep, I got tired. By the second day, the fatigue left. My body felt light. My physical energy was low, but my mind was alert and clear. My mood was serene.

My kuti had a concrete tile floor. They gave me a cotton blanket to sleep on – my bed was a thin blanket on concrete. I folded this blanket and I put my mediation cushion on it.

I placed a low table next to the cushion. It held a candle for light, a clock, and pen and paper to record times with minimal effort.

Early one morning, I sat down for my next sitting. I looked at the clock and wrote "3:10 a.m." I closed my eyes in meditation. After a month of fairly continuous practice, my mind didn't drift. I was relaxed and present with the subtle flow of phenomena.

After five minutes, I half opened an eye. The clock said "4:37."

Huh? 4:37? Subjectively, it felt like five minutes. I had lost over an hour. Had I fallen asleep and not known it?

Ordinarily, when we wake from sleep, the mind is groggy. There may be after traces of dreams or a sense of the passage of time.

However, I was not the least bit groggy before or after. There was no sense of time passage. It was like I'd time warped ahead over an hour.

I hadn't wandering off into daydreams, fantasies, or random associations. In fact, there were no thoughts at all.

My mind was luminous: exceptionally clear, present, deeply relaxed, minutely aware of the pushes and pulls of the subtle flow of experience, flooded with a quiet joy.

Later that day, Ajahn Tong and Phra Noah questioned me and concluded it was peaceful cessation.

Nuts

I experienced these blackouts or "peaceful cessations" in other ways. Sometimes, coming out of it felt like coming out from under anesthesia, in that I didn't know where I was for a few moments. At first, all I saw were colors, shapes, and textures. These assembled themselves into objects: floor, wall, table, and fan. These came together into a room. Then, I remembered I was in a kuti in Thailand. Then, I remembered feelings I had about being there.

All the time, my mind was incredibly clear and quietly joyful. Even the dark room seemed bright.

Later on, I'd start to reflect on how wonderful it felt and what it meant. One thought lead to another. One feeling triggered another. The clarity faded. Within a few hours, I was racing over hundreds of topics, thoughts, fears, aspirations, worries, dreams, and fantasies in dizzying confusion. I wrote in my journal that my mind had checked half the books out of the Library of Congress and was trying to read them all at once. I must be nuts.

My mind was picking fights with old enemies, worrying, obsessing. I couldn't stop it. My mind was a herd of stampeding buffalo raising such a cloud of mental dust I couldn't make out individual thoughts - just a rumbling mass.

It was discouraging. "Oh well, so much for enlightenment." I'd smile at my pretentions, relax, and go back to simple mindfulness. With that, things gradually calmed down.

Perception

Perception requires at least a little bit of effort or tension. You experience a sensation. You compare these sights or sounds or feelings to things you've experienced before until you recognize, "Oh, that's a chair" or "That's a tree" or "That's a backache." It happens very quickly.

Forming memories also requires a bit of effort or tension to store the perception for future reference.

When the mind is deeply relaxed, you can experience the effort to perceive and remember. You can relax the effort. Perception starts to shut down, like tunnel vision. Then it just ceases for a while.

That is peaceful cessation. It's also called the eighth jhāna or the realm of neither-perception-nor-non-perception.

When we fall asleep at night, the mind relaxes enough that we don't form gross perceptions or memory, but there is enough tension for faint perceptions and creating dreams.

Peaceful cessation is different from sleep or daydreaming in that the senses are awake, open, and present. However, the mind is so unreactive that thought, perception, and memory don't congeal.

Why?

I asked Ajahn Tong why we did this practice. What was the point? What use was it?

He smiled almost imperceptibly. Most Thai people are devotional in temperament. They accepted his instructions without question. I had a Westerner's temperament. I was curious and questioned everything. I think he enjoyed it.

He responded by talking about cooking a particular Thai vegetable. "The stem is the only edible part. So you hold the base of the stem with one hand, circle the fingers of your other hand just above the base, and pull the plant through your encircling fingers. The fingers strip all the leaves off the plant in one motion.

"The stem is your core purity. The leaves are impurities. Peaceful cessation strips the impurities away exposing your true nature unobstructed.

"That total stillness and openness is nibbāna."

Then he added, "It is mundane nibbāna because there are still impurities in you. They are just turned off. But eventually, they wake up and sprout new leaves.

"These new leaves are the thoughts and feeling racing through you. You feel like a beginning meditator again.

"So you clear those leaves. You keep doing this over and over until the leaves no longer grow. Then you are pure and liberated and no more disturbances grow."

"Maybe it takes a few months, or a few years, or a few hundred lifetimes. Who can know?"

Nibbāna

I promised to talk about the experience of nibbāna. Mundane nibbāna – peaceful cessation – is as close as I've come. I can only extrapolate from there.

I would like to shift from the experiences around nibbāna to the implications it has for us. We don't live in monastic communities. We live rather busy lives in this jumbled world. Even so, the possibility of nibbāna and the processes around it say something about how we might live and view life.

I'd be interested in your thoughts about this. Let me share one line of reflection.

Nuggets

One classical metaphor says that all of us are nuggets of gold – huge, valuable gold nuggets. Our essence is pure and radiant. Like gold, it can't be tarnished.

However, gold nuggets aren't pure. They come out of the earth a mixture of gold and other minerals.

Meditation, contemplative prayer, and other spiritual practices are fires that heat the gold until it becomes fluid.

As it melts in a crucible, the impurities rise to the surface. This dross, this gold scum, can horrify us. However, it is just a thin layer. It can be gently poured off revealing the purity below.

Then deeper impurities arise. You skim that off to reveal a purer purity. Subtler dross surfaces. You release that, and so forth.

Impurities

In Christianity, these impurities are called "sin," like the famous seven: lust, gluttony, greed, sloth, wrath, envy, and pride.

In Buddhism, the impurities are called hindrances. They include attachment, ill will, agitation, sloth and torpor, and doubt. In Pāli, the word for "hindrance" has a root meaning of "covering." Hindrances are dross that covers the gold – the clear, loving radiance within us.

Jesus might call them bushel baskets hiding our light.

Nothing to Gain

In other words, spiritually, there is nothing we have to gain other than what we already have. There is no place to go other than where we are. There is nothing we need other than what we are. Like a gold nugget, we don't need to find something valuable. We are gold already.

Spiritual process is not about gaining, getting, or achieving. It's about purification – bringing the dross to the surface so it can be released and our pure essence can be revealed.

Spirituality does not create purity. It reveals it.

Tightness

The central insight of Buddhism is that all impurities have one thing in common: grasping or tightness. Lust, gluttony, greed, sloth, wrath, envy, pride, attachment, ill will, agitation, sloth and torpor, doubt, and all the rest are just different varieties or ways we hold or push or tighten.

So the secret of happiness – deep, lasting, vital happiness – is nongrasping. That's what "nibbāna" means: relaxing. That's what it comes down to. Just relax.

It's not relaxing into the dross, the impurities, or the unskillful habits. It's relaxing into our pure essence.

Essence

And what's this essence? I suspect you've felt it. It's not esoteric. When you've been mellow and attentive with family or friends or refreshed and at ease next to the ocean, you may have felt an open, generous, clear love. Maybe you didn't feel it purely. However, you've tasted it. That is the tip of the iceberg. From there, it can expand many fold into its fullness.

What hides this joy, wellbeing, and vitality in you? What are your impurities? What bushel baskets hide your light? What are your favorite forms of tightening? Working too hard? Impatience? Stress? Worry? Wanting stuff? Self-criticism? Doubt? Not trusting your essence? What?

As we mature spiritually, whatever impurities are in us rise to the surface.

When they do, we can rejoice! Alleluia! Our craziness, our sins, our dross has risen to the surface where it can be seen. We needn't be frightened of it. That adds tightness to tightness. We needn't indulge it. That's just greed or lust or aversion – more tightness. Instead, just let it be.

Your essence is fine. Trust it. Like the duck resting in the ocean swells, relax.

In Buddhism, the secret of happiness is relaxing. It's not relaxing into the dross but into our pure essence.

The more we do this, the more we trust that clarity, kindness, and luminosity that is our essence. The more we trust that we are wisdom and love.

Simplicity

May 31, 2009

Presence

Imagine you've been hiking in the high Sierras for several hours. It was enjoyable and took effort. Now you've reached a mountaintop. Ah! You feel satisfied – maybe a little tired from the climb. You take off your daypack and sit down to rest.

The view is incredible. It's a beautiful day. You sit gazing over the panorama.

Your mind is still. Maybe a few thoughts or feelings drift in like, "This is nice." They flutter on the edges of your awareness. You aren't trying to meditate or anything, so you don't try to get rid of them. But you don't pay much attention to them either.

They are like butterflies that settle on a bush a few yards away. Perhaps you notice them. But you aren't inclined to jump up and run over for a closer look. You don't get out your wildlife guide to learn their history, life cycle, or favorite flowers. You just let them be part of the panorama.

Mostly you are quiet and present with the world.

I invite you to imagine being in this state right now. …

Perhaps for a moment we feel: Present. Clear. Empty. Natural. Simple.

But not for long. Soon thoughts sneak in like: "What's this about? I thought he was going to talk about simplicity. … Why doesn't that person over there sit still? Is it okay to move? … Am I supposed to be doing something? He said do nothing. How do I do that?… Is this done yet? …"

But for a few moments before these thoughts meander in, we were just present. Nothing particular going on. Mostly quiet in a natural, simple way.

Simplicity

I'd like to talk about this natural, simple, ordinary presence. I'd like to talk about simplicity – not as an idea or practice but as an experience.

In another sermon, I'll share practices that cultivate simplicity. But in this sermon, I want to focus on the experience itself.

This sermon is a continuation of a series on religious experience. As you may remember, in this series we distinguish between religious ideas or beliefs, religious practices, and religious experiences.

Most people define religion by beliefs or practices. But experience is far more important. By religious experience I mean deep connection with life.

This three-part distinction is essential in exploring the experience of simplicity.

For example, let's say we *believe* simplicity is good – good for the earth, good for our families, good for our finances, good for our stressed lives, good for peace of mind. And lets say we understand the *practice* of simplicity to be giving up things we'd otherwise enjoy. "Simplifying our life" means "getting along with less." We give up certain foods, drive less, buy fewer clothes and stuff, go out less often, or practice other forms of renunciation.

This may feel good on the surface – "I'm a good person for renouncing these things." But underneath, we may feel deprived, neglected, self-righteous, guilty when our discipline weakens, condemning of people who live extravagantly, and so forth. This leaves us alienated. It doesn't deepen our connection with life. It makes us grumpy and hard to be around.

So before we talk about specific ways to simplify, it would be helpful to articulate the genuine experience of religious simplicity that connects us to life rather than alienates us from it.

Samatha

Clues to it can be found in the two experiences I pointed to a few minutes ago –

the pause before the sermon and imagining sitting on a mountaintop after a good hike.

Tibetans call it "*samatha*" which means "calm abiding." The monotheistic religions might call it "the peace of God." Eckhart Tolle calls it "the power of now."

We could call it "simple presence" — just being with what is, in a simple way. Not trying to do anything. Not trying *not* to do anything. Just being here with ease and heart.

Let's try it now. Usually there are thoughts or feelings fluttering inside us. Usually we try to chase after them or (if we think of ourselves as spiritual) forcefully ignore them. But for a few moments let them flutter without paying attention to them, just like on the mountaintop. Relax your mind and heart. Drop into the present. …

It is so natural and simple that we miss it. And, even when we do notice it, usually it doesn't last more than a few moments.

Monkey Mind

Most often we don't drop into the present even for a moment. More often our minds are like a monkey loose in a grocery store:

He sees a bin of bananas, jumps in and takes a bite. Then he sees shiny apples. He throws the half-eaten banana over his shoulder and leaps into the apple bin. The apples fall out in all directions. As he chomps, he notices sweet grapes. And what's behind all those boxes on that shelf? He tastes and samples and tosses things around until the whole place is a mess.

This is called "monkey mind" – a phrase from parts of Asia that have lots of monkeys.

Here in North America, we don't have monkeys in the wild. Perhaps we need a metaphor closer to home. I like "raccoon mind." Raccoons are clever and have a proclivity for mischief.

I had a pet raccoon once. So let me share a little of what I know about them and how they reflect our minds.

Amy

I was twelve years old when I got my raccoon from friends at the Houston zoo. I called her "Amy."

Raccoons have a reputation for washing their food. If I gave her a piece of bread, she'd dunk it in water. The soggy mess was not appetizing, so she'd leave it aside. Amy was neat and clean, but in the process she made a mess around her.

She was also clever. She could take her cage apart. Once she broke out in the middle of the night. She knew we were in the house, so she climbed to the roof and dropped down to the air conditioner in the window of my parent's bedroom. The windowpane kept her out. So she dug out the glazing putty that held the glass in place.

All she wanted was to be with us, but in the process she wrecked the window.

My father was furious.

In those years I built a lot of tree houses – "tree forts" I called them. Amy climbed up to join me. One day, men from the electric company were working on the power lines by the tree. Amy saw them as a threat and confronted them. The three men weighed at least two hundred pounds each. But my little four-pound Amy bravely screeched and yelled at them to protect her and me from harm.

They were not pleased.

Another time, she took her cage apart and went out exploring the neighborhood. Later, I was standing in front of the garage behind the house. Amy came around the front, walked straight to me, crawled up my leg, up my back, and onto my shoulder where she stuck her nose down the back of my shirt collar. And trembled.

A neighbor called to complain that my raccoon had gotten into her garage. She had chased Amy around with a broom for 15 minutes to get her out. The garage was a shambles.

And Amy was terrified.

Raccoons have black masklike markings over their eyes that remind people of bandits looking for trouble. But when I held Amy, all I felt was sweet innocence. Her big, black eyes were shiny and filled with life and curiosity. She was clever and limber. Raccoons have five long flexible fingers. The Houston zookeepers learned not to use combination locks on their cages because the raccoons played with the dials until the locks opened.

Amy had this cleverness and curiosity. She just wanted to be happy and safe from harm. If she felt cornered, she'd fight to keep herself and me happy and safe. But underneath she was sweet and curious innocence.

Raccoon Mind

Our thinking minds are like raccoons — they may seem like masked bandits, but are really sweet and innocent. They explore endless strings of associations. We don't tell them to do this. Sometimes we try to stop them with a mental cage. But they usually open the lock or take the cage apart and wander off chasing their curiosity.

Our thoughts can be agile and smart without being wise. So we get into trouble – external trouble as well as internal messes. But any time I've had the privilege to see into the depths of someone's soul, I've always seen a core innocence.

Like Amy, our minds just want us to be happy and safe, and sometimes are willing to fight to get it. All of us want to be happy and safe. Every creature. We share this with every living being.

Freedom from Wanting

So let's look closer at how innocent raccoon mind creates a mess.

The mind's error is thinking happiness can be found outside itself. I might think, "I'd be happier if I could get one of those organic burritos for lunch." When I get it, I feel good for a while. Then it fades. I think, "Ah, it really did make me happy. I need more."

If happiness actually came from the burrito, then 10 would make me 10 times happier. But of course, eating 10 burritos is painful. So happiness is not in burritos. It's somewhere else.

There is a relationship between getting stuff and happiness, but not the relationship raccoon mind imagines.

The experience of wanting is painful. Wanting a burrito, a winning lottery ticket, a meaningful experience, an exciting relationship, and so on is disturbing. If we imagine having those things, the fantasy may mask the discomfort. But raw desire doesn't feel good. And it focuses attention outside so we may not notice the inner discomfort as anything more than an appetite-driven restlessness.

When we actually get the food or money or experience, two things happen simultaneously:

First, the desire evaporates. We no longer want the thing because now we have it. I don't want a burrito because I have one in my mouth. The graspy, gnarly desire relaxes. "Ah! Such a relief!"

And second, we come into the present. We aren't fighting this moment or looking to the future. We savor what is here. Happiness tends to arise when we are just with what is.

Raccoon mind confuses the lack of desire with having the object of desire. It confuses the blessed relief from wanting with having the food or CD or new clothes or new experience. It confuses the presence of awareness with the presence of the object of desire.

Of course, nothing lasts: food is consumed; money is spent; music that was so wonderful may become annoying with repetition; spiritual highs fade.

Then raccoon mind looks for a new object or new experience to attach itself to – a latte, sushi, a book, a walk in the park, a massage, or something more. Simple presence is displaced by a complicated search for a new object.

Knowing versus Realization

I suspect you know what I'm talking about. This morning I'm not telling you anything new. You know happiness doesn't come from things out there. You've observed life. You've read philosophy or spiritual poetry or meditated or prayed a little. Or a lot.

So we *know* this. But we may not have fully *realized* it. We keep looking despite ourselves. Habits have momentum. It is hard to step away from them for more than a moment.

This is where practices of simplicity come in. They help us realize what we know. They help us embody what we understand intellectually. They help us simplify our external environment so it won't stimulate the restless mind so much. We take some of the energy that we'd otherwise put into the pursuit of stuff and use it to notice what's here already. We do less so we can relax more into the moment.

In another sermon, I'll describe some of these voluntary practices. But before I close today I want to talk about involuntary simplicity.

Involuntary Simplicity

All of us stumble into simplicity from time to time. Maybe we don't choose simplicity, but simplicity chooses us.

I remember the first time I clearly saw the relationship between simplicity and happiness. I was 13 years old. In September of 1961, hurricane Carla swept off the Gulf of Mexico and over our home in Houston. Back then I enjoyed being outside: camping, hiking, riding my bike, visiting friends, building tree forts, going across town for art lessons. But torrential rains, winds over 100 miles per hour and falling trees, confined me indoors.

Inside, I enjoyed watching TV – *Gun Smoke*, *Maverick*, and *The Twilight Zone* – or playing with electric trains. But falling trees took out the power lines.

In the evening I enjoyed working on model airplanes or other projects in my room. But with no electric lights, this was not possible after dark.

So I began to follow the natural daily cycle of going to bed at dark and getting up with the grey dawn.

I could have gotten into pining for all those things I was missing. But it was so utterly hopeless to want those things that I just let go.

Besides, I was fascinated by the storm. It was raining sideways! The winds were so strong that a drop of water coming over the fence on the right side of the yard exited on the left without dropping an inch. I sat for hours looking out the big windows in the family room. Just present.

I had three brothers and a sister. Without TV to fight over or rushed schedules, we got along better than usual, even in cramped quarters.

After four days, the storm subsided. The electricity came back and everyone cheered. I pretended to cheer as well. Having TV and lights and music lessons was a good thing, right? I knew I'd be happier without TV, for example. But with it there I knew I'd want it anyway.

I remember a feeling like nostalgia for that simpler living.

Have you felt that? Perhaps you were caught for days in a snowstorm? Or an economic downturn reduced your cash so you bought less and found it easier? Or an illness relieved you of some obligations? Or wilderness camping meant you didn't have all the frills and frenetics of modern life?

What are times you remember simple living? …

Recall how this felt. What was it like? … Embody that feeling. …

I want to invoke this wisdom that we all have – this knowing of the value of simplicity.

Cluster

To be sure, involuntary or voluntary simplicity can be difficult and painful. I spoke with a family who had lost their home. They felt this had actually improved their life. But I'm sure there were times when it was very hard.

In my next sermon, I want to talk about approaching simplicity deliberately in ways that maximize the gain and reduce the pain. We'll consider three areas: simplifying stuff, simplifying experience, and simplifying the number of thoughts and opinions we cherish.

But before getting to specific practices, I wanted us to be grounded in the actual experience of simplicity.

It is difficult to describe. It's like trying to describe a breath of fresh air. Naming the concept is easy, but naming the feeling is elusive and subtle.

However, there are a cluster of qualities and feeling tones that have simplicity as a major component. These can point in the right direction. For example:

Gratitude: the experience of genuine gratitude is very simple.

Freshness. Naturalness. Ordinariness.

Ease: when we are relaxed, we feel simple; when we feel simple, we feel relaxed.

Presence: just being here in a simple, ordinary way.

Happiness: Nietzsche suggested that unhappiness is complex. True happiness is simple.

So as you make plans for next week or this afternoon, you can use these qualities to guide you toward simplicity and happiness.

Contemplation

With this in mind, let's close with a contemplation on simplicity.

Sit quietly and easily. Let the breathing relax. As on the mountaintop, drop into the present without trying to do anything.

I'll suggest some qualities. See what these qualities evoke in you:

Gratitude …

Ease …

Patience …

Freshness …

Ordinariness …

Happiness …

Simplicity …

Practices of Simplicity

June 14, 2009

In February of 2006 I entered Wat Phra Doi Suthep to begin meditation training in the Buddhist Thai Forest tradition. A Wat is the Thai equivalent of a monastery. Doi Suthep is located high in the mountains east of the city of Chaing Mai in the north of Thailand.

Thailand is a Third World country, but not without amenities. For example, the water at Doi Suthep is clear, clean, fresh, and cold. It comes straight out of a deep mountain spring at about 33°.

Doi Suthep also has a large bath and shower room. Each shower has two faucets. Each faucet produces cold water. When I asked about hot water, my hosts smiled because the Thai were too polite to roll their eyes and tell me I was goofy for thinking about exotic luxuries.

The air temperature on a February afternoon in Chiang Mai can reach 95° with 95% humidity. Sitting quietly in the shade I'd sweat. I had planned to spend two months in Thailand. I knew I couldn't avoid showers that long. So after more days than I care to admit, I ventured into a shower stall.

I put my hand in the liquid ice, pulled it back and shivered. Then I soaped, rinsed, and dried my hand and waited for the shivering to stop. Then I put my forearm in the cold, shivered, soaped, dried, and waited to warm a little. Then I put my upper arm into the glacial runoff.

Meanwhile an old man went into another shower, stepped under the running water and began singing softly. By the time I finished my second arm, he was happily clean and on his way. I checked his shower. Both faucets produced running ice.

After three weeks at Doi Suthep, I traveled south 70 kilometers to Wat Chom Tong. The young monk with whom I'd trained traveled with me. He wanted to recommend me to his teacher, a renowned meditation master named Ajahn Tong.

Wat Chom Tong is dedicated almost exclusively to meditation. Rather than a few dorm rooms, it has hundreds of single meditation huts called *"kutis."*

I was given my own kuti with a concrete tile floor, cotton blanket for a mattress, ceiling fan and a private bathroom. Well, the bathroom was a tiny closet without a door but it did have a toilet, sink, and garden hose with a sprayer head.

My kuti was on the far edge of the wat. Several hundred yards of buried pipes brought water to my hut. The hot afternoon sun warmed the ground and the water in the pipes. By early evening, the water was "lukecold" – slightly cooler than neutral. I could spray it on my back and only shiver for a moment.

I was so happy meditating in my little concrete kuti with a ceiling fan and lukecold garden hose shower. It was luxurious.

Simplicity

In this sermon, I'd like to continue our exploration of simplicity.

One of the benefits of traveling was meeting people like the old man humming happily in the icy shower – people who had a vastly simpler material standard of living, and yet were happier than the average American.

Another benefit was living for months with only what I could fit into a backpack. I found it freeing to live with so little.

A third and dubious benefit was returning home with an appreciation for the vastness of our material wealth. I was chagrined at how quickly I reverted. Within a week I was back to seeing mattresses, hot running water, refrigerators, stoves, air conditioners, central heat, private cars, television, stereos, drawers and closets filled with clothes, precooked food, lawn mowers, and on and on as necessities of life rather than exotic luxuries.

I know many of you have traveled more extensively than I and have your own stories and insights about simple living.

Previously, I talked about the experience of simplicity. In this sermon, I would like to talk about practices that cultivate simplicity here at home.

Skipping Stone

When I was a kid I liked to skip stones on lakes. If I threw a flat stone at the correct angle and with enough speed and energy it would kiss the surface and leap into the air again and again.

If we have too much stuff in our lives, our attention skips from one object to another without really enjoying anything. If we have too many activities, our attention jumps from past to future without settling into the present. If we have too many opinions, we end up thinking about how things should be without fully seeing how things are.

Happiness and ease flow from the bottom of the lake. They aren't found hopping over the surface of life. We have to slow down enough to settle into the depths.

Joy and ease are simple and uncomplicated. Having lots of things to do, stuff to manage, places to go, and opinions to consult make life complicated.

Practices that cultivate simplicity do two things: they reduce the amount of stuff, activities, or preferences so we have a better chance of settling into the present. They get the outward to resonate a little better with the happiness, joy, and ease in our depths. And they help us become more aware of our relationship to stuff, experience, and thought.

Clutter Reduction

Perhaps the most familiar simplicity practice is clutter reduction.

The hall closet has so much stuff in it that opening the door is dangerous. The garage has so many boxes, broken pots, toys, and old bicycle parts that it is hard to get the car in. The desktop has so many piles that finding the paper we want is like a "Where's Waldo" mystery.

At some point, we can't stand it any more. We spend a few hours sorting and tossing. Afterward we feel relieved. Simplifying feels great. We wonder why we waited so long.

Actually, we know why we put it off. The job is annoying. Besides there were those old newspaper clippings we imagined wanting someday; those pants we haven't worn in three years, but who knows; the fan that broke four years ago but will be perfectly fine when we get to it; and on and on.

Clutter reduction can take a little time and discipline. But for the most part, once we get started, it feels good. And afterward, life feels simpler, lighter, and easier.

Renunciation

A more difficult simplicity practice is true renunciation. This involves reducing or eliminating things or activities for which we have substantive ambivalence.

The clutter in the closet, desk, or garage was problematic. But we didn't actually enjoy the clutter. However, there are things or activities we genuinely enjoy that create problems for us. We feel conflicted about them.

Addictions to alcohol, drugs, foods, or video games fit this category. And there are less obvious attachments.

For example, (true confession time), I love long, hot showers. They are soothing and sensuous. I lose all sense of time as I linger in steamy bliss. But good water is becoming scarcer. And our gas-fired water heater uses nonrenewable energy. I want to live harmoniously with our environment. So I feel genuinely ambivalent about long hot showers.

Another example for me is math and logic puzzles. At the end of a long day swimming in a sea of relationships, it can feel refreshing to immerse myself in the abstract logic of a difficult Sudoku puzzle. If I'm tired and need to rest, 10 or 15 minutes can help me unwind. But I can get hooked. An hour later I may be blurry-brained as I work through another puzzle when it would be wiser to just go to sleep.

Some of you may have an ambivalent relationship to television. TV can be educational, diversional, and relaxing. It can also be trance inducing. Maybe you find yourself watching more than is useful.

Or maybe you are a political junkie. Being informed is a good thing. But you find yourself following details, opinions, and intrigues until you are more agitated than thoughtful.

To be clear, there may be things we enjoy that are not good objects or activities for renunciation. Perhaps you have a beautiful shirt you enjoy in wearing. In fact, you feel guilty for enjoying is so much – it seems so "unspiritual."

In this case, the simpler, wiser practice is to just enjoy it. It will wear out some day. Meanwhile, savor it while it is here.

Renunciation is only appropriate for deeper, more substantive ambivalences. I can help to take a moment and reflect on things that you enjoy but may be problematic.

If you'd like to feel less conflicted, renunciation may help if you approach it wisely.

It helps to be clear about where happiness and unhappiness come from. A popular delusion (which I spoke about earlier) is that happiness flows into us from the hot shower, TV set, good music, vintage wine, and so on. In reality, happiness or unhappiness *flows out of us* into how we greet various things and activities. Wellbeing and suffering do not reside in math puzzles but in me. They arise in how I relate to them.

When we renounce something, we drop or reduce it. This shifts how we relate to it. We might see it from a fresh perspective and with clearer awareness. True renunciation is not about getting rid of something because it is bad, but about clarifying our relationship to it.

So when practicing renunciation, it is important to be present with what we feel. Are there ways we feel better? Worse? What happens when we dwell on what we are missing? When we ignore it? What good and bad judgments arise?

After a significant amount of time, take the object or activity back into your life. How do you feel about it now?

Then go without it again for a while.

Since we have significant attachment, renunciation may require focus and clear intentions. But grim determination doesn't help.

Don't examine yourself through the suspicious eyes of an inquisitioner – "What's wrong with me?" Look through the curious eyes of a scientist – "Wow, look at that thought." "What a curious feeling." Be playful and compassionate with yourself.

It doesn't help to condemn our attachments. That puts more energy into them. Rather than hold on or push away, grasp or blame, just relax; develop a sense of humor and play with them until they lighten up.

The lighter we take our attachments, the less relevant they become. Judgment subsides and discernment arises. With this, the attachment to the object softens. That is the true renunciation.

Opinions

Another important area to consider is simplifying opinions. This is similar to taking a vacation from stuff and experience. But since thoughts are less tangible, we play with them differently.

We Unitarian Universalists don't like to be told what to believe. We like to develop our own beliefs and opinions. And we can get attached to these and want others to share our attachment.

To practice simplicity toward our cherished ideas, it is helpful to remember that *any thought we can articulate is not absolutely true.* Any idea we can put into words is not ultimate truth. Absolute truth can be experienced. But it cannot be reduced to anything as clumsy as thought.

It is not very easy to take a vacation from our opinions. They keep cropping up, despite ourselves. With a little discipline, we can turn off the TV. But the inner thought broadcasts don't have an off switch.

However, we can reflect on the opposite of our opinion and see if there is some truth in it.

For example, every Sunday morning we say, "We value the goodness in every person." This implies that there is goodness in everyone. Do you believe that? I do. I believe it strongly.

So let's consider the opposite. For example, "There is evil in every person." Is this true as well?

My definition of evil is the intention to harm. Have you ever been so mad at someone you felt the urge to bop them on the side of the head? That is the desire to harm – my definition of evil.

I think we all have the potential to cause intentional harm. I hope we don't use it. But it is there.

So, I believe there is goodness in every person. I also believe there is evil in every person — we have both capacities.

Another thing we say that we value here is openness and curiosity.

Are there times when being closed or defensive is good?

Let's say someone wants to punch you in the face. Is it good to turn the other cheek? In some situations, yes. In others, no. If you want a more peaceful world, passively accepting violence is not always helpful. The world may be better off if you dodge or stop the punch.

How about child abuse? Is that something we should be open to? Most often not.

Clearly, openness and curiosity are very valuable. But there are times when their opposite is also valuable.

Many of the problems we face in our country today were exacerbated by rigid political ideas: "No more taxes." "Regulation is bad." "The free market is best." "Self-doubt equals weakness." "Democracy means freedom to do whatever we want." "Making money is the bottom line."

Each of these ideas has some merit. And the opposite of these ideas has merit as well.

On an individual level, over and over I see how people can get a conceptualized understanding of how they think they should be as a parent, partner, or member of a congregation. They cherish their idea so strongly it causes unneeded difficulty.

Seeing how the opposite of a cherished idea can have some truth does not invalidate the idea. But it helps us relax our grip on it.

We drop out of the realm of ideas and into the real world. We come out of our thought and into the present.

This is a deeper level of practicing simplicity. Perhaps it is what Lao Tzu meant when he said, "See simplicity in the complicated."

Silence

There are many different ways to practice simplicity. I'll mention just one more. At the risk of sounding esoteric, let me describe ultimate simplicity.

You may recall the story of Elijah in 1 Kings. The Old Testament prophet had retreated into a cave. A huge storm came up. But the Divine was not in the whirlwind. An earthquake shook the ground. But the Divine was not in the rumbling. A massive fire swept through. But the Divine was not in the conflagration. Then a gentle breeze arose. Elijah emerged from the cave to find the Divine in that quiet. (1 Kings 19: 11-13)

At its deepest level, simplicity is about silence. There is a deep, vast, non-judging, wise, compassionate, silent awareness that is our essence. Not our individual essence – that is noisy – but our collective essence.

Simplifying the amount of stuff in our lives, reducing the pace of activity, taking opinions lightly, and so forth helps us soften the storms, earthquakes, and fires inside so we might notice this expansive, quiet, intelligence that is all of us. It doesn't draw attention to itself. It is silent even as it is heartful and clear.

It is usually obscured by our noisy self-identification and self-fixation. But sometimes we notice it in quiet, simple moments.

The quintessential practice of simplicity is to notice when we touch this silent awareness. When you sense it, all the other practices are superseded. You can drop them and just lean into the vastness.

If you think about this pervasive awareness, your noisy thinking obscures it. It doesn't fit into thought. Best go back to the other simplicity practices like clutter reduction, renunciation, or relaxing opinions.

But many of you have felt what I am pointing toward. When you notice it, lean quietly into it – like Elijah emerging into stillness. Be aware of this intimate yet non-personal awareness.

It is what we truly are.

Living simply is not about separating from the world. It is about emerging into it with a relaxed and clear heart.

Unitarian Universalist Spirituality

An Openness of Being

I found that the chief difficulty for most people was to realize that they really heard new things, that is things that they had never heard before. They kept translating what they heard into their habitual language. They had ceased to hope and believe there might be anything new.

— P. D. Ouspensky

... to make you wonder and to answer that wondering with the deepest expression of your own nature.

– Shunryu Suzuki Roshi

December 16, 2001

I landed in the Manchester, New Hampshire, airport the last Friday in May. I hadn't seen Erika, my wife, in over a month. We had a lot of catching up to do.

I asked her about the status of the house. It had been on the market since February. Lots of people had seen it, but we had had no offers. "Any action?" I asked.

"Nothing," Erika said. "In fact, no one has even looked at it for 10 days. The realtor says the market has gone flat. Nobody is looking."

We had hoped to have everybody and everything moved to California within a month. The cost and complexity of continuing to own a house on the East Coast was daunting. What could we do?

We had already done everything reasonable. We had fixed things that might put off a buyer. We had lowered the price a little. The house has some unique aspects – like a mother-in-law apartment – that might appeal to some people but not others. The realtor said it was just a matter of finding the right buyer. From the start, she had said it might take time.

We were running out of time. I was feeling desperate. But I could not think of anything more to do.

Then it occurred to me that the one thing I had not tried was prayer: ironic for a minister.

As we pulled out of the parking lot at the Manchester airport, there was a lull in our conversation. I closed my eyes (Erika was driving). I let my breathing quiet and my body relax. I imagined the crown of my head softening and opening. I let go of some of my sense of being a separate, contained person and allowed a feeling of alignment and connection with the cosmos.

In this light trance I thought, "If it is in our highest best interest, send us a buyer for the house. We could use a little help down here."

I sat with that sense for a few minutes. I didn't have a particular image of God or guardian forces or anything like that. Just blending with the universe a little and asking for some support if it was for the highest good.

Erika was not aware of what I was doing. It was just a break in the dialog. She said something about Damon, our son. I slipped out of that state and back into the conversation.

The next morning we were preparing to leave for Providence, Rhode Island, for the weekend where our oldest son, Nathan, was graduating from Brown University. Just as we were leaving the house, the realtor called. Someone wanted to see the house at 1:00.

A little chill went up my spine.

As we pulled onto Interstate 495, I thought it was certainly possible that this was just another couple that would look at the house and we'd never hear from them again. So I closed my eyes and went into that same light trance. "If the house is right for these people, please let them see this. If it is a good fit for them, help them know this."

Late Monday afternoon when we got home from Providence, there was a message on the answering machine. We had an offer on the house. It was complicated. The couple had a house that wouldn't be sold until December, so they couldn't buy ours now. But they loved it and wanted to lease it and buy it in December. It took us a week and a half and consulting a lawyer, but we ended up with a lease and a purchase and sales agreement with which we were all comfortable and confident.

Question

So here is the question: Was there any relationship between my "asking for help from the universe" and this couple's deciding to look at a house they could not purchase right away? Was there any relationship between my "asking" and the couple's falling in love with the place once they'd seen it?

My scientific head says, "Don't be silly. It was coincidence."

But in my gut and heart I don't believe in coincidence. Our Unitarian Universalism does not offer an explanation. I am not confident in anybody's explanation of how these forces might work. I don't believe in a personalized God whom I can convince to pull a few strings on my behalf. But I do believe that there was a relationship between my willingness to align and ask for help if it was in everyone's best interest and the eventual offer to purchase the property.

Can't Dismiss

Many of you will politely scoff at this. Others may nod your heads imperceptibly because you've had similar experiences which are hard to explain.

One of the reasons I can't dismiss it quickly is it is not an isolated example in my life. For example, I worked as a psychotherapist for about 15 years. Periodically I'd get a lull in my practice – my client load would be low enough that I began to worry about finances. I refused to hook up with HMOs: they seemed unethical in how they dealt with mental health. I was reluctant to advertise just because that's how I am. I'd have to wait for word of mouth. Sometimes the wait got too long for comfort.

Then I'd think, "Why haven't I put out a request to the universe for help?"

I'd close my eyes, drop into that light trance, and say, "If it is in my highest best interest, please send me a few clients."

Within 24 hours I'd have three phone calls. It was spooky. I still don't want to believe it. But it was reliable as long as my need was real and sincere.

How often can I dismiss these phenomena before the dismissal is more denial and prejudice than reason?

Others

When it comes to experiences which are hard to define in conventional terms, I know I'm not alone. For example, last winter I led a training group for the Ministry Circles facilitators. One evening I asked them, "What are some experiences that have touched you deeply?" I did not ask this in the context of things that are hard to explain. Just "What has moved you?" I suggested they think about it and come back the next week to share.

The next week, some people spoke of a time when they felt they were in communication with someone who had died. Some spoke of moments of merging with another person – not only empathizing, but in some tangible and mysterious way feeling they *were* the other person for a time.

Most of the experiences could not fit easily into today's rational scientific frame of reference. Yet these people are not wild-eyed, New Age fanatics. They are mature, reasonable, emotionally stable embodiments of Unitarian Universalism. Some are leaders in our church. And some were a little reluctant to speak about them in church because they ran counter to an unspoken orthodoxy. These were powerful experiences which had affected how they feel about life. Yet they were not confident there was room for them in church.

Reluctance

Have you had experiences which don't fit conventional explanations? Have you had experiences which conflict even with your own understanding? Have you experienced things you might feel a little reluctant to share here?

What does this say about us that some of the things that touch us most deeply are difficult to share in our beloved community?

One thing it says is that we need more small group settings, like the Ministry Circles, where it is easier to risk pushing the edges for the sake of sharing what has touched us. But this morning is not a commercial for the Ministry Circles.

Boxes

This morning is a plug for getting out of our boxes.

During my adolescence I spent a summer working in a depressed Hispanic community outside Durango, Colorado. We built an adobe clinic to get some medical services to those people.

To build with adobe, we mixed mud, sand, and straw in a specific ratio. We carefully picked out any stones or sticks and pushed the mixture into wooden boxes. When it was evenly filled, we turned the box over on the ground and, voila, there was a nice adobe rectangle. When it had dried in the sun for a few days, it could be built into a wall.

Many people's religion is like an adobe brick. They get a mixture of ritual, feelings, and thoughts and stuff them into a box of beliefs. They carefully remove any stony experiences that don't fit. And over the years, it hardens into a brick.

Continuing Revelation

Over the centuries in the West, the church built the box that was supposed to mold our religion. For example, one doctrine was "complete revelation." This says that spiritual truth has been completely revealed to man through Jesus Christ and the Bible. Two thousand years later we still celebrate his traditional birthday. Anything we need to know is set down in the Bible. There is nothing new that can ever be added: all we need to do is read the Bible. Our fundamentalist brothers and sisters still think this way.

So, when Galileo invented a telescope and saw moons around Jupiter, his observation and the instruments used to make it were sticks and stones to be removed from the mixture. The Bible said nothing about Jovan moons; therefore, they don't exist.

Early Unitarians developed a counter doctrine called "continuing revelation." It says that life, the universe, and truth are more dynamic. Truth continues to be revealed to us. A healthy religious life involves searching through our own experience, not just accepting an external authority. Revelation continues through us. We must engage in this quest if our spiritual life is to be alive.

We all nod our heads and say, "yes, of course." Some of you may not be familiar with the term "continuing revelation," but it makes intuitive sense to us.

Creeping Orthodoxy

And yet there is a subtle, creeping orthodoxy. Yes, even here.

The box for us is not church doctrine. The box is scientific, rational thought. Anything that falls outside of that is a stick or stone to be discarded.

There are a number of different kinds of experiences that fall outside the box. One of the most common is what Carl Jung called "synchronicity." Perhaps an old friend suddenly pops into your mind. You haven't thought about him for years and for no reason, there he is. So you give him a call. He says his wife just died and it is such a comfort to hear from you. You say to yourself, "What a coincidence," but inside it feels like more than coincidence.

Another kind of out-of-the-box experience is a moment of inner illumination. The ordinary haze of thinking dissipates and you suddenly see things differently. "Aha!" The interconnectedness of life suddenly is not just a scientific, ecological theory. It is a reality you experience as clearly as the sun on a clear day.

What do we do with these illuminated moments? Our first impulse is to fit them into the mold or toss them out.

If I'm a fundamentalist, I interpret them as God revealing Himself to me or touching my life with His hand.

If my bent is toward New Age thinking, I may interpret inner illumination as communication with my guardian spirit.

If I am a depth psychologist, I may decide a suppressed archetype is breaking through into my consciousness.

If I'm a scientific materialist who reduces everything to high school physics and biology, I'll dismiss it as a chemical imbalance: too many endorphins.

In other words, we humans have a conformity streak. We tend to push our experiences into the familiar structures of our consciousness. How we interpret luminous moments often says more about us than about life.

Conformity

I've seen too many things that don't fit easily into the scientific or Unitarian Universalist mind set.

I knew a woman who was depressed most of her life. At her memorial service, I had a strong sense of her presence and she seemed less depressed and more compassionately concerned about her family than I had known.

I know a college professor who, against all his instincts, was persuaded to see a certain palm reader. The palm reader told him that he was going to get very sick – there was a problem inside his head. But not to worry, in a year everything would be fine. He scoffed and dismissed the whole thing. Three months later the doctors discovered a brain tumor. It was operated upon and a year later he was fully recovered.

I know a man who prayed to the Hindu goddess Kali to purge him of his jealousy. The next day his fiancée (who knew nothing about the prayer) started an affair. He was overwhelmed with jealousy. He saw how incredibly painful and fruitless it is. It rose to a fevered pitch and then broke. It evaporated out of him. He found a deep sense of peace. The next day, his fiancée dropped the affair.

My mother once asked me what I saw in her aura. I said there was a dark cloud leaving her that had been moving away for about a day and a half. She became upset and said she'd had an attack that felt like angina two days before. It scared her so much that she did not say anything to anyone and tried not to think about it.

I know a woman who can sometimes turn her VCR on and off with her mind.

I once prayed for a house buyer and they showed up the next day.

I could go on and on.

The universe is a lot more complex and interesting than anyone's box.

Conclusion

This morning I am suggesting two different ways of using Unitarian Universalism.

The first is to use it as a more comfortable box. We Unitarian Universalists are rightly uncomfortable with ideas of supernatural intrusion into the affairs of the earth. But we also don't like to leave things unexplained. So for our Bible, we turn to reason and scientific explanations. This becomes our box. We replace the old church dogma with scientific materialism dogma.

The second and truer use of Unitarian Universalism is as a way to become more comfortable with bewilderment.

At our best, we retain an openness of mind and heart, what in Zen is called "don't know mind" or "beginner's mind." There are these wonderful, powerful experiences and we don't know what to make of them. At our best we retain a sense of wonder, awe, mystery, and "don't know." We cultivate an openness of being, if you will.

We don't throw away our beliefs in the face of one experience we can't explain. We certainly don't retreat into pre-rational magical thinking just because something is a little strange. But we also don't dismiss a phenomenon we can't make sense of. We don't try to make experience conform to our previous understanding. We don't try to control the experience by stuffing it into a box. We stay open and see what we can learn.

We are in the midst of the Christmas season. The essence of it is the wonder and awe of birth, of the strength of spirit that can shine through human form. Yes, I know. Christmas has been overrun by a commercialism that makes us want to scream. But the core Christmas spirit can still be found. It is an openness of being, an openness that allows for mystery and wonder.

So this morning, I'm making a plug for wonder and awe and openness of being: a plug for those things which we feel deep inside but are reluctant to discuss in polite society. I'm inviting all of you who may be in a religious closet to come on out. Probably all of us have experienced things we can't explain. Be willing to share what has moved you whether you can make sense of it or not. Be willing to acknowledge that your own experience in life may be a little richer than you may even acknowledge to yourself.

The universe is a lot more interesting than anybody's model of it.

Unitarian Universalist Maturity

March 7, 2004

An elderly woman in a blue print blouse sat next to the fish tank in Dr. Westerling's office. On the other side of the tank, a man with a briefcase studied a spreadsheet through a furrowed brow.

Across the waiting room a three-year-old rested one hand on his mother's knee. His chin was tucked in shyly as he gazed intently at the fish and the two grown-ups guarding them.

He pointed at the tank and looked at his mom with pleading eyes. She smiled at him and went back to reading her novel.

He studied the aquarium some more, tightened his lips, took a deep breath, and struck out across the room. Mom glanced up long enough to see where he was going, then returned to her pages.

He put both hands on the glass. The fish glided back and forth a few inches from his nose.

After a few minutes he ran back across the room on his toes, grabbed his mother's knees, and smiled from ear to ear. She absently stroked his arm.

He took up his sentry position again: hand on her knee as he assessed the territory. After a few minutes he had soaked up enough courage for another expedition into the wild territory of strange adults and magical fish.

Psychologists call this process "separation-individuation." We humans are not born with a sense of being separate individuals. Our identities are fused with the parents we depend upon.

As we grow, we experience two conflicting urges. One is for comfort, safety, protection, a sense of belonging, being part of a family, and community. The other is to strike out into the world, establish our uniqueness, our separateness, and our individuality.

In the waiting room, I could see that these urges battled inside the boy. He wanted to go see the fish. But his mother didn't. She was different. She wanted to read her book.

His mother didn't pretend she was like him and go to the fish. She didn't make him be like her by making him sit next to her and look at a picture book. And when he ventured off, she didn't pull him back to safety or cheer him on. She instinctively let him explore his individuality.

Tattoo

As we grow, the urge to explore our separate identity takes us farther and farther away from home and family. We explore independence on many levels.

When our son Nathan was 16, the only thing he wanted for his birthday or Christmas was money to buy a tattoo. My wife Erika and I told him we could hardly stand him permanently marking his body. But we recognized he had different values and was old enough to decide for himself. But he would have to do it on his own: we wouldn't give him money for it.

His girlfriend gave him the money for Christmas. He got a beautiful Celtic knot tattooed behind his right shoulder.

Of course the process doesn't always go so gracefully. Especially as adolescents prepare to leave home, things can get bumpy. It is too much to expect them to say, "Mom, dad, it's been great. Thanks for the love and support. But I'm grown now. Goodbye." It's too much to expect parents to say, "We love you. But you need to be on your own. We rejoice in this parting." Often there is angst, struggle, tears, and door slamming. A friend remarked she was looking forward to missing her son when he went off to school. Her son felt a similar ambivalence.

Nevertheless, one way or another, sooner or later, however imperfectly, most of us establish an adult, separate, individual identity. We discover something of who we are as a unique man or woman in the world.

Beyond Selfhood

Maturation does not stop here. As children, our task is to develop a healthy sense of a separate self. As adults, our task is to loosen our grip on our individuality, to realize how deeply interconnected we all are, to know we are part of a larger organism called humanity. As adolescents we understand the interdependent web as an ecological concept or philosophical idea. As mature adults we know it as a gut-level, heartfelt reality. One researcher, Jack Engler, says, "You have to develop a self before you can lose it." Those who do not fully separate and individuate do not have the foundation for deeper oneness. Those who hang too tightly to their Ayn Rand individualism never leave spiritual adolescence.

Religious Maturity

I want to talk here about religious childhood, adolescence, and maturity. Specifically, I want to explore what it means to be a mature Unitarian Universalist (or "UU").

"Well, aren't Unitarian Universalists religiously mature by definition?"

No. Of course not.

To be a regular Unitarian Universalist all you have to do is be clear about a few beliefs you reject, look like a tolerant sort of person, have a collection of buttons on various social justice causes, and go to church when you feel like it. It's not that hard.

We don't test religious maturity. And we like it this way. Judging someone's conscience or beliefs is distasteful to us.

Consequently, a few Unitarian Universalist are religious children. A lot are religious adolescents. And some are religiously mature.

How do you know if you are religiously mature? Last summer Daniel O'Connor, our minister in Kirkwood, Missouri, wrote a short letter to the *UU World*, our denomination's magazine. He suggested four criteria of UU maturity. They are honoring your religious roots, wrestling with life's big questions, challenging your own assumptions, and becoming an elder.[34]

Let's explore them.

---

[34] *UU World*, July/August 2003, p. 14-15

Honoring Roots

One sign of religious maturity is the ability to truly honor your religious roots.

We are born to parents we didn't choose, families we didn't select, socio-economic conditions over which we had no control, a mix of blood lines and genes we couldn't manipulate and faith traditions or lack of traditions that were not our choosing.

As children we tend to accept these without question. We don't have any other perspective for comparison.

Part of maturation is developing enough discernment and objectivity to evaluate our roots. Failure to develop this capacity leaves us in perpetual childhood.

Many fundamentalist and conservative religions say we are "God's children": not His adults but His children. They favor obedience over experimentation, faith in a higher authority over developing your own inner authority, conformity over individuality. They try to keep people in religious childhood. We Unitarian Universalists like to rail against them from time to time.

When I was growing up, the vast majority of people coming to Unitarian Universalism came from these traditional religions. They felt stifled, confined, or wounded by them. They were delighted by our openness, acceptance, and encouragement to think for themselves. We had one-hour church services followed by one-and-a-half hour talkbacks where everyone could express their disagreement. The emphasis was on what we rejected and didn't believe. This is the source of the jokes about praying to whom it may concern and UU evangelists knocking on doors for no particular reason.

In short, we were religious adolescents breaking out of religious childhood. This rejection, rebellion, and pushing away is an essential part of religious separation-individuation.

But maturation doesn't stop with adolescence (I hope!). Our religious upbringing was neither all good nor all bad. Black-and-white thinking is characteristic of childhood and politics. There are parts of our background we may need to separate from. But there are parts we can honor.

If you find little you can embrace in your roots, at least you can bow to them and thank them for teaching you to be passionate for something different. And I suspect most of our roots offered more than a bad example.

Big Questions

Another sign of maturity is having spent time wrestling with life's big questions.

Unitarian Universalism does not prescribe theology, metaphysics, or beliefs. But it is not because we think they are unimportant. Quite the opposite. They are too important to be prescribed. If we are alive, our perspective will shift, change, and mature over time. So we affirm the freedom to develop and explore our own beliefs.

But with this freedom comes responsibility to explore questions like: "What's the nature of God?" "What does it imply to say God exists or doesn't exist?" "What happens when we die?" "Is there an underlying order to the universe or is it fundamentally random?" "Is there purpose to your life?" "What will allow you to die contented?"

You don't have to have a specific set of answers or even be certain about your own beliefs. But when asked what you believe, you should be able to say more than "I don't believe what I was taught as a kid." A mature UU can enter into a coherent, thoughtful conversation about theological questions.

I think this is one of the reasons our Ministry Circles and Adult Enrichment classes have been so popular: many of you are hungry for a chance to explore.

Stretching

A third sign of maturity is stretching: no matter how you answer those big questions, you step outside your area of comfort and challenge your answers.

Some people come to Unitarian Universalism, decide what they think and sit down. They become obnoxiously self-confident in their unexamined conclusions.

So challenge yourself. If your beliefs haven't changed in 20 years, you may be religiously dead. If you don't believe in God, try sincere prayer. If you believe in God, contemplate a chaotic universe with no divine forces. If you enjoy an active life, try a silent retreat. If you love solitude, join a protest demonstration. If poverty upsets you, volunteer at Loaves and Fishes.

Whatever makes you comfortable, know that. It's good to have a home base. And, mature UUs continue to grow. They stretch beyond this comfort base to add depth, texture and humility to their religious lives.

Eldering

A fourth sign of UU maturity is eldering. True eldering has nothing to do with age. It's a feeling of ownership, responsibility, and caring that grows on you.

Part of this eldering is the financial support you give the congregation. We are in the midst of our annual pledge drive. Typical financial appeals go something like this: "Think about what this congregation gives you. It costs about a dollar a minute to keep us running. If you pledge $120 a month, you keep us going for about two hours a month. Think about this and pledge as generously as you can."

Notice this is directed toward religious adolescents. It is framed as fee-for-service: it encourages you to separate from the congregation and evaluate the goods and services you receive. Many give generously in this way. It's fine.

As you become an elder, the fee-for-service rationale becomes less important. You don't stand apart from the congregation enough to want to count and measure services. You know the value. The only question is, "Given my resources, what can I do to strengthen my religious home." You move from a sense of ownership and generosity and less from "what's in it for me."

Erika and I give five percent of our income. And it comes off the top rather than waiting to see what's left over at the end of the month. It feels good that way.

Of course eldering is broader than just money. Perhaps the first sign of emerging elderhood is when you find yourself saying "my church" rather than "the church." You think of this place less as an institution and more as a home.

There are other signs of eldering. You know you are becoming an elder when:

- You see something amiss and rather than think "someone should fix that" you think, "I wonder if there is something I can do."

- You notice someone has not been around for a while and you call him to see if he is okay.

- You feel less concern about being welcomed and more about being welcoming.

- You are aware of your particular gifts and find ways to offer them that help you and the congregation. You don't volunteer out of guilt but out of caring.

- When you need to rest, you don't get anxious, you just slow down and take care of yourself.

Being a UU elder is not so much about a particular amount of money, time, or tasks. It's about living an attitude: you look at the congregation and feel "I love this place and want to care for it."

So these are four sign of UU maturity: honoring your religious roots, wrestling with life's big questions, challenging your own beliefs, and eldering.

Welcome

If you want to dishonor your religious roots, ignore life's big questions, never examine your beliefs and take no responsibility for nurturing this congregation, then I say to you, "Welcome. I'm glad you're here. I hope you'll come back."

Nothing I've said this morning is intended as a "should" or "ought to." "Should" is the language of religious childhood.

In fact, it would be a little strange for someone to come here looking for a place to elder without even knowing the congregation. We all have times of need. I hope you feel nurtured here.

On the other hand, if you honor your religious roots, wrestle with those theological issues, challenge your own assumptions, and spontaneously elder because this place feels like home, I say to you, "Welcome. You are the lifeblood of this place. There is nothing magical or mysterious about what makes us thrive: it is your generosity, caring, guidance, and wisdom."

And if you feel somewhere in between, if this place feels like home in some ways and you want to deepen your religious life, you might want to look at these four areas: How do you relate to your past? How comfortable are you conversing about those big questions? What can you do to step outside of your conclusions? Is there some way your heart longs to give something back?

I say to you as well, "Welcome. I think you are in the right place. I'm glad you are part of this place because …"

In the Buddha's Footsteps: Sujata

January 15, 2006

Transcendence and transformation are very different spiritual paths. Transcendence is about rising above the pain, suffering, and limitations of this world and your life.

Transformation is not about rising above anything. It's about settling into the world and your life as they are. It requires making peace with the pain, suffering, and limitations that are unavoidable.

At first glance transcendence is far more attractive. Who wouldn't want to transcend his or her worldly limits? There is only one problem: it doesn't work. Ultimately transcendence fails.

Transformation is more work. Not only do you have to know suffering and limitations, you have to open your heart to all of it. Keeping your heart open and keeping good boundaries is not easy. But it works. Your sense of who you are gradually evolves.

That is my premise: opening the heart and keeping good boundaries. If this theme doesn't appeal to you, you might move on to another essay.

I'll introduce this theme with stories. I'll tell you about Siddhartha Gautama and a beautiful young woman named Sujata. But first I want to tell you about walking south a few miles from Bodhgaya – the place of Siddhartha's enlightenment – to a banyan tree where Siddhartha met Sujata shortly before his enlightenment.

Bodhgaya to Sujata

After breakfast on Tuesday morning, November 22, we went out the back door of the hotel, around the watchmen, passed two Tibetan monks washing their robes, through the tiny door in the back gate and up a steep incline. To the right, the road led south to the center of Bodhgaya and the Bodhi tree. We turned left.

That Bodhi tree is a direct descendent of the tree under which the Buddha was enlightened. The tree is surrounded by a park that vibrates with spiritual energy. The park is surrounded by tiny shops, vendors, dogs, hawkers, beggars, con men, food stalls, rickshaws, vegetable markets, cripples, tourists, monks, pilgrims, tailors, internet cafés, and on and on. It hums with entrepreneurial zeal and hustler charm. No doubt, the hustlers who had marked us were now waiting for us there or in front of the hotel.

So we turned left, taking a circuitous course around the hubbub and then south to the Sujata grove.

As we walked, we found the back streets far from empty: A *dalit* ("untouchable") woman boiled rice over a tiny fire on the sidewalk. A water buffalo chewed its cud in the middle of the road as traffic swerved around it. Four tiny kid goats slept in a peaceful heap on a huge pile of trash. A nanny goat grazed on garbage nearby. A rickshaw carrying about 30 chickens in tiny cages stopped in front of us. A man hopped down, grabbed three chickens by the feet, and carried them across the street to a tiny plastic covered eating establishment. Barefoot men in turbans piled mud bricks into walls and lashed bamboo into building frames.

On the far side of Bodhgaya, the streets were even more congested until we ducked into an alley heading due south. The alley opened into a wide, high-walled street with a half dozen people: abandoned by Indian standards. A dilapidated building at the end displayed a fresh sign: "Get your X-rays here."

I stopped beneath the sign. To the west, an old 12-foot wooden gate stood half open. Dingy, stained, and cracked columns and arches surrounded it. I realized, "This is the entry way to an ancient palace!" Sure enough, in the other direction was a large courtyard. A few cows, ducks, chickens, and dogs wandered amongst thousand-year-old statues and ancient rubble. A small woman balanced a woven basket on her head. Two men lifted water from an ancient well and dumped it on themselves. Clearly people lived here. It could have been a scene in a Mad Max movie as people scrabbled amongst remains of a fallen civilization.

Half a dozen barefoot children hopped over to us. Their clothes were dusty and the wrong size. One had an eye infection. "Rupees, rupees," they said.

"Hello," I smiled. "Namasté." I shook my head, "No rupees." Giving money to street kids trained them to be beggars for the rest of their lives.

They held up their hands insistently and whined, "Rupees, rupees, rupees."

I was tempted to either give them money or turn away. Instead I asked, "What are your names?"

"I'm Balaji," a boy said.

"Let me show you something, Balaji." I took a picture and showed them the image on the back of my digital camera. Suddenly, I was not a walking bag of rupees. "Take a picture of me!"

The kids laughed, chatted, and held our hands as they showed us the huge organic garden outside the palace gate and the poor ashram inside the crumbling inner palace.

They showed us through another massive gate that opened south on the banks of the Niranjana River. In the Buddha's time, the water ran clear and blue. That day, the river was a three-quarter-mile-wide strip of sand.

As we started across Balaji announced, "I have two brothers and a sister."

"You have good English," I said.

He smiled.

"Where do you live?"

"Ishlim."

"Where's that?"

He pointed across the river in the direction we were walking.

"Sounds like a nice family," I said.

"I had four brothers. Two died. My mother died too."

"I'm sorry," I said.

He shrugged. Then he put his hands on the shoulders of a boy next to him, "This is my brother, Mihir."

Other kids joined in the conversation as we walked past bristly pigs rooting in the sand, knots of teenagers huddled around gambling games, women carrying baskets or babies, and children playing. By now, we had over a dozen in our traveling retinue.

We climbed the far embankment, walked single file through the narrow streets of Ishlim and ventured out into the fields to the south.

I pointed to some trees in the distance and asked the kids, "Sujata?"

They all pointed to the grove: "Sujata!"

Three gleaming white SUVs packed with Japanese tourists rumbled toward us in a cloud of dust. And in the front seat of each, a man with a camcorder filmed us as they drove by.

"I just made it into a Japanese home movie," I thought.

A crowd of grim, sullen beggars materialized. Giving them rupees could stir up a riot. We smiled, shook our heads, and walked around to the far side of the grove with everyone following us like gulls after trawlers.

A small concrete open-air temple nestled up against a banyan tree. We took off our shoes and entered.

John, our leader on this pilgrimage, said, "I want to talk about this place, but I don't think I can in this noise. Let's meditate and see what that does."

As we closed our eyes, most of the people fell silent. Those who didn't were hushed by others. Spiritual seeking is deeply respected in India, no matter who you are.

Fifteen minutes later, a Japanese tourist arrived, set up a tripod, filmed us meditating, and left.

After about 25 minutes, John rang a bell. I opened my eyes. The walls and doorway were lined with faces watching us. But the mood was relatively peaceful.

John began to speak.

Sujata

Twenty-five hundred years ago, prince Siddhartha Gautama of the Sakya clan was the heir apparent of the small, prosperous kingdom of Kapilavatthu about 50 miles to the north of where we were sitting. In his late 20s, he realized that money, power, health, comfort, and the world itself were all transient. Everything passes. So none could bring lasting happiness.

So he left the palace, gave up his wealth, and became a homeless monk. He traveled south to the forested hills around Rājagaha. John pointed to the southeast. We could see the hills. For six and a half years, Siddhartha studied there with four spiritual masters.

They taught that transcending the material realm and entering the spiritual was the path to lasting happiness.

Siddhartha learned two methods of transcendence. One was cultivating deep, yogic trance states called "*jhānas.*"

Through ardent practice, Siddhartha mastered the jhānas. He learned they are profoundly blissful, they don't last, and when he inevitably came back to normal consciousness, he saw in himself all the seeds of greed, anger, confusion, hatred, and other forms of unhappiness. The jhānas gave no wisdom for dealing with the world. Transcendence failed.

At the same time, Siddhartha pursued a second set of yogic disciplines: ascetic renunciation. Ascetics believe there is a conflict between the material and the spiritual. Therefore, weakening the material should strengthen the spiritual. They denied themselves contact with women. They renounced wealth, prestige, power, and sometimes shelter, clothes and food. At one point Siddhartha ate only one grain of rice a day. When he touched his stomach, he could feel his backbone. He took ascetic denial as far as possible. If he went any further, he would die. In fact, he was starving to death. Yet spiritual fulfillment eluded him.

Siddhartha realized both sets of practices were flawed. Both failed.

So he left the hills of Rājagaha and traveled northwest. He got as far as the tiny farm village of Senani. There he collapsed under a tree. Too weak to move, he awaited death.

Meanwhile there was a beautiful young woman in Senani. Her name was Sujata.

Nature was central to the folk religions of that time. Each town had a central tree that housed a deva, or god-spirit, that protected the village and its people.

Sujata was overjoyed that she had married a good husband and become pregnant. She wanted to thank the tree with a traditional offering of sweet *kier*: a mixture of rice, milk, honey, and rose that tastes similar to women's breast milk.

As she approached the tree with a bowl of kid, she saw an entity. After years of jhānic practices and near starvation, Siddhartha didn't even look human. He was "out there." She thought the tree spirit had taken material form to accept her offering.

But as she came closer, she realized he was a dying man. Instead of giving the food to the tree, she offered it to him.

Siddhartha Gautama looked at her for a long time. Then he accepted her gift. In that moment, Buddhism was born.

In the 21st century, it may be difficult to appreciate what a radical act it was to accept the food. The spirituality of Siddhartha's time used fierce, male, warrior-like qualities to try to transcend the earth. It rejected the earth, the soft, the feminine, and the receptive. Ascetics were not supposed to have contact with women or eat sweet foods.

Sujata was beautiful and in her sexual prime. Accepting rice pudding that tastes like breast milk from a voluptuous young woman was as unacceptable in his time as the Pope visiting a prostitute in our time. When his ascetic buddies found out they were scandalized and disgusted.

His acceptance of Sujata's offering was not the desperate act of a dying man. It was a conscious choice of a different kind of spiritual path: the path of transformation. He no longer tried to transcend this world. He tried to open his heart to all of it and let it transform him. Turning to her was deliberate acceptance of the feminine and the earth. Statues of his enlightenment depict him sitting with one hand on his lap and the other touching the earth as if to say, "We are part of the earth. This is us. This is part of our path."

Sujata brought him food every day. When he was strong enough, he walked north, crossed the Niranjana River, sat down under a pila tree and vowed not to move until he awakened.

But that is another story. Under the banyan tree with Sujata, at the very spot where we sat, he realized what he had to do to become enlightened. He saw the path of transformation: opening the heart to all this and at the same time keeping wise boundaries.

The Return

When we had finished talking, we left money in the temple donation box and went to get our shoes.

Outside, the crowd had grown threefold. The communication system was very efficient. All the people in Bodhgaya who had marked us "just happened" to be in the Sujata grove that afternoon.

My heart sank when I saw Ashok. He was an 18-year-old young man who had approached me my first day in Bodhgaya. "I just want to practice my English," he assured me. "I don't want to bother you."

Ever since, any time I left the hotel night or day, he was waiting to talk to me. The second day he spoke about his school. The third he talked about being poor and hinted at how I might help.

On the walk back to town, Ashok casually told me he was studying hard for his upcoming exams. But it wasn't easy because he was poor.

"Yeh, right," I thought. "He lurks outside my hotel day and night. All he seems to study is me. And he's good at it."

Out loud I said, "Ashok, we are walking the path of the Buddha from Sujata to the Bodhi tree. I think I'd rather not chat right now."

He walked quietly next to me.

I still felt trapped. I thought about what John had said about keeping the heart open and keeping good boundaries. So I put my hand on Ashok's shoulder. "Ashok," I said. "I just want you to know that I'm not going to give you money for your education."

He flinched. I went on. "You know the Prajnavihara School?" It is a school that educates the poorest of the poor. We had visited the school the day before. The nuns who run it found that education could break the cycle of poverty.

"Yes, I know Prajnavihara," Ashok assured me.

"Do you know Sister Mary Lobo?" Some of you may have seen her in a PBS documentary about micro financing amongst the dalit ("untouchable") women: the lowest gender of the lowest cast. Her work has been remarkably effective in building self-esteem and confidence, as well as providing very practical help. We had spent the previous evening with her. She is a tiny woman with a huge heart, boundless energy, and an unnerving way of cutting through any con.

"Yes, I know Sister Lobo," Ashok said as he stepped back a little.

"We're giving a lot of money to Prajnavihara and Sister Mary Lobo. I think they can put our resources to better use. We aren't going to have any money to give to others. Besides," I took a breath, "we believe that giving money to people we meet on the streets doesn't really help in the long run."

Ashok looked a little unnerved. But he quickly recovered. He looked hurt except for his eyes. They looked calculating as he scanned me.

"I haven't asked you for money," he said.

I felt my heart clench. I looked at his sad face and hard eyes. "Good move, Ashok," I thought.

Out loud I said, "I know Ashok. I know you haven't actually asked me for anything. I just didn't want you to get the wrong idea."

He dropped back about 15 feet. His charm quickly returned as he struck up a cheerful conversation with another member of our group.

I sighed.

Namasté

By this time we were starting through a narrow alley in Ishlim. People were sitting in their doorways.

At the far end of the alley, a man with thinning hair unconsciously stood up. He looked at us with open-eyed amazement and the biggest grin.

I bowed slightly and said, "Namasté."

He looked startled that someone with Barnum and Bailey could speak. Then he put his palms together, bowed respectfully and said, "Namasté."

He spoke Hindi to his five-year-old daughter. She quickly put her palms together and bowed to me. "Namasté." Her eyes sparkled.

I paused and bowed to her.

Namasté is a blessing. It means "I see God in you. I see the light in you. May it bless you."

The exchange took 15 seconds. But they saw God in me. And I saw the light in them. They beamed as if I had made their day. They had made mine.

I can barely imagine what their life is like in that little mudroom in a tiny village beside a dried-up river in Bihar Pradesh, the poorest province of a poor country. I can try to imagine, but I know as little about their life as they can imagine about mine in Sacramento.

But for that moment, on a hot afternoon along the footsteps of the Buddha, we saw each other's essence.

As we approached the Niranjana River, I felt slightly euphoric. "I just love this place," I thought. "I don't know how to explain it, but I love this place."

Heart and Boundaries

That's enough of my adventures for now.

In order to survive without shutting down or going crazy in India, we had to do two things.

First, we worked constantly to keep our hearts open. The grime, pollution, scams, suffering, and deprivation made it easy to get lost in fear, anger, resentment, overload, or numbness. So it was important to feel all of it in the heart. This helped us open to the people around us. And there were many lovely, light-spirited folks like the man and his daughter. Without an open heart I would not have even noticed them.

Second, we worked constantly to keep good boundaries. The heart is potentially infinite. Our love needs no boundaries. But our time, money, resources, and emotional energy are limited. They are part of a finite world.

The path of transformation requires that we manage our resources responsibly. It requires that we keep good boundaries. Without good boundaries, India would have sucked us dry.

Keeping good boundaries is not an excuse for closing the heart. The path of transformation is not a balancing act. It is not a little heart and a little boundary. It is all of both. It is doing your best to keep your infinite love flowing and at the same time managing your finite resources wisely: open heart and good boundaries.

In this country, the path may not be as stark. But the issues are the same. How do you encourage your love to open to everyone and concurrently manage skillful limit setting? When you are dealing with family, work, the church, the political scene, how do you stay heartful and within reasonable bounds?

These are the questions to reflect on at another time. For now, if you like, hold this phrase in your chest, "Open heart and good boundaries." Particularly in difficult times, let it guide and inform you. "Open heart; good boundaries."

May it help us come together, deepen our lives, and actively love the world.

Namasté.

In the Buddha's Footsteps: Transformation

January 29, 2006

A girl with severe spinal scoliosis squats beside a culvert. She uses sand to scrub soot off tin dishes. Ten feet away a man in dingy white trousers (possibly her father?) sleeps on an empty bed frame beneath a tree as music plays softly over a portable radio in the dirt. A cow gazes absently at both of them. Through an empty archway a woman in a vivid blue sari scrubs clothes on a rock. There is no roof on the walls. Apparently several families live in these ruins of an ancient horse stable.

Our narrow path through vegetable fields goes past the girl with scoliosis. The local children walking with us have been friendly to everyone. But they don't acknowledge her. She doesn't look up.

Erika pauses next to the girl and says, "Hello." The girl keeps scrubbing. When Erika doesn't leave, she looks up anxiously.

Erika puts her palms together and says, "Namasté," a common blessing and greeting in India.

The girl beams. But she is at a loss to know what to do with the blessing or the attention. So she goes back to scrubbing. From the side we could see her face lit up in a smile.

Our days in India and Nepal were a kaleidoscope of snippets like this. What was that girl's life like? Living in roofless ruins at the edge of a field? Ostracized by peers for a deformity no one could afford to treat? Spirit ready to blossom at a touch of kindness?

I don't know if my impression are accurate or what to make of them if they are.

But that girl tears my heart.

Transcendence is different from transformation. The path of transcendence can be pursued with a closed heart. I can ignore poverty, war, stress, loneliness, oppression, and other earthly problems. I'm not trying to fix things. I'm rising above them. I can even close my heart to myself. I don't want to get sucked into my physical and emotional needs. I want to evolve beyond having any worldly needs.

There is a kind of secular transcendence that is popular in America. We push aside the discomforts of the world by focusing on some small aspect of the world. We become absorbed in TV, computers, stereos, books, music, food, alcohol, sex, sports, money, power, or other hobbies.

In describing Siddhartha Gautama's spiritual training, I mentioned deep yogic trance states called "jhānas." To master these, a yogi puts all his attention on refined mental states. He becomes absorbed in these. Secular transcendence induces a low-grade jhanic trance by becoming absorbed not in mental states but in a material object, project, or pursuit. When you get on your computer and 10 minutes later the clock says an hour has gone by, you've been in a light trance.

The jhānas are very sweet and soothing. Getting caught in our hobby or pursuit can feel wonderful in the moment. There is nothing inherently bad about this. If our nerves are jangled, spirits frayed, or emotions exhausted, it can be healthy and healing to take a break. It's like going to a health spa.

But we can't live forever at a health spa. As Siddhartha Gautama learned, the jhānas don't last. Absorption states – whether yogic meditations or secular hobbies – give a bit of respite, but no wisdom. They are like cotton candy: they taste good but have no substance. They don't transform anything inside or around us. At best we are refreshed but no wiser. Eventually we come back to the same old same old.

So, we can pursue the path of transcendence without an open heart. It works for a while but ultimately fails. It is more likely to be addicting than enlightening.

The path of transcendence can also be pursued with poor boundaries. "Hey man, we are all one. Need a shirt? You can have mine. I need some money? I'll take yours. We'll live in one amorphous love heap." Sometimes the loss of good boundaries can feel sweet and inspiring – like the 1960s hippies. But without reasonable boundaries, personal responsibility is lost. We live in a world of limits. We have limits. Boundaries are a way of honoring ourselves and the kind of world we live in.

Erika decided to try an experiment one morning in Bodhgaya, India. She bought two handfuls of half rupee coins: each worth a little more than a penny. She told me, "I want to walk through the center of Bodhgaya and give a coin to every beggar, cripple, leper, or person who asks."

"Wow," I said. "I want to watch. I'll take some pictures."

As we approached the center of Bodhgaya, I dropped back 30 feet and got out my camera. I took a picture as Erika put a coin in the first cup. But I only had time for four or five shots. A growing crowd surrounded Erika. They all had their hands out and some were pulling on her shawl and shirt.

I put the camera in my pocket and waded into the crowd. Together we gently extricated ourselves before a full riot started.

The people in that crowd had needs as real as the scoliosis in the girl by the culvert. There is more need, more poignant suffering in the world than we can address individually or collectively. If we try to take care of it all, we will quickly emaciate our resources and get swallowed up in the sea of suffering. And all to no noticeable effect.

So it is wise to manage our personal and material resources intelligently and skillfully. The heart and the spirit have no boundaries. But our time, money, and emotions are limited and need to be managed with care. In this world we need good boundaries if we are to be of any help to anyone.

Good boundaries are not an excuse to close our hearts one iota. We can't trade one off against the other and do a little heart and a little boundary. It's not "either/or." It's "both/and." The path of transformation requires us to open our hearts as much as possible *and* at the same time maintain good boundaries.

Keeping the heart open is often difficult. Many people saw us as walking moneybags. A good salary in India is $30 to $40 a month: less than a day's pay at minimum wage in this country. Many people saw dollars signs on our foreheads. It hurts to be seen as the object of someone's need or greed. Those projections often elicited our anger, fear, or hurt. Keeping our hearts open meant staying open to these feelings until we could see past them, greet a beggar with genuine warmth even as we said, "No rupees."

India is a wonderful place to practice an open heart and good boundaries because it is so stark and gritty. The issues were personal and in our face: we dealt with them or crashed. We all crashed at times.

In America, we deal with all the same issues. But the situation is subtler. Few if any of us in this room are wealthy by American standards. But we all know what it feels like to be treated as an object of money, sex, comfort, stability, advice, or something. Other people's projections onto us can be upsetting. If we get sucked into the projection or deny the feelings they trigger, our spiritual paths collapse. The open heart requires we work with our reactions until we can transform them and see past them.

And in America, the solicitation is not as personal. Rather than a man with one leg and stubs for fingers standing in front of you with an open palm, we get a brochure in the mail about the 20,000 homeless in Sacramento. This Christmas Loaves and Fishes served over a thousand meals: a new high. Or we get an email about the hundreds of thousands going bankrupt because they are sick and could not get medical insurance. Or we hear reports on TV about flood victims. The suffering is real but not as in-our-face as a woman carrying a small child asking for rupees to buy milk for her baby (this was a favorite come-on in Katmandu).

So we deal with all the same issues in our lives here in America. But if we close our hearts or have poor boundaries, the effects may be subtle enough to ignore. We slowly get depleted or callous or alienated or disenfranchised without realizing the role our hearts and boundaries play in this.

So we need to practice. There is no single right way to keep your heart open and have responsible boundaries. On our latest trip to India, we gave generously to the Prajnavihara School and Sister Mary Lobo: people who were not tourists, who were on the scene, doing effective work, and who we trusted would know how to use our resources to do the most good. And we said "No" to almost everyone else.

When I was in India a few years ago, I used a different strategy. Each day I set aside about a dollar's worth of small coins and gave them to curbside beggars, lepers, cripples, or others when I felt intuitively moved. When I'd gone through the coins for that day, I'd stop until the next day.

There is no one right way to practice generosity with wise boundaries. What is important is not that you find the "right" solution, but that you wrestle with both issues: how to keep your heart open and how to keep good boundaries in a callous and painful world where the suffering is very, very real.

We can practice this daily. Life is always presenting us with challenges: we can try to transcend them; we can ignore them. Or we can let them transform us.

For example: staying busy to avoid boredom. Is this transcendence, transformation, or neither? (Answer: transcendence because it pushes away or tries to rise above the discomfort of boredom.)

Situation: You get a request for money from the Environmental Defense Fund. You drop it in the wastebasket unopened. Transcendence, transformation, or neither? (Answer: Not clear. If you think "I don't want to deal with this," that's a kind of secular transcendence. If you let yourself feel the pull of the needs of the wounded earth but decide you don't have the money, that is transformation. You are letting the situation work on you.)

Situation: A friend is hurting. You have no advice to offer but just sit down to be present with her. (Answer: transformation.)

Situation: You make a hard decision to cut back at work because you are exhausted. (Answer: transformation.)

What are some other situations you have witnessed?...

Summary

To summarize, there are two major kinds of spiritual paths: transcendence and transformation. They are very different. I suspect some of you are uncomfortable with the word "spiritual" because, for you, it is associated only with transcendence. It is associated with trying to rise above the world rather than engaging responsibly; it is associated with closing the heart or not managing resources wisely. It is associated with escapism and addiction.

But for me, the word "spiritual" has more to do with transformation than transcendence.

Buddhism is a middle way. It is midway between trying to transcend the world on the one hand and getting lost in it on the other. Midway between pushing away and indulging.

Unitarian Universalism is also a middle way. We believe in engaging in the world, but hopefully with a higher vision and heartful perspective.

Closing

There are little girls scrubbing dishes next to the culverts in our lives. They may not be as obvious to the eye. But the open heart can sense them. Some want our help. Some only want to be seen so they can smile.

May we let life transform us. It's how we are meant to live.

Namasté.

Bright Faith

It takes a little faith to hold on. It takes a lot of faith to let go.

January 7, 2007

I'd like to begin a series of sermons on faith. But it is difficult to know quite where to start. So I invite you to listen to the word and see what it evokes in you. If you like you can close your eyes.

Faith — What feelings does this evoke? How does your body/spirit respond?

Faith — Do you relax and open up inside as you hear this word? Does your heart lighten?

Faith — Or does your body tighten a little? Do you want to pull away?

Faith — What memories, associations or images do you have with it? Where does it take you?

Faith — Are there a few words or a few sentences that describe mood, images or associations?

Consider feelings and associations, some have felt including:

- *Trust and confidence*
- *Comfort – faith as solace*
- *Ease – faith as safety*
- *Alienation – being an outsider or bring turned off*
- *Love and Inclusion – faith as embracing*
- *Cold – faith as weird doctrine*
- *Silenced – "blind faith" and the squelching of questions*
- *Hatred – faith as an excuse to blame or scapegoat*
- *Fresh and Vibrant*
- *Liberation and Opening*

Some of us grew up in faith traditions that felt supportive. Some felt silenced or alienated. Some grew up with no faith traditions and found this positive. Some long for spiritual roots. Some of us had mixed experiences.

As a congregation, I'd like us to explore faith together. But it is difficult to know where to start because we come to this topic from contradictory places.

It is tempting to avoid the word "faith" and come at the topic from a different angle. But faith, and the word "faith," are important to most Americans. If we avoid the term we leave it to our religiously conservative brothers and sisters to define it in a way that does not include this rich variety of experience. It unfairly sounds like many of us don't have faith. It makes it hard to talk to people outside our circle.

Before we begin, let's affirm that all our diverse responses are valid and valuable. When the person sitting next to us uses the word "faith," they could be talking about experiences very different from ours. If we hope to communicate with each other, we may need to acknowledge our personal take on faith and then let it go, enough so that we can listen carefully and empathetically, to truly hear each other.

Unfolding

To move more deeply into the topic, let me suggest that faith is a process of unfolding. Faith is not a commodity. It is not an object to hold onto. It is a process of opening up that goes through phases and seasons.

Most discussions of faith don't begin with faith itself. Most discussions begin with the faith object: "What do you believe in?" Do you believe in God? Or the Goddess? Or science? Or money? Or power? Or the human spirit? Or love? What is the ultimate object of your faith?

This discussion can be vaguely interesting. But given our variety of experiences and associations, it usually degenerates into nit-picking concepts and opinions: "How do you define 'God'?" "What is human nature?" "Tell me what you mean by love?" Quibbling over definitions has little practical value in our daily lives.

In truth, faith grows out of experience more than thoughts, ideas, or beliefs. Our deepest experience gives rise to our deepest faith. That which enhances our deepest experience deepens our faith. That which narrows, squelches, or attenuates our deepest experience narrows, squelches or attenuates faith.

That superstar Unitarian minister Ralph Waldo Emerson talked about "self-reliance." He wasn't talking about egotism or isolating ourselves. He was talking about relying on our deepest experience. Another great Unitarian minister, William Ellery Channing, pledged to his Boston congregation that he would never speak about anything he had not experienced himself.

We come from a tradition that relies on our deepest experience as the authority for faith.

Since our deepest experiences shift over time, the objects of our faith will shift over time. If faith doesn't grow and evolve, it is dead.

For example, if your deepest faith is in God, your ideas of God will change – perhaps radically change – over time. If you put your faith in God and you have the same ideas of God now that you had as a child, your faith is dead.

So I am not interested in us figuring out the ultimate object of faith or telling us what should be the ultimate object of your faith. That will take care of itself. It will reveal itself in our unfolding. I am interested in our faith process, our faith journey, our faith unfolding.

This journey goes through cycles that begin with bright faith or enthusiastic faith. With artful questioning, it matures into verified faith. And eventually it deepens into embodied faith – a way of living.

This morning I want to focus on the first phase – bright faith. In two weeks, I'll talk about verified faith and the art of questioning. The first week in February I'll speak about embodied faith.

Bright Faith

To get a sense of bright faith, imagine a long cold winter. The windows and doors and curtains have been closed to keep the cold out. The air inside is musty and stale. Everything looks dingy. Your mind feels a little musty and dingy as well.

Then, spring arrives. You open the doors and windows. A soft, fresh breeze inspires you to breathe deeply. You feel your mind clearing.

That is the feeling of bright faith. It is energizing, exciting, inspiring, and rejuvenating.

In 1989 while inducting Bob Dylan into the Rock and Roll Hall of Fame, Bruce Springsteen said "The first time I heard Bob Dylan, I was in the car with my mother listening to WMCA [when *Like a Rollin' Stone* played. It was] like somebody had kicked open the door to your mind."

That feeling of having your mind and heart kicked open is the feeling of bright faith.

The "boot" that kicks open those doors may be flamboyant. Or it may be as quiet as a book. When I was in college, a philosophy professor assigned Norman O. Brown's book, *Love's Body*. Brown wrote about the interrelationship between the physical, psychological, and theological. I was enthralled. I read his books, quoted him in papers, and I tried my wife Erika's patience talking about him ad nauseum. This week I found the book up high on my book shelf collecting dust. I probably haven't opened the book in 30 years. But back then, it kicked open my mind and filled me with bright faith.

A number of years ago Erika and I joined an off-shoot of EST called "Insight Seminars" – a kind of "EST with heart." The trainers had an uncanny ability to cut through our defenses and show us how to see ourselves starkly. Both Erika and I went through all three levels of training. We found it captivating and inspiring. We had bright faith.

Bright faith can be invoked in a quiet way by something as broad as nature. If after church, you spill coffee on your shirt, it can be upsetting: the shirt may be ruined. If, on a weeklong wilderness trek, you spill catsup on your shirt, it's no big deal. You laugh, wipe it off, and go on. Being in nature can loosen attachments and shift what you think is important. This enlivened perspective is bright faith. It draws many people to the wilderness.

Some people discover Unitarian Universalism and have bright faith in finally finding something that speaks to them.

In the spring of 1974, Ram Dass drove his antique sports car up my driveway. He was speaking at my church that evening. When I introduced him to an overwhelming crowd, I was the only one of 300 people wearing a tie. We spoke of spiritual yearning and insight that was more personal, more familiar, and more accessible than I'd ever heard. I thought, "He may actually know something about life. I've never met anyone who knows anything. He may know a little. I could learn from him." For the next few years I went to many lectures and workshops. I bought at least 50 tapes and listened to them over and over. I corresponded with him. I had bright faith.

Ram Dass brought a friend with him named "Krishna Dass" who led us in singing and chanting. I had never had anything to do with devotional practices before then. But I loved the singing and how it felt. It opened up a new way of using music and singing for me. For many people, immersion in music touches bright faith.

Bright faith can be as strong as a kick from a boot or as subtle as a nagging thought in the back of your mind that looks around and says, "There's got to be more to life than what I'm seeing."

Does this give you a sense of bright faith? Do you recognize the places in your life where you have felt it?

So What?

Bright faith is important because it can begin to take us out of who we thought we were and bring us closer to who we truly are. It can take us out of what we thought life was and closer to what life truly is.

Our understanding and experience is always smaller than the greater reality. We have more depth, more potential than we know. The universe is far more interesting, mysterious, and wonderful than we can guess in our wildest imagination.

Bright faith awakens the curiosity, excitement, and energy to explore new realms inside and around us. It can carry us out of who we thought we were. It can enlighten possibilities in life that were darkened before. It can lead us into more enriched lives for ourselves and more enriched ways of serving the world.

Yet, the difficulty with bright faith is that it leads us into unfamiliar and sometimes uncomfortable territory. We don't know our way around.

It is natural and wise to turn to someone, something, or some map of this new territory to help guide us until we get our bearings.

The dilemma of bright faith is: who do we trust? If we refuse to trust anything, we may stumble, fall into holes, or wander around in circles. But if we put faith in the wrong person or wrong map we may be led astray or walk down a blind alley or be taken advantage of. How do we know who or what to put our faith in?

The simple answer is: we don't know. We can't know until we have some deep experience in this area. If we try to figure it out, we may not have enough intellectual understanding to do competent figuring. If we try to intuit our way, our intuition might be fuzzy.

So what do we do? Do we run back to safe familiar territory and never learn? Do we risk getting lost?

I believe the deepest experiences we have are still our most reliable guide. If our experience in a particular area is shallow, the deepest we have is our most reliable guide. If we experience excitement or bright faith, I think it is wise to trust it and follow it. If a teacher or community awakens enthusiasm in us, listen to it. We may want to look inside and make sure it is our enthusiasm and not theirs we feel. But regardless of the catalyst, if the draw feels genuinely our own, go with it. It'll work out.

Sometimes we experience both enthusiasm and doubt. It feels wonderful and we have reservations. We feel drawn and want to hold back.

Ralph Waldo Emerson famously said: "A foolish consistency is the hobgoblin of little minds, adored by little statesman and philosophers and divines. With consistency a great soul has simply nothing to do."

I think we are better off letting our minds open wide. Our congregation's value statement says "We value openness and curiosity." Think of the inconsistency not as a hobgoblin, but as a guiding angel.

If you experience genuine doubt, don't let your enthusiasm overrun your doubt. If you do, bright faith can become blind faith. Bright faith is not blind faith. It has its eyes open.

But don't let doubt override your enthusiasm, excitement, and freshness. Don't let cynicism, reservation, or diminished self-confidence blot out your energy.

Let them both be there – the excitement and the questioning, the enthusiasm and the fear. Rollo May once called anxiety "excitement without oxygen." Give it air. Breathe into all of it. If you do this, sometimes the worry turns into excitement. Sometimes it points to a different direction.

Sometimes when we listen to the deepest pull, we honestly feel drawn toward money, power, prestige, or other religious no-nos. In this case, if we are listening to the pull inside us rather than the drone of advertising, we can still trust it. Money, power, and prestige are usually symbols of something deeper. If we are open to our deepest experience, a deeper draw will make itself known in time. Faith is an unfolding. Sometimes there is a bit of wisdom in dark territories.

When we let our deepest experience guide us, sometimes we *will* be led astray, follow false prophets, head in the wrong direction, bruise our knees and shins.

But when I look back at those times, usually it was worth it. If there was pain or difficulty, they seem small compared to what I gained. Do you know what I mean? Have you experienced this?

Even a false prophet may have useful wisdom. Sometimes the fastest course is to be led astray and then find your way rather than just stand still and go nowhere.

But don't take my word for it. Trust what I'm saying only if it resonates inside you. If what I'm saying enlivens something slightly or completely different, put your faith in what awakens in you.

Conclusion

Once that excitement is flowing, there is a way of investigating the experience that deepens the faith process and reduces the likelihood of wandering too far down a blind alley. This is the art of questioning. Skillful investigation is the second phase of the faith cycle. We'll explore it more in two weeks.

But first, it is important to follow bright faith long enough to have something new to investigate. Otherwise, we'll just keep asking the same old questions in the same old territory in the same old way. Where's the fun in that? Where's the gain?

So for this morning, I'll leave you with a few questions: What draws you? What excites you? A teacher, a book, an experience, a community, a nagging question in the back of your mind? What pulls you? Where do you feel it in your life? Is it in art, music, spiritual practice, new ideas, congregations, special programs, ways of serving? Where do you feel the draw of bright faith?

Faith and the Art of Questioning

January 21, 2007

Unitarian Universalism is not a rock to hold onto. It is a river to swim in.

If you want a set of beliefs to hold onto, if you want rules to guide your life in all situations, if you want a foundation for a spiritual fortress, you will probably be disappointed with us.

However, if you want to dive into the river and explore, if you think that what you experience and what you do is more important than what you believe, if you want to be with people who engage in this world to promote wellbeing for all, we may have something to offer.

Life itself is more like a river than a rock. Life is in flux; it changes, twists and turns, ebbs and flows. When a river encounters a boulder, the boulder may win for a while. But eventually, even the most massive stone is worn away by the currents of time.

Unitarian Universalism is about learning to swim in the river rather than climbing out of it onto a rock.

We are looking at faith not as a rock but as a process of exploring and questioning. For us, faith is a verb. In English, faith is a noun. But in Latin and Hebrew, it is a verb, an action, a doing. In *Pāli*, the language that first recorded the Buddha's talks, the word for faith is "*saddhā*." It literally means, "put your heart on." Deep faith pours itself into something.

There are three phases of the faith cycle: bright faith, verified faith, and embodied faith. Using the river metaphor, bright faith gets us off our familiar rock and into the water, verified faith teaches us to swim, and embodied faith helps us become the river.

First, let's focus on the first phase: getting into the river. Perhaps we encounter a new teacher, book, idea, experience, or community: something inspires us to dive into the river. Or a nagging suspicion says, "There must be more to life than my familiar habits," and we slip quietly into the water. Or maybe we are standing firmly on our rock when a big wave rushes down the river – a loved one dies, a baby is born, a relationship collapses, a life-threatening disease invades our body – and we are swept away by the flood.

Life, in its benevolence, won't leave us stranded on a boulder forever. One way or another we are pulled in.

The second phase of the faith cycle is learning to swim. As our faith matures, we learn to navigate effectively, even joyfully. One technique for learning to swim is the art of questioning.

If you see faith as a rock to hold, then questioning can be a problem. Questions loosen our grip and break up solid beliefs. Doubt threatens the rock of faith.

But if we see faith as swimming in the river, questions are helpful. The fewer rocks we carry, the easier it is to swim. We are more buoyant with fewer stones pulling us to the bottom. From the perspective of swimming, the opposite of faith is not doubt. The opposite of faith is despair: giving up and sinking to the bottom. Doubt and questioning make us stronger, more mature swimmers.

Hiking

Before getting into the specifics of skillful questioning, I want to offer another metaphor that focuses on questioning itself: the metaphor of hiking.

I love to hike. In a valley, I can set a course and head straight for it. I may swerve to cross a stream, but this is momentary. Most of the obstacles are human constructs: buildings, fences, property lines, and more. In nature, I can follow a direct course across a valley.

But what I enjoy most is hiking in the mountains.

The first time I climbed Round Top Mountain, I parked my car a half mile from Carson Pass around 8,500 feet. From the roadside, I could see Round Top rising up several miles due south.

But the trail led southwest and dropped into a forest where I lost sight of the mountain. Then it turned southeast and rose up to where I could see the mountain off to my right. But the trail turned left and headed northeast leaving the mountain behind me. Then it turned abruptly south for a mile or so to a beautiful lake.

Across the lake a quarter-mile was Round Top itself. But there was no way to get to the mountain from where I was. Even if I could get around the lake, the mountain rose straight up a thousand feet. I couldn't climb that.

So I turned my back to the mountain and headed west up a steep incline. I came to another lake with trails pointing off in various directions. One turned toward the mountain. I tried it.

The trail faded out completely. Soon I was walking over loose rock. From what I could see, the easiest climb was up the south face of the summit. But as I hiked, the slope got steeper and steeper, sliding off to a drop of 2500 feet.

I decided this was too dangerous and retraced my steps until I could go around the north side, scrambled over boulders, loose rock, and outcroppings and reach the summit.

High Altitude Spirituality

Spirituality is a lot like hiking: there are differences between low and high altitudes.

At low altitudes, we can see our destination across the valley and head straight for it. Low-altitude spirituality emphasizes the straight and narrow.

At high altitudes, it's impossible to travel in a straight line. In Christianity, this is represented in labyrinth designs. To get from the outer edge of the labyrinth to its center requires following a circuitous path.

Since travel is straightforward at low altitudes, simple, generalized maps may be perfectly adequate. But at higher altitudes, even detailed maps can be unreliable. There may be a trail on the ground that doesn't show on the map. Or there may be trail on the map that we can't find on the ground. Changing weather conditions have more impact in mountains than in valleys.

So even if we have a good map, it is important at higher elevations to ask skillful questions, to compare our map to our experience, to examine our assumptions, to investigate with an open and curious mind.

Practical

But the most important difference between low and high altitudes is the nature of the questions we ask. This may seem a little counterintuitive unless we think about it. At high altitudes, our questions are less theoretical and more practical. They are less concerned with metaphysics and more concerned with immediate, tangible reality.

At low altitudes, the big, generalized questions are enough: "What is my destiny?" We see our destination across the valley and head for it. But if we head straight for our destination at higher elevations, we may walk off a cliff. So we become concerned with practical questions like, "Which fork in the trail should I take?" "Is this map really helpful at this place?" "Was the footprint left by someone who knew what she was doing or someone who walked off the edge?" "Should I rest for a while or push forward?" "What's the weather like?" "Do I have enough water?"

At high altitudes, we don't have to ask, "What's the meaning of this mountain?" "What does this view tell me about life?" The inspiration comes from being there. We just absorb it. It is freely given by the surroundings. We just stop and take it in.

At lower altitudes we may ponder the meaning of life and come up with lots of theories. At higher elevations the vision and meaning are inherent in the situation. Rather than ask, "What's my ultimate destination?" we ask, "Which step will take me closer?"

Social Engagement

This hiking metaphor is not just about spirituality as an inward journey. If your spirituality is expressed through social justice, the metaphor is equally valid.

The path to greater peace, solving the drug problem, improving healthcare, or most other social justice issues is not straightforward. Like the mountain in the distance, we have a vision of where we want to go. But the practical path to it can be circuitous.

For example, "Just say no to drugs" is a simple, low altitude path. The sentiment is commendable. But the real world is not so straightforward. It doesn't fit into a sound bite. The war on drugs has done nothing to ease people off drugs. Today there are as many addicted people – a little over 1% of the population – as before the "war" was launched. By criminalizing everything, we've brought more money, corruption, crime, and violence to the problem. But it's done nothing to solve the problem. The solutions lie in education, psychology, and support systems. These are not as straight ahead as "just say no." They require high-altitude thinking. They require skillful questioning, testing, and seeing what works. But they work.

The war in Iraq is another tragic example of how idealistic thinking leads to disaster. "Free Iraq by using the military to overthrow a dictator and hold an election" was appealing in its simplicity. But by ignoring the circuitous terrain and by failing to ask practical questions, the war has created more suffering and danger.

So, whether we are talking about deepening our own lives or being a healing force in the world, the art of skillful questioning is essential to mature faith.

Artful Questioning

So let's look at a few questions.

Artful questions are not cynical, rhetorical, or defensive. And artful questions are not about vague abstractions. They are engaging and practical.

What are some of the questions you have found helpful in your life? As you recall these, here are a few questions I have found engaging and practical:

Next Step

I've already mentioned one of my favorite questions: "What's the next step on my path?" It may not be as helpful to ask, "How do I achieve world peace?" "Where do I find enlightenment?" or "How do people find God?" They are too big, too general, too low altitude. The more practical question is "What moves me on the circuitous path toward peace, toward God, toward freedom?"

Acceptance

Another question: "What needs to be accepted?" We know that pushing things away causes suffering in the long run. So ask, "In my life today, what needs to be accepted?" or "In this situation, what wants to be acknowledged?"

Expressed

Another question: "What wants to be expressed?" If you tend to hold back out of fear or politeness, it can be interesting to reflect on "What wants to be expressed in this situation?"

Silence

On the other hand, it can be helpful to ask, "Is what I'm about to say more valuable than silence?"

Question the Questions

The art of questioning also involves skillfully questioning the question. Rather than leaping immediately for an answer, ask what's behind the question.

Heart of the Question

If we are caught in a conundrum, we can ask, "What's at the heart of this question?" or "What is the motivation behind the question?" For example, the question, "What is the meaning of my life?" might be motivated by a spiritual yearning. Or it might be motivated by fear as in, "My life is a mess. What does it all mean?" If a question is driven by fear or tension, it may be wise to deal with that tension directly on its own terms: reflect on it, sit with it, explore it. Once the tension dissolves, the question may dissolve or come from a very different place.

Authority

We can also skillfully question our own beliefs: "What's the authority of this belief? Is it something I've experienced or been told? Where does this belief come from?"

For example, maybe we believe God directs our life. Or maybe we believe God is a figment of the imagination. It can be useful to explore where this belief came from in us. Bright faith, enthusiastic faith, even passionate faith is wonderful. But blind, unexamined, unverified faith is, frankly, immature. It's low-altitude faith.

When we see where our beliefs came from, we are less likely to say, "This is true for everyone," and more likely to say, "I have faith in <whatever> based on my experience or based on this reasoning or that authority." This is a nuanced, mature and sustaining faith.

Ways to Question

Finally, the art of questioning includes how you ask the questions.

Walk

One way is to take the question on a walk. Go for a stroll with the question.

Sit with It

Another way is to sit quietly with a question without trying to answer it. The Quakers call this "holding a question." Maybe we are wondering, "What do I do about my son?" or "Is it time for me to leave this job?" or "Should I read a book or join a protest next weekend?" Rather than try to figure it out, we relax and let the question sit inside. This is a high-altitude practice where we don't go after the answer but quiet down, become more receptive, and let the insight arise in its own way and own time.

A variant of this is to ask a question before going to bed and see if it shows up in dreams.

Being Questioned

Another wonderful way to work with questions is to go to a friend or Ministry Circle and say, "I'm struggling with this issue. I want you to ask me questions about it. Don't try to fix it or give me solutions. Just ask me questions about it."

Context

Another way to use questions is to shift the context. If we are wondering what to do with our life, we can ask, "What if I had a week left to live. What would I do then?" Just shifting the context can loosen up insight.

Another favorite of mine is to ask, "If I were wiser than I am, what would I do?" and then see what arises inside.

Other Questions

Those are a few questions I find engaging and practical. What are some questions you've found helpful?

Closing

To summarize, there is a relationship between faith and belief. We all have many types of beliefs. Maybe you believe the way to get the most out of life is to set a goal and go for it. Or maybe you believe in spontaneity. Maybe you believe God personally guides your life. Or maybe you believe the universe is impersonal laws. Maybe you believe you can get to work tomorrow without stopping for gas. We live with many kinds of beliefs.

If you believe faith is a rock to hold onto, then strong faith means a strong grip. You want to be able to wrap your arms around your faith and hold on powerfully.

If you believe faith is a river to swim in, you still want strong muscles – good swimmers have strong bodies. But they have a different kind of muscle. Swimmers' muscles are fluid and relaxed. They can stroke against the currents and they can relax, let go, and go with the flow.

If faith is a river to swim in, you dive into your beliefs, you question them, you try them out, you see which work and which don't, which can be verified and which can't. Swimmers don't hold onto the water. They go into it.

As you question and release your beliefs, some will float away. And some will stay with you, not because you've got a good grip on them but because you've embodied them. Your faith is not something you hold onto or try to sell to others. It is something you live.

Enjoy your questioning, your questing, your openhearted engaging, testing, and exploring. Enjoy the swim.

Embodied Faith

March 11, 2007

Faith is like breathing: we can't live without it, yet mostly we take it for granted.

For example, when you turned the ignition in your car this morning, how did you know it wouldn't blow up? Without some faith we'd have to take the car apart, check all the pieces, and put it back together every day before leaving the house.

Coming here for services requires enough trust to imagine something more useful than sleeping late.

To walk into this building requires faith that the wiring won't burn the place down around us.

Of course, we've started our cars a thousand times without losing our lives; we've probably been here on Sunday before and found something stimulating; the building has stood here for almost 50 years without burning down. We've got statistics that make our decisions seem rational and scientific.

True enough. Not all faith is blind faith. Not all trust is uneducated trust. Still, life offers no guarantees.

Faith is like breathing: we can't live without it, yet we mostly take it for granted.

We don't all put our faith in the same thing, to be sure. But we all put our faith in lots of things. Some people put faith in seatbelts and drivers staying in their lanes. Some put their faith in working hard, others in procrastination. Some put their faith in avoiding conflict, others in being quick to the defense. Some people have faith in a righteous God, others in a benevolent universe, and others in the absence of anything resembling divinity. Some people have faith in candor, others in playing their cards close to their chest. Some people put faith in money, prayer, intellect, feeling, Charles Darwin, divine intelligence, and on and on.

There is probably nothing in the known universe in which some humans, at some point, have not put their faith. Faith is like breathing: we do it all the time without thinking about it very much.

Breathing and Faith

This morning, I'd like to continue exploring faith as a process that is as simple, basic, and profound as breathing. This most mature stage of faith could be called "embodied faith," because its main expression is not words or beliefs, but how we live and how we embody. When our truest nature manifests in our behavior we have embodied our faith.

So let's begin with this simile of embodied faith as breathing.

In-Breath and Bright Faith

If you watch an infant breathe, you may see what natural breathing looks like. It begins with the in-breath: the belly rises, the chest expands, the pelvis tilts a little and the chin rises slightly. In full breathing, these motions extend subtly down the arms and legs in a wave that spreads through the whole body.

Similarly, faith begins with inspiration, which literally means "breathe in." In early January we explored bright faith – the burst of energy that comes from a new insight, revelation, teacher, book, new practice, community, or something that inspires us to try something new or venture into new territory or break out of stale patterns.

Out-Breath and Verified Faith

In physical breathing, the in-breath is followed immediately by the out-breath. The muscles that exert effort to draw in the air relax. In natural breathing, there is no exertion in the out-breath. The muscles simply let go.

The second phase of faith is verified faith – we loosen our grip on faith enough to question it, test it, to see if it is relevant. We previously explored verified faith and the art of questioning. We relax and investigate.

Pause and Embodied Faith

The third phase of breathing is a pause. There is a rest between the out-breath and the next in-breath. The body is no longer relaxing. It is relaxed. Nothing is happening.

In a moment, a new breath arises naturally out of the pause.

Embodied faith has a quality of stillness and quiet, like a pause or a deep pool. But it also has vigor and curiosity. Embodied faith is less like a phase of breathing and more like the whole breath process: the inspiration, release, and equanimity all combined together.

Variations

Few adults fully breathe physically in the way I described. For example, I was scared of my father for the first 20 years of my life. I had so much fear stored in my diaphragm muscle, that my belly often pulled in rather than expanded with the in-breath.

People who have had a lot of heartache may unconsciously pull their shoulders forward to protect their heart. This can prevent the chest from fully expanding.

People who are angry or stressed may hold it in the shoulder muscles preventing the head from moving naturally.

There are lots of ways breathing can be obstructed by cumulative life experience or medical problems. Similarly, natural faith can become obstructed. But breathing has two particular variations I'd like to explore.

Emphasize the In-Breath

What happens if we emphasize breathing in? It is impossible to breathe in without breathing out. We'd pop. But we can put more emphasis on the in-breath than the out-breath.

To do this, draw the breath in as deeply as you can and hold it for a moment. Then rather than relax, forcefully and quickly expel the air. And before the breath is completely expelled, suck it back in without a pause.

Go ahead and try that for a moment and see what happens.

You may get a little dizzy with too much energy. You may begin to feel a little anxious.

You are simulating anxious breathing. If you want more anxiety in your life, try this kind of breathing. It'll help.

Similarly, with too much emphasis on bright faith and inspiration – on breathing in – our faith can get stuck. Bright faith can become anxious, tight, dogmatic, fanatical. Without the letting go, bright faith becomes blind faith. It drifts into fear and holding. Fanatics are often afraid to face their own uncertainty and questions. They'd rather sell their beliefs to others than let down into their own gnawing doubts.

Emphasize the Out-Breath

In some circles, the word "faith" has become synonymous with bright faith or even blind faith. It's equated with doctrine, narrow-minded beliefs, specific deities, lack of intelligent examination, submission to authority, and even excuses for bigotry and hatred.

For some, faith has such a bad reputation that they'd like to get rid of the whole process and have nothing to do with faith.

This is like overemphasizing the out-breath. So let's see what this does.

It is impossible to breathe out without ever breathing in. But we can emphasize the out-breath by not allowing the breath to come in fully. Before the belly and chest fully expand, force the breath out. And then hold the breath out as long as you can. When you can't hold it any longer, take a quick half in-breath, then force the air out again.

Go ahead and try that for a moment; see what happens.

Your energy may decrease due to lack of oxygen. You may feel dull or lethargic. If you'd like to have more depression in your life, this is a good exercise.

Putting too much emphasis on verified faith and unskillful questioning is like putting too much emphasis on breathing out: we don't get much oxygen, vigor, inspiration, or aliveness.

In natural breathing, the out-breath is a release, not a forceful rejection of the breath. If we reject everything exciting or inspiring, we become cynical or jaded. We may be articulate about what we don't believe but become dull, lethargic, or inarticulate in describing what we do put our faith in.

Natural Breathing

Now, rather than leave you here, let's emphasize natural breathing.

Breathe in fully and deeply. Sometimes this requires a little effort. Then when the breath is full, don't force it out. Just let go as completely as you can. Let the out-breathing do itself. When the breath is all the way out, just rest. There is no need to force the breath to rest or to start the in-breath. Just let it rest and allow the body to start the next in-breath on its own.

Try that for a few moments.

That's what embodied faith is like. Little of value in life comes without some effort. Inspiration provides this energy gracefully and naturally. There is little happiness in life without the capacity to relax and enjoy. Release provides this. And there is little depth in life without the time and patience to look deeply. The stillness provides this.

Embodied faith encompasses all this – inspiration, release, and stillness – plus one more element: the content of our experience.

The content of our deepest faith is something that inspires us, something that we freely and openly question and release, and something that still resonates deeply inside us when we sit quietly.

Examples of Embodied Faith

This sounds like an oxymoron: putting our faith into something we let go of; feeling inspired by something we release. So let's look at a few examples.

When faith is young, we pour ourselves into one thing and let go of something different.

We might put our faith in God and let go of pursuing money.

We might put our faith into Unitarian Universalist principles and let go of traditional church doctrines.

We might put our faith into social activism and let go of passive grumbling.

We might put faith into expressing feelings and let go of thoughts. Or we might put our faith into thinking and let go of feeling.

We might put our faith into working out in the gym and let go of being a couch potato.

We might put our faith into one thing and let go of something else.

But as faith deepens, we find less and less need to hold onto anything. We may put a lot of energy into some things but not hold them so tightly.

Children

Consider: if we embody faith in our children, we give them our hearts. We give them love, guidance, and support. And at the same time we let them go. We let them be themselves.

If we just pour our energy into them without letting them go, we are controlling. That's not faith. We aren't letting their potential unfold in a natural way.

On the other hand, if we just let them go without investing ourselves, that is indifference, not faith.

If we truly embody faith in our kids we pour our hearts into them and let them be.

God

Another example: the 14th century German mystic, Meister Eckhart, once wrote, "God, please remove from me all images of God." He put his faith in God. He poured out his heart to God. And part of his faith was to let go of all images he had of God so that the divine could reveal Itself in Its own terms rather than his. He let go of God as he put his faith into God.

That is embodied faith.

Science

A scientist may not use language like "pouring out my heart" and "letting go" but goes through a similar process. She puts time and effort into inquiry and experimentation. Without this, there is just idle speculation. At the same time, a good scientist tries to poke holes into her own theories. Without the ability to let go of pet theories in the face of new evidence, there is science as dogma rather than science as discovery.

Getting There

Embodied faith sounds groovy, doesn't it? It's what we all want: walking our talk, living our values, embodying our faith.

What's the fastest way to get there? Let me offer a few thoughts.

There is No Fast Way

We have to go through this whole faith process: see what draws us, let the inspiration emerge in us, give ourselves to it, follow it, test it out, question artfully, and then pause and listen deeply to see what emerges from our being. This inspires us to go through the process again.

It takes time. Faith grows out of experience and experience takes time.

Mature Faith is Not About Certainty

I was writing a book several years ago and began to question, "Why am I doing this? Is it because I have something helpful to say? Is this just some big ego trip? What are my motives really?"

I stopped writing to reflect deeply. I couldn't figure it out. But as deep as I could go inside, I felt drawn to write. I had no idea if I could publish the book. But I was drawn to write.

So I did.

You may recall, the opposite of faith is not uncertainty. It is despair. Uncertainty, doubt, questioning, and testing are part of the faith process when we use them to engage more deeply.

Mature Faith Does Not Insulate Us From Fear and Suffering

Jesus, the epitome of faith, cried out "My God, my God, why have you forsaken me?" He had doubt, pain, and suffering up to his last moments.

According to the legends, his very last words were, "Into Your Hands I commend my spirit."

Faith does not shield us from suffering, but it changes our relationship to it. Fear and suffering are part of life in this world. Embodied faith does not try to futilely block out life. It embraces it all.

We Don't Get to Decide the Content of Our Faith

A church can't dictate your faith. Even you can't dictate your faith.

Some people come to Unitarian Universalism and say, "I can believe whatever I want to believe." Well, I'd like to believe the lottery ticket will make me a millionaire. Believing that doesn't make it true.

Mature Unitarian Universalism does not grow out of believing what we want to believe or rejecting what we don't like. It comes from trusting what we discover in our deepest experience.

In short, Mature Faith can be Messy

I have a deep and abiding faith in this congregation. When we are open with each other, the heart and wisdom we have as a collective is inspiring and verifiable. But even if I embody that faith perfectly, I know our process will often be messy.

Many people assume mature faith will be pristine, simple, and easy to put in a box. But real faith takes us into the real world with real people. And the real world is messy, ambiguous, and sometimes confusing. Deep faith is a magnet that draws us to engage in a particular way. The draw can be simple: to engage honestly, to be heartful, to relieve suffering, to deepen consciousness, or other convictions. But the outcome can be messy.

Don't be dissuaded by messiness.

Summary

Embodied faith is not a belief but a way of living.

It's not something we can figure out in our minds but can discover in our hearts.

It is not something we create out of will power but something we become, by learning to trust our deepest experience.

It is not something we can hold onto to protect us from life's travails, but something that takes us deeper into life in all its dimensions.

It is who we are when we embody our deepest passions, our curiosity, and our stillness.

Closing

I am not interested in what you believe. (I may be a little curious.) What I am interested in is what you put your heart into, how you live, and what you embody.

Our values statement is about embodied faith.

May we be inspired with love and courage.

May we embody openness and curiosity.

May we embody the goodness we find at our core when we are still enough.

May we embody these in each breath.

May it be so.

Namasté.

Relax

Now we are ready to look at something pretty special.
It is a duck riding the ocean a hundred feet beyond the surf.
No, it isn't a gull.
A gull always has a raucous touch about him.
This is some sort of duck, and he cuddles in the swells.
He isn't cold, and he is thinking things over.
There is a big heaving in the Atlantic,
And he is part of it.
He looks a bit like a mandarin, or the Lord Buddha meditating under the Bo tree,
But he has hardly enough above the eyes to be a philosopher.
He has poise, however, which is what philosophers must have.
He can rest while the Atlantic heaves, because he rests in the Atlantic.
Probably he doesn't know how large the ocean is.
And neither do you.
But he realizes it.
And what does he do, I ask you? He sits down in it.
He reposes in the immediate as if it were infinity – which it is.
That is religion, and the duck has it.
He has made himself part of the boundless,
By easing himself into it just where it touches him.
I like the little duck.
He doesn't know much.
But he has religion.

– Donald C. Babcock, *The New Yorker*, October 1947

June 8, 2008

I'd like to talk about relaxing. I'd like to talk about being a duck sitting in the ocean.[25] I'd like to talk about making ourselves part of the boundless by easing into it just where it touches us. I'd like to talk about relaxing even as the ocean heaves under us.

Summer is a time we like to relax. So I'd like to talk about the practical implications of relaxation. But first, let me suggest a religious context.

Religious Implications

I would suggest that enlightenment is the most natural state of mind. Divine illumination is the most natural state of heart. Goodness in action and generosity of spirit are the most human ways of being.

Orthodox Christianity has other ideas. The doctrine of original sin says we are born corrupt. Our natural state is depraved. We need the intervention of God, Jesus and the church to protect us. We need to be disciplined and controlled. If we relax, we'll all slide into hell.

In contrast, Unitarian Universalism puts its faith in the worth and dignity of every person. In this congregation, each Sunday we remind ourselves that we value the goodness in every person.

We Unitarian Universalists are not very good at blind faith — there is too much healthy skepticism in us. We like to test things and see if they hold up.

How can we verify worth and dignity? Where can we look in ourselves for this source of goodness?

Do we look to our thoughts? I don't think so. We all have enlightened thoughts at times. But we also have foolishness and chatter rattling through our brains. So thought can't be the source of goodness.

---

[25] This favorite poem of mine also appears on pp. 193, 253, and 332.

What about feelings? I don't think so. Our hearts don't always feel divinely illuminated. Some of our emotions are pretty ugly or petty.

Do we look to our actions? Nope. We've all done things we'd rather not admit. Looking around the world, we can see plenty of actions devoid of goodness.

If we want to verify goodness, we have to look deeper than thoughts, feelings, actions or even our intentions. We have to relax deep into the core of our being and see what's there.

If we are always controlling our lives, holding ourselves in check, hurrying to the next task we won't see what's underneath. We'll skip over the surface.

If Unitarian Universalism is more than empty words we repeat to each other, then we have to relax enough to see our natural state of mind and heart and action and being.

Is our core sinful and destructive? Or do we have worth and dignity? How can we truly know if we never relax and just be?

Spiritual Relaxation

Relaxation is important to a faith that claims to trust human nature.

However, the word "relax" means different things. So let's shift from the importance of relaxation to what it is in a spiritual context.

Holding Still

Spiritual relaxation is not the same as holding still.

Imagine 10 feet of water. A big pole rises up nine feet, eleven inches from the ocean floor. The top of the pole is an inch below the surface. The duck sits in the water gripping the top of the pole. If the ocean is placid, he looks restful.

But what happens when a wave comes along? He nearly drowns as the crest passes over him. He's thrust out of the ocean in the trough between the waves and plunged below by the next crest.

Gripping the pole holds him still, but it is more torture than relaxation. It resists the natural rising and falling rather than resting in it.

I have approached spirituality like it's a pole or rock or practice or idea to hang onto. Let me tell you a story.

Breathe Meditation

Years ago, I drove into Cambridge, Massachusetts, for an interview with Larry Rosenberg. Larry was the chief student of the Korean Zen master, Seung Sahn. He was also a senior *vipassanā* or "insight meditation" teacher.

I told Larry, "After years of practice, my mind still wanders a lot." He asked what I did to still my mind. I said, "I sometimes count my breaths from one to ten."

He said, "In our tradition, we don't need a lot of stillness before shifting to insight practice. If you can count 10 breaths 10 times, that is more than enough *samādhi*."

Unfortunately, Larry didn't appreciate the German blood in my veins and the compulsive streak in my personality.

So I went home to see if I could count 100 breaths without wavering. I sat on my meditation cushion next to a window in my attic: "Breathing in, one. Breathing in, two. Breathing in, three." If my attention wandered, I'd start over at one: "Breathing in, 83. Breathing in, 84. Breathing in, this is going pretty well. Maybe I'll get to 100. Oops. My attention drifted. … Breathing in, one. Breathing in, two."

For nine months I tried unsuccessfully to count 100 breaths. Then one morning I did it. I counted 100 without drifting.

Immediately I had a flash of insight: "This state of mind is a dead end." It was quiet. It was pleasant after a fashion. But it was a fake stillness, not a natural peacefulness. My mind was a steel cage. It was so tight; there was no space for wisdom, insight, or illumination.

And sure enough, as soon as I got off the cushion, all my old compulsions, fears, depressions, and foolish habits rushed back in.

Imagine trying to quiet your mind and open your heart by putting duct tape over your mouth and tying yourself into a chair. It would force you to shut up and sit down. But I doubt it would be conducive to wisdom or illumination or revealing your natural goodness.

Prayer

Some people approach prayer with similar foolishness. Jesus taught otherwise. In Matthew 6 he said, "When you pray, don't be fancy. Don't use a lot of words. Don't babble formulas over and over. Relax. Be simple, natural, and spontaneous. Say something like, 'Dad, not the earthly dad but the spiritual dad, let the heavenly be on earth. May we have food to eat each day. May we be generous and forgiving. May we see the eternal in the present.'"

The irony of the Lord's Prayer is that it was not supposed to be a formula. It was supposed to illustrate relaxed, spontaneous prayer. Yet today it is an endlessly repeated formula that doesn't even use natural language: "Our Father who art in heaven, hallowed be thy name. Thy kingdom come, thy will be done, …"

Repeated formulas can be comforting. But beyond this they are a dead end.

So spiritual relaxation is not about holding still or holding to a formula or holding onto anything. It is not about controlling, containing, or manipulating or changing yourself into anything you are not already. It is about relaxing into our core and being with what is here.

The duck "can rest while the Atlantic heaves, because he rests in the Atlantic."

Not Going Unconscious

Spiritual relaxation is also not about going unconscious. It is not about snoozing or drifting around in a haze. It is about being awake and aware.

Image the duck sitting down in choppy waters, tucking his bill under his wing, and going to sleep. He'd be relaxed. But it is unconscious relaxation. He could easily drown or be dashed onto the rocks.

Spiritual relaxation is not about sleep, mindlessness, or giving oneself over to unconscious impulses. It is about being both awake and relaxed at the same time.

Practical

In everyday life, things are more complex than meditation or prayer. But the same principle applies.

For example, on vacation if our schedule is too full, we may feel stimulated or distracted from our work-a-day routine. But without real leisure, there is no space for wisdom, illumination, or deeper kinds of wellbeing.

On the other hand, if we just space out or run on unconscious impulses, we may get rest. That's helpful to a point. Then it's a dead-end spiritual slumber.

So, let me describe an informal practice that is suited to summer leisure. It's called "guidance."

Guidance

Set aside a block of time when there is nothing you have to do. It could be an hour. It could be a day. If you accomplish nothing during this time, it's okay.

Then allow yourself to quiet a little. Be like the duck. If there're tensions inside, let them be. Invite them to relax if they are ready. Let down into the waves and rest.

Then ask a simple question: "What do I do now?" Don't worry about who you are addressing. Just ask, "What now?"

Suspend preconceived notions of what the answer might be. Empty out. Listen patiently for impressions. Feel with your mind; think with the body. The Quakers call it "holding a question." Don't grasp for answers. Trust they will come from a source wiser than your ego.

If, after "listening," you don't "hear" an answer, be content. Don't force the process. Relax. Just make up what to do.

Do this lightly. Don't make a big deal of it. Just listen and trust.

For example, I set aside some time one summer morning. I asked, "What do I do now?" The thought lightly went through my mind, "go for a walk." I walked out the door.

"Which direction do I go?"

"Left," was the first impression. So I went left.

"What do I do now?"

"Turn around." I didn't question it. There was nothing I had to do anyway. I just turned around and went back the other way.

"Now what would be best to do?"

"Sit on that boulder in the sun."

And so on.

As simple as this seems, it can be very rejuvenating, especially for those of us who tend to be over-structured. It can be relaxing to let go of being so in charge of our life. Let life be in charge of you for a while.

As you develop some familiarity with this process, you become more sensitive to the difference between the voice of old habit patterns and the voice of wisdom. You begin to learn how and when to trust the process. You can use it in more demanding situations: "Which job should I do next?" "Should I buy this or not?" "Would I be better off continuing or not?"

It is helpful to practice guidance in relatively easy situations first. Then when the waves get rough, the practice will be stronger and more likely to be trustworthy.

Cautions

A few practical caveats: Even if the guidance seems clear, on the mark, and appropriate today, it may not be appropriate tomorrow. There can be twists and turns, particularly if we are traveling through rough seas. At one time, it may be wisest to drop everything and leave for a few days. Another time, it may be wisest to pick everything up and push forward. One day we may need to be more assertive, the next let ourselves be led. One time we may need to exert control, another time to listen more carefully. "There is a time for every purpose under heaven" (Ecclesiastes 3). Today's wisdom may be tomorrow's folly.

A second caveat: We all carry repressed feelings and destructive tendencies. It may not be clear if we are drawing on these or on greater wisdom.

For example, we might ask, "What should I do with this mess?" The thought comes to mind, "Get out of here." That might be the voice of wisdom, or it might be the voice of fear. It may require discernment to sort it out. Just because something comes to mind through a mysterious route, doesn't mean it is wisdom.

In general, if the guidance leads to needlessly hurting others, if it inflates or deflates our ego, if it is coercive, dictatorial, or autocratic in tone, or if it clashes with our highest values, then it is probably distorted by repressed feelings. You may need to listen more deeply.

Self-Organizing Chaos

Before closing, let me introduce one other important topic: self-organizing chaos.

When we relax more deeply than usual, what happens? If we aren't used to meditation or silent prayer or just sitting quietly, what happens when we quiet down?

The endless stream of patter in our head gets louder. Maybe swirls of feelings well up. Or maybe we feel restless. "I can't meditate," people tell me. "When I try, there's too much going on inside me."

In short, we experience inner chaos. As waves rise, we may be tempted to stop relaxing and do something. Or to fall asleep.

This morning I'm suggesting doing neither. Relax without going unconscious. And be attentive without going tight.

If we do this patiently, there are times when the chaos self-organizes. Doing the guidance I described, I have often stumbled into magical moments.

I remember riding my bike one way and another, then walking through unfamiliar woods and sitting on a rock using guidance. Suddenly the sun came out. I looked down and a lizard next to me was tasting the air. A rabbit walked into the clearing and started nibbling. I felt like St. Francis.

Another time I walked through town using guidance and came upon an old friend I hadn't seen for years. We had a lovely reunion.

Ordinary magic can self-organize out of chaos when our intentions are heartful and we are relaxed and attentive.

It doesn't always happen. But it happens more often than when I plow through my daily routine with my blinders on.

These then are the three ingredients: heartful intention, attentiveness, and relaxation.

Meditation

To close, I invite you to close your eyes.

Be a duck.

Whatever comes up outside or inside, rest in the waves. Notice tensions. Invite them to rest. They've worked so hard. It's time for them to relax as well.

Let yourself be part of the boundless. Breathe with the infinite.

The ocean is big. We don't know where these waves come from or where they are going. Like the duck, we don't know very much. But we can still relax in the immediate as if it were infinity. Which it is.

Make yourself part of the boundless by easing into it just where it touches you.

That is religion. And the duck has it.

May we have it too.

Unitarian Universalist Spirituality: Finding the Soul

Be patient toward all that is unsolved in your heart and try to love the questions themselves. ... Live the questions now. Perhaps you will then gradually, without noticing it, live along some distant day into the answer.

– Rainer Maria Rilke

August 30, 2009

Last March my wife Erika and I spent a week meditating in the desert of southern California near Joshua Tree National Park.

At first glance the desert seemed barren. The only colors were light shades of grey: dusty greens, pale yellows, and tans. The only visible wildlife were a few birds floating in the distance sky. The only sounds were the wind whispering in sage and the crunch of my feet on the sand.

I found shade near a large prickly pear and tall sage. I sat and closed my eyes to meditate for an hour or two.

When I opened my eyes, the first thing I noticed were fresh tracks of kangaroo mice near my feet. I looked up and saw a dozen little birds the size of finches. They hopped around the bushes and bathed in the dust. Six feet to one side, two larger birds worked on a nest. Behind me another couple built another nest. Further away a roadrunner loped by in easy strides. I felt blessed to be in this exotic company.

When I moved, the animals stopped and looked at me. If I made no sounds or large movements, they soon relaxed and returned to their business.

But if I made noise or got up, they disappeared. In a flash there was nothing but a slight breeze in the brush and a raptor riding the updrafts a few miles away.

If I closed my eyes and sat still for 10 or 15 minutes, the menagerie of wildlife re-materialized around me.

I came to appreciate that they were there all the time. But they remained hidden unless I was quiet and still.

During last June's dialog service, the last question to arise was: "What is distinctive about Unitarian Universalist spirituality?"

It was a wonderful question because Unitarian Universalism as a spiritual practice is still emerging. Since we had used up our time, I only gave a quick answer. So this year, I'd like to speak several times on this topic.

This morning I'd like to leap in and talk about helping one another find our deepest, truest, most authentic self – what we call "inherent worth and dignity" or "goodness." I'll use the word "soul" to refer to this most authentic self we are seeking. Like a menagerie of desert creatures these deeper dimensions are both ordinary and exotic, amazingly gifted and naturally shy.

This has implications for how we relate to one another in ways that encourage soul dimensions to come forth.

But before going into specific community practices, we should lay some groundwork. We should explore this term "soul" and its quality of shyness.

Soul

"Soul" is a tricky word because it means different things to different people. So I looked it up on the Internet. I typed "soul" into Google and found some helpful definitions:

- Soul is the actuating cause of an individual life – as in "the soul comes into the fetus."

- Soul is a person or human being – as in "there are 250 souls in this room."

- Soul is one's consciousness and personality – synonymous with spirit, mind, psyche, and "self."

- Soul is the immaterial part of us that may survive after death or be reborn
- Soul is a music genre combining elements of gospel and rhythm and blues.
- Seoul is the capital of South Korea.
- Soul is a weapon-based fighting game series by Namco Bandai Games.
- Soul is a telecommunications company based in Sydney, Australia.
- … and more …

As informative as these are, I use the word "soul" differently. I don't use it to indicate anything metaphysical or speculative. I use it to indicate that we live divided lives. We have an external self we present to the world (or example: I'm a minister, you're a congregant). And we have an inner self that is much richer, nuanced, and multidimensional than shows on the surface.

Outwardly we may be boss or employee, teacher or student, parent or child or partner, citizen, patron, consumer. At best, these persona only partially reflect something deeper beneath the roles.

I use the word "soul" to refer to this "something deeper."

As much as we cherish these deeper dimensions, they are not always helpful. Reflecting on the meaning of our existence while driving through traffic may attenuate our existence in this world. Reflecting on our truest breadth and subtleties makes us less efficient in doing what needs to be done in our busy lives.

To help us navigate the external world, we adopt identities to encapsulate and protect feelings and thoughts that might throw us off stride or get us into trouble. (Do you really want your boss to know what you really think and feel?)

But if we can get so caught up in our identities that we don't exercise deeper aspects of our being, they may fade from awareness – life becomes flat, mechanical, or loses its meaning. Something's missing – we can't put our finger on exactly what.

We may not even notice this until something disrupts our routine – a loved one dies; we get seriously sick or injured; a relationship collapses; a job is lost; the kids leave the nest; our finances crash — and we find ourselves less resilient than we'd imagined.

Something along these lines may have brought you here this morning. If so, I say, "Welcome." You have come to the right place. I hope. Of course, we can't give you that meaning or depth. We make no pretense of having found "The Answer" or knowing "The Way." But if you are looking for greater vitality, depth, peace, or authenticity, there is a lot we can do to help and support each other.

Shy

To be supportive of each other, we must appreciate the soul and its natural shyness and tenderness.

We humans are creatures who choose to stand up on our hind legs, exposing our soft underbelly to the vicissitudes of the world. We do not have natural body armor or weapons. The soul is particularly soft and tender – unarmed and unarmored. This makes it sensitive, intuitive, insightful, and almost magically attuned to the flows of life around. We all have amazing gifts.

We are accustomed to thinking of the soul as a discrete entity. But as we settle into the actual experience of our depths, they may seem more like a menagerie of exotic creatures – a collection of qualities, deep flows, and energies within that don't actually coalesce into a singular entity.

Whether we conceive of it as an entity or a collection of qualities, the soul is naturally shy.

Like desert creatures, it may be difficult to find even though it is walking by our toes, sitting in a bush before us, or nesting next to us.

The soul observes us more than we observe it. If we blow the horn on our Harley-Davidson as a way to find it, we won't. If we go crashing through the wilderness yelling, "come out, come out," it is likely to recede into the undergrowth. It is wise to do so.

Examples of Shyness

Let me share an example of this natural tenderness and shyness.

I flew to Missouri earlier this summer for a two-week meditation. My return flight was delayed en route by thunderstorms. I didn't land in Sacramento until after midnight.

Erika, my wife, met me at the airport. She was bleary-eyed from a long day.

On the drive home she asked how the retreat had been. There were subtle and powerful experiences I wanted to share with her. But about all I said was, "It was quite wonderful." Late at night, bleary-eyed, driving down the interstate I felt shy about trying to articulate something so tender and powerful, even to my wife.

I suspect all of us have felt this natural shyness. When you want to share something that touches your soul, you may be reluctant to do it during a television commercial or when you have bumped into a friend in the produce section of the grocery store.

In *Walden*, Henry David Thoreau said his cabin was a fine place to talk about the bean harvest. But if there were important matters to be shared, he preferred to go outside and sit where there was more time and space.

Skills

So, to find our soul dimensions, we need time and space to let them emerge. And we need to relate to each other in ways that respect the wisdom of shyness.

So let's shift gears from general consideration to specific ways to encourage the soul to come forth as it is ready.

In a book called *A Hidden Wholeness*,[26] a Quaker, Parker Palmer, talks about a number of skills that respect the soul's integrity. I'd like to describe two specific practices particularly appropriate for us. Palmer calls them "not invading or evading" and "honest, open questions."

Not Invading or Evading

First, not invading or evading:

One way to invade or evade a person is to try to fix them, help them, advise them, or straighten them out. Fixing, helping, advising, or straightening obscure their subtle gifts.

When someone is hurting, angry or mixed up, our compassion may be stirred. We want to help. But wise compassion sees more than their surface issues. It sees what we Unitarian Universalists call their "inherent worth and dignity" – it sees their soul, their wisdom and wholeness.

The person may be so lost in their problem that they've lost touch with their depths. Perhaps we too get caught up and don't see them either.

If we rush in to help, fix, save, or advise we reinforce the illusion that they are helpless and need to be straightened out. We don't intend to be invasive. But we are invasive in pushing onto them the delusion that they aren't already whole. And we are also evading (or running from) them by not being present for their depths.

Unitarian Universalism can become a faith practice in that moment before we rush in. We recognize that we are not seeing their wholeness and wisdom. But we have faith that it is there.

Rather than rush in with a surface fix, we pause and patiently listen for their wisdom to come forth.

Like the desert creatures, deeper wisdom is often shy. If we are noisy, it retreats into the undergrowth and makes itself invisible.

Sometimes, seeing a person's difficulty can be so uncomfortable or agitating that we want to evade – to leave the room emotionally, mentally, or physically. Or we try to help them, not out of compassion for them, but to relieve our own discomfort. It would be kinder for us to relax into our discomfort and stay present.

Not invading or evading means listening with no agenda other than hearing what is truly going on. We are not trying to prove anything. We are just sensing with our mind and heart and being.

We call this "being present." It is one of the greatest gifts we can give one another: to not lean in or turn away.

---

[26] Parker Palmer, Jossey-Bass, 2004.

Exercise

Let's try it now for a few minutes. Turn to someone near you (or two people). Don't speak. Just be present for one another without saying anything. Be together silently with no agenda other than seeing deeply and being seen deeply.

You may feel some of that natural shyness. If you feel like diverting your eye for a moment, honor that. Then come back. Relax. Just be present.

Thank you.

That may be the greatest gift we can give each other.

When someone is baffled or confused, our greatest gift may be to just listen as they struggle to explain. If we silently attend, they may have new insights.

Describing a situation to a quiet, attentive human often allows natural wisdom to peek out of the bushes.

Honest, Expansive Questions

Other times people may be so entangled in their difficulties that they remain confused. Skillful questions may help.

Once we can be present without invading or evading, a second skill we can cultivate is the subtle art of asking honest, expansive questions.

An honest, expansive question grows out of faith — faith that the person has available wisdom and insight that neither of us may see at the moment.

An honest question is not a statement in disguise. "Are you angry at her?" is probably not a question but a statement. "Don't you think you probably should … ?" is instruction more than a question.

An honest question has no agenda. We aren't fishing for a particular response.

Parker Palmer puts it this way: "A dishonest question insults your soul, partly because of my arrogance in assuming that I know what you need and partly because of my fraudulence in trying to disguise my counsel as a query."[27]

Honest questions expand the exploration rather than narrow it. "Do you have a good lawyer?" is not very opening. It narrows to a legal concern.

Examples of honest, expansive questions might be: "How do you feel about the situation you are describing?" "What have you learned from the experience?"

In asking these, we truly don't know the answer. The question is honest and open-ended.

Settings

In this congregation, one of the places where we cultivate these skills is in our Ministry Circles. These are groups of four to ten people who typically meet twice a month for a few hours for the purpose of being with one another in a deeper, soulful way.

We also have other classes and groups and activities that may be helpful.

In fact, I think it is helpful to use these practices in many settings: small groups and coffee hour, mediations groups and Board meetings, with your children, your partner, your friends, and your work.

Caveat

Just to be clear: There are times when it is appropriate to help, save, advise, or set someone straight. There are times when it is important to ask leading, probing, or invasive questions. There are times when it is wise to evade a person or dodge a topic. There are times when it is impossible to give full attention.

However, as a culture we do these all the time. They do little to bring forth our sensitive, creative, intuitive aspects – the soul.

If we truly value the worth, dignity, and goodness in everyone – if we want more depth, soul, authenticity, and peace in ourselves and our world – then part of our spiritual practice must be encouraging our shy depths to emerge and mature.

Practice can be as simple as asking ourselves: "Am I being invasive or evasive?" "Am I trying to fix or advise or just be present?" "Is my question honest and expansive?" " Do I allow silence to open deeper levels?"

---

[27] *Ibid*, p. 132

Patience

There is a quality that encompasses all I've said: patience. Patience is not something we *do*. It is a quality we *become*. There is no way to "do patience." "Waiting patiently" is an oxymoron – waiting is looking for something to happen next. Patience is being with what is now. We are either doing waiting or being patience.

To be present without invading or evading requires patience. Honest, expansive questions begin with patience.

So let's close with a few moments of patient silence in which I invite you to sense your own soul or the deepest qualities you experience. Before we do that, I'd like to share a few words from Nikos Kazantzakis. Then we'll go into silence followed by a round.

> *One morning … I discovered a cocoon in the bark of a tree, just as the butterfly was making a hole in the case preparing to come out. I waited a while, but it was too long appearing and I was impatient. I bent over it and breathed on it to warm it. I warmed it as quickly as I could and the miracle began to happen before my eyes, faster than life. The case opened, the butterfly started slowly crawling out and I shall never forget my horror when I saw how its wings were folded back and crumpled; the wretched butterfly tried with its whole body to unfold them. Bending over it I tried to help it with my breath. In vain.*
>
> *It needed to be hatched out patiently and the unfolding wings should be a gradual process in the sun. Now it was too late. My breath had forced the butterfly to appear all crumpled, before its time. It struggled desperately and, a few seconds later, died in the palm of my hand.*
>
> *That little body is, I do believe, the greatest weight I have on my conscience. For I realize today that it is a mortal sin to violate the great laws of nature. We should not hurry, we should not be impatient, but we should confidently obey the eternal rhythm.*[28]

Closing

The issue is not living our lives.

The issue is letting our lives live through us.

---

[28] Nikos Kazantzakis, *Zorba the Greek*, (Simon and Schuster, 2014) p 120-121

Unitarian Universalist Spirituality: The Goodness in Everyone

September 20, 2009

Josie and the Turkey

I love the woodlands and meadows that stretch along the American River near our home. One afternoon I was sitting in a grove of trees writing. I looked up and noticed a wild turkey in a clearing about a 150 feet to my right. Her movements were angular and aggressive as she paced back and forth. After a minute or so she settled into some high grass. She was completely hidden except for her head which looked this way and that, like a suspicious periscope.

After a few moments, a big white dog with a red mouth came loping happy-go-lucky up a path. He was oblivious of the turkey. The turkey sprang straight into the air and came down toward him, talons extended.

Surprised by the ambush, the dog backed up half a pace and sat down. He outweighed the turkey about five to one. So his ears perked up and his eyes lit up as if to say, "Oh boy, look what I found!" He leaped at the turkey. The bird was faster out of the starting block and got about a ten-foot lead on the dog. The chase was on. As both animals came up to their full running speed, the dog was a little faster. He was closing in.

My stomach clenched.

"Josie!" a big voice yelled through the woods. Back near the clearing a man stood with fists on hips. "Josie! Get back here, Josie!"

Josie was too excited to notice, much less heed the command. He was only six inches from catching the bird.

The turkey spread her wings and took off. But she only flew a foot or so above the ground. The dog continued the chase. However, the turkey was a little faster in the air. When she had a ten-foot lead, she came out of flight and started running again!

Josie closed in.

A shrill whistle pierced the woods. "Josie, leave that turkey alone and get back here!"

Josie slowed down a little. He veered off the chase and ran toward his master.

The turkey turned and pursued the dog! She tried to peck his rear end!

The dog stopped dead in his tracks and turned around. They stood face-to-face. The bird's head was low. Her eyes squinted as she all but scratched the grounded menacingly. The dog was bright-eyed with delight. He leaped at the bird. The chase was on again.

The whistle shrilled, but Josie was intent on the sport. This time, when the turkey took flight, she rose higher and landed in a tree. Josie stopped below the branches and looked up wistfully.

Another harsh whistle. "Get back here, Josie!"

Josie turned with an "aw shucks" expression and trotted back to her master. The two of them turned their backs and ambled away.

From my vantage, I could not actually see the turkey in the tree. So I returned to my writing thinking, "That has got to be the meanest, stupidest bird I've ever seen. No wonder they call them turkeys!"

Five minutes later I looked up. The turkey was back in the clearing. But now her motions were graceful. I noticed some peculiar leaves or feathers blowing around her ankles. When I looked more closely I saw tiny chicks. They could not have been more than a day old.

Suddenly the bird was transformed from a stupid, mean turkey into a smart, courageous mama who, with instinctual love, had risked her life to distract the dog and protect her babies. My heart went out to her in admiration.

Of course, the bird had not transformed at all. The mama with her babies was the same creature that had taunted the dog earlier. I just didn't know the whole story. Nothing real had changed. It was just my opinion that had turned 180°.

I am convinced that when we don't see the goodness in another, we don't see the whole story.

Worth and Dignity

There are seven principles that we Unitarian Universalists have officially adopted to help describe our religious movement. You'll find them in the front of the hymnal. The first may be the best known and most often quoted. It says "We affirm and promote the inherent worth and dignity of every person." In our congregation we say, "We value the goodness in everyone." For me, this includes dogs and turkeys.

Last June during the dialog service, the question arose, "What is distinctive about Unitarian Universalist spirituality?" It was a great question because as a spirituality, Unitarian Universalism has not fully emerged. But it is emerging now and you and I and all of us can help it manifest. I'd love to hear your thoughts and feelings. Please send me an email or note.

Any emerging UU spirituality will include the worth, dignity, and goodness of everyone because this is so near and dear to our hearts. In a subsequent sermon, I want to describe a practice which cultivates the direct perception of the light of goodness in everyone – including dogs and turkeys, human or otherwise.

But before we get to that, it would be helpful to be clear about the difference between spirituality and philosophy or ethics. And it would be helpful to understand what this first principle is claiming before we try to turn it into a spiritual practice.

So, let's begin by looking at this first principle.

Controversial

The first principle may be the most widely quoted. And it is the most controversial.

People ask me, "What about rapists, serial killers, mass-murderers, child molesters? Am I supposed to believe there is worth and goodness in them? What about those politicians and leaders who cause so much harm?"

A good example for me is George W. Bush. He may be my least favorite president. In my view he started two wars (one out of pure ideological arrogance), devastated the economy, increased the chasm between rich and poor, undermined the social safety net, assaulted the environment, and promoted greed and self-interest. He left the world poorer, more violent, more dangerous, less caring, and more depleted than when he started. Where is the worth and dignity in that?

Our first principle doesn't say, "We affirm and promote the worth and dignity of most people" or "… of those we like" or "… of those who make us feel warm and cozy." It is simple, direct, and unrelenting: every person and everyone. If we don't see his or her goodness, we don't see the whole story. It encourages us to look deeper.

For example, George W. Bush's father was reportedly distant emotionally and preoccupied with politics and diplomacy. His mother, by her own account, was overly strict. His sister was chronically ill, and no one talked about it. Such a cold, harsh, non-communicative childhood environment could affect anyone. Perhaps if I knew his whole life story, I'd have a more sympathetic sense of him. I'd feel his worth and goodness.

However, I have no direct experience of George Bush. I have never met the man, shaken his hand, or looked into his eyes. I have no way of knowing the inner person.

Politicians, public figures, and criminals we read about in the paper are, in a sense, abstractions. All we know is what others tell us. We don't know the whole story of what's inside them. We have no way to measure the inner person.

To be sure, accepting worth and dignity in others doesn't mean everything they do is okay. Other Unitarian Universal principles call us to heal the world. They encourage us to stand witness or rise in protest against various actions and policies. We are responsible for our actions and may hold others accountable for theirs.

Gandhi said to the British, "You are good decent people. How could you be so terrible to the Indian people?" Similarly, we may be critical of people's ethical actions at the same time we affirm their inherent goodness.

This can be a fierce discipline. It is not for the faint-hearted.

Up Close

But where our first principle really comes home is not with distant public figures or hypothetical people. It is with those we have met up close: the irritating in-law, the tyrannical boss, the incorrigible teenager next door, the fellow congregant who pushes our buttons.

Charlie Brown famously said, "I love humanity. It's people I can't stand."

Think for a moment about the mean, stupid human turkeys in your life: the control freaks; the power hungry; the irritating; the manipulators; the overly needy; the self-centered. Think of those people who you are tempted to mentally toss into Universalist purgatory.

Unitarian Universalism encourages us to explore our actual perceptions of these people. Are we caught by surface appearances? Do we see their motivations, yearnings, and fears, their desire to be happy and safe? Have we dismissed them without taking the time to see their wholeness?

As we start exploring our perceptions, we have moved beyond Unitarian Universalism as a philosophy or ethical system. We have moved into Unitarian Universalist spirituality.

Direct Experience

So let's pause here for a moment.

"Spirituality" can be a confusing term because it means different things to different folks. Before getting further into a distinctively UU spirituality, it would be helpful to ask the broader question: "What is spirituality, whether UU, Christian, Hindu, Muslim, pagan, or any other flavor?"

At the very least I'd like you to know what I mean when I use the term. For me, spirituality is a way of knowing with the heart-mind. A mature spirituality includes practices that help cultivate heart-mind consciousness. But the core is a way of knowing through direct experience.

To give a trivial example, "What color is the sky in the middle of a clear day?"

You say, "Blue."

I ask, "How do you know?"

You answer, "I go outside in the middle of a clear day and look up. I see blue. There's nothing more to discuss."

I press: "What if we lived our whole lives at the bottom of a deep cave. Are there ways of knowing the sky is blue other than direct experience?"

You answer, "Of course there are."

For example, we could conduct physics experiments passing light through various media like glass, water, and air. Under the right conditions, light breaks up into component colors. From this we could conclude: when sunlight (which we've never experienced) passes through the atmosphere (which we've experienced a little) it starts to break up. The shorter wavelengths – the blue end of the spectrum – scatter more causing the sky to appear blue.

In other words, another way to know something is to carefully think it through to a logical conclusion. We call this "rational intelligence."

Are there other ways?

We might know because a person we trust has been to the mouth of the cave and reports that the sky is blue.

Or we might look it up on the Internet. Or check the Bible for references. Or have a vivid dream in which the sky appeared the same blue-grey as our lover's eyes.

There are lots of ways to know something. Some ways are more reliable. Some ways are more vulnerable to distortion.

Unitarian Universalist spirituality contends that the most reliable way to know is direct experience. The claim of a trusted leader or sacred text may inspire us. But that is blind faith – something we haven't seen directly for ourselves. Unitarian Universalists don't put a lot of faith in blind faith. We want to verify it in our own life.

Caveat

However, there is one important caveat: Direct experience is not infallible. If we lived our whole lives in caves, we could walk into the next chamber, look up and conclude the sky looks just like the roof of the chamber we've been living in – how comforting! Or we might find our way to the cave entrance and look up in the middle of the night or on a rainy day and conclude the sky is black or grey.

Ralph Waldo Emerson, probably the most famous Unitarian minister, said a "true preacher … deals out to the people his life – life passed through the fire of thought." We have a long history of the use of reason in religion. We may use our intelligence to decipher a map so we can find the cave entrance and see the sky for ourselves. We think through the effects of time and weather to help discern what we see.

In the woods, I saw an aggressive, dumb turkey. Later I saw a loving, clever, and courageous mama defending her babies. I used thought to sort out those conflicting impressions and conclude that my first impression was off because there were motivations I hadn't seen.

Or to give another example closer to home, imagine a newcomer in a fundamentalist church.

The preacher is talking about Jesus and how you can be saved if you believe in Jesus. His cadence is engrossing. The people are smiling and clapping and shouting, "Amen! Preach it brother!"

The newcomer is blown by the love radiating through the congregation. He feels joyful, tearful, and grateful to be there. "I love this love," he thinks.

The preacher sees his mood and says, "Brother, Jesus has touched your heart. Hallelujah! Jesus is trying to enter your life. Hallelujah! Do you love God? Do you accept the love of Jesus?"

He is touched. He's overwhelmed. "Yes, I believe," he says. "I feel the power here. I believe."

The choir sings louder. The preacher prays ecstatically. The people shout for joy. The newcomer feels renewed and uplifted.

And in the back corner of the church a visiting Unitarian Universalist crosses her arms suspiciously thinking, "What a bunch of bunk!"

It is not bunk! It may be a lot of things, but it is not bunk.

For this particular UU the problem may be phrases like "Jesus," "being saved," "God descending into your life," that are used to point to a type of ecstasy. These phrases clash with her intellectual belief system. So she's tempted to dismiss the whole thing.

But many people having such ecstatic experiences don't really care what they're called. The words don't matter to them.

And if that experience leads the person to go out into the world and help the poor, heal the sick, stand up for the oppressed, affirm and love all beings as God's creatures, then it is as authentic a religious experience as I know how to measure in this world.

However, a problem arises if the experience leads the person to believe, for example, that people with a different sexual orientation from him must not know God's love or are possessed by the devil. At the very least they are undeserving of the support of a God-loving society. The problem gets worse if he feels inspired to deprive some people of civil rights based on sexual orientation.

From our perspective, he's not affirming and promoting the worth and dignity of everyone. This doesn't mean his experience in church was *necessarily* false. But that it has been misinterpreted. He's missing something essential. He needs to look deeper.

Authentic Spirituality

So, we can distinguish between Unitarian Universalism as a thought experiment, philosophy, ethic, or idea- or belief-based religion on the one hand, and, on the other hand, Unitarian Universalism as a spirituality. UU philosophy may be content with physics experiments at the bottom of the cave. UU spirituality accepts nothing less than direct experience of the sky.

Authentic spirituality has three essential aspects: It is based on direct experience. It provides guidelines, precepts, values, or principles to evaluate our experience and see if we got the full picture or if we need to look more deeply. And it has simple, dependable practices that cultivate the ability to see the whole story – not just think it, but know it fully.

Spirituality is so much more powerful than ideas or ethics alone because it is simple and direct. Once you see the blue sky and validate the experience, you don't have to expend all the time and energy to think through all the laws of physics, properties of light. You just know, "It's blue. End of discussion."

Spirituality is so much more transformative because it touches many aspects of our being, not just our intelligence alone.

Cultivating a Generous Mind and Heart

So the question before us is: How do we cultivate the direct perception of worth, dignity, and goodness in everyone, including those we don't easily hold in our hearts?

This is not a philosophical proposition to be debated or a principle to be accepted or rejected. How do we cultivate direct perception that is as simple, clear, and compelling as the blueness of the sky in the middle of a clear day? You look at someone and see their goodness. Period.

If we look at someone and all we see is a control freak, an anger addict, a power grabber, a conflict avoider, or other forms of confusion, we only see part of the story.

For example, underneath the desire to control is usually fear – without fear, why would someone feel the need to control? Can we see this fear? Underneath anger often is hurt, abandonment, or feeling stopped. Can we see this? Underneath power hunger is greed. And underneath greed is a desire to be happy that has been misdirected. All of us want to be happy and safe. Can we see this?

Seeing the whole story means seeing this universal urge to be happy and safe and how it manifests in this person, skillfully or unskillfully. The nuances of how these play out are as varied and numerous as the people and creatures of the earth. This side of enlightenment, none of us will see the whole story in everyone.

However, we can hold the intention to see as much as we can. For me, this is what it means to affirm and promote the worth, dignity, and goodness of all beings – the intention to see both clearly and generously.

Sometimes the intention is enough to actually see the goodness. And sometimes it's not. We need the help of practices that cultivate this ability under difficult circumstances. This is where we'll pick up in the next sermon.

Closing

Several thousand years ago in his letter to the people of Corinth, Paul of Tarsus wrote, "For now we see in a mirror dimly, but then face-to-face; now I know in part, but then I will know fully …" *(I Corinthians 13:12, New American Standard version)* He suggests our perceptions are like looking into a mirror that is cloudy or dusty.

But just because our perceptions are distorted or partial doesn't mean they are wrong. It just means they are incomplete. The person may be power hungry, abusive, dissembling, self-centered, or whatever. That may be part of the truth.

Wisdom does not grow out of blinding ourselves to what we see. Wisdom doesn't grow from putting on rose-colored glasses and refusing to see unskillful behavior.

However, wisdom does grow out of being humble enough to take another look. We relax, clear the dust of preconception, and carefully and generously look until we sense the light within them. Then we will know fully.

May it be so.

Unitarian Universalist Spirituality: Radiant Heart

October 11, 2009

In a previous sermon, I described a wild turkey I saw attacking a dog that outweighed her five to one. The turkey nearly got herself killed. I decided she was the meanest, stupidest bird I had ever seen.

A short while later I saw her with a brood of one-day-old chicks. I realized she was a smart, courageous mama who had risked her life to protect her babies. I had misjudged her because I hadn't seen the whole story.

Our first Unitarian Universalist principle "affirms and promotes the worth and dignity of every person." It suggests that when we don't see the light of goodness in a turkey (bird or human) we probably aren't seeing the whole story. We need to look more deeply.

This morning I would like to offer a practice that cultivates seeing deeply through what could be called "generosity of spirit" or "the radiant heart."

This sermon is part of a series on Unitarian Universalist spirituality. Mature spirituality – Unitarian Universalist or otherwise – has three fundamentals: it is based on direct experience; it provides guidelines, precepts, or principles to evaluate our experience and see if we have the full story or need to look further; and it offers simple, dependable practices to cultivate that depth and clarity.

Unitarian Universalism does pretty well with the first two. We don't put much stock in blind faith — we trust our own experience more than someone else's claims. And we have values and principles we can use to verify our experience.

Our growing edge is the third fundamental: practices that deepen perception rather than just discuss how things should be. Historically, Unitarians and Universalists spent more energy breaking away from the excesses and imbalances of mainline religions and less in developing practices – or adapting practices from others.

This is changing. This sermon series is a reflection of this effort to develop practices that ground our ideals in transformative experience.

Practices

Effective spiritual practices are often quite simple, like going to a gym. We exercise muscles, and they get stronger. We exercise consciousness in a particular way, and it becomes more acute.

We don't need a medical degree or advanced knowledge of physiology to strengthen our biceps. In fact, if we put all our efforts into understanding anatomy and none into exercising it, our bodies weaken rather than strengthen.

Sometimes we aren't motivated to work out in the gym. Sometimes, the mind can come up with hundreds of spurious reasons to avoid spiritual exercise.

I wish we could develop physical strength without sweat. And I wish we could develop spiritual perception without effort. But it takes more time and intentionality than a few nice thoughts. We must engage our spiritual faculties if they are to become robust.

Varieties of Consciousness

This morning we are interested in practices that help us see the light of goodness deeply and clearly. Such consciousness is both light and penetrating.

When we're tired, stressed, frightened, or grumpy, our consciousness becomes heavy, course, and thick. When we look at others we are more likely to form critical opinions. We are more likely to be irritated by superficial flaws.

Conversely, when we are rested, in love, playing with grandchildren or enjoying our favorite music, our consciousness becomes light, clear and generous. If someone says something insulting, we are less likely to take it personally and more likely to think, "They've had a hard day." We can see their difficulty without getting hooked. We see through it.

Strategy

So, rather than wait to stumble into it, what kind of exercise cultivates this light, penetrating consciousness? Here is such a practice:

Before starting, think of someone for whom it is very easy for you to feel kindness and caring.

Phase one: Repeat short phrases that send love to this person: "May you feel safe." "May you have ease."

Phase two: Drop the phrases and send the feeling itself without words.

Phase three: Joy, kindness, peace, and other uplifted qualities radiate on their own in all directions to all people.

This practice can be done formally sitting in a quiet place. And it can be done informally in various family, work, and social situations. It is helpful to do both formal and informal practice.

Again, the three phases are: (1) simple phrases, (2) uplifted feeling, and (3) radiant heart.

Practice

Let's look at these more closely.

Spiritual Friend

Before beginning, think of someone who evokes in you this generosity of spirit. In some traditions, this person is referred to as a "spiritual friend."

Velma is one of my spiritual friends. She was a therapist I worked with for many years. She was a tiny woman large in wisdom. She could be tough. But she had a way of convincingly pointing out positive qualities in me that I couldn't see by myself. I feel so grateful to her that it is easy to send her kindness.

A spiritual friend might be a counselor. It might be that special teacher you had in third grade, or a mentor, or that aunt or uncle who saw the world in you, or a friend who always has your back. It could even be a grandchild. It can be anyone who evokes tenderness and the wish for his or her good fortune.

Children in their terrible twos, partners, people you find sexually attractive, and other complicated relationships are not the best choices. You may have a lot of love for them, but those relationships are complicated. For this practice, it is best to start with a simple, generous relationship.

Phrases

Phase one begins by repeating simple phrases that evoke generosity of spirit. You think of your spiritual friend as you repeat, "May you be happy," "May you have ease," "May you be healthy," "May you find peace." Any positive, uplifting quality is fine: "I wish you joy," "I wish you grace," "I wish you see who you really are."

After a while, the phrases draw up the actual feeling. At first, it may be fleeting. But with time and practice it becomes steadier. Eventually it becomes so strong that repeating the phrases feels relatively clumsy or crude.

Sensation

In phase two, you let the phrases drop. They've done their job. Instead, you focus on the feeling of lightness or joy, and send it to your spiritual friend without words.

If you are familiar with the Buddhist practice of *mettā* or loving kindness, this practice will be familiar. I draw on it because it is well honed and well suited to Unitarian Universalist temperament.

However, many Buddhist teachers in this country put too much emphasis on the phrases — just as many Unitarian Universalists put too much emphasis on thoughts and ideas. The phrases are simply a way of priming the pump, as it were. When uplifted sensations arise, let the words drop like a butterfly dropping its cocoon so it can spread its wings.

Radiate

As you continue to practice, the feeling or consciousness begins to radiate on its own with less effort.

In phase three, let go of exclusive focus on your spiritual friend and let your heart radiate in all directions to all people and creatures.

Everyday

From this place of a radiating heart, look at people and see what you see.

You can do this at any phase: the phrases, the feelings, or the radiance.

One of the beauties of this practice is you can do it any place: walking down the street, in conversations, during coffee hour, tucking the kids in at night. Whenever you think of it, send out positive, loving energy to those around you. Maybe you do it for only a moment before getting pulled back into the drama at hand. That's okay. It's a foot in the door – a reminder of a possibility. It will grow in time. Like doing push-ups, every time you do a little, the loving clarity gets a little stronger.

These qualities – joy, peace, wellbeing, and so forth – run deep into our essence. As you settle into them, you'll be more able to see the essence of other people. If they have fear, pain, anger, or confusion, that will be easier to see as well. But you'll also see their deeper yearning, light and wellbeing – the worth, dignity and goodness, if you will.

But don't take my word for it. Please. Try it out for yourself. See what you see.

Wandering Mind

I have described this practice as if it were a yellow brick road: You start with phrases and it gets lighter and more heartful until you are a saint walking through Oz.

I wish it were so.

Unfortunately we have this thing called "a wandering mind." One minute we are sending kindness and the next we are thinking about politics or dinner. Despite our most sincere intention, our mind has a mind of its own.

How you relate to the wandering mind has a dramatic effect on the quality of the practice and the quality of your life. If you try to shove your attention back to loving kindness or if you mentally beat yourself up for drifting, this shoving and berating will create more tension, agitation, and discouragement. These scatter the mind more.

So it is wiser and kinder to expect the mind to drift. When it does, just know it is doing what it is designed to do. Be kind to it. Be kind to yourself.

This morning we opened with a song based on a Rumi poem. The full poem goes:

Come, come, whoever you are.
Wonderer, worshiper, lover of leaving.
It doesn't matter.
Ours is not a caravan of despair.
Come, even if you have broken your
  vows a thousand times.
Come, yet again, come, come.

We sing this poem to describe welcoming all of us into our midst. But it could also describe welcoming our dear friend, the wandering mind: "wanderer, worshiper, lover of leaving." Don't despair. Though your intentions have failed a thousand times, it's okay. Come back. You are welcome.

To say this less poetically, when your attention wanders but you still feel the radiance or feeling or the phrases, don't worry about it. Ignore the stray thoughts. They aren't a problem. Stay with the practice.

But when you get completely lost in thought – I say "when," not "if," because you'll drift thousands of times – simply be aware of where your attention has gone. Notice. "Ah so."

Then relax. Release tension. Soften the body and mind and heart. *Relaxing is at least half of the entire practice.* Maybe even smile a little.

Then gently go back to the phrases or to radiating kindness.

Try It Out

Want to try it for a few minutes?

Ideally we'd practice for 20 or 30 minutes. But that isn't what you expected this morning. I want to honor that expectation.

However, if we try it for three or four minutes we might get our toes in the ocean and get a little feel of what the practice holds in store.

Take a moment to think of a spiritual friend if you haven't already – someone who evokes kindness in you. …

As you do this, I'll sing to set the mood. Feel free to sing with me as you are comfortable. Then we'll practice in silence together.

May you be free. / May you have joy. / May you delight. / May you have ease. (repeat)

Now use whatever phrases feel natural to you to send simple love and kindness to your spiritual friend. …

Thank you.

Namasté.

Tips

That's a taste.

Remember, this is a practice. Going to the gym and doing three push-ups doesn't give you huge muscles. Doing this a few times will not give you stable radiance.

However, you may notice flashes of joy or ease. Over time – months and years – these flashes grow longer and less dramatic until they're steady and quiet and obvious.

Let me offer two tips along the way.

Intention

Tip one: Sending kindness or wellbeing is not about trying to create a positive opinion. It's not about thought. It's about cultivating a clear and penetrating awareness.

This practice doesn't attempt to turn lemons into lemonade – or lemonade into lemons. It experiences sourness as sourness and sweetness as sweetness. Unitarian Universalism is about living in this world. This practice is about knowing this world clearly as it is.

If our minds and hearts are filled with tension or fear or opinions about how things should or shouldn't be, this distorts our perception. We don't see the world as much as projections of our tensions and ideas.

The consciousness that sees clearly is light in the sense of relaxed. It is generous in the sense of being open to all possibilities.

Lightness and generosity of spirit help us see the whole story, not just the surface and our reactions to the surface, but the story behind the story.

So this practice should not be confused with affirmations like "You are happy," "You are healthy" "You are peaceful." In truth, the person may not feel happy, healthy, or peaceful. Instead, we let them be as they are.

However, when someone we care about is unhappy, sick, or agitated, we may honestly wish them well. So we send a heartfelt wish, not wishful thinking: "May you be happy." "I wish you good health." "May you find peace."

Two People

Tip two: In the beginning send this generosity of spirit to two people and only two people – a spiritual friend and yourself. If you send kindness to all your family, friends, and co-workers, you will scatter your consciousness rather than allow it to settle and deepen.

And, be sure to send kindness to yourself. The person whose love we need the most is the person we spend the most time with: ourselves.

Courage

One hesitation I hear about entering this practice is fear it will make us more tolerant of violence and injustice.

However, the heart is the seat of courage as well as kindness. An open heart is both skillful and forthright.

If we have radiant hearts and we see someone slapping her baby around, we may be less likely to march over and say, "This is unacceptable. You're a terrible mother. Stop it or I'll do something about it …" and have the door slammed in our face.

We're more likely to see the whole story and say, "You seem tired and worn down today. How can I help you and your baby?" or "I'm worried that you will end up feeling badly about how you are treating your baby. And I'm worried about her as well."

And if she says, "Mind your own business," our heart may stay engaged. "This is painful for me to watch. For both your sakes, I'm going to intervene."

Sending love and wellbeing to people does not make us timid. It makes us wiser, more skillful, and more courageous. We may act less out of fear or anger or self-righteousness and more out of love.

Safe Landing

Another hesitation I hear is difficulty with the phrase, "the goodness in everyone." I could speak to this for a long time. But it may be easier to just use a different phrase. They are just words. There are many phrases that point in the same direction: "Everyone deserves compassion." "Everyone has inherent worth and dignity." "Seeds of goodness are in everyone (even if those seeds may be buried deep under the snow)." "All of us partake of the divine." "God loves everyone."

Find language that resonates with you. That is skillful practice – finding what works most easily.

On the other hand, if you're resistant to the direction of this practice – if the radiant heart seems naïve, if you are convinced that some people don't have the seeds of goodness or deserve compassion, if you aren't interested in exploring that conviction – then you are off the Unitarian Universalist spiritual path.

You are still most welcome here. We don't require adherence to belief. But you have wandered away from our guiding principles, precepts and practices.

Modern airports send out landing beacons. Aircraft with instrument landing systems use those beacons to determine if they are on an optimal landing course.

Ninety-five percent of the time, aircraft are actually off course — they are a little high or low or off to one side or the other. They use the signal to come back on course only to overshoot or go off again. And come back again.

The aircraft don't have to be perfectly on center to land safely – just close enough.

Any powerful spiritual path has the strength to pull us back on course when we drift. We don't have to be perfect, just willing to make course corrections.

However, if you insist that some people are just bad to the core, I fear you are at risk of not landing safely. The tension around that view can damage you and the people around you. Remember the lessons of history: What people have done when they see other people as bad is not pretty. Holding to a vision of good people and bad people sows violence – perhaps not intentionally, but it sows violence nonetheless.

However, if you are willing to notice the tightness, if you are willing to invite it to relax, if you are willing to send out kindness as best you can, then you are on course closely enough. You are bringing us together, you are deepening our lives, and you are a force for healing in the world.

*May we trust the radiance
that wants to shine through us all.*

Unitarian Universalist Spirituality: From Interdependence to Oneness

October 25, 2009

Our first Unitarian Universalist principle "affirms and promotes the inherent worth and dignity of every person." Our seventh and last "affirms and promotes respect for the interdependent web of existence of which we are a part."

These two principles are the most often quoted. They are near and dear to Unitarian Universalist hearts. They point to the sacredness of the individual and the sacredness of the collective.

This morning I want to focus on the seventh: the interdependent web.

This sermon is part of a series on emerging Unitarian Universalist spirituality. If Unitarian Universalism were just a thought experiment or philosophy, respect for the interdependent web could be adequate. It calls us to be good ecologists and environmentalists. It reminds us to recycle, be modest in consumption, and use energy wisely. It calls us to speak up about the upcoming climate treaty in Copenhagen, to network with those who share our values, and hold others accountable when their behavior is destructive. Respect is important.

But for spirituality, respect is not intimate enough. Respect can be cold and distant the way you might respect an ancient philosopher or scientific principle. We do want our spirituality to be intelligent. But genuine spirituality touches us more deeply than respect alone.

So our emerging UU spirituality carries our seventh principle into an empathetic connection with life, into feelings of wonder, joy, and intimacy with our surroundings.

So this morning I want to talk about moving from understanding interdependence to feeling oneness.

I'd like to talk about empathy as an agent that helps us move from our minds to our hearts. I'd like to offer a few practices that cultivate empathy with the whole of life. And I'd like to reflect on what this says about life's purpose.

But before I get to that, let me tell you a story.

Two Snakes and a Butterfly

On the first warm day of spring I was walking through the woodland along the American River near our home. Two snakes reared up out the grass eight feet from me. They were at least four feet long. The exposed creamy underbelly gave little hint as to species. But the triangular heads suggested venom.

They were outside striking distance, so I stood still and watched. After a few moments their movements revealed a diamond pattern and a rattle.

This puzzled me — rattlesnakes are usually shy of humans. I wondered if they were fighting each other.

But their motions seemed more affectionate than combative. They wound around each other, fell back into the grass, rose up again, wound, fell, and rose again.

I smiled. "They're making love," I thought. "They're so enamored with each other they don't even know I'm here."

I'm not particularly scared of snakes. But I had never felt so warmly toward rattlesnakes in the wild so close to me.

Snakes and humans and all sentient beings feel urges that lead to generating life. I don't know what snakes actually feel. But I felt a commonality with them. It made me beam.

After a while I moved on. There were lots of butterflies out that day – black ones with white spots. I didn't know their name. But that's okay — they didn't either.

I passed one on the ground on the edge of the path. He fluttered his wings without rising in the air – just moved through the dust a few inches.

I turned back for a closer look. His wings were dusty and ragged.

"Near the end of your cycle," I whispered to him. I wanted to reach down and touch him to see if he could take flight. But if I were a butterfly, I imagined a big, fleshy finger descending from the sky would not be pleasant.

So I just attended from a distance. His wings moved slowly with his breathing.

Butterflies don't live very long. Of course, from their perspective, they live full lives. From their perspectives humans are ancient creatures who live near eternity.

But one day, I, like the butterfly, will be near the end of my cycle. I'm past the middle of mine (probably) and not too near the end (hopefully).

I wasn't trying to empathize with the butterfly. How could I know what it feels? His nervous system was so different from mine. But I knew eventually life ebbs from both of us. In this, we are the same.

I walked down the path leaving the butterfly to die in peace.

The urge that starts new life. The ebbing of life.

As I gazed at the green woods and meadows around me, everything sparked because my eyes were moist. I felt touched to be part of it all.

Empathy

Empathy is the faculty that helps us feel part of it all. The word "empathy" comes from a German word that means "feel into." Neural scientists are finding this to be literally true.

In his book, *Social Intelligence*,[29] Daniel Goleman describes a man referred to as Patient X. Patient X's visual cortex was damaged. If you showed him pictures, he had no idea what was in them. His eyes and optic nerves worked fine, but without a functioning visual cortex, he was effectively blind.

However, if you showed him a picture of someone laughing and a picture of someone crying, he would tell you the first picture felt

---

[29] Bantam Books, 2006

happy and the second one sad. He empathized with the pictures without consciously knowing what was in them.

What was going on? To explain this, we have to look into neural anatomy.

We have a class of brain cells called "mirror neurons." They mimic or mirror what we perceive. For example, if we smile, MRI brain scans show a specific pattern of neural activity. If we *see* someone smiling, scans show similar neural activity. The mirror neurons cause our brains to mimic what we see. So we feel inside ourselves something akin to what we perceive another feels inside them. We resonate.

We've all experienced this. When we see a baby smile, we smile. When we see a baby frown, we frown. When we see someone yawn, we tend to yawn.

Mirroring happens before we are conscious of it. When we see the baby, we don't think, "He's frowning, so I guess I'll frown too." The frown arises without forethought. Then we notice that we are frowning and feel some measure of sadness inside ourselves.

Brain research shows that we have at least two sets of sensory circuits. One is relatively slow and gives us conscious awareness. When we see something, the information travels down the optic nerve to the visual cortex and from there to the prefrontal lobes where we process the information and become conscious of what we see. In Patient X, the visual cortex was damaged, so the visual information never got to the prefrontal lobes and conscious awareness.

The second set of sensory circuits is very fast. It bypasses the visual cortex and goes straight to a structure deep in the center of our brain called the amygdale. From the amygdala, it goes to the motor areas. Patient X felt his face smile or frown. He felt happiness or sadness even though he was not conscious of the actual pictures.

So we may think of empathy and oneness as a fuzzy mystical sense. But scientists are mapping the circuitry that amplifies empathy.

Empathy requires three things:

(1) We pay attention to another. If we aren't looking at the baby, we won't see the smile or feel empathy. When Patient X looked at the

pictures, he could empathize though he was consciously blind.

(2) We pay attention to ourselves. If we smile or frown but are out of touch with our feelings, we won't feel empathy or attunement because they arise inside us.

(3) We are relaxed. The amygdala is involved in many activities, including fight or flight. If we are preoccupied in other feelings or thoughts, the mirroring may be overridden. If we look at the baby, see the smile, but are preoccupied with a fight with our neighbor, the smile may not register consciously or unconsciously. However, if we are relaxed, we tend to feel inside us what we see in another. We "feel into."

Practices

Now, lets look at some practices that can be used to cultivate empathy, attunement, and oneness.

Radiant Heart

In a previous sermon when talking about the radiant heart, I described a simple practice that develops the three ingredients of empathy. (1) Sending kindness, joy, peace, or wellbeing to others makes us more aware of those around us. (2) The practice involves awareness of our feelings. It begins with phrases like "May you be happy. May you have ease." But as uplifted feelings arise, we drop the words. We shift attention from prefrontal activity – thoughts and words – to our body – the actual sensations inside. And (3) we relax to reduce the amount of inner distraction. Half to 90% of the practice is relaxing.

Since I described this practice in detail before, I won't elaborate now. But try it. I think you'll find sending kindness leaves you more at one with the world around you.

Hanging Out in Nature

A different kind of practice is hanging out in nature.

We humans evolved for hundreds of thousands of years in wilderness settings. Farming and especially cities are very recent inventions in evolutionary time. Our organisms are naturally attuned to the natural world.

When I go out for a long walk in the woodlands, at first my mind keeps returning to daily stress, pesky people, unfinished arguments, social plans, and so forth. But if I pay attention to the landscape around me, the churning begins to slow down. I settle inside.

The trees don't care if my pants are rumpled or my hair sticks out. The river doesn't have an agenda about who I am. The clouds don't have opinions about the events of the day. Maybe the birds, deer, and coyotes have some concerns about what I do. But their concerns are pretty simple and uncomplicated. Pretty soon I'm feeling simpler and less complicated.

Sages from Gautama Siddhartha to Saint Francis of Assisi to Emerson speak of the spiritual benefit of being in the woods and fields. Thoreau famously said, "In the wilderness is the preservation of the world."

Of course there is a difference between communing with nature and a pleasant ramble. If we do a power walk with an iPod plugged into our ears or jump out of the car, take a few photos, and drive off, the effect is not so soothing or attuning. To attune we have to (1) pay attention to what's around us, (2) pay attention to what's inside, and (3) relax.

Projecting

To take this one step further, rather than merely attend to nature, project yourself into it. This is like "walking a mile in another's shoes," only the other is an animal, plant, or landscape.

For example, you can sit quietly by a river or in your backyard. See what draws your attention – a tree, a bird, a hill in the distance. Then imagine that you are the tree or bird or hill. How does life look from that perspective? Imagine having their consciousness. Take a little time with this.

This is what happened to me spontaneously along the river when I saw rattlesnakes mating and the butterfly waning – I started imagining what it would be like to be them.

This intimate sense of connection is not to be confused with romanticizing nature or projecting human personality onto other creatures as in a Disney movie. Other creatures may have different nervous systems. What we feel in our bodies may not be the same as what they feel. It is more what we'd feel if we were in their position.

In other words, having an intimate connection with life around us should not be a temptation to go pet the nice rattlesnakes. The connection starts with respect: respect for the interdependent web and respect for creatures being what they are. It sees the ways we are different. And it goes deeper to recognize our commonality – the urge that creates new life, the knowing that we'll all feel life ebbing, the desire to be happy, and so forth.

Switching Places

If you want to take this even further, imagine what it would be like to be them seeing you.

For example, there is an old grandfather of an oak tree in the play yard behind our classrooms. In the photos of the building ground breaking ceremony 50 years ago, that same tree is looking over the fields, a few cows, and a gaggle of humans.

Go out and sit by that tree. Imagine what it would be like to be resting there all these years: watching people come and go and come and go and come and go. Watching the seasons move through their cycle – being in intimate contact with each one. Then imagine you are the tree watching you sitting there. What do you as an oak tree see in you as a human? What advice would you give this human?

Practicing

My description of these practices may not wow your intellect. They may not tickle your prefrontal lobes. They are, after all, pretty simple: You send out wellbeing or hang out in nature or imagine being a tree or a bird or a river. Like most spiritual practices, they're not complex.

Thinking about them may not do much for you. Doing them once or twice may be pleasant enough, but may not do that much either.

However, if they become a habit or hobby you do over and over, they can transform your relatedness from separateness to interconnection to attunement to oneness.

Purpose

And they may also shift your sense of life purpose. So let me say a little about this.

Many preachers say everything happens for a reason, even when it is hard to divine the reason. Many people say, "Life has given me a special purpose. My job is to discover that purpose and fulfill the destiny life gave to me."

This strikes me as a bit narcissistic. Given the vastness of time and space, why should I think there is some special attention given to me?

In my deepest meditation, I see no sign of this. Rather, I see us as pebbles on a beach. The waves wash over us simply because that's what waves do. And we happen to be there.

We are small fish in a very large sea of eternity. Or if you prefer, we are stars twinkling in a firmament of billions upon billions of heavenly bodies.

I don't think that everything in our life happens for a reason special to us. I don't think life gives us a purpose. This is why so many people can live unconsciously, wandering aimlessly until they trip and fall into the grave.

However, we can adopt a purpose and organize around it. This doesn't make it our destiny, only a direction that we have chosen.

Many people organize their lives around taking care of themselves. Our culture tells us to look out for our material, emotional, and spiritual needs and wants.

For thousands of years, sages of all stripes have counseled that this is ultimately unsatisfying. All living organisms change and die: people, snakes, butterflies, trees, even mountains — everything. Any place we imagine for ourselves in life eventually disorganizes and vanishes. If we focus just on taking care of ourselves, we may have fun for a while. But in the end, things just don't work out.

However, sages have also counseled us to adopt a purpose or organizing theme of serving the greater good.

Life itself goes on even if our place in it evaporates. By devoting ourselves more to connecting to the larger span of life and less to one organism, our sense of identity starts to shift from a tiny me to a larger us – from my life to life itself. This shift doesn't happen easily or quickly. However as we do these practices, our sense of satisfaction and wellbeing fixates less on one transient life and more on the wellbeing of all life.

Then, when our individual organism goes through change – the death of a loved one, the loss of a job, the collapse of health – we are less likely to see it as a total disaster and more likely to think, "Ah, look at how life is flowing through me now. Far out."

And when death approaches, we are less likely to hold on desperately to a deflating inner tube sinking in the ocean and more likely to feel gratitude for having been part of it all.

We are part of it all. Life may not give us a special purpose. But we are part of it all and can harmonize with it all.

That's what touched me walking along the river on that spring afternoon.

I heard a Tibetan Rinpoche quote Nietzsche once in what must have been a rare soft mood for Nietzsche. He said, "Suffering is complex, but happiness is simple." Walking through the fields I felt simple. I felt ordinary. I felt natural. I felt blessed to be part of this world.

I know all of you have felt that too. The simple truth is that we are all part of it all.

May we know the truth and live fully into it.

Blessed be.

Swimming in the Deep End: The Dark Side of Unitarian Universalism

January 24, 2010

John II Sigismund Zápolya was the first (and only) Unitarian Monarch in history. He was king of Hungary from 1540 to 1570. On March 18, 1568, he issued the Edict of Turda. Translated into English it reads:

His majesty, our Lord [King], in what manner he – together with his realm – legislated in the matter of religion at the previous Diets, in the same matter now, in this Diet, reaffirms that in every place the preachers shall preach and explain the Gospel each according to his understanding of it. *And if the congregation like it, well. If not, no one shall compel them, for their souls would not be satisfied. But they shall be permitted to keep a preacher whose teaching they approve. Therefore* none ... shall abuse the preachers; no one shall be reviled for his religion by anyone ... *and it is* not permitted that anyone should threaten anyone else by imprisonment or by removal from his post for his teaching. For faith is the gift of God and this comes from hearing, which hearing is by the word of God. (*Emphasis added*)

Kind of snappy, huh? Did you catch the drift of it?

The Edict of Turda has also been called the Edict of Toleration or more loosely the Act of Religious Freedom and Conscience.

In Medieval Europe, the most respected minds said, "Take care of your own. When you come to power, secure freedom for your people and your religion by suppressing others. It's the right thing to do."

The Edict of Turda was unique in declaring a person should not be abused, compelled, or "reviled for his religion" or "threaten[ed] ... by imprisonment or removal from his post for his teachings."

And it went on to declare a universal principle: "Faith is the gift of God and this comes from hearing." In other words, don't force belief upon others.

This was quite revolutionary for its day. Unitarian Universalists point to it as a seminal moment in our tradition: the first Unitarian king strived not for just his religious freedom but for the freedom and tolerance for all as a general principle.

By 21st century standards, the Edict is quaint and limited. It applied only to well-connected groups of the time: Catholics, Lutherans, Calvinists, and Unitarians. Jews, Muslims and Eastern Orthodox were "tolerated" but not granted legal guarantees. Pagans and atheists were considered deranged.

Nevertheless, it was cutting edge thinking in its day. It was swimming in the deep waters of the times.

The appeal to freedom, reason, and tolerance was so revolutionary it created a backlash. John Sigismund was replaced in a few years and the edict was revoked.

But it was a shining moment of which we are proud.

Freedom, Reason, and Tolerance

In 1925 Earl Morris Wilbur, the highly respected Unitarian historian, declared freedom, reason, and tolerance to be the hallmarks of our Unitarian tradition. Today in theological schools and pulpits across the country many Unitarian Universalists say our core is freedom, reason and tolerance.

We can see all three of these right there in that Edict of Turda in 1568.

However, they are no longer the deep end of the pool.

This sermon is part of a series on Unitarian Universalist spirituality and what it might mean for it to mature into the 21st century and beyond.

A lot has happened in 450 years. Collective human consciousness has evolved. Unitarianism evolved as well, but not as fast. We are no longer cutting edge.

So this morning I'd like to look at how consciousness has evolved. Then I'd like to look at the dark side or the limitations to Unitarian Universalist values in today's world.

Consciousness is how we think about and perceive the world and ourselves. It shapes what we value, what we consider important, and how we treat each other. I'll talk about mythic, rational, pluralistic, and integral stages of consciousness.

Mythic

In late medieval Europe, the leading edge consciousness was mythic or ethnocentric. It said, "It is important to stick together and take care of our own." "Our own" might be defined by ethnicity ("my people right or wrong"), religion ("my God right or wrong"), land ("my country right or wrong"), or something else.

It believed there was one right way passed down to us from on high. Our job is to live by those laws. It valued tradition, hierarchy, everyone in his or her rightful place, tidiness, moralistic teaching, and rewards in the afterlife. It's thinking was concrete and literal, like today's fundamentalists.

In the middle of the 16th century this and less mature structures of consciousness accounted for 99% of human beings. Today they account for 40% to 70% of the human population depending on which researchers you ask.

Rational

Traditional mythic ethnocentrism has obvious limitations. So, in the 17th and 18th centuries a new consciousness emerged that was more rational and complex and included more people in its circle of caring. We call this emergence the Western Enlightenment. It valued freedom, reason, and tolerance.

Rather than one right way, it saw many possibilities. It valued individuality over tradition and upward mobility over static hierarchy. It valued objectivity, modern scientific methodology, and self-determination. It laid the groundwork for democracy, modern medicine, critical thinking, and so forth. It was a dramatic shift into the modern age – so called "modernity."

Pluralistic Cultural Creatives

As powerful and successful as this rational modern consciousness was, it had a dark side that gradually emerged: materialism, eco-destruction, unequal wealth distribution, tyranny of the most ambitious, corporate personhood, and so forth.

So in the 1960s, another stage of consciousness emerged that was even more complex, compassionate, and inclusive. It was pluralistic and egalitarian. It's been called "postmodern" and its people "cultural creatives." It values feelings, communication, collaboration, inclusion of everyone, sticking up for the oppressed, ecology, and distrust of authority.

It brought us many gifts: the civil rights movement, feminism, ecology, and so forth. But it too has a dark side. We'll get to that in a minute.

Integral

In the last 10 or 15 years another consciousness has started to emerge which takes all the previous ones into a higher and deeper synthesis. It's very sophisticated in its caring. It's been called "integral," "integrative," "holistic," "vision logic." It accounts for 1 to 2% of the population today, according to research.

Unitarian Universalists

Today all the early stages and their value systems are alive and well in various places and amongst various peoples. But leading-edge consciousness has moved quite far in 450 years.

And in our Unitarian Universalist congregations we may notice these four consciousnesses.

We may hear concrete, mythic thinking: "there is one best way to govern this congregation," "one best way to organize this protest," "one best set of priorities." Anytime we hear strong "shoulds," "oughts" or absolutes, there may be mythic thinking.

And at times it is helpful.

We may also hear amongst us rational, world-centric consciousness. After all, our movement was born during the Enlightenment with a humanistic orientation that values reason, objectivity, innovation, and the trying of new things.

These people have an honorable and valuable place among us.

And we may also hear this pluralistic, egalitarian, communitarian way of thinking. I think it is our center of gravity, if you will. There are more Unitarian Universalists here than in other sets of values. It values the inherent worth and dignity of everyone in the interdependent web.

And, we may also notice a small but growing number of Unitarian Universalists who are integral-holistic.

Tradition and Trajectory

As the inner landscape of consciousness evolved over the last half millennia, the outer landscape has also changed. The human population has mushroomed — the planet is thick with us. Our technologies for saving and destroying life have grown rapidly. We've encroached on the ecosystem. Communication technology puts all of our conflicting value systems into uncomfortably close contact. The possibilities and the dangers are tremendous. The world is more exciting and more at risk than ever.

Frankly, today's world does not need our traditions. It needs our trajectory – our movement toward integral consciousness.

Our traditions of freedom, reason, and tolerance that were so cutting edge many centuries ago are still essential today. But they are no longer sufficient.

Our late 20th century tradition of green, ecofriendly, "feelingful," pluralistic egalitarianism remains essential and remains near and dear to me. But it too is no longer sufficient.

The complexities of our lives and the dangers of our world need the next emerging integral consciousness, which sees the value of all previous stages without being naïve and knows how to work with and integrate them in a holistic vision.

The world doesn't need our traditions. But it needs us and others to move into the next consciousness.

I suspect that most of the people in this sanctuary can think holistically – that is, think in several different systems at once. Most educated Westerners can.

But I suspect that most of us have value systems and make decisions out of younger, less embracing ways of thinking and feeling.

So if Unitarian Universalism is going to be relevant to the 21st century – if we want to deepen our lives in the world that is and be a force for healing in the world that is – we want to nudge ourselves along toward integral consciousness.

That is our trajectory.

Dark Side

How do we do this?

One way is to become more familiar with integral thinking and perception.

Another is to see the limitations of some of our past and current Unitarian Universalist values. This can motivate us to explore more complex, compassionate, and inclusive ways of thinking, feeling, and valuing.

So for the rest of this sermon, I want to look at the bad news of Unitarian Universalism. Many of us have seen or felt these limitations. I hope putting them on the table will encourage us to joyfully follow our trajectory back into the deep waters.

(If you want a more detailed exploration of the strengths and limitations of liberal consciousness, you may be interested in Don Beck and Chris Cowan's *Spiral Dynamics* or the writings of Ken Wilber.)

I'll briefly mention some of the limitations or "dark sides" to our cherished values. I invite you to reflect on where you see them in your life, in your family, in this congregation, in other groups you are part of, or in the larger world.

- Our value of including everyone can degenerate into tokenism. We may feel guilty if our collective profile does not statistically match the profile of the larger community.

- Our value of diversity can focus on a limited range of politically correct attributes, and limit diversity in other areas.

- Our desire to help the oppressed can slide into competition to see who is most oppressed. It can also encourage us to pour resources into our weaknesses rather than build from our strengths.

- Our compassion can give resources away without asking anything in return. This creates resentment in both the giver and the receiver.

- Our equalitarian sentiments can become suspicion of any structure or authority, making representative democracy difficult.

- Our urge for fair representation can give equal weight to the informed and uninformed, the involved and the disinterested, the competent and the incompetent alike.

- Our desire to get along can attract people who are conflict avoidant or conflict habituated.

- Our discomfort with judgments can make us less discerning and less able to make simple value judgments. For example: global cooperation and white supremacy. In the extreme someone might give them equal weight because all views are welcome.

- Our desire to see the goodness in everyone can lead to not holding each other accountable for destructive behavior.

- Our emphasis on the importance of feelings can lead to a "tyranny of the most disgruntled." For example, we are doing long-range planning. So we could take a particular issue, bring in experts, solicit suggestions and feedback, have multiple discussions, and reach a collective decision. Then someone comes along and says, "I haven't been paying attention because I didn't think you were serious. But I disagree with the group decision." So we stop and go through the whole process again. "Tyranny of the most disgruntled" means that anyone who expresses displeasure can stall forward movement.

Do these sound familiar?

Our values of inclusion, helping the oppressed, egalitarianism, compassion, diversity, inner feelings, getting along, nonjudgmentalism, seeing goodness, and more are wonderful and important. And they all have dark sides we have felt.

Dark Side of Acceptance

Let me share a story that illustrates how these can crop up.

Last June I went to the General Assembly, the annual gathering of Unitarian Universalist congregations.

One afternoon I sat with a small group of self-identified Unitarian Universalist mystics. I told them a question from a congregant had inspired me to think about emerging UU spirituality.

I was interested in talking with people who were immersed in our movement and who also had a mature spiritual practice. I wanted to hear their take on UU spirituality.

A man in the circle said he objected to the phrase "mature practice." He said, "The word 'mature' implies hierarchy – that some practices are better than others. Unitarian Universalism values inclusivity and not judging one person as better than others. I'm uncomfortable saying one practice was better, deeper, or more mature than another. They all have value."

His was a good point. However, I worry about confusing judgment with discernment.

I said to him, "In any field but spirituality, we easily acknowledge differences in maturity. A four-year-old learning to play the kazoo may have the same inherent worth as Yoyo Ma playing his cello but not the same musical mastery.

"Music, painting, carpentry, culinary arts, auto mechanics … in almost all other fields of endeavor, it is obvious that there are different levels of skill and proficiency.

"One person has a casual interest in playing the piano or sculpting or writing. Another person is drawn to devote time and energy to the art.

"Similarly some people are content with a spiritual practice that brings a touch of ease or wellbeing. Others long to see to the core of their being.

"If Unitarian Universalist spirituality is to be more than dilettantish dabbling, it will acknowledge differences in intentions, depths, stages and levels of practice and accomplishment.

"Without mature practice, those drawn deeper will simply go elsewhere. And many do!

"A mature UU spirituality takes someone's beginning interest and offers a path (or paths) leading to greater and greater insight, contentment and effectiveness in healing our complex world."

Thus ended my rant about some of the dark sides of liberal religion.

Freedom, Reason, and Tolerance

To be clear, I sincerely am not putting down our traditions and values. As we mature from mythic to rational to pluralistic to integral and beyond, the earlier stages are not discarded. They remain with us enfolded in a deeper synthesis.

For example, let's look one last time at freedom, reason, and tolerance.

To a young consciousness, freedom means, "I do my thing, you do yours: anything goes."

To a more mature consciousness freedom is integrated with responsibility. With freedom comes responsibility and with responsibility we find true freedom.

To a young consciousness, reason is cold, hard, disembodied logic. To a more complex consciousness, reason is one of many intelligences: cognitive, emotional, social, ethical, spiritual, and more. All work with each other: Reason without love is not intelligent. Love without reason is not compassionate. Reason without ethics is not intelligent in the long run. And so forth.

To a young consciousness, tolerance means, "I can put up with anything." As consciousness matures tolerance becomes acceptance, which becomes appreciation of differences and commonality.

As we learn to swim in deeper waters, the earlier stages and values are included in this broader visionary synthesis.

In fact, with integral consciousness and beyond, thought and joy come together in a delightful dance. So I close with words from Carmen Bernos DeGasztold:

[May we have] such philosophic thoughts
that [we] can rejoice everywhere [we] go
in the lovable oddity of things.
  Amen

Namasté

Swimming in the Deep End: Merging with the River

Now we are ready to look at something pretty special.
It is a duck riding the ocean a hundred feet beyond the surf.
No, it isn't a gull.
A gull always has a raucous touch about him.
This is some sort of duck, and he cuddles in the swells.
He isn't cold, and he is thinking things over.
There is a big heaving in the Atlantic,
And he is part of it.
He looks a bit like a mandarin, or the Lord Buddha meditating under the Bo tree,
But he has hardly enough above the eyes to be a philosopher.
He has poise, however, which is what philosophers must have.
He can rest while the Atlantic heaves, because he rests in the Atlantic.
Probably he doesn't know how large the ocean is.
And neither do you.
But he realizes it.
And what does he do, I ask you? He sits down in it.
He reposes in the immediate as if it were infinity – which it is.
That is religion, and the duck has it.
He has made himself part of the boundless,
by easing himself into it just where it touches him.
I like the little duck.
He doesn't know much.
But he has religion.

Donald C. Babcock (The New Yorker, October 4, 1947)

February 21, 2010

Walking along the American River I came upon a tiny cove. I sat down on some boulders in the place where the cove and the river met.

In front of me the main body of the river rushed by at thousands of gallons a minute. It formed standing waves and whitecaps.

But in the cove, the water stood still. Two ducks – a male and a female – drifted gently, picking bugs and other morsels of food off the smooth surface.

As I watched them, I noticed the water in the cove was not completely still. It drifted upstream. The river current flowed into the downstream side of the cove and pushed upriver. Leaves and twigs moved slowly toward me, then out into the main current.

The downstream rush rubbed against the upstream meandering spawning dozens of whirlpools. Some were as narrow as pencils. Others were as broad as watermelons. Some funneled down a hand span below the surface. Some were gentle depressions. Some were wide enough to hold three or four little ones inside. Some winked out in a moment. Others lingered.

The effect was magical. I pictured river spirits dancing across the water leaving whirls in their footsteps. I imagined, "What if the whirlpools and the river were conscious?"

If they were, the whirlpools would probably have little awareness of the river. Their attention focused inward on their frenetic turning. Occasionally they might glimpse the larger river-universe beyond. Occasionally they might slow enough to notice the flows in which they exist. But mostly they would be preoccupied with their own dance.

"The Duck" is a favorite poem of mine that also appears on pp. 193, 253, and 302.

The river, on the other hand, would be aware of the whirlpools. There was so much going on in the river and the whirlpools were so ephemeral that the river would not think the little swirls important. But it would have no problem seeing them.

As I watched, sooner or later each whirlpool drifted away, ran out of energy, spun itself out, and dissipated back into the river.

As it vanished, nothing was lost. The water of the whirls remained right there in the river. Even the energy that caused the spinning remained in the river though it was more dispersed.

Merging with The River

This morning I'd like to talk about a shift of mind and heart that could be called "merging with the river – a little bit."

In its big form, merging might be called a shift from whirlpool consciousness to river consciousness, from wave consciousness to ocean consciousness. But like the duck becoming part of the boundless, even this profound merge begins by sitting down in the waves. Like the whirlpool merging with the river, it begins when its energy relaxes and spreads out. For us, it begins when our identity shifts a little bit from the whirling inside to the currents that flow around us.

This shift of mind and heart is important not only for our own happiness but for our effectiveness in the world.

Unitarian Universalist Spirituality

This sermon is part of an ongoing series on deepening Unitarian Universalist spirituality. This morning I am less concerned with what UU spirituality has been in the past or is today than I am in what it could be in the near future.

However, it might be helpful to put it into a historical context.

Historical Context

Several weeks ago I spoke briefly about the mythic-ethnocentric consciousness that dominated medieval Europe. It placed little stock in the individual. It valued rigid social hierarchy in which everyone stayed in their God-given place.

The Western Enlightenment brought forth a very different consciousness that valued reason and scientific objectivity. And it valued individuality and the freedom to improve our lives.

Unitarianism was a child of the Western Enlightenment. If we look in the front of our hymnal, it is no coincidence that our very first principle "affirms and promotes the worth and dignity of every person." This is where we began.

As the medieval oppression receded in the modern era, individualism flourished. At times it not only thrived but ran rampant contributing to alienation, individual and corporate greed, environmental havoc and so forth.

So, by the mid-20th century – as we moved from the modern to the postmodern era – another consciousness emerged that was more aware of complexity, ecology, systems, and so forth. It saw that we might not be embedded in a mythic medieval hierarchy. But we are embedded in an interdependent web. The river surrounds us and flows through us whether we recognize it or not. We ignore it at great peril.

So it is no coincidence that our seventh and last principle "affirms and promotes respect for the interdependent web of all existence of which we are a part."

The first and last are opposite poles: individualism versus the web, independence versus interdependence, dignity of each person versus the reality of interconnection.

Today, most UUs value both. But we don't bring them together in the same thought. After all, they are separated by five other principles. They are like cousins who coexist but barely speak to one another.

Today, as we move deeper into the so-called "post-postmodern" era of the 21st century, the possibilities and perils are greater than ever. Population growth, rise of technology, stress on the environment, strain on democracy, dysfunctional economies, and so forth create more risks and opportunities than ever before.

To deal with these, the two cousins must get together. We must ask, "What happens when the dignity of the individual meets the reality of the web?" What happens when the whirlpool merges with the river? When the duck becomes part of the boundless ocean?

Clearly we don't want to go back to the oppressive medieval values or even further back to tribal fusion. The postmodern Romantics tried this until they realized that the life of the noble savage was not as noble as they'd imagined.

We don't want shallowness but depth. We want a consciousness that integrates the worth and dignity of the individual with a realization that separate individuals do not exist. Without the river there are no whirlpools. Without the web of everything there is no single thing. To pretend we can take care of our individual welfare without caring for the collective welfare is suicide – like a whirlpool trying to leave the river.

This shift of mind and heart can be hard to describe. But perhaps it can be illustrated by analogy.

Optical Illusions

There are two images in your order of service. The first is the familiar vase-two portraits illusions. If we see the white part of the image as foreground and the black as background, we'll see a vase. But if we see the white as background and the black as foreground, we'll see two faces nose to nose.

The second image may be less familiar – but it's fun. If we see the white as foreground, we see a woman's face. If we see the black as foreground, we see a cartoon of Bill Clinton playing the saxophone.

Three observations:

First: If we only glance quickly at an image, it is easy to assume we know what it is without seeing alternate possibilities. If, away from the image, I call it a woman's face and you call it Bill Clinton on the sax, we may each think the other is daft.

Second: As the images shift from a vase to two portraits or from a face to Bill Clinton, nothing in the external world changes. The ink on the page doesn't move. The shift is entirely in our minds. We change how we see, not what is actually there to be seen.

Third: It is difficult to hold both the woman's face and Bill Clinton in mind at the same time. As we become familiar with the image, it can flip back and forth quickly. But it's hard to hold them both at once.

However, it is not impossible. If we mentally step back and relax as we look at the image, we may be able to see them both at once. If our mind is tight, this is difficult. But if we are gently attentive, it is possible.

That is what this shift of mind and heart feels like: not shifting from one construct to another but shifting from one at a time to all at once.

More Than Parlor Tricks

This applies to more than parlor tricks.

For example, is it more important that we save the spotted owl or that we retain jobs for people in the logging industry? It is more important that we save the delta smelt or that we give farmers water?

Depending on our inclinations, it is easy to take one position or the other – black or white – and think the other positions are daft. But the real solution comes out of a relaxed, attentive, wider systemic view. If we cut down too much forest we'll have neither owls nor jobs. If we destroy the delta ecosystem, we'll have neither smelt nor useable water. Real solutions require seeing the health of the system as more important than any elements within the system.

When one part acts like it is more important the whole, we call it cancer.

Health care, the economy, terrorism, job creation, legislative gridlock – all of these beg for systemic, broad-view thinking rather than a black-or-white stance in one part of the system.

Untangling these issues would take more time than we have this morning. My point is that a shift to what's called "flex and flow" systemic thinking is vital to solving many very practical problems as well as to deepening our spirituality.

Merging Just a Little

But for now, let's return to how we perceive ourselves and the world around us – to how much we are caught up in our own swirling versus how attuned we are to the subtler currents flowing around us.

Let me give a few common examples of what I mean by this.

At the end of a tough week, you come home spinning inside. After a few day's rest – maybe hiking in the foothills or just hanging out in the yard – you aren't so wound up. You have a touch of peace. The way you experience yourself and the world has shifted. You've relaxed out of your spinning into a state that is not so tightly bound. You've merged a little.

Or imagine your young daughter running up and telling you a joke. From your personal perspective, the joke is dumb. But she laughs with delight and you find yourself smiling easily. The delight did not arise out of your whirlpool. Your sense of self eased and spread out to include some of the river around you – in this case your child. You feel her delight as your own. Your mind and heart merged a little with this other being – your daughter.

Or consider: When I first moved to Sacramento, I lived in an apartment complex down the street from the church. I especially enjoyed the hot tub privileges in the complex.

But one cool evening, the hot tub would not warm up. I was annoyed. It remained broken for several days. Finally one morning, I caught the manager and complained.

I left his office and drove down to the Samaritan Center in Oak Park. It was a street agency that helped people on the edge of homelessness. They were offering a free, pre-Thanksgiving diner and I had promised to help serve.

A 30-something woman named Anita and I spent several hours carving up a few dozen turkeys. As we worked, we dropped into casual conversation. I had two sons: at the time one was at Brown University and the other was in a charter high school. She had two sons: at the time one was in jail and the other was drug addicted. I had a wife. She had a husband who had disappeared years ago with a gang – she assumed he was dead. The suffering in her life was palpable though she spoke matter-of-factly with no trace of self-pity.

Later that day, back in the apartment complex, the hot tub still didn't work. I preferred that it work. But it no longer annoyed me. I simply smiled. After conversing with Anita, I was less wound up in this little problem and more aware of all the problems and gifts of life around me. My perspective had shifted. I had merged with the river just a little bit.

Merging a Little More

These shifts of mind and heart may not be profound. But they are movements in a profound direction.

Ralph Waldo Emerson wrote, "learn to detect and watch that gleam of light which flashes across [the] mind from within." In other words, pay attention to small glimpses of light, the touch of peace, the unbidden smile of delight, the glimpse of the river, the presence of the ocean.

When the worth and dignity of our individuality meets the interdependent web, our sense of who we are as separate entities becomes less demanding and more spacious. And the web of life feels less abstract and impersonal and more intimate.

And if we patiently follow Mr. Emerson's advice, with time we feel less like a whirlpool in the river and more like a river with whirlpools. Rather than being a duck sitting in the ocean, we become the ocean with waves and ducks within us. We flip from seeing peace to being peace, from sensing God to being God sensing us, from experiencing illumination to being luminous, from experiencing spaciousness to being space.

Next time I'm in the pulpit, I want to talk about these more profound shifts. The subtitle for that sermon is "beyond of self as we know it."

Happiness

But this morning I want to make sure we don't underestimate these smaller shifts of heart and mind, these more common experiences of merging a little bit. Their value can be seen as two different kinds of happiness.

One kind is whirlpool happiness. This arises from the thrill of spinning or the joy of riding the surf. This happiness comes out of excitement, doing, moving, thinking, and acting.

The other kind is river happiness. This arises from relaxing into a larger context, sitting down in the ocean, slowing down, easing up, mellowing out, and just being.

One is not morally better than the other. Sometimes life takes us for a spin, so it's great to be able to enjoy the energy. Sometimes life slows down. It's lovely to savor a slower pace.

But the two kinds of happiness are different. Spinning happiness can arise quickly. But it takes energy, so it doesn't last.

River happiness is always available. The life of the river and life of the ocean are always with us whether we notice it or not. When there is a lot going on in our lives, the peacefulness may be harder to see, feel or even believe is possible. This is because there is not as much energy in river happiness. It is mellower. And precisely because it doesn't require much energy, it can last and last and last.

The ocean is always here waiting for us to just sit down in it.

Like the duck, let's sit down in the waves rather than try to stop them.
Whatever is going on, may we just be as we are and be with what is
May we be less agitated about being agitated
　　less worried about being worried
　　less angry about being angry
　　less distressed about feeling stressed
　　less upset with being upset
　　less sad with being sad
　　less controlling of being controlling
　　less frightened of being scared
　　more patient with our impatience
　　strive less to strive less
May we sit down in the waves.

Swimming in the Deep End: Beyond Self as We Know It

Once you realize that the person is merely a shadow of the reality, but not reality itself, you cease to fret and worry. You agree to be guided from within and life becomes a journey into the unknown.
– Sri Nisargadatta Maharaja

March 7, 2010

> I remember once
> in a far off country
> it doesn't matter where
> or even when
> it had been a hot day
> and a lot of work to be done
> and I was tired
> I stopped by the road
> and walked across a field
> and came to the shores of a lake
> the sun was bright on the water
> and I swam out from the shore
>   into the deep cold water
>   far out of my depth
>   and forgot
>   for a moment
>   I forgot
> where I had come from
> where I was going
> what I had done yesterday
> what I had to do tomorrow
> even my work
> my home
> my friends
> even my name
>   even my name
>   alone in the deep water
>   with the sky above
> and whether that lake was a lake
> or the shore of some great sea
> or some lost tributary of time itself
> for a moment
> I looked through
> I passed through
> I had one glimpse
>   as it happened
>   one day in that far off country
>   for a moment
>   it was so[31]

---

[31] "The Lake" by Gael Turnbull, *There are Words: Collected Poems* (Exeter: Shearsman Books, 2006), pp. 211-212.

Moo Shin

Before moving to California I trained for eight years in a classical Okinawan school of karate called "Ueiche Rue." Ueiche Rue has a term, *moo shin*, which translates as "no mind." The ideal way to practice karate is in a state of moo shi" or "no mindedness." When sensei wasn't around we'd mistranslate it as "no brain karate."

But by the time I earned a 2nd and 3rd degree black belt, I and most of my fellow students knew what the term referred to, though we didn't talk about it much.

For example, Dan and I had come up through the ranks together. He was younger than I. But we were well matched in temperament and skill. We loved to spar freestyle together. We could throw everything we had at each other trusting that each of us could take care of ourselves without hurting the other.

We had to move and respond more quickly than we could think. If we planned, anticipated, or thought about what we were doing, it would slow us down. But if we stayed focused yet relaxed, attentive without thinking, the flow of movements came through us.

When it worked, moo shin was exhilarating.

End of Self

This morning I would like to talk about the end of self as we know it. Moo shin is an example of heightened awareness accompanied by reduced thinking. Without thought, self as we normally think of it fades. Such states can be a fountain of wellbeing, clarity, heart, and effectiveness.

As far back in history as we can see, saints and seers have alluded to an even fuller version of self-forgetting as key to the fullness of life.

The Hindu Upanishads date back three or four millennia. They describe yogic practices that reduce selfishness, greed, and self-preoccupation.

The Greeks called it *kenosis* or "self-emptying." The Buddha called it *anattā* or "emptiness of self."

The Christians called it "selflessness." This should not be confused with a maudlin self-denial or martyrdom. Selflessness is a light and loving loss of self-absorption.

The Sufis and Wiccans practiced spinning. Whirling requires relaxing and letting go in order to stay balanced.

The 13th century Zen master Dogen wrote, "To study the way is to study the self. To study the self is to lose the self. To lose the self is to be enlightened by all things. To be enlightened by all things is to remove the barrier between self and other."

Our own Ralph Waldo Emerson wrote: "Standing on bare ground, my head uplifted into infinite space, all mean egoism vanishes. I become ... transparent ... the currents of universal being flow through me."

Look back over the last few years of your own life and recall the most painful and the most uplifting moments. During depression, anger, or fear, our sense of self becomes dense and demanding. During times of love, inspiration, joy, or ease, our sense of self becomes light and transparent.

Befuddling

Nevertheless, the end of self as we know it can be a befuddling concept. Trying to think about *non*-self is like trying *not* to think about a white horse. "Who is this self who thinks he doesn't have a self?"

It is a difficult concept because it is not a concept at all. It is an experience. It is not a thing we experience but a way we experience things.

That moo shin flow of movement in martial arts is not a concept. It is an experience.

Gael Turnbull's poem "The Lake" doesn't describe a philosophical proposition but a way of perceiving.

The loss of self in sexual ecstasy is not an intellectual point of view. It is a feeling.

Flowing down the ski slope at high speed with your body attentive and your mind free of thinking is not an idea. It's a way of experiencing being.

The musician who loses herself in a performance is not lost in thought but immersed in a flow of sounds and sensations.

Merging with the divine in sacred dance is not a belief. It is a state.

These experiences are hard to put into words because they arise outside the universe of words.

Evoke

The more we evoke these states, the more their meaning and importance becomes self-evident. The less we recognize them in our own experience, the more explanations sound like gibberish.

So rather than explain them, I'd prefer we share them. Shortly I'd like to hear from you some of your experiences.

But I thought I owed it to you to share at least one of my deeper experiences. These have arisen first in the context of meditation.

A long time ago I adopted Buddhist meditation as my root path. It resonates with Unitarian Universalism, it suits my particular temperament and I've been lucky to find helpful guides.

William Ellery Channing was arguably the father of American Unitarianism. When he was being installed in the Federal Street Church in Boston in 1802, he promised he would only speak about things he had experienced himself.

So I speak about *anattā* or emptiness of self not because I think Buddhism is the only path or even the best path but because it is the one I can speak about most authentically.

Beginning Practice

I've described some of this practice on other Sundays, so I'll just summarize the early phases.

The flavor of Buddhism in which I have trained begins with familiar states that hold the self lightly. You send kindness, peace, or wellbeing to yourself or to one other person: "May you be happy." "May you have ease." "May you have joy."

Soon the actual feeling arises, if only for a moment. With practice, the feelings last longer and go deeper. In time, joy relaxes into a broader happiness. Happiness relaxes into a quieter equanimity. Equanimity spreads out into a great spaciousness. In that spaciousness normal thinking stops for short moments. As you attend to these short gaps in thinking, they get longer until thinking fades completely.

The Buddha called this the "realm of nothingness." This state has lots of subtle sensations, pulls, tensions, relaxations, vibrations, and movements. But there are no thoughts about anything outside the mind itself.

It can take months of intensive practice to stabilize in this place. Or if you are like me, it takes years. But last summer in retreat I was hanging out in the realm of nothingness for several days. I felt pretty good about it.

Jolts

Then after lunch one day, I sat down to meditate. But instead I began daydreaming. I was not spacious and clear but spaced out and cloudy. I took a deep breath, came back to the present. And drifted off into nah-nah-noo-noo land.

If someone peeked into my meditation hut, they'd have seen a serene Buddha. But if they peeked into my mind, they would have seen a swarm of butterflies.

Then a shiver startled me back to the present. "What was that?" I wondered, and drifted off again.

Another startle shook me. "Hmm. Curious," I thought and went back to fantasyland.

These jolts kept rising every three or four minutes until I became more present to my body.

Then I noticed a tingling in my feet. It got stronger and rose up into my ankles. Then the hair on my legs stood up. A slow-motion blast of energy rose through the body and subsided.

A few minutes later another wave passed through. The more attentive I was, the slower and deeper it went.

Finally a protracted tidal wave shook my body. My teeth rattled until they hurt. I laughed.

I cried. It rose and rose and rose in a crescendo until it exploded in all directions. And vanished.

I dropped into a nothingness that had nothing in it: no seeing, no hearing, not the subtlest ripple. Just spacious stillness.

Yet, that void had qualities. It was compassionate and loving. Without judgment or thought there was nothing left but love. It was strange. I'm familiar with feeling love from a person or from myself. But there was no me and no other: no subject, no object. Just soft, full compassion that was neither inside nor outside. It was everywhere.

And there was clarity: a sense of intelligence and knowingness without subject or object.

Staying out of the Way

That night Bhante, my teacher, asked how the practice was going. I described what I could.

He nodded and said, "Now your practice will get really interesting. But I don't think there is much more I can teach you. Your mind is starting to untangle itself. It knows more than you or I."

He was silent for a minute. Then he looked at me and said, "The only thing I can tell you is stay out of the way."

"What about distracting thoughts?" I asked. "Should I see and release them and relax as before?"

"No," he said. "Just stay out of the way. Take all you've learned about meditation in the past 35 years and forget it. This is different. Don't do anything."

Meditating with effort is difficult. But meditating without effort seemed nearly impossible. Nearly.

Over the next few days I tried staying out of the way.

If the mind went off into thought, I did nothing about it. Very quickly, the thoughts rose in a crescendo, popped, and left behind that intelligent-compassionate-stillness.

If the mind started to drift into dull drowsiness, I'd let it drift. Very soon, a luminous energy arose out of nowhere and brought alert, loving clarity.

It was fascinating watching how skillfully, intelligently, and kindly it straightened itself out if I could just stay out of the way.

I knew a little about the next stage of practice. I wanted to move into it. But I couldn't. I said to Bhante, "*I* can't enter the next stage, can I?"

He laughed. "Yes, you're right. As long as you identify with an I, you can't. The least amount of trying will block it."

So I gradually gave up trying. As I did it felt closer and closer.

Then it was time for me to fly back home to Sacramento.

I sat in the airport waiting for a connecting flight and reflected on the retreat. Some people might say I had experienced a deeper or higher or truer self. Some might say I had experienced God. But those are just words – semantics.

What I would say is there is an awareness that is larger, more loving and more intelligent than any concept of self that I've ever come across. And this awareness-love-intelligence is more intimate and more dispassionate than common concepts of God. It is not a concept. It is an experience.

And the experience is much more accessible than we imagine. I suspect all of you have felt a touch if not a full immersion in it. This intelligent loving awareness is what we are made out of.

Field Notes

This week as I reflected on what I might say to you about the end of self, I asked Erika, my partner, "What have I gotten myself into? A wiser person would be mute on this topic."

But I find it so helpful to hear about other people's experience that I want to encourage all of you to share more of your moments of depth, joy, uplift, or enlightenment. So I must be willing to do so myself.

I make no pretense of having mastered any path. So consider these comments to be field notes. From where I stand today, I offer three observations:

Many paths, One Mountain

First, not all paths lead to the top. But many do. And there are different elevations along all paths. So the mountain may look very different from different vantage points.

But still there is only one mountain.

To say this in terms of Unitarian Universalist spirituality: the root of "Unitarian" is "unity." There is a oneness to life even if it expresses itself in diverse ways.

Self Dissolves into Love at Higher Altitudes

Second, the higher we climb on any path, the less important our ego. This loss of self is not a descent into a cold and lonely void. Quite the opposite. It's a relief as we experience Emerson's "currents of Universal Being." We find ourselves acting more out of what is good and healthy for all those around us and less out of concern for ourselves alone.

To say this in terms of Unitarian Universalist spirituality: the word universal refers to universal love. Love is essential to the unity of life. This awareness-love-intelligence is the very substance of the mountain and basis of existence.

The Path Up This Mountain Is Not All Sweetness and Light

Third, we all have feelings and wounds we consciously controlled or unconsciously suppressed. As we climb higher and self relaxes, these float to the surface. We have to embrace and integrate these before they can be released.

A transpersonal psychologist put this succinctly: we have to have a healthy self before we can lose it. We can't rid ourselves of a self we don't like. We have to love ourselves before we can lose ourselves.

This makes for an interesting trip. It's not always an easy one.

Yearning

There is a yearning that motivates us to move up the mountain – to reconnect with that awareness-love-intelligence. It's a kind of spiritual homesickness:

A lone bird floats in the dusk light. There is a softness, a fullness, a sense of completeness, closure. A taste of grief, perhaps, at the waning of day's life. To open to this moment is to be touched by the movement of life itself – even as it fades.

Coming home is returning out of individuality and all its frenetic energy. The loss of self which comes with peace can be sad. The hand that held on so strongly for so long aches as it relaxes its grip. The merge may seem scary. We would avoid it if we could. But at some point it seems that that is all there is to do. So, we gradually let go.

Love begins to penetrate the aching. The boundlessness of the sea has been waiting patiently for so long. The hurt softens, dissolves. How could I have stayed away from this for so long? Yes. This is Home.

Unitarian Universalist Spirituality: Choosing Love

Jacob tricked his father into giving him the inheritance that should have gone to his older brother, Esau. To get his birthright, Esau would have to kill Jacob. And he was enraged enough to do just that.

Jacob ran for his life.

He found safe haven in a neighboring country. He took up shepherding. He married. He began to raise a family. He prospered.

He was tempted to forget about Esau and his past. But his heart nudged him to face his trickery and reconcile with his brother.

So he packed his tents, gathered his family, servants, and flocks and began the journey back to the homeland. It took weeks.

Late one afternoon they came to the Jabbok River – less than a day's walk from his old home. He set up camp for the night beside the river.

Then, in the dead of the night, Jacob awoke. The hair on the back of his neck was standing on end. There was something in the camp. Was it Esau come to kill him? Was it a wild beast? Was it a demon? Jacob couldn't tell.

So he roused his household and sent them across the ford of the Jabbok. Alone, unarmed, in the black of night and with no possibility of help, he went back into the abandoned camp.

Something grabbed him and threw him to the ground. Jacob grabbed its leg. Together they grappled in the dark. Jacob didn't prevail. But it didn't beat him either.

When the eastern sky turned grey with a hint of dawn it said, "Release me, for I must go."

Jacob said, "No."

The entity leaned over and with one finger dislocated Jacob's hip. Jacob realized it was much more powerful than it had let on! With one finger it popped his leg out of its socket. It hurt!

It said, "Release me, for I must go."

What would you have done?

Jacob said, "No."

"What must I do to get you to release me?"

Jacob answered, "You must give me your blessing."

The demon turned out to be an angel from God. It said, "Your name shall no longer be 'Jacob.' You shall be known as 'Israel' and from you shall descend an entire nation."

At that time and in that culture, that was the highest blessing one could receive.

So Jacob released the angel. It left. And Jacob limped into the sunrise.

– Genesis 32:24-32

May 2, 2010

River

Unitarian Universalism is not a rock you can hold onto. It is a river to swim in. If you are looking for an island in the stream to protect you from the currents of life, we won't be much help. But if you enjoy plunging into the river, if you want to be a stronger, more agile swimmer, we offer good company.

In the end, the rock is an illusion anyway. Life is change, flux and flow. Real life is a river, not a stone.

UU Spirituality

This morning I'd like to reflect on Unitarian Universalist spirituality.

But before I speak more about spirituality, I should share with you what I mean by "Unitarian Universalist." Anyone heard of that?

The root of the word "Unitarian" is "unity." Originally it referred to a unified or one-part God rather than a three-part Trinitarian God. We are Unitarians, not Trinitarians.

As Unitarianism expanded out of the Christian fold it came to mean a unity or oneness of life. We are all connected in the interdependent web. All are welcome at the table.

Universalism originally referred to universal salvation – the belief that a loving God wouldn't condemn anyone to eternal hell — we are all saved – universal salvation. As Universalism expanded it came to mean Universal Love.

A colleague once summarized Unitarian Universalist belief as: "A oneness of all life that has love as essential to that unity." I like that.

But Unitarian Universalism is not founded on belief. Beliefs are cheap. People believe the darndest things. What counts are deeds not creeds.

So a living Unitarian Universalist *spirituality* is not a set of metaphysical claims. It is not a set of beliefs about the river. It's a way of swimming. It's a way of engaging life that grows out of the experience of oneness and love. And it's a way of engaging life that cultivates oneness and love.

Fear and Love

The spiritual practice I'm offering this morning can be summarized in one sentence: "Hold your fears gently before you, and then choose love."

The word "fear" is used in the broadest sense to include fright, worry, stress, grief, despair, numbness, anger, self-righteousness, cynicism, spite, or any way we tighten against love or contract out of oneness.

This practice begins with fear because we want our spirituality to be robust. When the waters are shallow and the currents are slow, any old way of swimming will work.

But when we wake up in the dead of night with sweaty palms and ask, "My God, what have I done with my life?" … When a loved dies … When demons sneak into the body politic … When times are dark and waters are deep, … we want a robust spirituality that can guide us from fear back to Love and Oneness.

To do so, we can hold our fears gently before us and then choose love.

To see how this works, let's apply it in three arenas: how we relate to ourselves, how we relate to each other, and how we relate to the larger world.

We'll start with ourselves.

Ourselves

Asian meditation masters who come to America are often blown away by the amount of self-hatred they find in us. We take it so much for granted that we don't even recognize it.

So I invite you to reflect for a moment on aspects of yourself that you aren't so fond of. …

Is anyone having difficulty finding these? Let me help.

I have a magic hat. When you put it on, everyone within about 100 feet can hear your every thought. Who would like to be the first to wear this hat? …

Yes. All of us have petty gripes, self-doubts, secret fantasies, unkind thoughts, misdeeds, and embarrassments we'd just as soon others didn't know about.

How do we relate to these aspects of ourselves?

If we try to ignore them, they distort our life. They may grab us in the dead of night like Jacob or merely whisper from the shadows and drain our energy. If we want to cultivate oneness and love, we must find a way to welcome them.

Caveat

There is one caveat. At times, life can be so overwhelming that, like Jacob, it may be wise to get out of town for a while. Or, like Gael Turnbull, go for a walk in a field or swim in a lake until we can see through it all. We all could use meditation, prayer, yoga, or other disciplines to cultivate calm and clearness.

But these are not the goal of spirituality. They may be an essential beginning, but not a destination. The heart pulls us back into the river.

Jacob may have been tempted to stay in that peaceful haven and forget the broken relationship with his brother and his own trickery. But the heart pulled him back.

As love drew Jacob closer to home, fear intensified. He wrestled with that demon, but not to defeat it. He sought to hold it gently, to get a blessing, to gain some insight.

And with that bit of wisdom he limped into the sunrise to continue his journey home.

We could summarize the story: "Hold your fears gently before you so you can see them clearly. But don't follow fears' bidding. Instead, choose love and follow its pull."

Emanuel

I first heard this practice from Emanuel, a being channeled by a woman named Pat Rodegast.

(I may have just discredited myself by telling you I'm quoting a new age spook. This is great. Try the practice yourself and trust your own experience.)

I met Emanuel years ago at our Unitarian Universalist Rowe Conference Center in the Massachusetts Berkshires. Toward the end of the weekend, a couple asked Emanuel about their daughter. They said they had hurt her. They'd made some terrible mistakes they wished they could change. But now their daughter seemed lost to them. What could they do?

Can you feel that heartache?

Emanuel said. "Hold your fears gently in front of you and then choose love." He told them to first look at their fears about their daughter: that her life was ruined, that she would be forever distant from them, what this said about who the couple were, and so forth. If they couldn't see these fears clearly, they would distort anything else they did.

Once they could see their fears, they could choose love. In other words, set aside the history and their guilt and ask what is the most loving way they could respond to her now in her present condition? That would create the most loving environment possible for their child to heal *if she so chose*. That is the catch. It is not in our power to force someone to heal. That is their choice. All we can do is create a loving environment that allows them the freedom to choose.

Do you see how this works?

Relationship

This brings us to the second arena: how we relate to those around us. Let me share another story.

Ram Dass slouched in a courtyard in India. On the other side, his guru, Neem Karoli Baba, sat surrounded by Americans. A few were meditating. Most were laughing and having a wonderful time with his guru.

Ram Dass was not having a wonderful time. He was devoted to his guru, but he disliked these fellow Westerners. He hated their habits, their attitude, and their sloppy mannerisms. He stared down at his hands, trying to relax them.

He heard a shuffling sound and looked up. Sam was standing in front of him with a plate of food and an obsequious smile, "Maharaji told me to bring you this."

Ram Dass took the tin plate and threw it across the courtyard. It clanged against the stones. Food splattered everywhere.

The courtyard fell silent except for the sound of the plate circling around itself until it clattered to a stop.

Everyone looked at Ram Dass.

Then Maharaji motioned, "Ram Dass. Come here, Ram Dass."

He walked through the stillness and sat next to his guru.

"Ram Dass. What's the matter?"

Ram Dass poured out his heart: "I just want to be with you, Maharaji. All these people don't take their spirituality seriously. They're just here for the high. I hate having to be around them all the time." He began to cry.

Maharaji cried with him and stroked his head affectionately. He asked a woman to bring warm milk for him. They cried more.

Finally the tears subsided. He felt better.

Maharaji said, "Ram Dass. I thought I told you to love everyone."

"Yes, Maharaji. You told me to love everyone. But you also told me to speak the truth. And the truth is I don't love everyone."

Maharaji leaned over until his forehead touched Ram Dass's. He looked straight into his eyes.

"Ram Dass."

"Yes, Maharaji."

"Ram Dass. Love everyone. Speak the truth."

In the arena of relationships, a guiding principle is: Love everyone; speak the truth. We don't get to do love 70% and truth 80% and say we're doing 150%. We do both love and truth 100%.

If that seems too hard, great. That difficulty is a form of fear. We can hold it gently and then choose love. In other words, we can look at what we are afraid will happen if we open our hearts. Are we afraid of getting hurt? Of being abandoned? Of getting angry? Of saying something we'll regret? Of appearing uncool?

See those fears gently, kindly, and clearly. Then choose love.

It's been said that love without truth is not loving and truth without love is not truthful.

This turns relationships into a Unitarian Universalist spiritual practice that affirms and promotes the worth and dignity of yourself and the other person and the interdependent web in which we all relate.

This doesn't mean we like all people, only that we love them and speak the truth. The poet Kabir wrote, "Never put someone out of your heart. Do what you have to do. Yell at them. Scream at them. Throw them out of your house. But don't put them out of your heart."

In churches I have served, periodically someone says, "We have to do something about so-and-so."

I ask, "Have you spoken with them?"

They say, "Oh no. I can't speak with him. He's impossible." Or "I can't speak with her. She's scary." Or "fragile." Or "closed-minded."

I respond, "You have no choice. We are a religious community. We have to speak to one another in truth and love. This is our practice."

Sometimes we can't do it alone. That's fine. Get help. Get support. Get a mediator. But find a way to speak the truth in love.

We won't do this perfectly. It's an imperfect world. But going as deeply, honestly, and lovingly as we can is enough.

There is a collective intelligence that arises in a group that speaks with deep intention to be loving and truthful. We find paths through difficulties that none of us could ever figure out on our own. Speaking and listening with love-truth brings forth this collective intelligence.

Boundaries

There is one caveat: The more we open our heart, the more we must keep good boundaries.

I had a stark teaching in this the first time I went to India. My son Nathan and I were traveling together for several weeks. But in the first days we were thoroughly overwhelmed by the suffering of the beggars.

Our hearts wanted to respond. But it was totally beyond our resources to give all that was asked. When we tried to say "no," they didn't hear. They kept coming after us for more.

Nathan got so fed up that he shut down: "I'm not giving any more. Period."

I understood but was not comfortable with that solution for me.

So one afternoon I sat in a tiny square in the old city section of Agra, not far from the Taj Mahal. I noticed that the Brahmins could say "no" to the beggars without getting hassled.

Then I notice a tiny hand gesture. With his arms down and palm flat, he rotated his hand out as he said, "no."

The next time a beggar approached me, I said "no" and mimicked the hand gesture. It was like flipping a switch. The beggar stopped mid-sentence and withdrew.

It was like magic – I'd found the cultural body language to communicate clear boundary.

After that, every day I put a few dollars worth of rupee coins (that's quite a lot of money in India) in a separate pocket. When I was instinctively drawn to a beggar, I approached and gave a few coins. When I ran out of coins or didn't feel drawn, I said "no."

This allowed me to be generous of heart and still have good boundaries.

Our hearts have an unlimited capacity to love. But in this world, our bodies have limited energy. We have limited time, money, and other resources. To keep our hearts open, we have to respect these limits.

So if we want a heart that knows oneness and Love, part of our spiritual path is finding ways to respect our limits. Keep good boundaries out of love for those around us as well as love for ourselves.

The World

This brings us to the third arena: our relationship to the larger world.

When you look at the world, how many of you ever feel fear? Despair? Cynicism? Anger? Frustration? Grief?

How can we look at war, legalized greed, unequal wealth distribution, civil oppression, political polarization, grid-lock, polar bears breaking through thinning ice, the possibility of human extinction, so one and not be disturbed?

The horrors of the world are bigger than any of us can handle psychically or emotionally on our own. This is where we truly need each other. This is where healthy religious community is so important. We can cry together. Grieve together. Support one other. Find grounding and courage together.

Then we can look at the world with eyes that are clear and gentle and wide open. From that place we don't ask how fear drives us. We ask how love pulls us – how compassion draws us.

Some of us may feel drawn to protesting in the streets, some to raising joyful children, some to developing alternative technologies, some to creating life-sustaining communities, some to meditating to a deeper vision of the possible, some to writing poetry and music that help us connect with the beauty around us, some to just bringing moments of kindness into the world.

The interdependent web doesn't need any of us to do it all – only that each of us do what we are drawn to do in our deepest hearts. To keep our hearts open, agile, creative, supple, and responsive in this way, we need good boundaries and good support. Then our hearts open easily and gracefully and courageously.

When we share the depths of our despair and come out the other side, we find an incredible release of creative energy – sometimes the power to change our lives and the world.

Well, the power has been here all along – right under our noses. It is only fear and timidity that keeps us from trusting the power.

Adrienne Rich, the feminist poet, wrote:

> … *gentleness is active*
> *gentleness swabs the crusted stump*
> *invents the more merciful instruments*
> *to touch the wound beyond the wound*
> *does not faint with disgust*
> *will not be driven off*
> *keeps bearing witness calmly*
> *against the predator, the parasite*
> *I am tired of faintheartedness.*

Simple

Did someone tell you religion should be undemanding? Did someone tell you spirituality is easy? Was that person selling snake oil?

True spirituality is simple, but not so easy. But what else is there to do? So let's just get on with it:

Hold our fears gently, and then choose love.

Love everyone, and speak the truth because love without truth is not loving, and truth without love is not truthful.

Keep our hearts open and keep good boundaries.

If we do that, we may find hard swimming at times. And we'll find more inspiration, more love, and more fun than we ever imagined possible.

Everywhere we look we start to see oneness and love. The power we have been trying to harvest is busy harvesting us.

Namasté.

Indexes

Sermons by Title

Title	Date	Page
An Openness of Being	December 16, 2001	273
Anger	October 7, 2001	19
Atheism and the Wisdom of Uncertainty	September 28, 2008	222
Bad Reality, Good Reality	November 19, 2006	122
Being Who We Are: Playing Golf in Calcutta	September 25, 2005	81
Beyond the Storyline	May 20, 2001	15
Bright Faith	January 7, 2007	289
Compassion	November 11, 2001	28
Compassion and Anger	November 4, 2001	24
Conflict and Community	October 22, 2006	110
Conflict and Goodwill	September 17, 2006	106
Conflict and Ill Will	September 10, 2006	101
Consciousness and Morality	October 13, 2002	40
Contentment	November 12, 2006	118
Cultivating Happiness	June 10, 2007	135
Deep Connection	August 24, 2008	213
Deep Listening	October 16, 2005	86
Discontentment	November 5, 2006	114
Dying into Life	January 7, 2001	7
Embodied Faith	March 11, 2007	297
Ethical Lapses	February 22, 2009	160
Experiments in Truth	April 27, 2008	156
Faith and the Art of Questioning	January 21, 2007	293
Fallow Time	January 4, 2004	63
Fire Unbound by Longing	October 6, 2002	35
Forgiveness	January 4, 2009	244
Forgiving Others	January 12, 2003	49
Forgiving Ourselves	January 5, 2003	44
Generosity I	February 4, 2007	125
Generosity II	February 18, 2007	130
Getting Real	May 7, 2000	3
God and the Power of Surrender	September 14, 2008	218
In the Buddha's Footsteps: Sujata	January 15, 2006	281
In the Buddha's Footsteps: Transformation	January 29, 2006	286
Joy and Formless Wellbeing	December 14, 2008	240
Joy, Enjoying, and Being in Joy	June 6, 2010	167
Killing a Friend	November 1, 2009	165
Light Beyond the Scrim	September 24, 2000	175
Lines in the Sand: Creating a Self Through Boundaries	January 27, 2002	11
Little Mind, Big Mind	June 5, 2005	71
Love-Truth	October 15, 2000	179

Loving Kindness	February 11, 2001	183
Loving Your Consciousness	August 28, 2005	76
Mindfulness I: Wat Life	May 7, 2006	197
Mindfulness II: Transformation	May 14, 2006	202
Nibbāna I: Unbound by Longing	January 11, 2009	248
Nibbāna II: Nothingness	January 25, 2009	253
Nibbāna III: The Secret of Happiness	February 15, 2009	257
Of Sisyphus and Groundhogs	February 2, 2003	54
Our Divine Vulnerabilities I	September 16, 2007	143
Our Divine Vulnerabilities II	September 30, 2007	148
Our Divine Vulnerabilities III	October 14, 2007	152
Paradise and the Struggle for Harmony	October 19, 2008	227
Peaceful Heart	December 7, 2008	235
Practices of Simplicity	June 14, 2009	266
Relax	June 8, 2008	302
Remorse and Guilt	October 12, 2003	58
Resting in the Tempest	June 1, 2003	193
Sànùk: Fun	June 11, 2006	97
Seeing Simplicity	August 26, 2007	139
Self as Trance	October 28, 2005	90
Simplicity	May 31, 2009	261
Spiritual Eyes	November 26, 2006	206
Spirituality of Despair	January 6, 2002	31
Swimming in the Deep End: Beyond Self as We Know It	March 7, 2010	337
Swimming in the Deep End: Merging with the River	February 21, 2010	332
Swimming in the Deep End: The Dark Side of Unitarian Universalism	January 24, 2010	327
Taking Refuge	February 24, 2002	188
The Pursuit of Happiness	November 16, 2008	231
Unitarian Universalist Maturity	March 7, 2004	277
Unitarian Universalist Spirituality: Choosing Love	May 2, 2010	342
Unitarian Universalist Spirituality: Finding the Soul	August 30, 2009	307
Unitarian Universalist Spirituality: From Interdependence to Oneness	October 25, 2009	322
Unitarian Universalist Spirituality: Radiant Heart	October 11, 2009	317
Unitarian Universalist Spirituality: The Goodness in Everyone	September 20, 2009	312
Wise Speech	May 2, 2004	67

Sermons by Date

Date	Title	Page
May 7, 2000	Getting Real	3
September 24, 2000	Light Beyond the Scrim	175
October 15, 2000	Love-Truth	179
January 7, 2001	Dying Into Life	7
February 11, 2001	Loving Kindness	183
May 20, 2001	Beyond the Storyline	15
October 7, 2001	Anger	19
November 4, 2001	Compassion and Anger	24
November 11, 2001	Compassion	28
December 16, 2001	An Openness of Being	273
January 6, 2002	Spirituality of Despair	31
January 27, 2002	Lines in the Sand: Creating a Self Through Boundaries	11
February 24, 2002	Taking Refuge	188
October 6, 2002	Fire Unbound by Longing	35
October 13, 2002	Consciousness and Morality	40
January 5, 2003	Forgiving Ourselves	44
January 12, 2003	Forgiving Others	49
February 2, 2003	Of Sisyphus and Groundhogs	54
June 1, 2003	Resting in the Tempest	193
October 12, 2003	Remorse and Guilt	58
January 4, 2004	Fallow Time	63
March 7, 2004	Unitarian Universalist Maturity	277
May 2, 2004	Wise Speech	67
June 5, 2005	Little Mind, Big Mind	71
August 28, 2005	Loving Your Consciousness	76
September 25, 2005	Being Who We Are: Playing Golf in Calcutta	81
October 16, 2005	Deep Listening	86
October 28, 2005	Self as Trance	90
January 15, 2006	In the Buddha's Footsteps: Sujata	281
January 29, 2006	In the Buddha's Footsteps: Transformation	286
May 7, 2006	Mindfulness I: Wat Life	197
May 14, 2006	Mindfulness II: Transformation	202
June 11, 2006	*Sànùk*: Fun	97
September 10, 2006	Conflict and Ill Will	101
September 17, 2006	Conflict and Goodwill	106
October 22, 2006	Conflict and Community	110
November 5, 2006	Discontentment	114
November 12, 2006	Contentment	118
November 19, 2006	Bad Reality, Good Reality	122
November 26, 2006	Spiritual Eyes	206
January 7, 2007	Bright Faith	289
January 21, 2007	Faith and the Art of Questioning	293
February 4, 2007	Generosity I	125
February 18, 2007	Generosity II	130
March 11, 2007	Embodied Faith	297
June 10, 2007	Cultivating Happiness	135

August 26, 2007	Seeing Simplicity	139
September 16, 2007	Our Divine Vulnerabilities I	143
September 30, 2007	Our Divine Vulnerabilities II	148
October 14, 2007	Our Divine Vulnerabilities III	152
April 27, 2008	Experiments in Truth	156
June 8, 2008	Relax	302
August 24, 2008	Deep Connection	213
September 14, 2008	God and the Power of Surrender	218
September 28, 2008	Atheism and the Wisdom of Uncertainty	222
October 19, 2008	Paradise and the Struggle for Harmony	227
November 16, 2008	The Pursuit of Happiness	231
December 14, 2008	Joy and Formless Wellbeing	240
January 4, 2009	Forgiveness	244
January 11, 2009	*Nibbāna* I: Unbound by Longing	248
January 25, 2009	*Nibbāna* II: Nothingness	253
February 15, 2009	*Nibbāna* III: The Secret of Happiness	257
February 22, 2009	Ethical Lapses	160
May 31, 2009	Simplicity	261
June 14, 2009	Practices of Simplicity	266
August 30, 2009	Unitarian Universalist Spirituality: Finding the Soul	307
September 20, 2009	Unitarian Universalist Spirituality: The Goodness in Everyone	312
October 11, 2009	Unitarian Universalist Spirituality: Radiant Heart	317
October 25, 2009	Unitarian Universalist Spirituality: From Interdependence to Oneness	322
November 1, 2009	Killing a Friend	165
December 7, 2008	Peaceful Heart	235
January 24, 2010	Swimming in the Deep End: The Dark Side of Unitarian Universalism	327
February 21, 2010	Swimming in the Deep End: Merging with the River	332
March 7, 2010	Swimming in the Deep End: Beyond Self as We Know It	337
May 2, 2010	Unitarian Universalist Spirituality: Choosing Love	342
June 6, 2010	Joy, Enjoying, and Being In Joy	167

Made in the USA
Coppell, TX
30 January 2022